CW00546511

Ivor Gurney

COLLECTED
LETTERS

25

Ivor Gurney

COLLECTED
LETTERS

edited by R K R Thornton

THE MID NORTHUMBERLAND ARTS GROUP
& CARCANET PRESS
1991

Mid Northumberland Arts Group ISBN 0 904790 65 7
Carcanet Press ISBN 0 85635 941 6

First published 1991 in this edition by
The Mid Northumberland Arts Group, Leisure and Publicity Department
Town Hall, Ashington, Northumberland NE63 8RX
and Carcanet Press Limited,
208-212 Corn Exchange Buildings, Manchester M4 3BQ

Designed by Sue Richards
Typeset by Parchment (Oxford) Ltd
Printed by Short Run Press Ltd, Exeter

CONTENTS

ACKNOWLEDGEMENTS

I would like to thank all those who have helped in the making of this edition. The holders of the originals have been unfailingly helpful in making their material available and I wish to thank them warmly: the Harry Ransom Humanities Research Centre at the University of Texas at Austin for their letters to Blunden; the Berg Collection of the New York Public Library for their letters to Edward Marsh and one to Walter de la Mare; the British Library for their letter to Maurice Jacobson; the National Library of Wales for their letter to Iolo Williams; the Bodleian Library and Lord Bridges for the letter from the Bridges Collection; the Special Collections Library of the University of Birmingham for their letter to Francis Brett Young; the Gloucester Public Library, which houses the majority of Gurney papers in the Gurney Archive; to all of them and their staffs I am very grateful. I would also like to thank Michael Hurd for making available his transcripts from letters which have enabled me to get texts for letters which I can not trace. I have also been helped by scholars and enthusiasts past and present from Marion Scott, Gerald Finzi and Robin Haines to the makers of *The New Grove Dictionary of Music and Musicians*. Much work on which I have been able to build has been done by Michael Hurd, P.J.Kavanagh, and Anthony Boden and I have been continually indebted to them. I am grateful to students and colleagues for their willingness to share their discoveries and insights: to Joy King, to George Walter, to Liz Ward, to Mark Brown; and I hope that this work will help them in turn. I would like to thank Nigel Fortune and John Whenham for giving me the benefit of their wide knowledge of music and for preventing me from making more mistakes with the music, Simon Fox, the Librarian of the R.C.M. for useful information, Christopher Bornet for searching out information on Jacobson, Gordon Clarke of the Royal College of Organists for help in identifying Gurney's examination date, Jake Thornton for information on the war, Geoff Barnbrook for assistance with the computing side of the project, and George Stephenson for being the most patient and sympathetic of publishers.

Like all those who work on Gurney, I owe a major debt of gratitude to Penny Ely, Trustee of the Gurney Estate, not only for the permission to publish his work, but also for her great fund of information and encouragement.

To my wife and children, who have probably grown tired of my lengthy attempts to finish this book, apologies and love; they too have put a lot into it.

INTRODUCTION

The recent Summer Weekend of English Music and Verse celebrating the centenary of Gurney's birth indicated the dramatic scale of the increase in Gurney's reputation in recent years. From those gathered there it was evident that there was a pressing need for the publication of his letters. Scholars, musicologists, enthusiasts were all eager to have the texts in their hands, and I am delighted to be able to bring out this edition.

It is no surprise that there should be such an interest in the letters since not only do they substantially tell the story of Gurney's mature life and development, but they are intrinsically attractive; witty, generous, playful, committed, informative, and above all reflective of Gurney's enormous creative talent.

They are at times curiously self-conscious. In letter 117 he hopes that Marion Scott will be 'out of danger, and will soon be able to resume that correspondance which is inevitably fated some day to be the joy and wonder of my biographers'. He is aware of posterity. In letter 48 he circles a fingerprint with the suggestion that it be kept for 'posterities sake', and in letter 58 he wonders whether the night he spoke on 'Ghosts' will become famous. This is all part of his sense of mission and consciousness of his own abilities, which is mixed up with that other complex of ideas clustered around desert, reward, payment, and earning merit through suffering.

He often apologises for the selfishness of his letters, but they are remarkably unselfish. He is striking for the altruistic pleasure he takes in the pleasures and successes of his friends, whether Sydney Shimmin's chance to meet the Chapman family (see letter 63), or Herbert Howells' chance to write away from the demands of war (see letter 228), or what comes across as his genuine concern for Marion Scott's frail health. One incidental feature of the letters is the large amount of illness in Gurney's circle of acquaintance. The Scotts, the Chapmans, Howells, Shimmin all had serious ill-health. Not that Gurney did not, with his dyspepsia, 'neurasthenia', toothache, and 'cold in the stomach'; but for a man who is at times written of as needing our compassion, he appears very often as the one who offers comfort, cheer and reassurance to his correspondents.

For his fellow soldiers, this ability to sympathise and keep cheerful is one of his main features. 'I pass with my comrades as one who is willing to be friendly with almost anybody; looks depressed, but makes more jokes than anyone around here' (letter 64). In letter 177 he reports that 'as a personality I am rather popular in my company'. And the same playfulness is evident in many of the letters, from the highly avant-garde depiction of a strafe in music in letter 117 to his proposed 'symphony in Canon' to dedicate to Howells in letter 266.

Perhaps the playfulness and cheerful attitude come from his sense of proportion. He recognises the war for what it is and is always aware of 'another world but that of war' (123). Even when his own story begins to sound impressive he can come back on himself with 'Does it sound interesting? May God forgive me if I ever come to cheat myself into thinking that it was, and lie later to younger men of the Great Days. It was damnable' (250). Of course the interest in the narrative of the letters written in the army is to some extent qualified by the censorship both external and internal. In letter 126 he reports that the Censor has specially requested he shorten his letters; in letter 112 he comments that 'It is difficult in these letters to interest you and yet avoid trouble with the Censor'; but his self-censorship acts just as effectively to screen out certain sorts of experience from the letters.

This ban on describing the abundant material he had available is another of those forces which combined with the distance from a piano to throw Gurney into poetry as a major part of his letters. This collection of letters is extraordinary, if not unique, in the place that poetry takes in them. We can see almost the whole of Gurney's progression from imitator of Brooke to writer of his own strong-lined and distinctive poems. We see indeed the 'growth of a poet's mind'. Gurney had obviously always been interested in poetry, as one can see from the way he easily breaks into doggerel in letters 4, 8, or 10 for example; but his commitment to poetry deepens and achieves a new priority.

I have said before that the absence of a piano helped to push him towards poetry, and I have been told that this should not have made any difference to a musician, but the struggle between the two arts was a long one in Gurney's mind and, although he claimed to choose in favour of music, this does not always seem completely to match the case. In letter 57 he says that 'a sonnet comes far easier to me than a prelude'; but there is always the assertion as in letter 324 that 'music is my real path'. On the other hand, when there is 'quite a nice piano' available (see letter 192), he cannot bring himself to use it. It is perhaps as he writes to Sydney Shimmin in letter 325: 'If you are at all like me, you neither enjoy touching it nor leaving it alone'. The same spirit sends him to Edinburgh when he longs to return to Gloucester and away from Gloucester when he is placed in asylum there.

What is most important about this ambivalence in his attitude is that neither poetry nor music seems to have his whole attention and that he begins to appear as an author who does not like or believe in boundaries. The poems run into the letters (see for example letter 129), the words run into the music and the letters become poems in the asylum. They become part of some complex whole rather than differing genres.

I have not followed Gurney far into the asylum, however, for a variety of reasons. I have no intention to reinforce the idea of Gurney as the 'mad poet'; the letters from the asylum are very many and would have swelled the book to twice the size; they are repetitive and require a different type of editing and selecting from the earlier letters which seems to me to demand a study on its own. In bringing the letters down to the end of 1922, I have included the Barnwood group of asylum letters which I hope sufficiently illustrates the reasonableness of the decision. There is a complete change in self-awareness of the writer of those letters; yet I have been lucky in that the end of 1922 comes with a letter which, however odd, ends with a poem which magnificently and in characteristic Gurney manner searches for

> the sure
> Thought behind all motion that makes endure
> The swinging of the spheres and the good going.

The struggle to pluck such poetry out of his madness is the subject of another study.

Meanwhile I have attempted to place as accurately as possible the letters which we have. Sometimes this proves difficult when the whole subject of the letter seems to be ping-pong and cricket; but the datings can provide some important new understandings of Gurney's career, which will prove valuable in the task of writing a new biography of Gurney, which I have begun to work towards. The redating of letter 14 is a good example. Based on the dating of W.H.Davies' book and the date when Gurney passed his A.R.C.O. exams, the letter can now be seen to belong to 1914. What this means is that the 'Elizas' were not 'brought with him' from Gloucester when he began at the Royal College of Music, nor were they a surprising and sudden change of direction in 1912. What happened was that Gurney went up to the R.C.M. in 1911 and studied there for well over a year before a sort of a breakdown in the summer of 1913. He went to Gloucester and Framilode to recover, visited the Misses Levetus at Southwold and got back into College life at the end of 1913 before writing the 'Elizas' probably fairly close to the date of the letter in 1914. The 'Elizas' thus come at a much more credible point in Gurney's career, and there are many more minor adjustments one has to make to a Gurney chronology.

I have also included a record of the printed forms that Gurney sent. As Paul Fussell points out in *The Great War and Modern Memory* (1975), the Field (Service) Post Card with its options for deletion was the first widespread example of the modern world's characteristic document, the form, and its use and the dating can sometimes be a valuable clue as to Gurney's activities, banal and uncommunicative though it is.

What I cannot include are the letters to which Gurney was replying. This is a very one-sided correspondence and we have none of the letters from Howells or Shimmin or the Chapman family. Gurney was always very grateful for letters; 'like stars in a dark night' he told the Chapman family, and his response to Marion Scott is often full of warmth. He is 'very grateful to you for your letters – so full of interest and kindness' (143). 'You have given me just what I needed, and what none other of my friends could supply to keep me in touch with things which are my life; and the actuality of which is almost altogether denied me' (185). We have some glimpses of the sort of letter that Marion Scott wrote and of the care she took in revising her letters to get them right, from draft and corrected copies of two of her letters in the Gurney Archive at G.70.38 and G.70.64. It is worth giving a sample of the first, which is dated 19 June 1918:

My Dear Friend

Thank you so much for your letter, which should have been answer[ed] before this, but that the days have been so extraordinarily full that I simply I have not known where to turn or what to do next. And now I have the enclosed to send on to you from the *Westminster Gazette* for the 'Immortal Hour'. They have paid at their usual rate of 1/- a line, but I wish it had been more: 16/- seems very small to set against a lovely poem. Still it is at least 'a bird in the hand' so to speak – this little fee – & I hope it may prove the fore-runner of better luck in this direction. (I forget if I told you that I am wanting to try the *Spectator* with some of your poems, and have asked Lady Cynthia Colville for an introduction to St.Loe Strachey the editor:- failing that, Lady (Mary) (Trefusis) has promised me an introduction to Graves, the second in command.)

The *Westminster Gazette* very stupidly made out the cheque for 16/- in my name – & crossed it so that it had to be paid through a bank, so I am cashing it at my bank, and am sending you the money in postal orders, as I thought perhaps those would be easier to deal with if you are still in hospital than another cheque (made payable to you) would be. So I enclose two p.o's – one for 10/- the other for 6/-.

Miss Hunt evidently liked the 'Immortal Hour' very much, for she wrote to me most enthusiastically about it, and said how much you had gained in poetical technique; she was very keen about your poems in the College (Magazine) too. You know, you declare yourself you are not a real poet, but I'm just going to contradict you to your face, monsieur! – politely, (gently), but perfectly firmly do I contradict you! You *have* got the root of the matter in you. 'le musicien le plus poete que jamais' – I don't recollect exactly, but it seems to fit you. It is abundantly true that both in music and in poetry you have the real thing – you *are* a poet, you *are* a composer. You said in your letter, (apropos) of the account of H.N.H. that went to (Dr) Hull 'if only something of the same kind could be written of me – now in shame and despair – with so little done'. Ivor, it is the *quality* of work which is what counts in the end, and though you feel yourself that you have accomplished so little as yet compared to what you hope to do, you have done some songs which will take their place as part of the inheritance of England.

The letter is a mixture of the sources of stimulation for him: correspondence, newspapers and poetry, wherever it could be found.

We are lucky not only that Marion Scott helped to stimulate him into writing, but also that she kept the letters so carefully to allow us to get to know the man who can aptly sum himself up in letter 238: 'Author, Composer, Soldier-of-a-sort, and your humble sincere servant'.

R.K.R.Thornton, The Old Vicarage, Tibberton, 1990

ABBREVIATIONS

A.B.	Arthur Benjamin
A.H.C.	Alfred Hunter Cheesman
A.N.D.	Annie Nelson Drummond
A.S.C.	Army Service Corps
B.E.F.	British Expeditionary Force
C.B.	Confined to barracks
C.C.S.	Casualty Clearing Station
C.H.H.P.	Sir Charles Hubert Hastings Parry
Con.Camp	Convalescent Camp
C.V.S.	Sir Charles Villiers Stanford
D.C.M.	Distinguished Conduct Medal
F.H.	French horn
F.P.C.	Field postcard
F.W.H.	Frederick William Harvey
G.L.A.	Grand literary agent
G.O.C.	General Officer Commanding
H.E	High explosive
H.N.H.	Herbert Norman Howells
H.W.	High Wycombe
I.B.D.	Infantry base depot
J.W.H.	John Wilton Haines
K.R.C.	King's Rifle Company
L.A.	Literary agent or Lord Almighty
M.G.C.	Machine Gun Corps
M.M.S.	Marion Margaret Scott
MS.	Manuscript
N.C.O.	Non-commissioned officer
Ordeal	*The Ordeal of Ivor Gurney* by Michael Hurd
P.C.	Postcard
Q.M.S.	Quartermaster Sergeant
R.A.M.C.	Royal Army Medical Corps
R.B.	Robert Bridges
R.C.M.	Royal College of Music
R.L.S.	Robert Louis Stevenson

R.S.M.	Regimental Sergeant Major
R.T.	Radio transmission
R.W.	Royal Welsh
S & J	Sidgwick and Jackson
SASAWE	*Severn and Somme and War's Embers* ed. R.K.R. Thornton
Stars	*Stars in a Dark Night* ed. Anthony Boden
S.S.	Sydney Shimmin
S.W.	*Saturday Westminster*
S.W.G.	*Saturday Westminster Gazette*
S.W.M.	Society of Women Musicians
T.M.B.	Trench mortar battery
T.L.S.	*Times Literary Supplement*
TS.	Typescript
V.A.D.	Voluntary Aid Detachment

CHRONOLOGY

1890
28 August   Ivor Bertie Gurney born at 3 Queen Street, Gloucester, son of David Gurney, tailor, and Florence (née Lugg), 2nd of four children: Winifred (b.1886), Ronald (b.1894), and Dorothy (b.1900). Alfred Hunter Cheesman acts as godfather.

1890s   Moves to 19 Barton Street, house and shop.

1896   Purchase of family piano. Begins Sunday School at All Saints in October. Attends National School, London Road.

1899   Joins All Saints Choir; full membership on 3 December.

1900   Wins place in Gloucester Cathedral Choir and King's School. Taught music by Charles H. Deavin.

1904   Sings with Madame Albani. Begins to write music.

1905   Begins intimacy with Cheesman, and Margaret and Emily Hunt, who encourage his artistic talents.

1906-11
January   Articled pupil of Dr Herbert Brewer, organist of Gloucester Cathedral. Temporary posts as organist at Whitminster, Hempsted and at the Mariners' Church. Friendships with Herbert Howells (fellow pupil of Brewer from 1907), F.W.Harvey and (later) J.W.Haines.

1907   Sits and passes matriculation examination at Durham University.

1911   Wins open scholarship to Royal College of Music of £40 per annum. Cheesman provides another £40. Moves to London and takes digs in Fulham.

1911-14	At R.C.M.; fellow pupils Howells, Sydney Shimmin, Arthur Benjamin. Makes acquaintance of Marion Scott and Ethel Voynich. Taught by Stanford for Composition, Waddington for Counterpoint, Sharpe for Piano, and Drs Davies and Allen.
1913	Begins to write verse. Nervous problems and dyspepsia diagnosed as 'neurasthenia' by Dr Harper. Recuperates at Framilode and Gloucester.
1913-14	Writes the 'Elizas'.

1914

17-23 January	Passes A.R.C.O. examination with Frank J. Sawyer prize for second highest marks.
4 August	War declared. Gurney volunteers but is refused.
October	Organist post at Christ Church, High Wycombe where he makes acquaintance of Chapman family.

1915

9 February	Joins 5th Gloucester Reserve Battalion (the 2nd/5th) as Private number 3895.
February	Battalion goes to Northampton.
April	Chelmsford.
June	Epping.
3 August	Sends Marion Scott the first poem of *Severn and Somme*.
August	Back to Chelmsford.
August-March	Plays the Baryton in the band. Rediscovers Whitman.

1916

19 February	Battalion moves to Tidworth and thence to Park House Camp on Salisbury Plain.
25 May	The 2nd/5th arrive in Le Havre. Travel to Le Sart.
31 May	Into trenches at Riez Bailleul.
8 June	Return to Le Sart and on to Laventie.
15 June	Relieve the 2nd/1st Bucks in Fauquissart-Laventie Sector (relieved on 21 June)
27 June	Back at the front for a week. Billets in La Gorgue followed by transfer to Richebourg-St.Vaast.
6 July	Relieve Black Watch.
12 July	Relieve 2nd/1st Bucks (relieved on 15 July) and on to La Gorgue and Estaires.
19 July	In reserve at attack on Aubers Ridge.
August	Back to billets at La Gorgue.

9 August	In reserve at Wangerie, Masselot and Fort Esquin. Sets Masefield's 'By a Bierside'.
17 August	F.W. Harvey captured, feared dead.
28 August	At Clearing Station having teeth attended to.
13 September	Out of hospital.
27 October	Move South to Albert and the Somme.
Early December	In Rest Station for 'cold in the stomach'.
9 December	Temporary job with water carts in Sanitary Section (until late January 1917).

1917

11 January	Writes 'In Flanders'.
7 February	Battalion marches to L'Etoile.
13 February	By train to Wiencourt, near Amiens.
15 February	To Framerville; relieve French infantry regiment in Ablaincourt sector.
March	To Brigade Reserve at Raincourt. Writes 'Severn Meadows'.
18 March	Battalion follows German withdrawal: Vermando-villers, Epenancourt, Croix Moligneaux, Caulaincourt.
31 March	Vermand.
7 April	Wounded in arm; sent to Rouen.
30 April	Gets new number: 241281.
5 May	Begins training again.
18 May	Back with the Battalion; move to Arras front.
28 May	Inoculation against typhoid.
Early June	In the line before Guemappe for 8 days.
11 June	Out of the line.
23 June	Rest at Buire-au-Bois and training. Gurney crack platoon shot.
14 July	Sidgwick and Jackson agree to publish a collection of his poems.
15 July	Transfer to Machine Gun Corps at Vaux.
31 July	Third Battle of Ypres begins (Passchendaele). Gurney in reserve.
August	Gloucesters move to Buysscheure and into support trenches near Poperinghe on the 21st.
10 September	Gassed at St Julien.
16-21 September	In hospital, correcting proofs.
22 September	On board ship to England.
25 September	In Edinburgh War Hospital, Bangour. Meets Annie Nelson Drummond, a V.A.D. nurse.
6 November	Leave in London, High Wycombe and Gloucester.
15 November	To Seaton Delaval for signalling course.

16 November	*Severn and Somme* published.
1918	
12 January	Weekend leave in Edinburgh seeing Annie Drummond.
12-18	February Leave in Gloucester; father ill.
25 February	Examined for effects of gas and admitted to Newcastle General Hospital.
March	Moved to Brancepeth Castle, a convalescent depot.
28 March	'Beethoven' letter. Some sort of nervous breakdown.
22 April	Moved to Newcastle General Hospital and on to Seaton Delaval
8 May	Sent to Lord Derby's War Hospital, Warrington.
19 June	Suicide letter. Marion Scott visits him. Major Robertson reports that Gurney hears voices and wishes to be sent to an asylum.
4 July	To Middlesex War Hospital, Napsbury, St Albans.
4 October	Discharged; returns to 19 Barton St, Gloucester. Pension of 12 shillings a week (not a full pension because illness 'aggravated but not caused by' the war). Friends alarmed by his behaviour.
October	Munitions work until Victory day.
11 November	Armistice.
December	Stays in Cornwall with Mrs Voynich.
1919	
January	Back to the R.C.M.; taught by Vaughan Williams. Digs in Kensington. *Severn and Somme* reprinting.
3 March	Margaret Hunt dies. Gurney in Gloucester.
22 April	Farm work at Dryhill Farm, Shurdington.
May	*War's Embers* published.
10 May	Death of his father.
19 May	Living in St John's Wood.
September	To High Wycombe. Begins to stay with Chapmans. Organist at Christ Church.
October/November	Meets Shanks, Hodgson, Monro, Turner.
8 November	Visits Masefield.
1920	
February	Walk from High Wycombe to Oxford and on to Dryhill Farm.
May	Tries to set up in cottage at Cold Slad, Dryhill.
October	In London again, in lodgings in Earls Court. Meets Blunden and W.W.Gibson.
6 November	Gets Government grant of £120 a year from 25 September.

1921

6 February	Meets de la Mare.
April	Staying with aunt at 1 Westfield Terrace, Gloucester. Many unsuccessful attempts to get verse and music published. Formally leaves R.C.M.
July	Working in Cold Storage depot.
December	In contact with Edward Marsh. Playing piano at cinema in Plumstead.

1922

January	Playing piano at cinema in Bude.
May	Book of 80 poems sent to Sidgwick and Jackson; Gurney advised to correct and select.
3 July	Begins job at Tax Office in Gloucester; holds it for 12 weeks.
September	Committed to Barnwood House, private asylum in Gloucester. Pension raised to £2 per week.
8 November	Breaks out of Barnwood and is brought back.
21 December	Transferred to City of London Mental Hospital, Dartford, Kent, under Dr Steen.

1923

6 January	Runs away making for Vaughan Williams's house. Returned to Dartford.
	Ludlow and Teme (Carnegie Collection of British Music).

1926 — *The Western Playland (and of sorrow)* (Carnegie Collection of British Music).

1937

26 December	Death from pulmonary tuberculosis.
31 December	Burial at Twigworth.

1938

January	Gurney symposium in *Music and Letters*, vol XIX, number 1.
	A First Volume of Ten Songs.
	A Second Volume of Ten Songs.

1952 — *A Third Volume of Ten Songs*

1954 — *Poems of Ivor Gurney* ed. Edmund Blunden.

1959 — *A Fourth Volume of Ten Songs*.

1973 — *Poems of Ivor Gurney* with introduction by Edmund Blunden and bibliographical note by Leonard Clark.

1978 — *The Ordeal of Ivor Gurney* by Michael Hurd.

1980	*A Fifth Volume of Ten Songs* ed. Michael Hurd.
1982	*Collected Poems of Ivor Gurney* ed. P.J.Kavanagh.
1983	*Ivor Gurney: War Letters* ed. R.K.R.Thornton.
1990	*Ivor Gurney: Selected Poems* ed. P.J.Kavanagh.

BIOGRAPHIES

Catherine ABERCROMBIE (née Gwatkin)   Wife of Lascelles Abercrombie.

Robert Seymour BRIDGES (1844-1930)   Educated at Eton and Corpus Christi, where he graduated in 1867. Practised as a doctor until 1882, but after that dedicated himself to a variety of literary, artistic and musical projects, which included the editing of the poetry of his friend Gerard Manley Hopkins. His first volume of poetry was published in 1873; his *Poetical Works* appeared in 1912. His anthology *The Spirit of Man* (1916) was very influential. Appointed Poet Laureate in 1913.

Edmund Charles BLUNDEN (1896-1974)   Served in the Royal Sussex Regiment; became assistant editor of *The Athenaeum* until 1922. Taught in Tokyo and was Professor of English in Hong Kong from 1953 and Professor of Poetry at Oxford in 1966. Published *The Waggoner and Other Poems* (1920), *The Shepherd and Other Poems of Peace and War* (1922), *Undertones of War* (1928), *Collected Poems* (1930). Edited Gurney's poems in 1954.

Edward CHAPMAN was in 1913 Chief Clerk to the Goods Manager at Paddington Station. He and his wife Matilda (the Countess Tilda) welcomed Gurney to their house (St Michael's, Castle Hill, High Wycombe) when he became organist at Christ Church where Edward Chapman was Churchwarden. There were four children: Catherine (Kitty, b.1897), Winifred (Winnie), Arthur, and Marjorie (Micky, b.1904). See *Stars in a Dark Night* (1986) by Anthony Boden.

William Henry DAVIES (1871-1940)   Born at Newport, he became a tramp and went to America, taking odd jobs and travelling by 'train jumping'. While doing this, he slipped and his right foot was cut off. He returned to England, began writing, was befriended by other writers and became famous with *The Autobiography of a Super-Tramp* (1908). He wrote many books of verse, including *Songs of Joy* (1911). His *Collected Poems* came out in 1943.

Walter DE LA MARE (1873-1956)   Began his career as a clerk in the Anglo-American Oil company. Granted a Civil List Pension in 1908, he devoted his time to writing. Gurney would have known particularly *The Listeners* (1912) and *Peacock Pie* (1913). *Collected Poems* was published in 1942.

James Louis GARVIN (1868-1947)   Editor of the *Pall Mall Gazette* from 1912-1915 and of the *Observer* from 1908-1942. He sought for a resolute national war policy and is often a sounding board for Gurney's opinions.

John Wilton HAINES (1876-1960)   A solicitor with the firm of Haines and Sumner. His interests in poetry, collecting first editions and in botany put him in touch with a number of Georgian poets, and he often formed a stable point of reference to whom poets like Frost, Thomas, Gibson, Abercrombie, Kerr, Harvey and Gurney could refer. He published *Poems* with Selwyn and Blount in 1921. His son Robin became Trustee of the Ivor Gurney Estate.

Frederick William HARVEY (1888-1957)   Early friend and poetic example for Gurney, he was born at Murrell's End, Hartpury, and grew up at The Redlands, Minsterworth. He went to school at Rossall, trained as a solicitor, and enlisted in 1914 in the 5th Gloucesters. *A Gloucestershire Lad at Home and Abroad* (1916) was written in the trenches. He won the D.C.M. after an encounter with the enemy in No Man's Land, was commissioned, captured, and attempted to escape. *Gloucestershire Friends: Poems from a German Prison Camp* (1917) reaffirmed his commitment to his native county which marks his life and work. His most famous poem is the title poem of *Ducks, and other verses* (1919). Other collections of verse include *Farewell* (1921), *September* (1925) and a selection *Gloucestershire* (1947). See Anthony Boden's biography *F.W.Harvey: Soldier, Poet* (1988).
   Peter HARVEY and Edith HARVEY were cousins.

Herbert Norman HOWELLS (1892-1983)   Articled pupil to A.H.Brewer of Gloucester Cathedral, he won a scholarship to the Royal College of Music, where his teachers were Stanford and Charles Wood. His Mass was performed in 1912 in Westminster Cathedral, and his first Piano Concerto in 1913 at Queen's Hall. His first appointment as sub-organist at Salisbury Cathedral was cut short by serious ill health, but he survived to teach composition at the R.C.M. from 1920 until well into the '70s. He succeeded Holst as director of Music at St Paul's Girls' School (1936-62) and was King Edward VII Professor of Music at London University. His *Hymnus Paradisi* is considered his masterpiece. See C.Palmer's *Herbert Howells: a Study* (1978).

Maurice JACOBSON (1896-1976)   Pianist, composer and publisher. Composition scholar at the R.C.M. in 1916, interrupted by military service and resumed 1919-1922. Became director of Curwen's music publishers.

Sir Edward Howard MARSH (1872-1953)   With a small inheritance Marsh was able to collect pictures, to publish poetry and to help needy talent. He was private secretary to Winston Churchill for 23 years and was thus at the centre of the cultural and political scene of London. His association with Rupert Brooke, and his founding and editing of *Georgian Poetry* make him of great interest to Gurney. See Christopher Hassall's *Edward Marsh, Patron of the Arts* (1959).

Sir Charles Hubert Hastings PARRY (1848-1918) English composer in many forms including songs, church and choral music. Joined the staff of the Royal College of Music when it opened in 1883 and become director in 1894. Professor at Oxford from 1900 (resigned 1908) but stayed at R.C.M. all his life.

Marion Margaret SCOTT (1877-1953) Attended R.C.M. 1896-1904, being taught violin by Arbos. She remained closely associated with the College, helping to found the R.C.M. Union in 1906, editing the *R.C.M. Magazine* 1936-44, and being awarded an honorary A.R.C.M. shortly before her death. She was a founder of the Society of Women Musicians in 1911 and its President from 1915-1916. She published *Violin Verses* in 1905, wrote music criticism, led her own string quartet, organised concerts, and was for a time leader of Morley College Orchestra under Gustav Holst's direction. She wrote a book on Beethoven and many articles on Haydn, though she never completed her projected book on the latter. See Herbert Howells' 'Marion Margaret Scott' in *Music and Letters*, XXXV, p.134 and Kathleen Dale's 'Memories of Marion Scott', *ibid*, p.236.

Sydney Charles SCOTT (1850-1926) is her father. He was a prominent member of the Law Society and legal adviser to the Herbert Spencer Trustees from 1903. Stella is his other daughter.

Sydney Gordon SHIMMIN (1891-1968) Attended R.C.M. 1910-1915, when he left to join up. Served in R.A.M.C. Taught by Stanford, Sharpe and Walford Davies. Taught at Cheltenham Ladies College 1921-1958. Founder conductor of the Cheltenham Bach Choir in 1946. Honorary A.R.C.M.

Sir Charles Villiers STANFORD (1852-1924) Joined the R.C.M. from its opening in 1883 as professor of composition and orchestral playing. Professor of Music at Cambridge from 1887. Composed in many musical forms. Influential in the late 19th century renaissance of English music particularly in his post as teacher of composition at the R.C.M. Notable for his initial cutting treatment of slovenliness in student composition. Gurney wrote of him in *Music and Letters* V (1924).

Robert Hunter STEEN M.D. (1870-1926) Born in Belfast; Medical superintendent, City of London Mental Hospital at Dartford, 1904-25.

Ralph VAUGHAN WILLIAMS (1872-1958) Born in Gloucestershire and educated at Charterhouse, the R.C.M. and Trinity College Cambridge. Joined the staff of the R.C.M. in 1919. A leading figure in 20th Century English music. See James Day, *Vaughan Williams* (1974).

Ethel Lillian VOYNICH (née BOOLE, 1864-1960) A friend from Gurney's time at the R.C.M. before the war, Mrs Voynich was composer, translator, and novelist. Her music includes songs, and a Cantata in memory of Roger Casement. Her translations include *Chopin's Letters* (1931), *The Humour of Russia* (1895), and Stepniak's pamphlets. Her novels, of which the most often reprinted and translated is *The Gadfly* (1897), also include *Jack Raymond* (1900), *Olive Latham* (1904), *An Interrupted Friendship* (1910), and *Put Off thy Shoes* (1945).

Sir Francis COLCHESTER-WEMYSS (1872-1954) High Sheriff of Gloucestershire 1919-20, Chairman of County Council and Chairman of the Police Committee.

Iolo Aneurin WILLIAMS (1890-1962) Author and journalist, contributing to a variety of journals and newspapers. Published *Poems* (1915) and *New Poems* (1919).

Francis Brett YOUNG (1884-1954) Essayist, short-story writer, novelist and poet. Born in Worcestershire, studied medicine at Birmingham University. His *Five Degrees South* was published in 1917.

A NOTE ON THE TEXT

The originals of Gurney's letters are in a mixture of conditions. Some are neatly written in ink on good white paper, others scribbled in pencil on flimsy yellow paper in the trenches in France. Putting them into print inevitably tidies them up, and so I have not been reluctant to make one or two more tidyings. The introductory matter to letters and the signing off formulae have been standardised in presentation, but not in content. It is sometimes revealing of Gurney's state of mind to see how he changes a typical form of address. Titles of books, newspapers and magazines have been regularised to italic.

I have reproduced Gurney's idiosyncrasies of spelling, for example in his characteristic 'quartett' and varieties of Lloydd George (Welsh seems to have puzzled him), but I have signalled it with [*sic*] only when I thought there would be difficulty. Gurney's French I have left with all its inadequacies to indicate his attempts at it.

I have occasionally closed inverted commas or brackets when Gurney has failed to do so or left it to the end of a page to make his close. The layout on the page sometimes serves for punctuation which it is impossible to reproduce here so I have tried to reflect it as far as possible. Paragraphing in particular is difficult since at times he has only three or four words on a line and begins every sentence on a new line. Where his layout does not make it absolutely clear, I have followed the pattern of the sense.

Letters have been checked where possible against originals, but some of the letters which I have been unable to find have been copied from transcripts made during the writing of *The Ordeal of Ivor Gurney* and kindly supplied by Michael Hurd. These will in due course be deposited in the Gurney Archive.

It has proved impossible for the most part to photograph Gurney's musical annotations satisfactorily. They are often hurried and unclear; but I have transcribed what they seem to indicate complete with potential errors. Anyone wishing to work on the music in any detail should check with the original manuscripts.

At the head of the letters I have indicated how the date has been arrived at with a letter:

O indicates that the information derives from *The Ordeal of Ivor Gurney*;

G indicates that Gurney gives a date;

P indicates that the postmark tells the date (though there are occasions when the letters have been returned to wrong envelopes and this information can be misleading);

E indicates an unspecified editorial note on the manuscript;

S indicates a note by Marion Scott;

W indicates a dating supplied by George Walter, who is working on the chronology of the post war period and the 'Rewards of Wonder' collection;

KT indicates my own conclusion about the date. I am of course responsible for using any of the other information, and its use implies that I agree with it.

The sequence of letters from 234 to 239 shows some of the problems of dating, since I have placed them in a sequence which is slightly at variance with the dates attached. I would be pleased to hear of new evidence for dating which would help to clarify our picture of Gurney's life, but I trust that the main outlines will be clear.

Gurney's France

Ivor Gurney

COLLECTED
LETTERS

1 To Marion Scott   G.46.30.10

Summer 1912 (KT)   15 Barclay Rd, Fulham

Dear Miss Scott

   Thank you very much indeed for the concert ticket, which of course I used,
and which gave me a great deal of enjoyment. Do you know they are doing
the Trio we all have to fag through – Beethoven's String Trio in C mi – next
time? I enjoyed all I heard save the Scherzo and Slow Mov: of the Brahms.
Again, thank you very much. With kind regards

Yours sincerely
Ivor Gurney

2 To Marion Scott   G.46.30.11

Summer 1912 (KT)   15 Barclay Rd, Fulham

Dear Miss Scott

   I shall be delighted to come, especially as it is to be so informal – which
means I suppose, that there is no need to dress; for which and all other mercies
etc. I will do with pleasure what you ask about my music – you shall even be
allowed to handle the M.S.

Yours sincerely
Ivor Gurney

3 To Marion Scott   G.46.30.8

Summer 1912 (KT)   15 Barclay Rd

Dear Miss Scott

   I shall be delighted to come on Thursday, and to bring my Quartett, if it is
finished; which is a consummation devoutly to be wished, but to tell the
truth, the Young Genius does not feel very well and His brain won't move as
He wishes it to. But in any case, there are the first three movements all ready,
and you could have the parts on Thursday if you wished; in any case I will
bring them. Also some songs I should like you to see, done before I came here.
   Today I have been reading for the first time Stevenson's Letters Fourth
Volume. And oh! my delight to find that he himself said that Barrie was a
genius and his superior, and that he did not like *Tess*.[1] Hooray! The babe and
suckling is supported by the old hand. Someday I hope to find an opinion that
Jude the Obscure is worse still, which it is. Grimy nonsense.

1

Well, no more of this.

> With best regards
> Yours very sincerely
> Ivor Gurney

¹ R.L.S.'s letter of December 1892 to Barrie calls him a genius, and a footnote to a letter of November 1892 to Barrie says that R.L.S. did not like *Tess*.

4 *To Marion Scott*   G.46.30.1

3 December 1912 (P)   15 Barclay Road, Fulham

Dear Miss Scott

Thank you so much for the invitation, which I would like to accept, but can't – as Miss Bostock is having a last rehearsal at 6.15 and wants me to go. Certainly the rehearsal will not (if I can help it) be over in time. So the dinner and the sonatas must get on without me as best they can.

I don't think there is anybody I want to ask on Wednesday since Brahms is dead, and one or two more defuncters you may have heard of.

> 'The young man was too proud to make a fuss;
> He never forgot he was a Genius.'

> With kindest regards
> Yours very sincerely
> Ivor Gurney

5 *To Marion Scott*   G.46.30.12

February 1913 (KT)   15 Barclay Rd, Fulham

Dear Miss Scott

Thank you very much for your kind letter. I put off answering it, till I could say – I shall be at College tomorrow, which I shall be. But oh, so sick of everything, and by no means looking forward to work. I will allow anyone to say anything against my Scherzo, my slow Movement even, which shows to what depths I have descended.

But that should go when I get back my *Path to Rome*¹ again, and walked again from Putney Bridge to Hammersmith.

I hope people have been turning up to the Society's meeting better? I will make one of that happy throng next time.²

Did you hear Vaughan Williams' *Sea Symphony*?³ I crawled out of bed to hear it, and afterwards went back for three days more – but it was worth it. A Third is Nonsense, but the other two thirds simply great. Runciman says it is the finest work of that school he has seen. Well, well, this prattle must end.

So Good bye

Yours very sincerely

Ivor Gurney

P.S. On second thoughts, perhaps my V.S. *won't* be better than the Brahms. But who knows what the third thoughts may be?

---

[1] *The Path to Rome* (1902) by Hilaire Belloc was a favourite book of Gurney's.

[2] i.e. the Society of Women Musicians.

[3] First London performance of the *Sea Symphony* was in February 1913. See *Ordeal*, pp.34-5.

6 *To Marion Scott*   G.46.30.9

Summer 1913 (KT)   15 Barclay Rd, Fulham

Dear Miss Scott

Thus it turns out – My brain, heart, nerves. and physique are certified sound, but that I am overworked and quite run down. This after telling me I am quite able to work, and setting me to stare at blank paper till I was sick at heart!

Well, this six weeks of almost complete solitary confinement is over, and there is two months of abstention from music before me.

I'm glad

I've got to hate it.

Music, that is.

Please give my kindest regards to Shimmin, and to your people, and take them yourself.

Yours very sincerely

Ivor Gurney.

P.S. Sir Hubert, of course, was a darling.

I am *not quite* sure of the address, so send it to the College. I wrote a letter yesterday, which, if the address is incorrect, you will not receive.

7 *To Marion Scott*   Transcript G.53.57, *Ordeal*, p.44

May 1913 (O)   Lock House, Framilode on Severn, Stonehouse, Glos:

Dear Miss Scott

Please excuse pencil. I am (if I may say so) in bed a-writing this.

I am very sorry to hear of the rapacious microbe, and the spoilt holiday, and also of the dreadful indignity and pottiness of it all. Me also behold. A very little work did for me. After four days, I went to Dr Harper,[1] who gave me sealed orders for Homeward Bound (What writing!)

I have been here a week. And oh! what a difference. And oh! Framilode on good behaviour! What you want is sailing, I am sure. And if you came here I would give it you. Could you manage it? You and your sister in distress? As for cost – Bridgwater is not more than 50 miles I should think, and (but I speak personally) at least one lodger here pays but 12/6 a week! But lady friends of mine stay comfortable in a dear little cottage for 18/6 each. I don't suppose you'll come, *but why stay in Bridgewater*? Oh, I have a promise to go to Swansea in a coaster, perhaps Cork too! Come to Framilode, Fretherne, Elmore, Arlingham Saul! Framilode on the map is just where the Severn does this sort of antic

Yours v: sinc:
Ivor Gurney

[1] Gurney's doctor. In December 1922 Gurney wrote from Barnwood House an appeal to Dr Harper of Threadneedle Street, Piccadilly. See below.

8 *To F.W.Harvey*   G.61.394

Early June 1913 (KT)   15 Barclay Rd

Willy dear,

I was sorry not to have seen you before you left – the more so because partly through *Eyewitness* and the weather and a dry-up of thought, I had a most terrific attack of the Blues. However they are gone now.

Thank you very much for the Pome, which was just what I wanted; it was set the day after I got it, and the result is excellent for its purpose I think. Now what is Sonny's official name? I can't write to 'Sonny', can I? On Tuesday, I was taken to the Court Theatre [1] by a male and female fairy godmother, if so I may express myself, and saw *The Playboy of the Western World* – which contains the most beautiful love-passages in Literature. I have also read *Tess*, and agree with Bennett that it is in spite of the scene on Stonehenge and the death of Tess' child, a decadence from the others. Alec is not credible, neither is Clare; coincidence is wrested rather; it is in fact a flagrant piece of special pleading. But oh, Tess herself! Occasionally the characters talk like handbooks and irritating staid handbooks at that. Is there anything finer anywhere than Hardy's great scenes? Buck up, Willy my boy, let us have that great elver-fishing scene. You'll have to write short stories first though. In another three weeks I shall be at home, and then I'll give you summat to talk about. Priding Point to Bollo Pool, a Souwester, and a strong ebb tide, and a blue sky, and me taking risks in pure glory of soul and joy of heart and yelling and quoting and singing and hauling at the sheet with my foot brace [sic] against the gunwale, and breaking my arm with holding the tiller.

      O that will be
      Glory for me.

I do hope you get through your exam this time. It is bad enough to go in at all, but to fail at it....! Wow! To try at it again.....Woow! To....
Nunno! Notso!

The Irish Sea.

      The after glow slid out of Heaven,
      Heavily arched the vault above,
      Then round my bows, and in my gleaming
      Wake, dim presences 'gan to move.

      My boat sailed softly all the night,
      Through wraiths and shapes of mystery,
      But dawn brought once again to sight
      The friendly and familiar sea.

A Pome, refused by the *Eyewitness*[2] which should not be, as its author is a great admirer of Hilaire Belloc, and takes in the *Eyewitness* every week now. I have just got the Drinking Song to my satisfaction. How is your mother, the embodiment of dignity and maternal sweetness, to visualise a little. How's Eric, and the Motor-bike Merchant, and the young Varmin, also the young Lidy? I wish I were in the bosom of such a family at such a time and place. (Likewise the Aunt). But oooh. Framilode. One morning I will sail through Bollo Pool up to Minsterworth – an adventure, by Thunder.

    Ah, well, Willy, these be comforting things to hold in memory and prospect. I hope to share many such with you.

    Now a nice short story.....
Neglect not the toilsome sonnet.
Farewell.

Yours
Ivor Gurney

[1] The Abbey Theatre production of the *Playboy* opened at the Court on 2 June 1913.
[2] *The Eye Witness* was edited by Belloc and subsequently by Cecil Chesterton.

June 1913 (KT)   15 Barclay Road, Fulham

Dear Miss Scott

It has been borne in upon me (as the Dissenters say) that the letter I wrote you went to 192 or 193 or thereabouts; I believe I think I remember writing such an address – if so you will have wondered not to have heard from me. Well, I had a pretty bad time of it for the first 6 weeks, and then an increasingly better time of it; and I am still on the mend, thanks be to Goodness. And as for Framilode, who could do justice to it? I will simply say that from a small hill not a mile away from where I stayed (or 'stopped', as they say there) and this hill, lovely in itself, though tiny, and probably not 200 feet high, gives one a view of the Forest of Dean Hills on the West, the whole broad Severn on the S.W. Gloucestershire to the Southern Border on the S. And the whole line of Cotswolds on the S.S.E. and E. Likewise the Malverns on the North! Oh, what a place! Blue river and golden sand, and blue black hills – In fine weather, of course.

London is worse than ever to bear after that. Still, let us hope the Militants will blow it up soon.[1]

I hope everything has been going well with you all, and that I shall see you soon. But please don't expect any immortal imaginings from me yet. I am a pricked bladder still. So that Strauss may lie quiet for a while.

Yours very sincerely
Ivor Gurney

[1] Militants are Suffragettes.

17 August 1913 (KT)   19 Barton St, Gloster

Dear Willy

I am relieved to hear from Downing that the operation is some time in the past, and that you must be, or ought to be well on the way to health now.

I shall be very glad to see you again. You and M.H.[1] are in different ways my confidants, on whom it does me good to let leak all my bilge and waste water; or the chimneys through which I love to vent the smoke I cannot consume.

Did I tell you that Haines had seen Abercrombie? Who asked Haines whether he knew one named Harvey, who showed great promise. What do you think of a piece of blank verse I have wrought out?

The rough hewn rocks that Neptunes hosts defy
And stem the { tower-tall } seas; that granite mass
              { conquering }

The kindly haunt of tern and sailing gull
is set in sullen joy to mere inert
expectancy, blunt valour, 'gainst the boyish
charges and youthful splendour of ocean old.

Have you read *The Dynasts*?[2] No. Well then, quickly must you to't, as Captain Hook might say[3]. The verse is sometimes great, sometimes merely good, sometimes downright grey negation of poetry, but the whole characterisation and some of the scenes are colossally good. There is a tip top song on Trafalgar[4], better than Drakes Drum. Which I have set in my head.

Oh, about my health. A tiny bit stronger perhaps, but digestion very little better.

How long shall you be there? at Thanet? Why I ask is , that if you will be long enough there to make it worth while to send Chesterton's *Victorian Literature* and *The Call of the Homeland*[5] I will. Have you read either *A Gentleman of France* or *A Minister of France*, both by Weyman?[6] Very good both.

Violin Sonata in my head. How's yours?

My tears are near the top, and welly,
Because the devil's in my belly.
Oh, may I find some potent pill
To turn him out, or make *Him* ill.

Let me know about them Bookses.

Yours ever

IBG

[1] Margaret Hunt.

[2] *The Dynasts* (1903-8) by Thomas Hardy.

[3] In his last fight with Peter Pan in chapter 15 of *Peter Pan* (1911) Captain Hook cries despairingly 'To't again'.

[4] At the end of Part First, Act V, scene vii of *The Dynasts* occurs the song beginning 'In the wild October night-time' which is reminiscent of Newbolt's 'Drake's Drum' and which Gurney set in 1913 (see the 8 page manuscript at G.31.8.5).

[5] *The Victorian Age in Literature* by G.K.Chesterton was published in 1912. *The Call of the Homeland* (1907) is a collection of English verse, selected and arranged by Robert Pickett Scotts and Kath.T. Wallas.

[6] Stanley John Weyman (1855-1928) published *A Gentleman of France* in 1893 and *From the Memoirs of a Minister of France* in 1895.

11 *To F.W.Harvey*   G.61.389.a

17 August 1913 (P)   19 Barton St, Gloucester

Harvey, my dear chap

You don't know what Portway was today – you don't know! I could only sing for joy, and cry in my heart with pure happiness. Great black shadows, white violets, intensely blue sky, and a sun like wine to the soul.

Damn London!

I have found that Smith's have *On Something*[1] second hand – for 2/6; at any of their depots. With the money you'll save – get *Mrs Warren's Profession* by Shaw[2], paper cover 1/-. It – is – tremendous, not so much as a play, but as an eye-opener. Good God! is all you'll say when you finish it.

Well, 'oping to 'ave the *h*onour to see you soon.

I remain,

Sir,

Your humble, obedient, and respectful servant

Ivor Gurney

[1] Hilaire Belloc (1910).
[2] One of Shaw's *Plays Unpleasant* (1898), frequently reprinted.

---

12 *To Marion Scott* G.41.3

31 August 1913 (O) 19 Barton St, Gloucester

Dear Miss Scott

I am sorry not to have answered before to such a nice letter, but sorrow expressed let me proceed to a nicer one. How does Westbourne Terrace taste after Southwold? Does the stink of petrol compensate for the sea scents and winy air of the East Coast? I wot not. Shimmin and I are to go there on the 15th,[1] so I can check your answer carefully in the light of experience. I really am much better than I was, although the trail of the dyspeptic serpent is over me still. (Do you know, reading the Life of Beethoven, even Nohl's[2], does not reconcile one to indigestion?)

I hope the measle microbes have long ago been conquered by the phagocytes and lie bound in some gloomy cave of furthest remoteness. Also that your eyes may have been in a fine frenzy rolling[3] lately, in the throes of composition and the spurring of Pegasus.

Could you possibly let me have a look at Walford Davies' Violin Sonatas[4] next term, and early? I have fell designs on a V.S. and the pleasant consciousness of superiority which those Sonatas would probably give me, might be in the highest degree valuable. Observe – I do not ask it as a personal favour, but in the Service of Art, and to the special Glory of English music.

I have actually condescended to read a lady-novelist. Mrs Voynich. *An Interrupted Friendship* is without form and void[5] but not uninteresting, partly from the fact that one does not know who the hero is for a long time, and it amuses one to guess. But the *Gadfly*! Dr Johnson would not believe me, but I take my bible oath, I read it very carefully up to the capture of Felix, and read the rest in 15 minutes. Why ever did she lose grip in that way? Why did – – ? Why did – –? What made – – – ? Would – – – – ? It is the kind of thing one

8

would write in cold grey dawns after a substantial breakfast of cold beef steak pie and porter. But it really does strike me as an awfully fine book, in spite of the fact of the characters being non-attractive and a little puzzling.

Belloc, you will joy to hear, is writing a life of Napoleon which explains his journeys over half Europe.[6] Did you know there was a Scott on the Victory? Was he a forbear or relation of any kind?

Have you seen Saint-Saens' new work? If not, forbear; there is no fool like an old fool. It should be entitled 'Reminiscences of the Old Apprentices – Mendlessohn [sic] and Gounod' dedicated by the composer to the memory of the designer of the Albert Memorial.

I hope the Women Musicians will be more tractable this season. Likewise that everybody at 92 (is it) Westbourne Terrace is well.

Yours very sincerely
Ivor Gurney

[1] See next letter about the visit to Southwold.
[2] Karl Friedrich Ludwig Nohl (1831-1885) wrote a life of Beethoven which was translated into English by John J. Lalor in 1884.
[3] 'The poet's eye, in a fine frenzy rolling'; Gurney obviously knows Theseus' speech on 'The lunatic, the lover, and the poet' (*A Midsummer Night's Dream*, IV, i) whose perceptions have some bearing on him.
[4] Sir (Henry) Walford Davies (1869-1941) became a well-known composer, organiser of musical events, judge, and broadcaster. He was a former R.C.M. scholar, pupil of Parry, teacher of counterpoint at the R.C.M. 1895-1903 and superintendent of the choir training class 1910-16.
[5] Ethel Lilian Voynich (nee Boole, 1864-1960) published *The Gadfly* in 1897 and *An Interrupted Friendship* in 1910. Gurney's criticism quotes Genesis, I, 1.
[6] Belloc's *Napoleon* appeared in 1932.

---

13 To Marion Scott   G.46.30.14 and TS copy G.53.56

25 September 1913 (E)[1]   (Just about to quit) Southwold

Dear Miss Scott

Thank you very much. I should like to come on Friday; and I won't bother about evening dress; and I would like to hear the one or two things; and perhaps to show you a thing about Trafalgar.[2].

Yours very sincerely
Ivor Gurney

[1] On G.53.56 is the TS note: 'The envelope of this letter is postmarked 'St John's Wood N.W. 12.15 AM 25 SEP 13' The two Misses Levetus had spent the summer at Southwold and had invited Ivor Gurney and Sydney Shimmin to stay with them.'
[2] The 'Trafalgar' song mentioned in letter 10.

Early 1914 (KT)   15 Barclay Road, Fulham, S.W

Dear Willy

It's going, Willy. It's going. Gradually the cloud passes, and Beauty is a present thing, not merely an abstraction poets feign to honour.

Willy, Willy. I have done 5 of the most delightful and beautiful songs you ever cast your beaming eyes upon. They are all Elizabethan – the words – and blister my kidneys, bisurate my magnesia if the music is not as English, as joyful, as tender as any lyric of all that noble host. Technique all right, and as to word setting – models. 'Orpheus', 'Tears', 'Under the Greenwood Tree', 'Sleep' and 'Spring'. How did such an undigested clod as I make them? That, Willy, I cannot say. But there they are – 'Five Songs' for Mezzo Soprano – 2 flutes, 2 clarinets, a harp and two bassoons.

                    by Ivor Gurney. A.R.C.O.[1]

Yes, Willy, I got through that exam, and meningite my cerebralis if I didn't get Second Prize!

Well, well, a truce to my affairs. How do you get on? Have you written much? Doesnt not [*sic*] this sacred hunger for Spring nourish that fire in you? If it does not yet, get, as I have just got, Davies *Farewell to Poesy* [2] *Foliage* (his latest book) and *Songs of Joy* – the finest lyric poetry in English. God bless the day when Haines recommended that last book to the Gloucester library.[3] What a Treasury of divine simplicity!

Willy, dear, your photograph is on the piano not far from me as I write in bed. Have your confounded family given to it their august approval yet?

How does the daily round, the common task go? More slippily than formerly I hope.

Someone has donated me 25 golden yellowboys. Teewentyfive quid! And the bloody indigestion is slowly quitting! 3 hours writing today!! Dawn of hope!!! May be well by Midsummer!!!! Do Mullers Exercises.[4] Please do. I have more material for you. A little Irish boy is staying here, and lighting up the whole place for us. He has had a devil of a rough time for two years, and was quiet when he came; but now shows himself to have one of the sweetest souls in human body. Last week he sang me a delicious folksong I had never known before. It will go to Sir Charles tomorrow.

O Willy, to be well! To stroll around Redlands deep in the keen joy of comparing experience and the taste of verse.

Little scrap from *Foliage*
          I heard the voice of the soft brass instruments
          Led by the silver Cornets clear and high. [5]

Noble, is it not?

Do Mullers exercises!

How's Mrs Harvey, Eric, Roy, Bernard, Gladys, and the Aunt?

Spring! Spring!! Spring!!!

Play this on the piano (from 'Spring')

Dont think that your poetic gift will not develop because you have to be at the office most of the day. I do not believe it. There are too many examples to the contrary.

Remember – *Daily Telegraph* on Wed and Fri, and *Academy* every week, and *Bookman* every month.

Yours ever
I.B.G.

[1] Gurney took his A.R.C.O. examination between 17 and 23 January 1914, and would know the result by 24 January. He won the Frank J.Sawyer Prize for second highest marks for tests at the organ (184 took the examination and 20 passed).
[2] W.H.Davies, 1871-1940. *Farewell to Poesy*, A.C.Fifield, London, 1910. *Foliage*, Elkin Mathews, London, 1913. *Songs of Joy*, A.C.Fifield, London, 1911.
[3] This copy is still in Gloucester Library.
[4] *My System: 15 minutes' work a day for health's sake*, translated from the Danish of J.P.Muller (1905 etc).
[5] Lines 40-41 of 'A Strange City'.

15 To J.W.Haines   G.84.8

Spring 1914 (KT)   15 Barclay Road, Fulham, S.W.

My Dear Haines

I daresay you have been wondering why I was so very rude as to make an appointment – miss it and say no word. To which must be said that I had thoroughly tired myself out and spent that and two other mornings in bed. And that as I was out of Gloucester practically the whole after-Christmas time it was only too easy to omit calling; and departure day found me too busy to go. But believe me I was sincerely sorry to miss the walk and talk, even though my bloody-bloody head is thick and my naughty-naughty inside fractious. Harvey spoke of calling to see you but he had only 4 days and couldn't fit it in. But we talked of you and wished for battles of words on the little hill behind his house. But maybe he has written to you. A most interesting book is *Dramatic Portraits* by P.P.Howe.[1] They are exceedingly good criticisms and appreciations of everybody who is everybody now. Barrie. Shaw. St John Hankin. Pinero. Barker and the rest. It is his book on Synge which, so they say, is to remain the standard.

I hope you have gone further than asking about *My System* by Leiutenant

(Lieutenant, I mean) Muller. They – it – are excellent all ways.

When shall I – like you – rejoice once more in the skilful use of words and the joyful movement of the body? When shall I conquer Cranham Heights and hear the Maenads or glory in *Antony and Cleopatra* once again? I would like a letter in token of forgiveness.

Yours very sincerely
Ivor Gurney

How's the Missus and the Kid? Well, I hope?

[1] (1914) by Percival Presland Howe (1886-1944).

16 To Mr Edward Chapman G.45750

9 February 1915 (P)

[*Postcard*]

Private Gurney (5th Gloucester Reserve Battalion) sends you greetings.

17 To F.W.Harvey G.41.1

February 1915 19 Barton St, Gloucester

Dear Willy

Well, here I am, and a soldier, in your own regiment's 2nd reserve – to go to Northampton on Monday for the first Reserve.

I am glad you are pretty well now, a week should put you right; and make you happy. Tonight I have been reading the *Georgian Poetry Book*[1], and it is this that has made me write to you. Our young poets think very much as we, or rather as we shall when body and mind are tranquil. Masefield's feeling of beauty and its meaning strike chords very responsive in ourselves. I found myself remembering old things, old times together as I read 'Biography',[2] and it brought you very near. May 1925 see us both happy and revered by the few who count and know the good when they see it. Meanwhile there is a most bloody and damnable war to go through. Let's hope it'll do the trick for both of us, and make us so strong, so happy, so sure of ourselves, so crowded with fruitful memories of joy that we may be able to live in towns or earn our living at some drudgery and yet create whole and pure joy for others. It is a far cry for me, but who knows what a year may do? And I mean to touch music no more till I must.

The Sea, the Sea will be my home for a while, and the hard friendly life of that wrestle with that most untameable, unknowable element of God. Could we only do it together! Do you read much now, are you (most wisely maybe) letting yourself float on the stream of common consciousness; just living and taking the nearest thing as your present fulfilment? Do you look forward, or do you wear blinkers and cultivate short sight and a narrow perception? This is all rather blithering, but that book made me think of you and our common aims.

And I would give much for a couple of hours teadrinking and smoking with a piano and book-talk; but that's not yet, indeed it may be very far away, worse luck.

Good bye
Yours ever
IBG

[1] The first Georgian anthology, *Georgian Poetry 1911-12*, was published in December 1912.
[2] 'Biography' is John Masefield's only poem in the book.

G.61.392

18 To F.W.Harvey

February 1915

Pte I.B.Gurney, B Company,
2nd 5th Gloucesters, Northampton

Dear Willy

Well, here I am; hard worked and, apparently able to stand about 7 hours a day drill, praise be to God. I think it will be all right. If so, May should see me considerably better and much happier.

Today was a sailing day, and I thought of the day when I should first sight the Plate or Spain or even Ireland from the bow of a three master. And of that further day, when, all difficulties being removed, health and technique and inspiration restored, I should get an appointment on shore. And last, when I should be acknowledged great in Art by those whose judgement I value. Let em all come!

The Army biscuits suit me. Of course they are too hard for my poor teeth, but hot tea and patience helps one past all.

It was an experience worth the writing about, when we recruits stood at ease in the dusk while the 5th Gloucesters crowded around us with cries of welcome and recognition and peered into our faces to make sure of friends. It gave me a thrill such as I have had not for long enough.

I have already changed billet, and the chaps here are very nice indeed. Good men, which is a great point. But in this new democracy almost everyone is jolly, or tries to be.

Kipling's little 6d book on the new Armies[1] is very good. Hast seen it? Goodbye and best luck and health and willing endurance of all.

Yours ever
I.B.G.

[1] *The New Army in Training* by Rudyard Kipling (English edition February 1915) collected together a series of six articles first published in the *Daily Telegraph* in December 1914.

February 1915 (KT)   Pte Gurney, 6 Platoon, B Company,
                                            2nd 5th Glosters, Chelmsford, Essex

Dear Mrs Voynich

Well, here I am; a soldier of the King, and the best thing for me – at present. I feel that nowhere could I be happier than where I am, (except perhaps at sea) so the experiment may be called a success. What the future holds has to be kept out of sight, and indeed that is easily to be done where noone talked of the war until the last few days, and only now because the regiment of which we are the reserve has already been in the trenches and perhaps in action.

They are good sorts, most of these boys; and will surely fight as well as those who have already gone – though there is no word of war; nothing but a gentle grumbling about the rations or the sergeant major.

It is indeed a better way to die; with these men, in such a cause; than the end which seemed near me and was so desirable only just over two years ago. And if I escape; well, there will be memories for old age; not all pleasant, but none so unpleasant as those which would have come had I refused the call.

Now I am tired; but tired with many others. Hungry, but honestly so. And if I *must* grumble there is always a good reason somewhere. The army meat would make Falstaff misanthropic (and reduced [*sic*] his bulk.)

I hope your health is good now. Europe is not now a fit subject for sick people to read about, and if you are not well this must very much depress you. But here's the spring. And Framilode, Minsterworth, Maisemore and the Severn villages must be full of flowers and peace.

Your little garden must look well under these skies of the last week or so. Did you go to this three Bs festival? They did some great stuff.

I was glad to see that Verbruggen had taken liberties with the scoring of the Choral Symphony.[1] Have you read *The Undying Past* by Sudermann[2]. It struck me very much indeed, and I doubt whether any of our young men could touch it. It is German – very much so – everything so intense and volcanic and half-mad, except Hertha.

(This letter has been left more than a week and shall go now for fear it should be left for ever.)

Goodbye and best wishes
yours very sincerely
Ivor Gurney

[1] Beethoven
[2] *The Undying Past* (1906) is Beatrice Marshall's translation of *Es war* by Hermann Sudermann (1857-1928).

February 1915 (KT)   Pte I B Gurney, B Company,
2nd 5th Glosters, Northampton

My Dear Chapmen

Well, life is distinctly harder here than at Gloucester. 1st parade 7-7.45 Physical Drill. 2nd, 9-12.45 Drill 2-4.30 Drill Hard work too, but I hang on and hope for the best. I think I shall come through. If it tires me, it tires the other recruits also and so I don't care.

I was going to send my billet address, but that is forbidden, and besides I did not like my first billet and have now changed it. You may expect an army biscuit by post soon. Personally I rather like them, and though they are terrifically hard, hot tea alters that.

I hope everbody is well and out of bed, and – oh yes! did Arthur get his Sherlock Holmes, and has he liked them? I could not find the one supposed to be left at home.

How is the ping pong, and the hockey, and Moses and all? My thoughts go back to High Wycombe, and the ping pong tournaments 'and all' with pleasure, and the conviction that I should not be as well now if it were not for that.

I think there is no danger of my breaking down, and a large prospect of my becoming much better, thank the Lord, and paid a bob a day for it, too!

The Chaps at my billet (3) are very nice and we ought to have some good evenings together. How is Mr Ketchlee? Tell him to advertise for the Lost Tribes in the Agony column of the *Times*. If the Germans answer it, then of course his theory is wrong.

Goodbye

Your affectionate friend
Ivor Gurney

9 March 1915 (P)   Pte Ivor Gurney, 6 Platoon, B Company,
2nd 5th Glosters, Northampton

My Dear Chapmen

I should have replied to that P.C. but never got it. Some of my things have gone astray to a man in this Company named J. Gurney, and he forgot to let me have it. I have not yet thanked you for the writing case – which is charming, nor the pipe lighter, which is very useful on a march; especially in a wind.

I hope the family is all right now and jolly and revelling in ping pong tournaments galore. I am afraid you will not see me this side of the war. Leave is very difficult to get, and as I was such a short time at home it must be spent there; if I get any at all. Tomorrow the foreign service men do their firing; those who pass the tests may be at the front any time soon. Our first 5th (of which we are the reserve) may go at any time, and reserves are not kept waiting long in *this* war.

Our rifles are of Japanese make, but some others are to be served out for firing – the Lee-Enfield type.

No, I am not ill. Indeed they tell me I look much better; and indeed, I must be pretty strong for a neurastheniac. Yesterday I was on from 8.15 – 12.15, 3 – 5.30, 7.15 – 10 and then we had an alarm and turned out at 11 not to get back till 2.15.

The Ordinary day is

      6.45 – 7.30
      8.45 – 12.30
      2.00 – 4.30

This I do, and never am very tired, though during last night's alarm I marched in a sort of dream, but this fatigue was healthy and not nervous exhaustion. The food has been wretched, but now is better. Half my money has gone on extra food, chiefly meat, a substance considered in the Army to be composed entirely of fat bone and gristle. I buy bully beef when it becomes too annoying. We may leave here for Chelmsford any day; and from Chelmsford perhaps – who knows? – to the Dardanelles. There are rumours ...

Well, this is all about myself, but the details about army life are from the inside, and, chiefly, about the inside. I do not at all forget you – Pa and Ma, Kitty, Winnie, Arthur and the exuberant Mickie. Not by no means. But rifles, boots, buttons, need cleaning; coats need rolling, clothes brushing; and there are night operations, street pickets, fire pickets, and guards to be done.

May you all be happy and healthy and wealthy and wise – more so every day. Good-bye to all of you. Easter is near; and after then, I am no more organist of Christ Church – my official tie to High Wycombe will be gone, and there will be left that unofficial one of being your friend.

Yours affectionately
Ivor

(*On back of envelope:*) Would you like a hay band or a straw[1] – ? I've finished with mine.

---

[1] Country men unfamiliar with the 'left, right' of marching orders were reputedly given a hay band to tie round one leg and a straw band for the other. The drill sergeant could then call out 'hay foot, straw foot' instead of right and left.

8 April 1915 (P)   Pte I B Gurney, 6 Platoon, B
                                          Company, 2nd 5th Glosters, Chelmsford

Dear Howells

Well, if you and Miss Higgs could make out 'I Praise the tender flower' to
C H H P's satisfaction, you are very deserving of praise – I did not mean that
to be sung; there were corners to be rounded off, too. But still, if 'Edward'[1]
went well, I am content.

What had you done for the exam? Anything besides your suite? And are
you quite well now, and able to let fly with the nimble pen? And how is
Benjamin[2]?

As to whether I like soldiering. I am convinced that had I stuck to music,
complete health would have been a very long job. This life will greatly help.
Secondly, supposing I had not joined, and never attained my high aim in music
– I could not have forgiven myself. *Thirdly*, that if I get shot, it won't matter
to me what my possibilities (with health) might or might not be. *4thly*. That
the life, though hard, and the food scant and coarse, makes me as happy as I
can be made without a yacht and money. It is hard, and always I am tired, but
struggle through in a very much happier frame of mind than that I have had
for some time – probably 4 years. There's your answer, and longer than you
wanted I daresay.

As to chances of fighting – our first battallion is already in France. We fill
up gaps, and generally stop up holes in it. So that May or June may see us, and
myself, in the fighting line. The chaps are rough, but as a general thing good
inside. And never a word do they say about wanting to fight, or being in the
trenches. Their attitude is – We don't want to fight, but someone must do it
– the best attitude of all.

Will Harvey is already in France with the 1st 5th Glosters. Now I suppose
you are in Glostershire; and soon will see apple blossom and the pear trees
'praising God with sweetest looks'[3]. Sometimes my heart aches for Framilode,
and my little leaky boat; my gun and the ever changing Severn, now so full in
Flood. And through my thoughts when indigestion has lessened and left my
brain clearer, there runs the symphonic greatness of the 'Wedge' Prelude and
Fugue.[4] Curious is it not?

Work lately has been

    6.45 – 7.30
    8.45 – 12.45
    2.0 – 4.30

and occasionally night operations. One of which was 11 – 2.15 pm – am.
There was language! 18 carat, full blooded, above proof, purple verbiage, in
broad Glostershire.

If you can get hold of Masefield's *Philip the King*[5] read it. Besides 'Philip'
there is a poem named 'August' – the best of the war poems.

Well, Good bye and the very best wishes for all happiness.

Yours
I.B.G.

[1] Gurney's settings of Robert Bridges' poem and a ballad.
[2] Arthur Benjamin.
[3] Line 16 of Thomas Hood's poem 'Ruth'.
[4] Bach; called the 'Wedge' from the shape of the notes on the page.
[5] *Philip the King* (Heinemann, 1914). Masefield's 'August 1914' is the poem referred to.

23 To Edward Chapman   G.45750

8 April 1915 (P)

[*Postcard*]

I got your letter yesterday morning. It was such a pity. I should very much have liked to have seen you again – but there is a chance next week. I believe – *believe* mind, that we go to Epping Forest on Friday. I B G

24 To Mrs Matilda Chapman   G.45750

21 April 1915 (P)

[*Postcard*]

Dear Comtesse

Thank you for your nice letter. As for arrangements, they must be hopelessly vague. We are reported to be leaving here either on Sat: or Monday. I heard that the Captain told our platoon so today fairly definitely. If it is true (and I think it is) we return to Chelmsford, another 17 miles! But nothing – nothing is certain, but uncertainty. I B G

25 To Marion Scott   G.41.4

9 May 1915 (P)   Pte Gurney, 6 Platoon, B Company,
                                                2nd 5th Gloucesters, Chelmsford, Essex

Dear Miss Scott

Thank you for your kind letter, and the reminder of College life. It is a happy friendly life there -- at S.Ken – and if it were not for my unworthy body, I should have nothing but pleasurable memories of London. As for me –

18

I am well; in the sense that I am able to hang on in everything they have done as yet, but in the sense of feeling well there is improvement but nothing else. But fatigue from the body brings rest to the soul – not so mental fatigue.

Do you know that the Glosters have the second best roll of battle honours in the British Army? So it is. And though we are a rough lot in some ways, (and the Bosches will discover some of them,) we have no end of a good domestic reputation, so to speak.

The less that is said of our musical taste the better; but in full chestedness and knowledge of ragtime etc we excel. Our Colonel is Bathurst ('Benny') an M.P. Our Captain is Sewell of some note as a cricketer; S.African and Gloucestershire[1]. And our talk is rough, a dialect telling of days in the open air and no books. We do not talk about the war, although we have taken to looking at the casualty lists now our 1st regiment is in the trenches, and our friends are astonishing the fields of Flanders with strange talk.

And so Rupert Brooke is dead[2]; still he has left us a legacy of two sonnets which outshine by far any thing yet written on this upheaval. They are as beautiful as music. They are so beautiful that at last one forgets that the words are there and is taken up into ecstasy just as in music.

'These had seen movement, and heard music; known
Slumber and waking; loved; gone proudly friended;
Felt the quick stir of wonder; sat alone;
Touched flowers and furs and cheeks. All this is ended.[3]

But the *Times Literary Supplement* for March 11 quotes two in full; there you must find them. Galsworthy calls Beethoven's 7th Symphony the most wonderful piece of music in the world; (in the *Patrician*, I think;) and that is not so bad a guess. It holds at any rate the spirit of our armies.

Beethoven, Bach, Mozart, Schubert seem to be left high above war-mark, with folksong and Palestrina and our madrigals. I should think that Brahms chamber music is often insufferable now. But oh, to hear the 'Sea Symphony' again! How is Vaughan Williams? If he goes, and with Rupert Brooke dead, we shall have suffered severely enough on the side of Art.

It is possible that I may get leave this week end, and if so I shall probably come up to College on Monday morning (I must be on first parade (6.30) on Tuesday.) There and then I shall find out what Howells is doing and all the other little etceteras that I want to know.

Poor Concerto – so fine, so strong, so beautiful; when will you be done again?

I will let you know about my visit. It may be from 1 oclock till four on Monday (tomorrow week.)

Yours very sincerely
Ivor Gurney

[1] Lt-Col Hon Allen Benjamin Bathurst, D.L. (1872-1947), M.P. for Cirencester Division of Gloucestershire 1895-1906 and 1910-18. Lt-Col 5th Batt. Gloster Regiment 1908-13 and of 2/5th Batt. 1914-16. Cyril Otto Hudson Sewell was born in Pietermaritsburg,

S.A., in 1874 and died in 1951. He played for Gloucestershire from 1895 to 1919 and was
captain in 1913 and 1914.
[2] Brooke died on 23 April 1915.
[3] 'If I should die' and 'These hearts were woven of human joys and fears' were quoted in a
review of *New Numbers* in the *TLS* for 11 March 1915.

26 To Herbert Howells   G.3.7

14 May 1915 (KT)   19 Barton St, Gloucester

Dear Howells
    I shall not be at College till the afternoon. But hope to see you then – to sit
at your feet; both hearing and asking questions.

I.B.G.

27 To Marion Scott   G.61.28.a

14 May 1915 (KT)   19 Barton St, Gloucester
(on Y.M.C.A. 'On Active Service' paper)

Dear Miss Scott
    I have got leave, and intend to be in London on Monday morning; and at
College from 2 till 4 at least. I hope I shall be able to see you.

Yours very sincerely
Ivor Gurney

28 To Edward Chapman   G.45750

17 May 1915 (P)

[*Telegram*]

Shall be Paddington ladies waiting room from 4.15 – 6.30. Could you come
bring family Winnie anyway reply Paddington Ivor.

16 June 1915 (P) Pte Gurney, B Company, 2nd 5th Glosters,
Chelmsford, Essex

Dear Miss Scott

Thank you for your letter, and the kind things; not to say flattery.

The Library here possesses but one copy of Shakespeare's Historical Plays, and that'is out. But I should guess it to be either from *King John, Henry V*, or *Henry IV*. Certainly it is Shakespeare.

What date is the College at Home? I feel that I should like to come to it, and could probably do so. Tomorrow we march to camp, somewhere near Epping; but your letter would be forwarded at once. Stanford wrote to me a short time ago – very kindly but hieroglyphically. (?)

My health is still slowly improving; and as my mind clears, and as the need for self-expression grows less weak; the thought of leaving all I have to say unsaid, makes me cold. Could I only hand on my gift! Anyway, I have been rejected for second-reinforcements, and Territorial 3rd reinforcements will be late in going. The war however seems like lasting a year, and there is none of the exhilaration of battle in hot weather training. Still, I chose this path, and do not regret it; do not see what else I could have done under the circumstances; and if the Lord God should have the bad taste to delete me

'Deil anither word tae God from a gentleman like me'.

Anyway there's the Elizabethan songs, Edward, The Twa Corbies, the Sea, and Kennst du das Land – two of which seem to be lost and one a sketch.

Masefield is with the Red Cross in France.   John Drinkwaters new book seems to be good. Have you read any of Neil Munro's books? *John Silence, The New Road, Doom Castle*? They are very good, and exciting in the R.L.S. style.[1] What a fine speech was Churchill's, at Dundee. The man has pluck enough. *Land and Water*, Belloc's affair is optimistic but John Buchan thinks it highly probably [*sic*] that there will be another winter campaign – farther east though.[2]

One of the best signs of healthy taste at present is the significant fact that though Rabinadrath [*sic*] Tagore has been knighted, the critics I read did not pretend to be transported by his work – Not so much, indeed, as before the war[3].

Yours very sincerely
Ivor Gurney

[1] Perhaps Drinkwater's *Swords and Ploughshares* (Sidgwick and Jackson, 1915). Neil Munro (pseudonym of Hugh Foulis, 1864-1930) published *John Splendid* (not *Silence*) in 1898, *The New Road* in 1914, and *Doom Castle* in 1901.
[2] Belloc wrote a well-known series of war articles in *Land and Water*, a weekly periodical begun in 1914 to deal exclusively with the war; its circulation was over 100,000.
[3] Rabindranath Tagore won the Nobel Prize for Literature in 1913 and was knighted in 1915, though he surrendered the knighthood in 1919 as a protest against the Amritsar Massacre.

June 1915 (KT)   Pte Gurney, B Company, 2nd 5th Glosters,
                                                        Chelmsford, Essex

Dear Old Winnie

Thank you for your letter, and Dear Comtesse, thank you for the cake which is *good*, and dear Micky, thank you for *your* letter.

I am sorry you poor creatures that there has been such pestilence and famine among you. And so unseasonable a thing as rheumatism; which should go with winter and plum puddings.

I am writing this near Galley wood outside Chelmsford. We are on what is called anti-aircraft picket. That is – we are on the look out for Zeppelins etc. And at this time it should be exciting enough. We get out about 7.00 p.m. and stay till 6 a.m. In fine weather it is very good fun; both sunset and dawn are beautiful, and there is only an hour's guard each.

This will last till next Sunday.

Bayonet practice is over now, and we ought to have more firing soon.

How is Arthur getting on at cricket? Good scores and hat tricks I hope.

We are leaving here soon I believe, for somewhere near Epping perhaps.

Well, Goodbye Winnie dear and I hope the toothache is quite well now, and Daddies rheumatics.

Love to Everybody and no rheumatism or crocking up of any kind.

                                                Yours affectionately
                                                Ivor.

June 1915 (KT)

My Dear Winnie

I wonder how you too are getting on, you poor imp of misery. (This is a letter to a lady.) It is the patriotic duty of every English woman to wear a pack now, and I don't feel disposed to write politely to anyone who doesn't – and 60lbs at least in weight. But blessings on thee, thou art a blithesome thing, God wot. Would that it had been possible to have taught thy nimble forefinger the divine Beethoven, but the Gods willed otherwise. I suppose you are looking forward to Perranporth and to see the great Atlantic rollers in a perpetual siege and attack on our England. My spirit will be with you there, chasing the bunnies or quietly watching the 'sunshot palaces high' and breathing contentment with the common air. This seems to be a frightfully high faluting letter; but you will understand it, and it is such a restful thing, to high-falute. Many of our occupations are 'so low, my dear'. But this morning I sat hidden behind a table, on my beam-ends and had a high old time learning the Morse alphabet and reading the paper. This afternoon, now at this moment, was to be given to us as a time of peace, as we are to be out all night, but They (a malison on them!) could not let us be, and ordained a hut-inspection, and of kits etc. But Private Gurney did espy the orderly corporal in the next hut, and got him outside straightway to listen at the window; whence he is now writing letters in a wood a mile away from camp – even this to his amiable correspondent, Mistress Winifred Chapman, to whom he sends his love and best wishes.

Goodbye

Yours affectionately
Ivor B.

32 *To Arthur Chapman* G.45750

June 1915 (KT)

To the paleface Chief Arthur

Glass-eyes, the player on instruments, sends thee greeting. Prays the Great White Chief for thy welfare and desires to know the state of thy health. Announces that he has 4 or 5 loaded blanks which may arrive at Chief Arthur's wigwam at any moment, should an insurrection headed by Smith, the Rusher By[1] (the henpecked medicine man) or any such washout (keep that dark though. Destroy the missive). But really old man, are you all right now? Body, soul and spirit, and between the cracks?

Here there are no more blizzards, but Spring with the sweetest smiles, and so I hope you are cricketing – on the heath or elsewhere.

But I am sure you stood what you had to pluckily as befits an Englishman. Someday we will hunt together on Keep Hill, and gather many scalps to hang round our umbrellas. Till then, Farewell and Greetings.

Yours affectionately
Ivor

[1] Rev Rushby-Smith, vicar of Christ Church, High Wycombe. Mrs Rushby-Smith was the Choir mistress.

33 *To Mrs Matilda Chapman* G.45750

June 1915 (P) Chelmsford Essex

My Dear Comtesse

I am very sorry, but everything has turned out a failure. On the last two Saturdays I have been inoculated and on guard. And the few hours I hoped for either yesterday or today have not been granted. I should have written before; but camp has been very hard, and when there was any spare time it was spent on the flat of my back. Reveille 5 Breakfast 6.30 Dinner 1.30 Tea 4.30 - 5.0, and on all the time between those hours!

I am sorry not to have written, but always hoped to be able to let you know I was able to get a Saturday pass. Hope you will all enjoy Perran.

Yours affectionately

Ivor

34 *To Winifred Chapman* G.45750

June 1915 (KT)

My Dear Old Winnie

Bless you my child; yours was a nice letter for a war weary son of a gun to get.

I hope you will get your reward at Perran, and play endless exciting games of tennis; and have delightful cool – but not chilly – bathes, generally enjoying yourself as you deserve.

Well, it doesn't look much like seeing you for some ages yet. Before this week 1 man a company per week was *supposed* to go. This week leave is again violently smitten on the head (a frequent occurence with us) and may have succumbed to its injuries.

My fairy god-mother is most frightfully slack. Perhaps she is after the vote or Proportional Representation or summat new-fangled. I am, I hope I may say – a just man, a long-suffering and humble servant; (Don't this sound like Lloyd George) but even fairy god-mothers can get it in the neck. And this particular one has been asking for it for a pretty long time.

When will the days of peace and plenty and beaucoup ping pong once again return? Alack, man knoweth not. Nor young women either, in spite of their growing up, putting their hair up, putting on frills, and fine raiment, and generally startling and upsetting their humble adorers – of whom

I am

(Very affectionately)

one of the wormiest and most enthralled

Ivor

28 June 1915 (P) Pte Gurney, 2nd 5th Glosters,
Wintry Farm Camp, Epping, Essex

Dear Miss Scott

Very sorry, miss, but it couldn't be helped. They left me uncertain up to the last moment, and the leave was not granted, so I heard, simply through the carelessness of an orderly corporal. I hope that everything went off well in spite of the unfortunate hiatus.

Edward Thomas reviewed Brooke's poems in the *Chronicle*, and I got another sonnet out of that -

Now God be thanked that has matched us with this Hour

another very good one. It *is* curious how little great youthful-seeming poetry has been written; and sonnets seem especially fated to be the work of 'solemn whiskered men, pillars of the state'[1].

Well, here we are in camp, and a nice old mix up it is! Whatever is wanted out of the ordinary is at the extreme wrong end of the kit-bag. Everything has to come out, and at last in exasperation one stuffs things of hourly necessity in first, and language flows not wisely but too well[2]. This lengthens the act of cleaning up at least 250%. But this is good for me.

The unmentionable by-products who manage this brigade (there are the Bucks, the Oxford and Bucks and the Glosters here) give us reveillé at 5. Breakfast at 6. Parade at 7. Dinner at 2. Tea somewhere about 4.30 – 5.30. May this iniquity be remember [*sic*] at the last!

And such tea!

At present I am 'on sick' with lumbago, a horrid name. But this came just in time to prevent C.B. for a dirty rifle, which is thus put off, – may it be forgotten!

Land and Water is still very optimistic[3]. My thoughts go onward to the dim time after the war, and the politics in ten years time. Here is Belloc gaining a great following; who is a very strong opponent of the Party System, a Strong Anti-Socialist, and though once a Liberal M.P. with a strong contempt for it. He is certain to show large in public opinion, and there will be many and curious rows and large and generous bewilderment.

A 100 reinforcement went off on Friday to the front, and there was some excitement – 'some' in the American sense. The cheering was immense, overwhelming, cataractic. The only things that can give you an idea of that sound are either elemental sounds like the war of winds and waves or the greatest moment in music – the end of the development in the 1st movement of tbe Choral Symphony. Like the creative word of God.

I have discovered an original essay on Spring! In a book called *Southward Ho* by Holbrook Jackson in Dent's Wayfarer's Library – a good book[4]. There is nowhere to put books here – nowhere! Only in that comic-tragic kit bag, Gott strafe it. A slot machine is what I want, or a valet.

Do you know anything about our people in the Army? What has happened to Benjamin? Warren? And that person Brown whom I disliked so much.[5] What are they doing at rehearsal now? Will there be an Opera?

Please excuse writing and the pencility thereof, but nothing else is possible in camp.

With best wishes
Yours very sincerely
Ivor Gurney

[1] *2 Henry VI* has 'Brave peers of England, pillars of the state'.
[2] 'Of one that lov'd not wisely but too well'; from Othello's final speech.
[3] See letter 28 and note.
[4] *Southward ho! and other essays* (1914).
[5] Fellows at the R.C.M.

36 To the Chapman family   G.45750

29 June 1915 (P)   Pte Gurney, B Company,
                                          2nd 5th Glosters, Wintry Farm
                                                 Camp, Epping, Essex

My Dear Chapmen

We have been here in camp just over a week, and the whole time has been a rush, from 5 o'clock reveille to 9.45 Lights out. The chief thing is attacks and all sorts of company and brigade actions; this is why we have come into camp. The roads are horrid, bristly with shingle and pebbles which raise blisters in record time. For breakfast we have as a rule bacon; for dinner either what they call shackles (stewed meat) or roast meat; for tea, bread, margarine, jam, and 'tea', made in the same dixie as the shackles – very different in every way to the dainty meal held about the same time at St Michael's High Wycombe. No oatcake, no scones; likewise no ping-pong. If you would like to see a camp, one is allowed to bring people in on Sundays, when the camp deletes as much of its grease as possible, ameliorates its language, and relaxes the stern visage of war.

The Bucks, the Oxford and Bucks, the Glosters, the Berks and a few Engineers and RAMC are all here-abouts, and all affable to visitors. Camp open from 3 – 9.

Has Arthur made any great scores lately? And what has Winnie done? Micky I suppose is just as naughty and nice as ever all reared on the bounteous provision prepared by the Comtesse and made possible by the arduous exertions of the Count.

Our first reinforcements have gone – three days ago; and our second are ready to go; and so the Brigade gradually dribbles out to the Front.

Well, goodbye all you dear creatures in Buckinghamshire. Oh, does anyone want an exciting book about Scotland? *The New Road* by Neil Munro would suit.

Goodbye

Your affectionate friend
Ivor Gurney

37 To Herbert Howells   G.3.2

June 1915 (KT)   Pte Gurney, B Company, 2nd 5th Glosters,
                                                      Wintry Farm, Epping, Essex

Dear Howells

It couldn't be managed. One has to make such applications 5 or 6 days before, and so the chance was missed. I hope the estimable A.B. is all right, and not so sick of the Army as we are here; but poor privates may only guess at the riot of extravagance and debauchery which make up the lives of lieutenants and such folk.

At the moment of writing, I am lying precariously on the edge of a pool, watching for signs of khaki over a hedge half a mile away and cursing the army strongly and long. The aim of training troops is to make them as tired as possible without teaching them anything. Take em for a route march, stand em on their heads, muck about with em in any fashion so long as they get tired and sick of soldiering. It is an unintelligent affair for the infantry nowadays. If you do what you are told and have no objection to sudden death, that means a good soldier.

What are you writing now? Let's have another, simpler string quartett or V and P sonata. I would like to hear that bloated monstrosity of a Concerto of yours again though. Glad to see you were publicly recognised as the most deserving pupil. I hope the medal is not too large to roll or bowl to the pawn shop.

My health still improves very slowly, though if it had not been for 5 easy days (for inoculation etc) last week I should have come a cropper. They are mad as hatters here. Reveille at 5. Roll call and rifle inspection at 6. Breakfast at 6.30. Parade at 8.15. March or summat. Dinner 1.30 – 2.30. Bayonet Practice 3.30. Tea 4.30. So the meals come at 6.30, 1.30 about, and 4.30. O Generation of vipers! I joined to cure my belly!! May the Lord play dirty tricks in great abundance on such malapert cock-knaves. Please remember me to C.V.S., C.H.H.P., Mr Waddington, Dr Alcock and Dr Davies; who I suppose will still be splitting hairs while I am splitting cocoanuts[1]. How do the composition-cubs get on? Write me a newsy letter or at least P.C.

Yours etc
IBG.

[1] All R.C.M. staff: Stanford; Parry; Sidney Peine Waddington, teacher of harmony and counterpoint; Walter Galpin Alcock, teacher of the organ; Walford Davies.

9 July 1915 (P)

[*Postcard*]

Letter soon. Why did they take them
or
The drunken recruiting officer.[1]

---

[1] This message is on the reverse of a photograph of a group of untidy recruits, including Gurney. Reproduced in *Stars*, p.35.

---

39 To Mrs Matilda Chapman G.45750

July 1915 (KT) Pte Gurney, 6 Platoon, 2nd 5th Glosters, Epping

My Dear Comtesse

I am sorry that you have had so wretched a time at so unprofitable a game. It is hard lines on one who would like to live life to be cooped up in bed and see the clouds drift and do nothing and be nothing of importance.

Of course I forgive the lecture. It was deserved, though not so much as you think perhaps. The 'nice long evenings' are occasionally filled up by army duties, such as guard, street picket, night operations, fatigue. And last Monday we marched 17 miles, hunted for billets, and at 7.30, when I was about to go in, I was collared for duty and got two hours sleep, and on duty all next day. Besides, unlike yourself I hate writing. That 17 miles was with the pack – that is, about 40 lbs to carry.

We shall be here till Monday week, but whether I can get leave or no is doubtful. Of course I do not mean my 48 hours leave which would be spent in Gloucester – but leave till 12 at night. Not this Saturday anyway, but perhaps next. On Sunday I am on guard. Please thank Micky for her letter. It was just like the dear rascal, and I wish I were back to lose to Arthur and Winifred Emma the champion once again. I wish you all were not so good to me. I like my friends to be willing to give to me in proportion to what myself would give, and you are all too generous in affection and otherwise.

Hoping you are better now, with love to all
I remain

Your affectionate
Ivor Gurney

3 August 1915 (P)   Pte Gurney, B Company, 2nd 5th Glosters,
                                             (tomorrow to be) Chelmsford, Essex

Dear Miss Scott

I am so sorry about the bloodvessel; sufficiently exciting for one who had a
mind in favour of peace and whole organisms. But now it is more or less over
(as I hope) now you may reap some benefit. As how saith the sage – A
headache may seem a poor investment while in full blast, but when it is
slackening is worth a dollar a minute.

J.E.Patterson has written a book around Minehead, perhaps *Fishers of the
Sea*, or no – *Love like the Sea*; which I liked[1]. Perhaps you might. He has
power, but an amateurish trick of underlining his points which is irritating.

Belloc has a passage in one of his Essays; the one called the Views of England
I believe; in which he speaks of the strange and secret enchantment and the
haunted tides of all that Sou Western coast.

You did not at all bore me by your description of the West; if it had been
dull, probably I should have skipped it, but every word was read and enjoyed;
behind it all, the continuing aching current – 'Shall I ever sing it all'? Indeed,
England has been poorly off for musicians, or at least (I believe) for musical
output. Schubert so full of happy memories of orchards, and Mozart so clear in
spirit and expression like a Spring sky, cannot we produce these? The country
that produced the man who could write such a speech as
'Ye elves of hills, brooks, standing lakes and groves'[2]
could produce anything. Our young men must write on a diet largely
composed of Folk Song and Shakespeare.

The Sonnet of R.B. you sent me, I do not like. It seems to me that Rupert
Brooke would not have improved with age, would not have broadened, his
manner has become a mannerism, both in rythm and diction. I do not like it.
This is the kind of work which his older lesser inspiration would have
produced. Great poets, great creators are not much influenced by immediate
events; those must sink in to the very foundations and be absorbed. Rupert
Brooke soaked it in quickly and gave it out with as great ease. For all that we
have very much to be grateful for; but what of 1920? What of the counterpart
to *The Dynasts* which may still lie within another Hardy's brain a hundred
years today?

Thank God we leave camp tomorrow! In it we have suffered all the horrors
of slum life. They have driven us to distraction with parades and unexpected
unnecessary swoops on our (supposedly) free time. Rainy weather was our
only respite, and that on clayey soil how appaling! Shackles and over and
underdone roast. Execrable tea, margarine crying to Heaven and the Sanitary
inspector for deracination. Bread often fit for museums. Bacon virginal –
unspoiled pig. The Canteen was a bright spot, but a bright spot cherished and
administered by swindlers and rogues of nameless birth.

From this we go to billetts – not to grumble; not to grumble, but to make sacrifices before the altar of the Godess of Home, that estimable female who, like all her sex, is not allowed in camp.

What we are to do, what destiny confronts us the Gods themselves may well be to[o] confused to know in all the rumours excursions and alarms which surround those condemned for their sins to dwell in camp.

(This is a queer letter. Once more it is taken up and perhaps may be completed this time.)

What do you say, for an ending, to an original

To the Poet before Battle
Sonnet

Now, Youth, the hour of thy dread passion comes;
Thy lovely things must all be laid away,
And thou, as others, must face the riven day
Unstirred by the tattle and rattle of rolling drums
Or bugles strident cry. When mere noise numbs
The sense of being, the fearsick soul doth sway,
Remember thy great crafts honour, that they may say
Nothing in shame of Poets. Then the crumbs
Of praise the little versemen joyed to take
Shall be forgotten; then they must know we are,
For all our skill in words, equal in might
And strong in mettle, as those we honoured. Make
The name of Poet terrible in just War;
And like a crown of honour upon the fight.

Please criticise this very frankly, and with no eye on Wordsworth's 'September 1802', 'London 1802', 'It is not to be thought of', 'October 1803', 'November 1806', or any such. It is not meant to compete.

Kitchener reviews us on Thursday.

I am in the band – a new one – playing the baryton, a bass cornet arrangement. It is a fine instrument, and three days practice – even to me – are inadequate to do it justice.

Good bye and good-luck

Yours very sincerely
Ivor Gurney

Oh, what do you think of the Ballade to Beelzebub?[3] Barring one line, it is worthy of anyone. It was written by my best friend for the 5th Glosters Magazine, a trench paper. Have I not right to be proud of him? Is it not gorgeously *meaty*?

---

[1] John Edward Patterson (1866-1919) wrote both *Fishers of the Sea* (1908) and *Love Like the Sea* (1911).

[2] From Shakespeare's *The Tempest*, V, i, 33.

[3] The poem is reprinted in Anthony Boden's *F.W.Harvey: Soldier, Poet*, pp. 78-9

c.12 August 1915 (KT) Pte Gurney, B Company, 2nd 5th
Glosters, Chelmsford, Essex

Dear Mrs Voynich

It is long since I meant to answer your charming letter, but an evil time in camp smothered every social feeling I had; now that is over, 'Sweet Piety resumes her reign' and I can write friendly letters with some enjoyment.

I hope you are well, and finding some solace in your duties. You must find it hard to console aliens in England. They probably love England, and now they are aliens indeed. There was a letter in the Northcliffe *Times* not long ago from a lady who would make Bach an alien; a difficult job.

Well, we have practically finished our Training; have been inspected and are to hold ourselves ready to move. There have been rumours of India, but the wording of the announcement makes that very unlikely, though sweet to my mind. If I am to leave earth shortly, a trip to India would make no bad preliminary.

You spoke of the Jewish persecution by the Russians. The English papers are allowed to speak of it now; at least there was a strong condemnation in a book-review in the *Daily News*.

I was delighted to see Bourtseff is released. After all if he had advised assassination of the Tsar it was a pretty severe offence. All's well now I hope. But what torture is Poland subject to now!

The *Times* published a special supplement of War-Poems on Monday.[1] Did you see it? I think Hardy's poem is most likely to survive. It stirs me much more than it first did. On route marches now to occupy my mind, I am learning Wordsworth Sonnetts and the first lines of *Paradise Lost*, for which I can find no praise. It is too colossal. Too Bach-like.

'Him the Almighty Power
'Hurled headlong flaming down the ethereal sky
'In hideous ruin and combustion down
'To adamantine chains and penal fire
'Who durst defy the omnipotent to arms.'[2]

What sort of exultation must have possessed the man while he wrote that!
How like the introduction to Beethoven's 4th Symphony is

'Thou from the first/ wast present
'And with mighty wings outspread
'Dovelike sat brooding on the vast abyss,
'And mad'st it pregnant.'[3]

It is a curious comment on the English character that it takes rain to bring its musical side out. Our company had been all day on the range, and started for the 5 mile march back at 7-oclock – soaked to the skin. It was raining still and the sky gloomy with a sort of dyspeptic meditativeness. Why, we sang ourselves hoarse. A parody has appeared from nowhere; and it goes to the tune of 'Hark my soul it is the Lord'; which increases the joke.

'Sergeant-major, I can't shoot;
Give me back my civvy suit.
Put some shoes upon my feet,
Take me to the Monk's Retreat.' (a Gloucester inn.)

In fine weather they are not so easy to move. The English seem to have a great reserve of strength. I would rather be fighting Germans than English from what I know of both.

Have you read *Harry Richmond* lately? I like the first part of the book immensely, but skipped afterwards – copiously and vigorously. On the whole *Evan Harrington* pleased me more.[4]

War and Peace will hold me always in thrall. But next time I skip the chunks of History, and read about Pierre and Natasha. As for *The Return of the Native*, God seems to have arranged with Hardy to do his cunning-worst. But how rich are the country scenes! and some 'lovers of the Bard' talk about Shakespeare's peasants! May God take the flunkey out of their minds.

I am glad to say that my health goes on improving, but slowly. Still, now I know what neurasthenia *is*; I realise and fight it – a great step. If nothing serious happens to me, I shall have saved myself years by joining the Army. How far health is away now I cannot tell, but still, a long way.

How is Sidney? He has been disgracefully neglected by me, but I will write almost at once, and try and make it up.

Miss Scott I have written to several times – for me. Last time – oh bashfulness and blushes! – I sent her a Sonick, but with no great opinion of it. Wordsworth is too much of the master to read and allow confidence overmuch in oneself.

The Glosters march is good. It is called

We did 9 miles with a 50-60lb pack and after a sleepless night to it anyway.

Is D'Annunzio worth reading, if I could collar a book of his? He speaks well anyhow.

I hope the little lakelet and the trees – fruit- and aristocratic- are all doing well. You have done better than Belloc's boast. 'Let me get but 5 miles from a railway, and I will get as much peace as will fill a nosebag.'

With all best wishes

I remain

Yours very sincerely

Ivor Gurney.

[1] The sixteen page supplement of Monday 9 August 1915 contains on p.3 Hardy's 'Song of the Soldiers' ('Men Who March Away').

[2] *Paradise Lost*, Book 1, lines 44-49 omitting line 47 and with inaccuracies in the prepositions.

[3] Ibid, lines 19-22.

[4] George Meredith wrote both *The Adventures of Harry Richmond* (1871) and *Evan Harrington* (1861).

---

42 *To Winifred Chapman* G.45750

August 1915 (KT) Pte Gurney, B Company 2nd 5th Glosters, Chelmsford, Essex

My Dear Winifreda

Thank you for the P.C. and your letter which I never replied, miserable sinner that I am! Bless you my child for your friendship and thoughts of me. Now they have put me in our new brass band – on second-hand instruments – I shall have more time and in all probability become fat and lazy. ('Fat and well-liking' the Psalmist says).[1]

I hope all you dear creatures are happy and dirty down at Perran. Why have colds? Why have minor ailments? What use are they? What cash value do they represent? What relation do they bear toward the Eternal Verities? (Carlyle, whom some day you will read).

My landlady here curiously enough stayed at Perranporth years and years ago; she loves it, and likes to speak of it. She is an individual old girl, with a mind of her own, and very kind.

I was sorry not to see you before you went, especially as it is probably the last chance. I have had no leave for about 14 weeks, and no half-day leave since I saw you all. Kitchener has now seen and passed us. We are to be ready to take our places when wanted, and so the 5 days leave preliminary to going abroad has just started, and the first batch went today. I must at least see the Comte at Paddington when my time comes, which may be in about 3 weeks time.

Don't get drowned, or sucked down by shifting sands, or get battered to bits by those huge Atlantic rollers. How are the trout?

I hope to see you all again one day, sound in body and mind, and to give you all a hundred runs and beat you, or 49 points of 50 at ping pong and beat you; you half-Gaelic rapscallions!

Good-bye, Winnie dear, and increase in wisdom, stature and health, and tell me all about yourself when you write. No polite inquiries.

Yours affectionately
Ivor

[1] Psalms XCII. 13.

---

43 To Mrs Matilda Chapman

G.45750

August 1915 (KT)   Pte Gurney, B Company 2nd 5th Glosters,
Chelmsford, Essex

My Dear Comtesse

I am sorry that worries pursue you even down in Cornwall, and that the poor kids are not up to the mark. Perhaps it is all right now, and the sun is shining.

Why do you suppose that when you do not get a letter, I am 'cross'? Well, it is an old trick now, and a legitimate one; though doubtfully useful as you must realise that I don't take fits of *that* kind, anyhow.

I am glad to be able to tell you – that my mind is gradually becoming more sane and more happy. It is hard work, but now I realise to the full that it is chiefly my mind at fault, I push on that way; and feel more hopeful. But please don't praise me for my courage! It is my only chance of happiness and health.

You won't mind this bit of self-analysis I hope? It is better to do very little of it, though.

Don't overwork yourself and spoil your holiday; it is better and nobler by far to worry over other people than yourself, but why do either?

Have you got Browning at all? The second volume of Everyman is excellent; or did I give you that little red-covered volume? That is good too. You ought to get Wordsworth in that edition; it is first rate.

What must the sea look like? The sea – unbroken in force by any barrier for thousands of miles! What free grace and careless glory must show itself in such unhampered movements. Well, probably (by statistics and ordinary reckoning) I myself may take joy in it someday; when this tyranny is overpast.

They have made a brass band now, and for the present put me in it; on a [*sic*] instrument called the Baryton – a bass cornet – affair. I like it, though my lips are too thick ever to do it justice, perhaps. Still, practice may put that right.

Now go I to bathe in Chelmer; not an imposing river; nothing of the 'rude imperious surge' about it.

Good luck!

Yours affectionately
Ivor

34

September 1915 (S)   Pte Gurney, B Company, 2/5th Glosters,
                                                Chelmsford, Essex

Dear Miss Scott

Thank you very much for your letter which pleased me very much. It is
easier to take a letter bit by bit as you did.

The Glosters have no prospect of camping in Windsor Park; neither do they
wish it – Billetts are in every way better. Thanking you kindly; but it is
curious that some Essex troops have just gone there from Chelmsford.

I was glad to hear of Shimmin, and have wiped off a long standing debt of a
letter, and hope to hear from him soon, though that is undeserved. Tell him I
write many more letters now than once I did. He will get little enough sleep in
camp I am afraid. He must rest between tea and bedtime, if they let him alone
then.

But I had written before you sent your letter and it went to Marlborough
Road way.

Belloc's Essay on the Views of England is in either *First and Last*, *On
Everything* or *On Anything*.[1]

As to the *Dynasts* all you say is true; and what you say establishes it high
enough. You did not mention the songs though, some of which are
magnificent. His bad verse inevitably recalls Browning, to me. His good, is
splendidly direct. Milton could never have imagined the Dynasts; and at least
Hardy spares us that vile Latin-English, and Latin constructions. The puzzle is
that Hardy's sense of humour in some things so strong has not restrained him
oftener.

As to Faith.

There is an excellent article in this week *Saturday Westminster*, a paper of
which I am very fond. It is a review by Walter de la Mare, and is that poet's
confession of Faith. (There is also a charming poem on Bach, called 'during
Music'.) I repose myself on a blind faith that all evil is somehow unavoidable,
and therefore necessary, and that in the End a complete explanation of and
compensation for the least scrap of evil is to come. I hate all formal ceremonies
and Churches, and my master in all these things is Wordsworth, and my place
of worship his. (The article is not de la Mare's; but one called Religion and the
War. I wish you would get that number.) The important thing to remember
now is that there are no problems now that were not equally urgent two years
or 2000 years ago. A Faith which needs reconstruction now will need it often
again maybe.

Let us play – the 48.[2]

People who find their Faith shocked by this war, do not need a stronger
faith only, but a different one, without blinkers. The whole question is
summed up in the last line of the A^b Prelude. 2nd Book. There you will find a
complete and compendious summary of all necessary belief.

I count myself lucky to be in the band. Fancy getting an interesting job in the noble profession of Arms! There's something wrong within the state of Denmark. We made our debut at this (Sunday) morning's Church-parade with that first of all march tunes, 'Marching through Georgia' – bugles and brass. O, but it was hard work! The band is a soft job usually, but not on the march. Our chaps marched splendidly, as they can when they choose.

At present I am writing a ballad of the Cotswolds, after Belloc's 'South Country'.[4] And there are two sonnets which may come with this. I find ballad writing very grateful and comforting to the mind, and to praise one's own county makes it not the less joyous. Someday maybe I'll write music with not less facility. *I* call this hefty good verse. Yet it flows (as R.L.S. said) like buttermilk from a jug.

> When I am old and cannot bide
> The grimy townships more,
> When dreams and images will not
> Assuage my longing sore,
> I'll shake their (the towns') mire from my quick feet
> And shut an alien door,
>
> And get me home to my dear West
> Where men drive ploughing teams,
> And smell the earth, sing earthy songs,
> Drink careless, dance, swim streams
> Of Crystal, Jest with God; I'll have
> Dreams Substances not dreams.
>
> There in the creeper clad old houses
> Of beautiful grey stone,
> I'll have my friends, and make amends
> For bleak years spent alone
> Deep-snug in a black old chimney seat
>   Close to the hearth-stone.

I repeat, Madam, that strikes me as being a damgood piece of verse, and yet when I feel like it, it means the simple trouble of sitting down, opening my poetical pores and exuding as fast as pen will write – almost. But not so this.

Satan above the Battle

> Think you that he who made the skies was ever
> Able before to make a scene accurst
> As this one? Nay; now God hath done his worst,
> His keenest spite hath poured on Man's endeavour
> To live and dream – like Him! Nor would he sever
> His countenancing help from Man, nor burst

That bubble of Love, till those, his creatures, had first
Near equalled Him in might. O clever! Clever!
But, Son of God, and Man, what think you of this?
What is your Passion worth? Three days in Hell
Under protection. Poverty. Judas' kiss?
(O Sentiment!) Or can it be you came
Too soon? These taunting triumphs of Science....! Well,
That's all; but were I you I'd burn with shame.

Afterwards

Those dreadful evidences of Man's illdoing
The kindly Mother of all shall soon hide deep,
Covering with tender fingers her children asleep,
Till Time's slow cycle turns them to renewing
In other forms their beauty – No grief, no rueing
Irrevocable woe. They'll lie, they'll steep
Their hearts in peace unfathomed, till they leap
Quick to the light of the sun, as flowers strewing,
Maybe, their own friends paths. And thats not all,
When men who knew them walk old ways alone,
The paths they loved together at even-fall,
Then the sad heart shall know a presence near,
Friendly, familiar, and the old grief gone,
The new keen joy shall make all darkness clear.

In this band of ours I have discovered a delightful creature. A Great
broadchested heavy chap who has been a morris dancer and whose fathers and
grandfathers uncles and other relations know all the folk song imaginable.
High Germanie, High Barbary, O No John, I'm Seventeen Come Sunday –
whole piles of 'em. He is a very good player too and a kind of uncle to the
band. Chock full of an immense tolerance and good humour and easy to get on
with. 'I loved him for his great simplicity', and hope to be like him some day.
So strong in himself, set fast on strong foundations. Not likely to be troubled
with neurasthenia. He whistled 'Constant Billy' which I had never before
heard.

My leave starts on Thursday most likely – 5 whole days. O Cranham,
Minsterworth, Framilode, Maisemore. All of you love me and I return the
compliment. It is you that have poured into my as yet defective mould that
fluid of beauty which shall one day take form in me and make others aware of
your graces and sweet looks. Let but the Germans leave me alone, and in 5
years time the Lord Almighty may relax that critical brow with which he yet
regards me and decide not to delete me as yet. Gloster in September! Gloster's
fairy tower against the hills. September mists. Fruit picking in the orchard,

even that orchard from which my dearest friend has gone and is now on other work overseas. I send you a song which you have not yet seen. When you have finished, please send it and the letter to Sir Hubert, for whom it is meant. Meanwhile I am occupied on a march for the Glosters those inheritors of fame and a long roll of honour.

Do you not like Laurence Binyon's verses in the *Times Supplement*?[5] Those and Hardy's and Kipling's are the best of the bunch. Though I like Watson Grenfell and Noyes. Hardy's grows on one. Did you ever read his last book of Short Stories – *The Changed Man*?[6]

Have you read any of D F Lawrence? I have just finished an extraordinary book called *The White Peacock*, full of arresting studies of character and most essentially breathing of earth and clouds and flowers – though not a pleasant book.

Good bye yours very sincerely
Ivor Gurney

P.S. There are two important items of news. One is that I have just had a birthday – my 25th. The other that we had Zeps here about a fortnight ago. Two bombs were dropped on Chelmsford itself, both on or near the Glosters billetting area. The damage was perhaps 5£ worth. It cured an old lady of muscular rheumatism, indeed it made an athlete, a sprinter of her – she went down the street in her nightgown like a comet or some gravity-defying ghost. One of the bombs was terrifying and must severely have shocked the elm tree which it mostly affected. Our supply guard did a roaring trade in old iron, and if it ever occurs to some wealthy enthusiast to buy up the two bombs in bits for purposes of reconstruction, he will probably get prostrated either by worry or rage; some of the guard may also suffer prostration.

5th Gloucester Gazette

In Flanders

I'm homesick for my hills again -
    My hills again!
To see above the Severn plain,
Unscabbarded against the sky,
The highblue blade of Cotswold lie;
The giant clouds go royally
By jagged Malvern with a train
Of shadows. Where the land is low,
Like a huge imprisoning O,
I hear a heart that's sound and high,
I hear the voice within me cry:
'I'm homesick for my hills again –
    My hills again!

38

Cotswold or Malvern, sun or rain!
My hills again.'

F W Harvey.

[1] Hilaire Belloc (1870-1953): *First and Last* (1911), *On Everything* (1909), *On Anything* (1910)
[2] Bach's *Well-tempered Clavier*.
[3] Gurney slightly misremembers *Hamlet* I, iv, 90.
[4] Gurney only published the third of these poems, 'Afterwards', in *Severn & Somme*.
[5] See note to letter 41.
[6] *A Changed Man, The Waiting Supper, and other Tales* (1913).

45 *To the Chapman Family*   G.45750

15 September (P)   Pte Gurney, B Company, 2nd 5th Glosters,
                                                   Chelmsford, Epping

My Dear Creatures

It was good-as-gold of you to send me such a parcel of good things. Never have I felt such a sensation of overwhelming luxury and surprise of riches since (alas! many years agone; lang syne) I bought a penny lucky bag and discovered a real wooden monkey on a real wooden stick. The air cushion is not a present useful to me, but if we have to sleep out it will be a blessing unparalleled. The tin will do for baccy, stamps, stray sovereigns, maggots and beetles, small photos. What the handkerchiefs will do for is better left out. Praps some day I may find the need for soap.

I wrote a p.c. to Mr Chapman about a week ago, telling him that I should be in London at a certain time. Two days after I remembered that the address on the p.c. was Mr Chapman – Goods Manager. So that may have been the reason I did not see him. Perhaps he lost his post through the G.M.'s jealousy and so has left you down at Perranporth to live on rabbits till he can scheme some money or other. Perhaps he's dead of grief, all through an unfortunate slip. I'm very sorry if this is so; he was a man who, though enthusiasm would be out of place, was not altogether bad: he was not as black at some points as others. His chief use was to excuse, by the display of his imperfections, any tendency to gaucherie or villainy in his children. And a good excuse it was for them, on almost anything.

(Just for sentiment's sake I will light up, and accompany this letter with Winnie's etceteras pipe and baccy. Puff, puff! Thank you).

I am very sorry to have left this letter so long. It was very wrong when there were so many nice presents to thank you for. They are all in use, save only the cushion, or rather pillow, for which, thank Goodness, no occasion for use has yet arisen.

I am afraid that your visit to Perranporth is drawing to an end. But you must draw cold comfort from the fact that High Wycombe is a very nice place to live in. Compare it with any London suburb.

My best friend[1] has just got a D.S.M. and has been recommended for a commission, but his nerves are pretty shaky. When we are to go, no one knows, but from rumours it is not likely to be just yet. But what are rumours worth?

I should like a game of ping pong very much: it would appeal to me more than forming fours or other such manifestations of military glory.

My 5 days leave happened about a week ago, more than a week in fact; and the beauty of my own county astounded and enchanted me more than ever. As a friend of mine[2] has lately written -

> I'm homesick for my hills again,
>   My hills again!
> To see above the Severn plain
> Unscabbarded against the sky
> The blue high blade of Cotswold lie;
>   And giant clouds go royally
> By jagged Malvern with a train of shadows'.

Isn't it exquisite?

Good bye all you unfortunate people who weren't born there!

Yours affectionately
Ivor.

[1] F.W. Harvey, and it was a D.C.M.
[2] 'In Flanders' by F.W. Harvey

46 *To Mrs Voynich*   G.41.11

Late September 1915 (KT)   Pte Gurney, B Company, 2nd 5th Glosters,
                                                          Chelmsford, Essex

Dear Mrs Voynich

Thank you very much for your letter. I enjoyed it all, but have no comment to make on the earlier parts.

You say that Bach and Milton are first cousins. Maybe, but if heredity were a calculable affair, and supposing their fathers really to have been brothers, I should say that Bach's father must have considerably annoyed Milton's dad and vice versa. Oh the dogmatics – the blank stares at fun and humour – the self-absorption and the wide outlook – the difference in ideas on God and the Universe! The tolerant admiration on the one side and the slightly contemptuous fatheadedness on the other!

Milton is one of the great men not worth crossing the streets to speak to. Bach was worth a hungry pilgrimage to see.

Do you remember Shakespeare's 'native woodnotes wild?'[1]

I have not yet read *Samson*, though this is one of the things I firmly intend to tackle soon. In the extract you sent (It begins 'Among them he a spirit of mischief sent') one thing jars me a good deal – 'desire' and 'destroyer' for consecutive line endings is very bad.[2]

A tiny P.S. says that Meredith is not Hardy. Which is only slightly truer than that Hardy is not Meredith. Shakespeare never drew such women! Hardy's sins are chiefly the result of a narrow spiritual outlook, or a dryness of soul. Meredith's are mostly technical, and probably come from the striving of an original mind to be more original. (I don't wonder ... He lived in the age of Tennyson and George Eliot.) But his boys, his girl-women and his best men are superb. He never could have spoilt a book as Hardy has spoilt *The Return of the Native*, with sins against Art and Probability and all those feelings that make one lump the worlds experiences, and use laughter born of Tragedy, and that half cynical nobility and clearness of eye that forbid men to complain much. The book is perverse. Besides, most of Hardy's chief characters are essentially uninteresting in themselves. Stuck up against Egdon Heath they do well, but they leave Egdon Heath the pride of place. However we cannot mould our great men; we must take Hardy's peasant-characters as being what they are and be grateful. Why some people have the cheek to compare Shakespeare's country characters to Hardy's I cannot guess. They (S's) are sometimes good – even brilliant sketches, but no more. And if Meredith's prose is tortured, Hardy's is often that of the leading article, or the magazine writer – dessicated and non-committal.

Walt Whitman is my latest rediscovery, and he has taken me like a flood. One of the greatest of teachers. And as a poet, he among others has this enormous virtue – that when he has nothing to say, you may divine it a mile off. A marked copy may be read in half an hour; but oh, what gorgeous stuff it is!

One line (and fit for us today)
> 'And how the same inexorable price must still be paid
>   for the same great purchase'.[3]

> 'In the name of these States shall I scorn the antique?
>   Why these are the children of the antique to justify it'.[4]

(By the way, this reminds me that my mind-picture of triumph and restrained gloriously-trembling exultation is this chord on trumpets.

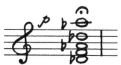

And that last quotation has it – that tingle of expectancy and jubilation.)
> On Death he says the supreme word.
> On the making of men also.

On the Open Air and its revelations.

And he is Democracy's own poet and prophet.

This line on the sea -

'Where the fierce old mother endlessly cries for her castaways'.

The titles of his poems will be a complete inspiration to a sensitive musician in tune with his spirit.

'Ethiopia saluting the Colours'

'To the leavened soil they trod'.

'Darest thou now O Soul'

'Thou Mother with thy equal Brood'.

'Out of the Cradle Endlessly rocking'

'Song for all Seas, All Ships'.

'Year that trembled and reeled beneath me'.

And the end of 'This Compost'. (This poem is all about the chemistry of Earth.)

One line runs

'Yet Behold ......

The summer growth is innocent and disdainful above all those strata of sour dead

And the End

'Now I am terrified at the Earth......

......

It renews with such unwitting looks its prodigal annual sumptuous crops.

It gives such divine materials to men, and accepts such leavings from them at last.'

Well, we're here still. If I hear definitely or almost definitely that we are to go to France or the Mediterranean, straightway shall I go in for a commission. It is best to get paid for taking risks. Meanwhile my instrument is not any other than the baryton, a kind of bass cornet, for we have not long formed a brass band, and I, moi-même am a performer therin. Great fun, it is, and my co-Orpheuses are all goodnatured and bottomlessly tolerant. My bridge playing has improved quite perceptibly since I left the company......

One word my company will give to the next Oxford Dictionary - and I love it. This word signifies (let me be lexicographical) 'One of small intellectual powers'

Twallet

Doesn't it sound like it?

This noun is, as you may guess, not infrequently qualified......

My best friend has just got the D.C.M. Also he has written this

42

I'm homesick for my hills again!
   My hills again!
To see above the Severn plain
Unscabbarded against the sky
The blue high blade of Cotswold lie,
And giant clouds go royally
By jagged Malvern with a train
Of shadows. Where the land is low,
Like a huge imprisoning O;
I hear a heart that's sound and high,
I hear a heart within me cry
'I'm homesick for my hills again,
   My hills again!
Cotswold or Malvern, sun or rain,
   My hills again!'[5]

That will be in anthologies hundreds of years hence, surely.

Well, my 5 days leave is past and over, and Gloster's delicate colours, long views and sea breezes are the whole breadth of England away. That soil bore me and must ever draw my dreams and for ever be home to me. It is to [be] torn up by the roots for me to live flatly in a flat marsh like Essex, where the air is stagnant and unalive. But if we stay here the eastern winds will give us sea airs – sharper than the serpents tooth.[6] May it come soon.

I hope you enjoyed your holiday with the Taylors. If I had been able to come along, we might have formed fours and squad and columns of platoons like the Guards, after a period of probation. But that was not to be. Your remark about the refugees pleased me very much.

(An inversion has just occurred to me. 'If I were God, how I would pity the hearts of men' – to (an angel-being's soliloquy) (cynical) If I were a man how I would pity the heart of God.) That was caused by your sheet on Poland. One has seen the dummy at bridge keep silence for some time while his partner seems bent on destruction, but near the end at some apparently-lunatic play he glances up with a countenance in which distrust has almost swallowed up belief. One can imagine the heavenly beings watching Poland, and secretly scanning God's inscrutable face .... 'Can it be smugness or may there be a purpose'? 'Certainly he has rounded some nasty corners, and his technique is perfect of course, but....' 'Can he have left things to a bureaucracy to manage'? 'The office boy's forgot....' 'He's wound it up and lost the key....'

The Budget seems to be a very good one, don't you think?

If I get any idea when we are to go to the front; or any idea we are not going to India, immediately I shall try for a commission. One may as well get paid for taking risks.

My health gradually improves, but it is hard to control the mind. I only hope it will be as quick in the right direction one day. Have you read any

D.F.Lawrence? *The White Peacock* is an early work I believe;[7] but, though it is black in outlook and is obviously carrying the world on his shoulders, he is very good at characterisation, and his feeling for Nature is superb.

Someone has lent me two of Tchekof's plays – *The Sea-gull* and *The Cherry Orchard*. The first I have read twice and am very struck with it – for its truth and its well drawn characters. I must read the other again before I decide, but it will probably not please me so much. (There is a lovely phrase in a review this morning, about our young men, who are continually pulling up their emotions by the roots to see how they are getting on.)

Hauptmann's *Sunken Bell* is good, but not not very good, I think.[8]

Well, that is all I find to say in this queer letter.

We are expecting Zeps tonight as there is a rumour of four somewhere about. But Chelmsford is a straggly place and probably not easy to spot.

They discovered a spy at Epping, and made one or two very interesting discoveries. One was that his garden shone phosphorescent at night with an arrow pointing to London.

I rail against Lady Fortune inasmuch as baccy the solace and reconciler to destiny is to be 2d on the ounce dearer. Nectar and ambrosia are untouched.

Here

I remain

With best wishes
Yours very sincerely
Ivor Gurney.

[1] From Milton's 'L'Allegro', l.134.
[2] 'Among them he a spirit of phrenzie sent' is line 1675 of Milton's *Samson Agonistes*; 'destroyer' and 'desire' are the endings of lines 1677 and 1678.
[3] From 'Beginners' in the 'Inscriptions' section of *Leaves of Grass*.
[4] From Section 4 of 'Starting from Paumanok'.
[5] Harvey's poem was first published in the *5th Gloucester Gazette*.
[6] The phrase is from *King Lear*, I, iv.
[7] Published 1911.
[8] *The Sunken Bell*, a fairy play in five acts by Gerhart Hauptmann, was translated into English verse by Charles Henry Meltzer in 1899.

47 *To Sydney Shimmin*   G.76.3.1-2

September 1915 (KT)   Pte Gurney, Band – D.Company,
                                                      2nd 5th Glosters, Chelmsford, Essex

My Dear Shimmin

I am very sorry you have been ill, old chap. It is hard lines to get misfortune on top of dull routine to look forward to more dull routine. Bless you, my child, but I hope it is getting all right, and that you have had not too bad a time.

If you can get up from Aylesbury to see the Chapman's they would be very pleased to see you, and make you comfortable for a time. Do try, when you are well enough.

The Hunts send you their very best wishes and hopes for a quick recovery. They are dividing their time between visiting relations and looking after sick people of all sorts, with a sort of garnish of sock-knitting and other similar frivolities.

How far off and faint the R.C.M. life seems to all this twaddle and tomfoolery! I daresay you must envy me, being in the band. At least I shall be able to do something that was not in me before; the baritone is a pleasant instrument, and not unlike the French Horn. Why should I not play the F.H. in Mozart and Haydn etc? Or why not a double concerto for Double Bass and Baritone by S.S. + I.B.G.? Would you like some books? There are any amount of good things lying unread (as I suppose) at home or the Hunts. Get somebody to present you with a minature [sic] score of 'Also Sprach Zarathustra' (?). It will calm you and give you something to think about; remind you of what drove you into the army – the Prussian Spirit so well exemplified in monstrosities such as that; a spirit so different in birth and action from our beloved J.S.' whose music entrances me more and ever more.

Have you ever read Wordsworth's *Prelude*? It is very Bach-like in places, and would, I am convinced, please you very much. The philosophy – O well, I'll not bore you with it. Try it yourself, without dulling descriptions. What do you think of this phrase, as expressing the artist's need for self-control, and the best way to get it; how to shut ugliness and introspection out of the mind, and set it free from all the devil's bonds and whimsies.

'Uphold
Intense desire through meditative peace.'

Howells, I hear is forging ahead, and doing good stuff. I hope to goodness they don't conscript him, or run him into anything in some underhand way. I wonder what has happened to Karg-Elert?[1] He will find it difficult to compose on potato-bread.

Miss Scott told me you were anxious to get to the front, and feel useful for somewhat. I must confess that as my health improves I feel more intensely the conviction that someday my mind will put out work not unworthy to stand with good stuff, and that halts me. What will happen to us is still uncertain. Rumour still says India, and I have always wished to see that old land of sunshine and dark iniquity. What can I tell you else? What is there in the Army to talk about? Nowt. I can only say that you must add to the gaiety of nations by arising from your bed and walking about with a pack to show your essential vigour.

Good-bye, old man, and excuse this stupid letter. Someday we will play Brahms together again, and *that* will make a subject for talk.

With best wishes
Yours ever
I.B.G.

[1] Sigfrid Karg-Elert (1877-1933), composer.

6 October 1915 (E)   Pte Gurney, The Band, D Company,
                                      2nd 5th Glosters, Chelmsford, Essex

Dear Miss Scott

Thank you for your letter, which contained much balm and unction for the wounded spirit, which has got an hour's C.B. tomorrow – most likely, anyway.

I'm glad you liked that sonnet; it gets to please me more than it did; better, at any rate than the soul-revealing poetic prophecies that manage to make their way unto the *R.C.M. magazine.*

Colles[1] face is that of a critic – Shaw's definition of a critic – one who cannot do, but teaches others to do.[2] Does he read Walter Pater? It is very easy for a man like that to throw sand in the eyes of the public – and nearly as easily into his own. How is he to know whether Heldenleben is music or not? He gets his opinion (unconsciously) from weight of opinion - which does not, Mr Colles, necessarily make opinion of weight.

The War News is thrillingly thrilling, is it not? Whether it is good or bad depends on what we had expected to do. Colonel Maude, who has always been optimistic, sometimes too much so, says we may have them at the Rhine in a month's time. And then, O Deutschland, Wonderful and Sittlichkeitish Vaterland,[3] show us then the mettle of your pastures.[4] Will you be able to stand the strain and suspense that the French have sustained in a mood of exalted irony? If only your civilians will hold out! But will they?

There is little to tell you about F.W.Harvey. He is, perhaps was, my best friend, and a man almost without blot. He has never had good health, and so has not yet been able to prove himself; war does not suit weak nerves either. Let's hope he'll get what 'our gallant soldiers' call 'a blight'; a wound bad enough to incapacitate, but good enough to come home with.

I am glad that you like the song. My own opinion is that only 'Erl-king' and 'Doppelganger'[5] equal or surpass 'Edward' and 'The Twa Corbies'. I tell you that anything beyond a temporary puncture will annoy me very much. As my health and spirits improve, so within me I find a store of poetry, an accumulation of pictures – dead leaves, Minsterworth Orchards, Cranham, Crickley and Framilode reach. They do not merely mean intensely to me; they are me, points from which my soul, as our armies at Lens and Champagne, will make irruptions and declare as I hope Music to be as much an English as a German art.

I have just finished a long letter to Mrs Voynich, chiefly about Walt Whitman, curiously enough.

Please keep this for posterities [*sic*] sake. [*He has circled a fingerprint.*]

USA must have been worth something once. Mark Twain, Emerson, Walt Whitman, Marching Through Georgia, and John Brown's Body all at the same time! The good of Whitman may be condensed in 20 pages, but O, what a score! He is either absurdly unpoetic; or a prophet, speaking high things in high words. A greater and more balanced (on the whole) than Tolstoi – yes, on twenty pages he is that; Just as Bach is greater than Mozart on the few bars that make up the 1st Prelude in the 2nd Book of the 48. Have you noticed that the climax of the F major Prelude (2nd Book) is made as follows

It is badly written enough, but you will recognise it. I have forgotten the barring.

[*There is no formal end to this letter.*]

---

[1] Henry Cope Colles (1879-1943), subsequently editor of the 3rd and 4th editions of Grove's *Dictionary of Music*.
[2] 'He who can, does. He who cannot, teaches.' One of the 'Maxims for Revolutionaries' in *Man and Superman*.
[3] Literally 'morality-ish fatherland'.
[4] Gurney is quoting from Shakespeare's Henry V's speech before Harfleur, III, i.
[5] By Schubert.

49 To Mrs Matilda Chapman   G.45750

22 October 1915 (P)
[*Postcard*]

Sorry not to have answered your letters, but ever since Monday we have been out on manoeuvres; and civilisation a thing unknown.

I have made application for Sunday leave, but shall not know till then whether I shall get it. If you knew what a time we have had this past 3 weeks you would not suspect any sane person of not wishing to get anywhere else. But I'm afraid you'll have to pay for it. I.B.G.

50 To Mr Edward Chapman   G.45750

October 1916 (KT)   Pte Gurney, Band. D. Co:, 2/5 Glosters,
                                                               Chelmsford

My Dear Comte (de Tilda)   = title of female successor
    The Comtesse your gracious consort has written me a charming letter all about herself (and myself), but happens to mention that you would like a letter

from me; and as it is rather important to me to keep in with you, I take the hint, though there is not much to say.

There was no train from London that night, and so after sleeping for an hour or two at a Soldiers and Sailors home – a most comfy 3^d doss – I went down to prison on the paper train at 5 a.m.

When we (for there were other daredevils besides myself) handed our passes in, the following dramatic scene occurred – from the Play 'An Escape from Gehenna'.

Act I   Hurried evasion
Act II   High Wycombe
Act III   Doss house in London Slums
Act IV   Handing the Pass In

Scene *Quarter Guard Room*

(Enter two men of doubtful mien and hangdog air)

1st Guard	Hullo!
1st Criminal:	Ah do! Where's the Sergeant?
1st Guard:	There
1st Criminal:	Thanks ... Sorry, Sergeant, to wake you up. Here they are.
Sergeant:	(Grunt ... Grunt ... Grunt ...) Ere, wot's this?
1st Criminal	
2nd Crim:	Wot's Wot?
Sergeant:	'Ere, wot's this?
1 & 2 Crims:	Wot's Wot? Sergeant?
Sergeant:	This! Wot's this? These are midnight passes
1st Criminal:	Ah, yes ... most unfortunate. *Most* unfortunate. Somehow or other there didn't happen to be a train after 8.30. They must have taken 'em off. Bit rotten, wasn't it ... We didn't mean to disturb you. Very sorry. Won't do it again. Quite a mistake.
Sergeant:	Ah ... Well you just get off into your billets at once. There'ud be a blushing row if anybody seen you.
1st Crim:	Oh yes ... thanks, Sergeant. Good morning.
2nd "	

Exeunt

Act V   has not yet come, and doesn't look like it.

It was good to get back to St Mike's again, bless it, and feel free and golopshus once again.

We went out on a brigade stunt, and got a dinner of bone splinters and hot water at 4 o'clock next day; so the impression of cloistral peace was heightened

48

by contrast. Curious that a rotten liver should be able to spoil everything save only memories ...

The Comtesse says you are in Wales, and have not yet seen the miracle-working gent who may be able to recall me, like Orpheus, from Hell. That doesn't affect me much .. I do not dare to hope much for fear ...

But if it is real, and not phantasmal and only a rosy dream, let the proof be forthcoming not too late. I may be snatched away of a sudden into some remote outlandish place outside England, but that is not immediately likely, though there are rumours.

I might also say that if there is another place, Cridlan that analyst etc. from Stevens [sic] Jammery[1] would be delighted to get it, and would if necessary get references from his uncles. He would certainly be very useful. Well, that's all about that – FOR THE PRESENT I hope.

Oh, but this is a grey unuseful unbeautiful waste, this Essex. No suns, etc, no colours. No beechy hills, no downs, no nothing, no kids to play with, no free cigarettes, no ping pong. No something that gives a romance and mystery to ordinary trees and hedges and houses in more fortunate parts. If ever I come to write music some of it will be around Totteridge, Keep Hill, and that Macbeth-like wood that lies beyond it to the south. Some of it also round the homelife which is so strong and sweet a stimulant to any sound art.

But this is rather gassy. Get me out of this. Let me know that I shall still be doing war-duty with a practical certainty of being some day able to do all that lies in me, some day, for the honour of England; which is very dear to me. Indeed, if I could feel certain that there never would be anything in me really worth the showing in music, the first thing I'd do would be to volunteer where they wanted me most. Though on that point even, I believe that the Railway Transport, if there is a chance to rise, will give me a fair run.

Please excuse this egotistical letter, but I can write no others that are not washy platitudes.

Yours affectionately
Ivor Gurney

[1] Stephens Jam factory in Gloucester.

51 *To Marion Scott*   G.41.13

October 1915 (KT)   Pte Gurney, Band – D Company, 2/5 Glosters, Chelmsford, Essex

Dear Miss Scott

Thank you very much for the jam, which looks very nice, but my uneasy conscience will not let me be – on the grounds that if I am unable to afford jam on 8/- a week, I can hardly deserve it to be sent. It would be best to send some money home for some Gloster jam, which, it is an article of creed with me, can hardly be equalled.

There was no train, as I expected, that Sunday night; and after a 3d doss which I very much enjoyed, arrived at Chelmsford at 6 a.m., but wangled the sergeant into saying nothing. In this sort of thing, as the Immortal Bard observes, 'there's nothing so becomes a man as modest stillness and humility',[1] with which I dosed the sergeant, to the desired end.

In a recollection of our conversation, I remember the subject ran from my being able to do railway work, to the discussion, or rather assertion that I could not imagine a one sided brain of any greatness. I hope that you did not suppose me so humourless as to refer even distantly to myself then, but my memory makes it seem very like it. We happened on one of the few things I think about on route marches, and which is an article of salvation with me. Carlyle has not put it too strongly in *Heroes*.[2] It is chiefly a matter of environment with the really great men what shape they take in their power; but with the smaller men, such as Wordsworth, I am not quite sure. Whether I could do railway work or not, which of course I *can*, referred not at all to this. What made me more sensitive to this is that I have just bought Wordsworth's life in Jack's 6d Home Series, and his colossal complacency makes one anxious. What a crowd they must have been – Wordsworth, Dorothy and Coleridge!

But how a poor wandering mind like mine must envy Wordsworth's strong self-sufficiency! How must his mind have been filled with those pictures that are the all-in-all to any artist! Here in Essex there are no sunsets, and no colour; no mystery in woods, no sense of other-worldliness. Nothing but common life in the light of common day. When my mind can escape from its imprisoning body, it reaches out desperately to the memory of Malverns purple and, later, black against afterglow, or Cranham trees transfigured to shapes of colour and form and seeming without substance, merely imagined, stuff of dreams. (Cotswold man beside me)

'Here's luck to the world as round as a wheel
Death is a thing we all must feel.
If Life were a thing that money could buy,
The Rich would live, and the poor would die.'

It is Fred Bennett – the morris dancer of old time, who is alternately telling stories or answering questions in broad Glostershire, and playing cadenzas and hymn tunes on his trombone – so things must be as they may as regards mistakes.

Redgauntlet is amazingly good where it is good, and the dull parts can be detected from a mile away.

I hope you like the Chesterton book I am sending. Some of the things are as good as could be – as The Grocer. Old Noah. The Song on Cocoa; all jolly and rollicking in good hefty English.[3]

Have I ever quoted a phrase from a *Morning Post* review on a book by some young 'naturalist'? It is – that 'our young men are continually pulling their emotions up by the roots to see how they are getting on.'

I hope you are not doing so much work as you were, and are now pretty well. To have weak nerves is rather like the sensation a strong man must have, struggling in treacle. You had better read the *Prelude* for a sedative. Or *The Excursion* as a soporific. Or the *Daily Mail* as a galvanic.

Have you noticed the Eastern (or N.E.) sky about 10 oclock at night lately? What there is about the stars to make them more impressive than any other object, I do not know. But the sight of Orion and the three stars near by moves me as much as Beethoven. How garish, how vulgar, how Raphael-Tuckish [4] the moon is to such, save only when it is a thin curve and seems a sort of star, or crescent out of which stars will be cut, or delicate scimitar for the making thereof.

In winter when the trees are naked, and frost binds all moist things with iron, and breath goes strangely up in vapour – then who goes out from the warm neighbourly comforting firelight and stands in mere starlight and earthy gloom, what a continual surprise, what a revelation of unknown purpose is his who turns his eyes upwards and sees that majestical roof fretted with golden fire! It is a strong assurance to man, that his mind, confronted with the sight of all those worlds, some of them thought to be dead, many dying, as even this our own; that his mind, I say, though humble before these unintelligible mysteries is exalted with an uprushing of fierce and tender joy, and strangely, of a pride in God's Handiwork, as if a private should view his Chief Commander's handiwork or a molecule take pleasure in the soft fantastic imagery on English autumn trees. (Copyright in U.S.A.) (Forget the Clamour.)[5]

Yours very sincerely
Ivor Gurney

[1] Again from Henry V's speech before Harfleur

[2] In *Heroes and Hero-Worship* near the beginning of Lecture III 'The Hero as Poet', Carlyle writes: 'The different *sphere* constitutes the grand origin of such distinction, ... the Hero can be Poet, Prophet, King, Priest or what you will, according to the kind of world he finds himself born into.'

[3] The poems referred to are 'The Song against Grocers', 'Wine and Water' and 'The Song of Right and Wrong', all first published in *The Flying Inn* (1914).

[4] Raphael Tuck published pretty postcards.

[5] The phrase is from Belloc's *Path to Rome*

52 To Herbert Howells   G.3.8

October 1915 (KT)   Pte Gurney, Band – D Company, 2/5 Glosters,
                                                                      Chelmsford, Essex

My Dear Howler

I am sorry not to have seen you for so long, but what time I have had in London has been either irregular or entirely unexpected, and so have made no appointment.

I hope you are forging ahead with epoch-makers, with a teeming brain and a full and happy mind; (the two are inseparable, I believe.)

As for me, behold a poor dyspeptic Tommy more sick than can be shadowed in words of the army; but with a kind of delirious joy at the back of his mind, because there is a chance of his getting a job in the Railway Transport at the front – opportunities to rise and 3/4 a day to start. I do not think, old chap, my health will improve much more in the army. I *must* have something to think about. That is, I am so far well as to try to shun the danger of introspection and self analysis. Two years of brain work and outdoor exercise would probably put me right. I cannot remember a time since schooldays when my health was better – anyway. You can imagine, too, what the hope of being able to praise England and make things to honour her is in me, as in yourself. You can imagine too what a conflict there is between that idea and warfare .... If only I could be convinced that there was nothing unique, nothing that was not easily paralleled in me, I would not care. But to be neurasthenic – To wonder what my capabilities are – to have patience only because, someday, there may come something to give joy to men and especially Englishmen .... to suffer all this in the thought-vacuum in which the Army lives, moves and has its being, is a hard thing. The hardest thought of all is that I am deceiving myself, that nothing especially worthy is in me; and that I should take a commission at once. The Railway job would allow one to remain in the army; to get some money; to rise if it were at all interesting; and not to run into any great danger. But anything – anything to take my all too subtle observation off myself.

Well, well; excuse the clamour – 'Forget the clamour', I mean.[1]

I say, old chap, I wish you would do myself and a lonely girl a favour. Harvey's cousin, Edith Harvey, is in London at some girl's club, earning her own living. Could you, would you send her some Concert tickets?[2] She is an interesting plucky girl, and you would get on well with her, I think. Please do this. Her address is

> Miss E.Harvey
> 11 St George's Square
> S.W.

Which is a girl's club of a new sort, where they are allowed to do exactly as they please without let or hindrance. Coming in at 2.a.m. with a latch key is nothing uncommon.

I often think of your Concerto and its strength and beauty. It is a work which must one day force itself on the atttention of a world whose mind, alas, must for some time be fixed on other things. Have you ever read Wordsworth's *Prelude*? There is nothing better for evoking those pictures in the mind which are the soil and seed of all art worthy the knowing. It is dull enough and egotistical enough at times but still is full of stimulation and packed memory.

How is Benjamin? Is *he* sick of the Army too? And your brother – still sick? Is he abroad yet? Well, I will leave this in hopes to see you again before long, some fine or otherways evening; but at present to the *Prelude* and to envy you, but, should this Railway business come off perhaps there will not be such cause. But say nowt about it! Please try to send those tickets. When are you going to write some Cotswold music? Oh, for a Symphony on *Henry IV*! You just look at it!

With best wishes

I suscribe and profess myself to be, Gracious Sir, your most obliged and humble servant

I.B.G.

[1] From Belloc's *Path to Rome*
[2] Howells wrote to her on 5th November 1915; see G.74.13.

---

53 To Mrs Matilda Chapman   G.45750

October 1915 (KT)   Pte Gurney, Band *D* Company, etc.

P.S. Have you the Everyman *Century of Essays*? If so did I give it to you? If not, *please* let me have it.

My Dear Comtesse

I wonder how you like High Wycombe now? The change from Perran must be great, but let it not blind you to the merits of High Wycombe, which are many.

Today is bright and bracing, and after flat and featurless Essex, Bucks would be Beauty personified. Walk you straight round Castle Hill and be glad of it. I hope you are pretty well and cheery after your long holiday – It was a long one you know; and you must not have wasted money by not feeling a jolly sight better.

You are quite wrong about my not wanting letters. I like them better than for years I have (a sure sign of improving health), and am glad of them. But I *don't* like wee bits from R.H. or A.E. Benson, and sentimental 'Wehmuthings'[1] to give you a Teutonism. They insult God and Man, either by refusing to see truth, or insisting on unimportant platitudes. I like letters to be about the people who write them. 'A healthy egotism' as our German friends would say. There is a distinct possibility that we shall not go abroad till March, which will make the chances of getting through all right quite large.

My mind gradually tranquillises itself, and more and more I see that a splendid teacher Wordsworth is for all sorts of men. When I can lie quite still in joy by the side of some stream or in a meadow for an hour or more, then music will come easily and well. Not till then. Happiness is in ourselves, and until this is a platitude to be smiled at for its obviousness, it is not possible for sensitive people to be happy. Come and let's be – together. At present, it is probable that I am in front.

I find I have been preaching. Sorry! But it is as much for myself as you. But ... does that make it any more excusable? I wonder ...

Yours affectionately
Ivor

Oh, Mr Smith has not replied to my letter. The one before was curt. Is this due to my attitude on Prophecy?

[1] 'Wistfulnesses' perhaps.

October 1915 (KT)

Dear Kids

How's Hockey? How's cats? How's dogs? How's football? How's Keep Hill?

I would very much like to share all these with you, but Lord Kitchener won't let me. Herbert Horatio Has the Hump. But really: Essex is a flat and unsatisfactory place, and now Autumn is in the air I remember High Wycombe, and how I went down there just about this time last year, and discovered a family which liked Bach and whose presents I am now loaded with. I take baccy from a magnificent sterling silver pouch-thing, light up a splendid Spring Model pipe, and recline on a lovely Latest style air-cushion, carefully dusting my trousers with an exquisite handkerchief embroided (as is the cushion) with my name, and am ready to sneeze in the most gentlemanly fashion into the most lady-like handkerchiefs.

Is Winnie going back to School? What will Kitty do? Is Arthur going to take a commission? Is Micky allowed to associate with other more respectable children?

How's Dad? With whom I used to settle the fate of Europe and the Universe with my feet pointing upwards to the skies, as the hymn says.

Mr Jack White is in the Naval Air service now, and has made trips into the empyrean (Gotcher!)

Oh, dear! but how sick we are of the army; and how we watch the placards for any indication of a near end to the war. Things are rosy just at the present, rosier than they were, anyhow.

It's Sunday, today, and were things different from what they are, I might be looking forward to clutching hold of about 6 pairs of hands and trying not to break my neck, *and* look affable! Do you remember how the Gadarene

swine used to run down the quarry at Keep Hill? Well, one day again perhaps
...

Good bye everybody

Your affectionate friend
Ivor

55 *To Marjorie Chapman* G.45750

1915 (KT)

My Dear Micky

I hope you have been doing no *very* naughty things lately, you imp of iniquity, you! How many times have you fallen in, and upset the whole household for clean clothes? How many dogs have you worried, you extreme example of wilful perversity? How many cats? Children? Mothers? Brothers? Aunts?

But indeed, I may be quite sure that it will take more than a European war, and a wetting to damp *your* spirits and stop *you* dancing. Go on then, be naughty and get muddy. It is not I that have to set things straight. They may scold, but I am far enough away not to mind so much; and all I want is a letter about it, and kisses at the end.

Draw me a picture, lady-artist. Make me a song. Play tricks – and – naughtiness all the day long.

Yours affectionately
Ivor B:

56 *To Marion Scott* G.41.9

19 November 1915 (P) Pte Gurney, etc.

Dear Miss Scott

I am so sorry about Sidney. He sent me a cheery P.C. which made me think he was well over the worst. Poor chap, he has not had the best of times.

As for the sonnets I shall be delighted to see them in the next number. In which, it may be safely prophesied that the verse alone will be worth the money.

I hope by now that you are much better than you were, and out of Cold's clutches, and more your own. If you [are] hard up for new things to read, remember the *Century of Essays* (in 'Everyman').[1] There is much solace and delight therein, and a ripping little essay by Dekker on Winter; which ends, 'When Thames is covered with ice, and men's hearts are covered over and crusted with cruelty, then mayst thou or any man be bold to swear that it is Winter.'

To end this note I send you a

Carol

Winter now has bared the trees,
Killed with tiny swords the jolly
Leafage that mid-summer sees
But left the ivy and the holly.
  Hold them high
  And make delight
For Christës joy that's born tonight.

All green things but these have hid
Their heads, or died in melancholy,
Winter's spite them all has rid
Save only ivy and brave holly.
  Give them place
  In all men's sight
For Christës grace that's born tonight.

Baby eyes are pleased to see
Bright red berries and children jolly,
So shout and dance and sing with glee,
And honour ivy and prickly holly,
  Honour courage
  And make delight
For Christës sake that's born tonight.

Christus natus hodie!
Drink deep of joy on Christmas day.
Join hands and sing a roundelay
For this is Christ's and children's day.
Christus natus hodie!
Hodie!

And now I have forgotten the corrections.

Very well, let it be 'Unstirred by rattle of the rolling drums.'[2] I do not understand the objection to it though.

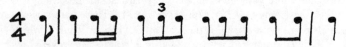

Just as

If England to herself do rest but true[3]

I'll guarantee to find a line of 13 actual syllables in *Paradise Lost*.

The other objection I cannot meet. 'Maybe' means maybe there. It is not padding. For instance Jones has a friend, acquaintance, or companion named Brown. Brown is stirred up by his young lady to enlist. Jones is engaged on War Work, tying up parcels at the Admiralty with odd bits of string which it is his business to untie and use to purpose. (as per instructions on Economy.) Brown, who becomes sick of the Army, lacks the courage to desert. Is shipped over to France in a cattle boat, and contracts a severe fit of sea sickness which is only terminated in an especially violent paroxysm, by a 29.6 shell.

Jones rises in the World, gets a string contract from Government, acquires fame from his superb collection of Knots (now in the Bruem, otherwise the Mittish Bruseum), obtains through influence a free pass, and goes, after the war, on a tour in Flanders. Is it not possible that he, maybe, 'maybe', mayhap to exterminate the solitary dandelion which has sprung out of the former friend and companion of his youth – Brown? I wot so.

Yours very sincerely
Ivor Gurney

[1] *A Century of Essays from Caxton to Belloc*, introd. Ernest Rhys, Everyman No.653.
[2] See letter 40 for the original form of the sonnet. It was printed in *RCM Magazine* vol 12, No 1, Christmas Term 1915.
[3] The line is from *King John*, V, vii.

---

57 To Mrs Voynich   G.41.15

November 1915 (E)   Pte Gurney, D.Company, 2/5 Glosters,
                                                    Chelmsford, Essex

Dear Mrs Voynich

Don't think I mind be[ing] slanged. A good healthy quarrel, on literary matters especially was and is always pleasing to my still unquiet mind. I take the truth about Milton to be – that he was the greatest of all our word-craftsmen. That, he was not nearly national enough. That, though he was self-critical enough as to rythm and form, he wrote the most detestable half-English; sounding more like a Bohn translation than anything else. (But see Belloc's essay on his chief merit – 'picturing'.) That, though his mind was huge in some ways, it was surprisingly limited in others. And that to the universal charity and often careless exercise of great powers that Shakespeare has, he can oppose only those characteristics which have nothing to do with good-fellowship. What has he to do with the Renaissance, or any rebirth of spirit? In spite of his political ideals. Beethoven became deaf and wrote the C#

minor Quartett and the Ninth Symphony. Milton became blind and wrote *Paradise Lost* and *Samson Agonistes*. His spirit was huge, but not generous, because he lacked humour, and its attendant qualities.

We are to go abroad before long I think; somewhen about January. As my health is improving, this does not please me. I am so far well as to wish to get back to music + (a big plus) football and long walks. This is a far cry from last Feb: is it not? I hope you have a similar, or rather, a better tale to tell of health: that you are indeed quite well. These cold bright days of winter are salutary and good for all sorts and conditions of men. Poor Sidney has had a hard time of it, but from his postcard to me he is well out of the worst. He shall have another letter in a day or two. Miss Scott too, is one of the unhappy band, but she writes cheery letters – if that has anything to do with health in *her*.

There was a chance, there is still a chance, of my getting a post in the Railway Transport Office in France, but oh, it has dwindled down to such a small one. So I suppose that I must take my chance and trust to the 'luck of the Gloucesters', a proverb in the Army. The 28th Foot fought the rearguard action at Corunna as the most trusted troops, so 'Q' says in a book called *Shakespeare's Christmas*[1]; and they are the 1st Gloucesters and famous as any, and as good.

My D.C.M. friend[2] is in England – in Glostershire – training as an officer, and no doubt invoking the Muse.

It is a fact that makes me think, that though I have had more training in music than verse, yet a sonnet comes far easier to me than a prelude or any other small form in music. Perhaps it is because I am compelled to think of and have more to do with books than music, but it is certainly true that arrangement of words comes with less effort than the other. But it is probable work would alter that.

Tonight there is a debate on 'Spooks'. Please goodness there will be something [worth] hearing about them. At present, all I know of them is very dull and hardly worth remembering.

How the A major Prelude (Book II) of Bach seems to be born of the spirit that makes Christmas Carols! The UnMiltonic candour, sweetness and childlike natural grace recalls the (Gloster) carol of 'A Virgin Unspotted'

Well, I'll away to the spooks. And end

With best wishes
Yours very sincerely
Ivor Gurney.

[1] Sir Arthur Quiller-Couch, *Shakespeare's Christmas and other stories* (1904)
[2] F.W.Harvey.

My Poor Dear Shim:

Miss Scott tells me you have had another relapse, and are again not at all well. I hope this does not mean that the pain has come back again. Cheer up! Bright days are in store. Horatio Bottomley Rouses the Government, and Rallies the Empire several times a week. Germany develops an Irish type of face on potatoes, concurrent with a strong desire for pigs which should do well with the Teutons, and the 2/5 Gloucesters may or may not be sent out before Christmas.

It is not a nice thought, that one day a prattling child may climb on his (or her) father's knee, and with quite innocent intention, ask 'Father, what did you do in the Great War'? But the Buxom Wife will intervene with the tactful 'Sssh! Sydney! (or Sidneia)' to save her adored spouse from confessing that he had the belly-ache.

God! What eternal years away the College life seems! Dammy! but life's a strange thing! Then the question of war with Germany was an academic, fit for the tea table, sandwiched in between lies, naughty stories, gossip, clucks of drinking, and calling for food. Now it is none of those things, pleasant to remember but an ugly actuality: taking with us the shape of the squad drill and saluting by numbers; bad enough – but worse to come. But I say, old chap, a most extraordinary thing happened last week. Through mere boredom and vacuity of mind I was led into promising to attend one of a series of weekly debates. It matters not that the promise was not intended to be kept. It was kept. The subject was 'Ghosts', on which I took, mostly against my convictions, a contrary attitude: reduced the meeting to a perspiring silence – and got Elected on the Committee. Me! On a Debating Committee! Let Deutschland tremble, for England is at last realising and using her greatest men. Who can say that night will not be famous? Not I!

I hope they make you pretty comfortable in your distress. You would be very useful here now. I bought in London when last there a duet arrangement of 3 of Mozart's Quintetts. First of which is the G minor Piano Quintett. (or is it Quartett.) It really is a wonderful thing, and effortless and in action all as easy as ball bearings or the Solar System.

It is very different at Band practice, which is beginning to bore me like billyoh. As a matter of fact, I believe my mind and body improve little by little constantly; but would to God that power would be given me from on high to wake up earlier. 'Tis truly distressing to miss 5 parades in one week, chiefly through that reason. I deserved the V.C. but, Lord knows how, they either did not miss me or someone answered my name, for the slimy dungeon has not yet received me.

Cheer up, if you need cheering up; if you do, cheer up for the essential virtue in the mere act of cheering up, which is beneficial in the highest degree.

Measure your smile and perform exercises to expand it.
Goodbye

With best wishes
Yours ever
I.B.G.

---

59 To Mrs Matilda Chapman   G.45750

December 1915 (P)   Pte Gurney, 2/5 Glosters, Chelmsford

My Dear Comtesse

I thoroughly expected to be with you today, but we are on Brigade duties, and have had so many extra things to do that I did not think it worth while to apply – rightly, as it turned out. But either next Saturday or Sunday will do I think. Probably Saturday – as I could stay till 10, if there is a train then. You say it is a pleasure to see me. I suppose it is difficult for a person outside the Army to know what a delight the mere being absent from quarters is. And when the return is to delicate food, white tablecloths, large, or largeish rooms, and such company as I can get at High Wycombe, then the feeling lasts as much as a week, and one is able to stand a whole 7 days without too much remembering the feeling of utter futility and waste of time that is the average thought of any educated man in Army life. I am not at all sure that we shall not be glad to get abroad – glad for a time anyhow; and that seems to be coming not long after Xmas.

Thank you, Madam; the food is better now. Indeed, I have left quite a lot lately. It is to be hoped your progeny (there's an expression to be applied to such children!) are either well or on the mend now.

As for Winter Trees – I believe, never are they so beautiful as now. Never are afterglows so far beyond words to describe as in Winter. And never is Teatime so lovely a thing to be looked forward to – or regretted most in the Army.

But I don't grumble. My health improves all the time. I am fit for double as much as when I joined 9 months ago. My mind can escape from itself a little. I think of music with some pleasure, and in another 6 months I ought to [be] able clearly to see my way to such health of mind and body as never before. Why not you, too? It is a question of thought and not overworking and Joy consciously created till the creation becomes habitual and spontaneous. And as for worrying – If the maker of Stars and Waters and Trees does not know his business, I am afraid that there is no one who can teach him.

Goodbye, and best of luck. O, I forgot to mention the Railway job. I am afraid it will be very difficult as there are only 612 of us. That is to say only 12 more can leave. But I never worry about possibilities, or hardly ever.

Yours affectionately

Ivor

[*On reverse of envelope Gurney has written* Letter and Mittens just received Thank you!]

60 *To Winifred Chapman* G.45750

December 1915 (KT)

My Dear Old Winnie

I am sorry you have been sick and at such an untactful time of holidays. Perhaps it is all better now. Bless you my child, I hope so. As for the photo, it simply hasn't arrived, and my laziness has prevented me writing to know why.

I hope to see you next Sunday, and it is fairly certain that I shall – or on Saturday.

What a funny Xmas this will be! Away from everything in the way of Children and ping-pong. Anyway, I shall be feeling much better this year than last, and not such a drag on the entertainment as then; for we simply must get up some sort of entertainment in this dead-alive unfortunate hole. Either 4 or 8 of us are plotting how to make believe that Army life may be made jolly around Christmas time. We'll do it, somehow. Unless they stick us on guard, or the extremely military operation of picking up paper. Anyway, I hope all you will concentrate all your phsycic [*sic*] faculties on having a damgood time then; and remembering me only to pledge me in the quaffing of huge tankards of beer, to the shouts of Waeshael! Let the ancestral hall of St Michael, and its stately keep and barbican echo to the sound.

Epic on the Celebration of the Mass of Christ

> Kinkering Kongs
> Do ping their pongs.
> And title-takers
> Get stomach achers.[1]

Tell tales all round again. Put your hand on each others backs, and count the shivers. Judge each ghost tale, not only by the frequency of the shivers but also by their duration and wobblyness.

Goodbye dear and best wishes

Yours affectionately

Ivor.

---

[1] Reference to the hymn beginning 'Conquering Kings their titles take' by John Chandler (1806-76), as in *Hymns Ancient and Modern*.

61 To the Chapmans   G.45750

December 1915 (KT)   Pte Gurney etc.

My Dear Old People

You'll not have me with you, I fear, just yet. Never mind, I don't care whether it's Xmas day or not, you shall have me with you before very long, as we are getting leave in bits. My bit will probably not be very long delayed. I only hope you racketty kids won't be at school when the auspicious occasion ausps.

Remember me in thy down-sitting and thy uprising. At the pinging of the pong, and the rendering on the tinkles. Sing you loud and lustily, and use your windbags bustily; prostrate yourselves every five minutes, reverently murmuring 'I.B.G.' and no doubt something will reward you; though the time be long-distant, and its connection with the act doubtful and hard to trace.

Bless you, my children
(From 60 downwards)

Your affectionate
I.B.G.

62 To the Chapman family   G.45750

17 December 1915 (P)
[*Postcard*]

Merry Xmas and don't forget last year's ping pong and beeeeastly wet, Likewise especially I.B.G.

63 To Sydney Shimmin   G.74.5.1-3

17 December 1915 (P)   Pte Gurney, Band. D Co. 2/5 Glosters,
                                                          Chelmsford, Essex

My Dear Shimmin

I am very glad to hear from other quarters that you are much better, and out of bed; even indulging in dietetic flights beyond brenmilk and brenburr. This is good news, and worthy of all men to be believed. There is a rumour also that you may be going to stay with the High Chapmen. May it be so, for you will enjoy yourself, if you emerge alive from so much petting and hero worship.

Your letter gave me great pleasure; and for once I took your advice on a matter of books, to the extent of buying that World's Classics Selection you mentioned (I have the first, selected by Peacock) and am just on reading it.

If you can go to High Wycombe, do so, old man; nothing could be better for you. If the combined energies of the Chapmen do not distract your mind from sickness, not even Hell will. (So you are safe either way.) Above all neglect not the honourable and galumpshious game of ping pong.

As for books – you ask for recommendations -

Poems of Today (Sidgwick and Jackson 2/6)

Century of Essays (Everyman)

Four Men – Belloc (Nelson 1/- and 2/-)

Scott's Novels. *Guy Mannering. Redgauntlet. Antiquary. Fortunes of Nigel. Rob Roy.* (Skip judiciously in all these)

Dickens *Pickwick. Nicholas Nickleby. Old Curiosity Shop.* (Skip etc) 1/- each

Algernon Blackwood *Garden of Pan*

Barrie *Window in Thrums. My Lady Nicotine. When a Man's Single. Auld Licht Idylls.* (all a bob)

Jacob's books; at least his short stories.

Mark Twain *Life on Mississippi. Tom Sawyer. Huckleberry Finn. Roughing It.*

Owen Wister's *The Virginian* (The Chapman's have it. Most strongly recommend)

Stevenson's books, including *Weir of Hermiston. The Wreckers* and *Across the Plains.*

But there is no need to buy most of these; to borrow them should be quite easy.

If you want more of our younger Poets, the two books of *Georgian Verse,* with *Poems of Today,* is what you want.

I read little now, and auction bridge (O game of games!) debating, a little music, and spending boring evenings with fools occupy me much. (O, you would enjoy much of Browning; say volume II in Everyman, and let me know if you get it. It wants selecting.)

For travels. A book by Tomlinson about S.America came out a few years ago. The title was perhaps by *Land and Sea.* Then there is Kipling's *Sea to Sea* (Read *Day's Work, Captains Courageous, Many Inventions, Rewards and Fairies, Traffics and Discoveries* as well.)

By Gum, I hope you do go to High Wycombe! We are to get 5 days leave, and I mean to spend a day of it at H.W. *when* it comes. May you be there. Then will I place my feet high up on the mantelpiece and smoke my churchwarden; deliver pregnant sayings of wisdom humourous and dry; fill my mind with the good fortune yet in store for us; feed myself on kindness and unselfish love; and altogether forget my stomach, music, the devil, and lastly but not leastly, the Army; that uncomfortable necessity.

Yours ever

I.B.G.

Bleshu, mein kind.

Late December 1915 (KT)   Pte Gurney, D Company, 2/5 Glosters,
                                        Chelmsford, Essex

Dear Mrs Voynich
     What a jolly letter!
     Thank you very much, and I hope you had an enjoyable Christmas in bed.
You must have had some exciting times in your war work, and some day I
shall be glad to hear more; though female furies are not much in my line, as I
prefer the more downright male in tantrums. But what a Xmas present for our
enemies! May he receive many such.
     We may quarrel about Milton, though my admiration for him is enormous,
– as a master of words; and God knows I envy even more the mastery of his
mind – but never about Bach. But the attitude towards Bach can hardly be
called by so cold a word as admiration, it is an enormous and partly
incredulous love; a wonder at such a wealth of wonderfulness and such a
control. A Bach hand grenade is worth a whole battery of howitzers of other
names.
     Shakespeare also.
     Do you know this – of Masefield?

> Here is a marvellous city, built of marvellous earth,
> Life was lived nobly here to give such beauty birth,
>
> Death is so blind and dumb Death does not understand -
> Death drifts the brain with dust, and soils the young limbs glory,
> Makes empires idle tales, and Fame a traveller's story,
> Death sends the naked soul to wander under the sky,
> Death opens unknown doors. It is most grand to die.[1]

I have sadly marred it, and omitted one line, but even then it must strike you.
     I shall be glad to be out of the army. The best thing for me is brainwork
again of some kind. I need something to fix my wandering thought in the
morning. My health is very different now to what it was, but even now a true
description of my mind at its best would be, not unhappy. Would two years
put me right now? I could walk 20 miles a day for weeks, and take pleasure in
music or verse after that. But *must* have work and movement not to be badly
depressed. At auction Bridge I am a cunning fiend, at least to such opponents
as one finds here. In the evenings I look with favour on the divine art of
Music; but in the afternoon I am a clod. Two years, think you?
     As for going abroad, there are rumours only.
     I pass with my comrades as one who is willing to be friendly with almost
anybody; looks depressed, but makes more jokes than anyone around here.
One who can play the piano above archangels, who can read anything at sight,
and makes (O wonder) classical music interesting; but has an itch, a positive

mania for arguing, and discursing on weird and altogether unimportant subjects. A good card-player, a good goal-keeper, a first-rate liar, (on occasions needful) and a friend of the 1/5 D.C.M.

Please use my Christian name when you write to me. I feel embarrassed. Private Gurney I know, and Ivor, but who is Mr Gurney?

Martin Chuzzlewit entrances me just now, and I have just come across a most delightful R.A.M.C. man who met Tolstoi in Russia. You would like him. He showed signs of drifting into a confirmed idealist at one time, but I think that will not happen now. You should have heard our folk song concert. And a priest (R.C.) who has heard the peasants sing all the Irish folk songs, nearly, I know. And the reader at Cardinal Newman's old place. And O, lots more – people you will never know. Lovable in themselves, and meaty stuff for the full artist there may be in me; If only once I can get to the stage of being able to think high and sustainedly for only two pages, as Prelude I Book II (the 48)! Then all the world shall have grace to know of the beauty of my County, of stars, and moving water, of friendship and the companionable solace of tobacco; all in little black dots of notes, and fiddle sounds and the harsher touch of the piano; but not in words, for towards Literature I feel slightly contemptuous. 'All art strives constantly to the precondition of music.'[2]

> Goodbye
> With best wishes
> Yours sincerely
> Ivor Gurney

[1] The Chief Centurions in Masefield's *The Tragedy of Pompey the Great* (1910) say the lines Gurney is trying to remember:

> Man is a sacred city, built of marvellous earth.
> Life was live nobly here to give this body birth.
> Something was in this brain and in this eager hand.
> Death is so dumb and blind, Death cannot understand.
> Death drifts the brain with dust and soils the young limbs' glory.
> Death makes women a dream and men a traveller's story,
> Death drives the lovely soul to wander under the sky,
> Death opens unknown doors. It is most grand to die.

[2] The quotation is a slight misremembering of Pater's 'All art constantly aspires towards the condition of music'; from 'The School of Giorgione' in *The Renaissance*.

65 To the Chapman family   G.45750

New Year 1916 (KT)

My Dear Chapmen

Indeed you are darlings of a special sort. The birthday book of my beloved William[1] is charming, and you know what I think of the oatcake and scones you make. But why have you not written in the book? Where are your birthdays?

I suppose the dangerous looking tin is a footwarmer? O individuals of great price. As for leave, and consequently coming to see you, I knows nowt. Not before Friday week anyhow, as far as I can see.

So please expect me on a visit either next Saturday or Sunday, but this is not certain. The Band has had some rough times lately, and one hardly knows what is going to happen. But Cheero. Leave cannot be long away; anyway not if the strong rumour is true that we are moving in February. Goodbye everybody.

Dad and the Lad. Mick and the Rest of the Click.

Yours affectionately
Ivor

[1] Wordsworth.

66 *To Mrs Matilda Chapman* G.45750

New Year 1916 (KT)

My Dear Comtesse

This kindness comes from all of you, but it bears the special mark of Tildaness upon it. Kindness follows me through life and I can say at least this for myself, that it bewilders me, and makes me shy. But you must be doing these things, I suppose. Thank you very much indeed.

As my letter says, the Fambly letter, I hope to see you soon and to get an oasis of green in this dreary-same life. But I keep pretty cheery, and have no doubt you are practising the noble art of keeping your pecker up. Anyway, let's all hope you will all keep well and happy in this coming New Year. What would not the end of the War and a week or so at Wycombe mean to me? Nevertheless, we cultivate the habit of slummocking along without worry and smiling at Life. Oatcake is no contemptible help to this, nor Wordsworth either.

Thank you.

Yours affectionately
Ivor

67 *To Marion Scott* G.41.20

1 January 1916 (P)   Pte Gurney, 2/5 Glosters

Dear Miss Scott

Thank you very much for your presents – the first of which was perfect; the second I am only regretful to have because most of the extracts are taken from the *Path to Rome*, a book I - have read.[1] But very much 'Thank you'!

I hear Sydney is with you now. Please remember me to him, and say that I hope he has received my last letter which was sent to Aylesbury. I hope he is getting better properly now. You shall have the songs right enough; but I hope to get leave in a little while, and to rummage them out, and perhaps retouch them. Would a fortnight be too long? If so, you shall have them before. 'Twa Corbies', 'Edward' and the Elizas; but not touched up.

Please let me have the Poetry Book when you have done with it. The markings were, almost, random guesses, or things I knew to be good. I hope to know it better before opinionising. How good our younger writers are. It is arguable that we have no great writers, but how good a foundation for another Colossus is this fashion of writing in clear direct and coloured English verses containing, as a general thing, no moralising, no recommendations save to love life, and to seize on its sweet moments when possible, and to make as many as possible; and still more to make existence a many coloured thing of joy. I hope you are getting strong now, and able to feel things more as you wish. Our poets should help an invalid who can feel. They have a divine dissatisfaction with blindness and spiritual inactivity that is tonic and stimulation.

(O by the way, I am leader of the Opposition against a Socialist Government, next Monday and have ordered Belloc's book on the Servile State[2] to make things hot for it.)

And I really feel, begin to feel, competent at last to feel and express dissatisfaction with Shakespeare. A great step. W.S. is not perfect often, but how much of the greatest things is perfect. Let us leave perfection to Tennyson and William Morris – in lengthy things, I mean.

The College Executive have held over my Schol: till the end of the war, which is very nice of them.

> But here go I walking common ways;
> Drab-souled things on every hand;
> A sulky mist is all its haze ....
> It's very dead desert this land.

Here I will wish you a happy new Year, full of keen experiences, and quietly joyful times of fallowness.

May the War end soon, and let us dream again, but nobly and to active ends. May England grow dearer, sweeter in herself (for we deserve better weather and more amiable smiles) and in our memories. And may the President of the Women Musicians be preserved to sanity.

With best wishes
Yours very sincerely
Ivor Gurney

[1] *A Picked Company, Being a Selection from the Writings of H.Belloc* has the right date (1st edition July 8 1915, 2nd edn. November 1915) but its preface notes that there is not 'any passage from *The Path to Rome* ... due to copyright difficulties'.
[2] Hilaire Belloc, *The Servile State*, 1912.

18 February 1916 (P)

My Dear Chapmen

After all, Harvey could not get leave, and so every part of my plan miscarried, and we never met. Well, well; so wags the world. Receive herewith the grateful wherewithal. This is chiefly to let you know that we are nearly certain to be off on Saturday to Tidworth that haunt of devils.[1] If so, it is not so far from Reading – and – consequently from the Merry Chapmen. Prepare to receive music and books forthwith.

Yours affectionately
Ivor

[1] The battalion went to Tidworth on Saturday 19 February, and then on to Park House Camp on Salisbury Plain.

69 To Ivor Gurney G.61.144

17 February 1916

Printed circular from the Royal College of Music Union

Dear Mr Gurney

It has been brought to the notice of the R.C.M. Union General Committee that some of the Members who are on Active Service may have experienced difficulties in arranging for the maintenance of their professional musical interests during their enforced absence, and may be glad to know where to apply in the event of their wanting a temporary teacher for their pupils, a reliable deputy to take over a position, or a responsible representative to gather any royalties from publishers which may accrue.

It has therefore been suggested that it might be desirable to form a Sub-Committee of the R.C.M. Union for this purpose, but before any definite steps are taken the General Committee has requested us to enquire into the matter, and to ascertain the views of Members on Active Service. It will be of the greatest help to us if you will kindly let us know at your earliest convenience what your views are, and whether such a scheme would be of any service to you personally. Replies should be sent to the Hon. Secretary (MISS MARION SCOTT) at the above address.

Yours faithfully,

Marion M.Scott	Harold Samuel
Mabel Saumarez Smith	Harold E.Darke

Gurney's reply on the reverse of the above circular :

Dear Committee

I have experienced no great difficulty in arranging for the maintenance of my professional musical interests, for at the best they were only slightly more than nil. As for requiring a temporary teacher, you could serve me little in this, but for any temporary pupils – at half a guinea a lesson of 20 minutes – I should feel most grateful. Your remark about collecting royalties happens merely to be ironic; and so does not give me anything like the pleasure the other offer does – that offer to provide a responsible deputy for my position. My position is at present that of a private in the 2/5 battallion of the Gloucesters, who are about to move to huts on Salisbury plain. Any deputy, trustworthy or otherwise, would be most gratefully welcomed, and fulsomely flattered, receive all my military decorations, and valuable insight into the best methods of mud-cleaning with vocal accompaniment.

Yours truly   Ivor Gurney

---

70 *To Marion Scott*   G.41.18

22 February 1916 (P)   Pte Gurney, D. Co 2/5 Glosters,
                                                                   Park House Camp, Salisbury

Dear Miss Scott

Thank you for your kind letter. Yes, the Elizabethan songs are good. They are damned good – and no apology. 'Edward' in the copy I sent you is almost complete, – anyway could be completed with that other, first script. But somewhere there is a fair copy, which may yet turn up.

You shall have 'The Sea' and 'I praise the tender flower'[1] before we go hence and maybe are no more seen; one or two more perhaps by Davies or Masefield.

In my best moods I feel, though at the same time recognising fully what the names of Beethoven and Bach stand for, that I have immense capabilities in me – if only I can make myself strong and tranquil, and are given time. I am not greatly afraid of Death. I am big enough to view great things in their true proportions, more or less, though not yet the smaller ones. Of all the written words of Man that help one to submit to Destiny I know nothing more persuasive than that part of *War and Peace* which tells of Pierre's captivity and his peasant friend. It is near the end, the first half of the last volume I think – stamped with genius and a high loftiness, Bach-like and as true as his Preludes and Fugues. Will you ask Mr Dunhill[2] why he has such a comparatively low idea of the slow movement of the Rasoumoffsky? To me it has enormous significance. It is full of stars and mystery, and provokes those questions never to be answered while flesh contains us. I will write to Howells in a few days. But if you see him first – tell him that the score of 'Spring' is not the final one, which is not yet found. But that the parts will show him what are the tiny but vital alterations – particularly the change of time is to be noticed.

Oh, this place is quite charming, and Huts are 7th Heaven to tents.

Yours very sincerely
Ivor Gurney

---

[1] Settings of poems by Davies and Bridges respectively.

[2] Thomas Frederick Dunhill (1877-1946), composer and teacher. He helped to bring Gurney's poems to the notice of the publishers; he also incidentally wrote a setting of 'The Fiddler of Dooney'. The Rasoumoffsky (then the standard spelling) are Beethoven's three string quartets opus 59, dedicated to Count Rasoumoffsky; Gurney is referring to the third.

71 *To Mrs Voynich*

G.41.19

Late February 1916 (KT)

Pte Gurney, D. co 2/5 Glosters,
Park House Camp, Salisbury

Dear Mrs Voynich

Thank you for your present, which gave me great pleasure – that brand being as I think the very best, and, worse luck, is not obtainable here. We are about 3 miles from Tidworth, in the middle of downs, a charming spot; far past our best hopes; and huts at worst are far better than tents, in winter at any rate; and who may deny that winter is here now?

More and more, though still not very actively, I feel the need for brainwork – Chess does all for me that is done as yet. I am very grateful for Chess; a noble and fascinating game.

The two camp pianos are distressing. One suffers badly from a disease, the opposite of aphasia. Its nervous system is so weak that some time must elapse before a note can be repeated. And may I pause here to repeat my firm faith that the slow movement of the C major Rasoumoffsky Quartett is one of the loveliest things in music?

How are your aliens? Some times I think that it would be nice to share your duties occasionally. We are firing and marking for a fortnight, which is an interesting and cushy job. It would tax Shakespeare's mind to conceive the monotony of eternal bayonet fighting, squad drill, and fatigue.

Isn't 'Vittoria Corombona' fine? (*The White Devil*) *The Alchemist, Cataline* and *All for Love* are very good too.[1] But the later Jonson comedies are impregnably dull.

Snatch of Shakespearian wit, from Pte Tim Godding. A Sergeant was going round collecting birthdays, (not for generous purposes.) and one man hesitated to answer. Said T.G. 'He don't know his birthday. He don't know his name. The sun hatched it.' Our men are far too fond of swearing, and quarrel, though not badly, on too small provocation; but they are a good lot, and are to be honoured. I believe we are not less in mettle than the 7th. Time will prove, and perhaps before long. Did you care for Henry James. If so, what books? With best wishes

I remain, yours very sincerely

Ivor Gurney

¹ Plays by respectively Webster, Jonson Jonson, and Dryden.

72 *To Herbert Howells*   G.3.33

Late February 1916 (KT)   Pte Gurney, D Co 2/5 Glosters,
Park House Camp, Salisbury

My dear Howler

Here am I, not so very long ago an invalid, cohabiting with 30 others in a small hut; to feed on the first thing that comes along – so be the canteen is shut – to sleep on bare boards, no paliasses; in damp blankets; rising at midnight to stoke fires, or fulfill the needs of nature; going forth into snowdrifts 8 inches deep, as they are now; reading Shakespeare and composing in a continual and profane noise; meekly obeying my spiritual and temporal pastors and masters; not at all unhappy, and remembering always my dear Cranham, Framilode, Minsterworth. I am sure either to be killed or cured by this, hein?

Well, about those songs, my benefactor. All's well with the Elizabethans save 'Spring' of which there is another score, as the parts testify. There is very little difference between the two, but one difference is important – the line or so where there is a change to 3/4 time for a bar or so – or indeed one bar only. I have just rewritten 'I praise the tender flower' also, in which you may make alterations as I am away from pianos. My brain is pretty clear now, however, at best, and I don't think there is much wrong.

Tidworth country, where we are, is supposed to be the nicest spot on the plain, and this is probably true as the lookout from D Co parade ground is not unlike Cranham, from which I suppose it is only about 50 miles direct. Here it is chalk, there limestone, but both look much alike at a distance, and woods are woods all England over. There is one horrid change however. Today the snow is 8 inches deep in places, and consequently there was no *Times*, no *Daily News*, my usual matutinal mental pabulum, as a really educated person would say.

I think we are quite near the front – the fighting line, but at least I have control enough of my mind to think very little of this. The only thought that disturbs me ever, is that all my continual striving and endeavour to become a fit and full man, ('full man' is Shakespeare¹) may be ended by a German bullet or bayonet. But then my belief in our destiny rises clear and strong and in spite of my sick mind, and by the help of the last volume or so of *War and Peace* I am calm again. Read it, boy, read it.

War and Peace & Shakespeare & Whitman & St Matthew & Wordsworth &

Plutarch is a pretty complete diet – mental pabulum.

These men are rough as a rule who swear frightfull;y, but are good men inside, and full of things for such as I to imitate. Floreat Gloucestriencis. 2/5, 7 and 9th. French inspected us last Wed[2]: a short kind faced gentleman.

Good bye

Yours

I.B.G.

[1] The *O.E.D.* attributes it to Bacon, who in 'Of Studies' says that 'Reading maketh a full man; conference a ready man and writing an exact man.' 'Full-mann'd' occurs in Gurney's favourite *Antony and Cleopatra*, III.7.51.
[2] Sir John French inspected them on 22 February; see *Ordeal*, p.61.

73 *To Mrs Matilda Chapman* G.45750

March 1916 (KT) Pte Gurney, D Co 2/5 Glosters,
Park House Camp, Salisbury

My Dear Comtesse

I was sorry to receive so sad a letter from you. One does not like to think of one's friends suffering, and for your complaint, I have of course a particular feeling. I hope that you are not eating too little; that is worse than eating too much by far.

Yes, we have left Chelmsford all right, we did so a fortnight ago; and have been literally freezing ever since. It *has* been cold, and most of us are wheezing and coughing when we are not standing at 'shun or other impossible situations. I might mention madam, that should you – I say, *if* you *should* happen to send a parcel of eatables, it would not be wasted. Also, if you could, would you get me another stopper for the valve of the air-cushion; the original stopper has got lost, and the poor cushion lies useless in my valise.

I hope all the kids are well and happy, occasionally playing ping-pong as a sort of sacramental remembrance of I.B.G. And E. Chapman, who will receive the most tremendous licking at chess next time we meet – with P – R4 K Kt to B3, K, B to QB5 etc.

I think we are not very far from going now. A man from the brigade office – who may know nothing says 3 weeks. I just dodder on and worry as my mind will let me.

This is a pretty place, far better than we expected, about 3 miles from Tidworth, almost in Hants. And Huts are far away better than tents. There is a stove going all day to toast things by, and make things look more cheerful, and the men are noisy and happy – they are bellowing popular songs, in a robust but sentimental fashion – a good lot of chaps.

Good-bye everybody, and cheer up, ma Comtesse. Always eat a good breakfast, a rule that I live up to now with considerable success. Your description of the concert made me wish a little for music, but not much as yet.

Good bye. Love to everybody.

Yours affectionately
Ivor

74 *To the Chapman family* G.45750

16 March 1916 (P)

[*Postcard*]

Thank you everybody. Letter coming. Meanwhile, please send Davies' *Foliage*, and please order R. Bridges' *Poems* in that shilling edition, like the one you keep for me. I think I might set one or two, and must have paper covers. And so, cheero – or Ipsi Pris, as we say.

Ivor.

75 *To the Chapman family* G.45750

20 March 1916 (KT) Pte Gurney, D Co 2/5 Glosters,
Park House Camp, Salisbury

My Dear Chapmen

Your parcel was very acceptable to a poor stranded mariner, marooned far from comfortable chairs and hot oatcake and scones; perishing cold, but among men whose cheerfulness not even the devil could daunt, and so, not complaining more than they of my lot.

We don't write many letters here. For myself, I hate the Army so much, and all the worrying little muckings-about fash me so, that I spend the evenings trying to forget all about it. There is firing going on now; I fired the preliminary course, but developed a bad cold, and a catarrh that kept me continually in galvanic movement, no doubt amusing to others, but annoying to myself. But it is merely impossible not to blame oneself in some measure for being unhappy among such men as these. Their vitality is marvellous, their spirits high and continually high.

I am sorry the poor Comtesse has not been well. If good works and a generous heart might make health and happiness, or had I anything to do with the distribution of felicity, she should do very well, but alas! it has little to do with me. I make her a present of our little Regulars back-badge, which we are extremely proud of, are to be allowed to wear, and to me are very pretty. More shall follow when it is possible to obtain them.

Thank you kindly for the book which is nearly finished, and then shall be returned, for my book-accommodation is limited, and would do better with you. Thank you very much for the cushion, but is the other one, my name worked thereon, to be wasted for a valve? Nay!

Goodbye, my dears, and bless you all, and again thank you for your cheering letters, like stars in a dark night. Winnie and Micky shall have letters soon. Greeting to the Arch-Power Ted, though he *did* beat me at chess! Yet will I be revenged – revenged.

Yours affectionately
Ivor

76 *To Marion Scott*   G.41.21

22 March 1916 (P)   Pte Gurney, D.Co 2/5 Glosters,
Park House Camp, Salisbury

Dear Miss Scott

The beginning of this letter is to commemorate Tim Godding – one of the most original people in all this regiment, a big word.

Here am I, sitting on my bed, against my kit bag, half-reading Carlyle, little soaking through to my dull mind, when I become aware that a boxing match is being arranged. Tim Godding will be obviously somewhere near the top of this. And presently, 'No, mate, I can't say as I can box, but Ive had – good hidings from one bloke and another ....'

Today also, when we were lying on our bellies, trying to load and reload and rereload with the quickness of those who get extra pay for it – though not likely to get the pay for those who have extra quickness – a skylark arose. Now Tim Godding has little bits of jargon, some of which I strongly suspect to be Hindustani. One of these is 'Ipshi Pris', a sign of high spirits, of salutation to a passing battallion or the crown of a joke; anything joyful. So Tim Godding half turned over, looked up to the first blue of spring -

'Ipshi pris, skylark; ipshi pris'!

One night also, after lights out, he, as is the usual course of things gave voice to the feelings of the hut – this time on the universal distaste for army life. 'Ah, let me once get out of this bastard lot, and they won't see Tim again. The – Germans can come and fight on our doorstep, and all as I'll say is 'Fight on, lads, fight on.' They can come and drag our old man out the front door, and I'll be up in the attic – washing me feet.'

It was also he who made answer to the doctor, when asked how he felt. – 'Bad all over doctor. Worse in some places than in others.'

Our address is Salisbury, but in reality we are 14 miles or so away. Tidworth is our habitation more or less, and on a sunny day, the view from our camp is charming. Army life is for me full of long blanks of tedium. Would that I were sound in mind and body, and able to take all in that is [to] be taken! Hard for an artist to go self-condemned to practical blindness and deafness through that which might be so fruitful to him! But on the whole I take it as a price to be paid for my education, and dodder on as contented as may be. But it is hard to long for beauty, and beauty obtained to remain unsatisfied – chronically discontent. But given time I think that my revenge on myself and circumstances shall be long and sweet.

Last Sunday Cridlan and I lay out on a down so like our own; but the first violet had not yet arrived, whereas the woods must be happy-eyed with them at home – in Glostershire where Spring sends greetings before other less happy counties have forgotten Winter and the snow. Where the talk is men's talk, and eyes of folk are as kind as the soft airs. The best roads in England, the finest cider, the richest blossom in the most magical orchards, beauty content in security, strength quiet in confidence controlled, blood mixed of plain and hill, Welsh and English; are not these only of my county, my home? And yet were I there the canker in my soul would taint all these. But at least I have reached the position of longing for work, and of blaming myself for part of my misfortunes at any rate.

Now we are allowed to wear our honour, the back-badge; and great is the joy thereat. Today is the anniversary of that great day in Egypt when the rear rank of the double line faced about and the Old Braggs – 28th Foot – repelled two attacks in blood and glory.

Of course you may quote from my song, and accept my best wishes for a successful address.

Yes, that A minor 6/8 movement is the one I meant.[1]

You ask me whether I will look at certain poems with a view to setting – after the war. The reason I do not write now, is not because there is a war on, but because I do not feel bound to write; when my mind compels me, then I will write; then and not before.

I am not altogether in agreement with the Russian attitude to Suffering. It is too passive.

In a review of Rupert Brooke's *Letters from America*[2], I found that Henry James had written to this effect, in the preface. 'I admire the British soldier. His mind seems to contain a moral hospitality to all the vagaries of fortune', etc. So it does. He grins nearly all the time that one might expect him to have little reason for doing so.

We are 14 miles from Salisbury, near Tidworth. If we stay any time I mean to visit Stonehenge.

Arthur Bliss a Captain![3]

A Captain!

!

There is no chance of coming to London; none at all. We shall see France, I guess, first.

I still read the *Times* Supplement with great pleasure. It is a good review. But don't read the leaders as a rule – don't heed Clutton's Brockings or Brock's Cluttonings. But I did read Andrieff's article, and that on Shelley, – both very good.[4]

The band is a washout.

And I am at present a Wesleyan, for the Wesleyan contingent is so small 'that it 'scapes the thunderbolt'[5] of particular Sunday inspections.

> With best wishes
> Yours very sincerely
> Ivor Gurney

[1] Of one of his own quartets.
[2] *Letters from America* with a Preface by Henry James, 1916.
[3] Arthur Bliss (1891-1975), composer and student at the R.C.M. in 1914; was commissioned to the Royal Fusiliers in October 1914, mentioned in despatches in April 1916, promoted Captain in 1916, wounded on the Somme in July 1916, transferred to Grenadier Guards in December 1917, gassed at Cambrai in November 1918.
[4] 'Shelley was with us' is the front-page article in the *TLS* for 24 February 1916, and 'God Save England' by Leonid Andrieff the front-page article for 2 March.
[5] 'Some innocents scape not the thunderbolt'; *Antony and Cleopatra*, II.5.77.

77 *To Mrs Matilda Chapman*   G.45750

March 1916 (KT)
[*Postcard*]

I forgot to ask you – will you please send me Davies' *Foliage* – or whatever its name is – the green covered book. And please send more *R.C.M. Magazines* to Mr Watson, 46 Juer St, Battersea, London S.W.

> My feet – the mud doth stick' em
>   Would I were at High Wycombe!
> In divers muds and mucks
>   Worse by far than Bucks.

[*Unsigned*]

78 *To Mrs Voynich*   G 41.8

April 1916 (E)   Pte Gurney, *B* Co 2/5 Glosters,
                                                   Parkhouse Camp, Salisbury

Dear Mrs Voynich
    Thank you again for your parcel, which made a redletter day for me – partly on account of the unexpectedness of sweets of such quality in such conditions.

Chocolate and chocolate-cream is all that we can get here. Mrs Taylor's[1] parcel made much the same sensation, and lasted longer; we get pretty well fed, though not quite on those lines. But O! when is the war going to end? My legs and head might change places most days, and I not know the difference. As to going to France, that is a matter of indifference to me. Let me go, get not too painful or undignified a wound, and return to quietness and a space for digestion, which space is now occupied by evolutions in marching order. Yet out of all this mirk and gloom there shines the gleam of 5 days leave on Monday! And the doubt whether I shall be able to enjoy it or not ,....... But Cranham, Framilode, Minsterworth, Crickley, May Hill, and the sight of Malverns .... The soft air and kind faces that go in my mind with the name Gloucester.

I wonder how you are getting on with your alien work. Have you had any more difficulties with female desperadoes? And how the garden is getting on, and the little pool.

How are Geoffrey and Julian? Salonika has been a rest cure for him, by all accounts. I wonder whether we might be sent there. But France is the ever present word with us. And yet – there is the youth of us of the 3rd line recruits lately drafted in; and even more on account of the Home service men of other regiments attached to us, which make a mixed lot. These draft men signed on only a short time ago, and are really no more than conscripts. Why have they drafted other regiments' Home Service men on to us? Why not our own?[2]

Tim Godding made a remark the other day, which might amuse you. Someone was poking fun at him, and Tim, patient for a time, got all his own back with 'Ah, mate, I was born too near a wood to be frightened with owls.' But he is a Shakesperian character, and I am sorry to have left him in D Company, though I am happy and more at home in B.

But O, O, O to get back to my music, and time for books and walks. All manifestations of energy are hard for me, but I'd manage more work now than ever before in my nerve-ridden existence. Have you no observations by a Distinguished Neutral Observer to comfort me withal – that Peace is near to view? How long shall the tyranny of Officers and Non-coms endure? When shall the advent of the orderly sergeant inspire no fear?

But Floreat the 2/5. They are a clean minded comradely lot whose cheerfulness and cork-like buoyancy fill me ever with admiration and love. Can there be mettle enough in the Germanies to meet this spirit if it be wide-spread?

Will you please send me Sidney's address when you write? Or before, on a P.C. to

19 Barton St

Gloucester

Bless his heart! I believe he hates it more than I.

Do you know, Madam, that hut orderly – the lighter of fires and washer up of dishes etc for the day – is an enviable job, and sought after by myself not least? And Wash house fatigue? And firing and marking from 7 till 2 a dream of bliss? 3 hours trench digging after! Excuse these moans. But I am as a bottle in the smoke, a mouldy pelican in a howling wilderness of monkeys.[3]

A miserable self analysis of a despised carcass-haunted spirit, or vice-versa. A being cut off from Civilisation by the fixed gulfs of Militarism and an extreme distaste for doing anything not forced on me. Hamlet in Khaki. A Macbeth without courage to Murder or fly.

Ah, well. They who funk Life have to pay! Perhaps I am lucky in paying hardly but more quickly than most in my position have to.

Anyway there is Tim Godding and many more, masters of life, and my unconscious kindly instructors.

My best wishes to the Spring flowers.

Yours very sincerely
Ivor Gurney

[1] Perhaps the wife of Franklin Taylor (1843-1919), the R.C.M. Professor of Pianoforte.
[2] Presumably because of the new policy of avoiding the wiping out of the men of particular localities.
[3] The bottle in the smoke occurs in the *Book of Common Prayer*, Psalm cxix; the pelican (not 'mouldy') in Psalm cii of the same; but Gurney is also mixing in the 'wilderness of monkeys' from Shylock's valuing of his ring in *The Merchant of Venice*, III. i.

79 *To Marion Scott*   Hurd Transcript and G.41.24

25 April 1916[1]

Dear Miss Scott

Thank you for your letter, and the praise of my song: which is in itself a complete vindication of all charges against the intelligence of woman-kind. But, joking aside: Mrs.Voynich tells me you are ill. Which news, if it is true, gives me great distress. It is hard for so plucky a person to be tied to house at best, and maybe bed. Hard lines, hard lines. And it is not with you, as with us, that you escape unpleasant duties by falling sick! With us in many cases, most cases, it is a looked for blessing. I await anxiously the time when either we go to the front, or I fall not too seriously ill. Cleaning up is wasting me away to a pale shadow. But what have you to look for in all this? Nothing but nothing. It is hard lines indeed. I hope you are able to read and so forth. In that hope there are two books, both of which you will agree are extraordinarily good of their kind. The Sonnets in *Friends* are some of the best modern sonnets I know. But you shall read and test all these for yourself. And in this connection – Gibson's – let me tell you of my happiest day on my lately-spent 5 days.

On the Tuesday, the second of the five, I breakfasted deliciously late, and after lounging about in a most unmilitary manner with the *Times* and *Daily News* I completed my toilet, got my bike and went down the noblest road I know – the Gloucester-Malvern road, where all the telegraph poles are down and great trees lying stricken and low forever. Through Maisemore, Hartpury, Corse Staunton – near the Malverns now – then into a pub, where I quaffed a foaming beaker of gingerbeer (price 2d) and turned off to Ryton, across roads puzzling on the map, but asking questions of my own courteous country men and women. Then as I neared Redmarley (O the good county) I saw the sight which had been my hope to see – Daffodils growing in the orchards and lovely-green fields smiling at the sun. Little knolls rising up continually on the unexpectant eye, deep lanes (and still the uprooted disinherited trees; not wasted to decay, I thought in consolation, but nobly overthrown by a noble enemy: 'a Roman by a Roman valiantly conquered.'[2]) and a soil coloured of a surpassing red, from which Redmarley gets its name. That little village set under the shadow of the Malverns and set with orchards thick and fair with blossoms and flowers. Cowslips, daffodils, bluebells, ladysmocks; all Shakespearian like the country – a perfect setting for the old comedy.

Then a wandering thought became firm. Lascelles Abercrombie and Wilfred Gibson both live at Ryton, near my way. I would go see their houses. And when I asked some pleasant smiling woman where Mr Abercrombie lived, I was told 'The second house on the left'. Then there came a dip of the road with a gorgeous bit of redsandstone rock jutting out on the road, then a double cottage with a sort of courtyard. I stood hesitating for long with my eyes fixed on its white front; made up my mind, went up and knocked. Let it suffice to say that I spent 6 very full hours of joy with Mrs Abercrombie, her husband is munition-making in Liverpool, and acquired a rich memory. I wheeled the pram, I did feats of daring to amuse the three children, and talked books and music with Mrs Abercrombie, the genius of the place; all set in blue of the sky, green of the fields and leaves, and that red, that red of the soil. Abercrombie is very interested in music too, and can read scores; his is a very wide versatile mind.

Then I left her with kind thoughts and words, westward to Newent and Dymock, to take supper finally at Minsterworth – but no laughter there now. Mrs Harvey being a widow, and her three sons in the army. But there was Bach for a while. Then out to the night and Venus high in the air and black vault studded with stars not so fair as she but dear to me; and most dear.

Here's a go! This is 9 oclock and the sergeant has just stricken us dumb with the news of 'Night operations 12.15 marching order.' 'Oh, the pain'! as our catchword runs. That gives you some notion of the way they work us now. I don't mind the hard work so much, but the cleaning!!!

I feel as if 'Heldenleben' were inadequate to express my feelings – pettily childish – O those buttons and buckles and boots! Hell to it, say I.

Goodbye, and please get well soon; it will gratify many people myself not least. And the photographs you shall have at once when they are ready.

Meanwhile I envy you the Rupert Brooke.

Yours very sincerely
Ivor Gurney

[1] This letter is dated 25 May 1916 by an editor on the ms and in *Ordeal* on p.221 note 22, but that was the day the 2nd/5th Gloucesters arrived in Le Havre. The Hurd transcript has ?25 April 1916. [*The Gloucester ms begins at 'on the map'.*]

[2] Gurney has substituted 'conquered' for 'vanquished' in this line from *Antony and Cleopatra*, IV. xiii.

80 To J.W. Haines   G.84.4.1-4

1 May 1916 (P)   Pte Gurney, B Company, 2/5 Glosters,
                                              Park House Camp, Salisbury

My Dear Haines

Thank you very much for *Battle*,[1] but curse this nib. To me it is not as good as Housman; some things appeal to me for setting, but not strongly. The first is pretty and 'Deaf' and 'Comrades' I like best. The last is good too.

But *Friends* has some real slap-up damned good stuff. Clear simple direct untortured thought and verse.

'I saw three pigs ariding' is as good as could be wanted.

The first four sonnetts, particularly the second. 'Tenants', that about the gold beater, about their house, and about the room lit by the winter sun, ending 'up on the bed of bridal birth and death'.

I say, sir, these are bloody good, keenly seen, directly felt, or, rather, vice versa. And cheero for Gibson. I lent *Battle* to my platoon sergeant for an experiment; and he particularly chose 'Comrades', which pleased me.

Here we still are, worked like horses, having quite narrowly escaped being sent as a division to Ireland; some of the Worcesters have gone I believe; and as fluent in speech as ever about the Army; but managing to snatch some illicit and forbidden joy in one way or another – myself by reading in bed after hours. I read the end of *Antony* last night, and confirmed my belief that it is the finest thing in Shakespeare.

What do you think of *All for Love*?[2] Did you read any account of that Asquith gathering of the poets to read their own things? There was quite a long account in that deplorable rag the *Weekly Dispatch*. Davies seems to have been the chief figure of importance, and Yeats of fun.

Good bye and thank you. Please let me know if anything small cheap and good comes out.

Yours v. sincerely
Ivor Gurney.

[1] By W.W.Gibson (1916).
[2] By John Dryden (1678).

2 May 1916 (P)
Pte Gurney, B Company, 2/5 Bat.,
Gloster Regt., Park House, Salisbury

Dear Howler

I was delighted to see your name down as one of the composers of new works for Westminster. How I should like to hear them! Have they spoilt the Cathédral with frescoes? There has been some correspondence about it, and I should like to know what you think.

Today is a perfect Spring day, and so I must think of Glostershire and Shakespeare, and envy those who may look on our county's radiant green and joyful blossoming. O the richness in the ride from Gloster to Newnham! Someday, someday....

What have you been writing this term? Something clear and English I hope. Does the war still obsess you? If so, you are, perhaps, less fortunate than your comrades in the Army, whose mind is full of pack and rifle, buttons and boots.

When you get back to London, ask Miss Scott for the two books of poems I lent her; you will probably find something to suit you. How I envy you the chance of seeing Shakespeare, a desire that is very strong in me. O to see *Antony* and to be thrilled once again by Antony's passion and the proud defiances of the great queen. If I must die think only this of me,[1] that I sincerely wish that what rag of a mantle I possess should descend on you, and inspire you someday to turn your thoughts to an Antony symphony.[2]

Do you know Miss Scott has been very ill, a near squeak this time apparently.

How is Benjamin?[3] Tell him, as a friend I send a blessing; as a lootenant nothing but kicks. Floreat Armae Brittannicae, et exerciti whose motto is Fed Up. Fed up.

Yours ever
I.B.G.

Mrs Voynich has whooping cough.

---

[1] Quotation of the first line of Rupert Brooke's 'The Soldier'.
[2] He didn't
[3] Arthur Benjamin (1893-1960), composer and fellow R.C.M. pupil; joined O.T.C. January 1915. Gazetted 2nd Lieut., 15th Battn Royal Fusiliers, May 1915. Proceeded to France, May 1916. Promoted Captain, 32nd Battn Royal Fusiliers 1916. Transferred to R.A.F. end of 1917. Made prisoner by Germans, July 1918. Demobilised 1919.

Soon after 2 May 1916 (KT)   Pte Gurney, B Company, 2/5 Bat.,
                                Gloster Regt., Park House Camp

Dear Haines

I meant to send a postal order immediately after I discovered that it had not been included in the letter. Now when there is time and I do recollect it I find that there is only 3/- left, and some one wants to borrow one of them. So please excuse me for a week.

And again, thank you immensely for *Friends*, an unforgettable book.

Mrs Abercrombie has just written me a delightful letter from Liverpool, where she now is, in reply to a letter asking for the home adress [*sic*] of the honey I had there; so that we have lost our local poets, and my county is so much the poorer. Dammit, it is a loss. Let us raise up a host, a horde, a legion of young poets all eager in praise of that Severn county of ours.

My town-pride received a shock yesterday – and my pocket. Cridland and I went to Salisbury, which took both of us by storm. The Cathedral is not so fine as Gloucester, but the surroundings thereof, and the town beat ours. So we fell back on the county and recovered our spirits. But really, if you have not seen it, there are many worse ways of occupying your time before death in delighting in yet another glory of England. It was shocking to one who is used to the clear eyes clear skin and generally good physique of our own fold to see the half starved faces of these Wiltshire people; but that I hope is more a result of bad former times than these present. I bought Cobbett's *Rural Rides*, in Nelson 6d edition, there and am getting on very well with it, he praises the look of our valley people, and hurt by the condition of the Wiltshire.

On my word, if there is anything left of me, part of every year shall be given up to the life of the country Inn, after the style of Borrow, Fielding and Cobbett, to say nothing of the I.B. (Immortal Bard.) Through a misunderstanding we had 6 miles to walk at 12.30 midnight, and by the greatest of good luck discovered a policeman, soft of voice, racy of speech, full of local knowledge and country pride, and of ideas in the making of which newspapers had played no part. He exhorted us at the end – we had been speaking of the Cathedral and the C. of E. – to 'Take care of the old things. We cannot make them again, and anything which has lasted a long time must have some good in it'. We were willingly delayed, and answered back at 2.30 a.m. Sergeant asleep, good! You shall have your willingly-to-be-paid debt soon. Maybe in francs!

                                Yours
                                I.B.Gurney

May 1916 (KT) 2/5 Glosters, Park House Camp

Dear Miss Scott

I hope things are going better now with you, and that you feel able at least to take a keen interest in things. From your letters it would seem almost impossible ever to dull that interest in you, but one cannot tell. A Brave pretence has to do sometimes. However if anything could stir a lethargic brain, I think Gibson's little book would do it as well as anything. There is no doubting Gibson's health anyway. So clear a vision and so musical a speech must belong to physical and mental well-being. 'I saw three pigs' is the very expression of spontaneous joy – to be found in folksong and in Bach preeminently.[1]

You mention Ian Hay and MacGill.[2] I had a glance at Ian Hay, and wished I could read it, but had to leave it. What I saw was very good indeed. Patrick MacGill I remember from reviews, and his *Autobiography* I very firmly intend to get hold of some day. By the way have you ever read W.H.Davies *Autobiography of a Super-Tramp*. It would delight you immensely by its simplicity and plain truth. (I am not sure whether you have read any of his verse. I could lend you *Nature Poems* and *Farewell to Poesy*. The best, *Songs of Joy* is lost.[3] The first of the Songs of Joy ends up thus

'Sing happy soul, thy songs of Joy,
Such as the brook sings in the wood
That all night has been strengthened by
Heaven's purer flood.')

The only poor thing about the *Autobiography* is the title. I hate 'Super' things. However England seems in little danger of becoming high-faluting these days.

[*There is no signature, but a p.s. fills the remaining space:*]
O please let Howells have the Gibson books will you? They ought to stir him up.

---

[1] *Friends* (1916). The poem is called 'Girl's Song' and may be compared with Gurney's poems of the same title written in an attempt to capture the same unspecified sense of apprehensive wonder and awe at life.

[2] Ian Hay was the pseudonym of John Hay Beith (1876-1952) who wrote many plays and books; his *First Hundred Thousand* (1915) is a narrative of the war. Patrick MacGill (1890-?) also wrote of the war in, for example, *The Amateur Army* (1915). He also wrote *Songs of a Navvy* (1911) and *Songs of the Dead End* (1912) and *Children of the Dead End: the Autobiography of an Irish Navvy* (1914). He was published with Gurney in *The Muse at Arms*.

[3] *Nature Poems* (1908), *Farewell to Poesy* (1910) and *Songs of Joy* (1911). The quotation is almost accurate.

17 May 1916
[*No address or perhaps even first page(s), but Park House postmark.*]

Your letter reads as though written by a radiantly healthy person, but you say Yorkshire is to[o] far to travel. You *must* have some go in you. I meant to ask you in this where Hindhead is; but today reading Cobbett's *Rural Rides* (in Nelson's 6d Library)[1] I came across it. Did you know that both Arun and Wey make their start near there? I love Arun, not for the sight of it, of which I know nothing, but for its name and for Belloc's continual affectionate references. Especially that in an essay on either Death or Rest. Methuen now publish a selection from him at 1/-. I forget the name unless it is *A Goodly Company*.[2]

We are certainly to be off soon. Next Monday or Tuesday will be the exact date most likely. All this leaves me merely indifferent, as I set the extra danger against the not having to clean buttons; and not being inspected every morning.

I mean to send with this a book on Keats by Edward Thomas.[3] I hope you will like it.

On Saturday the gods gave me a brief respite from servitude, and I snatched a space at High Wycombe,[4] after great gulfs of wasted time at Andover, Basingstoke and Maidenhead and Reading. From Basingstoke to Reading I travelled with a corporal of the Coldstreams, who had been out since Mons. He was the kind of man who would make an efficient and self-effacing member of a Church Council. Quiet voiced and quiet-eyed he exhorted us never to spare any Germans, never to take prisoners; and backed it up with some effective evidence. It would have been the queerest thing, before the war, to have seen this quiet man uttering the most bloodthirsty wisdom. He did not hate, bore no malice apparently, but merely was determined to kill every German he might lay hands on. One thing he told us was that the Prussian Guard at Loos was a very mixed lot and very inferior to the original. But dammy, I wish they would let me transfer to the Navy or the Air Service. This marching and futile stunting-about bores me. And if I am to die, who would not rather be dropped from an aeroplane than blasted up to aeroplane height from a hole?

Sir C.H.H.P. wrote me a cheery letter a few days ago, in which he expressed his surprise that the love of music had survived in his young men. It surely would persist in any whose love of music was not merely a varnish, or a justification for long hair. (And O, how they've clipped us!)

I must leave off now; there is a 'buzzer' parade. (They have made me a signaller now), and must be off.

Need I say how delighted I am to be able soon to afford my amiable female correspondents the delight of saying that they have recently received 'a Letter from the Trenches'?

Goodbye. Your letters interest me very much. You say mine interest you, but I'll be scalped with a jack-knife if they do me.

With best wishes for new energy and spirits.

Yours very sincerely

Ivor Gurney.

[1] In Nelson's Classics (1914).

[2] *A Picked Company* (1915). The essay 'On the Sources of Rivers' mentions Arun, but Gurney is referring to 'On Rest', which is about death and mentions Arun. It is from *On Everything* (1909) and is reprinted in *A Picked Company*.

[3] Edward Thomas, *Keats*, The People's Books (1914).

[4] Where the Chapmans lived.

85 *To Marion Scott*   G.41.17

Between 17 and 23 May 1916 (KT)   Pte Gurney 3895, B Co 2/5 Glos:,

61st Division, B.E.F.

Thanks Miss Scott for her letter which he took great delight in, and hopes for more of the same kind.

Here are Keats and Davies – the last is a poor specimen of his work, save perhaps for 'The Moon', and 'When on a Summer's Morn'.[1]

Belloc will please you enormously. What a bobs worth![2]

I misinformed you about the rivers of Hindhead. Arun rises there, but the other stream is unnamed by Cobbett. This joins the Wey by Godalming. These rise close to each other. Itchen and Wey come from a hill near Alton. You may get the whole of Cobbett's *Rural Rides* in Nelson's 6d Library, now 7d, in one volume; Or as Everymans in two, with better print, but the 6d is pretty and good. I am taking this to France. It is a series of records of rides taken to observe the state of agriculture after Waterloo 1821 etc. and written in a clear direct style.

I have just startled the hut by announcing as official information that we go to France as diggers out of unexploded bombs, with pickaxes.

Yours very sincerely

Ivor Gurney

[1] Poems in W.H.Davies, *The Bird of Paradise* (1914).

[2] Presumably the Methuen edition referred to earlier, which also refers to the rivers of Hindhead.

86 *To Mrs Matilda Chapman*   G.45750

22 May 1916 (KT)

My Dear Comtess

Thank you for your letter which shall be replied to when we get to France;

and we leave tomorrow night or Wed morning. Here are the cushions. Please get me a valve for the green one, and let me have it some time.

Yours affectionately
Ivor

Love to everybody.

---

87 *To Herbert Howells*   G.3.14

24 May 1916
[*Postcard with postmark of Park House Camp, Salisbury.*]

Dear Howler

Finis est, or rather, Inceptus est (?). We go tomorrow. Little Howler, continue in thy path of life, blessing others and being blest, creating music and joy, never ceasing from the attempt to make English music what it should be, and calmly scornful-heedless of the critics. Go on and prosper, and Au revoir.

I.B.G.

---

88 *To Marion Scott*   G.41.25

7 June 1916 (P)   [Pte Gurney, B Co, 2/5 Glosters,
                                                   B.E.F. *deleted by censor*], France

Dear Miss Scott

Your letter has just reached me, here, dans les tranchées. Where and how of course I may not say; bang in the front seats we are; so that when you read of a slight disturbance near Donawhere you may picture me standing gallantly to attention as near to the cookers as possible.

But O what luck! Here am I in a signal dugout with some of the nicest, and most handsome young men I ever met. And would you believe it? my luck I mean; they talk their native language and sing their own folksongs with sweet natural voices. I did not sleep at all for the first day in the dugout – there was too much to be said, asked, and experienced; and pleasure in watching their quick expressions for oblivion. It was one of the notable evenings of my life.

The French children are fine, a joy to watch for their grace and independence. Why our good friends over yonder should have called them degenerate only the devil who inspired their spiritual pride can explain. And the women. How different their faces are! How full of character. Some of the country we passed through was very beautiful – rather like the Stroud valley only far longer, and there was later a river, most serenely set in trees, long lines of trees.

We are of course trying to brush up our French, but it is not easy, for where we stayed the dialect was very broad, and instead of 'Oui' they uttered a sound like 'Waw'.

The food in trenches is curiously arranged, apparently. I don't know whether the A S C steal it, but nobody gets more than a third of a loaf ever, and as a rule only a quarter. This is serious to a battalion that has innocently trusted to the army and spent all its money, before knowing how fickle and uncertain is the day of pay. Where everybody is broke there is of course a certain consolation of comradry, but O give me any other reason to be thankful for this spirit which binds the Infantry into a happy band of brothers.[1] But who may resist French bread, and the inviting open door of cafes? Not I, I take my good thing where I find it, and excuse my weakness and extol my taste.

The night before we came in there was a heavy bombardment of these trenches so our debut narrowly escaped being extremely thrilling, but the telling of all this and much more must be postponed till that happy day, when I shall hold the listener with my glittering eye and bore him to shrieks and titters of apprehensive imbecility. Apres la guerre.

But these few days in the signal dugout with my Cymric friends are of the happiest for years. Out of the company to an extent we breathe the air of freedom almost forgotten. It really does not do for one who so much desires freedom as myself to think of the general conditions of the last few months. A waste of spirit in an expense of shame.[2] We are all sick of this continual – about[3] (Pray excuse the language; nothing else but that word does justice to the Army ways.) And these boys here, so friendly and good to talk to are – O well, in agreement with us. War's damned interesting. It would be hard indeed to be deprived of all this artists material now; when my mind is becoming saner and more engaged with outside things. It is not hard for me to die, but a thing sometimes unbearable to leave this life; and these Welsh God makes fine gentlemen. It would seem that War is one of His ways of doing so.

Best wishes for health
Yours very sincerely
Ivor Gurney

Your going to London sounds as if your health was improving. I hope so indeed. It is a hard thing to have an active mind and be helpless. Yesterday in the trenches we found it so; our minds were active enough, and we felt sufficiently helpless. There was a trench mortar strafe, and we had casualties. As I was in a signallers dugout, a bombardment means little else but noise and apprehension – as yet. But a whiz-bang missed me and a tin of Maconachie (my dinner) by ten yards; a shower of dirt no more. Good luck to us all. I have been told that I may say that we are with the Welsh. They sang David of the White Rock, and the Slumber Song, both of which Somerville has arranged.[4] And O their voices! I thank God for the experience.

[1] A memory of the 'feast of Crispian' speech in *Henry V*, both the general context of soldierly comradeship in France and the line 'We few, we happy few, we band of

brothers'.

[2] An adaptation of the opening of Shakespeare's Sonnet 129: 'The expense of spirit in a waste of shame/ Is lust in action'.

[3] The omission is Gurney's.

[4] Sir Arthur Somervell (1863-1937). Joined the teaching staff of the R.C.M. in 1894. Michael Hurd in *The New Grove* says his 'most important contribution to English music is to be found in his five song cycles.'

---

89 *To the Chapman family*   G.45750

7 June 1916 (KT)

My Dear Chapmen

Whom I greet with best wishes, most particularly Arthur and the Guvnor who are soon to attain the seldom honour of a birthday. Well, we were not out long before we had been put a Company at a time into the trenches. At least two companies, with two other regiments. And we had a strafe too, which caused a few casualties but not to me. It is charged against me that I did not open a certain letter. As a matter of fact, the cushion was never undone. When I received it I decided that it was too good to use, and better to wait till the other valve arrived, which of course I sent for late. Please do not think I do not read *all* letters, even sentimental and religious. Could you but see the rush for letters here, and the disappointment on the faces of the unsuccessful, you would feel pleased indeed. I would send you souvenirs, shrapnel and such like – but that's all forbidden now.

The news of a present of a watch is good. It will save me languishing in gaol perhaps for being late. The chap I depend on for my horology is nearly as uncertain as myself, and I was thinking of dismissing him soon. It would amuse you to see me trying to talk French, but at any rate I can get what I want without much trouble.

My dear people, all of you, the remembrance of that last stay with you is refreshing to one who sleeps in barns, but there are some consolations. The faces and comradeship of the Welsh Regiment we are now with were worth going far to meet, and they sing their old songs! Picture my joy.

I regret to say that the Army sees to it that one has enough money on leave by dishing out only 5 francs a week to us, and that irregularly. We get also but a quarter loaf of bread, but the French bread is excellent – in great round slabs. Very grateful after the drier Army bread is its dampness and yielding quality. The chocolate is excellent, and the people very kind. It is surprising to see everything as usual very well within reach of the guns. They used to shell the villages but do not seem to now. There is quite a fine church a few yards from me shattered but still noble, and under the shadow of it the estaminets are doing good trade – maybe with windows shattered, the children play; and the country a mile or so behind the firing line is green and peaceful as our Dear England's.

A Bon sante of all, but more especially of Messieurs Arthur and Le Pere.

Yours affectionately

Ivor

P.S. For goodness sake do not wait till you get my address – this would not be till 'apres le guerre'; may be a long time yet.

And you will be pleased to hear that we get letters pretty regularly, in or out of the trenches.

90 *To Mrs Voynich* G.41.28

June 1916 (KT)

Dear Mrs Voynich

I hope you are well now – from whooping cough and all other ailments that do afflict the wearied flesh, and able to play Bach, delight in meditation of your garden, or look after aliens, as most pleases you. I also am attending to enemy aliens, as you may guess... Being at this moment in the reserve trenches near Somewhereorother, after a stay in the front line and then in reserve. Here I went through the most amazing experience, it may be, in my life. We were told that our battallion was to go up for intruction to a Welsh battallion, and some of us feared a rough type. Well, up we went through the interminable communication trenches, watching the West when we halted, our minds filled with thoughts that are naturally the raw soldier's; reached our point, were detailed, and then – C.[1] and I crawled into a candle lit dugout, and so met four of the nicest young men you could meet, possibly. They knew folksong. And one of them sang 'David of the White Rock' and 'A Slumber Song', both of which Somervell has arranged, and both beauties[2] -

We talked later of Omar Khayyam, Borrow, Burns, Wordsworth, Oscar Wilde etc. etc.

A most amazing evening, as you must admit. I had but 3 hours sleep the night before, but sleep was out of the question on such an occasion. Some of them came from Welsh universities, one of them was a Yorkshireman. All of them good fellows, and as kind as could be to us new arrivals.

Most soldiers seem to think that the French are a lot of thieves; but that is probably due to the fact that we get paid only 5 francs a week, and that irregularly; and get anything from $\frac{1}{4}$ to a $\frac{1}{3}$ of a loaf as a rule; and things seem dearer than they are perhaps, and this feeling reacts against the keepers of estaminets. Up till now however such people as we have met have been very nice. Everything goes on as usual behind, and only just behind, the firing line. The children move gracefully, the farmers tend their fields, coffee is sold and beer in large quantities; and at evening soldiers stroll about under the lime trees in the shadow of ruined churches and roofs long ago wrecked – usually in a blind rage, it seems, by our neighbours the Bosches, only a few hundred yards away from where I write. We speak French well enough (C and I) to get what we want, but the talk here is fairly broad, I should say, and it is difficult to go much beyond that. Whether the faces of the French have changed with the war I cannot say; if not, then it was a horrible height of spiritual pride to maintain that the French were degenerate – or a very great compliment to the ancient state of France. There was a boy I saw – at the landing post – who stood in one of the most noble attitudes I ever saw as he watched us pass; and yet his face was not unEnglish. How is it that so few of us are dignified in appearance? Were we in the time of Tom Jones afraid of looking noble? Well, as the whole world sees, we can behave well enough; and the account of Beatty's squadron fighting against so great a superiority should stir us to all nobility, act word thought and appearance.[3]

'Let's do it after the high Roman fashion,
And make death proud to take us.'[4]

This is a queer war though. Guns are going in the distance, and every moment there is the chance of a strafe (we have had one, not a bad one) yet the note of the whole affair is boredom. The Army is an awful life for an artist, even if he has such experiences as we had with the Welsh. Either it is slogging along uselessly with a pack or doing nothing but hang about after – or boredom or hell in the trenches. Very little between.

How different the life of Richmond, save in sickness! There are gardens there and a broad river, a sense of security and houses whole and not shattered, with blind eyes. And one can forget the present deeds of les Boches, with the high thought of old Germany. Well, Goodbye and best wishes for all good fortune

Yours very sinceredly
Ivor Gurney

---

[1] Presumably Cridlan.
[2] See letter 88 above.
[3] Beatty's squadron met the German Grand Fleet in the Battle of Jutland.
[4] *Antony and Cleopatra*, IV.xiii.87-8.

Dear Mrs Abercrombie

Your delightful letter reached me yesterday, with the book; for both of which I thank you most sincerely. Comment on the book is withheld till later, which sounds official, but means that I will read it once fairly carefully, and after with the greatest attention, as is my custom when I find so good a first act as that of *Deborah*. J'en vous remercie, as we say in France (a la Mr Jorrocks, if you know him).

I could write you a long letter of the most immense interest – that is, there is enough material therefor. We were not long in France before we were in trenches, and in and through our first strafe. I saw no wounded myself, and therefore a bombardment is nothing but noise and apprehension to me; others saw more and dread more a repetition.

Well, we landed at one of the noblest – what do I say – the noblest town it has been my good fortune to see; I hope to speak to you of it some day. But we had not long to stay there or anywhere till we were marched here and put in trenches with another battallion for instruction. They were Welsh, mostly, and personally I feared rather a rough type. But, oh the joy, I crawled into a dugout, not high but fairly large, lit by a candle, and so met four of the most delightful young men that could be met anywhere. Thin faced and bright eyed their faces showed beautifully against the soft glow of the candle light, and their musical voices delightful after the long march at attention in silence. There was no sleep for me that night. I made up next day a little, but what then? We talked of Welsh Folksong, of George Borrow, of Burns, of the R.C.M.; of – yes of Oscar Wilde, Omar Khayyam, Shakespeare and of the war. Distant from us by 300 yards. Snipers were continually firing, and rockets – fairy lights they call them; fired from a pistol – lit up the night outside. Every now and again a distant rumble of guns reminded us of the reason we were foregathered. They spoke of their friends dead or maimed in the bombardment, a bad one, of the night before, and in the face of their grief I sat there and for once self forgetful, more or less, gave them all my love, for their tenderness, their steadfastness and kindness to raw fighters, and *very* raw signallers. Well, we had two days like that, and played Auction Bridge, talked, read, smoked and went through a trench-mortar strafe together.

Once we were standing outside our dugout cleaning mess tins, when a cuckoo sounded its call from the shattered wood at the back. What could I think of but Framilode, Minsterworth, Cranham, and the old haunts of home.

This Welshman turned to me passionately. 'Listen to that damned bird', he said. 'All through that bombardment in the pauses I could hear that infernal silly 'Cuckoo, Cuckoo' sounding while Owen was lying in my arms covered with blood. How shall I ever listen again ....!' He broke off, and I became aware of shame at the unholy joy that had filled my artist's mind. And what a fine thin keen face he had, and what a voice – for speaking I mean. Gibson may have had this same thought as he listened to the cuckoo this spring. Shakespeare also maybe –

O word of fear

Unpleasing to a soldier's ear.

But I can hardly write a coherent letter as you may guess. Never did I have such material, and never, O never was writing paper so dear; 1 franc 50 for this. A veritable horror of war!

It is impossible to read much in this new environment. *Antony and Cleopatra* in the dugout and Cobbett's *Rural Rides* in the vacant spaces before – not many of those. O yes, and F.S.Oliver's *Ordeal by Battle*, a striking book.

But could Mr Abercrombie see the little white puffs of smoke encircling the aeroplanes – Germans high, British low – Could he but see. Ah, poor munitioner, but ah, lucky not to be disciplined and driven.

By God, I want to come out of this safe, discipline my nerves and mind into a normal sanity, and do my best in some symphony to praise these men as they deserve; if it were possible. Nevertheless

'As the stars, as the stars they remain'

whether their praise is adequate or not.

I'll write no more, even to such an interesting correspondent as yourself. Partly because of the huge price of bearable writing paper, partly because of the amount legitimately to be said.

I send my love to the children, and assure them that when this is all over, they with the rest of children over there in Blighty will probably have no end of a good time. Not many sweets maybe, for we shall be poor, but ten dinners from men who have endured many things because of them and for England, of which they are a dear part in the mind. I hope Liverpool affords something to compensate for the Orchards and free small spaces of Redmarley.

Goodbye and best wishes and kisses and corollary endearments to the children.

Yours very sincerely
Ivor Gurney

92 *To Mrs Voynich*   G.41.29

June 1916 (KT)

Dear Mrs Voynich

Thank you for your cheery letter which contained bad news of yourself; and that is always a good thing to get and know of – blows of fortune taken as serenely as you have taken this; though I hope with all my heart that nothing will come of it. Herbert Howells told me you looked as though you had never had a day's illness in your life, so that there is very good chance of the microbe expiring in its lair, an ignoble unuseful death.

I wonder what you are reading and thinking of now. This morning that extraordinarily unequal collection *The Golden Treasury* came out of its hiding place, and served to astonish me once more with the lasting wonders of the 'Intimations' Ode. But what I want is a Marcus Aurelius, a small cheap one. Would you send it me? The Gospels annoy me by their emptiness, and the eloquence of St Paul though good enough in some places, is mere argumentative theology only too often. If there were only a pocket edition of the 48. What a blessing it would be to at least one fed-up soldier trying to make his mind serene. But that is a state not easily obtainable here, if the war had held off another two years, (which it didn't, Thank the Powers!) perhaps I might have leaked stoic wisdom at every pore; but even Walt Whitman would have been tried by all this racket and uncertainty, though afterwards, long afterwartds he might have used those things with profit. Anyway I have done pretty well, and kept pretty serene, while others have gone under. One of them being the identical person who made this gorgeous jest. A heavy strafe had just finished. Men were doubting whether it were yet all over, and if they might yet look forward to a new day. A voice broke silence wearily from the corner of this – signallers – dugout. 'By God, I wish all this were over.' Up spoke my man, then operating. 'So do I. I've been sitting here for three hours now, and my bottom's sore.' In the new day he looked for, he collapsed and is gone from us. Our battallion gradually goes down in numbers and up in honour. We have been praised by the Corps Commander, singled out of the whole division for notice. Which is good, and I am indeed proud of my steady quiet comrades. Who vanish one by one notwithstanding, while the rest of us wait our turn. As for news, you in England are far more fortunate than we. My self I love newspapers when my brain is watery, and none have I seen that is not a week old. In reserve however I was a hardened but often puzzled reader of *Le Telegramme*, *Le Journal*, *Le Petit Parisien*, *Le Matin*.

Well, it does not look like lasting many months, and I lie here meditating on strange and splendid revenges on Life – for my past life especially. If nothing happens, a couple of years will make me not a master, but a pretty capable and well-equipped apprentice to delight in lovely words, lovely sounds, and the friendly eyes of men. In beauty and comradeship wherever the seeking mind may find them. For the fine life is not got by denying oneself low pleasure but in desiring eagerly the high delights so many and so splendidly far off. Tolstoi is good, but Bach is better.

Your South-country house sounds very desirable. And I hope that in no great space there may be a foregathering there. To meet friends again, and such friends .....

Well, I am hoping for a nice blighty and to have that pleasure soon. But I hope still more for a speedy end to the war – a rest – and then work, for which I am more fit, more eager than ever in my life. Dammy it cheers me up to think of it even!

Goodbye and best wishes
Yours very sincerely
Ivor Gurney

What is Elgar's setting of 'To the Fallen'[1] like? Have you any idea?

[1] 'For the Fallen' was composed in 1915, put together with others as *The Spirit of England* and performed in Leeds in early May and in London from 7-12 May 1916 in concerts at the Queen's Hall organised by Clara Butt.

93 *To Herbert Howells*   G.3.27

14-20 June 1916 (KT)

My Dear Howells

How are you all this long time? Be good, and write me a long letter full of meaty things about College; a real gossipy letter full of all the little things I want to know – what you are writing now, whether Sir Hubert is lecturing, and if so on what subjects; how Sir Charles is getting on with his new pupils, how everything goes; what the gossip of the tea-room is, though there must be few indeed left to carry on anything animated.

Well, here we are in France, and almost at once shoved up into 1st line trenches, but where I write is reserve, in billetts, and surrounded by some of the attributes of civilisation, but not many. Thank the Lord you had a weak heart, my crescent genius; you cannot imagine to what a length of nervous tension we are driven. The Chinese knew a little of torture, and had an inspiration named 'Death by the Thousand Cuts', but amateurs they were besides the Grand High Inquisitors who run the British Army; which, while 'resting', has the natural aversion to wounds and death to a fear lest it should, by the anger of God, be left alive and physically fit to endure more of the same kind of 'rest' – how it hurts a man with a sense of word-values so to misuse words! It is almost as bad as 3rd grade neurasthenia.

But supposing I come at last through all this complete in mind and body, there will be some memories will remain. Our first night in trenches was one of the most surprising things that can ever happen to me. We set out I suppose about the beginning of the afterglow, and went eastward with the usual thoughts in our mind – at least I suppose so. In the communication trenches, which were very long, we had lots of opportunity to look at the West, and remember what lay under Venus; as Wordsworth did in a Sonnett written on Calais sands, beginning 'Fair Star of evening'; up we went, with now and again a bullet whizzing above us or a startling clatter of machine-guns in the distance; and then at last the trenches – 2nd and then 1st. We made enquiries, and then C and I crawled into a signallers dugout, and so made the acquaintance of 4 of the nicest people that ever you could meet – and educated. They were absolutely first rate chaps. Unlike some men out here, they didn't try to frighten us with noribble [*sic*] details, but gave us as much help as possible in getting hold of ordinary routine, and in making us feel as much at home as possible. I had no sleep for 36 hours. We talked of books and music. And they sang – Glory be – 'David of the White Rock' and the Slumber Song that Somervell has arranged.[1] What an experience! I have also got hold of an adress of a man who is rather noted for his knowledge of these things. If there is anything left of either of us after the war, I shall attend to it myself – if not, you will write to him and find out.

E Kemp
109 Madeline St
Pontyquaith
S.Wales.

He was busy at the time, and I shall most probably not see him again in France. Such a chap would not only give you his songs but give you other names of other singers also. Lest your pride in your name should become overwhelming, I must tell you that a day or two after, we were put in for instruction with a much rougher crowd. But most men look well in steel helmets, and they had the reputation of being a daring crowd. I have also had the experience of seeing a most beautiful city, about which you also must hear someday, perhaps visit. There is precious little jerry building in France, and all the village roofs are red like the Sussex Roofs. And in an easy walk from the front trenches all the normal life of farms and villages goes on as well as possible except for the shortage of men. They cultivate very well here too, leaving very little grass land.

Write me a letter old man full of news and Fashnable Fax and Polite Annygoats, as Thackeray called them.[2]

Remember me to everyone.
Yours ever.
I.B.G.

[1] See note to letter 88 above.
[2] Title of section of *The Yellowplush Papers*.

94 *To Herbert Howells*   G.3.28

21 June 1916 (P)

Please hand letters out I haven't any Envelopes
My dear Howells

Your letter reached me just before going into the trenches, where I read it last night with great pleasure, and, I trust, profit. It was good to get a letter so gossipy, and remindful of home, the R M C, and, not least, my friends – our friends. On whom be Peace. (May it be soon on us also.) I am glad to hear of the new Quartett, and considerably flattered by the dedication,[1] which is the first of a considerable bunch in the future, from admiring comrades, and worshipping disciples. If you could write a Quartett inspired by Chosen, I can only conjecture how Framilode would move you did you know it as I know it to be – the most magical and fascinating of places. Then Crickley Hill, a magnificent conception. Cranham, especially Portway; little Minsterworth, Redmarley and the noble Malvern road. Someday perhaps .... But there is much to see, and there are three walking tours – in France, Wales and the lakes, that simply cry for fulfillment. By a walking tour I mean something accomplished without a pack – not carrying one's possessions like a snail, at a snail's pace.

You are right about the Elizas. They need a String Quartett or Quintett very badly, and should it be 1 flute, 1 clar:, 1 bassoon and a harp? Anyway the news of their approaching production gives me great pleasure. The selection of artists satisfies me wholly; and the piano accompaniment is perfectly adequate. I look for a huge increase of membership of the W.M.S. They are to be congratulated on their President, and she on her taste, and all deserve completest success. Please remember me to Idwen Thomas, who sang these things so well – how many ages ago. Surely I am a different creature since then? Ah, Howler, there will not be much the matter with me a year after the Army sees my back. –

> 'And joy shall overtake us like a flood
> When everything that is sincerely good
> And perfectly divine
> With truth and PEACE and Love' shall shine

once more on this poor distracted Europe of ours. And the swiftness[2] of the Russian victories have given me much hope. In this connection, please O please try and get last Sunday's *Observer* (June 12th or thereabouts). The leading article is a perfect exhibition of pusillanimous twaddling and a kind of sneaking shamefaced hope that the war will not last 4 years after all, as it might be worked out on blackboard by fainthearted blitherers. I believe it will be all over by September – even if I am over too. And that will annoy me; partly because I feel that when I have renewed and trained my spirit there is work for me to do, and partly because the New England – the New World will be so terrifically interesting. Your faith in the Survival of the Fittest as exemplified in me gave me pleasure, and renewed my own quite strong hope, but when you go on to include so many others, I feel that there is not a dog's chance for any of us. Curious. Keeyurious. But anyway on that subject my mind is pretty tranquil, and on that subject (compared with others) rests, as in a harbour. Which is Marcus Aurelius – a great old boy.

How do the girls behave at College now? Is there any new air of dignity on them – or do they frivol and sing Coningsby Clarke and Landon Ronald with the same delight as formerly?[3] What do they talk about now? Do they like Bach better?

By the way, have you heard or seen anything of Elgar's setting of Binyon's 'To the Fallen', that noble poem? How has he done it? Don't forget to reply to this. I envy any man who can set that properly

'They went with songs to the battle, they were young'
'As the Stars, as the Stars they remain'
'Age shall not weary them, nor Time condemn'
'We will remember them'

These little scraps stick to my mind and thrill me. It is a great poem.

If you would hear anything of life at the front, I am afraid that at present I have seen too little to qualify my description of it as a damn dull life. It is for me – 'an expense of spirit in a waste of shame'[4] save only for the glorifying touch of danger. One marches heavily burdened, cursing one's Fate, from the rear circuitously to the front, reaches ones post, and hopes for fine weather. I am a signaller, holding on to that name by my eyelids and teeth, and that is an infinitely softer job than the ranks, which nearly drive me mad for its monotony, lack of elementary commonsense living, and for what men like you and I must feel as insults repeated continually. But it is much better out here than in England – save only for the 'Rests'. Which if they be rests, bear the same relation to Rest as you know it, as a demisemiquaver to a breve. However there is the great consolation of being allowed free in the villages to go where one pleases.

It is sweet to think what a revenge of Joy I will have on Life for all this. For all this grey petty monotony, I will gather all the over-strength of spirit so hardly earned and force it, coax it, lead it to the service of Joy for ever. And as Masefield points out in his wonderful little book on Shakespeare, no mind but a supremely happy is able adequately to brood with Pity and Anger on Tragedy.[5] From the mountains one must look in the valleys and know their secrets, not dwell therein.

Sing Happy Soul, thy Songs of Joy
Such as the brook sings in the Wood
That all night has been strengthened by
Heaven's Purer Flood.[6]

By the way, those Welshmen I spoke of were a *very* exceptional lot. It was originally mostly from Bangor University. Another lot we met with soon after were not of much account. Gossip I prithee, Gossip!

Yours ever,
I.B.G.

---

[1] 'To Chosen Hill, and Ivor Gurney who knows it'; see letter 106 below.

[2] The word is either 'surtness' or 'switness' which I take to mean either 'sureness' or 'swiftness'; the context favours speed. The Brusilov offensive was the most successful Russian attack of the war, capturing over a third of a million German prisoners.

[3] Sir Landon Ronald (1873-1938) was conductor, pianist and composer; his song 'Down in the Forest' is his best remembered piece; Principal of the Guildhall School of Music 1910-38. Robert Coningsby Clarke (1879-1934) was a composer of songs and settings of Henley, Masefield etc.

[4] Shakespeare Sonnet 129.

[5] *William Shakespeare* (1911).

[6] W.H.Davies, last stanza of 'Songs of Joy'.

June 1916 (KT)

My Dear Old Winnie

Thank you for your jolly letter which I enjoyed very much, with all its bits of news and gossip. Bon. And I am glad to hear about Kitty's great success in her new sphere of existence.

And, from my influential friend the Comtesse de Tilda how Arthur is getting on at le creeket. Bless his little heart. Stap me, but tis a sprightly youth. Also it pleases me that you are so much in request as a vocalist. My dear kid, continue you in the straight and narrow way, take as pattern the high example set you by my good friends the Rushby-Smith girls and it will give me the greatest pleasure, apres le guerre to confer on you the famous order of the Icy Glare.

I suppose Ping Pong is still impossible for you. Alas this is a horrible war. And they don't give us enough bread in it, confound 'em. He asked for bread and they gave him a stony look. Oliver Twist would have a bad time out here I fear.

How is your frail body, too weak to bear all the strain as yet your spirit would put upon it? Anyway go on steadily: someday it will stand a lot. My jaws for instance have developed terrific crushing powers, absolutely unimaginable to the ordinary low down civilian.

Arthur and Micky shall have letters very soon, and but for the fact that another letter is overdue and these will go off tonight, they should have them now. Meanwhile, cheer up my estimable female, and hope for the end of the war which chiefly bores me. Though two nights ago it was sufficiently exciting. There is difficulty in showing where we are placed but opposite Lille will do maybe. Micky shall not have to wait long for a letter from Laventie as we are in reserve for a time. Goodbye mes chers enfants. Expect me to tea on Sunday.

Yours affectionately
Ivor

21 June 1916 (P)

My Dear Comtesse

You are as kind as ever, and your scones as good. It was delightful to get them, and they were eaten with great rejoicing in a little (signallers) barn at the back of a farm in Northern France – somewhere. But – may I say so? – While we are in reserve, in the villages, we can get everything almost we can afford. Tobacco is *much* cheaper than in England. The war taxes do not apply in Army canteens. Those cigarettes, which may have cost you 8d, would cost

4d here. Soap and Cold Cream about the same price as with you. And then there is the enormous postage! We buy French bread – excellent stuff, and cakes. And chocolate is cheaper than the English. It is not nice to say so, but it is better to make presents of food in *money*. The more so as we get the benefit of the exchange. This is bad to say, but everybody out here agrees. The more so as they pay us 5 francs only, instead of 10 as in England. Bread is all we are short of – the A S C steal it – and out of the trenches that is easy. *And we are not allowed to carry extra stuff outside haversacks* and in those there is no room.

Well, what of the Russian news? All the puling pessimists and the toadies of Germany swept away by one fact – that the Russians got through in 9 hours at one place. This is great – glorious. We will no longer think by rule and measure a la Garvin, but according to our faith – freely and with courage.

The two souvenirs I send were picked up in a ruined bank next to a ruined convent here in this town – where we live in comparative peace so short a distance behind the firing line.

I hope the kids will like them. Arthur and Winnie will make best use of them I think.

I am glad about Kitty, and believe the life will suit her. She has company and some definite interesting new work to do; and what colossal sum the 2/5 would give for that happy fate. God only knows. The motto of the British Army is 'Fed up, but carrying on'. Winnie must be proud she is so much in request. She is the kind of lady who will some day make herself useful if not even indispensable in all sorts of ways.

Micky is at present une chere petite diable (feminine in this case) and unforgettable in any case. By the way I have already written you a letter. I hope you got it? I know that one letter has reached its destination HEAVILY CENSORED, so that the official eye is On Me.

The Katharine Tynan verses are perfectly charming in that War Poetry cutting. Sweet, original and truly felt. The rest – n'importe. I did not read the slip on Women's influence on Men. Il est vieux jeu. Arthur is making scores of C.B.Fry size now I hope. He will make a good bat, but don't let him tear himself to pieces as a bowler, and shove him in the slips as a fielder. *Don't* forget. The news about Mr Rushby Smith is astonishing but I bear up.[1] Go and do thou likewise.

Now I go for half an hour to a cafe where French may be painfully learnt at the cost of two cups – charming people.

Goodbye everybody

Many happy returns and may I be there to share the next.

Yours affection.

Ivor

Congrats to the Gov: and Arthur

---

[1] The Rev Rushby-Smith was appointed Canon of Oxford.

21? June 1916 (KT)

Ideal Parcel would contain matches.

Dear Miss Scott

Thank you for the amount of general interest in your letter, your pretty verses and the news about my songs, which has given me great pleasure. Of course you can use them. The Piano accompaniment is quite adequate, but as to the sacrilege of ever having a piano instead of a harp – well, I think it would be an admirable substitute. I never thought at all about the harp quality save in one or two places, but merely the getting of a background for tunes or counterpoint. Well ....

I like your gray Mayday altogether – save only 'invisible like Fate', which is out of the picture. And people under counterpanes do not naturally enough suggest the labour of climbing the sky at all. Apparently he dived under the bed clothes and started work – an unusual proceeding. But I like this sonnett.

As for the other

Line 3 Verse one seems to me awkward. Why not 'on' for across? (*On* and *run* I suppose.)

Line 3 Verse 2 don't suit me at all.

But do let's have some more. (Have just received letter thank you.)

There is a gentleman in Mark Twain, who used poetry, statistics, pathos, bathos, blasphemy etc to prove his case; and won it. Write letters of this sort – anyhow letters. Run wild letters. Cockeyed and topsy turvy letters. Anything but the ordinary polite correspondance. For which I have no polite uses.

I hope this poetic outburst means that you are on the mend, and likely to be able to do more according to your desires before long. This has been a vile washout of a Spring, whateffer, look you! Today has been fine, but the sunset is closing with stormy looking clouds and cold breezes. High up in the air like harmless gnats British aeroplanes are sailing – but No Germans – and ever and again as they come round in their circles lovely little balls of white fleece, or dark fleece or occasionally ruddy, gather in their track and up above and below. But they take about as much notice as of so many peas. They go round and come back to the accompaniment of thumps like a soft tap on the bass drum when distant, or a loud tap on timpani when near.

Being in first line trenches in a soft part of the line is easily the best thing that falls to our lot out here. But lately, I have had a very soft time, being newly made (6 weeks?) a signaller, and being on an out of the way Post with two others. 'Cushy' is le mot juste. It is like Heaven to be away from our sergeant major, who, I am glad to note is not quite such a Prussian in the trenches. Give me signalling, first last and all the time. Had I but known before, O the drudgery I should have escaped!

What Ho, for the Russians! Surely that means the war is highly likely to finish soon, even quite soon? It is the Great Test, and Mr Garvin is tying himself into knots to swallow all his pessimism in time to be there first. Hey

for Hilaire, who has Faith and doesn't emit noisome darkness like a squid –
'but in the first does always see the last.'

Stap me, but it's cold!

The naval news is great. I could wish no more. We had to force them into action somehow, and did it by sacrificing the cat squadron.[1] Bien! There are men like them – proud of them – ready to do the same. Only Fritz will find some difficulty even in coming out for a bolt back.

The books I mean to lend you will arrive someday.

> *Songs of Joy* (if it can be found)
> *Nature Poems*
> *Farewell to Poesy*
>   and
> *Foliage*

All very good Davies, especially the first. There are some more too, if I can remember them. Yeats' later plays. Masefield's book on Shakespeare.[2] One or two more also.

Madam, I distinctly remember that months ago you offered to send me a parcel, if the need arose. Well it – well *has* arisen. They give us quarter of a loaf in the trenches, where men may stay (1st line and reserve) a fortnight. This deserves pity – for there is no means of getting any but by taking it up, and they do not, if they can help it, allow us to carry extras. (Some day you shall hear my candid opinion of the British Officer.)

To speak very personally now –

My feelings about my being connected with the whole affair are

(1) It is a weird queer war – this, against unseen enemies.

(2) That I have really no part in it. I wake up with a start from my dreams of books and music and home, and find I am – here, in this!

(3) That I have as little fear as anyone I have seen around me. Partly because I am more or less fatalistic; partly because my training in self-control not yet finished, has been hard enough. Partly because I possess an ingrained sense of humour. (A whizzbang[3] missed me by inches over my head and exploded ten yards from me – and the impression it gave and gives me now is chiefly of the comic.)

(4) The conviction that prayer is no use to me.

(5) The fineness of the men. (The officers *may* develop.)

(6) My increasing love of music.

(7) An absolute belief (not so very old) that once out of the Army I can make myself fit. (Trench mortar starts.) (But does not stop the Cuckoo, which cannot be far from the battery.

 and so on.

(Queer! it is a deuced queer thing.)

(8) The conviction also, that in a hand to hand fight I shall be damned dangerous to tackle. A useful one to have; but I hope to God that He has a nice

blighty ready for me and that there will be no need of such vulgar brawling – greatly against my taste as it is.

And now here's the end of my letter (Bang! Bang! – Phutt! Phutt!) and here's to the end of the war – now I must believe not very far off. (Shell goes down the chromatic scale from

Good bye,
Yours very sincerely,
Ivor Gurney.

Letter 2

Your book – my book has just arrived, and it is finished. Only to increasing certainty that Davies was once an exquisite poet – of which time he has now but occasional memories, and that he knows himself to be failing in power and is bitter at the knowledge. I happen to know it is true, from private information, but anyone who knows his earlier work must feel sad. He is now – merely a 'boom' 'Tramp-poet'. And yet – 'April's Charms', 'The White Cascade', 'The One Singer', 'Come Thou sweet Wonder'.....[4] These are bon, but alas, after *Foliage* he is practically Na pooh. Thank you very much for so charming a present.

Thank you also for sending the *Times Literary Supplement*, but I have one sent already. However both are passed on, and read with enthusiasm by one and another.

Tonight an aeroplane has been sailing high up in the blue – right over the German lines, and occasionally leaving at his back a flock of tiny white clouds; looking so innocent as they unfold, that unless one has caught the tiny flash of the explosion it is perfectly impossible to think that these are anything but the tiny clouds of Summer W H D loves to sing of. I might be a good soldier could I forget music and books. Indeed I try to fill my still-sick mind with thoughts of these. Which makes a strange combination, as you may imagine.

A sense of beauty is every hindrance to a soldier; yet there would be no soldiers – or none such soldiers had not men dead and living cherished and handed on the sacred fire.

I.B.G.

[*P.S.*] If you will send me a parcel, will you please send it when you receive a PC with 'telegram' untouched, a sign that we are either going or have gone out to trenches?

---

[1] Another reference to Beatty's squadron.
[2] *Songs of Joy* (1911), *Nature Poems* (1908), *Farewell to Poesy* (1910) and *Foliage* (1913).

Perhaps the Yeats book is part of the 1908 *Collected Works* or *Plays for an Irish Theatre* (1911). John Masefield's *William Shakespeare* is from 1911.
[3] 88mm German gun.
[4] These are from *Child Lovers* (1916).

22 June 1916 (KT)

Dear Miss Scott

Still another interesting letter! Please don't expect such a one from me as the weather is very dull and sultry, and this is a small room with 8 signallers lying low from fatigue. However, interesting things have happened. We have come into reserve now, having gone through a strafe which a machine-gunner who had been through Loos said was worse than Loos while it lasted – which was for $1\frac{1}{4}$ hours. And it left me exalted and exulting only longing for a nice blighty that would have taken me away from all this and left me free to play the G minor Prelude from the Second Book of Bach. O for a good piano! I am tired of this war, it bores me; but I would not willingly give up such a memory of such a time. Everything went wrong, and there was a tiny panic at first – but everybody, save the officers, were doing what they ought to do, and settled down later to the proper job, but if Fritz expected us as much as we expected them, he must have been in a funk. But they behaved very well our men, and one bay filled with signallers and stretcher bearers sang lustily awhile a song called 'I want to go home' very popular out here, but not at all military in feeling. The machine guns are the most terrifying of sound, like an awful pack of hell hounds at one's back. I was out mending wires part of the time, but they were not so bad then. 10 high explosives were sailing over the signaller dugout and the bay where I was in front of it. A foot would have made a considerable difference to us I think. They burst about 30 yards behind. Their explosives are not nearly so terrible as ours. You can see dugouts and duck boards sailing in the air during even in a trench mortar strafe (Toc Emma Esses – signallers' talk). Theirs of course do damage enough, but nothing comparable. They began it, and were reduced to showing white lights, which we shot away, and sending up a white rocket. Floreat Gloucestriensis! It was a great time; full of fear of course, but not so bad as neurasthenia. I could have written letters during the whole of it. But O to be back out of it all! We had a gross casualties or more – some damned good men among them. Two chaps especially, whom I hoped to meet after the war. The writing in the latter part of this letter will be very bad – myself having come off the worse in a single handed combat with a bully-beef tin; but the bandage looks interesting.

Out of the window we can watch men making hay in a fashion reminding us distractingly of Home. They are easily in range of the smallest field guns. Les bons Francais! There is a delightful girl who with her mother runs a cafe in

Laventie, evidently born to be the mother of dauntless men.

Here follows

The Song that Signallers Sung and Stretcher bearers of C Company, when the great guns roared at them, and the Germans thought to attack.

My dear lady, I am pleased with myself. They tell me I was nearly recommended for a D.C.M. or something or other that was done chiefly by other men. But all through I had time to wish I had chocolate, and wonder whether so much baccy was good for me. I may be chronically introspective (and this is a shocking life for that) but as little fearful as a stolid cow. It has given me still further confidence that once I get back to work my mind will take proper paths and let me be happy. You see I don't expect to get knocked about much, and don't intend to go on bombing stunts if I can help. I have forgotten what my other letters contained, but anyway will repeat that your choice of singer and player for my songs gives me great pleasure. I would not wish any other.

I hope your health is still improving, still surprising the doctor. Keep on and hope like the BEF. Did you see R.Bridges' Sonnett on Kitchener?[1] Tray bong. And here is a poem on Pain by Morley Roberts from the *Saturday Westminster* It is a good poem I think woflille [?] and one worthy of its subject. But O that G minor Prelude! It sticks to me in solemn moments.

I tell you what, mamselle; when I return to England I am going to lie in wait for all men who have been officers, and very craftily question them on several subjects, and if the answers to my questions do not satisfy me, they may look out for squalls. This is deadly serious. Talk of the need of 'dithipline' won't suit me.

Yours very sincerely,
Ivor Gurney.

[1] Bridges' poem 'Lord Kitchener' was collected in *October and other poems* (1920).

22 June 1916 (G)

June 22

My Dear Comtesse

No present could have given me more pleasure than this one. The very best, and 'twill no doubt save me much trouble.

We have just come out of trenches after a strafe that a man who had been through Loos described as being worse than Loos while it lasted. Well, it is as well to do the thing properly. I am glad to be out of it, glad to have been through it, and the Glosters are a good crowd, bless 'em. But it seems doubtful whether I should ever see High Wycombe again. I think 6 inches or so lower would have given much opportunity for damage to 10 high explosives, which burst about 30 yards behind us. I had my eye, or part of it round the corner of the bay, and it was a fine sight. Also I was as cool as now, writing this letter. This suits me, but it don't put my belly right, or make me less introspective, confound it! All I wished for was to play the G minor Prelude from Part II – Bach, when it was all over. But there was only those brick biscuits to chaw. I hope my generous benefactress you are pretty well and kicking fairly strongly. I hope for a nice blighty to come and see you all before long.

Yours affectionately
Ivor Gurney

22 June 1916 (G)

My Dear Arthur

Go you on and prosper, and rise from the 'not out 0' to the 'not out 20'. Then from 'not out 0' 1st eleven to undreamed of heights. It only means coolness with you, who have all the other gifts, necessary for big scores. You should have bits of shrapnel and so on, if it were allowed to send them, but the official foot is hard down on such little presents. Lying in my dugout or funkhole the other day, I became too bored to read serious stuff, or write letters; so turning my attention to the few filthy magazines strewn around, left by the last visitants, I became aware of a thrilling boys tale of 3 scouts who apparently played the very deuce and all with the Germans. It was so absolutely unlike the real thing that I read quite a lot of it, and laughed a great deal. At present it is chiefly – sticking it; with the prospect of a big bust soon. Machine guns all going at once are the terrifying things, and I don't like 'em.

Everything goes well with you I hope. You've got brains enough to do the lessons they will give you, if you take it coolly and don't worry. The only way I can clean equipment and rifle (and O how I hate doing that silly old job over and over again) is to do the first thing – any 'first thing', and let the rest sort itself out.

Here is a song our men sang when the last strafe was at its hottest – a very popular song about here; but not military.

> I want to go home, I want to go home
> The whizzbangs and shrapnel they whistle and roar
> I don't want to go in the trenches no more,
> Take me over the sea
> Where the Alleman can't catch me.
> O my! I don't want to die.
> I *want* to go home.

Not a brave song, but brave men sing it.

Yours affectionately
Ivor.

---

101 *To J.W. Haines*   G.84.5.1-2

22 June 1916 (KT)

My Dear Haines

Well, how are things going with you? Have they called you up yet? And if so, where are you training? I will not insult you by asking silly questions about how you like it and so forth – to be a strong silent man with outbursts of appalling profanity when the limit of endurance is reached; or to take everything as a joke; are the only courses open for chaps like us.

Well the Whatsisnames – our gallant regiment – have been in it a damn sight more than ever they expected, by the Lord. We are hardened veterans, fed up to the neck, muddy to the eyes, for the weather is execrable. And like Justice Shallow we have had losses. Two of the nicest chaps in the whole crowd killed. And of our very best lieutenants more gone than I like. So it goes with us. I pray for a nice blighty very sincerely, but take all possible steps to prevent my getting one, as is the manner of men.

Have you seen *Child Lovers*, W.H.D.'s new book? It has some good stuff in it – but he would do well to shut up shop. He is merely reminding us of what he used to be, and a sad reminder at that. Perhaps the war has unsettled him, he may feel that such verse as his is not wanted. One wants a condition of full-circling active peace to produce *Songs of Joy* I suppose.

Mrs Abercrombie sent me *Deborah*, which I like immensely, except the

Gabriel Hounds, which are poor tykes not worthy the poetic license. And the blank verse, also very fine, is hardly often enough simple. It is too skilled, too educated. One must have a background of simplicity, it seems to me, and then those exact descriptions, those seizing expressions will have room enough and weight enough behind them to drive home. But how good the storm is! And the marsh! And Barnaby! Well, I have written Mrs Abercrombie to all these effects, hoping that she will not mind.

About simplicity – to return – I was struck as much as by anything in the play by a speech of Deborah's -

'I was wondering why you came'.

That is ordinary speech; and there should be metres, yards, tons of it more than there is. The lack of it makes one feel that his blank verse style is not due so much to his character but to his education – like Strauss.

So much for *Deborah*.

One thing that runs continually in my head out here is L.Binyon's 'To the Fallen' which delights me ever more and more. Did you see Bridges' Sonnett on Kitchener? That was fine too. I believe that to be one of the most melodramatic things in this funny bug War of ours. I would not believe the news at first – it sounded so like the obvious rumour.

Oh, but it's raining like blazes!

What ho, les Russes! Who have given us the 'x' we have [been] looking for. How long will the war last, do you think? Not very long now, say, end of September?

Yours very sincerely
Ivor Gurney

Oh the chaps are behaving very well. And we got praise from the Corps Commander just lately.

Bravo us!

The officers? Oh, well, – some ... the rest will improve. We had one strafe which a man in the M.G.C. told us was worse than Loos while it lasted.

Given from Our Bombstore Somewhere in France.

---

102 *To Sydney Scott*   G.70.3

Late June 1916

Dear Mr Scott

The postcard which must have reached you by now was hardly adequate thanks for good baccy where nothing but the very foulest Army issue was obtainable; and many men have blessed your name. I should have thanked you before but for different happenings, and beg you to think that the sender of cigarettes to men miles away from anywhere must necessarily be well thought of – regarded with respect, and even affection.

And thank you very much for your kindness in introducing my verses to Dr C.Morgan, who ought to be a very useful advertiser. 'Quoted by Dr C:M:'. Why, (to be rude) it may be 'cribbed from by Horatio Bottomley next!

I hope before many months to thank you in person.

Yours sincerely,
Ivor Gurney.

103 To Mr Edward Chapman

G.45750

29 June 1916 (KT)

My Dear Mr C.

Nothing, as your acute intellect will perceive, has yet happened to me. I am still all in one piece, but a bored, humiliated, altogether fed up piece of humanity, who looks for the end of the war to deliver him from bondage. And just as I reach this, it turns out that a German aeroplane is soaring over us, and so our anti-aircraft guns are potting and sending lovely little white fleeces of cloud high up against a quite perfect blue. But Fritz when he attempts these daring feats takes good care to fly as near Heaven as he will ever get, whereas our men fly low and saunter along – a cheering sight.

When you write, as I hope you will, please send me some facts about munitions. As how a piece of waste land, chiefly distinguished for its fine vein of sardine and pineapple tins, has now been turned into the most amazing group of works turning out by thousands of tons a day shells of the most remarkable destructivity. Any little facts like this, or the Rev Horatio Bottomley's prediction of the close of hostilities in June before last; anything like this will bring a smile to the wasted lips of a soldier. But don't breathe a word of anything nasty happening after the end of August or else you will run the risk of extreme unpopularity with the gallant defenders of your country.

I hear that you are frightfully busy and so out of mischief. What would I not give for the chance of good clean honest work, instead of the aimless mucking-about! I envy Kitty[1] with all my heart, so do all we. She seems to have done very well, and to be 'busy, well, and jolly ...' Oh squirms from the Gallery! Almost two years ago I was driving a tedding machine with the Severn, May Hill, Malverns and Cotswolds to look at. But all these joys have descended upon the women, who seem quite capable of doing the job. I wish they would tackle this one. No.3895 is always ready to resign.[2] With best wishes.

Yours affectionately
Ivor Gurney

[1] Kitty was in the Land Army.
[2] Gurney's first army number.

108

29 June 1916 (G)

Dear Miss Scott

Nothing to do – a signaller's confession – so I start another letter to you, though there is very little to say – except continuous artillery action on the Western Front, which has up till now left me unscathed, and still able to see the fun of things – such as it is and they are. There are no exciting tales this time save of shells bursting uncomfortably near our billets in reserve. That was nasty, and made one feel as if les Boches [*sic*] were taking a mean advantage of us; but they are getting hell these days and don't seem to [be] able to find our guns. Soon I suppose, the curtain will shut down on our Western doings and you will hear no more of our little gang for sometime. I should like to hear how my songs went and so forth, before we go over the top. It is an eternal mystery to me how I managed to write such sunny things when my mind was 'covered with thick darkness as with a cloke.' But as Masefield says in his book on Shakespeare, none but the serene of mind can contemplate tragedy and not be shaken.[1] So that my turn for Tragedy will yet come, when my natural state of mind is Joy – 'Freude, Freude' –

I hope when you were convinced that the little dust up in the North Sea *was* a victory that you turned to the 'Sea Symphony'.

> And out of these a chant for the sailors
> Fitful like a surge.
> Thou sea that sucklest the race in time, that
> Fate can never destroy or Death dismay.
> Indomitable. Untamed as Thee.[2]

O the gorgeous stuff!
And

> Picked sparingly without noise by Thee, old Ocean,
> Chosen by Thee.

I shall be extremely rude to God Almighty if he takes me away from all this, just as I am breaking the egg so to speak. After dinner I am a clod; no spark is in me; but on fortunate mornings and after ten, I feel that there is stuff in me. But hold! Such thoughts are not for me. But only those of the Roman Marcus Aurelius and Epictetus the Greek, and our own Little Willy –

> 'All places that the eye of heaven visits
> Are to the wise man ports and happy havens.'[3]

Only the eye of heaven don't visit us much now, and the mud is somethink chronic, and a nasty yellow in colour at that. Our dugout stinks of buried vittles somewhere. I myself am lousy – moi qui vous parle; and this majestical canopy fretted with golden fire[4] is a washout in grey. But we go out to 'Rest' in four days time, and the amount of work we shall have to do will keep me from thinking anything but strictly military thoughts, or thoughts which if translated into action would certainly bring me into contact with the military authorities. But up here I don't shave, and, in this weather, Don't wash over often. But the Hun is at the gate, and Civilisation is a dream merely. I am quite sure that if man were left to himself, he would finally relapse into a most dreadful state of general disreputability, horrible to behold. It is the kindly influence of woman that has produced, or did produce so short a time ago, that crown and very top of civilisation, the oiled sleek and well-defined-shapely crown of the nut. The carpet slipper. The Temple Classics. The blanc-manger and all that is most lovely and of good report in our uncertain existence.

Only the Pipe is of man's own appointment, that dear rank foul companion of difficulty and danger, that goes with the great victory and the forlorn hope; that greets dawn with the sentry and the wide-eyed wakers after the strafe; that watches the sun down and the gnatlike aeroplane sailing blithely amid bits of fluff – some dark, some cloud-white, some gorgeously crimson with the falling day. That astonishes and annoys with its guggle the expectant lookers for death, and soothes with taste and smell the night-signaller tired of intellectual stunting with that horrid bore of Milton's, On Christmas Day.

(Oh, but there's a perfectly stunning gun letting off Hell and Damnation (see the jump there?) a few yards away it would seem from the pit of my stomach, and I wish it would stop.)

Bored, Fed up, Full to the neck, is my motto tonight. And would that I were on a mine-sweeper (!!! Bang) earning more than a bob a day, and though only a shipboy

'and cradled in the rude imperious surge.'[5]

O Hell. What a noise! I can't write with that going!

Later

After I finished that little scribble, I had to go up to the front line for message running, and my first, or no – third – message, took me out of the firing line just in time to escape the most hellish strafe, which did the most incredibly small [*a page break here seems to have broken off the flow of the sentence, but the description continues*] All heaven seems to be falling on top of us, and when it is all over, our senior major, who looks as if taken direct from George Morrow,[6] reports 'a little heavy gunfire', there are some dugouts to put right, and in this case no casualties worth the speaking of.

I am no expert, but it would seem as if there was absolutely no comparison between the German explosives and ours. We get frightened enough, but they have all the terror and a very good and sufficient reason.

And now I have your note and an offer to send a parcel – most willingly accepted. Please send it in 3 days time after getting this. I think that will be the best thing.

Our men are still behaving well, and are still able to 'gag' with straight faces and to some purpose. For instance last night, after the strafe had just finished, some weary eyed Signaller spoke the mind of the dugout. 'I wish this were all over.' The man on duty, a nervy-to-a-degree but plucky gagster, laughed at and loved, and one of my beloved few who have kicked and still do kick whenever possible against the Army pricks 'So do I. I've been sitting here 3 hours and my behind is sore.' An immortal joke, I think. But that's them. Jokes in unexpected places. Our men will gag before the Judgement seat and before the throne of Heaven, and not in the most refined language either, and smoking a fag the while. Last time we were in trenches to amuse myself I wrote a more or less, chiefly more, obstetric Journal – The Somewhere in France Gazette, which has caused great delight. But then, I always was a rude person, and these things come naturally to me. Music and lewd nonsense and using words. Well, I am summoned hence. Goodbye.

Your sincere friend,
Ivor Gurney.

Saturday

My beloved gagster has come a cropper and gone into hospital with a breakdown. Another of my friends not to see for a space. This was the result of a short but perfectly horrid strafe last night, and I feel depressed today, partly on account of a strained back caused by stretcher bearing last night – one of our best men; hit in many places but none serious.

Things have started to move. The big advance has begun and all things are now ready for the great Bust. On the top of that comes the news that the Russians have attacked Hindenburg and taken 10,000 prisoners – huge news, and soothing to my jumpy nerves. I need music, which means Bach, very badly; and won't be happy till I get it.

A fleet of aeroplanes on reconnaissance has just returned from a dawdle over the German front lines, with shrapnel bursting round so as rather to resemble the pinpricks on cardboard that one afterwards connects up with wool; reminiscence of childhood. Or thickly populated fly-paper. This is the ordinary manner of our aeroplanes at evening, who stroll over in the casual way that men use after dinner, smoking cigars and feeling pleased with themselves, not caring very much what the unimportant rest of the world think or do. A reassuring sight. 'Gerontius' has run very strong in my mind of late – the solemn and noble priests music especially

in the name of Christ who died

And

that shall be poured on thee

very beautiful that

part. There is a bunch of glorious poppies perched as if they meant to astonish and delight one, on a little green knoll just back of the firing line. Blue through the rift, or one of Walt Whitman's letters from God.[7]

To England – A Note

I watched the boys of England where they went
Through mud and mire to do appointed things.
See one a stake, and one wire-netting brings,
And one comes slowly under a burden bent
Of Ammunition. Though the strength be spent
They 'carry on' under the shadowing wings
Of Death the everpresent. And hark, one sings
Although no joy from the grey skies be lent.

Are these the heroes – these? have kept from you
The flood of German beastliness so long?
Shall break the devil's legions? These they are,
Who do in silence what they might boast to do.
In the height of battle tell the world in Song
How they do hate and fear the face of War.

Ivor Gurney.

[1] See letter 94 above.
[2] Gurney's memory of part of the first movement of the *Sea Symphony* by Vaughan Williams, 'A Song for all seas, all ships' with Whitman's words.
[3] From *Richard II*, I.iii.275; Gaunt's attempt to find consolations for his son's exile.
[4] *Hamlet*, II.ii.318ff; 'this most excellent canopy, the air, look you, this brave o'erhanging firmament, this majestical roof fretted with golden fire, why, it appears no other thing to me but a foul and pestilent congregation of vapours.'
[5] *Henry IV, Part II*, III.i.20; Henry's apostrophe to Sleep:
　　　Wilt thou upon the high and giddy mast
　　　Seal up the ship-boy's eyes, and rock his brains
　　　In cradle of the rude imperious surge.
[6] George Morrow (1870-1955), book-illustrator and contributor to *Punch*.
[7] See Whitman's 'Song of Myself', section 48.

Early July 1916 (KT)

My Dear Shimmin

I could have sworn I wrote to you a few weeks ago. I could have sworn it. And now Mrs Chapman lets me know that you did not know of my going abroad. And I could have laid my last hapenny (a frequent possession of mine) that I sent you a field postcard, or anyway a P.C. from Park House. Forgive my neglect though I am sure something came from me to you c/o Mrs Taylor.

Well; my man, here we are, and have been in 1st line and 2nd line trenches and reserve, and what the cynical call 'Rest'.

The stay in the first line is one of the most memorable things that have ever happened or will happen. For there I came across four delightful set of[1] men who could sing their own old songs, the Lord be good to them. David of the White Rock and the Slumber Song both of which Somerville has taken.

Imagine though, mon vieux getting this on so momentous an excursion as that! They *were* fine chaps. Mrs C: tells me you wish to come out here. I don't know what conditions you RAMC live under, but here they use the infantry in such fashion as to make us lose all our self-respect. Driven about from pillar to post, we can but envy the ASC and such services, and wonder, when *will* the end come? Would to God I had joined with you! Who have not to 'Rest'! 'Please make me a good boy and send me a nice Blighty' is the prayer of every private in France.

Mon cher vieux, what a foregathering we shall have when all this is well over! Everyone seems to be a little optimistic now, don't you think? But the Army has such strong desires, that it runs from complete fatalism to highest active hope in a day, and back again, and through all the grades in a night.

News, O Royal Musician, and Royal Medician also – the Women (no need to elaborate) are going to do my Elizabethan Songs. More power to their feminine elbows. (But not in pp passages!)

My Dear Shim: dish me out one letter – long, of many sheets small-written – garnished with news – spiced with gossip, served with lots of S.S. Send it now. Do it now, at ONCE. We thirst after epistolary matter as no hart after that chemical combination known as H_2O. Goodbye

Yours ever
IBG

[1] Written over 'Welsh', which is heavily deleted.

5 July 1916 (KT)

[*a P.S.*] This is the 9th. A green envelope doesn't turn up, so here goes in the ordinary way.)

Dear Miss Scott,

The parcel has arrived, and is being put to its proper use with the proper speed. The cake is excellent. Tray bong. J'en suis tres oblige. If you have not sent the other parcel by the time you get this do not trouble till you receive another F.P.C. The fact is , that in this last 6 days in the trenches, we had such a devil of a time that I felt that if parcels were to come at all – if 'tis to be done, then twere well it were done quickly. We were made a cock-shy of for the artillery, and so have really been a part of the advance. One strafe lasted 2½ hours, and gave me a permanent distaste for such. We were under fire every day, and nowhere was safe. In the post where I was for half my time, there were twelve dugouts. Four have been smashed, the cookhouse a mere melancholy ruin of its former greatness, and the bombstore not what it was. Souvenirs are plentiful round there, ...

I hope you are pretty well now, and that going to the concert did not harm you at all. Your being able to be there sounds encouraging. Herbert Howells' 'programme' was quite charming, was it not? His English is usually quite tortured and topsy turvy, but that was clear and gets just the effect needed. I did not know my song was to be done. It was quite like old times to see 'Sea wrack' down again. I must have heard the thing 4 times at least. But of course 'The Twa Corbies' is a man's song, if there were any left to sing it, and that's all the comment Sir C H H P will get when I write.

And thank you very much for your programme.

Well, the advance, or the preliminary advances has or have begun, and things have gone very well up till now. O may they so continue. There are surely great hopes now of an early advance. Up in the trenches one is liable to get only the big news and the wildest rumours. One needs good ones – of the latter, I mean – to keep one's pecker up sometimes. But the chaps stuck it like good ones, and I am proud of them. Pity it is that whatever happens to me, it will be difficult to meet them again. The world is large, but I do not want better comrades than these, and these are going by degrees. [*The censor has deleted about four lines here which begin* If a fresh battallion *and containing the words* we shall be a minus quantity.]

But look here about that parcel, and my pencil moves decidedly quicker at the thought of it.

Here's how. (And I've lost my well prepared curiously conned syllabus.)

Fowl. (since you insist on such a lofty height.)

Cafe au lait. (Tin, you know?)

Cake. Stodgy and Sustaining.

Tommy's cooker and tin of refills (can't get this here somehow.)

Lemonade crystals or powder or such like.

114

Chocolate. (*Plain*)   *One book.*
Biscuits. *Oatmeal.*   cheap.
Tin of Butter.
Any old *interesting* papers.
A candle or two (somebody's always short.)
Acid Drops. Peppermint Bulleyes Toffee or such.

And if you must leave something out, the fowl may be proscribed, on the ground that it is proteinous matter, and we get tons of such. If one desires to eat 4 pounds of meat a day 'tis easy done. But bread... Never have I had more than a ¼ loaf, sometimes less, and the tale of my woes on the subject has ascended to the Lord Almighty with no result, so I appeal to You.

I should have remembered about the matches. A piano would also be acceptable, but is not insisted on. One must not push about trifles. We could get some of this on reserve but not here so well. Part of the cake is lying on the first part of this letter so excuse grease marks.

You said some time ago, that 'Helen of Kirconnell'[1] would do well to set. She is a fine wench but too long and repetitious and her limbs too much in evidence to be easy in surrender.

'O Waly waly', I have designs on, but not yet.[2] But have you heard Elgar's setting of 'To the Fallen'? Is it anyway worthy of the poem? I *would* like to set that! One of the best things I know 'in memoriam'.

Our sergeant-major has softened to all the world, and that includes even me, who went to him and asked him where the biscuits and cheese were; in a strafe; his mind being then set on less mundane matters. And so, in the trenches, I never shave, wash late in the day if I please, and wear horrid looking sandbags round my legs because of the mud. When the S.M. tackled me about looking so like a scarecrow – or rather ... 'Come, come, Gurney, look more like a soldier for the Lord's sake.' 'Well, He doesn't seem to be doing much for *my* sake, and anyway I'm not a soldier. I'm a *dirty civilian.*' He has taken to being more pious and is careful of the words he utters. Whereas I delight in expressing contumelious opinions of the Lord Almighty, and outlining the lecture which I have prepared against the Last Day. He is surprised that the 'coal box' [3] did not fall in *my* bay, but I reassured him that there was a worse thing laid up for me, and that left him somewhat cheered.

But, in the name of the Pleiades what *has* a neurasthenic musician to do with all this? One looks at the clear West and the evening stars, and thinks of Minsterworth, book talk and music in the quiet room there; and then the guns begin; and after, one's friends are taken away, some still and some cheerful at a blighty.

O cuss it all though, I am glad to have been through it all, and will keenly enjoy telling others about it after.

And O the Somme – the valley of the Somme round Amiens! A delight of rolling country, of a lovely river, and trees, trees, trees. Apres le guerre, it must be that I write of the piffle under the name of Rupert de Montvilliers Fortescue-Carruthers or some such name, to rake in the good gold in exceeding abundance, to see the earth and the glories thereof, and develop a paunch. But for all these there is as yet no opportunity.

Well the weather has improved now, and I hope will give you a chance of getting strong and fit to do something of what you want to do. O Kind President of the Women Musicians – forward baggages that they are.

Someday I will write out on some dirty scraps of manuscript I always carry with me, my setting of Davies' 'The Sea', which you would like, I think. Will you send me a penny manuscript book or some MS in the parcel – an extremely well devised one my committee say.

NO PROTEIN

is the soldier's motto. Another tin of cafe if you must, but no bully!

> Underneath yon auld dugout
> I wot there lies a khaki lout
> An' naebody kens what he does there
> But the ladye wha' sent the parcel fair.

Your sincere friend
Ivor Gurney

Literary Supplement.

Shrapnel makes a horrid clatter.
Trench mortars at a little distance sound
like footballs well blown up bouncing hard.
Coal boxes and H.E.s give a horrid crunch,
quite like a back tooth coming out.

To the Fallen (E.S.)

Living we loved you, yet withheld our praises
Before your faces

And though our spirits had in high in honour,
After the English manner

We said no word. Yet as such comrades would
You understood.

Such friendship is not touched by death's disaster,
But stands the faster

Nor all the shocks and trials of time cannot
Shake it one jot.

Besides the fire at night some grey December
We shall remember.

And tell men unbegotten as yet the story
Of your sad glory.

Of your plain strength, your truth of heart, your splendid
Coolness – all ended.

How ended! And the aching hearts of lovers
Joy over covers.

Glad in their sorrow, hoping that if they must
Come to the dust,

That such an ending as yours may be their portion
And great good fortune.

That if we may not live to serve in peace
England – watching increase –

Then death with you, honoured and swift and high
And so – Not Die.

I.B.G.

Here is a bit more, since the green envelope has not turned up as expected.

I hope the doctors have not forbidden work, or come down very heartily on you. You may be playing Bach at this very moment, now as I envy you the very possibility. This morning I was to have played hymn-accompaniments on the piano for our Wesleyan brethren, but suddenly they moved us, and there is filling sandbags instead; not an inspiring job though conversation may be easy and general throughout.

If you could come here where I sit, you would see little but English looking scenery, though flat and not of the best, and ruined houses, some still red-tiled, or partly so; some blind eyed and lacking scalps and other useful organs and appendages. War is a nasty job, and even a summer's morning like this cannot hide the evidences of war, even if there were no thumping of the guns to remind one.

Do you know anything of Lascelles Abercrombie's work? *Deborah* seems to me to be a very fine piece of work, more especially the first two acts, and he *can* write blank verse; rather of the type of 'The Bishop orders his tomb at St Praxed's', or Yeats, in a certain mood. Here is a passage which may apply to us outcast art-lovers.

Deborah

'For us, with lives so hazardous, to love
Is like a poor girl's game of being a queen.
What good are all these marvellous desires

That seem to hold life in mastery? They are
Dreamt things only. Men make no more of them
Than a hawk would make of a spider's mesh, when life
Is fearfully desiring towards death.'

Surely you will agree that this is good clean blank verse, compact and truly English? It is quite a representative quote. There are lots as good.[4]

By the way did you know that Howells has written a new Quartett – Miss Scott says a very good one – dedicated 'To Chosen Hill, and Ivor Gurney who knows it?'

---

[1] An anonymous ballad, to be found in Scott's *Border Minstrelsy* and Palgrave's *Golden Treasury*.
[2] There is no evidence he ever set it.
[3] A low velocity German shell from a 5.9 inch howitzer, emitting black smoke.
[4] Lascelles Abercrombie (1881-1938); *Deborah* (1913). In *The Poems of Lascelles Abercrombie* (1930) the lines, spoken by Deborah near the beginning of the first act, are on p.457.

107 *To Marion Scott*   G.41.31

17 July 1916 (G)

Your parcels received, and thank you very much also letters including one written on the 14 of July. I am always glad to have your letters – and parcels – but I am afraid you must expect little reply. There is too much to do just at present, and letter writing is off. However till something real comes off in this part of the line, we should always be able to receive letters here.

Anyway please write.
July 17
I.B.G.

Dear Miss Scott
You have many gifts, but the chiefest most shining one must be your power of flattery, which is most extraordinary. The flattery up till now has arrived chiefly in the form of letters, but here's parcels now... Tray bong, and thank you very much. I had had practically no parcels from anybody until our 6 days strafing, and then it struck me most forcibly that if I was ever to bleed my friends, now was the time, and so entreaties and commands went out to the four winds, but chiefly that sweet and moist West Wind which has responded so well.

The fowl and the plum pudding are still hidden in their lairs, but the chocolate and biscuits are in a position favourably to be reported on. And it was nice too to get the *Evening Standard* packed up with the rest. I do adore newspapers in certain moods. For frivolling time away they are incomparable. The cafe au lait was also your own thought. Also tres much bong. Why was the *Daily Telegraph* one page sent? For the College awards? Or for the review of Colles' book?[1] The insect sachet would be worth a trial, if you please to send it, but I warn you that it has vigorous and determined antagonists.

It is not cold that curtails ablutions but a feeling of moral washedoutness, and the chance of getting a sniper at you or a whizzbang has some part in it. The particular post I am at now is however safe enough in day time.

You can do what you like about the Sonnett. (More flattery about the *Westminster*!)

I wish to goodness that some powerful genie would hale me over to your place to hear Howells' things. His concerto is a glorious piece of work, and one exultant bit has haunted me quite a lot lately.

1st movement

But all the concerto was an eye opener to me, and since then everything of his I could get at has been carefully looked over. But his songs don't appeal to me much. They seem to me to be the old cleverness rather than the new matter – merely atmospheric sketches. Of course pedants and fools will some day say that the war brought him out. Damned nonsense! It may someday bring his pupils out, but not himself. When will the concerto get another hearing? That and the Sea Symphony and Gerontius are our best things as far as I know. Compare any one of them with the St Antony Variations! So stiff, so full of sense of duty, and 6-hours-a-day spirit. Not that I would run down Brahms, who is very much revered of me.

As for my photo, everybody knows more about it than myself, who haven't the faintest notion about it, save that it was taken in the afternoon when I always am a clod without any feeling but heaviness.

That story of the Sea Battle[2] was very fine, and I am reminded of a Stevenson essay where he speaks of the mutineers of the Bounty singing God save the King as they are being left on some unknown islet.

So you are still Confined to Barracks? Hard lines. But it may cheer you to know that the courage proper to such situations is exactly that which keeps men in the trenches, and holds them cheerful. It is a grey sort of virtue to use, but shining to watch.

(When's the war going to be over?)

I asked for a book to be sent in the parcel. That means any sort of a book. A twopenny box in London would give me acute joy, but if you are debarred from such, Nelson's 6d Classics would be more than excellent. What a washout most of the *Golden Treasury* is! As for the period of Pope, the selection is simply lamentable. Only the Elizabethan and Wordsworth period have much real stuff in them. Could you steal a small dirty copy of Shelley or Keats and send it me? I have tried to get these in the penny Poets, but they must be out of print. The Everymans are too big, or my pack too small. *Macbeth* is with me, but there is too much real tragedy about to find it pleasant. Milton I can read, (and have) particularly the Ode on Time which is terrific. Oh! I know! Walt Whitman. I want him badly, worse than all the rest. Palgrave makes me feel what a lot of good stuff I miss by reading anthologies. However he is wearing away, starting alas! at the Elizabethan section, and will soon drop into a ditch, or meet an ignoble death in some fashion or other.

Have you read the Kipling Submarine articles?[3]

O why did I join the Army! Though I suppose that joining the Navy means staying there, which the Lord forbid!

You will envy me when I tell you of my full confidence that I could manage 5 or 6 hours work a day now. Tis so, but – shall I get the chance? So wags the world, with ladies eager to fight, or conches,[4] and gentlemen who would (Like Happy Starkey) play pretty music, bored to an abysmal melancholy by the mere thought of a bayonet; and yet in trenches with the rats and family friends. It provokes the thought that the world is a jigsaw puzzle that the L.A.[5] has not managed quite to success.

(Shakespearian irony 'With what I most enjoy contented least.'[6])

I myself when frankly a crock was anxious enough to die in the breach; but now – only half a crock, – one's ideas alter. I am merely at the beginning of a proper view and managment of things. Send me a Walford Davies work to protect my bosom, but then they might use Strauss..... Supposing instead of a strafe, they played Heldenleben at us ....

(What a horrid imagination.)

There is little to tell you. We thought we were out for a rest, but were yanked up here by the scruff of the neck here to bide for a space. But on the whole it has been quiet, very quiet, and the sunsets have been only too remindful of home.

You speak of Mr Garvin. I hope, I do hope, trust and truly hope, that cavalry will not be used on the Western Front; it will break his heart to defeat the Germans by such crude and speedy devices.

Tell me when you next write what is your opinion of events, if you have one. How near are things to breaking etc. Can Germany hang out as long as Mr Garvin? Are our armies fighting well? What *is* the internal situation of Germany? I thought Mr Scott might know a little of all these.

I hope you don't mind my asking for those books. *Any* old editions will do if small. If I disappear, you will have the benefit of a generous glow at kindness done to a valiant defunct; if not, I hope to repay you for them, and for your kindness in worrying about my songs. The books I want could be got in Charing Cross Road for a shilling in half an hour, if only I were there. O Charing Cross, uninteresting, and artistically —- awful, what is there above the bond of books that keeps you so alive in my memory? Is it the friends who have walked there with me, or the faces of men seen in my walking? Is it the adventure of finding so much so worthy to buy, and having so little to buy it with? Do you, like Minsterworth, really possess a soul to live, albeit a grimy and vulgar soul? Or was it the stars above you or the evening sky before the fear of Zeppelins douted your brilliance at nightfall? However, I love you, and sympathise, for Charing would make me Cross.

Na pooh, fini, I've run dry.

O, Doughty's *Travels in Arabia* or such like is a very much praised book by such as can discern.

With best wishes
Ever your sincere friend
Ivor Gurney.

[1] Henry Cope Colles (1879-1943) wrote *The Growth of Music* (1912-16) as well as a Jubilee record of the R.C.M. in 1933.

[2] Jutland.

[3] *The Fringes of the Fleet*, a series of six articles written for the Ministry of Information for publication in England and America about the smaller units of the Navy. First published in *The Daily Telegraph* in November and December 1915 and collected in 1916.

[4] i.e. conscientious objectors.

[5] Presumably the Lord Almighty rather than Literary Agent.

[6] Shakespeare's Sonnet 29.

108 To Mr Edward Chapman G.45750

27 July 1916 (P)

My Dear Count

(that is if you *do* count) I snatch a peaceful hour at 1 a.m. to assure you that those cigars were far better than anything I could have made from parcel-wrappings. Indeed, I will go so far as to say that they tasted as if they had been really bought at a shop, had it not been war-time, and if homemade, do (or did) you great credit. They tell me you have taken up Bowls, which seems to show that you recognise your status and disabilities at last, and will soon be content to yield up the reins into your son's hand – a promising youth of considerable military reputation.

You have not submitted any further names of offers of appointments to my judgement, so suppose that there are no further offers. Or is it that there are too many?

Well, well, I will not condemn unheard.

Things are moving out here as you may have heard lately. Do you happen to know whether our Nobs consider the thing satisfactory? I thought you might have gathered some notion. War don't suit me, sir, and I don't care who knows it, unless the Kaiser gets trying any of his tricks. And to hide in holes from flying whizzbangs and gradually to approach the state of doddering grandmotherliness is not my idea of Fun. But here's the job ready to my hand, and what must be done, shall be done. Though selling chip potatoes in Hell seems to us occasionally to have merits superior to this life.

Well, someday I may return to a life with kids in it, and flowers and a real white tablecloth, and more cigars.

Meanwhile Cheero, my giddy Goods Manager.

Yours affectionately
Ivor

July 1916 (G)

My Dear Comtesse
(Whack! there goes another mosquito!)

It was delightful to get your letter tonight, and to renew my aquaintance with pleasant memories.

I am glad that Kitty seems to have dropped into her proper place, and in a nice direction too. Syde is quite unknown to me, however. Daddy I hope is as expert at bowls as at Chess, though if he has been boasting, I withdraw all that. He sent some good cigars though. It was all of a good parcel that. The oatcake was a Creation, an inspiration of high degree. The cake was good enough, and the tallow candles of a taste the most delectable. Cigars too, thought I. Cock ye up! thought I! Wha's the warl' comin' tae? (I believe that may pass). Luckily it got to me in the trenches, and so there was no need either to carry it, or eat it hastily. Also, we have been out of civilisation so much that I am quite wealthy – for me. In trenches one cannot buy, and then parcels are as manna of the best make.

What a pity it was you missed the songs. I knew myself very late, but thought the letter might just scrape home in time to give you notice. There nearly was a disaster about the singer, but not quite – thanks to H.N.H. and Miss Scott, who hung on like valiant limpets.

But how can one concentrate one's mind on higher affairs when those beastly mosquito's are gradually biting one to a shadow? It's no possible wumman. But thank you for your letter. My intellects wanted something restful and homey, and your letter supplied the want. St Thomas a Kempis is a ruddy unmitigated bore. I am afraid High Wycombe will receive some bad news soon from this way. If you send me a book ever, let it be small. I ask no more, so low and humble have my desires become. Pity the poor egotist!

Love to everybody.

Yours affectionately
Ivor

July 1916 (KT)

My Dear Shimmin

I suppose you are still in England, and sick of it. This is deadly enough, but I am not sure that being in England is very much better – that being merely another form of an abominable nuisance – the Army. Here it is difficult enough to keep any self respect, but there impossible I should think; unless you can get a piano and use it sufficiently to make yourself feel that you are a musician with a poor hobby – again, the Army. It is raining outside depressingly, the damp heat is depressing, and I have a suspicion of toothache and more of a cold in the head, so you will understand that my temper is not of the best nor serenest: especially as I have been talking to an Artillery signaller and wishing that Fate had led my steps into that service, and not into this. There is at least a little interest in the ordinary work, and an O P's job is not at all bad, I should think. However it was not to be, and isn't.

Have you anything to tell me of the Taylors? The beggars never write, not one of 'em. Is Mr Taylor going 3rd class passages in his liner on his Company's behalf for appearance sake? For I suppose passengers are short. I heard from Mrs Voynich not long ago, who was near the Isle of Portland, and liking it very much, with affectionate references to skylarks, who are not among my favourite insects. (They are dropping rifle grenades just outside here. These make a horrid feminine scream after bursting, and are rather disturbing things, especially about tea-time, which social feast it sadly disturbs. They are getting thicker, and one has just dropped with a bash on the dugout, or very near. Aerial torpedoes likewise.

You are aware that my Elizas were done in the Great Babylon. So was I aware, and, to use the 2/5 expression for being annoyed, it hurt my cory. If my teeth weren't sore I should grind them; as it is, to strop them seems to be the best course. What infinite ages and wide continents away the R C M seems! We shall be a different crowd to foregather there; who are left of us, and when it happens. But as to music, it is probable that I have learnt more about music in the last $1\frac{1}{2}$ years than the previous four, being increasingly in better health, though not very brisk and jolly. Do you find this too? Have you still that tired feeling? Or can you hammer at Bach by the glimmer of the midnight lamp? Being in the Army makes one of necessity feel mean, but a few consolations like long walks, occasional leave, and music take off the keenest edge of it. It is even impossible to get back to hear the Quartett dedicated to me. If it is really, as Miss Scott says, Howells' best work – better than the Concerto – it must be a surprising concern, and I feel very flattered. Can you get leave to these pleasant places? Think of the Chapmans down at Perran Porth! Cliffs and the Sea. Clouds and reflected blue. The Lord favoured us with a double rainbow yesterday, but did not please my critical mind altogether as being too gaudy. The news is good, eh? The Russian steamroller seems to have taken the bit between its teeth, and mixing up the Germans as I my metaphors. And as for the Somme, I suppose we make them lose at least equally; for by all accounts, our shells are perfectly devilish. Goodbye, old man, and if there is any news let me have it.

Yours ever
Ivor
Gurney

27 July 1916 (P)

My Dear Miss Scott

Two days ago I wrote you a letter full of grumbles about different things, but was ashamed on re-reading it, and this is the outcome.

You write very interesting letters, and noone, either from the script or the matter, could guess that an invalid was the author. I did not know you had pain as well, thinking it to be an illness of weakness chiefly at any rate. I hope it is getting on satisfactorily and as rapidly as can be expected now.

Thank you very much for all the trouble you are taking and have taken about my songs. Evidently the performance would have fallen through had it not been for you and HNH, whom may the gods reward!

I am glad you like those verses. Here is another set. It is simply too much trouble to ponder and reconsider. These things have to be written rapidly out here. This life takes away one's virtue altogether, or seems to. A Wet Rag is solidity itself compared to my moral and physical feelings. (Crrunch! Jack Johnson[1] on the right.) We moved very soon after I got your last letter, and it has got lost somehow, somewhere. But the other letter got here all right. Or is it the first I have lost?

It is good news to hear that Dr Allen has come across Howells, and I wish him the luck he deserves of it. I wonder if I shall ever hear 'my' quartett? Or see Chosen Hill again? Somehow one never loses hope, and England may yet see me swanking round with long hair and a symphony under my arm. (Another Crunch. O Sound of Fear. Unpleasing to a soldier's ear.)[2]

I am glad the photograph has pleased you. Myself I know nothing of it, save that it was taken in the afternoon, which is my chief indigestion-time; and nothing on earth could make me look cheerful then. But anyway it was taken a day or so after my Redmarley visit – a memory of great joy – and I probably felt more gay than I looked. Your offer of parcels is most grateful to me. *And* books. There is Nelson's 6d Classics, Cassell's 6d National Library, and 8d Classics, and Everyman. Also Stead's Penny Poets – a most useful edition – in which I would like Keats, Shelley, and Tennyson, also Browning and Walt Whitman if you can; but those are out of print I think. Also I want a Supplement to the *Golden Treasury* in a small edition. There is one in Everyman, but a smaller would be preferred. You see the reason of my liking for the Penny Poets? There is no verse pleases me better than the best of present day stuff though. We may have no great poets, but poetry so saturated with the very spirit of England has not been written before. When I try to call up a certain Autumn Evening at Minsterworth years ago, and now worlds away, it is our younger poets who give me help. Shakespeare and Shelley also but not so strong. Keats is sometimes good in that way.

You must not think we never get bread. It is very seldom that we get less than a quarter loaf and sometimes it is a third. We are not quite so badly off as you seem to think. There is meat in great quantities, but one gets very tired of meat. O for a salad, green white and red, with real dressing, and proper bread and butter! It is a great thing to have few desires, and those easily satisfied, but when the best of my desires are in their very nature impossible to do anything with, the ground seems to fall away beneath one and leave one dangling in mid air above the pit. My moral and mental fibre is that of the old grandmother, without the advantage of quiet and an old age pension. Could I but think that either were to be obtained! (Here I must work in a page of my discarded letter somehow.)

The machine gunners manage to make their job interesting by 'playing tunes' on their guns. As thus. After the ordinary casual shots and steady pour, one hears

Which always sounds comic, and must, I imagine require some skill. Here comes the other sheet.

The infantry have to make all their fun, but, bless their hearts, there is a considerable amount when one adds it up, but their musical taste is simply execrable, and they are given to singing the most doleful-sentimental of songs. One of the worst of which is a lamentable perpetration called 'For he's a ragtime soldier,' which they love to sing on the march after being relieved. We are all fed up. How fed up you must gather from the fact that anyone who mentions home is howled down at once.

(O, of course, do as you like with the memorial verses.[3]) But Gloster, like Troy in Masefield's poem[4], has become a city in the soul.

We sit together and brood till someone suggests some fitting way of dealing with the Kaiser. Then people brighten up and conversation becomes general, but not polite. The universal opinion out here is that the Navy has a soft job. One does not expect the Navy to agree, but do not you? Their dangers are mostly silent ones, and do not obtrude, and the great presence of the Sea is about them; and furthermore there is the great change of Sea and Land for them, who can, in a manner, return home every so often.

I came across Benjamin's people the other day, and was very much struck by their friendliness and childlike-ness. We got on very well together. And what a physique!

I wonder what you will think of these verses, the first effort at rhymeless verse that my humble muse has managed. Be candid, I do implore you. It is my one intellectual pastime barring only this same of letter writing, and I am too fed up with other things to be annoyed at a slating. Why need you give me your own opinion? Why not call yourself Our Poetry Expert? Your letter would take on an added importance, and receive greater attention. O what is the opinion of the success of this offensive? Of course, we have gained ground, but is it a real success, answering expectations? And worth what we have spent on it? You will probably have been able to get some general opinion on this matter.

Today, one of our men received a packet of army cigarettes containing a lady's name and address, and got me to write a letter to her; which I did in my best, most high-falutin Stevenson-to-Mrs-Sitwell style.[5] I wonder what she is like, and whether this is the beginning of a romance, or merely the beginning and end of a puzzle. Her name is nice; Margaret Black; and her address is Medway St Westminster. Perhaps she is heir to great estates, or perhaps she used to take in washing. Westminster is such an inclusive sort of place, and it is difficult to get much from the handwriting. Do I stand on the threshold of great events? If not, look out for a 'Lonely Officer' in the Agony Column of the *Times*.

There is nothing but burbling in my mind, nothing but an empty ache for Maisemore and Framilode and Such.

The *Gazette* I send will probably interest you quite a lot. F.W.H. is my friend of whom you have heard. He is sometimes ungrammatical, but increasingly a poet. And the 'Dorothy' you have also heard of – for her speed, her lovely great sail and most of all for her leaks.[6]

Good bye
With best wishes,
Your sincere friend,
Ivor Gurney.

[*a P.S.*] Will you please send me a copy of Masefield's 'By a Bierside'. I want to set it. And M.S.

Little did I dream, England, that you bore me
Under the Cotswold Hills beside the water meadows,
To do you dreadful service, here, beyond your borders
And your enfolding seas.

I was a dreamer ever, and bound to your dear service
Meditating deep, I thought on your secret beauty.
As through a child's face one may see the clear spirit
Miraculously shining.

Your hills not only hills, but friends of mine and kindly,
Your tiny orchard-knolls hidden beside the river

Muddy and strongly flowing, with sky and tiny streamlets
Safe in its bosom.

Now these are memories only, and your skies and rushy sky-pools
Fragile mirrors easily broken by moving airs
But deep in my heart for ever goes on your daily being
And uses consecrate.

Think on me too, O Mother, who wrest my soul to serve you
In strange ways and fearful beyond your encircling waters
None but you can know my heart, its tears and sacrifice
None, but you, repay.

The *Gazette* will come when we are out of trenches.

[1] German 15 inch gun named after the black world heavyweight boxing champion because of its black smoke and power.
[2] An adaptation of the song 'When daisies pied' at the end of Shakespeare's *Love's Labour's Lost* where the note of the cuckoo is a 'word of fear,/Unpleasing to a married ear.'
[3] i.e. 'To the Fallen'.
[4] Masefield's 'Fragments'.
[5] Stevenson wrote many enthusiastic letters of romantic/platonic kind to Frances Sitwell (afterwards Lady Colvin).
[6] Harvey's poem on the 'Dorothy', the boat he shared with Gurney, was published in *A Gloucestershire Lad*, p.9. Gurney is referring to the *5th Gloucester Gazette* to which Harvey frequently contributed and where the poem also seems to have appeared.

12 *To Marion Scott* G.41.33

1 August 1916 (G)

My Dear Miss Scott

I have already written half a letter and lost it, but writing to you is less a trouble than to anybody almost, and that is a great compliment – I think – from me.

Your parcels have arrived, and, though they must have cost some money, and trouble, I hope you will not think this was wasted. You have my deepest assurances that the pleasure caused by your kindness has been considerable. The days have been very hot lately, the lemonade very cool. And people in the bays sleeping before stand-to have taken great joy in peppermints and bullseyes.

The Cooker is the observed of all observers[1]; a marvel. And quite another and more sumptuous thing from what I had expected.

The reason I dared to ask for all these things is – we have been so busy and so much in the trenches, that it has been impossible to get these things ourselves, in the towns and villages. As for our canteen, the only thing one is certain of getting, is bootpolish, and perhaps batchelors buttons. This is an apology for having asked for so much.

But now – the books.

Shelley was very nice to get. Keats I haven't touched yet. But O – Walt Whitman! I never dreamed he was so good. It is true that in most cases his poems are not really so much poems as raw materials for such, but dammy, it has annoyed me to find so much in so tiny a book. I will go so far as to say that no present has ever given me so much pleasure; though that is not to say that a little boat and a month at Framilode would not be even much more acceptable, but now I speak as one of the foolish persons.

Pip is a jolly book, and full of good descriptions of sport, which I always liked. (O, what would a clean hit for four feel like now?) But there is [no] need to send me such – *unless you have already bought them for your own use.* One can only read them once, then hand them on. True, a lot of men see them. But Walt Whitman – why he has after some fashion renewed me, and while he makes one more unwilling than ever to die, noone can more feelingly persuade as to the beauty of Death. (But there is more in the lost letter which may yet be found. It will be wise not to repeat.)

While I remember. Cushy rhymes with bushy, not rushy.[2]

We have been having a quieter time lately on the whole, but never give the Boche much chance to keep quiet, and he returns the compliment. Men go one by one, some with nice blighties, some with the Eternal Discharge. But on the whole we are a cool lot. Some of us, including the subs, amazingly cool. I have an unresting imagination which never ceases to suggest danger, which when it comes, does not greatly affect me; but some of our men have all the gifts of courage, and humility with 'fundamental decency' piled on the top. There is one little sergeant who is the unconscious hero of an epic, which will end with *his* duration, or the war's.

O what a lot! What a lot! But I would like a turn with some Scots we just met once. They were fine indeed.

It is difficult in these letters to interest you, and yet avoid trouble with the Censor. I would like to tell you where we are and when we managed to get more than a general mention in 'the rest of the front', but it can't be. And on the other hand, humour and things humorous are either impossible to show in a letter or too long to write of. But there *is* fun, occasionally. What there is to see, and see with joy – is, men behaving coolly with white lips, or even unaltered face. Men behaving kindly to one another. Strained eyes and white faces yet able to smile. The absence of swank of any sort – among the men. The English virtues displayed at their best and least demonstrative, and musical taste at its lowest, worst. I would not have missed it for anything, and wait for my Nice Blighty with satisfaction, pride, and trepidation, lest the Almighty may have misunderstood my wishes in the matter. They talk about a Trade War after this. Will not the fact that so many Englishmen have become masters of Life have a bearing on this, in spite of the calculations of our Economic Experts?

Since men who do so much for England have at last come to see what they love in Her, and what they would have Her be, and what they themselves desire to be – Since these men if they return are to do the work and to shape England anew, will they not have something to say on all the proposals for night-schools that are to make us the Swots of Europe, thereby dethroning Germany from that proud position, and all the schemes to make them merely the builders of a huge trade? Are we to provide statistics to please the heart of the *Times* Economic Supplement leader writer! By heaven, I think not!

In my dugout there is placed very prominently a photo of a place that stands for delight with all Gloster men. It means a good tea, clean air, feminine society, a good row on a pretty stretch of river, Beauty and leisure to enjoy it; Home and all its meaning. I lead weary men into this commodious residence, and show them this pennyworth of poor printing. They cannot speak, or do so in such phrases as – 'That hurts my cory.' 'My God, my God!' 'What a life!' or more explosively, 'How *Long is* this = War Going to *Last?*' The first phrase is an obscure one to many, to me even.[3] But our men use to say 'That'll hurt his cory' when they would indicate that such a one will receive annoyance of some kind – from coming too late for tea, to just missing a Blighty. And here I break off for chocolate. Which having found I resume. Don't send any more books just now please. Unless (see previous underlined caution) they are absolutely not wanted and are meant to be handed round. And for the rest I must thoroughly steep myself in Whitman and the wonderful boy (comparatively) that is Shelley. He is rather too facile an exquisite poet for me as a rule. Though I know myself to be too grown up at present.

You send me an exercise book, which may yet contain my Collected Poems. But it was music M.S. I meant, to write out the 'Sea' poem of Davies – and me.

My mind so takes that other letter for granted that I have forgotten to say, what the other letter said at length, how disappointed I was to get no letter with all this manna and nectar and honey. Other people may send parcels and letters. But *you* send letters and parcels, which is a prettier speech than deep emotion commonly drags from me. And indeed B Co Signallers are under the stress of deep spiritual emotion tonight. (It is 1.45 a.m. Aug: 1st) They started with cafe au lait, passed an hour daintily with biscuits and weak tea, and have only now finished their felicitations on the lemonade.

They do not say prayers, I believe, nor know your name, save as Fairy Godmother; but were both these things so, you should be mentioned, yes, even in the Lord's Prayer (amended version, on account of luxuries.)

And have I thanked you for the trouble you have taken about my songs? Was that in my *last* letter, or my *lost* letter? Well, you will understand the feelings of a youthful composer, making his bow; at a distance maybe. I had almost resigned myself to never hearing anything of my own things. It is long since I troubled much about them; but here you come reviving my hopes and vanity in the most delightful fashion. (Squeals and moans from nose-caps.) (By the way, the cafe au lait was hit by a shell splinter this afternoon. But luckily this was noticed and disaster averted by a mess tin.)

I could talk with you for hours, but blithering along in this fashion on paper will probably bore you horrid. But please write whenever you can.

Shouldn't I just like a talk on 'This Compost' or 'A Sight in Camp'; on the man who could write Bach like openings like

'Word over all, beautiful as the sky'
or
'To the Leavened Soil they trod calling I sing for the last.'
or lines like
'They were purified by Death, they were taught and exalted.'[4]

No, I don't want to lose all this.

There are so many parts for an ambitious young man to play, from disciple of Walt Whitman, lover of common men, to the composer of 9 (Immortal) Symphonies, all English every bar. And what about sailing?

My other letter has inquiries about your health. I hope to find it and include it with this – but if not, I hope everything goes as well as possible with you. If pluck could do it, you would long ago have been rudely and annoyingly robust. May your phagocytes do their damndest, is the wish of

Your sincere friend
Ivor Gurney

[1] *Hamlet*, III.i.163.
[2] He uses the word in letter 97.
[3] 'cory' is either trench French or joke Latin for heart.
[4] From 'Reconciliation' and 'To the Leaven'd Soil they Trod' from Whitman's *Leaves of Grass*

113 *To Marion Scott*   G.70.4

1 August 1916 (KT)
[*This is an adjunct to a letter, probably to 112, but it is not the lost letter mentioned.*]

Your letter came after this was finished. Thank you for it. But it is time this letter went. Yes, I have received all you have sent. And the best of all is the Whitman and the Browning: two first-rate books for this affair.

Your emendation is a good one, but, excusez, not needed. More polished, but directness is the note of the poems.

Besides in my version the emotion, after two sharp endings, crescendos

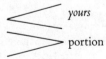

Your version has portion as climax.[1] But toss up, or decide anyway you please.

It is not very much to me, for so little trouble went to the making. I wrote that and another and half another part of one evening. And if you care to take the trouble of correction etc and thank you.

Very sorry about the mumps, but there was a man in the land of Uz who had a Job with boils, that must be your meagre consolation.

Your letter contained apologies for dullness that was not there. Please write again soon. Shelley is a wash out out here, as a general thing. I will try Keats next. But W.W. and R.B. are really the two. Please don't send any more for a bit. And then s'il vous plait, and by your leave, don't you think 1 vol of Pepys Diary a good idea? But you must guess at my gratitude for all these gifts. Goodbye and thank you again.

We are in rest at present, and require no assistance such as in the trenches to support the burden of existence. Another letter will be very acceptable without such aids to appreciation anyhow.

[1] He is referring to l.21 of 'To the Fallen' (later called 'To Certain Comrades') sent in letter 106. Final version in *Severn and Somme* is the smoother 'An ending such as yours may be their portion'.

---

114 *To Mrs Scott*   G.61.36

7 August 1916 (G)

[*Field Service Post Card deleting all but the messages*] I am quite well, I have received your letter dated *and* Letter follows at first opportunity *and signed and dated.*

---

115 *To Mrs Scott*   G.70.5

August 1916 (KT)

Dear Mrs Scott

Your news is a bad surprise, and I was very sorry to get it – more sorry than I can say.

It is very hard to be ill or partly ill for long, and then to fall seriously sick. However, I hope the news is better now, and that Miss Marion is well out of danger, and likely to remain out. But what can be said, if this is not so? We have not been real friends very long, but since I have been in France, her letters have been one of my looked-for pleasures. If these came no more, there must be a distinct gap; not to be filled up.

Please accept my deepest sympathy and best wishes for a speedy recovery.

Yours very sincerely

Ivor Gurney

Thank you, or at least Miss Stella for the verses.

August 1916 (KT)

My Dear Winnie

I did not write on your birthday.[1] Too many things cropped up for that. But it was remembered; the first since Arthur's that is set down in the book your revered Pa bestowed upon me. And now you are down at Perranporth, listening to the sea. Possibly bathing in it. 'Fore Jove, a lucky wench! No bathe for me this lovely morning but a dip in an old biscuit tin – such terrible hardships do our heroes undergo. But don't let this disturb you. Please enjoy yourself double for both of our sakes. And let the others follow your excellent example. Let your sand castles outdo the windiest vapourings of Sir Walter Scott, and your mud-pies outdo those of the Ritz or Carlton.

And tell me how the rabbits get on, and if they are still cannibalistic in their nasty habits, which is distressing.

In my next letter, which will be to Micky, there will be found a collection of be-yutiful drawings or stupendous epics; I have not yet decided which. However it is for me much easier to say 'The cow stands on four legs' than to depict the animal caught in the act. I can do the four legs with tolerable success. It is planting the cow on top of them that bothers me. The man who invented cows was a clever chap, and should be heartily congratulated by the Affiliated Society of Cunning Milkmen. Ping pong is more na pooh than ever I suppose. But wouldn't a hard wet sand table look well with little celluloid balls dancing about it? I wish I were with you to experiment, and to run races on the sand or to take down Arthur's pride at le criquette.

Yours affectionately
Ivor.

[1] Winnie's birthday was 10 August.

16 August 1916 (O)

Dear Miss Scott

The address on the label of the packet of M.S. is shaky and would not impress a real expert in such matters, but it seems to be yours, and so I guess that you are out of danger, and will soon be able to resume that correspondance [*sic*] which is inevitably fated some day to be the joy and wonder of my biographers. That is, if my biography is not fated to be one line in the casualty list, with the wrong number and a J instead of an I – as is set forth on my identification disc. I hope you have not been having too evil a time of it though, and that this is the last attempt at dissolution for a long time. It would be a pity to depart now – when all things seem coming to fruition, and Mr Garvin becoming more and more optimistic in spite of the price of paper. Well, cheero O. Ipshi pris, as the 2/5th say.

Halt of a day.

I have just finished a setting of Masefield's 'By a Bierside', and this will come to you either now or when we get back out of trenches. I hope you will like it. I will praise it so far as to say that I believe there was never anybody could have set the words 'Death opens unknown doors', as it is set here. The accompaniment is really orchestral, but the piano will get all that's wanted very well. It came to birth in a disused Trench Mortar emplacement, and events yesterday evening gave one full opportunity to reflect on one's chance of doing this grand thing. Did you see an article on Trench Mortar Tennis in *Punch* of a short while back? That is very good.

Last night I got letters from the whole Scott family. At least, they got here then, but did not reach me till this morning, having mysteriously been discovered in the Cook House. But everything is queer here. I feel like a cinematograph shadow moving among dittoes.

It is bad to hear that you cannot sleep. Read Dr Johnson's works, or Addison's, which are nearly as bad. If these are inutile then parts of the *Excursion* might meet the needs of the case.

The fear of death in sickness is widely different from that in a strafe. The most of us do not fear death very much. Hardly at all, in fact. It is hearing the shells and mortars soaring down to wipe you out, and the spiteful gibbering of the machine guns which *may* get you that does the trick. If a hypochondriac in the last stage of depression were to stand by a river, having fully made up his mind to drown himself when his waistcoat would come off; if a boy were to throw a stick at such he would dodge it. It is the same instinct that makes war dreadful, but, by a merciful dispensation, relieves the flat boredom of living among sandbags.

This letter is a spasmodic affair, and has already been interrupted 3 times, but we get on.

I have made up my mind to adopt that alteration you suggested, and had already written a letter to Mr Dunhill to say so, but envelopes being na pooh, it had not gone. However it shall go. The title should be To Certain Comrades (E.S. and J.H.)[1]

Mrs Voynich has sent me M Aurelius and Epictetus. The last is a game old boy, and I should dearly love to watch him in a strafe, but M Aurelius is a pious swanker in comparison, though he says some lovely things. Epictetus remains among the persons decidedly worth getting to know, perhaps after the next strafe.

If you were to send a parcel in anticipation of that happy date .... I regret to report that the signallers show signs of being, metaphorically speaking, fed up.

Keats certainly was no end of a poet. If he had lived? And Schubert? Well, no one can say. (If the violet were not so frail ...) But from the little foreword to 'Endymion' Keats would have been a fine man, and he left 'St Agnes Eve' – a joy for ever. and 'La Belle Dame' and the Cortez sonnett. He went 'before his pen had gleaned his teeming brain'[2], but there's enough to make a fine show in an anthology. Shelley wrote well too. Someday I must set 'Rarely Rarely comest thou' and that Invocation which begins, white hot, with 'Light of Life, thy lips enkindle'.

Walt Whitman is my man however, and I want to write in music such stuff as 'This Compost'. Every day my mind gets less sick and more hopeful someday of sustained effort.

What news! What a change since May! Let us unchain the optimists, and disport ourselves in the realm of the Ideal. In which the Germans must find increasingly their consolation, but not their rations. (Do you remember John Baptist's advice to soldiers?[3])

I wonder whether any up to date fool will try to depict a strafe in music. The shattering crash of heavy shrapnel. The belly-disturbing crunch of 5.9 Crumps and trench mortars. The shrill clatter of rifle grenades and the wail of nosecaps flying loose. Sometimes buzzing like huge great May flies, a most terrifying noise when the thing is anywhere near you. There are better things to treat though, and among them are sunsets such as the last, which would have coloured my thoughts had it not been for the greasiness of the duck-boards. Life is an aggravation unless the duck boards are dry. (There are fine opportunities in an Ode to a Duckboard.) There was also a double rainbow – a perfect thing of its kind. But rainbows always look as if a child had designed them in crayon, garish and too shapely.

Please thank Mrs Scott and Miss Stella for their letters, and ask them how soon the war will be over. They forgot to say..

Goodbye and best wishes for a quick recovery. This may have been what has kept you weak for so long. O, have you read any of the Askews' books?[4] They are a feast of delight. There is one here with a gorgeous strong silent duke of Jovelike power. An amazing duchess of the most astonishing beauty, who, poor thing makes numerous abortive attempts at adultery. A patient but occasionally insuppressive wife. Spiteful Cats galore. Latest dresses. Magnificent scenery. Snobbery and Indignant Virtue. Golly what a feast is *The Tempting of Paul Chester*!

Goodbye
Ivor Gurney

PS.

Today is changeable, rather cold and windy. I should have been out on the hills or riding round by Huw Bridge to Tewkesbury, if .... Short views, monsieur, short views!

This letter will go today I hope, and find you getting on at a surprising rate. I am glad not to have lost a most interesting correspondent. I recommend to you a book which was reviewed in the *Westminster*. It is a book of (French) poems by Marcel (?) Claudel.[5] A poet whom France has just recognised as he is. What was quoted was very fine to me. He speaks of his dead countrymen 'set in the ground like corn.' A most beautiful way of reference to the number of deaths and the virtue thereof. The publishers are the 'Editions de la

Nouvelle Revue, Paris', or something like that. The price is 1 franc for 3 poems. I feel sure it is worth getting, and he is a man of whom, so one tells me, much will be heard. I wish I could hear Howells' best work, my Quartett.

I hardly think of music at all, but stick to books. My friend Harvey, who is now a lootenant in this battalion has just lent me the *Spirit of Man*; and I am now browsing therein. Masefield is quite right. 'Life is *too wonderful* to end', and the better part of me is on fire adequately to praise it before I go. O please excuse the dirtiness of the M.S. but mud abounds here, and I always manage to find more than most people. And it is a horrid clayey muck that sticketh closer than a Flag seller.

On rereading my letter, I find myself thinking that my references to Mrs Scott's and Miss Stella's kindness in writing are rather curt. This was not intended at all.

> The careless writer
> And swift inditer
> > Often omits
> > To fill in bits
> Would make the prophetic obscurity
> Of his meaning and writing lighter.

[1] The poem was published in the *R.C.M. Magazine* Vol 12, No.3, Midsummer Term 1916.

[2] Gurney quotes from Keats's 'When I have fears'.

[3] In Luke 3, 14, John the Baptist tells them: 'Do violence to no man, neither accuse any falsely; and be content with your wages.'

[4] Alice and Claude Askew published over 90 books in the first quarter of this century. *The Tempting of Paul Chester* was published in 1908.

[5] Paul Claudel's *Trois Poèmes de Guerre* were published by the Nouvelle Revue Francaise at 1 fr.

---

8 *To Herbert Howells*　　　　　　　　　　　　　　　　　　G.3.26

24 August 1916 (KT)

My Dear Howells

How's a' wi' ye? I hope you are going strong on the Muse, and that ideas flow strong. Do my share as well, do double turns; for I tell you that here I feel altogether out of place – as if in some horrid long-drawn out dream that will not vanish. Your letter was a very generous one, and cheered me up, partly to feel that one so frank should have such gifts. You *must* do well, must do great things, for you have self discipline and staying power besides all the rest, and a high ideal. Continuez vous, mon ami. It is hard lines not to be able to hear my Quartett, for Miss Scott is the author of the good news that it is your Best Work, and this means a lot to me for I remember very well what your Concerto was – is.

Continue my child.

I have had rather a blow lately, and need music to express my feelings, and let off steam. F.W.H. is almost certainly dead, and with him my deepest friendship, as far as that does pass with death; a very little with me. He went out on patrol alone, and has not returned, an unworthy ending for so fine a spirit, who should have died, if his destiny were to die in this horrible anonymous war, hot in the battle, in some hopeless-brave attack.[1] But this was not the purpose of the Will for him, and none can say well or good to it; but it is bad to see one's friend to go from one's bodily touch with so little sign or cause for pride. What he would have done with his life it is hard to say. For he was a spirit absolutely beyond the reach of any earthly power to satisfy. Restless, set on other things, discontented in a fashion both evil and very good, but increasingly good, and less and less evil. He had all the gifts save only serenity, and whether he could have attained that is solely the question. Peace to his spirit! Someday you must remember him, if that is not possible to me, for not many knew him anyway so well as I and his generosity, and his heart of kindness to all men. His flaw, his only fault of nature was that cursed one of introspection: that and that only. Not a bad fault as towards other people, but a great misery to ones-self. However my dear Howler, I feel convinced that could I only get back to the work which is mine I could myself get rid of most of it in no very great space of time.

These are great days, my son. Against a huge evil there has risen up a huger force of good, and the world, knowing itself to be saved, must endure the utmost misery for the sorrow necessary in and inevitable to the fighting of evil. It is doubtful whether artists can gain a full enough view of all this drama for generations yet. Do not attempt anything that your spirit does not feel bound to meditate upon, but go your own way in trust and clear confidence; for you were born to a great end. Probably also to great difficulty and discouragement, which will merely be the cause of a greater achievement, since you are what you are – a brave spirit. If the Will designs to blot me out before I can do also what I would – I am content, but may such gift as is in me descend on you, and make your love of Earth and Men deeper. I wish no more. Which will show you that my mind is cleaner and steadier, than heretofore. Death would have no vestige of terror, if this only could be granted; and if not, well you are big enough, it seems .....

You will be pleased to hear the Glosters continue to do well, and are taking honours and getting commended more than any other battallion in the division.

The note of our men is not cheeriness. It is ordinarily a spirit of comradeship, sustained and real. Not much laughter, but many smiles. A hunger for the news of the end of the war, and an unflinching determination to stick it until Our Peace is obtained. No kind of hate of the Germans, but a kind of pity mixt – on account of the terrible power of our explosives, and their detestation of the German mind. A fixed grey-coloured nobility of mind that will last longer than hate and fury, for it is subject to no after effects of exhaustion or lethargy of spent force.

And O Howler! The French women and children! What features! What carriage! What pride of race! And the young French boys who come home on leave are soldiers of a proper appearance. We are obviously civilians in uniform, but they are the real thing. And no French man or Frenchwoman has been in the least discourteous to me at any time. In England, if one went in to a public house, one would have to be careful of one's language, careful not to offend people. Not so here. One just talks – and there you are.

Write me another letter, old man, Meaty and full of news. with special reference to our revered Benjy.[2]

Goodbye. A la bonne chance.

Au revoir et bientot
Yours ever
I.B.G.

[1] Harvey's account of his patrol and capture on 17 August can be found in his *Comrades in Captivity* (1920).
[2] Arthur Benjamin.

19 *To Marion Scott* G.41.35

24 August 1916 (P)

My Dear Miss Scott

I hope you are still improving, and getting on as well as becomes an English woman in these times. You may have written to me, but I am at a hospital miles away from the lines to have my spectacles and teeth mended, and to drink as much coffee as my interior may be induced to receive. Unfortunately we are kept within the camp, and one's efforts are necessarily confined in their sphere. Anyway there well probably be your parcel waiting to go into the line with me, when the time for return comes.

Do get on well though, and write me those interesting letters which are part of such joy as I can get here. They are the proper kind of letters too, properly commixed of news and intellectual brilliance. Continuez, mon amie, or rather m'amie (I suppose.)

I am writing in a canteen, temporarily transformed into a lecture room, subject being Prussia, the soldiers listening very attentively. Would they have been so attentive 3 years ago? I wonder!

The thing that fills my mind most though is, that Willy Harvey, my best friend, went out on patrol a week ago, and never came back.[1] It does not make very much difference; for two years I have had only the most fleeting glimpses of him, but we were firm enough in friendship, and I do not look ever for a closer bond, though I live long and are as lucky in friendship as heretofore. He was full of unsatisfied longings. A Doctor would have called it neurasthenia, but that term covers many things, and in him it meant partly an idealism that could not be contented with realities. His ordinary look was gloomy, but on being spoken to he gladdened one with the most beautiful of smiles, the most considerate courtesy of manner. Being self-absorbed, he was never the less nobly unselfish at most times, and all who knew him and understood him, must not have liked him merely, but have loved him. Had he lived, a great poet might have developed from him, could he only obtain the gift of serenity. As a soldier, or rather as I would say, a man, he was dauntlessly brave, and bravery in others stirred him not only to the most generous recognition, but also unfortunately to an insatiable desire to surpass that. His desire for nobility and sacrifice was insatiable and was at last his doom, but his friends may be excused for desiring a better ending than that probable, of a sniper's bullet in No Man's Land. There is only one thing to make me glad in all this, which is – that I saw him a few hours before he went out, and he lent me his pocket edition of Robert Bridges' *Spirit of Man*, a curious collection, but one well worth having, and a worthy memory of my friend. I need no such remembrances; if the Fates send that I live to a great age and attain fulness of days and honour, nothing can alter my memory of him or the evenings we spent together at Minsterworth. My thoughts of Bach and all firelit frosty evenings will be full of him, and the perfectest evening of Autumn will but recall him the more vividly to my memory. He is my friend, and nothing can alter that, and if I have the good fortune ever to meet with such another, he has a golden memory to contend with. A thing not easy.

I am anxious to hear what you think of my setting of Masefield's lovely poem. Do not spare criticism. Once I could not write away from the piano; that was written in the front line. Indeed I am becoming fit for my job – by which, as you know, I do not mean fighting. Our front has been fairly quiet, but that term will not exclude raids or bombardments, or the unwelcome irritations of Trench Mortars. These things often make me horribly afraid, but never past the possibility of making jokes; which must be my standard of paralytic fear. (I tell you, should we return to the R.C.M., it will not do for Sir CVS to act the python to our rabbits. We live in holes, but only for protection against Heavy Artillery, and his calibre I fear is not as huge as other more modern calibres.) Tell me something about our College people.

O horror! Mr Dunhill sent me the proof, and after the bother of coming from trenches it cannot be found.[2] Please let him know the *only* alteration is the one you suggest – 'an ending such as yours' etc. Not the very trite schoolboy alteration of the second All ended to How ended! Or at least, let him do so in proper journalistic style with

all ended ....

HOW ENDED !!!!!!

or something of that sort. Printed in red, with vari-coloured exclamation marks; and a huge sforzando fff in brackets; with a foot note to emphasize the point, and a mention thereof in the editorial; also an increase of price for the

Magazine Supplement – my photo with a huge laurel printed thereon.

These are great days now – in England. But in France, they are either —- awful or —- dull. Ours is the latter lot, which means less horror but also less chance of a blighty. I still expect to come through, but then, who doesn't? – out of the line.

'Our Cheery Wounded.' You don't say!

Mr Garvin ventured to speak of a 15 months possibility last Sunday. But the French papers have a more optimistic opinion, when they condescend to hint at it. Gustave Herve does not think she can last another winter. O that it may be! Anyway, we can stick it, and will, since now we understand Fritz and his cloudy soul.

Goodbye and best wishes for Exuberant Vitality

Yours very sincerely
Ivor Gurney.

¹ See previous letter and note.
² The proof was of 'To the Fallen' which was to be published in the *R.C.M. Magazine*. His objections are misdirected since he had himself written 'How ended'.

---

120 *To Mrs Voynich*   G.46.32.3

28 August 1916 (G)

Dear Mrs Voynich

My twenty-sixth birthday finds me at a Clearing Station having my teeth attended to. I wonder where the twenty-seventh will find me? I hope – in England, consuming such wonderful chocolates as you sent me. They were very tray bong, and deserve mention in dispatches. You are to be envied, being near Cliffs and the sea. I do not care for skylarks – you may have the whole tribe, but your telling me the French name for them came in useful a day or two after, as we marched past an Estaminet with 'Alouette' printed for all the world to see and wonder at. The French are a lovable lot, and a holiday in France, a walking tour especially, could not be bettered as a cheap escape from war-thoughts, if there are any, just after the war. (Apres le gore, our men say; as a joke, and not a bad one.) The French are so courteous, so easily interested, and obviously such a fine-tempered race, that j'en suis fervent. It is possible to imagine them destroyed, but not conquered. We are probably the finer and more miraculously achieving, when we are put to it; but the French will be sooner stirred to great ends than we – as allies we are ideal, and have a suitable enemy to call out our best. And how well and lovingly they build! France will not erect ugly little tinpot churches all over her tiny towns, but will have one great church worthily built in an open space. Our men do not speak well of the French towns, but all their comminations and cursings come down to the simple ground-objection that there are no picture palaces. They will remember

139

the quiet grace of these farms, and towns and villages when, apres le gore, they reach their own badly built, evilly-conceived, wilful-carelessly planned conglomerations of houses, and see vistas of grey depressing slate roofs, and terrible fever-visions of desirable villas.

Well, the thought of la belle France has run away with me somewhat. I hope you are much better now, and at least able to work, and please yourself in creating. Do you so much regret leaving Richmond? All London save only the City and the Embankment might, almost, fall through to hell without a word of regret from me. You surely cannot mind being far from (Cobbett's) 'Wen', since there is Dorset, or some such county to live in? But perhaps it is that friends cannot get at you so easily, and that is a strong objection; even though I might feel that with a pound a week, one might live in France for ever, and use one's friends, and think of them, merely as things to write to and pour out one's impressions upon. I hope this indisposition does not weaken you much; and that it is merely indisposition and an illness taken in time – even over by now; but that is much to hope.

You must have gathered from all this rigmarole that up till now I have been able successfully to dodge flame and steel[1] – even nice blighties have eluded my anxious search. There is something that one ought perhaps to be grateful for, in that my mind is very much more serene than it was and my health altogether better. Perhaps two years ....

My best friend went out on patrol some weeks back, and has never returned. I am glad to say that we accidentally met on that morning and he lent me R.B's *Spirit of Man*. Mine for always I suppose now. Unless that event occurs which will dissolve such rights of ownership, or desire. For it is a good book, though very far below what it might be. Why all that Shelley and Dixon, and Hopkins or what's his names of the crazy precious diction? About one third of the book is worth having, some of it foolish merely. The Greek stuff is sometimes nonsense. The French trite and dull. Where is Wordsworth, Stevenson, Whitman, Browning? And why not more Tolstoi? The Yeats things are good, but he has omitted rare stuff, as Kathleen ni Houlihan, the Fiddler of Dooney. One would not expect Bridges to include any Belloc; he is an old man; but the book would be better for it. You are right about M.Aurelius. He is mostly a washout. The only thing truly worth preserving is the 'Dear City of Zeus' passage. Epictetus has humour and more courage, but it is a waste of time to read more than the Manual. The whole of E: is there, save the 'custard with a hook' sentence. Anyway, are all of them, Whitman, Christ, Epictetus not included and summed up in the mind of Bach? Perhaps not some of Whitman, but add Beethoven and there you are. Having read these two philosophers once, it should never be necessary to read them again. They have one 'tip' to give, for which I thank them, and so – farewell.

Rondel (is it?)

on next page.

140

Nor flame nor steel has any power on me,
But that its power work the Almighty Will.
Nor flame nor steel has any power on me;
Through tempests of hell fire I must go free
And unafraid, so I remember still
Nor flame nor steel has any power on me,
But that its power work the Almighty Will.

(Yes, I note the two 'powers'; but perfection is not a thing I value, but only Truth and Beauty.)

A French-woman told me that les civils expected the war no more than we did, and that les civils say, that if there were a God, he would go into the trenches and finish the War. Les soldats think otherwise; and anyway, to see the French faces and to look into their eyes, is to be sure that whatever France thinks she thinks she will have no part for ever in the Prussian type of Atheism or religion.

What news! What a time to live in. And, if it must be as a soldier, What a time to die in! And for what a cause! Il faut a ecraser les barbares. And then perhaps les barbares will remember and serve Europe again after their own great fashion. But a thousand years might well run before even the charitable forgive, especially as Germany will so easily forgive herself; if she ever manages to reach that spiritual height. However we propose to try to help her there.....
Au debout de 1917. Hé quoi? (If there is such an expression.) With best wishes for present and future

Yours very sincerely
Ivor Gurney

[1] This phrase is picked up in the poem he includes later, which may well itself owe something to a poem he had read in his recently-acquired *Spirit of Man* : number 427 in that book is Grenfell's 'Into Battle', which includes the lines:

> Nor lead nor steel shall reach him, so
> That it be not the Destined Will.

---

121 *To Marion Scott*   G.70.11.2

Early September 1916 (KT)

My Dear Miss Scott

I am still detained, and so have not received any news of you, but hope that you improve in health and, if it were possible, wisdom every day. Voila les petits nouvelles! I have also two childrens books of French soldier songs to send you, which shall soon come.

Have you read *Le malade imaginaire*?[1] It must be great fun on the stage, and to read it is a great pleasure even to so poor a scholar as myself.

I know nothing about Les Monologues,[2] but it may interest you as being what it is.

Goodbye. Good luck

Yours very sincerely
Ivor Gurney

[1] By Molière.
[2] There is a pamphlet called *Les Monologues de la Tranchée* in the archive: G.61.397 and a letter of 13 September 1916 contains simply *Les Monologues de la Guerre*, No 25.

September 1916 (P)

My Dear Miss Scott

Still here, and not having sent any word to the battallion on account of the uncertainty of my stay, still without letters. However, I shall believe that you are getting better rapidly now, and have more pleasures than belong to a sick person. Now they have made me billet-warden, which sounds grand, and is grand; as it leaves me time and enough to spare for reading. No new books can come to me now, as my finances have dwindled down to 20 centimes; 2d, quatre sous. No *Petit Journal* or *Telegramme* (the local authority) after today. However, when I was in the full tide of opulence with ten francs, I chanced on a little bookshop with little 10 and 15 centime editions of Moliere, De Vigny, Voltaire, etc. More to come tomorrow; but alas! nothing it is to me what comes. However I am just Enjoying *Prometheus Bound* in a French Translation;[1] in prose – an excellent way to read Greek masterpieces, if only the translation is faithful. Aeschylus is certainly a person of great power; but what is Prometheus a symbol of? Tell me if you can. Is it a forerunner of the Christ idea?

I am anxious to know what you think of 'By a Bierside'. Two days or so should bring me to your letter. Meanwhile, let me tell you that if on the word dumb (4th I think: 4th beat) the accompaniment is not dumb, it must be so. I believe it to be some stunt though. It is meant for contralto, and I am afraid the accompaniment suggests orchestra very strongly. The harmonium in the chapel has several teeth missing, and some of the stops are mere outbursts of insensate fury. A few words back I was interrupted by hearing voices and seeing 3 grinning faces against the green leaves outside. Then Jean came a boy of about 16, with delightful manners and a nice voice, and the French knack (O that I had some of it) of being able to be interested in anything toute suite. O what a walking tour in France might be made! Last night I saw the first Frenchman suspicious in the way that Englishmen are. It was easy to let him alone.

In the square of this small town here, there is set a church some 30 years old, far finer than anything of ours would be likely to be. Les apaches quarrelled with les curés and burnt the old church down. The old one can hardly have excelled the new. The Frenchwoman who told me this, also told me how les civils of France expected war as little as les Anglais. No one spoke of war, then the papers spoke a little of it, and then the Germans ... and the end of all things it seemed. The Patrols of Uhlans came very near here, and war is not merely an affair of bullettins to this folk. Those who are left in civilian habits work very hard. The land is cultivated beautifully, and waste ground one sees none at all. There are no such fields as we see in England.

La Francaise, spoken of above, was a woman who had obviously suffered., and was very devout. She told me that les civils were not friendly to the curés. Their idea of it is, that if there was a God, he would descend into the trenches and the war would finish. 'If no fine, No Dieu, no God.'

That is the French kind of Atheist, a type that Belloc insists is not an atheist at all, save by the force of bad reasoning. They are very devout, and feel their religion much more nearly than les Anglais. The sacred pictures hung in houses are very superior to ours. The boy of this house here asked me what the news was, and on my turning up the title *Le Petit Journal* at the top of the paper, he would have nothing to do with it, as against the Faith and les curés. There is practically nothing said on these subjects now, but it rests ready to come to light at the end of the war; and the Socialists still mean to make things hot; the civilians that is. They may be disappointed in finding a nation of comrades for the old quarreling nation, and a returned Army anxious for peace.

What queer wrinkled jolly old faces the old country-men have!

Your letter just received, and enjoyed. I am very sorry you are still so feeble and frail and worn and sad. But hope that in the week that has elapsed an enormous improvement has taken place. Getting well at Hindhead is a different proposal from getting even half well in London. I hope to have stirring bullettins from you soon. Cheero, ipshy pris!

Commendatory remarks on song and poem noted. You are right in the blame too. It bears no comparison with Walt Whitman, being orthodox measured verse, unrhymed. Any fool can do better than WW, save at his best. Who may equal him then, or what better teacher is there?

Will you please show the song some day to Howells and CHHP? If so be I do not so myself.

O, the parcel was very well conceived. Tray bong. *Tray* bong. Biscuits excellent indeed. Sweets worthy of special praise. Books a joy. I might have asked for them, they so fitted in with my desire. Tray tray bong.

Now is the feel and smell of autumn sweet in the trist air (I think that will excuse itself.) And everything drives me to think, O if I were only back now at my old job! Well, how long will it be before I am? This fortnight's rest has showed me that now I am happier than ever in my life, or anyhow, for a long time. It was 3 years ago, I first got hold of myself and started dragging myself out of the mire. Since then everything has gone well with me, and this gives

143

me hope that my earthly destiny does not end for a long time. But unmaimed? Ah, that I do not know. Indeed, my thought is that I shall not come out scot free, but with a lasting mark, and a purpose to fulfill. (Is IBG also among the prophets?) This last year has been fruitful to me, and if I do escape as I am, nothing I believe can stop me, since my mind is calmer every day, and more ready to accept the inevitable. Some day I may attain to serenity and a vast patience, and then ... We'll see how much one has to 'learn' of Form, Ideas, toujours les idees. This autumnal morning stirs in me all those thoughts which shall someday crystallize into the 'English Preludes.' That setting of Masefield was written in two sittings, almost without effort, and only the first part had been premeditated upon. My verse also is almost impromptu. You see what invalids almost past any feeling but self pity may arrive at? Voila, donc. Voyons. Verrons. Here also I wake up to a sense of wonder as to why you like getting letters from me. Since they are nearly all soliloquies about myself, with interjected propitiatory remarks about the state of my kind correspondent.

> Who peers in his own anatomy
> Will dread the smallest shade, and flee.
> But he who keeps his eyes turned *out*
> 'S a blooming nut or thereabout.

(New Blake.)

Now's the time of year, or soon will be when Books become more precious. Gone will be the long garish uncoloured evenings of high summer, and for the overmastering light of the sun, the glow, the lovely golden glow of the lamp on cottage blinds, at tea time. Then the essayists, Walter Scott, *Pickwick Papers*, Tolstoi, *Huckleberry Finn*, *Poems of Today*, Belloc, Algernon Blackwood, *Travels in Russia*, *Sentimental Journey*, Pepys, Boswell, *Tom Jones*, *Autobiography of a Super Tramp*, Hardy, Stevenson, *Roughing It*, Meredith (in doses.)[2] O all these mix well with the memory of the autumn twilight, so blue, so gracious, so full of memories and thronging presences, and – at best it is a dingy London lodging for me. Not that I should be depressed by that. All these things are part of my mind; and, I do not doubt, of yours.

Write again soon, and be of good cheer.

Your sincere friend
Ivor Gurney

[1] Probably *Prométhée délivré*, trans. Tola Dorian (1912).
[2] Algernon Blackwood (1869-1951), author of short stories, Laurence Sterne's *Sentimental Journey*, Henry Fielding's *Tom Jones*, W.H.Davies' *Autobiography of a Super Tramp*, and Mark Twain's *Roughing It*.

13 September 1916 (P)

My Dear Miss Scott

Thank you for your letter and the postcard, which is very fine, and you are to be envied; the more so as, both from your writing and matter, you seem to be getting better. Well done, and stick at it.

Here I am beside a French canal, watching the day, and remembering with an ache what Glostershire is in such a season as September, and with whom I usually spent the best of it – with Will Harvey. The sunsets and afterglow are lovely now and behind their joy lurks ever the fear .... Which I cannot put aside, as it is my only hope to train my mind to think of such things for the music that one day may come out of such a saturated mind, full of sunsets and the smell of earth. Well one must pay something for being born in an heroic age. An age of continent shaping, when foundations are set afresh.

I am out of hospital, just out of it, and going into the line very soon, for which I am not sorry, as the chief delight in the Army remains for me the coming out of danger, which means in this connection reaching a place commanded by every sort of gun except trench mortars and field artillery; however they let us alone, for which mercy God and German fear of reprisals be thanked. I see by the French papers that Prussia is about to call the boys of sixteen to military service. Surely this is the last straw; the women will hardly stand that. And a copy of a broadsheet intitled 'Hunger' now being circulated secretly, a most significant document if authentic.

Peut-etre six mois, peut-etre moins. But that should do the trick. And to hammer them too hard to let them retire without disaster; in which connection please note the glorious bit of luck in having Hindenburg made chief! France has suffered badly enough, but the faces of the women show one how very far off she is from yielding. They do not adopt men's costume, or get photographed by the *Daily Mirror*, but do the work, and say nothing; cultivate every square inch of ground that needs it, smile and do their hair prettily.

Last night I saw the queerest way of catching fish that ever was. We were walking by the canal noticing how many fish were on the surface, and it struck us they might be ill. We met some Frenchmen who said 'Oui' and 'malade' and 'usine' which explained the matter. One of them then let down a string with a noose at the end dangling from a stick, so that the noose was just in the path of a young pike drifting in an aesthetically lazy way down stream, and yanked him out with a bash. It was very funny to see, and gave us thoughts of trying the same game on the Germans. Fancy yanking Hindenburg out of the front line one fine unsuspecting morning! The French stoves are worthy of this crafty way of catching fish; I must draw a diagram of one for you. Not a scrap of heat can be wasted. They take up room, but as the French don't litter their houses with useless stuff, this doesn't matter much.

You may be right about the extra bar in the song, very likely it is so. About binding the song more closely, that may be so too; but I cannot alter it out here. I need to play things over and think – for the present – about alterations; and then leave it, and return. Anyway it is good enough. The repetition of that figure in the orchestral version would insist bar after bar on a different thread of the counterpoint, or at a different octave as

then at an octave higher and so forth, with trumpets especially at the loudest with accented notes. The piano version can be made significant enough. There should be another bar at the beginning – the C major chord to be played twice. You please me in saying that it gives you the impression of looking down at a bier. In my mind I saw a picture of some poet-priest pronouncing an oration over the dead and lovely body of some young Greek hero. No song writer ever wrote a better phrase for Beauty than the one at the beginning. At least I begin to fulfill some part of my desire – to see and tell the ultimate truth of things, and especially of the primal things; what H.Belloc calls 'sacramental'.

Yesterday, some misbegotten fool took all my books and burnt them. They were in a sack and too near other rubbish sacks for safety as it seems. This includes the French war songs I had promised. You will have to wait for them till I can get back into 'rest' again. We are just going up again and will be on business for a little while now. Old Pepys is a great man, really a great man to be so absolutely interested in everything interesting. Of course he is funny, but that is not the final impression left by the book. While in hospital I had a lot to do with a friend of mine in the R.A.M.C. who visited Tolstoi about 1902, and loved him very much. He flew into a tremendous passion with an American Pastor who was dilating on what America was doing for the poor. Curious that even an American pastor should choose such a subject for a long discharge of gas. In hospital there was a Warwick man who described in the gravest tones, how a German officer on a raid against them while bombing dugouts, bombed the bomb store and blew himself to bits; an event which seemed to me very funny indeed – for War.

If Howells gets called up it will probably be for clerical work only and may we not think it? not for long. It is probably bluff anyway.

The article in the *Times Literary* on the Navy was very good.[1] Noyes isn't bad, but no more than that, and 'Drake' never impressed me. I read a great deal of Kipling's *Fringes of the Fleet*[2] in a shell hole, during one of the most annoying times we have had. It was during heavy fatigue, and the Bosches spotted us and let fly with heavy shrapnel and 5.9s.

Just received two delightful letters from Shimmin and Mr Taylor, who turned up trumps with a letter about mountain climbing. Curse me, though, they both talk about Bach in a most disturbing manner, and remind me there is another world but that of war; a thing one usually realises, when the bottom of one's mind seems to fall out suddenly with the horror of it all. But those times are very rare. Thank the Lord. Sidney says you are getting on wonderfully; perhaps the operation means permanent health for you. Cheer O!

In books, after a careful survey, I find myself reduced to Wordsworth's *Excursion*, and a few blitherings from the 'Pastor' have reduced me to a state of 'wet' melancholy. ('Wet' is B.E.F. for half-witted.) I bought that book from a 2d box in Putney, and the excruciatingly mild engraving at the beginning alone is worth the money; but not to me. It is lucky that some of my books were distributed, and can be begged back. But Alas! Walt Whitman and Browning are na poo. However there is a luckful wight that has W.W. him must I cajole.

Books recommended for an invalid.

By Land and Sea – Tomlinson[3]

Dumas *Memoirs*

Huckleberry Finn. Tom Sawyer. Roughing It (Mark Twain)

Nicholas Nickleby. Pickwick.

London Voices – Keble Howard.

A Book of Stories by Andrieff (?) not very long published. (Or the author might begin his name with a V. Pretty indefinite!)

Tolstoi's *Short Stories*, especially the Prisoner in the Caucasus.

Stevenson's *Wrong Box. New Arabian Nights. Kidnapped. Treasure Island.*

Davies' *Autobiography of a Super Tramp* and *Beggars*. All these, or nearly all, if you belong to a library. Arnold Bennett's *Burned Alive, A Great Man, Those United States, Paris Nights*. Yoshio Markino's books – *A Japanese Artist in London* especially. Up in trenches we are not to be allowed to send any letters now. So write whether you hear or not from me.

Yours very sincerely

Ivor Gurney

[1] 'The Tradition of the Navy', the front-page article of the *TLS* for 31 August 1916.

[2] See note to letter 107.

[3] The only unfamiliar books will be Henry Major Tomlinson (1873-1958) whose *The Sea and the Jungle* describes a voyage up the Amazon; and Yoshio Markino (1874-?) whose book mentioned here appeared in 1910.

124 To Marion Scott   G.61.29

13 September 1916 (P)

[*A copy of* Les Monologues de la Guerre, *No 25 in the 'Collection du Success' published by Les Editions Modernes of Paris.*]

16 September 1916 (KT)

Dear Mrs Voynich

I am glad you like 'Steel and Flame' or whatever its name is. The second line and its repetitions shall be – 'But that its malice work the Almighty Will.' Compree? Tray bon, eh? I did not guess you would think it so good, as this life does not leave me energy enough for concentration or meditation, and I have to write tout a coup. (Is that right.)

(I take your letter as it runs.) It is good news to hear you are so much better, though not yet London-well. Perhaps in the course of time you may arrive at the giddy heights of being allowed to live in East End slums – but this is a high ideal and not so easily attained.

I am sorry to hear about Mr Voynich, and his crack on the head, which I hope is alright by now. Who knows whether like John of Jingalo it may not release in him a flood of energy? (But that is a rude comparison.)

I hope that, if you do write a book, it will be about your aliens. Surely there is most interesting stuff to be got there? Why it thrills me to write one myself, although I never spoke with one; and already in my mind's eye I see the phenomenally successful reception and the reviews – of *my* book, not yours.

Perhaps you may see Miss Marion Scott soon. If so, she has a copy of Masefield's 'By a Bierside', which I would like you to see. (I crow over it, a confession.) At present I ruminate rather hopelessly over Binyon's 'To the Fallen' – one of the best things in the English tongue. But it is very big and very long for a baritone-and-piano setting.

Have you seen any reviews of Maeterlinck's latest book, and if so, what do you think of the ideas it sets forth? There was a gorgeous piece of writing in last week's *Observer* – a review of GKC of Masefield's Gallipoli. Also a hopeless piece of precious pedantry by Alice Meynell – whom may the simple things of life give simplicity. I would very much like a talk with you about *The Spirit of Man* – some day – apray le gore. Miss Scott has introduced me to Aeschylus, of whom I will say that *Agamemnon* and *Prometheus Unbound* are very great works, and of Blackie the translator that he had something very like genius.[1]

The stars are glorious now, but this land is lowlying and misty. A wind is needed here as not in my own county. (My own county! What a dream it is! Like Troy in Masefield's poem, Gloucester has become 'a city in the soul'.)[2] I suppose I may someday hear star-music again

and

And what with Tanks and British pluck and French valour and German funk –
perhaps at not so distant a date. What think you? Are you optimistic?

With best wishes
Yours very sincerely
Ivor Gurney

[1] *The Lyrical Dramas of Aeschylus*, translated into English verse by John Stuart Blackie,
Everyman's Library (1906).
[2] See letter 111. Masefield's 'Fragments'.

---

126 *To Marion Scott*   G.41.39

29 September 1916 (P)

Dear Miss Scott

Today the R.C.M. magazine has come, and so I have renewed old
memories; but O, curses on my losing the proof![1] Bad grammar, bad
punctuation. The bad grammar is, if I do not mistake, the result of a
correction by one possessed of more blue pencil than wits. '*Nor* all the shocks
and trials of time cannot' – O Lor! Thank you very much for the letter and
book, both of which were very welcome. It is not ingratitude that makes me
say now that the second half of Walt Whitman is probably the best.

Ah, dear mamselle would you were only right in what you say about my
health and work! The sad fact is, that I do not know what it is to feel well,
and what work I do has to be done in spasms very quickly over. But —- were I
to get back now at once, things would very quickly improve.

It is good news you are still getting on well. Keep it up. Also that Howells
has been rejected again. He has sent me two part songs; words by Blake. One
of which is absolutely and perfectly exquisite – the 'Shepherd'. This is truth
and Beauty. It is now *quite* perfect, some day he will see that a little more
might have been got, but always he must feel a pride in it. And what restraint!
A wonderful thing. The other is pretty, and clever; hardly much more, but
delightful to listen to.

I had an interesting letter from Mrs Voynich today; she also is doing well, it
seems. Please let her also see the Masefield setting, though when you please, at
any time.

My letters in future will not be so long; by special request of the Censor;

but do not you stint. Perhaps in my next letter I may talk about Aeschylus, but not in this. Going into the ranks is a strenuous change from signalling. I shall feel much better for it, having become horribly unfit and fed-up with all things. Thank you, yes; I am better now.

Allow me to indicate that with my change of occupation and of the season, a corresponding tendency towards substance rather than luxury in such parcels as you might feel inclined to send. ... (A mine of ours has just gone up. Nothing much.)

Cafe au lait is a necessity.

Would you mind sending a copy of Binyon's To the Fallen? I might have a shot at that, though not easy to make a song of. However I might try.

I saw a scrawl on a barn door a few days ago. It will interest you I think. 'Where is my wandering Boy tonight?
       Neuve Chapelle' (and date.)
That's all, and pretty grim at that. The Autumn sunsets here are *very* disappointing. The land is low and exhales mist, which blots sunset and night skies. It spoils even Orion hanging high over the parapet at stand to in the morning. Goodbye. With my next letter you shall have FWH's book. Ah, his name is a part of Autumn – and a Gloster Autumn – to me. And the falling of leaves has one more regret for me for ever.

Yours very sincerely
Ivor Gurney

---

[1] Gurney's dismay at seeing the text of his poem in the *R.C.M. Magazine*, Vol 12 No 3 for Midsummer Term 1916 was dismay at a line he himself had written.

127 *To Marion Scott* G.41.40

2 October 1916 (P)

My Dear Miss Scott

I am very sorry to hear your bad news, and that your sister is fallen sick. This is very hard lines, and you all must feel very worried. I hope this second sickness will have as fortunate an outcome as the first.

I am very relieved to hear about Howells' exemption; the monotony alone would kill him in a week. It is better to look on at this war, especially now the great events are coming on; when headlines will approximate, and the past two years of slow agony be forgotten in a more glorious and poignant struggle. Gustave Herve says – if the Lord will only grant us 6 weeks of fine weather we can look after the rest ourselves.

You are lucky to be on the Downs in Autumn. What will the Souwesters be like?

I am glad Harold Darke liked the song so much, and shall be very interested to hear what HNH and Sir Hubert think of it; in spite of the 'local colour' on the M.S: but the mud is atrocious about here.

Yes, the news about Harvey is very tray bong.[1] He is probably safer there (at this stage of the war) than anywhere; and so 'everything in the garden's lovely', as the music-hall song saith.[2] It is a wonderful piece of luck though. His brother has gained the Military Cross at the Somme. His other brother is on one of the Tanks; a remarkable family, with a sister quite ready to do the same.[3]

Have you seen any Reviews of Maeterlinck's latest book? It seems to me just what is wanted, at a time when the world may fairly be said to be shaming God.

The Setting of 'The Sea' you shall have some time or other. All those books of W H Davies I had promised to lend you seem to have vanished; my books are wide spread now, and God knows where some of my dearest are. The dirty battered copy of the *Path to Rome* is still at home.

It is interesting to listen to the German squeals now, and to watch the Strong Silent Prussian becoming garrulous on people's unkindness. It is late enough to become humanitarian at this time of day.

It was very queer to see the title of the poem in the *Times* of Sept: 29th. Vous comprenez. But it is not much bon as a poem though.

A Frenchman with whom I have often talked – a peasant with an interesting face and most courteous manners – told me yesterday that he earned in a day of 12 hours, a franc and a half! A wife and two children would be an appalling luxury, were the woman not French, and so infinitely capable. He longs for even a small German retreat, which would give him back his farm. The people here say that France was very happy and well governed before the War. Can you imagine an Englishman saying as much of England? Soon we shall be in a place where I can find something to send you – since the Monologues interest you. If possible, I will get the Children's songs again.

FWH's book did not contain much of his best work. It was meant to get him in the public eye while it was still open to such things. There is some perfect work, some good, some pretty good, some slipshod and downright bad. But 'Flanders' is a star.

Well, I will say again that Miss Stella has my best wishes and the rest of you my sympathy.

I do not believe the End of the Great Troubles is far off, and maybe the term of smaller woes as well. The whole of mankind almost seems to deserve well at present, and the remorseful charity of God may stretch even to appendicitis. Why not ? After all, pluck is the chief thing, and I am sure the Scott family does not lack a full share of that quality.

Goodbye your sincere friend
Ivor Gurney

[1] Harvey had been captured, not killed as Gurney had previously thought.
[2] Sung by Marie Lloyd, words by J.P.Harrington.
[3] For details of the Harveys see Antony Boden's *F.W.Harvey: Soldier, Poet* (1988).

8 October 1916 (KT)

Pas de contraband/ Lectures pour tous/ De la musique De la litterature etc etc etc[1]

Dear Miss Scott

We are in rest, and at present I myself am in quiet, with a sore foot that has compelled a little respect, so here's a letter. I do not know whether the packet sunk the other day had any of my letters on board, but I hope not. There will be bloody fighting if the Germans sink our parcels; if you have sent one I have not received it yet; let us hope frightfulness has not been carried to so extreme a limit. All the things you send arrive in good condition, thank you; and the coffee tablets sont plus convenables que le café au lait. I find now that I have forgotten to ask about your health, (of which H.N.H. reports most favourably) and your sister's; but the reason is that I take your letters as they run.

You will understand however that I *do* hope everything goes well with both of you. H.N.H. says you look like becoming stronger than ever. Tres bien. I expect to hear the same news of Miss Stella soon, who I expect, as an energetic person, is tired of being sick, by now.

I am sorry to have forgotten the punctuation of 'Strange Service'. Everything I do is done in a sort of determined fury after doing nothing, and something is always omitted. Comma after 'service', after 'beauty', after 'airs', after 'being'. Should it be '*your* uses consecrate'? (I can't help the bad grammar.)

Thank you very much for the trouble you are taking about these things. I must admit it would please me to see my verses in Osborne's book.[2] Now I have reached your corrections of my punctuation, and approve. You may always alter things like that. As they say in plays, I rely on your discretion.

Vehews on the Setting of Poems

Really, I haven't any. If I can set 'La Belle Dame sans Merci' well, the reason is; that there is something in me of Keats, able to live in the same atmosphere as that in which he wrote his poem; only – being musician, to have told my thoughts in another language. They must not be Keats' thoughts only, but mine also. It is not always necessary to read a poem through to start setting it. When one reads in Elroy Flecker –

'High and solemn mountains guard Rioupéroux.'[3]

One may start there at once. Sometimes it is necessary to be wary and forethoughtful, as when setting 'I praise the tender flower',[4] but that is a difficult poem – to set it adequately is a 'stunt', I think. So is to set 'By a Bierside'. It would not do to try to set anything very big, like 'By a Bierside' at once, perhaps. But who knows? I had only the first two lines in my mind, or perhaps three, when I began to write, and did not finish till my idea was complete. I did not trouble about balance or any thing else much; it came. And after 5 years or so, I will write sonatas in the same way. The points of vital importance are

(1) A *Poem*; that is a collection of words that have inexplicable significance, and gives one visions and vistas. And

(2) You. (the right 'you'.)

Being almost devoid of patience, I am always in a hurry to get the first verse done, but that is a thing Time will correct, I hope. You see, all this amounts to 'I don't know', and one usually has to be satisfied with that for an answer. N'est pas?

Last night's sunset was a thing would have stirred the devil of War to fine emotions and intangible longings. God's mind stirred from its late gray calm, and sprang to life in great masses of clouds and streams of colour against a windy-clear West. Even a soldier might be moved.

The Verdun victory is a very great one, do you not think? The Marne; the Thiepval-Contalmaison-La Boisselle day –; and Verdun. Belles victoires! By the way, do you know anything of a General Bohem, or of Notre Dame de Bohem. The girl at the farm here claims proudly a descent from this man who came to France 'after a Revolution'. Please do find out if possible. It would please her very much, and they are nice people. They asked if the English speak much of their dead, and were astonished, almost incredulous to hear it was not so. I saw in *Public Opinion* a sort of article on the spiritual attitude of the men out here which was very good.

The truth is, as Hardy says, that the English fall back on stoical fatalism; and whatever it is they believe, it is not Christianity. They go to Church, and desire something spiritual, but it is nothing the Churches give them. They are fine, but self-reliant not relying on God.

This is a pretty place; flat, with some poplars, and always the same cultivation and red-roofs. Never a vulgar building to be seen, as usual. And O, the twilights of late! Que Dieu soit loué! Of course, Minsterworth has been in my mind; and with Minsterworth, Bach and F.W.H., whose book the Doctor – in Spite of Himself – has lost. God reward him! But how good to see the poplars against the clear west! There's a great Autumn wind raging outside, and freezing my feet in this barn. *Le Matin* and *Le Petit Parisien* flap about helplessly, and the chickens' feathers ruffle up. A day to love, and to walk the Cotswolds in.

How the leaves must be flying on Cranham, and up and down and round in swirls on Portway! Painswick Beacon will stand as high and immovable as ever, and Birdlip too; I can do without them. But O for the wild woods and the leaves flying!

Your sincere friend
Ivor Gurney

Robecq

Apres le guerre is over, the minds of English boys
Will turn to thoughts of England, as a lover to his love,

Where peace is crowned and shining, with never a battle noise,
   And death not screams above.

And we shall drink our fill of a never fathomed quiet,
Love among friends deeper far than before,
War shall be the battle of winds and woods in riot
   Or seas on sandy shore.

Some may desire forgetfulness[5] of any thought of France
Some wrapped in home thoughts of France will not reck,
But I shall ever dream how the poplar shadows dance
   In the sun at dear Robecq.

Now I must love her because she brings me near
To thoughts of my own home, leagues on leagues away
But then – for that Robecq for beauty must be dear
   For her fair fresh look of day.

Strangely made are we, flesh and spirit, soul and body,
One lagging backwards, one aspiring high
But Robecq is part of this whole strange compounded
   Until the day I die.[6]

[1] This note is for the censor who had complained of the length of Gurney's letters. See letter 126.
[2] *The Muse in Arms*, edited by E.B.Osborn (1917), published Gurney's 'Strange Service', 'To the Poet before Battle', 'To Certain Comrades', and 'Afterwards'.
[3] Flecker's poem 'Riouperoux'.
[4] Robert Bridges' poem, set by Gurney in 1912 and published in Volume 3 of Gurney's songs (1952).
[5] 'Forgetfulness' is deleted but no word is substituted.
[6] The first line of this last stanza had ended 'spirit, body and soul' and the third line rhymed 'this strange compounded whole', but Gurney altered them.

129 *To Marion Scott*   G.41.42

10 October 1916 (P)

My Dear Miss Scott
   Your letter of one sheet with the good news of your sister has just come; I am glad that affair also is turning out well. Perhaps Europe, like you two, will be 'better after it'. (Have you seen the reviews of Maeterlinck's latest book?)
   Yes, you are right; weather and trenches no bon at present.

I am sorry not to [have] acknowledged your parcel, for which thank you very much. The sweets solaced the night hours of many sentries. The ration was three acid drops. (Further reference to further gifts.) Another lyrical masterpiece next journey. This letter is dangerously long already.[1]

Did you read G.K.C.'s review of Masefield's 'Gallipoli' in the *Observer*? O, it is a noble piece of praise. There are giants in our land, and in France; by the line he quotes of Peguy (?) Thanks very much for L.B. Not *too* easy!

[*The following page is completely deleted in favour of the preceding replacement, but it was posted with the letter.*]

My Dear Miss Scott

I hope your sister's illness is not bad, and that she is already past the worst of it. Anyway, there is little sense in worrying that you can do so little to help. You will do well to take advice in that matter from me, for I am a past master in the art of worrying, so much so that long ago I lost interest or enjoyment in it, and take it as a matter of course, – a dreadful fate.

I hope you are getting on well still, and having designs on your book, stronger every day in your mind; with the increasing need for scope that would make it an encyclopedia. May I point out that the songs of – alone would furnish sufficient material, even though so few.

Could you send me a copy of Binyon's 'To the Fallen'? Perhaps I might have a shot at it.

Yesterday, I found a letter to you from me in my pocket, which must be at least a week old. I know, or think I know that one was lost which was meant for you, and rewrote it. I hope to goodness it is the lost one in my pocket, and not the rewritten. It has a reference to Neuve Chapelle.[2]

I had a letter from Mrs Voynich a week ago, which gave great praise for a thing I sent to her. Have you had it?

> Nor steel nor flame has any power on me,
> Save that its malice work the Almighty Will;
> Nor steel nor flame has any power on me;
> Through tempests of hell fire I must go free,
> And unafraid; so I remember still
> Nor steel nor flame has any power on me
> Save that its malice work the Almighty Will.

Which is all very well; but what about Mud and Monotony? And Minnies[3] and Majors?

Your naval officer was very cautious. The French papers are, also. But the extracts they give from German papers, and the comments on the Chancellor's speech, give one to hope much. If I had £20 – a large supposition – I would bet the end comes ... by the end of November £5. By Christmas £10. By End of Feb £15 and by August £20. You will not convince me that such already panicky losers will hold out long. If Hindenburg has reserves Rumania will hear of it soon. If nothing happens – then no reserves. I am not convinced that we could not get through at the Somme, if we chose.

You must be enjoying Hindhead now. No Man's Land is in the last degree desolate, and nothing could seem sadder that the old willow tree I shoot at during Stand to. There are no Germans and one must shoot at something at Stand to. It was partridges that a corporal discovered two days ago. He shot 3, but as he had to wait till evening again, the rats got one more than he did. No bon.

Trench dialogue
Cook drops bacon in the mud.
(Cook) –! – – –!!! –!
(Passer by, sympathetically) No bon, eh?
(Cook). Compree me explique no bon?
(Passer by.) Na pooh fini, eh?
Cook Wee, no – bon at all.

Such accomplished linguists our gallant soldiers have already become.
Or.

Trench Dialogue no 2
Entitled   *Rations*
        Missing, apply A S C
Prometheus Unbound (off duty.) General expletives.
Chorus (Sympathetic silence).
Prometheus No Bon! No Bon!!
Chorus Don't compree.
Prometheus Compree no grub?
Chorus Whatt!!
Prometheus Compree no – grub?
Chorus (dejectedly) Me compree. Wee, Wee.
(Goes off to spread the news.)
Prometheus He comprees! *And* me.

These are the real Trench dialogues. The Spurious may be told by their unlikeness to these models, so Greek in their perfection of form.

Harvey's book is too much in request here to send it yet. Bide a wee, s'il vous plait.

May I request that your next parcel be more substantial with a cake and some sort of paste. Anchovy lasts a deuce of a time.

> Summer is over
> And the delicate taste
> Of the sweet and dainty lover

Is turned to the common desiring of fish paste.

Will you send me, sometime, the 6d Edition (Nelson's) of *Wild Wales* It is a wonderfully companionable book, and long, beautifully trench-fittingly long; although one skips so much in Borrow.

156

Best wishes to you, and for the quick return to health of *all* the invalids.

Your sincere friend

Ivor Gurney

[1] This is a first page to substitute for that deleted below.
[2] Letter 126.
[3] Minenwerfers, or trench mortars.

---

130 To Marion Scott   G.41.44

19 October 1916 (P)

Dear Miss Scott

Please excuse the state of the proof, just found.[1]

Thank you for both your letters and the tray bong parcel; for which you shall be thanked at length.

The unrhymed poem should be called, or may be called 'Dreams and Action'.[2] There is also the sonnet about the men in trenches, and 'Nor steel nor flame'.

Osborne is a 'Morning Post' man, of that pestilent class of politics but bon critique.

Merci, the news of your sister delights me.

Your sincere friend

Ivor Gurney

[1] Probably the proof of Gurney's 'The Fire Kindled', to be published in the *R.C.M. Magazine*.
[2] See next letter where its final title 'Strange Service' is fixed on.

---

131 To Marion Scott   G.41.43

19 October 1916 (P)

My Dear Miss Scott

Yesterday I sent off in an illicit way a letter to you, with the two poems – 'To Certain Comrades' and the unrhymed one, on whose title I am still undecided. 'Dreams and Action'? No, I prefer 'Strange Service'. Osborn is the 'Morning Post' man, and quite a good critic.

At present I have it in my mind to write 15 or 20 more, and chiefly of local interest, make a book and call it 'Songs from the Second-Fifth'. Compree tray bong?

Thank you for your letters which are a great pleasure to receive. Also the parcel, which was a well conceived finely carried out piece of work. But to save trouble, may I inform you that a good hard plain cake of Cook's will do just as well as the biscuits and fancy cake. My ideas are not grand, being that a parcel should consist of something to eat and something to make drink. Cake. Bulleyes. Coffee tablets, (as being more convenient). Anchovy paste, because of its enduring qualities. And perhaps there would be no need of currant loaf? Though that was welcome. When I first asked you for parcels, it was just before a stunt, and we were kept on half-rations, which may account for an impassioned note in my appeal. Oh well ....

I have just decided not to send a letter written before I receive yours, and consequently only now say how glad I am at the news of your sister's good progress; may it continue – and your own – and that of your book, perhaps we shall all be free and flourishing soon.

There is little in my other letter that needs mention, except a reference to a glorious review in the *Observer* of Masefield's 'Gallipoli'; in which GKC, the reviewer aforesaid quotes the following sentence – 'Happy is he who dies for his earthly city, for it is the body of the City of God.'

Thank you so much for Binyon's lovely poem; I am ashamed to have used such a title as To the Fallen after his use of it.

Winter is coming on, and things are becoming harder. I suppose the average amount of sleep is about 3 hours a day – very little more, sometimes less. Myself, I have had 2 hours in 48. Listening post is grisly: lying still in a puddle near our wires – 1 hour off, 1 hour on all night. How we shall welcome the shortest day. Next letter I will give you a faithful account of an average day, in the life [? *illegible word which does not look like life*] of a private.

If you have tears prepare to shed them then.[1] Rumours of changes and [*word deleted by censor*] are flying round. I wish that the censor would allow me to tell you of the little happenings in this quiet part of the line. I do hope to meet my friends again, if only to tell them of all the things which are so appallingly uninteresting to go through, and so interesting to be told.

Our men are really fine on the whole, and really do impress me. But to be fine out here it is absolutely necessary to forget everything of the past, and if one talks of home to think of it as a picture in the mind only – a gorgeous phantasy.

Have you read 'Mr Pepys on the Great War'? What I saw in *Truth* was first rate. Goodbye and do write when you are able. It is good to come off some clammy duty to find a friendly letter awaiting one. With best wishes – all round

Your sincere friend
Ivor Gurney

[1] *Julius Caesar*, III.ii.174.

October 1916 (KT)

Dear Howler

An answer to your letter soon. Meanwhile, please do one of our men a favour. Write to Sidgwick and Jackson, publishers of F.W.Harvey's book *A Gloucestershire Lad*, and ask them to send the 2/s cloth to

> Miss K Upton
> 57 Duke St

2/6 enclosed   Chelmsford

> Essex

S'il vous plait, m'sieur

Yours ever
IBG

25 October 1916 (G)

My Dear Miss Scott

I am very glad you both go on so well; please continue, and continue to please. (I had written 'breathe', because they are talking about gas-drill behind me). We are in reserve now, living in huts, and harried by inspections and the awful crescendo of brightness in buttons and buckles. This last is most dreadful to me; surely if any deserve blighties it is musicians! Captain Barnes has one. O lucky, lucky beggar!! *Wild Wales* has come, (yours is a good joke) and has already given me great pleasure. If one has the gift of skipping, it is a most companionable book – full of interesting people. That poem of mine was meant for a triolet – but I know none of the forms; not even the sonnet, to say off at once, without hesitation. However, what I wanted to say goes all right in its bastard form, so let it stand, but O for 'serenity'. Your own triolet was very neat I thought.

I am sorry to hear of the accident to Sir Hubert, which is bad news, since he is so little able to stand shocks.

The Binyon poem is too long, too big, I fear, for any setting I could give it, but perhaps, perhaps......

FWHs book seems to have disappeared in the lending. But bide a wee. Before I start my usual discussion, let me ask you not to stop writing, if you do not hear from me, as there may be little time for writing for a bit.

I promised to tell you something of the life in the trenches. Our last orders were as follows. – From Stand to 5.30. Stand Down, clean rifles 6.0. Breakfast 7.30. Work 8.30 – 12.30. Dinner 1. Tea 4.30. Stand to 5 – 5.30. Stand Down. Then Ration fatigue. Listening Post. Sentry. Wiring-Party. Some of these last all night. One is allowed to sleep off duty – but not in dug outs. And the average, now the cold weather has come, and rain, is about 3 hours sleep. Out of trenches, there are parades, inspections, chiefly for shortages; and fatigues. RE, Pioneer, and Ration fatigues for battallions in the line. The life is as grey as it sounds, but one manages to hang on to life by watching the absolute unquenchability of the cheerier spirits – wonderful people some of them. After all, it is a better thing to be depressed with reason than without.

When confronted with a difficult proposition the British soldier emits (rather like the cuttle-fish) a black appalling cloud of profanity; and then does the job. A pal of mine just returned from England – Cheltenham in fact – tells me that the people there are quite resigned to the war lasting another year and a half; and also quite resigned to any sacrifices we may be called upon to make. Tres bien! It is the war spirit, also Zeit-geist.

The weather here is melancholy, except for an occasional nippy morning of bright sunshine.

Bad news from Roumania and good from Verdun and the Somme[1]. I suppose this war will appear much about the same as Christmas 1914, till the trumpet sounds, and the walls fall! It seems like a Sunday Pictorial serial, also. Please tell me the opinion of any responsible people who open their mouths to you. Howells memory does him credit, and makes me compliment. I am not sure you are not right about the figure being repeated after 'Death opens unknown doors'. It may mean a couple of extra bars. About the extra bars that Howells finds – I should need a piano to find that out. The 4 Es must stand, even if the lady should need 4 trumpets to back her up. She is supposed to make a row like a brass band there. This only is admissible beside the repeated notes, and it is from an unwilling writer

It is most grand

Compree?

They have loaded us up with all sorts of extra clothing for winter – leather jerkin, vest, body-belt, Lord knows what all. I am afraid books will be too much of a responsibility and encumbrance. Anyhow *Wild Wales* will last me for months and months. And there are the Greek plays. *Agamemnon* is very fine, and the man does know how to translate.[2] I suppose that Blackie is that Greek professor whom Stevenson sat under, and who professed years after never to have seen the young man's face. I wonder how R.L.S. would have come off in the Army, had he lived now and been fit. Very queerly as a whole, I fear.

Well, may both you and your sister continue in the right paths now, and be blest as you deserve. Sickness no bon. Dinner up. Me down.

Moi explique that Anglais soldiers plenty fond of dîner. Not necessarily Army dinner though, for his thoughts float fondly back to the days of long ago. Yesterday we had pudding; clammy lumps of cold damp flour congealing and hanging together strongly by the force of malice. Goodbye best wishes

Your sincere friend

Ivor Gurney

[1] Rumania declared war on 27 August and had ceased to exist as an independent power on 6 December when Austrian troops entered Bucharest. The French were retaking lost ground at Verdun and the British slowly forcing the Germans back at the Somme,
[2] See note on letter 125.

134 *To Herbert Howells* G.3.16

30 October 1916 (P)

My Dear Howler

Yon was a nice comradely letter to receive, and of a good fat satisfying length. It was good to get it, and I can stand many such without a shrink (if there is such a word.) First let me congratulate you on having got rid of that tiresome Arts exam, which is a fine thing to be rid of. The rest should be very easy to you. By the way since you have taken French, have you read *Le Malade Imaginaire*? That's great fun, and easy to read.

Now to take your letter bit by bit.

Yes. FWH, is well, but hungry. Tray bong! No more to be said, except – since I am freed from supposing him to be na pooh, I have only to worry about not being na pooed myself, in order to meet him again.

All nonsense about the rhythm of war. Dr Davies has said that the noise of guns etc etc. But then it is only what one expects him to say. Some of the guns have a fine noise; but nearly all is of an insensate fury – too savage and assertive to be majestic. The noise of a Minnie[1] hitting the ground is of a most horrid nature. One does not realise how sensitive the earth is. A 'dud' shell may be felt easily a half-mile away. And then the outburst of a minnie explosion! The earth spouts up to a great height, and dugouts rock. It is a horrid sensation to hear a shell coming over you. If it is anywhere near, one feels it in the back of the neck, until it bursts, perhaps 25 yards behind, or even 50. Up till now however, we have not experienced the biggest shells; that being a pleasure to come.

A mine explosion is like a minnie-concussion many times magnified. The ground jumps exactly like a nervy person in a fright, the dugouts rock and the candles fall. Our Co has gained a piece of parchment for steady behaviour in trying circumstances of the sort. (An uncommon honour.) Very lights are very beautiful affairs, especially the German, which glide up in a perfect arc, and burn perfectly also. It is embarrassing to be in No Man's Land waiting for one to fall, as it seems, on top of you. To stand up at wiring, like living pictures, is more interesting than amusing, when Very lights begin to fly.

(O, in future, number of Brigade and Division must *not* be mentioned in addresses.)

I am glad Dr Allen is properly impressed by you, and I hope that Oxford will soon have a chance of hearing my quartett. It was very interesting to read about the dons and so forth. Their cobwebs and superstitions. The subjects they set for essays.

You say pretty things about 'By a Bierside'. I cannot agree with you about the repeated Es. Somehow they will have to sound like an immortal challenge after the recital of deaths damages and wrongs to man. If the Es are impossible, then

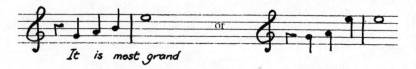

It *is* a surprise to hear that Elgars symphony is to be done. It has all the faults you mention. And all the good points too. Yet

is a phrase of joy (from the first movement) which often recurs to me.

Your account of evenings at the Taylors sticks pins all over my inner consciousness. In the language of the 2/5. It hurts my cory, whatever that is.[2] S.S. has probably received a letter from me by now. But O for Clifton Hill! We have to form hard places – callosities – in our hearts against such thoughts.

Yours ever
I.B.G.

[1] A minenwerfer or trench mortar.
[2] 'Heart', from 'cor' or 'coeur'.

---

135 *To Marion Scott*   G.41.46

8 November 1916 (P)

Bach and the Sentry

Watching the dark my spirit rose in flood
On that most dearest Prelude of my delight

The low-lying mist lifted its hood,
The October stars showed nobly in clear night.

When I return, and to real music-making,
And play that Prelude, how will it happen then?
Shall I feel as I felt, a sentry hardly waking,
With a dull sense of No Man's Land again?

Sawgint

His name it is Sparrow,
He looks but a boy.
He's a terror, a wonder,
A Treasure, a joy.

His men would go gladly
Through water and fire
To roll up the Bosche in
Barbareous wire,

If Squidge were in front
Of the bloodthirsty band,
Though rows of fat Germans
Near filled No Man's Land.

And if he were missing!....
The General would swoon,
And horrible faintness
Attack his platoon.

The Kaiser would shout,
And shove Little Willie –
'There's Sparrow hit out!
Go on! Knock 'em silly.'

Maisemore

O when we swung through Maisemore
The Maisemore people cheered,
And women ran from farmyards
And men from ricks, afeared

To lose the sight of soldiers
Who would 'fore Christmas Day
Blow Kaiser William's Army
Like mist of breath away.

(The war it was but young then!)
And we were young, unknowing
The path we were to tread
The way the path was going.

And even less we thought
As we marched across the bridge
How the thought of Home would linger
In our hearts – as Maisemore ridge!

When the darkness downward hovers
Making trees like German shadows
How our hearts turn and return
Times and times to Maisemore meadows

And Aubers ridge that Maisemore men
Have died in vain to hold....
O how the burning thought desires
Maisemore in morning gold!

O when we marched through Maisemore
Past many a creaking cart
We little thought we had in us
Love so hot at heart.

The Colonel

Keen, cool, and alert, he sits his horse
Without a touch of swank or Army Tosh;
    A figure and face of force.
One who would get his way as a matter of course –
Just the man to put the wind up Brother Bosche.

Song

Ah, tell me not the spirits of the trees
Are silent since the young men went away,
Stir not but watch their silent images
Mirrored in still clear water all the day.

O tell them how the homeward come desiring
Victors of death do seek them everywhere.
(This is the news should set their hearts a-quiring)
Wandering with cries about the scented air.

Requiem

Pour out your light, O stars, and do not hold
Your loveliest shining from earths outworn shell –
Pure and cold your radiance, pure and cold
My dead friend's face as well.

Requiem

Nor grief nor tears should wrong the silent dead,
Save England's; for her children fallen so far
From her eager care; though by God's justice led
  And fallen in such a War.

Requiem

Pour out your bounty, moon of radiant shining
On all this shattered flesh, these quiet forms;
For these were slain, so quiet, still reclining,
In the noblest cause was ever waged with arms.

Acquiescence

Since I can neither alter my destiny
By one hair's breadth from its appointed course;
Since bribes nor prayer nor any earthly force
May from its pathway move a life not free –
I must gather together the whole strength of me,
My senses make my willing servitors;
Cherish and feed the better, starve the worse;
Turn all my pride to proud humility.
Meeting the daily shocks and frozen, stony
Cynical face of doubt with smiles and joy –
As a battle with Autumn winds delights a boy,
Before the smut of the world and the lust of money
Power and fame could yet his youth destroy;
Ere he has scorned his Father's patrimony.

The Signallers Vision

One rainy winter dusk,
Mending a parted cable,
Sudden I saw so clear
Home and the tea-table.

So clear it was, so sweet,
I did not start, but drew
The breath of deep content
Some minutes ere I knew

165

My mother's face that's soother
Than autumn half-lights kind,
The softly-smiling sisters
Who keep me still in mind,

Were but a dream, a vision –
That faded. And I knew
The smell of trench, trench-feeling,
And turned to work anew.

30 November 1916 (P)

Dear Miss Scott

Have I yet thanked you for the parcel sent to me? If not, please receive here and now my grateful thanks. It was a splendid one all ways save for the lamentable omission of a cake.

Also with this exception, sympathy for the reason; which is a sad one for everybody.

You say nothing about the health of any of you. I hope this is a good sign? The mails come very irregularly now, probably, I should say, on account of the remining necessary after the raid. We are moving about now, staying occasionally for a few days at some obscure country place or other, but having wretched weather, and a little beautiful weather; and sometimes perfectly wretched billets.

We manage to exist though. The management pay us pretty regularly, but where we are moving there are none of the big cups of cafe au lait for deux sous. The people are meaner, perhaps because more poor, and one sees tumbledown barns with walls of mud and straw (And lives in them too.)

It takes a hard time in the line to make one appreciate that there are advantages in being here. Perhaps we shall have reason to see this soon, and long for a return to villages like these. But O, the mud! I believe the French English we use is quite common. A lot of it is anyway, and there is not much when you reckon it all up. Only it fits well in with common uses. Soldat Anglais knows what he wants; it is not a wide range of wants, and to any additional parly-voo, he answers Ah, wee. Only that and nothing more. Save perhaps, Mercy boko.

Is the French warloan the success it was expected to be? One hears that the French say they are tired of it all – 'I gave so much to the last loan; my brother has been killed. If I give to this; perhaps my son also'. But this is hardly a sign of breaking and the French are 'tenaces' [1] also. One recognises everywhere, that the war is very long, and that much blood has been shed.

I saw a perfectly lovely wood the other day, and beyond it, what I should take to be a fine specimen of an old camp – which would be difficlult to take today. How horrible to have written that last sentence about a beautiful ridge of earth!

> We scar the earth with dreadful enginry;
> She takes us to her bosom at the last;
> Hiding our hate with love, who cannot see
> Of any child the faults; and holds us fast.
> We'll wait in quiet till our passion's past.[2]

Your talking of London things interests me greatly – but what Dr Davies thinks of my songs will not touch me much. I would like to know what Vaughan Williams thinks – apres le guerre – apres l'âpre guerre (to make my first French pun. I hope it is correct.)

The glory of autumn is already passing, and the sorrow of dying things descending on us. We take no longer joy in the colour of leaves, but in the smell of the brown earth, and the newly unveiled tracery of small twigs against the bright sky. Then it is possible for a moment to forget the sadness of the dying year, and to remember only its beauty and austere romance. If Youth has dreams still left, frail vestiges of dreams they must be, it is good to hope that in disillusion they will partake of and show something of the Autumn loveliness and bare unsupported pride of Winter trees. Fine writing is all I am fit for – and not much of that.

Your sincere friend
Ivor Gurney

---

[1] i.e. tenacious.

[2] This impromptu was published in *Severn & Somme*. See letter 149.

37 *To Winifred Chapman* G.45750

December 1916 (KT)   Addresses in future only name, co, reg, and
                                                    B.E.F. France

My Dear Old Winnie

Still a war on! and I still in it! How I envy Kitty, and her rise in wages! It is really an achievement though to have stuck at hard work and got a rise. And I congratulate her very much. Cheero!

You must hurry up and get strong and fit and well: do stunts on the parallel bars, and lift dumbells by nervous convulsion only. On such meagre routine do the great thrive. Dear kid; it is a different sort of life now to the December of two years ago. Ping Pong between the lines has been stopped, and I no longer play accompaniments for the Germans. Soon they will stop us inviting each other to tea. The German spy system is excellent. Wonderful! They manage to find out when any oatcake arrives for me, and if I do not ask them over, invariably raid before they think it all gone, I will spend the last drop of my blood to defend the last crumb of La Comtesse's oatmeal.

I thought of you on All Hallows eve,[1] (Hallowmas Eve, isn't it?) and imagined you performing some strange Gaelic rites of memory and sanctification. I hope you had 'Sweet Polly Oliver' or the 'Bay of Biscay' in memory of one not yet needing rites but only remembrance.

The soap I am using now, but not the baccy. The oatcake had but a short life, but an appreciated one. Goodbye and Love to everybody.

Your affectionate friend
Ivor

[1] 31 October.

---

138 *To Marion Scott* G.41.48

7 December 1916 (P)

My Dear Miss Scott

I have written a whole letter to you and lost it. Let me write a scrappy one now to tell you that I received your parcels (both) and letters at odd dates, and that they were all of the greatest comfort and assistance. The post is most irregular but things arrive. As for writing letters – there was a whole fortnight passed without a chance of sending a letter off and little of writing one.

On all verse questions I ask you to judge. Do as you please, and thank you for the trouble you are taking about it all. All I have sent you is my own. Use what you like for the *R.C.M. Magazine*.

Please, please send the socks. They ought to be just the thing.

I hope you are all getting better, and feeling able to work to some purpose. How does your book progress? As to the sentence of mine you wish to use, use it by all means. I could write a book on the sentence, which I have forgotten – almost. How would this do.

'The true aim of the artist should be to perceive the divine significance of tiny things, that rightly seen, 'link one in some way to one's immortality' as Hilaire Belloc has said. What has the pedant to do with the firelight or the morning blue? He is merely playing with the machinery with which other men have striven to express the inexhaustible wonder of life – That is equally seen in the huge Alps and the small violet. In the wide sea and the tiny rain pool.' There is so much to say that, in this letter, I cannot find room. Permit me therefore, characteristically to indulge in a monologue.

My dear friend, we suffer pain out here, and for myself it sometimes comes that death would be preferable to such a life. Yet my chief thought is that I have found myself unfitted for Life and Battle, and am gradually by hard necessity being strengthened and made fit for some high task. I suffer so because of my self-indulgence in the past, and some part of my temperament. This thought upholds me, as it upheld Peter in *War and Peace*, and I try to accept whatever comes with patience – to take it with smiles is years away from me – and to feel that I am fulfilling God's purposes. The task is hard and myself weak, but the thing must continue, and may leave me ready to accomplish some great work for which I am intended. All this is to say – that I blame myself much more than I used to, and pray for patience.

We need it too; in face of the Rumanian news. Whatever can be the reason of so surprising a disaster?[1] It beats me completely.

I have received no letters for a few days being in a Rest Station for cold in the inside, going quickly now.

I will write again in a day or so to say more than can be said here. Please keep on writing, your letters are my chief link with music and my real life; and it is a great help to me to feel that my work is not altogether forgotten.

I do not know what those lighters you sent are like. As I was coming to this station I left them with my unfortunate companions to use. We had had no bread for a week. Send substantial things please now; We are out of civilisation. Standard Bread? Yes, if you please.

Another letter very soon, but it is very cold in this tent, and I must walk about. I hope that this cold weather wont hurt you and your sister. You deserve to be well by now, and able to do what you want.

Goodbye with best wishes
Your sincere friend
Ivor Gurney

[1] Austrian troops entered Rumania on 6 December 1916.

139 To Marion Scott   G.41.49

9 December 1916 (G)

No letter for days

My Dear Miss Scott

I have received all your most interesting letters, and now my two parcels also. Thank you very much for all. We need something of the kind now – now that the land is a sea of mud, and thoughts as grey as the weather. I wish I could remember all the questions you have asked me. However, as to the verses question, decide yourself. 'So hot my heart desires' is legitimate enough, and the line is not original probably.[1] Compare A E Housman's 'How soft the poplars sigh' [2] Or hundreds and thousands of other such. About everything else, do as you please; not caring overmuch for correctness, but setting more intention on colour and the conveying of truth. 'How hot my heart desires' is nearer fire and passion than 'So hotly my heart desires'. In 'Strange Service' – 'and uses consecrate' may stand. I *never* keep a copy of these things. I get them off my chest, and send them to you. So it is wise in you to quote in full when you make suggestions, for I could not repeat 'The Fire Kindled' as you have it for any money. Only – I remember the end, which was that poem's reason for being. Did you see W B Yeats reviewed again after so long a silence?[3] By Heaven, there must be some fine verse in that book.

'Suddenly I saw the cold and rook-delighting heaven', absolutely electrified me. It was glorious to read it. (Quoted in full in the *Sat: Westminster*). If you have not read it, I will send you a transcript in my next letter.

Really, we have little time for writing letters lately, and if any were written the officer would not receive to censor them. So my chief pleasure vanished; and as for music!

After 'Death opens unknown doors', your suggestion that the chief figure should be used is probably right. Anyway

Sketch for H N H

As to all publishers arrangements – that shall be in your most kind care, and thank you very much. All I have sent you hitherto is mine, only I want badly to write an 'All-Hallows Day' and 'A Salute', but cannot get time to think, and am not big enough for what I want to say.

I hope your book goes on well, and that you are strong enough to take joy in the writing. As to my sentence you wish to include, I am afraid that my sentences are too hurried and altogether-scribbled to bear quotation. Wait till next letter. Or 'What the artist needs is not so much technique, as a greater appreciation of beauty so generally overlooked. Why should not the violet be considered as the chief work of God visible to us? And yet it is the bunch and the coloured vase that must make up most people's mental idea of that lovely thought of innocence. The Artist must learn to feel the beauty of all things, and the sense of instant communion with God that such perception will bring. 'To feel Eternity in an hour'. Blake knew that to attain to this height, not greater dexterity, but greater humility and beauty of thought were needed. And the composer must judge his work by this standard – that his work be born of sincere and deep emotion sufficiently controlled by the intellect to be coherent and clear. And if his thought be deep and worthy, who shall say it will not shape its proper expression? Which is not quite what I want.[4] Do as you will.

Tonight we have had cafe au lait, our little circle; seated round a tiny hut fire; surrounded by the abomination of desolation and by day depressed by the sight of a piteously ruined church tower; once a glory. And amazed by the sight of a hanging statue. The weather is grey, but thank the Fates! not rainy and we are grateful for this small mercy.

Please go on writing in your usual fashion; your letters giving me great pleasure; and don't expect any regular reply from me. None knows what the next day may bring forth.

There is some chance of leave soon.

After all, my friend, it is better to live a grey life in mud and danger, so long as one uses it – as I trust I am now doing – as a means to an end. Someday all this experience may be crystallized and glorified in me; and men shall learn by chance fragments in a string quartett or a symphony, what thoughts haunted the minds of men who watched the darkness grimly in desolate places. Who learnt by the denial how full and wide a thing Joy may be, forming dreams of noble lives when nothing noble but their own nobility (and that seemed tiny and of little worth) was to be seen. Who kept ever the memory of their home and friends to strengthen them, and walked in pleasant places in faithful dreams. And how one man longed to be working to celebrate them in music and verse worthy of the high theme, but did not bargain with God, since it is best to accept one's Fate when that is clearly seen.

This has been discovered, and is now to come to you.

I am on a temporary job now, as I may have told you, and consequently have a little more time to myself. But there is no sun, and the whole outlook is depressing.

No letters have yet arrived (Dec 9th.) but perhaps tomorrow. If I send a F.P.C. with nothing at all crossed out, please send to me Pte Gurney attached to Sanitary Section, 61 Div H.Q. Or please do so in any case. Perhaps my letters have been returned to England. If so please send 'em again. It will not take long to forward letters if I am recalled soon. The sign of recall will be everything crossed out on a F.P.C.

What news of Rumania! What a tragedy! No words can show what a disappointment this is to all our hopes. How – how has it happened?

Good-bye, and best wishes for all good things and health most of all.

Your sincere friend
Ivor Gurney

[1] Published in *Severn & Somme*. 'The Fire Kindled', l.20.
[2] Housman's *A Shropshire Lad*, LII, line 8.
[3] Gurney quotes the opening line of 'The Cold Heaven'. Although this had been published in collections as early as 1912, Gurney is probably referring to its publication in *Responsibilities and Other Poems* (1916).
[4] Gurney wrote 'want I want'.

140 *To Winifred Chapman*   G.45750

December 1916 (KT)

My Dear Winnie

Here is a tiny note for you which may get to you by Xmas Day, or long before, or long after, as the case may be. Anyway enjoy it, my dear enemy (at Ping Pong). Alas! I know not if the sport of ping-pong still flourishes anywhere in the land.

Lately, I have shirked much on account of a disturbed interior. RAMC, Rest Station, and now on a job – a comparatively nice one to do with water-carts. This is all very well, but I have had no letters. Please write to me. Private Gurney 2/5 Glos. attached Sanitary Section 61st Div HQ. That will reach me I think.

I wonder how you have been lately with all this grey unpleasant weather. No bon! no bon!

And Arthur and Mick both of whom shall receive the polished epistle. Cheero!

There will be no long walk for us this Xmas – but there is a good chance of leave soon, and then who knows what wonders may happen? Yes, Leave. When? Don't know, but a good leave – no skimpy allowance of a day.

My dear kids there will be joy then and much galumping, even though they be meatless days, and only 3 courses.

Does the New Vicaw appreciate Mrs Chapman's excellent scones? I hope he has not taken my place – in the slippers only large enough because of the holes. Don't let him have any oatcake. I have heard and met so many Scots lately on this job, that I have tasted oatcake quite often in fancy lately.

O to do so in reality.
Bon O Bon

Yours affect:
Ivor

---

141 *To Marion Scott* G.41.50

22 December 1916 (P)

My Dear Lady of Courtesies

It is some time since I heard from you, which is not as I desire. Does this mean you are ill again? I hope not, though the weather might give one to suppose so. Here's the sun this morning; the first sun for weeks, to give us all hope.

Everyone talks of Peace Conferences now, and the wildest rumours go round; but for myself, next August seems likely to give us the first real chance of Our Peace – without Conference. Still – thank the Lord – I am on my Soft Job, and today my batt: goes into the line; to stand in frozen mud to the knees; to live 15 hours in the dark of every 24, staring and waiting; and collecting souvenirs. To come out so fatigued and fordone that only the knowledge that they must be left there for hours and hours keeps them from dropping in the sludge – that and some last grain of pluck and pride.

I spend 8 hours a day tramping about in mud and half frozen water, but keep pretty fit notwithstanding. Thoughts of music and verse not many. Yet there is

To An Unknown Lady

You that were once so sweet, are sweeter now
That an even leaden greyness clouds my days;
A pain it is to think on your sweet ways,
Your careless-tender speaking tender and low.
When the hills enclosed us, hid in happy valleys,
Greeting a thousand times the things most dear,
We wasted thoughts of love in laughter clear
And told our passion out in playful sallies,
But in me now a burning impulse rages
To praise our love in words like flaming gold,
Molten and live for ever; Not fit for cold
And coward like-to-passions Time assuages.
Nor do I fear you are lovely only in dreams,
Being as the sky reflected in clear streams.

And
(2)
The Strong Thing

I have seen Death and the faces of men in fear
Of Death, and shattered terribly ruined flesh,
Appalled; but through the horror coloured and clear
The love of my county, Gloster, rises afresh.

And on the Day of Days, the Judgement Day,
The Word of Doom awaiting breathless and still;
I'll marvel how sweet's the air down Framilode way
And take my sentence on sheer down Crickley Hill.

I have missed your letters, which however may turn up at any moment;
address, Pte Gurney 2/5 Glosters attached San: Section 61 Div: HQ, to be
received with great joy. The gossip of music and verse helps to keep me alive.

Today, the weather cleared and the sun showed. Begging your pardon
ma'am, but I am lousy to a degree, and had a 4 mile solitary walk for a bath I
did not get. But saw some lovely things and was renewed to some extent. O
the pain of remembering what might be!

Lately I have met lots of Scots, on my watering-cart job; and I have liked
them very much indeed. O but it was good to hear the tongue of Sir Walter
and Burns and RLS. A Scot and I were shivering in the bitter wind, and silent.
Till at last I was struck with a memory, turned to him and quoted 'I'm sure
it's winter fairly';[1] we both laughed and parted friends. To see their strong
faces and free walk is a great pleasure to me. They are the first of peoples. O to
be up late reading *Rob Roy* or *Kidnapped* or *Weir of Hermiston* again; smoking
Three Nuns or Chairman and drinking pints of tea!

I shall probably not be returning to the Batt for a fortnight, then there may
be a chance of leave. If so, I shall certainly spend a couple of days in London,
probably three.

That was an excellent essay on T Hardy in the *Times Literary Supplement* a
little time back.[2] And hardly anybody could have disagreed with it.

Will you please send me another insect preventer? And the silk socks?

How is your old cook getting on in her new state? It would be interesting
to hear if she manages to feed the brute into decency.

How good it would be to read *The Path to Rome*, *My Lady Nicotine*,
Boswell, *Guy Mannering*, *Under the Greenwood Tree*, *Hamlet*, *Friends*, Rupert
Brooke and *Huckleberry Finn* again. I will be a great devourer of books
when.....

I hope you and Miss Stella will be robust and Christmassy by the Day. Good wishes to you all.

Your sincere friend
Ivor Gurney

[1] The last line of the chorus of Robert Burns's 'Up in the Morning Early'; the chorus is said to be old.

[2] 'The Poetry of Mr.Hardy' was the front-page article in the *T.L.S.* for 23 November 1916, a review of the Golden Treasury Series *Selected Poems of Thomas Hardy*. Particularly relevant to Gurney are statements like: 'his great strength lies ... in the amazing insight and sympathy with which he shows how the historic doings of kings and generals affect the private soldier, the citizen in his shop, the man behind the plough'.

---

142 To Mrs Voynich   G.46.32.2

December 1916 (KT)

Dear Mrs Voynich

It was kind of you to send such a jolly nice parcel – a perfect sweet parcel. We are now altogether out of civilisation – and were so then, and the advent of such chocolates is decidedly an event. The letter was very acceptable also – a link with the things I long to return to, and which it is better save at such moments to forget.

I hope your health continues to improve, and you becoming more able, in not quite able, to do all you wish to do.

It is strange to turn from the gray monotony of doing continually things I hate doing, to talk of things that draw the best of me, and talk me out of myself.

I had a long talk with an RAMC man who knew Tolstoi, and runs well in his pleasures with me, – It was like a glimpse of Heaven; so sorely needed for a dyspeptic fish out of water. We talked of Tolstoi and Bach and Rupert Brooke, and the end of the war. I saw Heaven opening before my eyes and the lovely angels of Books and Music, Music and Books, sending all kinds of pleasant greeting and welcome .

I have come to the state where I know how good a Shakespeare Sonnet is, but cannot wrap myself in it, and cannot dwell on the lines to taste their sweetness; no not even in that beginning 'That time of year thou mayst in me behold',[1] which has always shown me an exquisite quiet sunset sky of winter, peaceful and serenely grave. Do you remember what happened to Peter in the Retreat? (*War and Peace*) I try to put myself in his place, and so fit myself for the task I wish to accomplish. Very well, but how much longer?

My letters now are all soliloquies; I can offer nothing better: a cuckoo, cuckoo with a very minor third, from sodden woodlands hopeless of the spring.

One is ashamed to complain for so many men take things smiling almost till the moment that they drop. Indeed it is a great thing to be in company with such men, and to imitate them as far as my waning will will allow. How much beter than four years ago anyway!

What a fatheaded sort of letter this is to send to a friend! Please excuse it, this being the best I can manage. We live in a gray waste of time, in a gray wasteful business and in gray discouraged days without sunshine. Duty is a gray thing also, and cheers very little if it upholds.

At present I am on some duty connected with water carts, out of the Batt: which makes a change.

Well the best of possible Christmases to you. Will Xmas day be a meatless day I wonder? May the kind Gods forbid! Let our homefriends celebrate it with great hunks of roast and steaming pudding. The spirit of Joy may the better descend upon us here.

Yours very sincerely
Ivor Gurney

[1] Shakespeare's sonnet 73.

143 *To Marion Scott* G.41.51

27 December 1916 (P)

My Dear Miss Scott

I have just received your luxurious parcel and your most welcome letters – on Xmas Day! Bon, tres bon.

All day long I was out hunting – for our little gang, scouring the town with our small combined funds; there was a glorious wind though, and I like hunting, but O it was a pleasure to get back and find your big square envelopes awaiting me. There seems a long gap between the last and these two (15 and 17.) If you sent a letter with an *Athenaeum* cutting I never got it, but today my sister Dorothy has enclosed it with her letter. They are all very impressed, but I doubt if the 'A's general reader is.

Thank you for the reception given to my monologue. I know my letters are nearly all about myself, and far too full of 'I's, and am very grateful to you for your letters – so full of interest and kindness. If your book is full of your spirit it should be a success; but then, that is the trouble – to translate feeling into words. I hope to be an interested grateful reader, say next October. The feeling in the Army is – that we can break them directly the weather gives us a fair chance. Incredible rumours of peace go round; officers give instructions that if Peace is declared, no undue commotion shall be caused. Men say 'it will be over soon'; but for all that, the Army, in spite of the scandalous things thay say about the men running things, is full of spirit, and knows itself superior to the Allemans. As for the Scots – O it is a joy to meet the water-cart drivers and attendants of the 51st division. The Scots are certainly the finest of races, and the hardiest. Not one of the Scots has caused any trouble. With most men I find myself trying to find a form of address, but not with the Scots. Who are stronger of Nature but do not waste any time in unnecessary display. 50,000 Scots would beat any other 50,000 men, I feel convinced.

I am chummy with two Scots Engineers who recite Burns and sing me O why left I my hame, and Ae waukin O, which you probably know.

O what wonder there is in life, what places to be seen, what men women and children to meet! If God is as decent as some of His creatures we shall be someday well content.

You are mistaken in supposing me to have been ill. This would have been so if I had continued where I was, but a few days in the warm put me practically all right, and now I am expecting a call to return at any moment, and it has been a Soft Time here. Only the first part of Bridges verse impresses me, and the trim Newbolt does not stand against the gaunt stark greyness of Whitman, being derivative and specially-requested, so to speak. The last movement of the Symphony has indeed some beautiful music. 'Bathe me O God in Thee' is hoarse with the last deepest emotion of a great and simple mind saying as nakedly as might be its inmost thought.

Your 2nd letter

Here is the Yeats.

> Suddenly I saw the clear and rook-delighting heaven
> That seemed as though it burned, and was but the more ice;
> And thereupon imagination and the heart were driven
> So wild that every casual thought of that and this
> Vanished; and in their place came thoughts out of season
> With the hot blood of youth, of love crossed long ago,
> And I put all the blame out of all sense and reason
> Until I cried and trembled, and rocked to and fro
> Riddled with light. Ah when the ghost begins to quicken,
> Confusion of the death-bed over, is it sent
> Naked upon the roads, as the books say, and stricken
> With the injustice of the skies for punishment.

177

Colour has come back again into the world and into my soul, and I am more alive. I can stand anything but the pressure, the slow grind of monotonous pain, and the weather has been all that lately. Write again soon please. Prattle, pretty creature, prattle. Letters out here are a ration and not correspondence. Leave is not at all unlikely to come before the end of January.

Now I go to my Scots. Last night I kept them up till 10.20 without knowing it. Tonight I must be more careful.

I hope you are not tormenting yourselves in England because of us. That can do no good at all. We wish you to remember us, but no [*sic*] so as with pain.

> Goodbye
> Your sincere friend
> Ivor Gurney

---

144 *To Winifred Chapman*   G.45750

New Year 1917 (KT)

My Dear Old Win

Still here and not there, as is perhaps to be expected. No leave yet, that is to say; but who knows? I may arrive home from office tonight and find a telegram 'Will you come and teach me how? Lloyd George' (reply half-prepaid). Or 'Do stop them, old man – Wilhelm' (not prepaid) lying on the hall table. This might mean quite a few days in Blighty, in which case I shall hurry at once to St Micks (Collis castelli – Castle Hill) and present my never-for-one-single-phsycological [*sic*] -moment-to-be-forgotten Winifred with the one souvenir I have – the tattered remains of a G. pocket book – if it lasts till then.

I hope Christmas went off all right and fine – that Daddy was not grumpy and La Comtesse grumpy at his grumpiness. I trust you danced the roundelay and Fa-la-la-ed to any extent. Stap me, had I been there, would not I have taken part in these innocent revels? Yea, by the to [*sic*] old Pig of Brixham, marry, so would I!

And how's Arthur and how's that little imp of restlessness Micky, the human Soap-Bubble? How many goals has Arthur the Hope of his Side managed to score?

I want to know all Mrs. It is port wine oatcakes and chews of bacca to me. Hogmanay was happy and rowdy just round here – happier than it was in Scotland the men come back from leave say.

Well I hope High Wycombe put some go into the parting kick.

Good bye

> Yours affectionately
> Ivor

4 January 1917 (P)

Scots

The boys who laughed and jested with me but yesterday
So fit for kings to speak to, so blithe and proud and gay,
Are now thoughts of blind pain, and best hid away....
(Over the top this morning at the dawn's first gray.)

O if we catch the kaiser his dirty hide to flay,
We'll hang him on a tall tree his pride to allay;
That will not bring the boys again to mountain and brae....
(Over the top this morning at the dawn['s] first gray.)

To think – Earth's best and dearest turned to red broken clay
By one devil's second! What words can we say?
Or what gift has God their mothers' anguish to repay?....
(Over the top this morning at the first flush of day.)[1]

[1] Printed in *Severn & Somme*.

146 To Sydney Shimmin
[*Transcribed from a very faint xerox copy supplied by Robin Haines; present whereabouts of the original unknown. Words in square brackets are faint and difficult to decipher.*]

Early January 1917 (KT)

My Dear Old Shim
    That it did not need a gift of chocolate to keep you in remembrance, I will show by writing before it gets here. (Privates giving gifts of chocolate! Toity-toity, as the ladies in books used to say.) Thanking you all the same, and hoping that I shall have [head] mouth and pipes fit to manage [it] when it does arrive.
    [Here] I am still extant, first edition [book] I am and unique. The Cold upset my belly and other parts that may be veiled under a descent [*sic*] obscurity (as they usually are actually) and that has landed me into a Soft Job, just for the present.
    Your kindly female relative – Mona by name – has been more than good to me, in fact, I may go so far as to say she has been Better.
    The Cake was Best, the only drawback being there was no Wurst – Sausage.
    Did you see that Marie Wieck is dead?[1] (Clara Schumann's sister) Poor old

girl, she has been knocked into the middle of the next now, at all events.

I think my foot has gone deep into it? Into what? Something particularly noisome. Cos why? Mrs Voynich shows distinct signs of making me confidant as to her new novel and cantata. No bon, je n'y desire pas. And yet ..... I may acquire much kudos as a brake or deterrent. What with all the other little circumstances though, I think I stand in danger enough already. However I can *never* have enough chocolate. Compree bon? Do not, je t'implore, show this letter *too* much, *too* often nor indiscreetly. Prenez Garde. Keep off the grass, the Old Man Said.

This is a skittish letter, i'faith, gadzooks! But then this is a soft job.

Please give all kind messages to the Taylors from me, retaining part of each for your self.

Yours ever
IBG.

[1] Marie Wieck (1832, d. 2 November 1916), half sister to Clara Schumann.

---

147 *To Marion Scott*   G.41.53

7 January 1917 (P)

My Dear Miss Scott

With an effort of will I make myself to leave off searching (unsuccessfully) and turn to letter writing and itching. Sorry to mention this, but it is my whole mental horizon at present.

Well, everything sent by you has arrived save the brown loaf parcel; but that's not to give up hope yet.

To take your letter as it runs – I am glad my poetry expert will take such trouble with my verses – but this time do not much agree. If she thinks I shall alter a passage which will delete 'the cold

And coward like-to-passions Time assuages',[1]

(the one thing that really pleases me in the Sonnet) she is mistaken. And 'rages' is only out of the picture because the picture is a sonnett. This has too many thoughts to be perfect, but that does not prevent its being not a bad poem.

'Rages' is strong but not excessively so. I wished to write 'a burning passion rages'; but wanted the word elsewhere; which would have been hotter still. The line and a bit quoted are, if you will believe me, quite Shakespearian. (You put commas in which are not needed; are bad, in fact.)

You are right about Crickley Hill not sounding well. Believe me, the view makes up for it, and I wrote from the viewpoint rather than the name. (Severn Plain, May Hill, the Welsh Hills, Malvern, and a little bit of Cotswold.)

But stick an 'on' in line 1 verse 2

'And on the Day of Days, on the Judgement Day.'

The part of your letter that pleased me most is that concerning the *Gloucestershire Lad*. Mrs Harvey will be delighted, and I will write to her to tell of the fame he has attained. Yes, you are right, the ballades are splendid. (I am surprised you do not like the French forms.) Is it not strange he finds it hard to write sonnetts? And that no sonnet finds place in the *Glostershire Lad*?

Mrs Harvey sent me a small Anthology, called *A Selection of Poems* – Sidgwick and Jackson, price 6d.[2] It is worth more than that for K.Tynan's 'Flower of Youth'. Some things are annoying in it, but a good six pennyworth is there. Harvey has 'In Flanders', and 'If we return', by which they show taste and discretion.

I should have liked to hear your lecture. There are many good war poems. Harvey, Binyon, Rupert Brooke, Wilfred Gibson, and so I have been told, G K Chesterton's 'Wife of Flanders'.[3] (Get that last book of verse by GKC. It will be worth reading, like his article on Wilson's note. He writes like one inspired, at his best.) And then there's Hardy and Captain Grenfell. Could you send me Binyon's 'To the Fallen' again? I have lost the verses, just as I felt some stirrings in me.

Meanwhile here are three new things (four, with 'Scots'.)

(O, the Unknown Lady is really unknown. She's but a figment or a dream of passion.)

Purple and Black

The death of princes is
Honoured most greatly.
Proud kings put Purple on
And vestments stately.

Though they have lived such life
As God offends;
Gone fearful down to death,
Sick, without friends.

And in the temple dim,
Trumpets of gold
Proclaim their glory; so
Their story is told.

In sentimental hymns
Weeping her dolour,
The mother of heroes wears
Vile Black – Death's colour.

Who should walk proudly with
The noblest One

181

Of all that Purple crowd -
'This was my son'.

Song and Pain

Out of my sorow have I made these songs,
Out of my sorrow;
Though somewhat of the making's eager pain
From Joy did borrow.

Someday, I trust, God's purpose of Pain for me
Shall be complete,
And then - to enter the House of Joy .....
Prepare, my feet.

Communion

Beauty lies so deep
On all the fields,
Nothing for the eyes
But blessing yields.

Tall elms, greedy of light,
Stand tip-toe. See
The last light linger in
Their tracery.

The guns are dumb, are still
All evil noises.
The singing heart in peace
Softly rejoices,

Only unsatisfied
With Beauty's hunger
And sacramental thirst -
Nothing of anger.

Mist wraiths haunt the paths
As daylight lessens,
The stars grow clearer, and
My dead friend's presence.

The soft job has given me opportunity to contemplate yesterday's lovely afternoon and evening and today's perfect sunshine, and these are the outcome. (Have you heard anything of Osborne? Probably a refusal from your silence. N'importe. Nitchevo.) Today I heard cries of 'Hello, Peter'! (my nickname from 'Widdecombe Fair') and looked up to see my company going up on fatigue; not so large as it was. I have met some fine people, by God. It sometimes seems worth it all now, and after the war, it will have seemed supremely worth while. It will have given England another topic of conversation other than the weather! But I made my fastest friendship on record with two Scots Engineers lately. One of them was fine indeed. He recited To the Haggis, Tom O'Shanter, the Daisy; and sang Ae Waukin O and John Anderson, and McGregor's gathering very well.

And then on Hogmanay – New Year's Eve you know, the pipers up in the village burst out in welcome for the New year with a glorious tune that set us all aching to dance.

'We've been happy a'thegither'

Over and over it went. (After the guns had finished distributing presents of iron rations.) They *had* been happy a thegither, and the night resounded with it. Alas the private festivities of my pet Engineer did not altogether agree with him and next day he was 'very poorly' as Gloster folk say. However, after the war I hope to see Sapper Ritchie again, and get folksongs off his father. O bonny Scots, apres le guerre! Que le guerre soit maudit!

I have received no letters from any College person save Shimmin lately, with an offer of chocolate – which is alas as yet only an offer.

I long to get back to consult the friend who guided me to *Friends*, and perhaps get some other useful information from him. Much do I long for good clean verse of this time! Shame though it is to bring it to this mud, it lifts my soul above the mud to read such stuff – Shakespeare's Sonnetts are too remote and so need too much of an effort. Yeats' new book is called *Responsibilities*, and the piece of verse I sent you comes from that. Harvey is too depressed to write at all now. Poor chap, it is no bon to be prisoner. It was good to get a note from him though, my first, and to see his queer handwriting again.

Your sincere friend
Ivor Gurney

[1] See letter 141 and *Severn & Somme*, where the poem under discussion, 'To an Unknown Lady', was published.
[2] *A Selection of Poems from recent volumes published by Sidgwick and Jackson* (1916)
[3] 'The Wife of Flanders', collected in *Poems* (1915).

148 To Marion Scott   G.41.55

11 January 1917 (G)

Sent with 'In Flanders'.

My Dear Lady of Courtesies

Here is what is meant as a courtesy from me; I hope you will be able to decipher it. This valuable fragment dates anywhere between April 1916 and now. Or is it September or August 1915? Goodness knows. However, here it is, cast up with the flotsam and jetsam in more or less permanent form, with – Wae's me – another orchestral accompaniment, dammit.

Well, it drew me out of lethargy for a space, and was no more trouble than an ordinary fatigue. Surely it reflects the words?

But on the other hand, ought there to be a figure to bind it together? and (my usual thought) is it Oldfashioned? And though undoubtedly music in places, is it Immature? Or will its freshness carry it off? Is it fresh? My Hamlet mind revolves its usual course – From the desire to set, to – the being too lazy to set, to – Self Castigation, to – the Beastly Bother of Setting, to – Half Disgust, to – Carelessness, to – Will it be Elation? All is Vanity, and until another decries my stuff I care little for it.

Please do not trouble about the Binyon verses; I having just received a copy. Beautiful stuff, which must be cut; and where? And altogether rather difficult to do. Wait till I have a month with the 48 and the songs of Schumann and Schubert and the often heavy Brahms. 'What! is *that* The Great Song – ? Then let Me Show Them!' Then starts the aforementioned round. – Heaven forgive me for my envy-inspired motives! I write from anything but Joy in the Making. More monologues!

Your sincere friend
Ivor Gurney

17 January 1917 (P)

My Dear Friend

Your letter of Jan 7 has just arrived, and its bee-yutiful compliments. 'Scots' seems to have been quite a success, since there is no sort of incident connected with me that brought it out – it was the talk and the tales of the men who won the victory in November (was it?)[1] Here is a case of 'trying it on the day' crowned with success.

As for the little 5 line poem,[2] it is the fact that, had you sent it to me as another's, and asked my opinion; I should not have wondered. I never remembered seeing it before, until next day; when the memory of an impromptu came to me – it was merely part of a letter, and went clean out of my mind after it was sent.

I never got your letter with the *Athenaeum* slip – it will turn up some day, no doubt. The parcel turned up today, smelling strongly; the mice have been nibbling at it nevertheless. Thank you very much, and for the candles, one of which is burning to light my writing. (O the name for the 5 lines might be Mother of All. Or no – simply 'The Mother'.)

By the time you have received this you will probably have had 'In Flanders' a day or two, and I am very interested to know what you think of 'Communion', which seems to me to be one of the most successful of all, if not, with 'Serenity', the most successful. Really, the book has filled up lately, n'est ce pas? And if they give me but a little time in the Batt: to myself; or if the nice Blighty comes along; or if the spring weather comes along and finds me rejoicing in it – The Complete Opus 1 of my Poetical Works (Or will it be 'Poetical Remains'?) will be on view. What is the minimum required? Please tell me; for if there had not been this rather mean definite end in view, I doubt whether I should have written above a couple of things this last month. So queerly are we made.

The Yeats poem was bound to impress you, it being one of the greatest things in the language – greater than anything Milton ever wrote for instance – so strong an advantage has English English over the Latin. When I come to my own self in Music, at least I will attempt to use all the strings, and not to harp upon a few, however nobly they may be used. In fact (Look out now!) Milton may be compared to one who should use the Old Modes or the Pentatonic Scale only; and a similar poetical comparison could not be made of Bach, for instance, who used more than his nobility to make up his Art.

I say, things are moving in England now! They'll move here pretty startlingly too in the Spring, if the lessons of Verdun are valuable at all.

We go back to the Batt: very soon, and I think it would be best to arrange the Field Postcard dodge again. No, I will be firm. Write to the Batt: from now please. since it is almost dead certain a week will see us gone.

Here is a bit of the 'Framilode' thing I meant to send you whole. Please be honest, and tell me really if you like it, as a long effort bores me, and I am tired of it. However, if your august approval is warm enough, I will try to continue with Afternoon – the Sands, and (O Lor!) Sunset and Afterglow. Then (O Jehosaphat) Night and the Stars. But it is a big Job. Don't send me on it unless you think it well worth while; and pity my lethargy, not to say laziness.

Framilode the Queen

1

The tanned faced Vikings venturing the open Sea
Were not so full of glory as was I
When the wind played treacherous boisterous tricks on me
Redfaced with rudder-hauling, nowhere dry
(Shaving the sandbanks barely
By God, right over – nearly)
Filled with the noise of water, sight of the sky.
I loved it all, despite all wise folks warning
That they'd wake up some morning,
And find my body over there on the mud.
The song of waters rushing sang in my blood,
Prudence and the tattle of gossips scorning
Since Danger was so noble high and jolly
Why Prudence might go hang with Melancholy.

2

I remember mornings when the clouds went sailing
Like great sea-galleon ploughing the foamless blue
All dazzling white, and wondered who at the railing
Pondered the course, and managed the wild crew.
Whether he went in faith onwards and on
Where never yet the keel of ship had gone
Or took familiar paths all captains knew
Sometimes cloud-castles seemed to endure an age
So strong in show
One thought they would outweather any rage
Although but snow.
Then lovely tiny flocks wandering the heavens
Sixes and sevens.
The piping shepherd, careless of Time and speed
Took never heed
Into what azure nooks his flock might stray
So he might play
His rapt hearts musing deeper than words could say
Out on the sweet day
Or cirrus clouds, stretched like the Milky Way
Gladdened the day.[3]

I have seen yesterday's English papers today. Never were they more optimistic, and the neutral comments on our note are favourable enough surely.

Garvin's article of Dec 31st (was it?) was very fine, and atones for his attitude of last April and May. but it is extraordinary how the minds of people have turned towards the light since December 1st. Perhaps it was not only German approaches brightened them up, but also their beginning to see the conquest of Roumania in its proper light – as an episode, and a revenge.

> We who have watched the darkened East so long
> Hungry for light, now know that Dawn is near
> With the huge Climax. Heedless of doubt and fear
> We fill our minds with the New Battle Song,
>   'Victory'.

We are sanguinarily tired of it all though. I met, of course, most of the the the water cart drivers and attendants – Infantry, Artillery, Engineers and RAMC – and talked to many during the time when Germany was reported to have opened Peace Negotiations. They more than half believed that Peace was near – the wildest rumours spread – until the news of our rejection came, and they settled back into the old lethargic mood of waiting, a little more depressed than usual. But for all that, they are absolutely confident of victory once we can get at them. And, whatever they may say, have confidence in their chiefs and in England. But don't question men just come from trenches. Or Artillery men whose pet horses, flogged so often out of the mud, have at last stuck there through weakness and been shot to save trouble. Ask ASC men, RAMC (or T.U.) or Staff Officers.

Your sincere friend
Ivor Gurney

> (Noctes ambrosianae?
>   or Deorum?)
> *The Estaminet*
>
> The crowd of us were drinking
> One night at Riez Bailleul
> The glasses were a clinking,
> The Estaminet was full;
>
> And loud with song and story
> And blue with tales and smoke, –
> We spoke no word of Glory,
> Nor mentioned 'Foreign Yoke'.
>
> But yarns of girls in Blighty;
> Vain, jolly, ugly, fair,

Standoffish, foolish, flighty –
And O but *we* were there

Where never thuds a Minnie,
But Minnie smiles at you,
A-meeting in the spinney
With kisses not a few

And of an inn that Johnson
Does keep; the 'Rising Sun'.
His friends him call Jack (Johnson)
He's Gloster's only one.

We talked of poacher's habits
(But girls ever and again)
Of killing weasels, rabbits,
Stoats, pheasants, never men.

Although we knew tomorrow
Must take us to the line.
In beer hid thought and sorrow,
In ruddy and white wine.

When we had finished drinking,
Though still was clear each head,
We said no word – went slinking
Straight homeward,(?) into bed.(?)

O never lads were merrier
Nor straighter nor more fine
Though we were only 'Terriers'
And only, 'Second Line'.

O I may get to Blighty,
Or Hell, without a sign
Of all the love that filled me,
Leave dumb the love that filled me,
The flood of love that filled me
For these dear comrades of mine.

[1] The first battle of the Somme ended on 18 November.
[2] 'The Mother', published in *Severn & Somme*. See letter 136.
[3] I have not recorded the crossings out and alterations here, and have inserted six lines
from the next page before the last two lines, as Gurney indicates.

18 January 1917 (P)

My Dear Friend

Thank you for your letter and the trouble taken in writing out those poems
– most interesting to read, but not seeming to me to be great. I like the
'Dying Patriot' hardly at all; the Old Ships has some very fine stuff in it,[1]
'Set the crew laughing and forgot his course'
is very suggestive – gives one an Odyssean feeling and visions of blue seas,
golden sands and tanned men bathed in a light of old adventure. And the end
of course is beautiful indeed; Brangwyn in verse?

I wonder whether the three sets of verses including 'Communion', have
reached you. It is doubtful whether the book, if book it comes to be, can ever
have for title 'Songs of the Second-Fifth', since there is so little of the
battallion in it. The number of things mounts up – it is over twenty now.

By the way, do you know much of Yeats' verse? If not, it will very well
repay you to read *Poems* (his first, I believe) and *Poems 1905* (I am not sure of
the title.)[2] In the first he is often annoyingly mystical and fluffy-haired – if you
understand me – but still; there is the close of *Countess Cathleen*, 'The Fiddler
of Dooney', a 'Slumber Song', and other things not clear in my memory. In
the second, the plays *On Baile's Strand*, and *The King's Threshold* will lift you
bang right out of yourself. There's the man who can write blank verse, fluid
poetical and English all at once. Also a song called 'Kathleen na Houlihan' is
very good. These two are all I could get hold of of all Yeats' books.

(O Abercrombie! what would you be without Yeats?)

Have you read Synge's *Aran Islands, Deirdre of the Sorrows, Well of the Saints*?
I can recommend these. His other plays I do not know so well.

Masefield's *Everlasting Mercy* is well worth reading. So is *Pompey the Great*
they say. Wilfred Gibson has written shoals – but see the two books of
Georgian Verse.

Thank you for what you wrote about FWH. I have written to his mother
quoting some of it.

   Song

  Only the wanderer
  Knows England's graces,
  Or can anew see clear
  Familiar faces.

  And who loves Joy as he (Who loves fair Joy as he?)
  That dwells in shadows?
  Do not forget me quite,
  O Severn meadows.

Your brown bread parcel came three days ago on the 7th. It was tres bon. Bread and biscuits first rate and most acceptable; particularly as the rations did not turn up one day. How good it was to get bread not dust dry to eat. What is in the stuff to keep it grateful to eat?

West Country

Spring comes soon to Maisemore
And Spring comes sweet
With bird-songs and blue skies,
On gay dancing feet
But she is such a shy lady
I fear we'll never meet.

Some day round a corner
Where the hedge foams white
I'll find Spring a-sleeping
In the young-crescent night
And seize her and make her
Yield all her delight.

But there's a glad story
That's yet to be told.
Here's grey Winter's bareness
And no-shadowed cold
O Spring, with your music
Your blue, green, and gold!
Come shame his grey wisdom
With laughter and gold.

All these lispings of childhood do not prevent terrific strafing on the left, Where Hell is apparently combined with the angry gods to make things thoroughly uncomfortable. On the whole, we do well to be here. The proper soldier's morality is in general to do what his comrades would do; in the case of Soft jobs to stick to them.

I say, I would like to get hold of some Verhaeren. He seems to have hold of an artistic dogma that is my foundation stone, and perpetual starting point – that simplicity is most powerful and to be desired above all things whatsoever. Not to be afraid of modernity of theme is again another great virtue. Well, another man to read on leave ... (And Stacpoole's 'Villon' too.)

Would you mind telling me candidly sincerely as possible, what you think of my things were they collected in a book and compared to F.W.H.'s? Personally, I think there is nothing of mine so good as 'Flanders'. And also, perhaps, 'If we return', but outside those, I think my things are better on the whole and more poetical. Do you think there is too much regret in mine? His book has a fine spirit, is mine too much the confession of being unwillingly a soldier? Is there too much of a whine? I would not be out of it – right out of it – for anything; this gives me a right to talk and walk with braver men than myself and an insight into thousands of characters and a greater Power over Life, and more Love. But if I get knocked out – with the conviction sometimes of being able to write the finest sort of songs – then 'deevil a ceevil word to God frae a gentleman like me.' But it is not good to let this appear since the forfeit of Life is paid by the noblest so often. After all (I take pride in it) there are not many chronic dyspeptics writing verse at the – . I think this is a title of Pride, and gives me excuse to be a little selfish.

Henderson's declaration to the *Tribune*'s reporter was a fine one. Surely we are really first Ally now, at last? France must be first in honour, but more depends on England than on any of us now. And the Tsar's proclamation to the Army and Navy – what a stroke! O it is a great time, and pain is the price thereof, and in any case a damned hard time for musicians.

What shall we do? Combine a picture palace with a church job? Or dress as a monkey and turn the handle? Or dress up as Germans to tour in a band?

Behold, I show you a mystery.[3] We shall live by correcting each other's proofs, in a Home for Mutual Admirers.

Your sincere friend
Ivor Gurney

Book progressing plenty bon?

[1] Both poems by Flecker.
[2] Yeats' *Poems* (1895) includes his early work but is not his first. Gurney is also probably referring to *Poems 1899-1905* (1906).
[3] 1 Corinthians. XV.51.

---

51 To Herbert Howells G.3.15

18 January 1917 (P)

My Dear Howler

Thank you for your jolly letter, and for your various kindnesses. Truly when leave comes, shall we meet again and discuss the best means for raising English music out of the depths. My remedy is to get conductors to play my things, but that may be too drastic for thinking on, even.

I hope the Gervase Elwes stunt will be successful.[1]

It does not do to think on music overmuch – the means for satisfying my desires being quite impossible to obtain here – so I have turned my mind to the Sister Muse and have manufactured a little lately. Something must always come from me when circumstances are not overwhelmingly depressing, and at present they are tray bon, considering everything.

I am sorry my verses are not lyrical enough for setting; if I have another 3 weeks of this perhaps Beauty will touch me to real Song – it would be nice to write a cycle for you.

What are you writing now, and what intending to write? Torment not your conscience uselessly, but settle down like a good boy and let us have something really Bon. Your character did not need some sort of training as did mine, and there is not much that would have benefited you, and a great deal of pain and discomfort to escape. (Also you have not a belly not to be put right.)

No, take what you can get out of Western beauty, and tell it out for all man (someday) to hear.

You seem to say that my songs were done at Oxford. Surely you meant at the Women Musicians affair in London? I know nothing about any other performance.

Personally, I do not yet feel much more able to write first movements – that is, to build – but that is simply lack of energy, I think; which Time will put right. I hope so; I would like to run races with you.

O Kerhistopher! What would an evening at the Taylors with plenty of biscuits and China Tea and Bach and Battles over again! What would that be like! We'll play the Organ things most bon as a duet! And make the most brilliant conversation scintillating past the ordinary intelligence. Potted Meredith, Browning in Little, Shakespeare in Short. (I pause to breathe – and scratch.)

Write again, my estimable tympanist. I take a kindly interest in your welfare.

> Best of luck
> Yours ever
> IBG.

[1] A planned recital by Gervase Elwes.

---

152 To Marion Scott G.41.56

19 January 1917 (G)

My Dear Friend

Thank you for your two letters; including one that had gone astray.

HNH is a faithful friend to lug my comps: round the country a la Commercial Traveller; it may mean an extra couple of lines into the *Gloucester Citizen* notice – with luck. I am sorry to hear the cold has pulled you back a little, but that should not be unexpected.

It surprises me that you like 'Song and Pain' best. It seems the least of those three. However, Compree this?

Time and the Soldier

How slow you move, Old Time;
    Walk a bit faster!
Old Fool, I'm not your slave....
    Beauty's my master!

You hold me for a space....
    What are you, Time?
A ghost, a thing of thought,
    An easy rhyme.

Someday I shall again,
    For all your scheming,
See Severn-valley clouds
    Like banners streaming.

And walk in Cranham lanes,
    By Maisemore go....
But, fool, decrepit Fool,
    You are SO SLOW!!!

And this?

Influences

When woods of home grow dark,
    I grow dark too.
Images of strange power
Fill me and thrill me that hour,
    Sombre of hue.

The woods of Dunsinane
    I walk and know
What storms did shake Macbeth,
That brought on Duncan's death,
    And his own woe.

Strange whispers chill the blood
    Of evil breath.
Such rumours as did stir
Witch and foul sorcerer
    On the lone heath.

No power have these on me;
    I know too well
Their weakness to condemn.

193

Spring will exorcise them
With one blue bell.

How many do *you* think the book will need? It will include the two sonnetts already printed in the *R.C.M. Mag*, and, if you have it, a Christmas Carol I wrote some time ago. As to the arrangement if you will let me have a list of what there is – when the time comes – I will write one, and you can correct it as you please, who have the copies. Sidgwick and Jackson would be tray bon. There will also be a Preface.

Later.   19th of January.

O tis cold! but this barn is pretty strawy, and my oil-sheet is over my legs, and I go straight on. Merely through boredom I have turned out another masterpiece today. Also having seen the *Observer*'s appreciation of Ledwidge's description of the robin's note as being like tiny cymbals, I looked for a robin, found one, heard it – and don't agree, altogether. He must have thought a lot to have written that description – it being too out of the way to be spontaneously observed. Now please turn back to the the back of page one, where further grace will flow from my pen.

I think everything you have sent me has arrived now. There are no stragglers left. Binyon's verses, for which I thank you are here also, but – O I need a piano; though two verses are pretty well settled in me. For the sum of one franc I got an hour on a faint toned piano yesterday; but that was not good enough, and there was no Bach, my fingers were stiff and my mind wandering always.... there was not much pleasure in it; even though it was my first chance of hearing 'By a Bierside', which contains even more of 'strangeness' than I had thought. (As to orchestration, if it comes to that HNH has absolute yea-or-nay-say.) By the way, what did Ernest Walker say of my songs, if indeed he said anything?

Poor Folk

We wonder how the poor get on in England,
Who wonder how the troops get on in France.
We're better off than many folks in England,
Although we've got to face the Great Advance.

We've troubles too – the mud, beer not worth drinking,
Sleeping in filth, and feet forever wet;
But women lie all night thinking and thinking
Thoughts that they hug with fear, and would forget.

We waste good food at times – Why some poor people
Work day and night for what we'd never miss.
Lengths of land and water to cover a steeple
To keep it from them... Yes, a bad thing, this.

Oh when at last there comes the Judgement Day,
I'll ask of God some questions that he must
Answer me well, Or I'll choose rather be
Some free spirit of Hell, or merely dust.

As how the poor who fight so well in France
Die with a smile for England in some ditch,
Seem never really to get a proper chance -
Their wars and justice made for them by the rich.

Well, the Soft Job is behind me almost now; we are away behind the line, and going back to the Batt: may mean leave soon. And the full joy of leave in Blighty will be tasted by me when that is sometime gone; more strangeness than Joy lies in the present of such things. And yet – Hot baths – breakfast in bed – tablecloths – books – late reading ¬ Bach – Great walks – Renewing friendships – Talks of books – hunting second hand bookstalls – a sight of St Pauls again and to lose oneself in being in London .... Strange that [such] things should not always be; and stranger that a stroke of the pen may give these back again, though but for a short time; now I hope you will not feel the cold too much and soon will meet a Spring February alive with shy smiles. O to see 'Severn valley clouds like banners streaming'! These are no vapourings but the mere truth. They are as galleons to the London wherries, or huffles, as I think the real name is. Au revoir.

Your sincere friend
Ivor Gurney

O surely the book would do best to appear before the end of the War?

153 To Marion Scott

G.41.57

1 February 1917 (P)

My Dear Miss Scott

Yes, back with the Batt: and doing the old dreary work, purposely designed to the breaking of hearts that the mud could not break. God reward the old sweats who run Army training in some suitable fashion of agony!

I have not had a letter from you since two came together – one a returned letter (O the name of the Sestet is 'Serenity'.) But that was not long ago. We have shifted about a lot since then, but this is a permanent stay, I think, for some weeks. The Black Prince did some stunt not far away, but one is too fed up in the Batt: to take walks for history's sake.

By Jingo but it is cold! The cocoa dregs freeze in the mess tins in this old house, and most of us sleep almost in full kit. Somehow our contrived

Chimney is not a success, and the smoke is occasionally overpowering. But what of it? There are six Gloucester-or-near and one Northener, and on the whole despite the appalling language things go very smoothly with the crowd of us.

There is Ozzy, who has the sweetness of an angel, the Stretcherbearer corporal; certainly of Welsh blood, and certainly one of the nicest of men. There is Don, never depressed, a corporal who mocks at all things military, and keeps his place because of his pluck, and would certainly have had no stripes in the first B.E.F. (Old Sweats Gang.)

Ac Emma, who is Brigade Bomb Store keeper, a lance corporal of extremely great powers of profanity.

Jem – who is really a nut. An old schoolmate of mine. Rather like Dick Swiveller in talk, and most india-rubbery as to feature. There is always laughter where Jem is, and usually at the Army.

Joe who is a lance corporal and Military Medallist. Also a bore, and the cleanest, most willing burnisher and brusher up in all the Company. (Curse him!) but a good sort. And Dicky,[1] a small Northern corporal of terrific energy and pluck, with the most wonderful eyes. His face shines with courage and chivalry, but as an old pit hand, his language .... is not to be taken seriously.

O, a good lot. And it will be nice to meet them in the after days, and talk over our past miseries together.

There is no Literary Supplement this week. Too much cleaning has dessicated my poetic vein. But that's not to be wondered at – I must have turned out about 15 in the last two months.

How are you all now? This weather is cold but the sun is a gift to men tired of grey skies and mire. At least there are hard roads here and promiscuous trees, and French beer and some sort of cafe, and eggs and chips and a canteen.

The letters from Sir Hubert (and Sir Charles?) did not reach me. I'll write to them and ask them to send them again. Herbert N Howells Esq shall also receive a letter, but I believe I have answered his after some fashion. Likewise the Hon: S Shimmin. It is extraordinary how tame-looking the German prisoners working on the roads are! And a joy to notice how untamed the French. But to tame the French would be no easy job; the Bosche would have had a rough time of it. Men, women and children always the same – that is, always different.

Ah, but this sunlight, this cold, and these elms remind me so vividly of Minsterworth, and are so sharply different to the present business that I cannot get used to them. They and I are out of place.

Goodbye and all good wishes

Your sincere friend
Ivor Gurney

---

[1]This is Richard Rhodes; see letters 180 and 185 and Gurney's poem 'Dicky' in *War's Embers*, all of which stress his eyes.

3 Feb 1917 (P)

My Dear Shimm:

It was a bon thing of you to send that tin of chocolate to me, and I takes it as such, my lad. Not much of it was eaten as chocolate, but drunk as cocoa – not at all bad. But that was in a good dugout, on a bon job. Now I am back with the Batt: in the hope of getting leave: but not being a good cleaner-up, chances do not seem especially rosy for me. I wonder what music you have been playing lately, you lucky devil, you! And I wonder too, when we shall play Brahms Symphonies and Bach's Organ Works together again?

'Time you old Fool, Walk a bit faster', as the poet said. The weather is bright here, but hellish cold. Water bottles freeze in billets, and knees tremble – as mine are trembling now; a bad writing table, distracted knees.

I think very often of a foregathering at the bon Taylors, with a good fire, a good tea, good friends, and good music. O beyond words, bon!

What are they doing with you now? Are you washing floors and things, or cleaning things and floors?

At least, you are not lousy, like us poor unfortunate chatty people out here. Don't try too hard to get out of England. Experto crede....

And if you think you might get more interesting work out here – you might; but then you mightn't. Why risk it?

Goodbye, old man; there might be leave for me soon. I wonder whether we might find ourselves in London together.

Yours ever
I.B.G.

3 February 1917 (P)

1st Letter
My Dear Friend

I am sorry you are again down – it is very hard to be sick, even when the weather gives one the best excuses; nothing, I know, will affect your kindness; and perhaps this be the sort of 'flu' which will allow you to write and direct your affairs. I understand that you have sent me *Friends*, if that is so something has delayed the book, for I have not yet received it. Indeed, I did not mean you to send it me; it was easy for me to afford it had I wished and taken the trouble.

(I write without your letter) It pleases me that you are pleased with my latest output. Tell Herbert that the Malverns in 'Flanders' *are* the Malverns. As I stand off from the song, the hills swim in sunlight like that, to the plucking of harps and a sustained sound of wood and strings. And somehow,

the thing does seem to hang together, n'est ce pas? And today the *R.C.M.*
Mag has arrived. I like Arthur Benjamin's article very much. Margaret Gatty
may go hang,
But

        What the
                Constellation of Orion
has Bellows' compositor or the censor done to my poor poor 'Fire Kindled'?
Now could I drink hot blood,[1] and that of the compositor. May he be
                      put in the Infantry, for much grief has he put on
me, unfortunate scribbler that I am! God help me , I meant no such thing.
What has happened to my Heine-ending? Did it reach you too illegible, or
was I mad, or have I unconsciously altered it since?[2]
      Never mind.
Verse 2. (alterations of my own and not before indicated)
      And Cranham, Cranham trees,
      And blaze of Autumn hues.

      Verse 4   (Ditto
    The star of afterglow,
    Venus, on Western hills;

Verse 5 – no comma after bastions.
        Last Verse
   (1)
   (2)
      But these are not my rivers ......
      And these are useless dreams.
[*written up the side of the above alterations* and no 'O God', but simply 'God' – a
swear not a *prayer*].
    'Strange Service' is all right, and I am pleased with it.
    No 'But' in verse 4. 'Forget the clamour'. You at least, Honorary Secretary
shall get no blame but only praise and thanks. Thank God, they have put me
on a canteen job, and this was as well, as a week's 'ranks' nearly killed me.
Never was a worse 'sweat'! Keats or Shelley could hardly make so conspicuous
a failure in all that relates to kit, or equipment. I warn you that, if possible, I
shall try to get a soft job. 9 months trenches is enough, or liability to trenches.
It seems to me I have the right if anyone has; certainly more right than most
men in these jobs. C'est n'est pas magnifique, mais *c'est le guerre*. It remains
only to make a success.
    Second letter straight on.

                            Your sincere friend
                            Ivor Gurney

[1] *Hamlet*, III.2.408.
[2] The last explanation is the most likely; I have found no original manuscript, but Marion
Scott's transcript (G.64.11.26-7) is probably accurate.

3 February 1917 (P)

2nd Letter
My Dear Friend
I find I have not yet mentioned Gervase Elwes' letter and your hint about Mr Dunhill.[1] Thank you very much for both, and I will certainly right [*sic*]. I am a person of poor knowledge of what to do; by turns shy and overbold and acting by impulse, I need advice on such matters, thank you.

Today I was left alone in the freezing wet canteen to guard the beer; and the Muse took pity on me and gave me something to beguile the time.

Hail and Farewell

A German bullet wounded him,
    They brought him down to die.
Far-off a bugle sounded him
    'Retreat', Goodbye.

Strange, that from ways so hated,
    And tyranny so hard
Should come this strangely fated
    And farewell word!

He thought, 'Some Old Sweat might
    Have thrilled at heart to hear,
Gone down into the night
    Too proud to fear!

But I – the fool at arms,
    Musician, Poet to boot,
Who hail release; what charms
    In this salute?

He smiled – 'The latest jest
    That Time on me shall play.
And watched the dying West,
    Went out with the day.

The stars have been wonderful lately; great blazing symbols of mystery that make me think of Beethoven – and the end of the war; when I may think of Beauty without apprehension.

Verse 3 of 'Fire Kindled'.
    May Hill that Gloster dwellers
        'Gainst every sunset see;

And the wide Severn river
　　　Homing again to the sea.

　I hope you will not be too headachy to read and that luck will bring you the
Yeats books to fill up the blank spaces. Have you read Francis Thompson's
Selected Poems? It was he who could write
　　　The peaceful moon that nothing does but shine
　　　Swings all the labouring surges of the world.[2]
Beethoven?
　　Goodbye and best wishes for health, or at least a comfortable sickness.
　　　　　　　　　　　　　　　　　　　Your sincere friend
　　　　　　　　　　　　　　　　　　　　Ivor Gurney

[1] Gervase Cary-Elwes (1866-1921), tenor.
[2] Thompson's *Sister Songs*, part the second, where 'innocent' replaces 'peaceful' and
'Moves' replaces 'Swings'.

157 To Marion Scott　　　　　　　　　　　　　　　　　　　　G.41.60

　3 February 1917 (P)

My Dear Friend
　　The boys are nearly all asleep – eight of us in a room, say, 14 feet by ten,
with a large stack of wood, a fireplace and equipment. Outside it is bitterly
cold; in here, not so bad; and good companionship hides many things. A
miner, an engineer, a draper's assistant, a grocer, an Inland Revenuist, and a
musician among them. ('Retreat' sounds)

　　　　　　　　　　　　　　Firelight

　　　Silent, bathed in firelight, in dusky light and gloom
　　　The boys squeeze together in the smoky dirty room.
　　　Crowded around the fireplace, a thing of bricks and tin
　　　They watch the shifting embers, till the good dreams enter in

　　　That fill the low hovel with blossoms fresh with dew
　　　And blue sky and white cloud that sail the clean air through.
　　　They talk of daffodillies and the bluebells' skiey bed,
　　　Till silence thrills with music at the things they have said.

　　　And yet, they have no skill of words, whose eyes glow so deep.
　　　They wait for night and silence and the strange power of Sleep,
　　　To light them and drift them like sea birds over the sea
　　　Where some day I shall walk again, and they walk with me.

But O, cleaning up! I suppose I get as much Hell as anyone in the army; and although I give the same time to rubbing and polishing as any of the others, the results – I will freely confess it – are not as they might be. Today there was an inspection by the Colonel. I waited trembling, knowing that there was six weeks of hospital and soft-job dirt and rust not yet all off; no, not by a long way. I stood there, a sheep among the goats (no, vice versa) and waited the bolt and thunder. Round came He-Who-Must-Be-Obeyed. Looked at me, hesitated, looked again, hesitated, and was called off by the R.S.M. who was afterwards heard telling the Colonel (a few paces away from me), 'A Good man, sir, quite all right. Quite a good man, sir, but he's a musician, and doesn't seem able to get himself clean.' When the aforesaid RSM came round for a back view, he chuckled, and said 'Ah Gurney, I'm afraid we shall never make a soldier of you.'

It is a good thing they are being converted to this way of thought at last; it has taken a long time. Anyway the R.S.M. is a brick, and deserves a Triolet.

> He backed me up once;
> I shall never forget it.
> I'm a fool and a dunce
> He backed me up once
> If theres rust I shall get it
> Your soul, you may bet it
> Yes all sorts and in tons ....
>   He backed me up once
> I shall never forget it.

(Triolet form quite forgotten. Please let me have it.) I fear there will be little writing till this tyranny be overpast.

I am glad you are pleased with your first Chapter, and shall be very interested to see it someday, Someday. Meanwhile le permission n'arrive pas, Curse it. I left the soft job only to get leave, and if the fates have landed me into an orgy of cleaning without the leave ..... May the frost have their potatoes, as Don says.

I am interested to see how you compare poetic forms to Musical. It will mean what I love anyway – A Good Jaw.

Please don't expect anything of any setting of mine of 'To the Fallen' until after the war – and after that. You see, most of my (always slow) mind is taken up with trying not to resist Things, which means a passive unrhythmical mind and music. Wait till I know Wagner and Bach thoroughly, and have a better digestion.

Jem tells a tale of how he wore one of those sachets until he found that, though the rest of his clothes were pretty good, the sachet was quite – athletic. But toujours le gagster – Jem.

Fire went out long ago, while I was hammering out 'Firelight'. It is too cold to think, write or read. Then sleep. O if I could but dream such things as would mean escape for me. But I never dream, one way or the other. Please excuse writing.

Your sincere friend
Ivor Gurney

7 February 1917 (S)

My Dear Friend
    Your great letter was received with joy this afternoon,[1] and I sit up late by a candle, well within reach of a wood fire cunningly stolen, to show you I appreciate your criticism and praise.
    Also, your putting aside your influenza to make so huge an effort in epistolation, or whatever the word is. (Epistlery. Epistolification, etc). I am sorry you are sick; even though there is some excuse to be found in the severity of the weather. Cheer up, the operation will make you or break you I feel sure, and flu might be anybody's fate.
    Thank you for all the pretty and stern things you say. I relinquish 'Framilode' with pleasure; if there is a whole after-the-war for me, little enough verse will I write again – most, *most* probably, I know which is my chief game. 'Time and the Soldier' I think will improve on you: it is W.H.Davies, but stronger; and one of my best. You are right about the roughness of some of my work; there is no time to revise here, and if the first impulse will not carry the thing through, then what is written gets destroyed. One virtue I know little of – that is, patience; and my mind is Hamlet's a wavering self-distrustful one, though quick and powerful at its times. Will Peace bring me peace, though?
    The four line thing was impromptu.[2] Would 'The Dawn' suit it, as title? 'Serenity' you have received. The first line is 'Nor steel nor flame has any power on me.' Alack, *Friends* has not arrived! My grief; but still there is a chance of leave. What I said about trying to get a soft job is absolutely sincerely meant. Two years in the ranks, almost 9 months in France, is quite enough for one who loathes the life as I. Who has better right? And who desires Glory less? But the chief reason is, that no man in the company would blame me, but only envy. And anyway, here I am still, though at present in a haven of peace as odd job man at the canteen, which suits me very well.
    Only, it is undignified to go to frantic lengths for such a job.

Pain
[*Rough draft of 'Pain' followed by fair copy as follows:*[3]]

Pain, pain continual, pain unending;
Hard even to the roughest, but to those

Hungry for beauty ... Not the wisest knows,
Nor most pitiful hearted, what the wending
Of one hour's way meant. Gray monotony lending
Weight to the gray skies, gray mud where goes
An army of grey bedrenched scarecrows in rows
Careless at last of cruellest Fate-sending,
Seeing the pitiful eyes of men foredone,
Or horses shot, too tired merely to stir
Dying in shellholes both, slain by the mud.
Men broken, shrieking even to hear a gun ...
Till Pain grinds down, or lethargy numbs her,
The amazed heart cries angrily out on God.

Which is also an impromptu – the first of Sonnetts 1917, 5 of them, for
admirers of Rupert Brooke. They will make good antitheses; but the note of
the rest will be quite different; this being the blackest.

It must be late – I will fill a last pipe, and finish this.

It would seem that 'Flanders' *ought* to have some binding figure, and yet – I
think it is all right there. But what of the change from D to D minor, B^b
minor, C minor, in about 3 bars? Ask Herbert please, and give him my best
wishes and kindest regards when you see him.

I must to sleep.

Goodbye
Your sincere friend
Ivor Gurney

O, it is West Country not County.

[1] Gurney is replying to Marion Scott's comments particularly on his letters of 17 and 18
January.
[2] 'We who have watched the darkened East so long'. See letter 149.
[3] The most important changes in the text are from these draft lines:
    1.2 'To all men, even the roughest; but to those'
    1.8 'Not caring whither their feet are tending.'
    1.11 'sucked in' for 'slain by'
    1.12 'And worst, men shrieking ...'
    1.13 'drugs' for 'numbs'

159 To Marion Scott   G.41.67

9 February 1917 (P)

My Dear Friend

At the present moment I am sitting – Here there is a bang, quite an
explosion, from a bully beef tin which somehow has got into the fire, the
stains on the paper are the result – in front of a big fire, a roaring monster and

am as hot as is comfortable. It is cold enough outside, but here .....

Soon we are off back again though, and this bon time as canteen attendant comes to an end. Unfortunately my desires are so great, and disposition naturally so unquiet, that these things serve chiefly to make me remember what things might be.

I hope you are on the mend now, your letters show no great signs of sickness. If you cannot move about much physically, then may the book move with increased speed towards its end. You also are baulked in your desires, which may by repression gather strength and become fuller and deeper in the end. You deserve it, anyhow. Please remember that this is a winter of records.

Friends has arrived at last, to the surprise of the postman for I was most affectionate. There is indeed some most beautiful work in it. What could be better than 'The Old Bed'? Thank you so much; no present could have pleased me better – a slim masterpiece.

I am glad you found no trace of unmanliness about my verses. Perhaps one or two later poems will help also.

When I wrote 'Compree this', and then 'Influences' and the other, it was merely the soldier slang term and had no special meaning. Pain there is enough, and I suppose it is not untrue that I suffer in proportion to sensibility. However, putting aside what was or was not possible, I chose rather to be musician than soldier. If there is a future for me I shall reap the gain. Anyway, what must be, will be.

The next sonnet I shall work on has for Octett, thoughts on the loveliness of life, and for Sestett, how, if one must leave these things, then a death in arms for England is not so bad. That shall say all I think, and it shall stand last in my book.[1]

I am delighted to hear Herbert's opinion on 'Flanders'. He shall have a letter on the strength of it. And even *touched* by your enthusiasm.

You are right about 'Poor Folk'. Wait a bit. I think these two disgracefully dirty scraps of paper I am sending contain two of my best things, and Hail and Farewell stands pretty high, and what will you think of Pain?

Tres bien about 'To Certain Comrades'. My preference is first of all Sidgwick and Jackson as publishers. They do print well, and good stuff. Arnold and MacDonald all right though. No chance of leave just yet.

I have taken quite a lot of trouble about 'Beauty'.

What an article is that on Keats in the *Times*. Good man that.[2]

Best wishes for health and work

Your sincere friend
Ivor Gurney

[*Page spattered and stained; hence the note at the top.*]
    Bully beef at fault

Beauty

I cannot live with Beauty out of mind.
I search for her and desire her all the day;

Beauty, the choicest treasure you may find,
Most joyous and sweetest word his lips can say.
The crowded heart in me is quick with visions
And sweetest music born of a brighter day.

But though the trees have long since lost their green
And I, the exile, can but dream of things
Grown magic in the mind; I watch the sheen
Of frost, and hear the song Orion sings.
Yet O, the star-born passion of Beethoven,
Man's consolation sung on the quivering strings.

Beauty immortal, not to be hid, desire
Of all men, each in his fashion, give me the strong
Thirst past satisfaction for thee, and fire
Not to be quenched .... O lift me, bear me along,
Touch me, make me worthy that men may seek me
For Beauty, Mistress Immortal, Healer of Wrong.

After-Glow   to F.W.H.

Out of the smoke and dust of the little room
With tea-talk loud and laughter of happy boys,
I passed into the dusk ... Suddenly the noise
Ceased on a sudden, left me alone in the gloom
To wonder at the miracle hanging high
Tangled in twigs, the silver crescent clear.
Time passed from mind. Time died; and then we were
Once more at Home together, you and I.

The elms with arms of love wrapped us in shade
Who watched the ecstatic West with one desire,
One soul uprapt; and yet another fire
Consumed us, and our joy yet greater made;
That Bach should sing for us, mix us in one
The joy of music and the sunken sun.

Bastard form though.

[1] This sonnet became 'For England', and was number 1 of the five 'Sonnets 1917' placed at the end of *Severn & Somme*.
[2] The lead article in the *T.L.S.* of 18 January 1918 was called 'The Promise of Keats', a review of Laurence Binyon's edition.

13 February 1917 (P)

For England

Though Heaven be packed with joy-bewildering
Pleasures of soul and heart and mind, yet who
Would willingly let slip, freely let go
Earth's mortal loveliness; go wandering
Where never the late bird is heard to sing,
Nor full-sailed cloud-galleons wander slow;
No pathways in the woods; no afterglow,
When the air's fire and magic with sense of Spring.

So the dark horror clouds us, and the dread
Of the unknown .... But if it must be, then
What better passing than to go out like men
For England, giving all in one white glow?
Whose bodies shall lie in the earth as on a bed,
And as the Will directs our spirits may go.

February Day

Winter, are you young at heart?
Winter, is this you indeed,
That put aside your usual staid
Cynical demeanour clean apart?
You, you that seemed afraid
To smile at all, now like a maid,
Nay, Spring herself, sweet Spring, your daughter,
Laugh out in light, Gaze on the water
To see yourself so sweet arrayed
From dawn to dusk without a start.
O Winter is this you indeed?
For once, you took of Time no heed
Nor feared the prude, but joyed in laughter.
Where once you made poor children bleed
At chilly fingers and sore heart.
O Winter is this you indeed?

February 1917 (KT)

Dear Mrs Voynich

Thank you very much for your letters and parcel – which came in rather a God-forsaken place where bread was most difficult to obtain; one had to wait for it, with plots.

You are very lucky to be so successful with your work; it makes me heave sighs like a Stokes gun[1] to think of it. And to walk in nights of storm not controlled by any military authority, free to set Villon to music or watch the moon as your desire leads you. O to feel my hair – longer than now – blown by big winds of the Belloc kind. (See 'On a Great Wind'[2]).
And to see
    'Jagged Malvern with a train of shadows'.

What is the cheapest edition of Villon? Is there one in Dent's French series (after 'Everyman'?) Or one smaller still? There ought to be something cheap in paper, some common French publication.

What difference will America's attitude make? They say today that she has declared war but the paper only speaks of broken relations.[3] Que le guerre fait finir bientot.

            You hold me for a space – What are you, Time?
            A ghost, a thing of thought – an easy rhyme.

            And I shall once again,
            For all your scheming,
            See Severn-Valley clouds
            Like banners streaming,

            And walk in Cranham lanes,
            By Maisemore go ....
            But, Fool, decrepit Fool,
            You are SO SLOW!!!

Round us here are earthworks and impressive earthworks that I thought were ancient Gaulish; but today un petit garcon m'informait that they were of Soixante-Dix. So my dreams of old battles have partly evaporated. There is a big rock here, and the village nestles thereunder. Some of this country is well worth painting; but not like Cornwall, and Blighty is a far dream.

Go on and prosper in your work, for it is nice and encouraging to know

that someone is hard at it. As for leave .... Congestion is the only talk now.
    With best wishes

Yours very sincerely

Ivor Gurney

[1] The British trench mortar.
[2] The essay is from *First and Last* (1911) and was reprinted in *A Picked Company* (1915).
[3] Woodrow Wilson severed diplomatic relations with Germany on 3 February; America declared war on April 6th.

162 To Herbert Howells   G.3.29-30[1]

13? February 1917 (KT)

My Dear Howler
    It is too bloody cold to write almost in this barn, but you having been sick and polite to my 'Flanders' barge, deserve a note longer than this will be.
    I hope old chap your health is not more shaky than the weather might excuse; our promising young genius must not fade away as a flower; we have not enough seeds.
    And thanks for playing Commercial traveller to me. By the way has Allen seen your Concerto? Very much I wish to hear that again, being bon and far from na pooh fini encore.
    Here the country is fine and marked with 1870 earthworks. A huge rock towers out above the town which being interpreted is the Star. Quite a revelation of beauty after grey desolations.
    What stunt are you on now? I wait for the Violin Sonata clear fairly simple with the romantic slow movement singing of Western things. Show us Tintern and sunset across the Malvern and Welsh Hills. Make us see the one evening star among the trees. And the Scherzo of the String Quartett – a great Spring Wind blowing the hair of the exultant traveller wandering without purpose save to find beauty and to be comrade with the wind.
    O to be back with you .....
    Well, what is Germany's game now? What will come of the clash of the Tirpitz and Bethmann Hollweg parties?[2]
    General January has fought for us, though a hard master he was, but le General Fevrier is even more terrible.
    I want you to see a thing just sent by me to Miss Scott, called either 'Beauty' or 'Winter Beauty'. It has two lines you will like
        'Yet O, the star-born passion of Beethoven,
        Man's consolation sung on the quivering strings.'
    Pencil bust. Time to feenish.
    Good luck
    Plenty tuck

Tunes in the noddle
For Concert-stück.

Yours ever
Ivor Gurney

[1] The envelope is marked 29-30 but contains only one letter.
[2] The parties that sided with Admiral Alfred von Tirpitz (1849-1930) and Theobald von Bethman Hollweg (1856-1921), the German Chancellor.

163 *To Marion Scott* G.41.64

14 February 1917 (P)

My Dear Miss Scott

Now we are nestled in a village under a huge rock; or so it seems, after much regular country: the place reminds me of Birdlip and Crickley, but O tis ruddy cold. The fates have been kind to me, and still leave me as canteen attendant; which means that though freezing one has time to oneself, and are off thesé confounded cleaning parades which so gnaw at my life.

How are you and your influenza now? There can be little gadding about for you anyway, yet who knows what February may bring – that sometimes is so kind and smiles like Spring. Well, good luck to both of us, as I fancy cold is little good to either. And your book, tient-il? If you can sit up and refound musical literature, things will not be so bad; it would be like a Nice Blighty, which I do most heartily desire the Lord to send myself. Anyway do not get too ill to write.

I hope the rest of the family is tres bon, and appreciative of the 'fine nipping air'. And Herbert, how is he? There is some slight recollection in me of having written to him. I wonder whether it is correct. (Yes, it is.) There is more literature in this letter, but not yet. The literal translation of the pretty name of this place is The Star, and there are earthworks all round, remains of 1870. Soon we go up again to the trouble; soon Fritz will be hurling high explosive compliments at us with gusto, and we close to the parapets. Well, tres bien, if there is no soft job, the hard one must do, but the first is better.

The title of the book I would prefer to be 'Songs from Exile, or Songs from the Second Fifth', as subtitle. That is the real title, and besides, the second needs writing up to which I am unwilling to do.

Home Sickness

When we go wandering the wide air's blue spaces,
Bare, unhappy, exiled souls of men;
How will our thoughts over and over again
Return to Earth's familiar lovely places,

Where light with shadow ever interlaces -
No blanks of blue, nor ways beyond man's ken -
Where birds are, and flowers; as violet, and wren,
Blackbird, bluebell, hedgesparrow, tiny daisies,
O tiny things, but very stuff of soul
To us ... so frail ... Remember what we are;
Set us not on some strange outlandish star,
But one love-responsive. Give us a Home.
There we may wait while the long ages roll
Content, unfrightened by vast Time-to-come.

Servitude

If it were not for England, who would bear
The heavy servitude one moment more?
To keep a brothel, sweep and wash the floor
Of filthiest hovels were noble to compare
With this brass-cleaning life. Now here, now there
Harried in foolishness, scanned curiously o'er
By fools made brazen by conceit, and store
Of antique witticisms thin and bare.

Only the love of comrades sweetens all,
Whose laughing spirit will not be outdone.
As night-watching men wait for the sun
To hearten them, so wait I on such boys
As neither brass nor Bosches may appall,
Nor guns, nor sergeant-major's bluster and noise.

These Sonnetts, For England, Pain, Homesickness, Servitude, and one other;
are intended to be a sort of counterblast against 'Sonnetts 1914', which were
written before the grind of the war and by an officer (or one who would have
been an officer.) They are the protest of the physical against the exalted
spiritual; of the cumulative weight of small facts against the one large. Of
informed opinion against uninformed, (to put it coarsely and unfairly) and fill
a place. Old ladies won't like them, but soldiers may, and these things are
written either for soldiers or civilians as well informed as the French what 'a
young fresh war' means. (Or was it 'frische (joyful) Krieg'. I can't remember,
but something like it was written by the tame Germans in 1914.)[1] I know
perfectly well how my attitude will appear, but – They will be called 'Sonnetts
1917'.

Friends is with me, and is as a friend. I love the book and have written to
Gibson saying so. He is a man who would well be worth meeting. Belloc,
Masefield, Yeats, Gibson, Kipling, Tomlinson – O have you read Tomlinson's
By Land and Sea? It is a travel book about S.America. Bon, in the extreme.[2]

What do you think now of Germany's chance of collapse ......?

I hope I have not offended you anyway by my outburst about 'The Fire Kindled'. I had thought it better in my mind than it really was, and the shock made sparks. Some of it I don't remember at all.

Go on and prosper and be kind; and tell me when to turn the lyric tap off. It spouts freely at present, but I desire to see my only book of verse in the dignity of print.

Meanwhile, Mamselle I am your most obliged servant

and sincere friend

Ivor Gurney

[1] 'Frische' might mean 'cathartic', as some of the German writers before the war were hoping.

[2] Henry Major Tomlinson (1873-1958) wrote *The Sea and the Jungle* (1912), which fits the description.

164 To Marion Scott G.41.75

14 February 1917 (P)

My Dear Friend

Thank you so much for your letter of the 5th of Feb: I think everything of yours has come so far; quite a lot came close together, comments on song etc etc. It is still intensely cold here, but the sun is warm (when the canteen attendants see it anyway) and the afterglow is always beautiful.

The order of the Battallion work is someways as follows. Reveille at 7. Parade at 7.45 for some footling inspection, but always clean as to chins and buttons and boots. Parade again at 9 for the sort of drill recruits do, this lasts till 12.45. In the afternoon, usually nothing. Every other night, night operations of some comic sort. Lights out at 9. Most of the spare time till now has been in cleaning, always cleaning equipment. For anyone with more sensibility than the yokel it is a life infinitely full of pain. Whether the wind blows gales of icy needles with the temperature below zero; always the same. And no fires now, in most billetts: From this, you will gather that 'Rest' is merely a technical term.

If you will take the trouble to copy out all those things one by one, please do so, and thank you – but don't write shorter letters because of it.

I shall be content if you attend to all matters of punctuation, and merely ask my opinion on doubtful points. The name, as I have said is

Songs in Exile

or Songs from the Second-Fifth.

The first poem will be To Certain Comrades; the last poems, the five sonnetts. (Perhaps an Envoi also. Any poem you think needs correction, send on, and fear nothing. And mix up things as you please, for I know you can be trusted.

211

The (pretty long) preface is nearly ready, please get it in unless they firmly refuse to have it. But – if you do all this, punctuate as you please, and take no notice of any marks of mine.

Under the Greenwood Tree is perfectly charming, and very Shakespearian in feeling I think. Hardy is a marvel.

I see Tolstoi's *Cossacks* is published in the Worlds Classics; how good the review in the *Times* was![1] Do you see the likeness between Tolstoi's sense of beauty and that of Beethoven? So constantly do I feel the two in company ....

With these beautiful days it becomes more of a loss to feel music and books so far away, and my county. And the days slipping past so quickly in which I ought to acquire technique and get rhythm into my mind. Once I get back, for a while I will simply reek songs; mere exudations; while I study hard Wagner and Rachmaninoff and the Russians; also the 3 B's and Folk Song for pleasure; and Chopin for piano technique.

But, Time, you are so slow
and hold the secrets of doubtful things not yet disclosed.

You will please supply indignation to the description of the ordinary routine here; and understand why the words are calm....

Yet we are mostly volunteers and not prison-conscripts. Toujours le même, I believe, everywhere now. And nobody seems to care, as the song says. [2]

Good-bye and good-luck with the influenza.

Your sincere friend
Ivor Gurney

[1] The *T.L.S.* reviewed *The Cossacks* on 1 February 1917, p.55.
[2] 'I'm a little prairie flower' or 'No-one cares for me' perhaps.

---

165 To Marion Scott   G.41.65

15 February 1917 (P)

Preface

This book stands dedicated to one only of my friends, but there are many others to whom I would willingly dedicate singly and in state, if that did not mean the writing of 40 books of verse and dedications; a terrible thing for all concerned .... So that under the single name and sign of homage and affection, I would desire such readers as come to me to add also – To my Father and Mother; F W Harvey, (also a Gloucestershire Lad;) Miss Marion Scott, whose criticism has been so useful, and she so kind; in spite of my continued refusal to alter a word of anything. The Vicar of Twigworth; H.N.Howells, (and this is not the last time you will hear of him;) Mr Hilaire Belloc, whose 'Path to Rome' has been my trench companion, with the 'Spirit of Man'; Mr Wilfred Gibson, author of 'Friends', a great little book; many others also; including

Shakespeare and Bach, both friends of mine; and last but not least – 5 Platoon, B Co, 2/5 Glosters; who so often have wondered whether I were crazy or not. Let them draw their own conclusions now, for the writing of this book it was that so distracted me … This is a long list, and even now does not include old Mrs Poyner, that was so jolly and long-suffering; nor my boat 'Dorothy' now idle in the mud; though a poet sung of her full of glory at Framilode.

Even as I write the list becomes fuller, farther extended, yet a soldier must face pain and so it remains shorter by far than might be.

I fear that those who buy the book (or, *even*, borrow,) to get information about the Second-Fifth will be disappointed. Most of the book is concerned with a person named Myself, and the rest with my county, Gloucester, that whether I die or live stays always with me; – being so beautiful in itself, so full of memories; whose people are so good to be friends with, so easy-going and so frank.

Some of the aforementioned people I have never had good fortune enough to meet in the flesh, but that was not my fault. I hope they will forgive my using their names without permission. Ah, would they only retaliate in kind! That is however not likely, as I never was famous, and a Common Private makes but little show.

All the verses were written in France, and in sound of the guns, save only two or three earlier pieces.[1] may well be indulgent to one who thought of them so often, and whose images of beauty in the mind were always of Gloucester, county of Cotswold and Severn, and a plain rich blossomy and sweet of air – as the wise Romans knew, that made their homes in exile by the brown river, watching the further bank for signs of war.

Compree Ballad also

Ballad of the Three Spectres

As I went up by Ovillers
In mud and water cold to the knee,
There went three jeering, fleering spectres,
That walked abreast and talked of me.

The first said, 'Here's a right brave soldier
That walks the dark unfearingly;
Soon he'll come back on a fine stretcher,
And laughing at a Nice Blighty.

The second, 'Read his face, old comrade,
No kind of lucky chance I see;
One day he'll freeze in mud to the marrow,
Then look his last on Picardie.

Though bitter the word of these first twain
Curses the third spat venemously;
'He'll stay untouched till the War's last dawning,
Then live one hour of agony.

Liars the first two were. Behold me
At sloping arms by one-two-three;
Waiting the time I shall discover
Whether the third spake verity.

Feb 1917

Not so bad, eh?

By Gum, what will all the Good People of Gloster think of the Ugly Duckling they have hatched? There will be Some Surprise, what with one thing and another if the Tome appears. Roll on that time as soon as possible.

Good luck with the flu

Your sincere Friend
Ivor Gurney.
Sunday night

---

[1] Gurney is obviously transcribing this from a rough draft and omits some words. The final version adds here: 'This should be reason enough to excuse any roughness in the technique. If more reason is required, people of home, and most of all people of Gloucester'

166 *To Marion Scott* G.41.62

17 February 1917 (G)

My Dear Friend Feb 17th

Here we are, back in our little holes; with strict instructions not to show our heads above ground; in Reserve in fact – deucedly uncomfortable; and expecting to become still more so. To get to this haven of rest we had a 6 hours march with twenty minutes halt, perhaps. So, as you may imagine, there is no literary supplement this week. Nobody has any water; there may be none for 12 hours or more, and bully beef and biscuits and a little bread provide the wherewithal for philosophers and soldiers to exist. For God's sake write letters, no-one knows how long this will last. Well, long enough I have existed upon hope, and why not now? And why should we not be cheerful, since this is better than the first line?

Farewell, Canteen, thou not un-appreciated, but not over-appreciated Home to me; thou wert at zero too oft, but there was freedom in thee and a fairly interesting occupation. Fare thee well. And only the day before yesterday, I was asking myself whether I ever should be able to write a good long movement, or how long it would take! O Evening Dreams!

Sir C.H.H.P.'s two letters have arrived, and very nice too. But niceness makes me yearn.

Sidney's Sister also came up with a good one: (I hope she wrote with cleaner hands than mine).

You see, I am so over-wrapt up in myself that there is little thought left for other people, but all the same it seems to me that you are sick or sickish with influenza. Soon I hope your book will begin to swell in spite of all drawbacks, Flu or Female Musicians; and soon I hope, too, to be able to see it myself and let fly torrents of praise or vituperation. Duggy Haig seems pretty confident, and Germany must be having the worst sort of time; but O books of any kind seem a long way off.

As for my own – *Friends* is with a Trench Mortar Man. *Wild Wales* and R Bridges' *Spirit of Man* are with me. The rest are in the care of a Frenchwoman at Laventie, and someday I must send for them. Anyway, who could read Aeschylus now? *Under the Greenwood Tree* is with the Sigs.

Harvey's book is now known to be with the Brigade Major, so there is a chance of getting it still.

The French are on rations now, and their soldiers don't like it - the only drink about here being wine at 4 francs the bottle. They are a much more cheery lot than ourselves though; I cannot say what they are like in trenches, but out – they are quick to smile and move about quicker than we. All the German prisoners I have seen anywhere save at Havre seem very tame creatures and not at all savage creatures.

In the mind of all the English soldiers I have met there is absolutely no hate for the Germans, but a kind of brotherly though slightly contemptuous kindness – as to men who are going through a bad time as well as themselves. Occasionally – as last night – you get nasty remarks about Lloyd George 'Fighting to a Finish' – at home, but not often. The whole thing is accepted as a heavy Burden of Fate. I have never been able to accept anything that way myself, and can only envy those who have such an attitude. Best luck with all sickness

Your sincere friend
Ivor Gurney

---

167 *To Marion Scott*   G.41.68

23 February 1917 (P)

My Dear Friend

Soon we are to be at work again – after the Rest – that is we go into trenches; for myself there are not many regrets, for Resting is a tiring business, and though being shelled is not pleasant, yet the escape from death gives in itself some slight interest in life. Anyway, Spring's first signs cannot be so far off now, and the cold relaxes a little. I hope you are progressing towards health now. Do you not get sunshine? There is hardly a cloud here, and the sun shines its very best sometimes. April will dispel the last sign of illness in everybody save the Allemagnes.

I am glad you like 'Firelight', and as you say it ought to be popular.

If a full stop is substituted for the semicolon at the end of line 2, verse two, the sense will be clear, I think. Bluebells', it is, not, bluebell's. If you will send a complimentary copy of the *R.C.M.M.* to Miss M Hunt, 54 Wellington St Gloucester that will be very bon; Also another, if there is a spare one to Mrs Chapman, St Michaels, Castle Hill, High Wycombe, Bucks.

I don't think there is any need to send me the original of 'The Fire Kindled', I not being enough interested really. What I want to do with this book is

(1) To leave something definite behind if I am knocked out

(2) To say out what Gloucester is, and is to me; and so to make Gloucester people think about their county

(3) To have *some* good stuff in it, whatever one may say about the whole.

(4) To make people realise a little what the ordinary life is.

Anyway it was good fun, writing; and gave me something to do.

'Hail and Farewell' I think will stand; it is impossible for me to try and perfect these things save after 6 months of life and peace and beauty. Would you prefer (the first draft):

> But I – the fool at arms,
> Musician, poet to boot,
> What joy for me, what charms
> In this salute?

You are right about the dots in 'Pain'; alter as you think.

As for the 'Elizas', your choice is all right, yet I rather wondered you should leave out 'Orpheus' and include 'Under the Greenwood Tree', but this will not worry me. Herbert's letter has not arrived as yet.

As for leave, that is possible. but probable? Soon? Je ne sais pas.

I am sorry you have lost a good friend, and by so foul a thing as cancer, and I hope you will not feel separated too much. Never yet have I lost any real friend, and so it is a guess to me how another may feel, but Death is a very little thing, so long as dishonour does not lie there.

I wonder how F.W.H. has got on in his prison lately ..... My thoughts of England are first and foremost of the line of Cotswold ending with Bredon Hill, near Tewkesbury, and seen with him. Or the blue Malverns seen at a queer angle, from the hayfield, talking when War seemed imminent, and the whole air seemed charged with fateful beauty. For illness I can feel strong sympathy, but Death means not much to me. Either I do not care much, or I care a great deal and am not separated.

'To the Poet before Battle' is all right.

Alter line 12 of 'Afterwards' to

216

'The troubled heart shall know a presence near'.
The first word is 'Those'.

Here are two more with this, one of which you may have already received; I send it again, being doubtful.

As for the evening of 'Firelight''s concoction, I will do my best to find out; it was about two days after I returned to the batt:

It sometimes puzzles me what you find to interest you in my letters, since what is not verse, is either about verse or myself. You support all this very bravely, and deserve better things; but so much it means to me to cling to verse, the one interest (now cafe au lait is not possible) left to me in life, and so good to talk about it, that I fear you will have to suffer yet more.

All I can think of is – What an unholy waste of time this is, what a lot I have to learn and how long it will take me to learn to write one good sonata movement; to satisfy C.V.S.

As for my comrades – after the war I can be interesting about them, but not yet. Goodness knows I am fond of them – some of them; but I cling to life by deliberately trying to lose myself in my thoughts of other things; trusting to some innate pluck in me to save me at moments when pluck is wanted. This is not the way to make a soldier of oneself – just the opposite in fact; and increasing sensibility must balance the advantage gained by concentration of thought on other things. But though I were sure of saving my life if I altered, and losing it did I not, still I should be the same; having set all on the future.

Forgive all this egotism, and may your book and you prosper cheerily. Continue, flourish and triumph, and put up a little longer with my cockeyed epistles.

With best wishes

Your sincere friend
Ivor Gurney.

Afterglow   to F.W.H.

Out of the smoke and dust of the little room,
With tea talk loud and laughter of happy boys,
I passed into the dusk. Suddenly the noise
Ceased with a shock; left me alone in the gloom,
To wonder at the miracle hanging high
Tangled in twigs, the silver crescent clear -
Time passed from mind, Time died; and then we were
Once more together, in quiet, you and I.

The elms with arms of love wrapped us in shade,
That watched the ecstatic West with one desire,
One soul uprapt; and still another fire
Consumed us, and our joy yet greater made -

217

That Bach should sing for us; mix us in one
The joy of firelight and the sunken sun.

Jan 1917

Praise

O Friends of mine, if men mock at my name,
    Say 'Children loved him',
Since by that word you will have far removed him
    From any bitter shame.

23 February 1917 (P)

My Dear Friend
    Back in trenches, and in the thaw, with water gladly releasing itself from
the hold of the frost. One can only wait for times to take one's boots off and
dream of the past – and the future. I have received your letter speaking of
'Beauty' and 'Afterglow'. I think I made the correction 'ceased with a shock'
instead of 'sudden'. What do you think of the substitution of 'firelight' for
'music'? It seems to be the more full of point – to sum up the beauty of
afterglow and firelight too; does not Bach's music do so?
    It delighted me to hear you are so much better, and I hope you are now well
away with your book. Take an extra pleasure in the work for my sake; but do
not forget to write letters. It is hard to say when I shall be able to write a long
letter again – the conditions are against it. Please tell Sir Hubert I have had his
two letters, and thank him for them, but say the reply may be delayed a little.
    Has 'The Ballad of the Three Spectres' thrilled you as I wish? Is it Border-
Ballady?
    Strange to write about pleasant things like music and books here!
    Desolation to the devil's wish, and a grey sky like Satan's hopelessness in
Paradise Lost – 'O Sun to tell thee how I hate thy beams' or something like
that.[1]
    Goodbye and best wishes

Your sincere friend
Ivor Gurney

[1] An accurate quotation of *Paradise Lost*, book IV, line 37.

4 March 1917 (P)

My Dear Friend

Here is an odd letter written in the filthiest of hands but the best of intentions. The mail has not arrived for two days, but tomorrow may bring something from you.

Today I have been thinking of what might be instead of what is. The conditions for us in support are not so bad as in the front line, because we can move about, and we manage to get a fire going with damp wood. The thing is not to suffer things without a sense of revolt; to accept as much as possible. And to forget the past – unless in the way I try to view it; as a means to write songs. And if I come out of this alright, there are two priceless lessons learnt – the first, that the price of almost anything that one desires worthily, is only Pain; ('only agony, and that has ending')[1] and the knack of getting on with people, which I have developed out here to a much greater extent than heretofore. So I fix my mind on these two possessions of mine and think what they will mean to me in the future. Long ago I decided that to accomplish what I wish was worth a great deal of pain and was ready to undergo it. Perhaps the last 6 years will be found sufficient by the Master of Beauty, and he may think fit to set free in me unknown forces of beauty to gladden men as some have already gladdened myself. With my heart comforting itself with these things I try to accept mud and cold feet as prices, prices; and wait for my repayment. And if a soon end is meant for me, and my hopes are destined not to be fulfilled here, then though disappointment lies in that and very keenly, yet who can say what lies beyond? Only – waiting for ever, and hardships, and doubt are heavy burdens – and maybe time be not long.

Now I feel better, having 'unpacked my heart with words', though music would suit me better – the G mi Prelude in the 2nd book for example. Or my book of 'English Preludes' of which only the name is yet in existence, even of thought.

There are no more verses; the sonnet 'England' not having taken shape, and anyway that needs quiet and some comfort – but chiefly quiet.

You see this letter is all about myself, but you must have learned to expect that by now, and let me but once out of this little of my thought shall be said in words; and there will be things beautiful and comfortable surrounding one to absorb the mind.

Nevertheless, though this is My Letter – so to speak – I will spare a word to say that it will please me greatly to hear you are well out of your sickness, and well on with your book. O to answer a query – I have no certain Dearest Prelude. Perhaps the E major 1st Book (*my* arrangement – *not* Bach's) or the C major or G minor or A^b or F major from the 2nd Book. I do not know the B^b minor (2nd book.) Surely the 48 is the wisest of all the works of man? It trains one like the noble touch of Pain; yet who could understand Bach without having suffered? The song at the close of Masefield's *Good Friday* is beautiful, is it not? I saw it in the *Times*.[2]

Good-bye, and best wishes

Your sincere friend
Ivor Gurney

[1] Quoting from Brooke's sonnet 'Peace'.
[2] Masefield's play *Good Friday* was reviewed in the *T.L.S.* of 8 February 1917, p.66. The reference to Masefield continues the theme of Gurney's letter since Masefield also writes of the 'Wisdom that comes from Agony'.

---

170 *To Marion Scott*   G.41.71

5 March 1917 (P)

My Dear Friend

Thank you so much for all your kindness. And I am delighted you are able to scrape and bow again – this is very good news. I hope to receive more of the same kind now the warmer weather – *should* be here, but of course it *is* warmer, though not comfortable. There is an enormous number of points to answer, and I will try to get through them straight away as they come up in your letters.

Very well – a baritone for 'By a Bierside'. You are right about 'For England' and 'Home-sickness'. I will alter 'For England'. 'February Day' I may think it worth while to alter and keep.

Does it matter very much if someone has used the title 'Songs from Exile?' How would 'Remembered Beauty' or 'Beauty remembered' do? I shall wait a little and think, for a good title is important. 'Songs before Dawn'.[1] Anyway, you have a perfect right to do what you like, except alter. You may cut out anything you think is not worthy if there are enough to make up the number. At present it is too cold and muddy to write. Perhaps in a fortnight......

Preface

The name of dedication is Margaret Hunt. The name that puzzles you is Mrs POYNER. (Sidney knows her.) 'Gloucester people' are the two words omitted.

Name to be signed at end of Preface is Ivor Gurney. I write B in my name only because I like writing Bs.

'To Certain Comrades' may stand as it is. The lines should be printed so that the initial letters are under each other. Compree

Living —
Before —

And though our spirits etc

Punctuate as you please all the way through the book – but never too much.

220

Curse the pronouns; my feet are too cold.

Do as you please with the merely pretty 'Carol', but it would do to dedicate to Micky Chapman. So let it stay.

I want to write my last Sonnett, but that refuses to come, so much is there to say.

The grammar of my book is, technically speaking, often shaky. Never poetically, I say what I want to say.

Sidgwick and Jackson first. Elkin Mathews second, is my best chance and choice. If these publishers cannot sell, then none can.

There is a lyric in my mind – just the beginning. 'Starlight in Water'.

> Starlight in water stirs the secret dreams;
> Starlight in water;
> Starlight in water troubles hidden deeps;
> Starlight in water.

Goodbye and good luck and thank you.

Another letter soon perhaps. May it contain the last sonnet and the correction of 'To England', also 'Poor Folk'.

sincere Friend
Ivor Gurney

[*The letter also includes Marion Scott's transcription of 'To England – A Note' on which she writes: 'Will you please put any punctuation marks you want? Should there be a hyphen in 'ever-present'? H.N.H. and Harold Darke did not catch the full drift of last two lines of sonnet when they read it, but no one else has failed to understand, I think. Still, I mention this in case you want to touch up or revise the lines.' Gurney has altered 'mire' to 'water' in line 2, 'The flood of German beastliness' to 'The power of primal savagery' in line 10 and has written alongside the poem 'Reference to singing "I want to go home", in a strafe.'*]

[1] Gurney has also crossed out 'Beauty in the mind' and 'Yesterday and'.

171 *To Marion Scott* G.41.76

7 March 1917 (G)

My Dear Friend March 7

Still in trenches, still in the mud, and watching lucky – and some unlucky – people going out with trench feet, and men almost weeping for exhaustion and sheer misery, stuck to the knees with some distance of torment still to traverse. Why do not I fall ill? God knows! The soul in me is sick with disgust, and hospital now would be a good stroke of business. The unfortunate part of it for me is that the ordinary and best way to face these things, is to face them; whereas my mind, by inclination and long training can only try to turn away and remember such things as a certain Spring evening at

Minsterworth when all was gold save the shadows of golden trees black on the ground of orchards; and F.W.H. was with me.

Here is the Alteration. Will it do?

> Where never the late bird is heard to sing ...
> And (or for) England's image must indeed be slow
> To fade. How shall dull her sombre glow
> Of Autumn sunsets, or the fire of Spring?

Song of Pain and Beauty

O may these days of pain,
These wasted-seeming days,
Somewhere reflower again
With scent and savour of praise.
Draw out of memory all bitterness
Of night with Thy Sun's rays.

And strengthen Thou in me
The love of men there found,
And eager charity,
That, out of difficult ground
Spring like flowers in barren deserts, or
Like light, or a lovely sound.

A simpler heart than mine
Might have seen Beauty clear
Where I could see no sign
Of Thee, but only fear.
Strengthen me, make me to see Thy Beauty always
In every happening here.

Please write anyhow. When we get back in rest, I may be able to think more clearly, and see exactly what I want to say in my final sonnett. And O, for the days when, with cigarettes biscuits and milk all round me, and a good fire and a piano, I shall joyfully attempt to say what is in me in music.

I am glad they are going to do my two songs.[1] Vaughan Williams wrote me a friendly little note, in his queer writing. We are to know each other afterwards... Afterwards; toujours apres le guerre.

They are shelling this place, but no-one takes any notice, being too fed up. Fires are forbidden in daylight, but it is better to die by a fire than live without one.

And as for snipers, who cares for those. Why yesterday one of our heavies landed 6 shells about 30 yards on our left, just behind our own lines. Cheerful

Tommy Atkins takes not much notice; it is only a Bairnsfather incident.[2]

Your sincere friend
Ivor Gurney

I hope the violin is progressing?

[1] Herbert Howells wrote to Marion Scott on 14 February 1917 that he had brought forward 'In Flanders' and 'By a Bierside' at a lesson with Stanford, who 'at once said they *must* be done at the second orchestral concert this term'. Taylor seemed likely to sing them.

[2] Charles Bruce Bairnsfather (1888-1959), cartoonist, who was at the height of his popularity in the first World War for making comedy out of grim reality.

172 *To Marion Scott* G.41.70

10 March 1917 (G)

My Dear Friend   10 March

The short letter in reply to your three long ones is in my pocket, but not for long. Tomorrow morning will see it off, I think.

We are out at last – the longest time we have ever done in trenches, and a pretty bad time some of it was; but anyway it is now a thing gone and swallowed up, there is no need to recall it.

Your three letters were a great pleasure to receive; they seem to keep me in touch with the things I love, and what I hope to be. Occasionally the heart in me almost dies with the strain of endurance, and the long waits and the work in the mud; then it is your letters are as stars in the night or blinks of sunlight – promises of blue.

When the war is over shall I ever write as voluminously again? I doubt it, hoping in my mind to say all my thoughts out in music, and so to write nothing but short notes, to anybody. O the happy time when, after a hard course of strict counterpoint and fugue, my brain begins to move, and sustained thought is possible to me. (Pause to scratch.)

Now to start your letter of the 25 Feb.

I am delighted that your sister has found some war work suitable to her abilities, though of course you must miss her. Please 'convey my congratulations' as the papers say.

The news about Herbert Howells pleases me tremendously.[1] He is lucky in all circumstances; it was another glimpse of blue for me. To live in such a close for such a purpose is not far off from reasonable perfection.

As for 'In Flanders' – of course he would do it well, bless him. I am glad he went to Robins wood Hill; the view there is absolutely magnificent. Do you know, standing off from my song, I can now see that the very spirit of my county is quick in the song. Gloster itself shines and speaks in it. It is as if, on the long night work, some kind spirit of home visited me, when I think of it. And the end of the song is exactly like the 'high blue blade' fading away to distant Bredon just above Evesham ... Surely it is impossible that God will not let me say all this out in music? Joy has been so far from me save in moments of exultation; so long has life been a fight against pain and depression; that now I am stronger and can make some sort of Joy, it would seem too cruel to fulfill me elsewhere, where my own places would be but names, even if names despised in the light of the new beauty. But no – not ever despised, for Maisemore and Framilode are part of the stuff of me, ineradicable, not to be removed.

By all means show my verses to C.V.S.

I am very glad that Osborne[2] has replied at last. Would it be any good to send him later stuff? 'Scots', 'Communion', 'Time', 'The Three Spectres', 'Severn Meadows'? all among my best stuff; and 'Hail and Farewell'. But this is your affair. If you think the chance worth the trouble ... It is late of course, but he might soften. Do just as you please; with approval either way.

The *Musical Times* has not arrived, and they say there will be no mail for 6 days!! You may quote from my letters if you like, but always they are written at top speed – except for chat-hunting pauses -

Your parcel arrived, and was here last night when we arrived. And the candles came in most useful. It is a fine parcel, and the whole thing shows the touch of an experienced hand. Thank you so much. These things make a difference in a desolate land. However in a day or two the Div: Canteen will be established near here, and the Reg: Canteen will go stronger. Cigarettes one can almost always get. Usually some chocolate. Everything else doubtful. Sometimes, famine.

There, your three letters are finished.

Will you please put Herbert Howells, not H.N.Howells, in the Preface?

Did you see Laurence Binyon's Poem 'Gallipoli' in the *Observer*? Surely this is a glorious piece of work? I will read it well again though, but at present it seems to me full of fire and splendidly vigourous and full-winged.

What do London circles think about the probable termination now? Will it be long after cessation of fighting before we return etc? Do tell me what people think. It will always interest. And is the War Loan a huge success really?

Your book I hope is getting on now, in spite of all drawbacks – weakness, letter-writing, troubles by land and sea; I only wish it was possible to see it in growth, and give you such help as is possible. And the violin, does it get easier for you, and the trials more satisfactory?

There is no verse for you, but that is not to be wondered at! After a week or so perhaps ... You cannot think how ghastly these battlefields look under a grey sky. Torn trees are the most terrible things I have ever seen. Absolute blight and curse is one the face of everything, and the mind must be weighted with the sights and smells and deadness of everything. And this is almost marsh, and easily gets waterlogged easily.

Goodbye and best wishes for all good things

> Your sincere friend
> Ivor Gurney

Punctuate as you please. Don't trouble to copy out for that.

[1] See next letter

[2] E.B. Osborn was to review *Severn & Somme* for the *Morning Post*. His knowledge of Gurney's association with Gloucestershire, music and Harvey, shown in that review, derive from Marion Scott's having shown him some of Gurney's work in connection with his anthology *The Muse in Arms*.

173 *To Herbert Howells* G.3.5

11 March 1917 (G)

My Dear Howler

Your appointment pleases me immensely,[1] and when the letter reached me, in a crowded dugout, full of men weary of labouring in the mud, it was as light in the darkness. How well I remember that exquisite Close with the Cathedral so delicate and yet so strong soaring like a pure desire. It gave me hope also for myself that one of my friends had had good fortune – the pleasure was a little selfish, so far selfish; and I thought how I might return to College and come down one day to see you, full of joy at work accomplished and anxious to see yours. And 'Lady Audrey's Suite'. Of course you deserve all these things, but your getting them must nevertheless be received with welcome at the start. Well done! go on and prosper; and take all the joy out of life you can. It has been very good of you to score and rescore my songs; I could wish for no better hand. Do as you will with them in the details. You know how hard it is to settle tiny points away from a piano, and particularly for a slow minded cuss like me. You have all my trust. But, old chap – Ain't my song pure Gloster? Standing off from it, I can see the whole plain and the tiny dear places – orchards, roads winding through blossomy knolls – as clear as they really seem in that crystal air. The memory has comforted me in the long blank spaces as if it had been the work of another.

The verse tap has not been running very freely lately, we having had the longest time so far in the line and in the most appalling mud. Well it can't last for ever, and a determination and fixed will toward Beauty such as mine must have its reward somewhere.

Yes, the writing was R.V.W.'s, and a nice letter it was too. Nothing much to tell you of it, save a wish we should meet after the war. A hope which I share, as you may think.

By the way have you read Cobbett's *Rural Rides*? I think you would like it, though just an Itinerary undertaken for the sake of agriculture. But its quality of English would please you. The more letters you write the better I shall be pleased. Miss Scott's letters are most valuable things to me, as they talk of all the things I try to remember, and so give me something to feed on. And she is a most valuable critic although I take so little notice of her advice. I hope someday you will set a cycle of my songs, or at least a group of songs; I hope they attract you that way. And a couple of guineas a time from a successful composer is not to be sneered or snorted at .... And all the while I am thinking about the Close, and you set somewhere in it, and Bach's majesty and passion filling the nave .... O take double joy for my sake, and tell me something of it that I may share again.

Goodbye and best wishes.

Please remember me to Dr Alcock[2]

Yours ever
I.B.G.

[1] The address on the envelope explains the details: 'Mr H.N.Howells, Assistant Organist, Salisbury Cathedral.'
[2] Walter Galpin Alcock (1861-1947), organist at Salisbury Cathedral and teacher of the organ at the R.C.M..

174 *To Marion Scott*   G.41.77

20 March 1917 (P)

[*This letter consists of Marion Scott's transcriptions of 'Maisemore', 'Robecq', 'Sawgint', 'Serenity' and 'The Colonel', with Marion Scott's questions about punctuation and layout and Gurney's minimal corrections and terse replies, of which the most important is 'Do as you like about punctuation'.*]

175 *To Marion Scott*   G.41.72

22 March 1917 (P)

My Dear Friend
    More verse.

> *June-to-Come*   to F.W.H.
> When the Sun's fire and gold
>   Sets the bee humming,
> I will not write to tell
>   Him that I'm coming,
>
> But ride out unawares
>   On that old road,

Of Minsterworth, of Peace,
    Of Framilode

And walk, not looked for in
    That cool dark passage.
Never a single word;
    Myself my message.

And then; well ... O we'll drift
    And stand and gaze;
And wonder how we could
    In those Bad Days

Live without Minsterworth;
    Or Western air
Fanning the hot cheek,
    Stirring the hair;

In land where hate of men
    God's Love did cover;
This land ... And here's my dream
    Irrevocably over.

Hark, Hark, the Lark   to F.W.H.

Hark, hark, the lark to heaven's gate uprisen,
    Pours out his joy ...
I think of you, shut in some distant prison,
    O Boy, poor Boy;

Your heart grown sick with hope deferred and shadows
    Of prison ways;
Not daring to snatch a thought of Severn meadows,
    Or old blue days.

Trees

The dead land oppressed me;
I turned my thoughts away,
And went where hill and meadow
Are shadowless and gay.

Where Cooper's stands by Cranham
And grey stone houses smile,
Where motion, joy-inspired,
Eats up the measured mile.

Beauty my feet stayed at last
Where green was most cool,
Trees worthy of all worship
I worshipped ... then, O fool

Let my thoughts slide unwitting
To other, dreadful trees; ...
And found me standing staring
Sick at heart – at these![1]

Your letter of March 4 has reached me, and as usual has been a great pleasure. Also a note from Herbert and a letter from C.V.S. Let me see; have I thanked you for your parcel? Letters went off yesterday, but were surely written long before that came. Anyway let me thank you now. The bread was as much appreciated as ever. Some of the tea tablets have gone, but they shall be kept for trenches again. The candles were a great blessing. So *was* the cake. In the trenches, in a way, we get enough to eat, but that is reckoning meat and cheese; toujours bully, tous les jours, and one sickens of it, and dreams Paradisally of Cottage loaf and butter .... There were not quarter enough biscuits even. So you see how welcome anything like that bread is.

There was one night we stood to for 5 hours, and then carried rations up, in equipment, through the mud; in places, and many places, such as would stick a tank fast. It took us 8 hours there and back, and – well, I may force my neurasthenic soul to Joy one day by dwelling on contrast.

Your remarks on Pain and Death are very good and true. But.

If this does not mean I can do great work for English music, then it is waste to me. I should years and years ago have done with living but for that thought – of making Musical History for England, and out of Gloster stuff.

The *Observer* of March 4 has frightened me. Said he – Well into next year? It seems to be a question of getting at the Germans, but what of the German desire to surrender? Is Germany never to crumple up? Never? With so much good blood spilt? Is her organisation, which preserves morale, never to be badly disturbed? And is Germany at home always to remain quiet? Well, none can say, but it seems to be reasonable that if we overmatched the Germans last year we can crush them this, Running away or no running away

Especially as the submarine campaign seems to be a failure, and we hammering at Bagdad almost.[2]

'In support' is a term of variable meaning. Here, in conquered ground it meant ration-carrying and fatigues a kilometre from the first line. Later it meant sleeping on dugout steps, but here 9 men in a tiny dugout; But – good fires; Lots of wood – our salvation. Tea leaves were boiled 3 times, and we managed a hot drink 3 or four times every day.

Do as you like about Miss Saumerez Smith and the *R.C.M.Mag*. I will speak of your *Musical Times* article, when I have digested the poems a little more.[3] Anyway it is one oclock and time to sleep, though there has been good sleep

228

lately.

Thank you for all your kindnesses every way. I hope you will like these verses.

The final sonnett will not take shape.

Your sincere friend
Ivor Gurney

[1] Gurney seems to be composing as he writes here, particularly in stanza 3: he deletes a false start of 'At last', moves 'my feet' before rather than after 'stayed', deletes 'the' in front of 'green' and rewrites the last two lines of the stanza from

Most lovely Gloster-worthy ....
And then, I, fool, O Fool

The cramped revision necessitates a note below indicating 'dots after worshipped.'
[2] The failure of the submarine campaign was not obvious until May. Baghdad was captured on 11 March.
[3] Marion Scott's Presidential address delivered before the Society of Women Musicians on 2 December 1916 was published under the title 'Contemporary British War-Poetry, Music, and Patriotism' in the *Musical Times* for 1 March 1917 (No.889, vol.58), pp.120-123. She quotes Geoffrey Howard's 'England', W.N.Hodgson's 'Before Action' and Gurney's 'To Certain Comrades'. She also uses Gurney's stories about the Welsh singers and the singing of 'I Want to Go Home'.

176 *To Marion Scott* G.41.73

23 March 1917 (P)

My Dear Friend

Your letter of March 8th has just arrived. Thank you for it and all the kindness shown therein.

At present we are having a very soft time after our three weeks in the line – the softest time we have yet had; and we have deserved it too. Lots of fires, enough money and a fairly satisfactory canteen; I, alas! no longer in it! Sleep, a few inspections, some cleaning up; in fact, a far softer time than you had about March 7th. Comradeship nourished on dangers and parcels and hardships shared, discussing Blighty, past, present and future. Copious letter writing, a little roadscraping, and mild weather to frowst in, sweating round far bigger fires than Nature called for.

Yes, 'Purple and Black' is meant for you, and your pleasure pleases me. The sonnett to come at the end of the set will not – deposit, what is the word? (Sediment appearing from a chemical mixture.) 'For England' comes first, then Pain, then Servitude, then Exile, then the last.

The ommission [*sic*] of two words is unfortunate – in your address, I mean [1] – but it does not spoil the poem, for anyone can see something has been dropped. The whole address is very interesting, I think, and must have given great pleasure. Do you know, my opinion of the other two things quoted, is not very high? The first I like little, the second is good G.K.C., but not *very* good .... slightly precious. What does 'his' refer to in verse 2? Why 'catastrophes'? Why 'benison'? I don't like the sun's sword, and yet admit the whole thing is likable and memorable. But still my dear Belloc and G.K.C. do so much better.

The first poem is so empty though – the man uses words without feeling their meaning -

'And full of little lanes all dense with flowers'

is a dense line itself.

The chief criticism to be directed against my own things is – too many 'and's'. That will sum up in a nutshell my chief defect.

Now will you do me again another favour? Yet again? Verse is necessary to me, anyway, and I am convinced that all that is necessary to set myself forward on a new course and to get new ideas (since I cannot get to Blighty and drink from the fountain) is new books. And small ones.

Will you send me Freeman's latest book 1/- [2]
>   Tolstoi's *Cossacks* (World Classics *Pocket Edition*) 1/3
>   Modern Lyrical Masterpieces (Gowan's and Gray) 6d
>   Soldier Poets (the book you quote from) 2/-
>   Harvey's *Gloucestershire Lad* 1/6
>   *National Song Book* (Paper) 9d

I hope a shilling will do for postage. Getting them about with me will probably mean kit shortage but that I can bear. Also, if the *Morning Post* reviews any verse and quotes some of special interest, will you cut out the review and send it me.

You shall have a 10/- note with the next letter. I have the necessary money now but prefer to wait till we are paid again as this would leave me quite broke.

Robert Bridges' *Spirit of Man* is with me, but I need modern verse now. It is difficult in these circumstances to live out of the thought of the present day, and Milton is absolutely impossible. Anyway the *Spirit of Man* is only half as good as it ought to be.

O if I were at home tonight – I think it would be *Guy Mannering* till very late, or early... Or a Yeats play ... Or *Poems of To Day* – Or *The Mayor of Casterbridge*, or *Kidnapped*, or *The Path to Rome*, or *Life on the Mississipi*, or *Montaigne* or *The Dynasts*, Or God knows What All. But these are disturbing thoughts .....

Goodbye

Your sincere friend
Ivor Gurney

[1] Marion Scott had quoted first from Geoffrey Howard's 'To England' and second from W.N.Hodgson's 'Before Action', printed in *Soldier Poets*, pp.46 and 61 respectively.
[2] Gurney has deleted '*Imagist Anthology* 2/-' and 'Ledwidge's latest 2/6 (?)' and added a later note alongside this list: 'Delete – no room must wait'. He mentions a book by John

Freeman (1880-1929), probably *Presage to Victory and other Poems of the Time*, noticed in the *T.L.S.* of 1 February 1917, p.59, and *Soldier Poets: Songs of the Fighting Men* (1916) ed. Galloway Kyle. He was aware of the titles and prices from the *T.L.S.* lists of new books and reprints.

77 *To Marion Scott*   G.41.78

23 March 1917 (P)

My Dear Friend

Things are beginning to move, and no one knows when may come the next opportunity for writing. I have just recieved your letter of March 11th, and a rumour hastens me on to answer it. Your letter to Osborne is a model of tact, business-method, discretion, savoir-faire etc etc. Do not consult me about these things, but do as your far more experienced judgement may lead you. But don't I wish he had some later ones!

I am glad that your article has been postponed, and you set free to do as you will for a little. And it is very good news that you are able to play sonatas again, and with a sympathetic pianist. It gives me a feeling of sharing your good-fortune to read of it; may your strength increase and give you hours a day of it.

> *Concerning Verse*
>
> *Requiem no 2.* Either comma or dash after 'England's'.
>
> *Requiem no 3* 3rd line
>
> For these were slain, so strangely still reclining.
>
> Is the 'Song' worth reprinting.
>
> The 'homeward-come' in verse 2
>
> the last word in line 3 is a-quiring.

Should the word 'could' in 'Acquiescence' last line but one be 'can'? (I don't care for any of these things much. Just padding.)

Well, that finishes the replies to your letter. One parcel of yours I have received – not yet the other; all the letters have arrived, and all given pleasure. O to return to England and my friends! Such joys are there as are dangerous to imagine at present; not all at once will my mind and body become sound, but it cannot be so very very long before Joy becomes 'used to me'. And as for piano technique, 3 weeks will give me all since my brain is so much clearer.

The new state of things entered upon by the German retreat[1] may mean little letter writing. This is the reason why I hasten to reply, though never have I felt more acutely the inadequacy of words. Last night and this afternoon have been so beautiful that my mind has been filled with Blighty thoughts. But consider what a queer past I have to look back on! Either I am a great musician or a chronic neurastheniac! There is nothing outside it, for the visible world is hardly to be seen by me unless music hallows my spirit with beauty and toughens it by the necessary work. You will be glad to hear

231

however that as a personality I am rather popular in my company. It pleases me this, as so I know myself nearer Walt Whitman's perfect man; equal to shepherd and President; equal and familiar. O the joy to be able to go into a little Cotswold inn and drop into conversation with the nearest man! And that, compared with my tongue-tied shyness of 3 years ago. And if not here, then in the Shades I will be friends with men contemptuous of the fate to which some Power has doomed them, jovially drinking in some phantom pub over doubtful tales and unprintable denunciation of the Infernal N.C.Os.

You patient correspondent, though you make no complaint, how should you not be tired of the continual self-analysis which makes up the bulk of my letters! And yet those letters are the safety-valves of my discomfort. It is a cheap amusement – grumbling – pleasing the writer and leaving the reader to read or not as she pleases. I absolve myself therefore from half the blame, take the other half if you please. Once I etc etc there will probably be little of discontent in such few letters as I may write.

We have all been overeating to make up for our three weeks in the line, and indigestion has brought a mood of spiritual blight - penitence for unknown faults, elegiac, moribundish, Symphonie-Pathetiquish mood. O but one night walk round Cranham would dispel all this. Will you please keep on writing though you may not hear for a bit. And as for that final sonnet .... Bless you, there is not a patriotic man in the whole B.E.F. And how should I - poet, musician, fool-at-arms ....?

Goodbye and many sonatas. Unless I write very soon, those verse books off.

Your sincere friend
Ivor Gurney

[1] German forces retreated to prepared positions on the Hindenburg Line between 25 February and 5 April 1917.

178 To Marion Scott

G.61.40

24 March 1917 (P)

[*This is a standard Field Service Post Card signed* I.B.Gurney *and dated March 22 with all deleted except* I am quite well, I have received your letter dated 13 M *and* Letter follows at first opportunity.]

179 To Marion Scott

G.41.79

24 March 1917 (G)

My Dear Friend
It is too dangerous to move towards my valise, where your letter lies; there

being too many men looking for seats, and the fire being too comfortable.

Your apologies for your letter were not needed; it was by no means a dull letter; but your thinking so seems to show that you must have been tired or not well when you wrote it. I hope you are well however – as well as can be expected, and expecting to become still better.

The news that my poor versifications are to be shown to R.B: gives me no pleasure at all. I did not want technical criticism, being quite aware that good stuff does not come out of such a one as myself in a hurry. It would need quiet and continued thought – whereas the things that are finished as quickly as possible: often finished in one go; things like the 'Signaller's Vision' are meant to appeal to such people as are in this room with me – not to the experimenters in Greek metres. However your second letter having arrived, and the chance of an interesting meeting for you being there made apparent – all I will say is, that at present there is neither Time nor energy to do what might be done. The final sonnet seems fated not to be written; we being on short rations and hard work. Thank you for copying out Drinkwater's poem, which makes me feel small. It is beautiful; someday I will drown myself in such.

(This is March 24th by the way) I am afraid one of my letters has got lost. Have you received some verses beginning 'O may these days of pain'? If not, directly you say, I will write them out again, being rather proud of them.

Well, what thundering interesting things are happening now!

O if I but knew German! Lots of newspapers, some quite late have come my way; and a book of short stories about Military Life - supposed to be humorous. *Simpllicimus! Berliner Tageblatt* etc etc. There is no room for souvenirs, as the opportunites for getting them later will probably be only too numerous. You cannot imagine the amount of work behind his lines; he must have worked very hard.

I hope you heard my songs on the night, and will be able to tell me of the extraordinary effect they had on the audience .... How strong men wept like children etc.

Our mails arrive very well still. I hope they will continue to bring your letters, though my replies may be short and infrequent. I enclose something which looks like a complete description of a German private but don't know.[1] I found also about a dozen pcs, one of Nuremburg, which provoked sadness that we must never visit Germany. Anyway the place I want to visit now is Blighty. 'Blighty is the place for me' as the song says.[2] Goodbye, Good health and Good luck.

Your sincere Friend
Ivor Gurney

---

[1] These items are missing, perhaps not passing the censor?
[2] 'Take me back to dear old Blighty'.

25 March 1917 (G)

My Dear Friend

This, the next night to that in which I last wrote (Doesn't that sound pedantic?) seems to offer opportunity for writing; so here goes.

Today we have been salvaging above swamps and a canal, both a heavenly blue in the clear sunshine; and that was warm as the day went on and the sun went down the sky. This poetical start means nothing – digging and short rations leave me little energy for writing; hanging on to my companions' courage. I strive to forget what has been and might be; and leave such thoughts to the marches and late evening. But here's an emendation for 'Firelight'.

'Till Silence thrills and murmurs at the things they have said.'

It is a hard life the soldier's – especially for one given to dreaming. It is strange to me how great a part the mind plays in every affair of the body. Always concentration is the secret; and where there is usually concentrated dislike .... How would Hazlitt have got on I wonder?

I see in today's *Daily Mail* that food regulations are to be made more stringent. Is it really serious? Or a right precaution? What a time our poor villagers must be having! I don't like to think of some of my Framilode friends, to whom the price of bread is a real distress.

I think that verse in 'Poor Folk' may stand. I find it difficult to alter, and the sense is clear – just space and its difficulties to make food of no avail.

Mrs Harvey has just written me one of her charming letters, in which the good news comes that F.W.H. is getting his parcels, and that his book is in the 4th edition.

There is a blazing fire going in this partially ruined house every night; no dislikable man; common troubles; and common subject of conversation; grub, Fritz, and Blighty – (I cannot imagine why there is not a huge capital G there!) and we rub along as well as can be expected. What an education it is for me - and would this last moralisation were but truly felt! As for leave, it is a dead thing till October. There is no chance of it at all. But ever the thought of Nice Blighty haunts the mind.

Here is a little tale for you.

One of the finest little pocket corporals that ever breathed went out on patrol, mistook his direction in the dark, and was shot when about to enter the enemy lines by mistake. His fate was unknown for a fortnight or more; but here in these changes one has discovered a grave with a cross, Corporal Rhodes, 2/5 Gloucesters. And so certainty comes, and a momentary warmness towards Fritz; who must have loved his beautiful face and thought of his own beautiful youth wasted in the tragic tomfoolery of war.

I hope the book goes well in the midst of whatsoever distractions may surround you. Perhaps before so many months I shall get a look at it, or hear you playing confidently the great musings on Life and High Praise. Soit.

Your sincere friend
Ivor Gurney

I believe the long line in the 'Song of Pain and Beauty' is quite all right. it is like 3/4 after 2/4.

---

26 March 1917 (G)
[*In same envelope as previous letter, dated 5 April 1917*]

My Dear Friend

Another letter has arrived, again very welcome, and again keeping me in touch with the things that mean life to me.

It was kind of you to send those things to be read. Who knows? through all the exalted names connected with my book, perhaps I might perform the incredible and make money out of the book.

Well, it is nice to hear of people liking these things – it pleases me in this waste of living,

My last letter that reached you did take a time. Everything is upset. The canteen is empty save of cigarettes. Rations are very scanty; we are all of us weak as rats and badtempered. And hard-worked. But

We have managed to make a nice billet out of the gaping remains of a room, and, there being any quantity of wood, have had huge great roaring fires to sit round. The remains of our platoon is very chummy; no one quarrels, though arguments are fairly common in high voice. And after all, though we have our troubles, they are woes in common, and the little better and more grub arrived tonight is a common joy.

Next to me is a man of the 7th Gloucesters who was wounded when that splendid battallion got cut up at Gallipoli. I don't think it will be ever possible to tell you much about these people, but they are all part of me, stored up in the novelist part, and an influence to fulfill my music with humanity.

By the way 'In Flanders' was not written in the trenches, but at Crucifix Corner, if you know where that is.

I am afraid the final sonnett does not stand a chance of getting written. The sooner the book is printed, the better I shall be pleased. In that case Sonnett 5 will stand thus

England the Mother
(then at the bottom of the page)
This sonnett will not shape itself, probably because there is too much to say. I hope however to say out my thoughts in music – someday.

235

This is to get 5 pieces corresponding to Rupert Brooke's. It is simply not possible to screw anything out of myself at present.

This is a barren land, of flowers, that is. Once it was rich cornland, and is not much scarred by shell holes; but O my county; what tokens of your most exquisite secretest thoughts are now appearing under the hedgerows. On the march not many days ago we passed a ruined garden, and there were snowdrops, snowdrops, the first flowers my eyes had seen for long. So I plucked one each for my friends that I desire to see again, and one for Gloucestershire....

What has happened to the *Times Literary*? It does not arrive now, though the others come as usual. Has it finished?

The list of books is cancelled just for now. The *Spirit of Man* still accompanies me, though past its best days.

Mrs Harvey has just written me a charming letter. Will is well; and getting his parcels, and well on with a new book, thank Goodness; so that is good news of him. The Minsterworth rabbits are having a luxurious time in my absence.... O your two parcels arrived all right; unfortunately when we were paid and could also get biscuits; but for all that they were most welcome. The cooker things have been most useful not in cooking, but in starting fires when wood was damp. We expect they will be more useful soon. Mr Scott's parcel has not arrived, but these things are very irregular. (By the way, your first parcel was waiting when we arrived after a four hours march from trenches. Nothing to eat ... and to see that waiting is as a great revelation of light.)

Please thank Mr Scott for taking my things to be read. I hope their success gave him pleasure. How is Miss Stella Scott getting on? Well, I believe; she looking a capable lady altogether. I hope your domestic affairs are not too dislocated. A talk with Mrs Scott on Russia would be very interesting now;[1] and as for your Audrey, I have never been able to forget her, and her Puckish smile. With best wishes

Your sincere friend
Ivor Gurney

[1] To discuss the Russian Revolution.

---

182 *To Marion Scott* G.70.11.1

29 March 1917 (G)

March the 2- something. Wednesday
My Dear Friend

Here we are seated round a roaring fire in the open air, waiting to move up into new ground, and though doing nothing seems to content my companions, it bores me. So here's just a note.

Well, what is London's opinion of everything now? It is a queer state of things. And Mr J'accuse[1] has been suggesting queer things about the Kaiser, and everything is queer. We are relieved about one thing. The shortage of grub was due to our ration train smashing – we were afraid it was to continue till October – in which month, so we are told, leave will next be given.

I hope your book and your violin playing go on well; you may haul yourself up to health by these means. I wonder which gives the finer sense of power – control over a piano or a violin? Perhaps by this time next year we may be able to test that – on my sonata, of which only the clefs on the first lines are written. And there are 3 other songs to go with 'By a Bierside', and 'In Flanders', and my English Preludes to look forward to. Some more Robert Bridges. 'To the Fallen'. O no-one knows what is to come; perhaps a nice Blighty before long .... Please send any interesting reviews the *Morning Post* may give, or articles worth reading.

With best wishes

Your sincere friend
Ivor Gurney

[1] Someone writing in support of truth under the pen name derived from Zola's famous letter.

---

183 To Marion Scott   G.61.34

31 March 1917 (P)

[*Standard Field Service Post Card signed* I.B.G. *and dated March 30 with all deleted except* I am quite well, I have received your letter dated *and* Letter follows at first opportunity.]

---

184 To Marion Scott   G.41.83

1 April 1917 (G)

My Dear Friend   April 1st

This is the right day for such a business, if it were not so bitter, and surely a jest-day should not be so dull? Well, here it is, and fatigues are over, and this queer billet echoes and reechoes with the sound of tin whistles and mouth organs, just issued; and the lilt of some Scottish tunes our crack players are rollicking though make life a little alive and worth living. The billet is a family mausoleum owned by a duke and spared among so much ruin because payment has been made to the Germans – 17000 francs, they say.

I am sorry to hear you have been unwell, ill, again, and rejoiced to know you have got over it so much more quickly than a few months ago would have been the case.

You have had far worse weather in England than in France, where there has been quite a lot more sun than with you. Much of the severe frost was absolutely clear as to the sky. This morning was quite beautiful, though it turned to rain later.

I hope by the time this reaches you, you will have started spurted [sic] with the Spring, which must be somewhere near by now.

Thank you very much for the accounts you have given me of the performance of my songs. It interested me and bucked me up very much. But Mr Taylor seems remarkably like a dam-fool; it was good of you to wrestle with him, but difficult to convince a man who held such 'movie' views on the 'Bierside' ending. The first part of the song is of course a raphsody [sic] on beauty, full of grief but not bitter, until the unreason of death closes the thought of loveliness, that Death unmakes. Then the heart grows bitter with the weight of grief and revelation of the impermanence of things – Justice and Strength turning to a poet's theme. But, anger being futile, the mind turns to the old strangeness of the soul's wandering apart from the body, and to what tremendous mysteries! And the dimly apprehended sense of such before us all overpowers the singer, who is lost in the glory of the adventure of Death. But that's all summed up by asking what the foremizzentopmast did I write 'ff' [for] if it were as this Taylor man suggests.

I will think about your suggestion as to 'Pain and Beauty' but do not yet agree. (The 'or' in verse 2 should be on line 5. Is it?) The long line should have something of the same effect as the 3 line in Fitzgerald's Quatrains.

We have not had so bad a time lately, nothing like trench conditions, at any rate, though hard work and not enough food (or at any rate, food not seeming enough) have made us all weak, and upset our insides. I should put this down to the peculiarities of my own stupid constitution, did not men of farming and similar trades also complain. I believe a great deal is due to the dulness of the life, which makes every one look to meals more than ordinary; but anyway they are bound to work us; it being as certain as anything that only going keeps us going. We should all relapse into neurasthenia were we not driven. Considering everything, especially the callousness to certain things such a life must develop, the men are marvellously good to one another, and surely much finer than ever they were, bless em.

I am glad London takes a more optimistic view of things than Mr Garvin – who has always been in the right when things went wrong, but not right. I remember his dolefulness about last May.

Lord, what a hell of a row in here, and what a crush! But I remember how quavery your writing was, when you were sick and still wrote. And not any of the alarums and excursions shall disturb me. But were I only at home ransacking books for verse to set.

The baccy parcel arrived last night, and we were all most grateful; everybody was short or bankrupt; and the cigar things were most grateful to us stranded wretches. (They are singing 'Annie Laurie'. O the joy of it!)

238

I fear I can send you no money yet, but if you would send the paper covered *National Song Book*, and the small selected *Browning* in Walter Scott's edition they would be most useful. The latter is 1/6 I believe. I believe *The Spirit of Man* is sucked dry for me, and my thirst for good verse; and short, is very strong.

The day has been springlike on the whole, and last night's sky was gloriously tragic; I sang 'In Flanders' to myself, facing the West, alone in a lately ruined house, spoiled by that unutterable thoroughness of the German destruction; and was somewhat comforted thereby. That has all been said for me in 'In Flanders'. What you said about the sense of being out under the stars, in 'By a Bierside' is obviously Cooper's Hill. O times! O saisons, O chateaux!

Goodbye for now

Your sincere friend
Ivor Gurney

185 *To Marion Scott*   G.41.80

2 April 1917 (G)

My Dear Friend

Tin whistles and mouth organs still going hard, and we waiting for dinner and moving afterwards, for a company of ours took two more villages last night, and we shift also of course.

We have been hard worked, but still and all the same, this open country work is preferable to trench life. This place is quite pretty, very pretty; and this morning I saw, at first dawn, one mystical star hanging over a line of black wood on the sky-line; surely one of the most beautiful things on earth.

I hope by the time this letter gets to you you will be trotting about in real Spring sunlight; it is cold here as yet, but no man may foretell of April's whims.

I told you of the death, a little time back, of one of our most looked to corporals. Well, that was before the advance. About a fortnight after the movement started, we heard his grave had been discovered; and after tea one evening the whole company (that was fit) went down for a service there. Quite a fine little wooden cross had been erected there; the Germans had done well; it was better than we ourselves would have given him; and on the cross was

'Hier ruht ein tapferer Englander,[1]
Richard Rhodes', and the date.

Strange to find chivalry in the sight of the destruction we had left behind us; but so it was. They must have loved his beauty, or he must have lived a little for such a tribute. But he *was* brave, and his air always gallant and gay for all his few inches. Always I admired him and his indestructibility of energy and

239

wonderful eyes.

I am sorry to hear about the shortage of pianos, that may affect me and my tinklings.

April 4 or 5th

I thought we were going over the top tonight, but it has been postponed – a state of things which will inevitably lead to soul-outpourings. My state of mind is – fed up to the eyes; fear of not living to write music for England; no fear at all of death. Yesterday we had a little affair with a German patrol, which made me interested for 5 minutes; after which I lapsed into the usual horrid state of boredom. O that the Nice Blighty may come soon! I do not bear pain and cold well, but do not grumble too much; so I reckon that cancels out. One cannot expect to have everything, or to make one's nature strong in a week. It snowed like anything yesterday, but today has been quite beautiful, and I have strolled about chatting of Maisemore Wood and such-like things of beauty. Your Kampote blocks came in very useful – what were left of them, and a warm drink now and then is salvation indeed; after the drink I settle down to think of the delightful cosy comfortable teas I will have one day, and of the music to follow; trying so to forget my feet. What an April! Well, we have had some bon fires not so many days back.

My dear friend, it has been very kind of you to write to my friends as you have, and I know they are grateful. It is something to know that my father realises his trouble and sacrifice have not been all wasted. He has been only too good always; especially considering the difference of our temperaments, and my long wasted time. Surely my life must lead to something. Surely the apprenticeship has almost passed?

I am afraid there are no poems again. The conditions are against it, but, thank Goodness rations are better now.

My friendships are mostly queer ones, and this is queer, but believe me, a very valued one. You have given me just what I needed, and what none other of my friends could supply to keep me in touch with things which are my life; and the actuality of which is almost altogether denied me. Well, perhaps it will not be long before I am back again, and having tremendous jaws about your book, and seeing you get stronger, and watching Audrey grow up, and seeing what her smile grows to be. Here we are called up.

Goodbye.

Your sincere friend
Ivor Gurney

Next day

Our Q.M.S. has told us that the 61st are mentioned in despatches. Is this true I wonder? We have risen a little in our own estimation if this is so; one does not wish to belong to a washout division. This morning was beautifully sunny, and daisies are poking their heads out here and there – without steel helmets! O the Spring, the Spring! Come late or early, you must give hope ever to the dwellers in the house of flesh. How does your frail tenement get on? I hope it is warmer and sunnier with you now, and you playing on your violin, revelling in sunlight of earth and music.

¹ 'Here lies a brave Englishman'.

186 *To Sydney C Scott*   G.61.35

11 April 1917 (P)

[*A printed postcard form. On the address side is printed:*]
This postcard is already addressed to the friend who sends you this parcel.
Please be sure to return this postcard to your friend.
It is important that you should send this postcard back as soon as possible because the sender is naturally anxious to learn that the parcel has arrived safely, and that you are pleased with it.
[*Alongside this is printed:*]
The smokes sent with this postcard were supplied by the Tobacco Fund by Martins Ltd, 210, Piccadilly, London, W.
[*and below it in a type box*]
Weekly Dispatch/ Tobacco Fund,/ Carmelite House,/ London, E.C.
[*On the reverse is printed:*]
This postcard acts as a Receipt for this parcel and **should** therefore **be posted** as soon as possible to the sender of the parcel.
But at the request of the Authorities,
In thanking the donor, please do not mention your unit.
[*Gurney has written as follows:*]
   Thank you so much for your present, which came most opportunely. Things are rather inconvenient here, but a letter shall arrive thanking you also for your kindness about my verses. Meanwhile – just Thank you
                                                                                        Ivor Gurney

187 *To Marion Scott*   G.70.22

11 April 1917 (P)

[*This is Army Form A.2042A, a Hospital Redirection Card:* On the admission of a Soldier to Hospital this card should be filled in and forwarded to his next-of-kin. *Gurney has filled in, in the appropriate places* Pte Gurney, B.Co, 2/5 Glosters, *but there is no entry in the space provided in the phrase* has been admitted into No   HOSPITAL, British Expeditionary Force. (Letters should be) addressed as above.) *In the place where he is told to* Indicate here briefly nature of wound or sickness *he has written under* 'Wounded' Bullet in arm   *and the*

241

188 *To Marion Scott*   G.41.85

14 April 1917 (P)

My Dear Friend

Well, I am wounded; but not badly; perhaps not badly enough; as although kind people told me it meant Blighty for me, yet here I am at Rouen marked 'Tents'. I do not yet give up hopes, but very few boats have been running lately; none at all for some days; and the serious cases go first of course. It was during an attack on Good Friday[1] night that a bullet hit me and went clean through the right arm just underneath the shoulder – the muscles opposite the biceps, to describe them more or less accurately. It hurt badly for half an hour, but now hurts not at all; I am writing in bed with the arm resting on the clothes merely.

Well, I suppose your letters will be lost to me for a little; please send them to me when you receive them.

I hope you are well now, inspite of the awful April weather.

There is a gap of two days between the writing of the two pages. I can send you no address; we are being shifted about too much, and everything is doubtful. Apparently the hospital boats have been and are almost completely held up, or else I might have had a chance for Blighty; though there is no real damage to my arm, not enough to please me.

Alas! Alas! there are hardly any books here! And the life is made up of hanging about waiting to be shifted again. Now if I could find some real hard reading to do – something to distract my mind, all might be well; or if I had some MS and a few books of verse, I would turn out something in spite of the flatness of my mind. O well, hopes are not yet gone.

Will Harvey is getting all his parcels, and has a new book of verse almost ready. This is good news; and it will be very interesting to see the difference betwen the two; for of course there will be a difference.

Though this Spring is cold and inclement, I cannot keep out of mind what April had meant for me in past years – Minsterworth, Framilode, and his companionship. And my sick mind holds desperately on to such memories for Beauty's sake; and the hope of Joy. 'By a Bierside' came from two evenings above all others: one most magical afterglow at Framilode when I was alone; and the evening before I rode in late to find England had declared war. Great billowy clouds hung over distant Malvern, and the poplars, black against the glowing West, sang music unto me, which someday I may fit myself to sing to others – but not yet; not in these conditions, when Pain rules so much and so continually in the sight of one who bears Pain hardly, supporting his courage by other examples. Still more analysis! Yes, but you are kind and infinitely patient and it does me good to 'moan', as the Army word is.

My total cash is 3½d, so you see that in spite of my credit of about 175 francs, I can buy nothing in the way of books. Two *Daily Mails* will finish my literary purchases. So, if I can send you an address, please send me some small books of verse, and Tolstoi's *Cossacks* (Worlds Classics – Pocket Ed). I wonder whether at last I might try Housman's *Shropshire Lad*?

I will write again in half a shake.

Your sincere friend
Ivor Gurney

(I write with my perforated arm, so you see not much is wrong.)

---

[1] Good Friday 1917 was the 6th April.

---

189 To Marion Scott   G.41.82

17 April 1917 (P)
[*Postcard marked* 'Y.M.C.A. ON ACTIVE SERVICE.']

Dear Friend

Still at the Base. No certain address. No certain tomorrow. No luck. No money. No damage to my arm, save a hole. Yet, had the boats been running, I might have got to Blighty. I will write a letter tomorrow. I hope the weather has been as good these last two days with you as with us.

I.B.G.

---

190 To Marion Scott   G.41.86

19 April 1917 (KT)   55th Infantry Base Depot/ France

My Dear Friend   Monday

At last we are more or less settled, and I can send you an address to write to.

How are you, I wonder, in this extraordinary weather mix-up? If you are not well, there is surely no reason for despair; if well, then you should have great hopes indeed; for indeed the conditions are no bon.

All hopes of Blighty vanished very soon. Men who had been marked 'Blighty' for a fortnight unwillingly got better and were shoved out to make room for other men. No boats are running, and that is the end of it. Had the Spring been fine it would have nearly broken my heart; to have missed so much by so little.

Not that there is much the matter with my arm; half an inch either way now .... Well, it could not be and was not, and there is the Line to look forward to in a little. As for verse, we have been altogether too harried for me to get any calm, and anyhow I seem to have run dry. Also my inside has not

243

been as placable as it might, though that will bring me little advantage indeed compared with my painless wound. It is good to be with a crowd of men who are admittedly illused – this makes a community of interest, and humour appears.

Please send your letters on when they return to you; there seems to be a gulf fixed between thee and me, but that should be bridged now.

It was very kind of you to write to my friends about the success of the songs, and I assure you they are very gratified. My poor father has had to wait long enough for any visible signs of success, and he is very pleased about it. A pity it was you could not be there, since you have had so much to do with them and taken such trouble; we will share the regret, since I have also some reason to complain.

What a tremendous victory the Arras affair was![1] Mein Gott, what a blow! Surely even Mr Garvin must perk up his head and chirp? Did any – ordinary – body expect such a one-day victory?

Who is running the Carnegie affair?[2] How delightful to see the 'London' Symphony is to be published, and there is 'my quartett' also, with the hills in it and the wind blowing through – so I please myself by thinking.

How is H.N.H. getting on? Perhaps even now there is a letter being returned to him. O well c'est le guerre, and curse le guerre and all to do with it, that has cheated me of my letters and made an unprofitable hole in my arm.

Will you please give the enclosed note to Mr Scott?

With best wishes, for health, and literary and musical activity

> Your sincere friend
> Ivor Gurney.

[1] The taking of Vimy Ridge was indeed a one-day success, but the battle as a whole got bogged down as usual.
[2] The Carnegie United Kingdom Trust was established in 1914 and began its musical publication scheme in 1917. Howells' piano quartet in A minor was the first work published under its auspices, and they also published Vaughan Williams' *London Symphony*

---

191 *To Marion Scott*   G.41.84

? April 1917 (KT)

My Dear Friend

Well, and how is all with you, in spite of the cold and clammy wind? I hope that your day includes hours of violin and book-making by now, and begins to resemble your desire a little. O well, the Victory which seems imminent should help you a little. This writing is pretty shaky – more from cold than anything else, though my fingers are rather stiff today. The orderly told me in confidence it might be three weeks before I was in training again. So there is time to write yet.

What news though! Today, peeping surreptitiously on another man's paper, I see the French have got 10,000 prisoners[1], which must hurt Hindenburg slightly. And soon perhaps Spring will gain her victory and flaunting glorious banners sweep the last rearguards of winter in flight to the North.

How is my distinguished coadjutor H.N.H.? Bless him, he with you have made my tiny triumphs possible. Did Sir C.H.H.P. really say my song was the most tragic thing he knew? If so, what an enormous praise! I shall be very proud of that, if it is so; and could desire no other or higher praise.

To resume next day. A kindly doctor has given me a week's No Duty, and there is a recreation room with quite a lot of old mags, and a few books; so I shall manage to exist, but O for some hard headwork and long walks!

Yesterday someone was playing the rather good piano in the Recreation Room – toshy stuff played quite well. It was difficult to stay in the room with so many desires awakened and so poorly satisfied.

> Music pours on mortals
> Her beautiful disdain,[2]

which is one of the few scraps of Emerson worth knowing; and I got it from the *Times L.S.* which arrives no more, since apparently Northcliffe will not bother with small fry. Would you mind sending your copy, unless you keep them for reference? It is a valuable thing and the extracts are stimulating.

This is a most beautifully situated camp – surely there can be no harm in saying what so many people know, that the 55th Inf. Depot is at Rouen – and there are some very noble pines not far from this tent. I hope to get a pass out of them before I leave here, and to see so historic a place of memories; was it not here that William the Conqueror saw his future wife washing in the courtyard?

Last night after lights out I had a long talk with a Cotswold man lying next to me – of his ambition to be a gardener; of Cotswold gardens; of the beauty of those churches; of certain jolly old masters-of-life there; of old songs; of the joy of life there in those homely and friendly-seeming houses of grey stone with so wonderful an array of flowers round each. I could hear music that I should make mixt with the older music respiring from his talk – language of Shakespearian comedy – and set myself to wait a little longer, and perhaps not so very long either.

I hope you are getting well, even if only to enjoy the warm weather when it comes. After all the cold and wet are hard on German spuds as well as Allied. But I should like some verse not yet known to me, especially as there is a good chance of being here 3 weeks or more.

With all good wishes

Your sincere friend
Ivor Gurney

---

[1] In the second battle of the Aisne (16 April-7 May)
[2] Quoted in the *T.L.S.* for 25 January 1917, p.38

21 April 1917 (P)

My Dear Friend

> 'Never so intense
> I felt the pang of beauty's innocence
> Earthly and yet unearthly'.

This phrase I have just found in a poem of Binyon's, and it seemed a good thing to send it you. There is not much else there, but the whole thing is interesting enough to send you.[1]

Weather cold today, but not rainy or any wind to pierce you, so you may be travelling London streets to-day, these perhaps soon to be decked out with flags, perhaps; if England have not restrained emotion too long to unfreeze at once. It will be very interesting to see what happens to our people, and probably joy will not express itself much till the Boys Come Home. And I shall return to quiet places and bathe myself in beauty till the power of earth should heal me and restore my courage.

Perhaps if there were some verse here and some MS, I might write something here; not willingly, but the effort would do me good, and it might mean some time not wasted. There are any amount of old Magazines here; which is a blessing; old *Cornhills*, *Scribners*, *Harpers*; but desultory reading becomes at last the most fatiguing of boredoms and one longs for something hard to chew.

One or two classics are there – *Esmond*, which is a very minor affair. O our Victorian masterpieces![2]

There is quite a nice piano in the Recreation Room, but that is not yet for me, and anyway it is a mixed pleasure to attempt to play from memory things which the hearers do not care for; and a pleasure also that reminds one to[o] much of Joy not to be Pain. (Cotswolds man on right talking like a Hardy novel of horses and pigs and being called up.)

Your sincere friend
Ivor Gurney   55 I.B.D.

---

[1] Gurney encloses a cutting of pages 512-3 of *The Canadian Magazine* reviewing *The Anvil* by Laurence Binyon, primarily by quoting 'Fetching the Wounded' from it. Gurney quotes from the end of the first paragraph. Though Gurney picks out a rather idealistic piece, the type of description and the form of the rest may have impressed, and even influenced him.

[2] Thackeray's *Henry Esmond* came out in 1852; 'perhaps his masterpiece, and probably the greatest novel of its kind' says a biographical dictionary guardedly.

24 April 1917 (P)

My Dear Shimm:

I wonder what has happened to you; has some little side-convulsion of war thrown you over on to these shores yet? Are you jolly well fed up in Blighty or merely bored in France? (It will not take long to reverse things.) Perhaps you may have heard about my little encounter with the Beastly Blondes and the consequent hole in my arm; had only the boats been running all would have been well, and I drinking sunlight and sweet air in Blighty, Blighty. All down the progression of dressing stations etc sweet murmurs sounded in my ear of Blighty, and already could see apple blossom on the Gloster orchards: yet now ——— behold me in No 55 I.B.D. and wasting whole precious days in doing nothing in a melancholy fashion.

Well, well, let us hope for the end of the whole business, and hang on.

What shall I say next? My favourite topic – grub – seems barred, for Blighty seems to be in somewhat of the same mess as we. Have you had any music-making lately? Can you settle down to it when you get the chance? I can't. Stiff fingers and brain and imperfect memory soon made me leave off. Well, not forever – non moriar omnis.

There is a horrid great gap of over a fortnight in my correspondances, which is like losing a sense, or having one's communications cut.

Old chap, I went into the Cathedral here two days ago, and stayed awhile in the perfect peace there. It was so still and beautiful that Bach's music mingled with the sunlight and bathed my mind with peace, with only the joyful thought of Tea to disturb it.

Good luck, my bonny man

Yours ever
I.B.G.

24 April 1917 (P)

My Dear Howler

How are you now, my dear collaborator, in your quiet Cathedral close, so far from the noise of War, but not its influence? I also, but with a souvenir in the form of a bullet hole in the upper arm. This would have got me to Blighty in happier times but there was no luck for me – here, at No 55 I.B.D. and hanging about regretting the wasted days, which might be filled with so much, so much.

I hope you are forging ahead with some new thing or other, and well and not too occupied in other business. These are holidays, you should have some time to yourself now; have you been to Winchester yet? Or, in a smaller way, have you rummaged those second hand bookstalls in the street, not far from the Cathedral? I myself bought nothing there, but rummaged nevertheless; later buying several 6d Nelsons at a book-shop not far off, before the return to servitude and the bleak plain again.[1]

Is the time far off when we shall meet, and discuss all these things in a proper fashion? What does Hindenburg think, I wonder? Or even more important, Nivelle and Haig?[2]

Well, we are all starving now, tout le monde. Soon the troops will be collecting up scraps of bully for the folks in England, 'Comforts for Civilians'. 'Remember the Kiddies' and so forth. As *Punch*'s lieutenant wrote 'I seem able to think only of Europe and my belly – nothing between', and here there are only old mags: and toshy novels to read; not that my intellect is fit for anything much stronger. But O those damned Minsterworth orchards, and what they might be singing to me! I am glad you climbed Robins wood. Coopers Hill is better, but then one cannot have everything. Good bye

Yours
IBG

[1] Salisbury Plain, where Gurney did some of his training.
[2] Commaders-in-Chief of their respective armies.

---

195 *To Marion Scott*   G.41.88

30 April 1917 (P)

My Dear Friend

Your letter of April 18th-22nd and the *Cossacks* etc have arrived, and that is all I have had as yet. More may arrive, for my address has been left at Con: Camp and sent to the Batt: Let em all come.

I am sorry you have such a queer and inconvenient illness; after all, German Kultur or the results thereof may very well cause an Englishwoman to break out in spots. What will you do? Can you get a kind of permission? The blessed nuisance of it all is that all substitutes go up in price like rockets in the air. And this morning, 40 big ships reported sunk. We shall pull through, I have no doubt, but it is a mess. This morning the doctor has given me Duty, which will tell you what the official verdict is. Apparently the beastly bullet hit absolutely nothing at all profitable – and as to escaping serious damage, I am too near to the event to feel grateful.

Sunday

I am supposed to be on Church parade but owing to the fact that my ripped coat has not been replaced, I am here writing this letter.

Yesterday evening the two *Poetry Reviews* and the *Times Supplements* arrived. Thank you very much, especially for the first, which is just what England needed – a magazine devoted to the interests of weak but sincere verse. Local poetry, local poetry is Salvation, and the more written the better. And how good to get such beautifully printed stuff out here.

I am very sorry to hear about Sydney's illness and will write to him at once. Poor chap, he has not had the happiest of lives; but after the war he will have gained wisdom, to limit his desires, and to accept facts, thereby gaining the fullest freedom possible.

I knew about the Carnegie business, and have written about it I think. It gives me great pleasure that H.N.H. should gain even so little a recognition, but where is the Concerto to be done again? Also the publication of the London Symphony is the best of news. About Bantock I am always sceptical. He is diffuse and ineffectual, and needs a great deal of material to make any effect.

(Oh, yes, my number is 241281 now.)

I suppose all your plans are held up; your book tugging at the leash so to speak, but not getting on. It is a thousand pities, but there you are; the better weather ought to make a large difference to you whether you stay in London or go to Dorset.

The Shropshire Lad and the MS have also been gratefully received, but once again I feel rather incapable of setting them. Such precise and measured verses are too easy to set; do not give the scope that R.Bridges' songs offer one. One can only set them, say, a little better than Hermann Lohr or Maude Valerie White can;[1] for their abilities are quite up to setting such poems. Compree? By the way, my subtle mind infers from the silence about R.B. that his judgement was not favourable, which does not surprise me. Such a master is not pleased with the amateur.

Doesn't the *Poetry Review* go for Abercrombie though! I am rather glad, hating by nature the obscure, and, pace Mr Masefield, being doubtful even of Sir Robert Ross.

So Edward Thomas is dead. This is a great loss; but this I think I have already written about.

The *Cossacks* is good stuff. Thank you so much; when one has read (Yes, I got hold of these) such a parochial masterpiece as *Esmond*, and such a thin finicking piece of work as *Travels with a Donkey* within three weeks of this book, it gives one's national pride a severe shock. One may put the case as – Tolstoi might have preferred man's life in the open air to that of a writer, but Thackeray that of a clubman – a Thorough Gentleman. Dickens had twenty times his genius, and, but for humour, he was small.

The *Poetry Review* may start me writing again; such imperfection in print is most encouraging. Please rush my book into print as soon as possible. If that sonnet can be done, it shall be. But continual disgust has sterilised me. However Spring really has been here for ten days now.

With all good wishes for health etc.

Your sincere friend
Ivor Gurney

[1] Hermann Frederic Lohr (1871-1943) made his name as a composer of ballads including 'Little Grey Home in the West'; Maud Valerie White (1855-1937) was a composer whose memoirs can be found in *Friends and Memories* (1914) and *My Indian Summer* (1932).

196 To Sydney Shimmin   G.76.8

30 April 1917 (P)

My Dear Shimmin

I am very sorry to hear you have fallen sick; the consolation is that afterwards, as Miss Scott says, you may be better in health than for three years past. Damned hard lines, O suffering broken mortal.

I also have been hardly treated by Fate, as you may have heard: a bastard bullet (as the Australians say) went clean through my arm with no other result than making me howl and getting me out of the line for a month, for that's all it's likely to be. So near to Blighty, yet with such a great gulf fixed between for such as I. There is good news about Howells anyway. About anyone else there is no news, though the letters floating about France (three weeks of 'em) may contain summat.

And down at Framilode though Spring has come late violets must be already showing in the sheltered places, and glorious mornings with great tides and elvers in them to be caught, fried in bacon-fat and eaten in stringy chunks. I suppose you are not too ill to read, unless the operation has only just been completed, and you a shattered mangled wretch with not so much cerebral strength as would do even for Charles Garvice or the soul shaking Silas Hocking.

The news is good, isn't it? Perhaps before many months we shall resume living again, and the past will become more rosy than it seemed when you and I were in the Army and chronically fed up. And at the worst the possible Fed-upness of Peace will be a pleasant change, hein?

Good luck old chap and best wishes,

Yours ever
Ivor Gurney

4 May 1917 (P)

My Dear Friend

Your letter of April 24th is here to answer, and this morning *Responsibilities*[1] has turned up. It is too generous of you really, and of course far too good a book to keep out here; so that directly I think they have put me on a draft I will send it back to you. The glance at it seems to show it an immensely interesting book, obscure, and unaccountably failing and only just failing to be great poetry time after time. What will the next one be like? Is it Transition or the end of him? After the War I shall be only too pleased to resume possession, but as to taking it up the line that is not possible.

I hope you are getting fit now – bedroom life must be terrible in these blue and momentous days. You have had a rough time since the similar days in August 1914. Perhaps you have been affected by some evil in the air, some potent and maleficent influence? Who knows? I don't believe it , but then this is only a letter, not an affidavit. The Herrick poem is very beautiful, and makes me long for the time when after a long tramp out towards round and about Staunton and Corse – on the way to Jagged Malvern, I shall return tired and full of memories to set up singing in my mind – and then Mr Herrick, we shall collaborate to some purpose.

I see Austen Chamberlain gives no official hope for peace before November. Then surely, having collared the guns, we shan't be long?

Also another kind friend has sent me *Soldier Poets*, in which there is precious little of value but much of interest. Julian Grenfell's 'Into Battle' is of course, easily the best. Geoffrey Howard's 'Without Shedding of Blood' E Melbourne's 'Before Action', 'Back to Rest', Victor Ratcliffe's 'Optimism', Robertson's 'We shall drink', Sorley's translation from 'Faust'. The curiously alive and unequal 'Charge at Neuve Chapelle'. The last two verses of 'To my People' of Wilkinson's.

(Have you seen any verse by a man named Sassoon? I remember having seen quite good stuff.)

You may send my things to Erskine Macdonald if you wish.[2] The *Poetry Review* is a first rate pusher. Why cannot I write now? Don't know, but I believe after this long frowst and feed up, the line will give me beaucoup ideas. No more strength had I than some decrepit rat, or seemed not to have, when we went up for the attack. But since being here, I have cherished my belly most generously, too generously some time, and hope to have a little spare energy for a month. In future however, I refuse absolutely to have any parcels sent. It is absurd and impossible to ask for them. And now the warm weather has come, we shall do very well.

After another dip into Yeats, I find myself still more impressed. It is not a great book, there are not more than a few things that one will remember; but it is a most valuable book for a young poet; most stimulating, swift and high-hearted. And though one cannot deny its occasional obscurity, after reading

Soldier Poets it seems strikingly original; though the strain is occasionally apparent of the care that roots out the obvious and worn phrase, and will not be too easily pleased with first sketches. You will find that when I come to work again I also shall show much greater scrupulousness than before. It was simple lack of energy that kept me from revision, and the only method possible to me was to write for a minute or two at top speed, refrain from tearing it up, and return to the charge after some space of time. It won't be so, afterwards.

Will you please accept the grateful dedication of 'By a Bierside'? I don't think it would have come to birth but for you, and your receptivity, and the chance of its getting a hearing through your insistence. And as to verses, there would probably be a very small crop had you not seemed to expect them from me; especially so as F.W.H. is in Germany.

O Robert Ross or whatever his name is – the *Poetry Review* man – is all bosh. Pope or Gray in the solidity of his good lines - ungoverned transcendability. A type of a different kind from Ella Wheeler Wilcox, but no better. Give me Walt Whitman.

What do you think of George Butterworth?[3] The friend of Vaughan Williams ought to do well, but toujours I am sceptical about the lasting value of most English music. It is the ploughing of the ground, the preparing, and while one is grateful, there is too much as a general thing of excellence that so many clever people arrive at with their well trained intellects and healthy minds and instincts.

Tonight to the pine wood. But to the bathhouse now and to wash clothes etc etc.

Tomorrow I start training, a good thing; you get frightfully slack doing nothing.

Your sincere friend
Ivor Gurney

[1] W.B.Yeats's book.
[2] The publisher
[3] George Sainton Kaye Butterworth (1885-1916). One of the most promising of his generation of musicians. Gurney seems unaware of his death in action on 5 August 1916.

198 *To Marion Scott*   G.41.90

9 May 1917 (P)

My Dear Friend   Sunday
I hope you are doing fairly well now – today is the first cold day for some time, and judging by the way the long-frozen trees have flourished in it, invalids should do pretty well; and the Gardens are not so very far from you.

All this week I have been down for training at the Bull-ring, as they call it –

Napoleon's parade ground, a bare white sand and shingle space set among hills and surrounded by pines. It is a fine place, but a nasty job. Perhaps I may be here for another week yet, and then up to the chance of Glory and another Blighty, a real one this time. My arm is quite well now, curse it.

Do as you will about my book. Will
'To Certain Comrades   and other Verses' do?
As a title, I mean. Not so bad, I think.

I had a letter from Sidney the day after I wrote to him – a plucky calm letter. It is over now, the second operation, I suppose, and he steering a clear course if a slow one towards health. Anyway, he stands a chance of escaping all this, which is a good thing.

The things I like best in Yeats, as yet, are The foreword in italics; The Grey Rock; The Two Kings; September 1913; To a Friend; The Witch; Mountain Tomb; To a Child Dancing; Memory of Youth; Friends; Cold Heaven; (as you may imagine) That the Night Come; A Coat; A Woman Homer sung; The Consolation; No Second Troy; Reconciliation; King and No King; The Mask; Upon a House Shaken; These are the Clouds.

Jolly good stuff these, and excellent chiefly for young poets interested in method.

Monday

Yesterday I managed to get to Rouen again, and was for a brief two hours and a half my own master. It really is a fine town, and a great rock which stands smiling and huge just out of the town and on the river is very impressive. I did not go to the Cathedral, whose iron spire struck me with increased horror; a dreadful thing. St Ouen has a very much finer spire.

Look here, did I give H.N.H. the dedication of 'By a Bierside'? I seem to remember something of it; and if this is so, I am afraid you must try and live without it. Cuss, I do get mixed up so in my wandering mind.

Still nearer to the line now – which may come any day. All kind of rumours fly round as to the actual whereabouts of the Batt: but noone really knows.

I have been reading Conrad's *Chance*, only to get tired of all that analysis, and not being able to get to the end. *The Mirror of the Seas* is Conrad's best, as far as I know. Otherwise Kipling infinitely surpasses him. Conrad is a good artist, but to me seems not to have much original genius. (But our acquaintance is not extensive.)

Now I am about to steer off for my chess-pupil, who has beaten me in one game – the first! On Saturday, I satisfied my vanity by flummoxing him completely; may it be so again.

I hope you are getting better now. Can't you get some kind of dispensation, or absolution from maize?

With best wishes

Your sincere friend
Ivor Gurney
Please keep on writing.

On second thoughts I have decided to send you the enclosed doleful production. You see I have shaved now, but cannot smile to order. I believe however that my ordinary expression is somewhat happier.[1]

I.B.G.

[1] The probable photograph is in the Gurney Archive (G.5.10.18) which is dated May 1917 Rouen in Gurney's hand. The photograph is reproduced on the dust-jacket of *SASAWE*.

199 *To Marion Scott*   G.41.91

11 May 1917 (P)

My Dear Friend   Wed:

Today there is nothing to do, save to laze or wash clothes, to enjoy the blue of the sky and regret the waste of precious time. Still the weather keeps fine though it rains occasionally, and yesterday morning was bedraggled and cold. I hope you are having this length of sunny days as well, and are getting good out of it. Perhaps already you are looking forward to more violin playing and hearing of music, or to writing your book or wielding the rod of power as President. Alas, most of the world is now engaged in doing things it doesn't like. Small specks of discontent in the huge whole, but rightly discontented and not to be appeased but by the turning of things top-side uppermost again.

I have read the *Hour Glass*[1], which is good, but far, far too sudden for me – like Masefield's *Tragedy of Nan* with its bloodstained pudden-knife. Also in the library here *Cynthia's War* by Mrs Sidgwick, a light novel which pleased me, save for a picture of Germany which hurt; the heroine marries a decent German, so depriving the Fatherland of its last chance.

By the way, are the Russians in a state to make a strong offensive? And if so, when will they be ready?[2]

Last night we were talking after lights-out, chiefly about the merits of town and Country life, as exemplified by Liverpool and Bourton-on-the-Hill, hotly discussed by a clerk and a keeper, both convinced. I like these arguments and usually start them. Someday I also must live in a little grey stone Cotswold house, with one largish room for the music room; with a garden to flame in summer against the cool greys and greens of house and trees and hedges, and there invite my friends to tell me of the great world and what goes on there between the mansions and the slums. O for a garden to dig in, and music and books in a house of one's own, set in a little valley from whose ridges one may see Malverns and the Welsh Hills, the plain of Severn and Severn Sea; to know oneself free there from the drill-sergeant and the pack, and to order one's life years ahead – plans, doubtless to be broken, but sweet secure plans taking no account of fear or even Prudence but only Joy. One could grow whole and happy there, the mind would lose its sickness and grow strong; it is not possible that health should wait long from such steady and gently beautiful ways of life. The winter's hardships should steel one, the spring bring Joy,

254

Summer should perfect this Joy, and Autumn bring increase and mellowness to all things, set the seal of age and ease on things not before secure. I grow happy writing of it - in a life where one keeps healthy not through Joy, but by simulating motions which Joy might bring; quick walking for fear of the drill sergeant, or, better but only by a little, for the sake of Conduct, an arid outlook and thankless motive for doing things well.

I *may* be here another week still. Directly I send a PC you will know I have flitted; anyway after next Monday it would be safe for you to write to the Batt:

With best wishes.

Your sincere friend
Ivor Gurney

[1] Yeats' play.
[2] The Russians, in the midst of revolution, were unable to mount an offensive until July.

200 To Winifred Chapman   G.45750

13 May 1917 (KT)

My Dear Winnie

I hope you have received the cards I sent a few days ago, and like them. Also that you poor creatures are not absolutely starving in poor old Blighty. They will soon prohibit the sending of cakes out here, and about time if all tales are true; you must be a nest of walking skeletons.

Are you all pretty well, now? The weather is certainly not cold, anyway, and you can get out. Do you play games ever? How is the Comtesse, worker of miracles out of oatmeal and plain flour? and Daddy with his weight of natural cares? How is Arthur doing at cricket? As for Mick, I never could believe her sick till the mourning cards were issued, and she is probably as naughty (and nice) as ever.

They are chucking us out at any time now – Hup the line: Hover the Top and the best of luck. Tuesday must see us off I think, so please write to the Batt: in future. The next wound I have will bring me more luck, or else I shall have cutting remarks to make to the Lord Almighty. How are the Christ Church people – His special delegates and assistants. And how is the Pet Lootenant[1] doing in France?

I have lost your mascot that you put in my overcoat. It had stayed there carefully cherished until Good Friday Night when we went over, and since then – well I shall be lucky if I see ever a thing again.

What must the High Wycombe hills look like now! Great clouds of miraculous green, green that looks alive and gifted with a voice.

Here endeth the last letter from the Base.

Yours affectionately
Ivor

[1] Lt. Wildsmyth

13 May 1917 (P)

My Dear Friend

Your letter of 4th May has turned up (this is a Friday) and thank you very much for it. I am so glad you are getting better now, and are less decorated; and that the Spring has come on you with such a rush: there is a perfectly beautiful orchard not a hundred yards from here, where a nightingale sings in the soft aired darkness.

As for the Pomes – cuss 'em.

Today I have been vainly trying to wreak some more on an unsuspecting public, but it was no go.

I think 'Strange Service' would be a good title; as for omissions and order do what you please.

As for Robert Bridges – it is obvious to me that he is one of the two poets of standing who would like the book least, William Watson being the other. One might as well submit Brahms early works to Cherubini. Of course the technique is rough, but the book is sincere and interesting and original. I never claimed more, though one or two things ('Purple and Black', for instance) may live.

Miss Dorothy Dawe and Herbert Norman Howells ought to be very happy together,[1] since both are generous people and fond of natural things and simplicity. I give the whole affair my approval, even though they have in no way consulted me on the matter. H.N.H. shall have a letter, which I hope will bore him as little as his bore myself.

Poor old Sydney. I do hope the Shimmin Civil War will soon cease. Bless his simple heart, he deserves good luck. I have just turned aside to number the things, chiefly by size. If you care to alter anything, please do so.

I do hope biscuits will hold out for your sake, and wish I could send you Army biscuits, some of which are excellent. (But shall we get them in the line?)

The date of our departure is probably Tuesday, by the way.

Well, here's some sort of arrangement of my verses, chiefly set as to size. I think it will do but don't care a cuss. There may be one or two more things, but please don't wait for them. Get it into print as soon as possible.

It is not in me to write decent letter, being too distracted by that confounded orchard, and perhaps by the heat. A soft day today, and all wasted. I intend to waste few days when – the time comes. With best wishes

Your sincere friend

Ivor Gurney

[There follows a list of poems in Marion Scott's hand with numbers in circles written before them by Gurney.]

List of Poems

- (1) To Certain Comrades
- (4) To the Poet before Battle (Sonnet)
- (6) Afterwards (Sonnet)
- (7) Carol
- (12) To England – A Note (Sonnet)
- (8) Strange Service
- (9) Serenity
       [Robecq *deleted*]
- (2) The Fire Kindled
- (3) Sawgint
- (14) The Colonel
- (5) Maisemore
       [Song: 'Ah! tell me not the spirits of the trees' *deleted*]
       ⎧ Requiem: 'Pour out your light, O stars'
       ⎨ Requiem: 'Nor grief nor tears'
       ⎩ Requiem: 'Pour out your bounty'
- (15) Acquiescence (Sonnet)
- (10) The Signaller's Vision
- (13) Bach and the Sentry
- (11) The Mother
- (18) To an Unknown Lady – (Sonnet)
- (16) The Strong Thing
- (17) Scots
- (20) Purple and Black
- (19) Song and Pain
- (27) Communion
- (25) Song 'Only the wanderer'
- (21) West Country
- (22) The Dawn
- (24) The Estaminet
- (28) Time and the Soldier
- (29) Influences
       [Poor Folk *deleted*]
- (23) Firelight
- (31) Hail and Farewell
- (30) After-Glow (Sonnet) To F.W.H.
- (33) Beauty
       [February Day *deleted*]
- (26) Ballad of the Three Spectres

257

(32) Praise
(34) Song of Pain and Beauty
(35) June-to-Come. To F.W.H.
(36) Hark, Hark the Lark. To F.W.H.
(37) Trees
Sonnets 1917.
(38-41) For England, Pain, Servitude, Homesickness.[2]

[1] They did indeed marry.
[2] This is essentially the shape of *Severn & Somme.* Apart from those deleted above, 'Sawgint', 'The Colonel', and 'The Dawn' were omitted from the final volume; 'Beauty' was renamed 'Winter Beauty'; and Gurney added 'Letters', 'Strafe','Spring. Rouen, May 1917', 'Song at Morning' and the final sonnet 'England the Mother'.

202 To Marion Scott   G.41.93

18? May 1917 (P)

My Dear Friend
Your letters of May 8 and March 29th have arrived today, so I will rove at random through them. Well, you shall have the dedication of 'By a Bierside' whether I have already given it or not. (Have I not the precedent of Beethoven's C# minor Sonata? And dammy shall I be outdone by a – no, I won't say that; he was partly Dutch.)[1]
I am glad London is so beautiful in this late but passionate spring; what must my country be like!
For Kipling's new book – All I know is 'Regulus' which interested me enormously, and of which I have already spoken. The poem is not bad; its use of words is lacking in the last touch of poetry, but it is good stuff for all that. Masefield is decidedly deteriorating. Like me, he lacks concentrated thoughts; also – how often does he make a good line? Still I saw a quotation in a review which was good.
            'Is all this lust
    A chymic means by warring stars contriven
    To bring the violet out of Caesar's dust?'
Do as you please about my verses always.
    End of Preface
All the verses ......two or three earlier pieces. This should be reason enough to excuse the roughness of the technique, and if more reason is required by the Critical Master of Words (who is rightly angry at clumsiness and botched work,) or the Arty Quibbler, (may he be poleaxed!) I would say, that it is my Royal Pleasure that it should remain rough – this book; with all its imperfections on its head. Say, O Quibbler, could You write with an empty belly and various internal disturbances? Not You; your exquisitely chiselled phrases need a velvet jacket and a crowd of imbeciles to bring them forth. Just

258

go to Ablaincourt next November and have a look at it. (Don't forget your pack.) You people of home, and, most of all, you people of Gloucester, may well be indulgent etc.

And then at the end

And if you *won't* be indulgent – why, dammy, I can do without you! I shall survive, though not as a poet perhaps.

'Hark Hark the Lark'

Put a hyphen between blue days, if you like.

Trees

> Where Coopers stands by Cranham,
> Where the hill-gashes white
> Show golden in the sunshine,
> Our sunshine – God's delight.[2]

You flatter me with the permission to smoke a pipe in the Music Room. After over-smoking for so long you will find it difficult to stop me – if I can afford it. God's pity on the poor! Baccy, once 5d, now 10d!

Well – tomorrow – off we go. To what? Well, I think I shall come through alright in the end, but first, a pretty severe and painful wound. I do not set up to be soothsayer, but the night before my last public appearance as an active soldier, I said to a friend of mine, 'I think – and do not know why – this is to finish me for a time; how or how long I do not know; but it seems to me that God had decided my limit has been pretty well reached, and I am to have a rest. I don't feel I shall see Blighty, but simply that I am to be out of it for a bit'. And this seemed almost certain to me; though when we went up in that sleet over the ploughed field, I did not care very much what happened.

Now, however, having omitted no opportunity of 'feeding my face', I am stronger and ready though not anxious to try again. And here goes. This is the only premonition I ever have had, not being a fanciful creature – in that way, at all events.

There may be two new things in my next letter.

Anyway, please prosper and let me know of it. Letters in the line are worth much fine gold. As for writing back, I don't know what chances are now, but still have three green envelopes left, so sometimes you shall hear from me.

O Curse the war, it is No Bon, and War in Spring is bad taste of the vilest description and radically damnable.

With best wishes

Your sincere friend
Ivor Gurney

[1] Beethoven's father was Dutch. The Sonata in question (Opus 27, number 2, the 'Moonlight') is dedicated to the 'Damigella Contessa Giuletta Guicciardi'. Opus 27, number 1 has a different dedicatee.

[2] Gurney has revised the last line from 'But ghastly at night'.

18? May 1917 (KT)[1]

My Dear Howler

So you've been and done it![2] Shall I congratulate you? I don't know, since before me there seems to lie two fat biographies, both of Herbert Howells.

The first opens at a passage

'At this time the composer's powers, already great, were doubled by the most fortunate act of his life: the engagement to and subsequent marriage to Miss Dorothy Dawe, a singer of miraculous endowments. From this time onwards his record is one blaze of great works and huge accomplishments. The first 14 symphonies, the great (Sanscrit) Te Deum, for the opening of the new lavatory in the Dead Language Section of the British Museum; the noble setting of the genealogies in the Old Testament; of the great Bradshaw Opera, the epic of railway life; and the whole of his masterpieces up to Op 462 which begins his Middle Period, was inspired by the remarkable lady whose exquisitely chiselled nose rendered beautiful sounds which otherwise would have been painful; for she preferred to sing through this organ only. etc etc

And

We must here, with regret, but extenuating nothing as is our business as honest chroniclers, set down the record of the sad fact that blighted this great life; that drove a despairing man to the false comfort of spirituous liquor, and that of becoming a Plymouth Brother; bleared his eyes and upset his digestion; and in a word set his feet on the dark path that was to lead him to spiritual damnation as Harmonium Professor at the Royal College of Music. He became entangled in the fatal web of fascination spread by an unknown contralto of doubtful attainments and tone quality.

O there's more of it, but I'm off up the Line tonight, and can't bother.

Still, O the best of luck to my bonny Herbert and Dorothy, Dorothy and Herbert. May you be blessed as you deserve, may you arrive at all felicity. And may I arrive soon and share it.

Carnegie ought to give you a Free Library for this.

But why don't you write to me? Your letters are as light in the darkness or as a third of a loaf instead of a quarter, up the line. And you must have other news.

And look here; I have totally forgotten whether I dedicated 'By a Bierside' to you. If so, it is hereby reft away from you and given to Miss Scott. If I had given it you, old man, please don't mind; Miss S: seems glad to have it and you can write your own masterpieces dedicated to yourself. And she has been as good as gold about everything. And if you are angry, write to say so; you won't get anything out of it but to give me pleasure by your letter – up the line, where there is little pleasure. How is the amiable Benjamin? O God, what would a reunion mean, down in that basement tea room! What would it mean to talk about things that interest me once again, and to talk freely?

They have given me a new number and badge of servitude -
241281
I hope all goes smoothly and not too busily at Salisbury, whose close must
be a wonder most high at present. Best wishes to both of you.

Yours ever
Ivor Gurney

[1] Although the envelope is postmarked 30 May 17, this is the redirection from Salisbury,
and the content of the letter dates it earlier.
[2] Gurney mentions Howells' engagement in letter 201.

204 To Marion Scott   G.41.94

18 May 1917 (G)

My Dear Friend[1]   May 18

The Observer has just come, and J.W.G's remarks on the probable length of
the war (almost exactly true) seem to lead me on to write a letter – to have a
good moan in sympathetic company. It is the bloomingest nuisance that a
thing so well intended as the Russian Revolution can so upset things.

I hope you are getting properly well now, and have had a look at the pink
and white world outside London – that you are beginning to enjoy yourself, in
short.

As for me, I am back with the Batt: alright, but the Batt: is back also,
practising attacks. (Today I was twice a 'casualty' ... Is there anything in it?)
So there is no need for anybody to worry just yet; as the present is taken up by
the process of Feeding you up, preliminary to serious business. (This process is
no way related to excess of food.)

I am glad that my song had not been dedicated; it should have become yours
anyway. Also that you are pleased with the little photograph. I may as well
tell you that the expression is not intended for determination but for
carelessness, instead of the ordinary grim desperation.

Outside here men are cleaning up their equipment for sheer want of
something to do – a dreadful state of mind, only possible in the Army.

By the way, how is that young boy violinist and composer of whom Sir
Charles and Herbert thought so highly? Noone has mentioned him to me.
Where is that Welsh girl who sang my Elizas once? I ask after her because of
the kindness I bear to the Welsh by reason of Herbert, the 13th
R.W.Fusiliers, Borrow's *Wild Wales* and, also, herself, whom I liked. And of
course Mrs Harvey is Welsh.

If the Bosches hit an arm off me I will get the largest pension I can and go
tramping the country, sleeping rough or with strange and wonderful tales
attracting hospitality. And the first walk I shall take shall be Dymock,
Newent, Ross and into Wales, to end at Chepstow after meeting names met

in Malory; names known it would seem a thousand years ago in some forgotten life stronger in charm than their realities of houses and trees, almost. These journeys must be made alone for the greater part, for friends are often busy, and who will hire an actor to make up as one's friend, to act the part, to have learnt 'the probable range of subjects', and to 'quarrel by the book'? No, they must be solitary for the most part, but only the fool is sorry for that when nothing but his foolishness prevents him finding friends at each resting place, and, if the wind is moving, between them? The modern composer must be a church organist and exalt forms and ceremonies all his days, not for bread (for that would be some excuse) but to wear a boiled shirt, and not to disappoint snobs. Looking at this blossom, it seems to me his choice is not a poetic one; for though tramps have been called lousy, the use of the term implies that there are some free, but who is free, of Britain's army? (The Navy is alright, I suppose.) Who will deliver us from the body of this death?[2]

You may like to know that in that mausoleum in which we slept two months ago, there was concealed – something which has sent the whole shute to glory. Good thing it had been set for a long time.

Best wishes

Your sincere friend
Ivor Gurney

---

[1] Included with this letter is a cutting from a newspaper of a poem called 'A Litany of Life' by S.H. It is a fairly empty rhetorical poem of four 4-line stanzas, but its picture of life as a 'dream of Life upon the bed of Pain' may have had some influence on 'Spring 1917 Rouen'.
[2] Romans vii. 24.

205 *To Marion Scott*   G.41.95

24 May 1917 (G)

My Dear Friend   May 24
    There is some more of this; would you like to have it? At any rate it will fill up. We are travelling still, and insteps are a thing of the past and 'our calves will develop terrific'.
    I hope you are still getting on to health.

Your sincere friend
Ivor Gurney

Spring 1917 Rouen

I am dumb, I am dumb!
And here's a Norman orchard and here's Spring
Goading the sullen words that will not come.

Romance, beating his distant magical drum,
Calls to a soldier bearing alien arms,
'Throw off your yoke and hear my darlings sing,
Blackbirds' (by red-roofed farms)
'More drunk than any poet with May's delight,
Green alive to the eye, and pink and white.'

Joy's there, but not for me;
And Song, but shall I sing
That live as in a dream of some bad night,
Whose memories are of such ecstasy
And height of passionate joy, that Pain alone
Is born of beauty in cloud and flower and Tree;
Yes, and the great Cathedral's towering stone.

To me these are but shadows
Of orchards and old meadows
Trodden before the dawn
Trodden after the dusk ...
All loveliness of France is as a husk;
The inner living spirit of Beauty gone;
To that familiar beauty now withdrawn
From exiles hungering ever for the sight
Of her day-face,
England's;
Or in some orchard space
Breathless to drink peace from her calm night.

How shall I sing, since she sings not to me
Songs any more?
High rule she holds for ever on the sea
That's her's, but dreams too might guard the shore
Of France, that's French and set apart for ever.
A Spirit of Love our link of song does sever.
Had it been hate
(The weakest of all sworn enemies of Love)
We should have broken through or passed above
Its foolish barriers;
Here we must bow as to established Fate,
And reverently; for, comrades and high peers,
Sisters in blood,
Our Mothers brook no rival in their state
Of Motherhood.

But not for ever shall our travail last,
And not for ever we
Be held by iron Duty over sea.
The image of evil shall be overcast,
And all his willing slaves and priests of evil
Scattered like dust shall lie upon the plain,
That image ground to dust, utterly level
With unregarded weeds and all as vain.

The oppressed shall lift their hearts up once again,
And we return ...
Not to scarred lands and homes laid in the dust,
Not with hearts hard to sights that sear and burn,
But with assured longing and certain trust,
To England's royal grace and dignity,
To England's changing skies, rich greenery,
High strength controlled, queenly serenity,
Inviolate kept by her confederate sea,
And hearts resolved to every sacrifice.

We shall come home,
We shall come home again,

[*The next page is headed* 'Continuation of Spring Rouen May 1917' *and transcribes the last eleven lines above before continuing:*]

Living and dead, one huge victorious host -
The dead that would not leave their comrades till
The last steep were topped of the difficult hill,
The last farthing paid of the Great Cost,
The last thrill suffered of the Great Pain.
Living and dead we shall come home at last
To her sweet breast,
England's; by one touch be paid in full
For all things gray and long and terrible
Of that dread night which seemed eternity.

O Mother shall Thy kisses not restore
Body and lifesick soul? Yes, and set free
Songs and great floods of lovelier melody
Than Thou didst give
When we those days of half-awake did live.
And Joy must surely flower again more fair
To us, who dwelt in shadows and foul air.
We'll breathe and drink in Song.

Spring shall blot out all traces of old care,
Her clouds of green and waves of gold among
We shall grow free of heart and great and young -
Be made anew in that Great Resurrection,
Perfect as is the violet's perfection,
Perfect as she
Who sanctifies our memory with sorrow,
Hugs, as a mother hugs, the thoughts that harrow,
Watching for dawn, hungering for the morrow
Lone oversea...

I am dumb now, dumb,
But in that time what music will not come?
Mother of Beauty, Mistress of the Sea.

06 *To Marion Scott*   G.41.96

29 May 1917 (P)

My Dear Friend

It is a lovely day, and there is no parade for us, we having been inoculated last night. And O, the sense of wasted days and Beauty! It is senile decay I have much more than typhoid, but there is nothing but hard work given for this.

I hope you are having the same weather and getting better now with a full biscuit supply, and thoughts turning ever stronger to work.

Yes, place 'Sawgent' and the 'Colonel' side by side if you wish. Include the Requiems if you want to. Do what you will with the 'Fire Kindled'. Put the extract in before 'Trees'. And do as you suggest about the last 1917 Sonnet. Do as you please, simply that.

Have I written about the bad news of H.N.H.? It gave me quite a shock, although, if there is too much work attached to the Salisbury post, he had better leave. Will he grow out of these troubles?[1] Meanwhile he must act as Razor to Uncongenial Grindstones, razors stropped on Red Tape. I hope poor old Shimmin is out of it now; when this is finished I will write to him.

I believe you are wrong about Masefield's Sonnets. They are lacking in continued music and halt every now and then in a fashion strongly reminding me of my own defects.

Number V is good.[2]

'His youth is April and his manhood bread' I like.

But as a general thing they show the strivings of an amateur to do perfected work. He must go to sea again and not write till he must write. His inspiration is now literary whereas before it was Life.

There is a big mail to come today; may it bring a letter from you, for not even this continual staleness can dull my pleasure in your letters.

Well, here is a song – the words of which you know well enough. I think it is all right now, and will go with the other two songs very well. This kind of thing is all I can do at present – things without technique and not much thought – mere wordsetting; and that is always easy to me. You may say what you like of it and not disturb me, save of the first three lines, which are as a glove to the words.[3]

Marcel Hutin in yesterday's *Echo de Paris* wrote that he had information which increased his confidence in a near and general offensive by the Russians.

Will this do?

England the Mother

We have done our utmost England, terrible
And dear taskmistress, darling Mother and stern.
The unnoticed nations praise us, but we turn
Firstly, only to Thee – 'Have we done well?
Say, are you pleased?' And watch your eyes that tell
To us all secrets, eyes sea deep that burn
With love so long denied; with tears discern
The scars and haggard look of all that Hell.

Thy Love, Thy Love shall cherish, make us whole,
Where to the power of Death's destruction is weak,
Death impotent by boys bemocked at, who
Will leave unblotted in the soldier-soul
Gold of the daffodil, the sunset streak,
The innocence and joy of England's blue.[4]

---

[1] See next letter.
[2] The sonnets in *Lollingdon Downs* (1917). Gurney quotes from number VII.
[3] There is no song with this letter but he is probably referring to a setting of Sir Walter Raleigh's 'Even such is time', two manuscripts of which have the date 1917 on them. See also letter 212.
[4] There is no signature on this letter.

---

207 To Herbert Howells   G.3.31

29 May 1917 (P)

My Dear Howler

I am more sorry than I can say to hear that you have had to leave Salisbury. Such a job in such a place! And then, with a troublesome heart, to be called up for clerical service, this is hard lines; especially when you might be doing your own work, so much more profitable for England.

What a spavined broken winded crowd the Soldier Poets of Erskine
MacDonald are! Not much to set there! Pious aspirations to verse for the most
part.

Well, here are letters to be collected.

Yours ever

Ivor Gurney

---

208 To Sydney Shimmin   G.76.14

29 May 1917 (KT)

My Dear Sydney

I was glad to hear from you, but sorry the second operation was not over;
surely by this time the thing is past? You have had shocking bad luck for years
and years, and the time is come when your luck should change.

I liked your tune very much; charming and fresh – but the last bar seems out
of place; a little too ornamental for the rest, I think.

Your kind sister sent in response to a passionate appeal a brilliant number of
Punch. 'The Mudlarks' particularly attracted me. *Punch* is better than ever it
was.

Poor old Howells has got into it now. Dam foolishness, but what does one
expect from the Army? Wherein is neither Justice nor Sense but only Carrying
On.

We are in a lovely village, and today – O most rare Joy – have had nothing
to do. That is, 'nothing' in an Army sense. And only the tattered remains of
the *Hundred Best Poems* and *The Shropshire Lad*; both too well known. I think
Browning is the best War Poet; since there are so many tales in his work, and
so many characters. You have offered to send me something; setting aside
where you are to get the money – being in Hospital – I should very much like
the Second *Hundred B Ps*, and *Modern Lyrical Masterpieces*, both from Gowans
and Gray, both 6d. These would give me great pleasure. And profit, but that
doesn't matter.

Cheero. Bellies will not always be troubles.

Yours ever

I.B.G.

Again I have lost – that is I do not well remember your address.

4 June 1917 (P)

My Dear Friend

Fritz's aeroplanes are ever so high above us, and shrapnel is bursting round them; shrapnel which never seems to fall anywhere. This is an old and stale game to us, would there were here in our place men who would be interested in such things. The weather is still almost cloudless and may is on the hedges, foam on green bosomy waves.

The post today may bring a letter from you, which I will wait for before inquiring after your health.

The title 'Severn and Somme' might sell the book a little better. It sounds like a John Bull poster, but otherwise there is nothing objectionable about it. Severn people might buy it if Somme people don't; my French not being equal to translation of works as delicate of language. At present my desire is to get the thing off my chest, and my chest out of Khaki.

(Please excuse dirt.)

Your letter of April 2nd has arrived. There is nothing that requires an answer or a reference I think. Thank you for it all the same for its interest.

We are going out for an all night and next day stunt, Heaven pity us! Still we expected it – on Rest.

Mrs Harvey has not heard from F.W.H. since late February, but his book has arrived.[1] How we would have argued about that book – what discussions strolling about Hygrove by the pines and in the Orchards! Curse it, there's 'nothing left remarkable beneath the visiting moon'[2] for me, save a hot time to come. I could do him a lot of good now, since I have learnt by writing. (Have you received the Yeats book yet? I did not send it myself, but left it with another.)

Next Day.

They say Fritz has retreated again, and if this is so, more marching, more road making, short rations again. May General Russky be right about victory coming by Autumn.

The Cossacks is a fine book; too small to be a great one – but accurate and life like. One can't help thinking that such a life is going on there, while in the Victorian books one is continually reminded of the fact that 'this is not Life but only a description'. And by such gentlemanly people too!

I will take a huge dose of Russian stuff apres le guerre. Some of the short stories of the lesser known writers are extremely interesting. How often, I wonder, did Thackeray really look at life? He shows at his best in the *Book of Snobs* and *Travels and Sketches* (is it?)[3] – things related more to books and form than actuality. In fact he was an artist at one remove from things; the opposite of W.H.Davies in *The Autobiography of a Supertramp*, that most fascinating of records. Brahms music at its not-best shows the same thing also – the mind of a man as satisfied in his study as in the open air. There are not many things that make worthy art. They are, Nature, Homelife (with which is mixed up

Firelight in Winter, joy of companionship etc.) The intangible Hope (which means all music only can hope to express), Thoughts on Death and Fate. And there are no more. It is right, as R.L.S. wrote, for a young man consciously and of purpose to regard his attempts as Art only, but this is a half stage, and should soon end; if the young man has anything to say.

End of the Treatise.

Your sincere friend
Ivor Gurney

[1] Harvey's *Gloucestershire Friends* was published by Sidgwick and Jackson in 1917.
[2] *Antony and Cleopatra*, IV.13.67.
[3] Thackeray's *Book of Snobs* (1847 as *The Snobs of England*) and *Sketches and Travels in London*.

10 *To Marion Scott* G.41.99

6 June 1917 (G)

My Dear Friend Sent a week after June 6
Your letter of the 25th has just reached me.

A letter to you has just been posted but still I write. You, of all my friends, write the most interesting letters; and, a most unusual thing, there is always something in them to comment on or reply to. A thing of strange and enormous significance.

You seem to be getting better, which is a meet right and sensible thing to do. Please continue.

So I have a new service to thank you for – the preparation of the book for printing. I had clean forgotten there was anything more to do.

It interests me to hear about people's preferences in (yes!) *Severn and Somme.* The prophet must always be annoyed when a friend tells him how much better slippers and a churchwarden become him than the splendid mantle, and so, your sister's liking for the 'Estaminet' does not please me. I see Siegfried Sassoon has published now. Do try to see it, and if you can do so, spot a poem on the subject of a man unconscious from the time of his being wounded till he was in train in Blighty; then recognising what part of the scheme of things he saw by the advertisements. It is very good; and came out in the *Sat: Westminster*.[1] I see Osborne calls him a great poet.

My second premonition is not vivid – probably only a pious opinion, a hint of the price I am willing to pay.

Russia still seems to strengthen. Perhaps the first successes of her offensive are needed to complete the cure. And Italian news is great news.

I am glad you like the photograph; your liking it may embolden me to send it to others also. I had twelve; one you have, 5 have got spoilt in my pocket and have been dumped, the rest I still have myself, till such time as the spirit moves me or carelessness to send them off.

Your description of Frederick Bridge's[2] organ playing amused me very much. Would I were back under the old boy! He was my counterpoint master, and it is my chief excuse for weakness therein.

O to be back cracking my head over Orchestration and Fugue and the Mass, the Mass! I foresee a quarrel even at this distance about that last, which must be got through. Shall I ever be able to outmanoeuvre Sir Charles? For argument does not long continue to be polite in the Army. Well, well, civilisation may yet touch me to gentle speech.

The time of the scarcity of letters is near at hand, I think; which is also that where most information and material is found.

Will people continue to write letters when Peace comes? Or retire and take a well earned rest behind huge fortifications of PCs after the Field Postcard fashion?

Peace

I'll write no letters in that happy season
When Peace illumes the world like the Sun's Lamp.
Laziness will be in part the reason.
But – shall *I* pay a penny for a stamp?[3]

No, no, it cannot be! And if some female
Is soft enough of head to lose her heart
To Me, she'll have to settle as to the Mail,
And pay for both. I'm damned if *I* shall start!

Your sincere friend
Ivor Gurney

---

[1] Sassoon's *The Old Huntsman* was noticed in the *T.L.S.* on 24 May 1917, p.251 and reviewed on p.259.

[2] Sir John Frederick Bridge (1844-1924), organist of Westminster Abbey and Professor of Music at the R.C.M. and University of London among his other energetic activities.

[3] On Gurney's letters from France he would write 'On Active Service' across the top left hand corner of the envelope and they would be sent free.

211 To Marion Scott   G.41.98

8 June 1917 (G)   [*On paper headed* 'Y.M.C.A. On Active Service
                        WITH THE BRITISH EXPEDITIONARY FORCE']

My Dear Friend

We have been in the line, or thereabouts, for over a week and this is my first chance to write; unfortunately for material, no letter has arrived during that time in the clear firm handwriting I have learned to associate with you. The letter I sent off yesterday had been written many days ago.

Being in the line does not conduce to letter writing, as Fritz strafes all day in a monotonous, tiring, stolid, pedantic manner – most annoying to the Sensitive Soul.

I hope this gap of a week in our Historic Correspondence does not mean you are sick again. This would be too hard lines; especially now, just as the food stocks are improving and men are chortling over the submarine returns.[1] And the weather has been so lovely it seems to give you no excuse for misbehaviour in this way. Also, on average, it is past your time of expectation for luck.

Miss Saumerez Smith has written me a very interesting letter – which means that it flatters me – and when we get out of the line I will see to it that her good intentions go not unrewarded – if even by only a Field Postcard.

Well, then; let the book's name be 'Severn and Somme'. Please cut out 'The Colonel', and please alter (in 'Westcountry') 'no-shadowed' to 'no-shadow', which is far better. Publish as soon as possible. Mr Dunhill is very kind about the whole thing, and deserves mention in despatches.

Let me say, while on subjects literary, how charming I think your phrase is: 'the golden-green illumination of young leaves'; for that is seen and felt.

I heard from Shimmin, poor chap, who sent a tune he had come on in the night watches. To have three relapses into flu is no good fate, and appendicitis is no longer fashionable. Please the Fates he may soon be through with it – but not in time to come out here.

Can we ever be cast together again, we miscellaneous crowd of sick musicians? And only I, of all the bunch with stories to tell; if I care to tell 'em.

It is time to stop perhaps, as all the paper I have is three sheets of this kind brought from Rouen. They say there is a mail in however, and if this is true there may be some word from you to me.

With best wishes

Your sincere friend
Ivor Gurney

Letter 2 June 8 [*in same envelope*]

I am glad you like the new things. The song wants brushing up, but nothing more. As to the Sonnet; yes, there should be a comma after 'utmost', and one after 'impotent'. I think you will get used to 'among' in the other poem.[2]

As for the 'Preface', I think you are right to leave out anything that may offend Robert Bridges. I had not thought how that sentence might affect him. As to the stay-at-home poets taking anything as a gibe – I only wish that Fate would make me one!

It is good news that you are getting better; may this continue. but may your father and Audrey be soon flourishing again. Why cannot I have laryngitis instead? It would be useful to me.

271

Goodbye, for they are collecting letters.

Your sincere friend
Ivor Gurney[3]

---

[1] The increase in food imports was a direct consequence of the convoying system, introduced on 30 April, which drastically reduced loss to U-Boats.

[2] In 'Spring. Rouen, May 1917'. Gurney obviously liked the construction since he used it again in 'The Incense Bearers'.

[3] The letter also contains a cutting from the *Westminster Gazette* of 2 June 1917 with a story by Caradoc Evans, 'A Widow Woman in Sion'.

212 To Marion Scott   G.41.101

11 June 1917 (G)

My Dear Friend

Out of the line once more, but for once, not hungry, for the Lord and the A.S.C. have been kind to us, and liberal gentlemen have bestowed cake upon me.

I have heard from Mrs Voynich, who tells me you are not able to walk as yet. This is hard lines my esteemed correspondent, but you have courage enough to win through I feel sure.

How are Mr Scott and Audrey? H.N.H. wrote me a long letter, and interesting. He says that the end of the Raleigh song is not so good as the beginning. This is true, but I do not agree that it needs rewriting. Though the details are hardly considered there – that being only a sketch I have sent you. If he decides to orchestrate it, he may do as he pleases, use a free hand. In my head is 'On Wenlock Edge' waiting to be written, and the details of that will be far more difficult.

Yes, the College Mag: and the *T.L.S.*s have arrived. I am sorry I forgot to thank you. If there are any complimentary copies please send them to Mrs Chapman and Miss Hunt.

It is good news you are going to Sevenoaks, where there is clean air untainted with petrol, and where an invalid has reason to get strong (Your letter of June 7th has gone to the making of this, I should have said.)

Today there are orgies of cleaning, and men brush and polish frantically at brass and leather. The weather is beautiful, and there is plenty of water to wash with, so we are not unhappy. Also there is plenty to eat. And in estaminets plenty to drink, but ah – Les pauvres Anglais; one charges half a franc a small glass for vin rouge, 3d a glass for doubtful beer in small measure, and so on. Matches are scarce now, but I have been lucky, and the men who smoke cigarettes only are in a bad way. French biscuits are very inferior things; there cannot be much flour of wheat in them.

Rondels. (is it?)

(1) *Letters*

'Mail's up'! The vast of night is over,
And love of friends fills all one's mind
(His wife, his sister, or his lover.)
Mail's up, the vast of night is over,
The grey-faced heaven Joy does cover[1]
With love, and God once more seems kind.
'Mail's up'! the vast of night is over,
And love of friends fills all one's mind.

(2) *Shortage*

Good God! No Jam! No Bread!! No Butter!!!
Whatever are we coming to?
O desolation, anguish utter -
Good God! No jam, no bread, no butter.
I hear the brutal soldiers mutter,
And strong men weep as children do.
Good God! No jam, no bread, no butter!
Whatever are we coming to?

(3) *Paean*

There's half a loaf per man today?
O Sergeant, is it really true?
Now biscuits can be given away,
There's half a loaf per man today;
And Peace is ever so near they say,
With tons of grub and nothing to do.
There's Half a Loaf Per Man today!
O Sergeant, is it Really True?

(4) *Strafe* 1

I strafe my shirt most regularly,
And frighten all the population.
Wonderful is my strategy!
I strafe my shirt most regularly;
(It sounds like distant musketry.)
And still I itch like red damnation!
I strafe my shirt most regularly
And - frighten all the population ....?

(5) *Strafe* 2

The 'crumps' are falling twenty to the minute.
We crouch, and wait the end of it, – or us.
Just behind the trench, before, and in it,
The 'crumps' are falling twenty to the minute;
(O Framilode! O Maisemore's laughing linnet!)
Here comes a monster like a motor bus.
The 'crumps' are falling twenty to the minute;
We crouch and wait the end of it – or us.

I wonder if the proofs are with Sidgwick and Jackson yet. That will interest me, and also (when the time comes) to know what Gloucester people think. Last night I read some to a friend of mine, and was surprised to find how little I cared for them, and how remote they seemed. As for Spring 1917, it is as I thought long dull, and unvaried.

    Later
This letter had better go now, as it has waited long enough.
    There is a chance of my getting a transfer to the M.G.C., which is plus bon, and does not involve sticking people.
    With best wishes

Yours sincerely
Ivor Gurney

[1] I have transposed lines 3 and 5 in accordance with a note at the top of the page.

213 *To Marion Scott*   G.41.102

25 June 1917 (G)

My Dear Friend   June 25 or there abouts
    That raid was a pretty terrible, and so I suppose, must bring about reprisals; on Crefeld, say, where F.W.H. now is. A ghastly business, and a true pride to the Prussians.
    Please tell Mr Scott I am sorry to hear of his laryngitis and of my hopes of his soon recovery. Also congratulations on being the centre of the circle – a position which magicians, yes, even those powerful men, found safest in their incantations.
    And if he could or would send me some more baccy .... It is the mere truth that our men find it very difficult to get cigarettes of any kind, and very sincere gratitude would be returned for anything smokable. Cigarettes, that is. For the pipe smoker is more fortunate, usually being able to beg, buy, or steal something.
    I gather from your letter you are able to walk now – as far as Hyde Park and

back that is. Tres bien; it is the prelude to mountain climbing in the future. Sevenoaks ought to do you much good, and, so I hope, Mrs Scott too, distracted with naughty servants and ration schemes.

Thank you for the suggestion as to dedicating something to Mr Dunhill. Whichever you please, then.

We are still out of the line, and now in a charming village, where there are roses, roses; honeysuckle not fifty yards from me, cheaper drinks, orchards, little hills (but not young sheep) and houses tinted white, or pink or pale blue; very charming against the green, the continual leafage of French villages. I think the English papers were never quite so optimistic as at present. Whatever Russia may do. Messines.[1] The Fall of Tisza. The Swiss riots, seem to me very significant. Belloc says the end may be quite near – his word is 'decisive issue', rather.

Thank you for the *Times*; they are good to get, so much to think about is in them, and the world seems full of interesting books just now.

Has the Yeats book arrived? If not, I will write to the proper people about it. It must not be lost without effort. I know, however, that post is very slow sometimes.

It seems to me this sunny evening that it would be most pleasant to come back to England the admired of all admirers (but not the glass of fashion) and secretly enjoying the petting one may anticipate to repel people with sour looks. To hear strings again, strings that can tear the heart out of any mystery. To ramble round second-hand bookstalls begriming one's eager hands, returning with wonderful finds bought chiefly for cheapness' sake. To be a civilian. To watch the changing English sky. To read the *Academy*, the *Nation*, the *English Review*. Ibsen, Tolstoi, Hauptmann, Romain Rolland, Shakespeare, Conrad, Fielding, Cervantes, Galsworthy, Granville Barker, Synge. Kropotkin's *Mutual Aid*. Gretton's *Modern History of the English People* again. Belloc. Stevenson. Scott, E.V.Lucas again. To see gray stone and Cotswold gardens. To be continually drinking tea, and playing Bach of evenings. To be free and interested, in a word.

Well, well; Time may bring all these, and more; since I am more patient and receptive than I was – and less sick. 'I'll do, and I'll do, and I'll do'.[2]

And what have S and J's decided, I wonder. Well, news of that should come soon.

Erskine Macdonald has had quite a burst of publication, did you see?[3]
With best wishes

Your sincere friend
Ivor Gurney

[1] Messines was a preparatory action to the third battle of Ypres.
[2] *Macbeth* I.iii.10.
[3] Erskine MacDonald the publisher.

25/26/27 June 1917 (G)

My Dear Friend   June 25 or 26

Well, I hope Sevenoaks pleases you and suits you, so that you will be trotting about like a four year old before long, and without any particular effort. This is most English country save for the tall trees lining the high roads, a thing not English but universal (as to high roads) in the France we have seen. And always the villages are woody.

We are having not so bad a time, save for the cursed cleaning. A diet of white hot brass buttons in Hell is what I wish those givers of orders, and to sit at table on fiery bayonets.

No news from S and Js. Well, well; it's little that disappoints me now; I have learnt to do without the things I want, if not to bear up against trifling things of annoyance.

The French papers seem to expect a Russian offensive soon.

How is your esteemed family? Mrs Scott with her fatigue, and Mr Scott with laryngitis?

                                                                June 27th

Your letter of June 23rd has arrived, to give the usual pleasure. As usual, I will wade through it from this end to that. I am glad you like 'Song at Morning'; and the only change is 'owl-witted bat-eyed fool' instead of vice versa. As for Sidgwick and Jackson you are hereby once more given leave to do as you please in all those matters; though I should like alterations to be submitted. As for Cap'n Stratton,[1] I shall want some more MS please; and on that might perhaps summon up energy enough to set 'On Wenlock Edge'.

There are thunderstorms all round this evening, and soon it will be necessary to move from this supporting tree and take refuge in the barn, wherein are creeping things innumerable etc etc.

Had I some books, it would not be so dead here, but so much of my belongings were lost at Vermand, when I was wounded – *Wild Wales*, the *Spirit of Man* etc etc, and I saw little at Rouen that struck me. However in response to my frenzied appeals I hope some of my books will be here tout suite.

How is Audrey now? And the nationally-striving Miss Stella?

Tonight I had an engagement to play auction bridge, which is often thrilling, but the Will has decreed that some at least of it is to be spent in washing haversacks and valises, so with the conclusion of this comes that melancholy performance; it seems better to stave it off for another page.

The French papers are protesting against this sort of thing, and well-known men write articles of various kinds which may extort promises not meant to be kept.

Really, this country is most delightful and very English. One could be at home here; one could get peace in these orchards; with a cottage, a piano, books, and friends to come on visits; a garden to dig and be proud of, enough money to go (though modestly) to England and Paris now and then. But these are the old dreams, with the old foundations in middle air.

Did I refer to Mr Dunhill in my last letter? Please dedicate anything you please to him.

With best wishes

Your sincere friend
Ivor Gurney

[1] 'Captain Stratton's Fancy', a setting of a poem by John Masefield, was published by Stainer and Bell in 1920.

---

215 *To Marion Scott* G.41.104

1 July 1917 (G)

My Dear Friend

I am glad you are enjoying yourself among natural things, instead of hoping for health in smoky London, where the air that should be such a joy is petrol laden and dusty. Really, I do not see why you or Mr Scott should be bound strictly by food regulations, having done your best and suffered by it – for conscience' sake. But that is the B.E.F. view of a probable shortage some time or other. Anyway, Devonport's rules must have exceptions.

I have told you about 'Cap'n Stratton's Fancy'.

Thank you for the *T.L.S* s. The article on Tolstoi was very interesting.[1]

It is hard to live a fine life in surroundings like this; not impossible, but nearly so for myself; who need intellectual work to steady me; good solid hard grind all the morning; and a long walk in the afternoon. And then – who can talk with me, as teacher? For I love better to learn than to teach. And since Music and books and my friends are not this life, therefore Life itself lacks the vital impulse and natural joy. One has to ignore so much, that only one capable of magnifying and concentrating on such pleasures as there are is at all comfortable, I do not say happy. It is the same with you too, I suppose; longing to do so much and so cruelly tied, so thwarted.

Tonight I have reached the happy state of being broke – nothing can touch me farther. My desires are automatically lessened in all directions save only that of newspapers. One obtains freedom and a view from on high; chocolate becomes a vanity, unwholesome also and hard to digest. Smoking becomes a real pleasure and rare. Also one reaps the reward of past generosity and may be surprised by a treat at any moment.

Yes, we have Summertime all right, and, if we turned in at the official hour would lose half lights. But we don't.

Tis cold and sunny and July 1st today. I hope all of you will get really well, and soon, in not-so-distant Kent.

Today the guns have been muttering fairly loudly; you also may have heard. Best wishes

Your sincere friend
Ivor Gurney

[1] The front-page article in the *T.L.S.* fo 21 June 1917 was on 'The Young Tolstoi', a review of the first volume of *Diary of Youth*.

216 *To Marion Scott* G.41.108

8 July 1917 (P)

My Dear Friend

It is delightful that you are living so pleasantly, and these surroundings should have a good effect on your perversely behaving body.

This village is still delightful and today the weather is perfect.

Two days ago, I had a dinner of salad and deux pain-beurres. It was perfectly wonderful to have such a dainty meal after aeons of shackles (Englished – skilly: stew.)

Your parcel has arrived, and thank you very much for it. Especially the lemonade powder and the fruit, which are summery things; but do not suppose that the cake, cheese, biscuits and OXO go unappreciated.

I am sorry about Mr Scott, and only hope Lord Rhondda may be able to do something for him, and that a proper holiday may be found possible.

Gloster county is packed full of beautiful things, and pink dogroses of the most delicate miraculousness find place therein. Also wild strawberries by the million; and would I were on Coopers Hill looking over to Malvern and Wales while easing my back at times. O God, that goes too deep though.

We are having really a pretty easy time now, and tí ́ means Over the Top, I think. Well, let come what come may as the Victorian said, I shall have had my day. (And a – poor one at times.)[1]?

Alan Seeger's poems must be interesting. I like 'I have a rendezvous with Death' very much.[2] O Sincerity, what had you to do with Elizabethan prattlings like 'My true love hath my heart' and 'Tell me where is Fancy bred'![3]

I have no change now, but next letter shall contain a 5fr note to be applied to the purchase of Ralph Hodgson's *Poems*, for you. So if you like to order it, the money will arrive in time (Macmillan 3/6). I remember 'facing a difficult hill, with sparkling and delight'. Or would you prefer the *Second Book of Georgian Verse* which (I suddenly remember) contains (I think) that 'Song of

Honour'?[4]

A Frenchwoman told me she never heard French soldiers sing half so much as English. This pleased me, and indeed 7 Platoon has been songful of late. 'Whitewash on the Wall', 'Everybody's Happy in the Old French Trench', and Ragtimes galore ('Charlie Chaplin's Walk' being favourite), 'Rolling Home', 'Old Man Brown he had a little farm'. I hope to play 'em to you soon. Meanwhile

       Vive les Russes!!!
       Et les Ecosses. (Scotts.)

                     Your sincere friend
                     Ivor Gurney

[1] Perhaps a reference to George Borrow, *Lavengro*, ch.92: 'Youth will be served, every dog has his day, and mine has been a fine one'.
[2] 18 lines of this poem are quoted in a *T.L.S.* review of 28 June 1917, p.307.
[3] By Sidney and Shakespeare.
[4] The quotation is from 'The Song of Honour', though *Georgian Poetry 1913-1915* has 'hopeless' for 'difficult' and (though I think this is wrong) 'sparking' for 'sparkling'.

217 To Marion Scott   G.41.105

12 July 1917 (P)

My Dear Friend

Here is the wherewithal for Ralph Hodgson, nay he long delight you. (Or the *2nd Georgian*.)

I hope you are still basking in peace, reading and writing and looking at clouds and flowers. Also that Mr Scott is better, and will not have to trek from his premises, like some unfortunate solicitors.

'Captain Stratton's Fancy' is half written and may be finished tomorrow. Last night I went into the county-town of this district, and O Joy – happened on *Round the Horn before the Mast*,[1] in which I am now revelling. Also on a French book on the English Army, which is chock full of kind things and Beelzebubbish hard words.

Thank you for the *T.L.S.* I am always delighted to get it - that being a meaty paper.

Did I tell you – we had a concert troupe here, and its violinist played a most exquisite minuet, doubtless by Bach. It was too wonderful, and one could hear Bach in the quiet dusk and full night. These things are always part of Minsterworth's charm for me, but even so, the picture of the College Hall golden in the artificial light was very strong in me, and

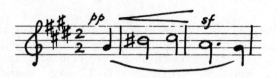

Best wishes

Your sincere friend
Ivor Gurney

[1] He probably means *Two Years Before the Mast* (1840) by Richard Henry Dana (1815-1882).

218 To Marion Scott   G.41.106

15 July 1917 (P)

My Dear Friend

Your letter of July 7th has just arrived.

I am sorry you are sick again, but this will be the final lookback, and a short one, on your journey towards health. And glad that your father was out of the mess in London. (Have any of our fine buildings been hit?)

Is Mr Scott's laryngitis pretty well yet? As to remembering numbers, who has a worse memory than my own? And yet, if one thinks of numbers in the Army way; 24-12-81; it is far easier.

As to Mr Dunhill – Tray bon. Wery well.

I thought you might like to put some names and dates below my verses. (If the Censor doesn't object.)[1] All written up to the end of October may be mixed up between Fauquissart, Laventie, La Gorgue, Merville. November – Robecq, Neuvillette, Bouquemaison. December, (my soft job) Crucifix Corner. January, etc. Gapennes, L'Etoile. ('Song of Pain and Beauty' – Ablaincourt. February or March.) I remember Harvey had trouble with S and Js, and had to tickle them up; this has just emerged from my queer memory. Macdonald, I think would have decided sooner.[2]

Last night there was a pure colourless October Sunlight, and I could smell apples in the Minsterworth orchards, and feel for a moment that soon we should go in and company with Bach, to talk of books and things of peace. How later I should go swiftly under the night towards Orion, home; there to smoke and read myself sleepy and not to go upstairs till just this side unconscious-ness.

The News. The News. Que pensez vous de tout cela?

Again the Miracle breaks all bounds, and Russia is strong; again the German dovecots flutter; more strongly than ever before.

Peace in the Balkans; Secession of Austria; Belgian coast and the North of France reconquered. All before Noel? Je le pense, m'selle.

Tomorrow 'The Old Bold Mate'[3] will come to you. It has been a grind to write it, please excuse the writing so scrappy and obviously hurried. The whole thing was more distasteful to me as it might have been the writing of something I loved, and even then I find it hard to settle all the details, which is the real meaning of setting stuff on paper.

Beaucoup journaux ici – a day late, to be sure, but reading 5 papers a day one gets a general idea .....

Did you mention leave? Well, it is nice to hear someone mention it....
Good luck

> Your sincere friend
> Ivor Gurney

[1] Gurney's sense of place insisted on this location of poems. When he annotated a copy of *Severn & Somme* now in Gloucester Public Library, he carefully noted the place; it is not clear whether the Censor or Marion Scott kept them out of the book.

[2] S and Js did not get the manuscript until 9 June 1917 when Frank Sidgwick wrote to Dunhill hoping that Marion Scott would send the manuscript and noting on the same letter that she had done so.

[3] 'Captain Stratton's Fancy' has as the last line of every stanza a variant of the line 'The old bold mate of Henry Morgan'; hence its variant name.

219 To Marion Scott   G.41.107

15 July 1917 (G)

My Dear Friend   July 15

Here I am in the billet instead of being at Church Parade. C of E is on my Identification Disc, but only for burial purposes; the Wesleyan chaplain is so good I prefer to go there for spiritual sustenance.

Still we are here, but expect to move in about a week's time. Alas the orchard!

I hope you are well again, or, at least, up to your former state of health. How did your father come off in raid No 2? Reprisals are horrid, but sooner or later we must come to them, before all our solicitors are wiped out. And what about Clements Inn?

The international situation is beautifully interesting now, n'est ce pas? And you must bow your head and lift up your heart to Russia. According to information filtering from Germany the Kaiser is afflicted with 'une grande neurasthenie' and who can wonder? But still, as yet Germany does not reproach her leaders with having committed a crime, but only with not having succeeded. Beaucoup angoisses encore.

They asked me to write something for the 1/5 Gazette, which I did, at some length. Let 'em print it if they please. It has much historical information about Gloucester. Perhaps you may receive it one day, perhaps even the sketch may come with this.[1]

Did you ever get a letter with a couple of verses about writing letters after the war? Called 'Peace' I think.[2]

The woman at the house here is very good to us. We are lucky in our billet. With one pain beurre and 4d of (once) skimmed milk a day I can dodge the Army dinners very well. Also she lends me the paper every morning that comes by Post two hours before the marchand arrives lui-meme. In France they have no posters (yet the *Cont: Daily Mail* has) and the marchand toots skilfully and compellingly on a horn. In France also they have a stove which wastes no particle of heat. Someday I will draw one for you. They have no silly snobbish front parlour but a sensible big living room you go straight into. *No* pianos at all. The lady here was surprised at our activity and tunefulness, and said les soldats did not move about much and did not sing. One for us! She knows folksongs, but refused to sing until after the War, when she will be bien content a chanter. Dear lady, so will I.

I have a book to send you in a week's time *La Machoire Carrée*, a book about the English Army.[3]

The Cossacks is with the R.A.M.C. now, and probably enjoying itself, for there are good men there. *Guy Mannering* too.

I would like to read Tolstoi's Diary that is now being brought out, he was an interesting, interested and supremely alive old boy.

Good luck

Your sincere friend
Ivor Gurney

[1] See next letter, which may or may not have come with this letter.
[2] See above, letter 210.
[3] By Henry Ruffin and Andre Tudesq, reviewed in the *T.L.S.* of 10 May 1917, p.218.

220 *To Marion Scott*   G.41.100

15 July 1917 (KT)[1]

> Here Rome held sway for centuries[2]
> Here Tom Jones slept
> Here Rufus kept
> His court and here was Domesday born
> Here Hooper, Bishop, burnt in scorn
> While Mary watched his agonies.
> O Christ, O God, what deeds of shame
> Have here been done in thy Love's name
> What fires are lit of what dread flame[3]

Time out of mind these things were dreams
Mere tales, ⎧ not touching the quick sense
⎩ grey phantoms of old time
Yet walking Gloucester History seems
A living thing ⎧ and an intense
⎩ and a sublime
For here and now I see the strength,
In passing faces, that held at bay
Proud Rupert in an arrogant day
Till Essex' train bands came at length
And Power passed like mist away[4]
Courage and wisdom that made good
Each tiny freedom, and withstood
The cunning or the strength of great
Unscrupulous Lords; and here, elate,
The spirit that sprang to height again
When Philip would conquer the wide Main
And England, and her tigerish queen.
⎧ Countenances here
⎩ Here faces full of an antique grace
And beautiful smiling comely look
That Shakespeare saw in his own place
And loved and fashioned into a book.
Beauty of sweet-blood generations
The strength of nations
Hear the passion-list of a fervent lover
The view from Over
Westgate Street at Night, great light, deep shadows,
The Severn meadows,
The surprising, the enormous Severn Plain
So wide, so fair
From Crickley seen or Coopers, my dear lane
That holds all lane-delightfulnesses there [5]
(O Maisemore's darling way!)
Framilode, Frampton, Dymock, Minsterworth,
You are the flower of villages in all earth
Whatever those may say
That have been cursed with an unlucky birth
Poor blinded multitudes[6]
That far from happy woods,
Like these, in towns and hovels make their stay.
If one must die for England, Fate has given
Generously indeed, for we have known
Before our time, the air and skies of Heaven
And Beauty more than common have been shown,

And, with our last fight fought, our last strife striven
We shall enter unsurprised into our own.[7]

There are a few lines at the start you shall have next time.

[1] See letter 222 for the beginning of this poem promised 'next time'. Scott transcript G.64.11 has a note 'written at Buire-au-Bois' July 1917.'
[2] Gurney has deleted two lines:
      Here is the inn Tom Jones he slept at.
      This is the town Prince Rupert leapt at.
He seems to have been composing as he wrote.
[3] There is a difficulty reading this line. The line was first written as 'What torment of what blasphemous fires', then altered to 'What flame of what tormenting fires'; the multiple crossings out of the second word make it difficult.
[4] Gurney seems to offer 'In King's' as an alternative to 'And' at the beginning of the line; 'mist' is written over 'breath'.
[5] The alteration of 'From Crickley, or from Coopers' to the present version of the previous line probably caused the alteration of 'seems' to 'holds' in this line.
[6] Having deleted 'Not near these happy' Gurney first wrote 'stunted' for 'blinded'
[7] This magnificent last line replaces the deleted 'As to a land/ As of a right we enter into our own'.

---

221 To Marion Scott   G.41.100

15 July 1917 (KT)[1]

My Dear Friend
    They have attached me but 5 minutes agone to 184 M.G.C.; that's my address for a bit, probably permanently, unless I turn out a dud.
    This is a far, far better thing than I have ev-er done,[2] and when one thinks of the Winter....
    True, it is a pity to lose so many good friends, but I console myself by thinking how many of those would have jumped at the chance.
    Thank you for the papers, very much.

                                      Your sincere friend
                                      Ivor Gurney

[1] The next letter locates within half an hour the summons to the Machine Gun Corps and the telegramme announcing that Sidgwick and Jackson's would publish his book. The telegramme (G.41.124) is date-stamped 14-7-17, but the letter dated the 15th above does not respond to the telegramme
[2] Sidney Carton's speech in Dickens' *A Tale of Two Cities*, bk.III, ch.15.

22 July 1917 (P)

My Dear Friend

Well I got your letters, your telegramme and the summons to the M.G.C., all in one crowded half-hour of glorious life.[1] Never was I so flabbergasted to get anything Postal as that telegram. Who could it be from, and what about? Its being French in form put me off, the flimsy blue after our larger yellow.

Well, S and J have not made the Great Refusal. I take this as an omen.

I hope your courage and humourous tenacity will meet with its reward; and I cannot see why this should not come – after the War; perhaps; perhaps not now.

As you will concerning Mr Dunhill.

I have heard that they have heard from Harvey, who is still pegging on. That's all I know.

When the summons came to 'proceed' to the M.G.C. it was rather a wrench. I have many good friends there, and (I am proud to say) those showed real regret at my leaving; though most thought I was lucky to get the chance; as they nor I do not like the thought of sticking Germans, forbye the chance of getting stuck. And it is a far more interesting game, a better fed; one does not do fatigues; one usually gets a dugout in Winter; does not go into the front posts, which in winter are feet deep with slime and water; and, as I have said or hinted, is a safer service on the whole. Since I have never really reconciled myself to the thought of sticking a man, it is a release also. As I am in No 1 Section of 184 M.G.C. which goes in with the Glosters, I shall not be cut off at all, really, in the line. Isn't this good luck?

Well, to return to my book. I hope you will triumph and get joy therefrom, since you have done all the dirty work. I doubt whether it would have been written but for you. ('A most valuable document', say the biographers.) If you would care to adopt any more of them please do. Dedications are yours for the taking.

Here is the beginning of 'The Old City' (that is, Gloucester)

Who says 'Gloucester' sees a tall
Fairfashioned shape of stone arise,
That changes with the changing skies
From joy to gloom funereal,
Then quick again to joy; and sees
Those four most ancient ways come in
To mix their folk and dust and din
With the keen scent of the sea-breeze.
Here Rome held sway for centuries etc.

This is dedicated 'to all Sons and Lovers of Caer-glow, Glevum – Gloucester'.

Don't send any books please, for a consignment of my own has just arrived.

Have you any books of Belloc's Essays? Just try *First and Last*, *On Everything*, *On Something* or *Hills and the Sea*!

Do as you please about *The Georgian (2nd) Book*. I don't know it at all.

The boy who had *Friends*, (in the T.M.B.) was sent to Blighty – sick – so there goes what I did not lose when I was wounded. When a man is wounded in hospital, all parcels are divided among his section – a thing I agree with, but greatly regret for some things. The Taylors also had sent me *The Mirror of the Seas*.[2]

Wild Wales was my most constant delight until I was wounded and lost everything worth having in my kit. It is a coloured book, full of friends, long to remember. There is no time for more, if you are to get this. I rather envy you the fun of correcting proofs. Again

> Do as you please.

I believe that soon, you may hear Our Guns.[3] Germany seems pretty visibly upset already, don't you think?

I hope Mr Scott may escape by miles any bomb-dropping. It must be horrid – it is, for though only two were dropped at Chelmsford, it was not nice.

Goodbye, good luck.

I suppose

(O this is so timid)

Sidgwick and Jackson
cannot be
made to fork out   ever so little?

No? well I thought not.

> Your sincere friend
> Ivor Gurney

[1] The phrase is from the epigraph to Chapter 34 of Sir Walter Scott's *Old Mortality*, stamped on the front covers of some school version of Henley's *Lyra Heroica*. 'One crowded hour of glorious life/ Is worth an age without a name.'

[2] *The Mirror of the Sea* (1906) by Joseph Conrad.

[3] The preparatory barrage for the third battle of Ypres began on 18 July.

---

223 *To Sydney Shimmin*   G.76.12

23 July 1917 (P)

My Dear Shimmin

I hope that second operation is over now old chap and you able to go forward slowly but unhindered to health. Mrs Voynich I know has been to see you, (and says rude things of the place,) who tells me you look pale and thin, which is not to be wondered at. But perhaps you will be able to 'fat up' now. ('Fat up' is Huckleberry Finn.) Only come through all right, and the fruit of all this pain and resistance continual will come to you, and show in your music.

My address is (name) attached 184 M.G.C., so you can guess what has happened. It is far more interesting than infantry work, and one can take a more impersonal interest in the slaying of Huns, like the Artillery. I count myself lucky, but did not do so just as I left, for there are many fine people in the 2/5 and I am proud to remember them as friends, bless 'em.

Sidgwick has accepted my book. I hope that soon you will be able to see it. But think of the agonising pleasure I miss – correcting proofs! Curse it, O curse it, my infant child shall be (what? Baptized, confirmed?) without my having anything to do there; a thing to rend the fond parient's throbbing heart.

How is your sister? She sent me *Punch* and another paper but no personal word. I hope she is all right, and now a virtuoso - with the two forefingers anyhow.

How are the much-bethought-on Taylors, too?

I am reading *Quentin Durward* – a perfectly gorgeous meaty 10 course dinner sort of a book. O to write music so coloured and ordered and strong! Scott is an increasing grant in these days, to me at any rate. As for our polite and well-skilled Thackeray, I am no ungoverned enthusiast there.

Germany is in an interesting state now, n'est ce pas? But what dull slaves they are, or rather have been!

With best wishes for interest now and health soon

I remain

Yours ever
I.B.G.

---

24 *To Marion Scott*   G.41.109

27 July 1917 (P)

My Dear Friend

Your letter of terms etc has arrived.[1] Thank you for it. It seems to me you have done very well, but still – that is no reason why you should not try to do better still, since publishers are our lawful prey and natural enemies. Personally (again) when the book was written there was not a thought of making money behind it, but chiefly an occupation and mind exercise. For all that, I really do not see why the book should not pay, though I do not expect any very laudatory reviews in the *Times* etc. You have won the preliminary skirmishes anyhow.

My own opinion of the book is, that it is very interesting, very true, very coloured; but its melody is not sustained enough, its workmanship rather slovenly, and its thought, though sincere, not very original and hardly ever striking. For all that, the root of the matter is there, and scraps of pure beauty often surprise one; there is also a strong dramatic sense. Where it will fail to attract is that there is none, or hardly any of the devotion of self sacrifice, the splendid readiness for death that one finds in Grenfell, Brooke, Nichols, etc. That is partly because I am still sick of mind and body; partly for physical, partly for mental reasons; Also because, though I am ready if necessary to die for England, I do not see the necessity; it being only a hard and fast system which has sent so much of the flower of England's artists to risk death, and a wrong materialistic system; rightly or wrongly I consider myself able to do work which will do honour to England. Such is my patriotism, and I believe it to be the right kind. But how to write such poems as 'If I should die' in this mood? (Also, I am not convinced that poets believe what they write always. Brooke was a sincere exception, but then, he was lucky; he died early in the war. So often poets write of what they wish to believe, wish to become, as one prays for strength and virtue not yet obtained.)

Golly, what a lecture! Serves you right.

Well, I have been thinking. To all appearances, the War looks like ending between July and September 1918. So my resolution goes, and there probably will be another book. So look out! But angels and ministers of grace defend us,[2] another year!

I should like a talk with you, and yet would a talk be sufficient? For one forgets so easily things which one knows too well. Details wearisome to write but interesting to hear. Men I have met. A boy of twenty who was an expert amateur conjuror, a great lover of Boswell's *Johnson*, a lover of machinery, who had read and admired (Cary's and Dore's) *Dante*, also *Paradise Lost*, (though he knew that he did not understand them; a rare modesty;) the common soldier's attitude to classical music and literature; his cheerfulness, his loose talk, his petty thieving, his nobility; his songs, his literature; his absolute acceptance of any rumours of 'Conferences' concerning Peace; his grumbling at his own country, his admiration of Fritze's, and especially Hindenburg; his (lessening) contempt for the French; his activity, his sanity; his praise of and scorn of wanglers; his cleanliness, his hate of being considered as Tommy, or of being thought a soldier, or patriotic. He is a queer and lovable character. Not in twenty talks could I tell you what I know.

We had a concert here last night. Really, some ragtimes are most exhilarating. 'Missisippi', 'Dixie', 'Alabam', 'Charlie Chaplin's Walk'. The one about the amorous shopkeeper also. I hope to play you these someday. They are not 'Georgia' nor 'Sambre et Meuse', but I know worse music.

So you have decided to call the book 'Strange Service', which is a very exact description of the feeling that made the book; it would sell better as 'Severn and Somme' perhaps, but that is your business; you are my War Cabinet but far more subtle than the real. (What a justification for the old cabinet principles all these changes are! The *S.Westminster* and the *Nation* have been fully justified.)

Do you think there will be much more fighting this year? Shall we not wait for U.S.A., or the collapse of Germany?

Be happy and get well. You are hereby appointed G.L.A. (Grand Literary Agent) with double salary.

With best wishes

Your sincere friend

Ivor Gurney

I hope Mr Scott's laryngitis is nearly gone by now.

P.S. How many complimentary copies?

---

[1] The terms were ten per cent on all copies sold after the first 500 and up to 2,000, fifteen per cent from 2,000 to 10,000 and 25 per cent thereafter. See *SASAWE* pp.111-12.

[2] Another quotation from *Hamlet*: I.iv.39.

225 *To Marion Scott*   G.41.110

27 July 1917 (G)

My Dear Friend

I think you have done very well, and hope you have enjoyed the wangling, (as is not improbable, I think.) They *are* good terms for a first book; from such a publisher, and you are to be congratulated on your strategy. Do as you think fit about a Colonial and a Cheaper edition; I leaves it to you, pardner.

'The Old Bold Mate' has gone, after much procrastination. Sorry - waiting for favourable opportunities means long waiting in the Army; the thing was written 10 days ago.

I am glad you are flourishing, and hope Mr Scott will soon be on the same good way; but that will do for his letter.

We have moved – to a flat land of continual cultivation; whose cottages are cleaner than those of other parts; where one may see windmills with the old new delight and pride in man's cunning and masterful mind; where churches are a landmark and houses loom large; a country of faint continual haunting charm almost entirely of man's fashioning. A Scarlatti, early Mozartish atmosphere restful and full of home-sense, and heart-ache.

It is good news that you have Sassoon's book, which sounded interesting and sincere. Please tell me about it. Nicholson, I should say, may become a big man someday. He is new and speaks of real things. and has the knack of saying much with few words – a vital test. The difficulty with myself is that, once in England and once with a healthy mind, I shall for ever chuck the Muse of Verse (if she was ever mine to chuck) and grind hard at Music.

And the signs of the Times are – that there will be very sufficient opportunity for another book; and you talk of playing Sonatas with you! My halidome! Gadzooks!!

By the way, did I dedicate 'To an Unknown Lady' to anyone? I do not remember, but, for its title's sake, it must not be dedicated at all.

Why not let S and J have the 5 triolets and the 'Song at Morning'? There is lots more to come. The next volume or tome will begin with 'Gloucester', and – O let us live dangerously and give much for the money. Please dedicate something to my sister Dorothy, also Winifred, who deserves something; being a good sort, though I never remember her existence, save when she writes. Father and Mother are provided for I think.

The Immortal Hour

I have forgotten where the pleasure lay
In resting idle in the Summer weather,
Waiting for Beauty's power my spirit to sway;
Since Life has snatched me up and flung me hither,

Here where the day's routine goes dully on
So evenly, so greyly that the heart
Not notices nor cares that Time has gone
That might be jewelled bright and set apart.

And yet, for all this weight, there stirs in me
Such music of Joy when some perceived flower
Breaks irresistible this crust, this lethargy,
I burn and hunger for that immortal hour

When Peace shall bring me first to my own home,
To my own hills; I'll climb and vision afar
Great cloud-fleets, line on line, up Severn come;
When Joy's great flame shall cleanse the stain of war.[1]

Question and Answer

What shall I say, O soldier unforgotten
And friends most dear, but fallen, when they shall ask
'How died our sons that were in pain begotten,
Whose boyhood's making was our daily task?

And what have you to comfort our most lonely
Our undivided anguish, what word to tell?'
Soldiers, what can be said, what told but only
'Your work was nobly ended; they died well.'

This is for the next book, not this.
May you soon be fiddling away on better bread than ever, and with better news to please you.

Your sincere friend
Ivor Gurney

290

[*In the same envelope is enclosed:*]

Battered Souvenir enclosed[2]

My Dear Friend

Just a note to say I have received your letter of July 24, and thank you for it. (It is only the 27th now!)

Yes, I think with you that Sidgwick and Jackson have treated us very well, and you have no need to chivvy them very much more. What a magnificent scene for a play that would make; a quiet party in England listening to guns so far off, yet powerful enough to make doors rattle! It could be made Shakespearian.

It is surely a good omen for sales (*and* reviews) that a firm like Sidgwick's has closed quickly with the book and offered good terms? Adsit omen! Also it is something pleasant to think around; and with publication and the appearance of reviews a different pleasure. Sidgwick, being called up, is likely to appreciate the spirit of the book more than Osborne – who hasnt been! By the way, what about that Anthology?

Meanwhile, all good wishes.

Your sincere friend
Ivor Gurney

[1] In the last stanza, line 2, 'welcome' became 'vision'; Gurney deleted 'And feel Joy's flame cleanse the last stain of War' in favour of the last line as printed.
[2] Nothing is enclosed.

---

226 *To Herbert Howells*   G.3.6

31 July 1917 (P)

My Dear Howler

Time deals astonishingly with you, and to my sense has treated you very well; considering all circumstances, quite wonderfully, and your friends rejoice at it, I among them. Don't be raided, my man, or go down very deep when the row starts.

Not since I was first out here have I had such a soft time as since the April affair[1] – only once in since then! However, that no doubt will have to be paid for.

You know by now what I am, and what the address is; in case you do not, here goes – (Name) 2/5 Glosters attached No 1 Section 184 M.G.C. B.E.F.[2] (All cheques cashed by sanitary man.)

What's happening I wonder (as did you) when these guns are hammering, or, what is going to happen? I should guess it would be an attempt to outflank Lille north and south.

How is your heart now? Let's hope the New Tribunals will deal more wisely and gently than the old. Don't do too much. Forge ahead slowly till

Time settles your erratic innards.

Well, you must know that Miss Scott and myself have passed the first most dangerous channel with my book, and soon I hope will be bearing strongly out to sea with Publication (and after, soon or late, Oblivion.) on the port bow, and Reviews to starboard. By Heaven, though, what stuff there will be to set apres la guerre! What Names! Brooke, Sorley, (I have not read him) Katharine Tynan, Nicholson, Sassoon, Gibson, John Freeman, Laurence Binyon, F.W.Harvey, Masefield, and ......(but not for me,) Gurney....Apres la guerre, toujours l'apres! O how much better than to seek through Palgrave and Bullen for something not wishy-washy yet settable!

So an Elegy of yours has greatly taken Dr Allen? So much the better. There is the Mass, the 'Chosen' quartett, the Concerto, the Suite, and this well in the public eye. What of 'Sir Patrick'? Dr Allen is a man of courage, I am glad you have got in touch with him.

Best wishes from your fellow pupil and envious writer of the list above.

Ivor Gurney. M.G.Corper.

[1] When he was recuperating in Rouen
[2] Gurney obviously wanted Howells to take notice, as he added the address again on the back of the envelope.

---

227 To Sydney Shimmin   G.76.11

31 July 1917 (KT)

My Dear Shims

You send good news, and I hope the last news of illness. Go on up to Blackpool and be happy. And, soon may we both evanish from the Army sphere altogether.

Howells has indeed had good luck; which is another uplifting thing; these are good omens and I hang on to them.

How is your sister Mona? She hasn't written lately. General Brussilof still persists in believing that the War will end this Autumn. Bless him! What will our next smack bring? The first attempt to break through since Loos?

You have heard perhaps of my Tome, now accepted by the high and mighty Sidgwick and Jackson. They will fork out too bless 'em. Nowt up to 500, 500 – 2000, 10%: 2000 – 10000, 15%; 25% thereafter. I call them good terms to an unknown scribbler for fun, and flattering to the vanity, bound to be highly developed, of a musician-poet, (or rather versifier.) There is something for you therein, but what it is escapes me.

And there are to be Proms again! England has really done well; there is no hate in us. Tirpitz' whiskers stir the wrath of any honest man, but were he shaved it would be a loss for our comic papers. (I believe the *Punch* cartoons get worse and worse).

I am glad Mrs Voynich came to see you, and Mrs Taylor, who I hope has laid in a stock of Brown Biscuits and China Tea pour l'apres guerre, when I intend to be strictly at peace.

By the way my address is (Name) 2/5 Gloster attached 184 M.G.C., B.E.F.

Write again to your disconsolate co-scholar, and keep heart up; and a set of healthy innards.

Yours ever
I.B.G.

3 August 1917 (P)

My Dear Howells

You are indeed queerly treated of the gods to be cast up again so high after so great a fall. £150 a year as sub-editor and at such a job![1] O bon! (By the way, in February they raised my yearly emolument from 18/4/0 to 22/5/0.[2]) And your elegy! And your Folk Song Quartett....

However the nobility of my spirit is such that it is more rejoiced than envious. I wish they would do my 'Bierside' with your 'Elegy' however.

But don't, don't worry or overwork. Get a photograph taken of the fair Dorothea in her mood of placid imbecility and gaze thereon several times a day.

My book is nearly settled for. Soon it will be altogether out of my hands, and the scorn of the great world. Naked it shall go out against armed critics and an indifferent crowd.

What are you writing now? Miss Scott says 'The Moor' of Hodgson is well worth setting. Why not look at it?

The news is good enough, but still .... when will it all end?

What does Gloucestershire look like now? Ungratefully the same, I suppose. She keeps her beauty for every wandering comer, but still I think does not forget her sons. Some of whom hope to make a little money by describing her beauties.

Will no-one do your Concerto again? That has been rather a shock to me, that such a fine piece of music should appear and attract so little notice. Still, cheer up; for if the worst comes to the worst you shall get a word in my Biography.

Good luck

Yours ever
I.B.G.

---

[1] Howells had been contributing articles to the *Athenaeum*.

[2] i.e. eighteen pounds four shillings to twentytwo pounds five shillings.

3 August 1917 (P)

My Dear Friend

It is certain you must have heard the guns lately, for they have been labouring terribly, and you should hear them as well as we can hear.

But it is M.G. mechanism which has up till now engaged my attention, not the dodging of shells. However, we can hardly remain neutral as this is probably the Big Push.

There are several Scots and men of the North in this section, and it is delightful to hear soft voices against the harsher English. Our instructor was a Scot, frae nearby the Forth, and he is a remarkable man. Talk of concentration, of patience! His remarks on mechanism are endued seemingly with the authority of Fate. Nothing draws him from the point. I feel a poor creature beside him, for while my mind wanders from heaven to earth, from earth to heaven, he has one idea only, the present idea. Terrible to offend, he is pleasant enough to those who bow down to his judgements. A fine chap, but doubtfully useful as a household pet. But the Scots surely are finest race on earth; taking them all round. But they must find it hard to learn languages, since foreigners frequently say things one does not expect. (Curse them!)

We have just heard that all first objectives on a 50 mile front have been taken. I wonder what this means?[1]

Russia seems about to settle down a little; the essential death penalty should make a great deal of difference to anarchy, and as to the retreat it seems to be in order, and to be engaging German troops fully enough to satisfy us on the Western Front.

'The Course of the English Novel' is a very good article I think.[2] In the Novel as in the Play, English genius rebels against perfection and turns rather to Content rather than Form. And our critics of Music must take note, must beware of requiring that from Englishmen which may not be the truest national expression. Our best works of Art are interesting because of the sense of open air in them and a surpassing human interest. As Belloc says somewhere, A man who reads *King Lear* feels as though he had been out all night on the empty uplands in a great storm. Such things must move us more for ever than perfection; a good aim, but a bad desire; and so, it seems to me, a work of Art never should be greatly praised for its perfection; for that should set off its beauty, and its beauty or truth should be the chief impression on the mind. To praise a thing for its faultlessness is to damn it with faint praise. (Please don't tell Sir C.V.S. or R.B.) But all this has no connection whatever with my own work.

I suppose one of the bitter-sweet musings of your weakness is your book; (this lecture recalled it to me.) and I hope indeed soon you will be able to start on that and your fiddle; for when that stage comes you should not have to wait long.

There was no mail today, but perhaps tomorrow may bring straw for my bricks.

Meanwhile all best wishes

from your sincere friend
Ivor Gurney

[1] The third battle of Ypres; they gained five miles.
[2] The front-page article of the *T.L.S.* of 19 July 1917 has this title and is concerned with the primacy of content as against form.

230 *To Marion Scott*   G.41.114

3 August 1917 (P)

My Dear Friend

Please don't send me anything to sign. Wherefore, and why?

You have full power over all matters of business connected with *Severn and Somme*, to be published by Sidgwick and Jackson, after the manner of which you have written. Trouble not the Master.

I am glad you are come to such exalted company; may you find much spiritual benefit therefrom. Also you may be cured of some heterodox opinions that may have formed, though how Miss Austen would like that I cannot say. As to omissions; 'Pain and Song' may very well come out, 'Dawn' also. But I could wish 'Sawgint' to be retained because of the man it talks of. 'Communion' I am fond of, and think that S and Js are wrong.[1] As 'The Dawn' is to be ommitted please give Winnie Chapman one of the new poems, 'Letters' if it is not already given.

There! that's business over! I would thank you again for all the trouble you are taking, if I did not think you take pleasure also in the struggle.

It is good news you can walk so much more now. It is very good news. Perhaps recovery will be quicker now; indeed I hope it will go at a perfectly sickening speed, so as to annoy people who have come to consider you as an invalid. Personally I have not so thought, but until the War ends and proper feeding begins you may get on slowly.

Why the shade of Chopin does he haunt me? Today my head has been full of Chopin's F mi Fantasie. I wish it would stop.

The News I know is big, in half an hour I shall know more definitely from *Le Matin*; but what weather!

I am writing a golopshusly thrilling thing on your hearing the guns. it needs only a little spit and polish, after which it will descend from the operating table and come out on life by itself.

Best wishes and thanks

Your sincere friend
Ivor Gurney

Rumours of Wars

On Surrey hills today
Women stand and hear
The guns at work alway,
Horribly, terribly clear.

The doors shake, on the walls
The kitchen vessels move.
The brave heart not at all
May soothe its tortured love,

Nor hide from truth, nor find
Comfort in lies. No prayer
May calm. All's naught. The mind
Waits on the throbbing air.

The frighted day grows dark.
One dare not speak. The gloom
Makes bright and brighter the spark
Of fire in the still room.

A crazy door shakes free...
'Dear God'! They stand, they stare
At a shape eyes cannot see
And the blank darkness there.

She knows, and must go pray
Numb-hearted by the bed
That was his own alway....
The throbbing hurts her head

July 1917

---

[1] 'Pain and Song' (or 'Song and Pain' as it was called) and 'Communion' did not come
out; 'Dawn' and 'Sawgint' did.

---

8 August 1917 (P)

My Dear Friend
   Your letter of July 31 and August 1st has arrived, and thank you for it.
   I am Glad Will Harvey has written to you, and hope it is not the last of
your acquaintance. That he 'is too mouldy to write' is a sad thing to read, but
a brave thing to write. He is naturally subject to melancholy, and himself only

in surroundings that suit him, and so must have a bad time anyway. Perhaps it may be the slow accumulation of small dulnesses that have affected him. I hope it is no worse.

As to *Severn and Somme*, I have another criticism to make, in spite of your vigourous defence, (which of course you *would* make, being G.L.A. for the same; there's a nasty one!) that is, outside the one line 'Fragile mirrors easily broken by moving airs', [1] I do not recall any line of real beauty. Answer that now. Perhaps by now you have 'Camps' or 'Works of War', or whatever I called it and 'Rumours of War' will reach you soon. And after surely some autumn poems of Minsterworth. The spirit is stirred by a wind uncontrolled, and moved by disconnected memories queerly rising up from the past; usually those thought on most often, but not always.

As to the attitude taken by certain writers to the present time and to their land; don't forget that this usually represents what they wish to think, and on some rare occasions actually do. These are intense moments and live in memory afterwards when the exercise of writing is sometimes used to recreate an emotion. As for F.W.H.'s 'Though unto me you be austere', it is obviously, (I will underline) *obviously* a poetic exercise, not a very good one. It is not a sincere expression anyhow. You are right about the state of my mind. So am I. It is a sickness caused by real surroundings now, not by imaginary. A great step as you say.

The weather is rotten; our usual luck of weather in offensives.

The *Times* article was not at all bad. I have seen one famous battlefield since my return from hospital much of it was hardly scarred and thick with flowers. Surely there can hardly be a lovelier colour than cornflower blue? It is the colour of Mozart, of Schubert in lighter moods.

Your story of the chalk uncovered is really very stirring. I hope we shall read some more on this subject. Perhaps the guns heard so plainly in Surrey, may not be the coast guns, but those on chalk – Arras way perhaps. But where the particular strata lie will be an interesting tale to hear.

Russia appears to be getting better, n'est ce pas?

We shall see some exciting things when the Rhine Bridges are kept broken, and a 50 mile sector of the front dominated by aeroplanes. Also, a huge attack on Kiel and the German munition towns. It might start in January and last till – Spring, or the collapse of Germany. It is the best way.

Best wishes

Your sincere friend
Ivor Gurney

[1] From 'Strange Service'.

8 August 1917 (P)

My Dear Friend

Here is the letter all right, and I think you will find it strong enough. The signature of the witness is plain enough too, and that of a Harley St man who prefers life with a Batt: he likes than life at the Base or in hospital – a fine man.

Thank you so much for all the careful trouble you have taken about these worrying details, of which I am grateful indeed to be relieved.

I have forgotten all about dedications. No, I am afraid that you had better not have more than F.W.H. But take any two of them, whichever you please. Also, will you give another to E.Hunt, making two? I am afraid the whole thing has been done carelessly, but let it go. The people who have more than one are yourself, F.W.H. and E.H (now). Are there any more? You shall have the second book. Please give T.C. (or is it M.C. = Mrs Chapman another making two) will you? Please thank Mr Scott for his help also. It has saved me some trouble and perplexity. The envelope for S and J was marched over by two or three muddy feet, but it is still serviceable and must serve.

Now you have been given almost complete control over all things literary connected with me. Just send the cheques and reviews (laudatory.) You need not explain things at too great length, for this takes up much room in your letters. If you are found out in any rascality, I will blister you immortally with a satire. Or write to *John Bull*.

Goodbye and many thanks. 'Now the labourer's task is o'er',[1] save the pleasant one of correcting proofs.

Your sincere friend
Ivor Gurney

Copy of letter to S and J

Dear Sir

Miss Scott suggests to me that it would be better to send you a letter giving her full authority to do whatever she may please to do in regard to *Severn and Somme*.

The situation is – since it is difficult to attend to business matters out here, and since I myself would infinitely prefer to dodge such matters; and since also Miss Scott is kind enough to manage these for me, I am merely grateful and willingly give her a free hand. I hope this will reassure you.

There are some new dedications to insert, but beyond these alterations or insertions the book will stand as it is. Of these things Miss Scott will tell you.

Please send the proofs to her, as, if they came to me – Lord knows where they might travel. My present address is Pte Gurney 2/5 Glosters attached 184 M.G.C. B.E.F. Permanent address – c/o Miss Scott, 92 Westbourne Terrace, Hyde Park London W 2. And so I wash my hands of *all* business arrangements while I am in France.

Yours sincerely
Ivor Gurney

[1] The first line of a hymn by John Ellerton (1826-1893)

233 *To Marion Scott* G.41.117

8 August 1917 (G)

My Dear Friend

Tonight I saw small birds settled together on a telegraph wire, and that was surely sign enough of Autumn, 'that leads on Winter and confounds him quite,' and us; but this Winter will be better than the last.

I can take a huge bound volume of reviews with me, reading it in day time hugging it at night. For exasperation may make one forget the cold and – there may be pleasure as well.

Tonight I have sent you a parcel of books. One belongs to Margaret Hunt; will you please return it to her when read? There is a sketch book of mine which you may like to have. *The Shropshire Lad* (your gift), a *Wild Wales* of my own, and a French book you may like to have also. What I have lost though! That precious lot which was stolen from me at Laventie last year, and what went west at Vermand! Including my beloved *Spirit of Man* that Will Harvey lent me in August. Quel dommage!

> *August 8th*

A letter from Mr Scott has just arived, so has 15 francs, so I must have some books. I will keep these till all I can suck out of them has been sucked, and then send them to you. Well, will you please send me *A Gloucestershire Lad* and *Five Degrees South* by Francis Brett Young (1s – Secker.) and John Freeman's last book, a shilling one I think; whose name I do not know.

The review of Nicholson's last book has just appeared in the *S.W.*, and curiously different to the *T.L.S.* review, as often happens.[1] The *Westminster* treats him as a curious animal who may become poet, and praises chiefly a thing the *Times* does not mention – 'Testament'. A queer thing.

By the way I think of rewriting 'Beauty', which has the seeds of a much better poem in it. There are two-three rather heavy sonnets of which I am doubtful. 'Hail and Farewell' should begin 'The destined bullet wounded him'.

[No further pages in this letter.]

[1] Gurney more than once gets Robert Nichols' name wrong by calling him Nicholson. Nichols' *Ardours and Endurances* and two other books of poems were reviewed in the *T.L.S.* on 12 July 1917, p.330.

299

14 August 1917 (P)

My Dear Old Shimmin

This is very bad to hear this news of your sister; and strange too, for who could have expected anything of the kind?

I suppose her breakdown was due to overwork, and if so she has as truly died for England as any the most brave soldier of the line. Destroy the letters please, there is no use in returning them.

I can say no consolatory things, for words are vain; if you cannot get peace from music nothing will suffice.

This letter I hope will find you at the Taylors, and recovering now and able to take interest in things. Don't let this depress you. Play Bach's G minor Prelude 2nd book or the F major from the 2nd also.

Goodbye, all good wishes.

Yours ever
I.B.G.

14 August 1917 (P)

My Dear Friend

The rain pours down then ceases to leave the wide breadth of blue and great clouds of thunder on the horizon. Queer weather, but nothing to do with guns.

I hope you are getting well steadily, and are not much worried by the vagaries of the weather; and indeed cheered by the episcopal small-talk thereon.

Poor Sidney has received a bad blow, and it seems to have affected him a lot. Strange to hear of Death from England.

Dear Old Charlie wrote to me (you compree C.V.S.?) a nice letter, illegible, but jolly. One of his remarks was such as only a superannuated civilian could write – he wished he were out here. Marvellous experience etc etc. Perfect civvy blither, which may be true, but is chiefly the product of ignorance, not nobility.

I hope you have received my letter with the bloodcurdler about the guns. Also your enfranchisement as agent. Free powers unlimited, don't bother me.

Mrs Harvey has just sent me an unnecessary but bon parcel, but alas! there is no F.W.H. book in it. Shall we astonish the Age together? If we could only have a week with one another, hearing and asking questions.

'Beauty' is being rewritten; and must be made coherent somehow. In that notebook I sent you you will notice X X X on some pages that are interesting.[1]

The Nicholson poems quoted some weeks ago in the *Times* are good direct stuff. The *S.W.* rather slangs it – but I remember to have told you all this. I look forward to my papers with great interest, and lately have been pasting poems quoted in reviews in a notebook similar to that you have. Had I but started sooner, there was a *Public Opinion* with 4 complete Masefield Sonnets. The *Times* review of Hodgson and Sassoon. However what I have is interesting and often read. One must have something modern.

Best wishes

Your sincere friend
Ivor Gurney

[1] 'Beauty', printed in *Severn & Somme* as 'Winter Beauty' was sent in February 1917; see letter of 9 February 1917, and the revisions in letter 236.

---

236 *To Marion Scott*   G.41.120

14 August 1917 (P)

Winter Beauty

I cannot live with Beauty out of mind;
I seek her and desire her all the day,
Being the chiefest treasure man may find,
And word most sweet his eager lips can say.
She is as strong on me as though I wandered
In Severn meadows some blue riotous day.

But since the trees have long since lost their green,
And I, an exile, can but dream of things
Grown magic in the mind, I watch the sheen
Of frost and hear the song Orion sings,
And hear the star born passion of Beethoven;
Man's consolations sung on the quivering strings.

Beauty of song remembered, sunset glories,
Mix in my mind, till I not care nor know
Whether the stars do move me, golden stories,
Or ruddy Cotswold in the sunset glow.
I am uprapt, and not my own, immortal....
The winds of Beauty swinging to and fro.

Last Verse as you know it.
Jan-Aug 1917.

Camps

Out of the line we rest in villages
Quiet indeed, where heal the spirit's scars.
But even so, lapped deep in sunshine and ease,
We are haunted for ever by the shapes of wars.

Green in the sun they lie, secret, deserted,
One takes the air in peace, one wanders slow
Where once the bright steel rang, the red blood spurted
And brave men cowed their terrors long ago.

By day there life was easy, but at night,
Even now, one hears strange rustlings in the bush,
And straining tensely doubtful ear and sight
The stealthy moving ere the sudden rush,

And flinches from the spear. War's just-bright embers
That Earth still keeps and treasures for the pride
In sacrifice there shown, with love remembers
The beauty and quick strength of men that died.

Who died as we may die, for Freedom, beauty
Of common living, calmly led in peace,
Yet took the flinty road and hard of duty,
Whose end was life abundant and increase.

But – when Heaven gates wide opening receive us
Victors and full of song, forgetting scars,
Shall we see to stir old memories, to grieve us,
Heaven's never-yet-healed sores of Michael's wars?

August 17

My Dear Friend

Since you have not mentioned 'Camps', I gather that I forgot to send it, or that some post has gone down. Anyway there is a nice long letter from you, and this may do as an answer. Dedications – to Dorothy Gurney. To Winifred Gurney. Whichever you please. I rather wish I had not thought of those cursed dedications. What do you think? Why not take all out, save only that to 'Certain Comrades', and one for yourself? I wish you would. As it stands, invidious distinctions and beastly bothers abound. To Certain Comrades, to those determined. Anyone to you. And that sonnet (Afterglow?) to F.W.H., no more. 'The Immortal Hour' may stand as title. In the last line thereof let 'pure' stand for 'great'.

You write of Marlborough; was he great? I know only Macaulay and

302

Thackeray, but all I gather from them in his praise is, that he was a great master of war. And 'English to the core'? Mean Churchill, husband of Sarah Jennings?[1]

In 'Question and Answer', 'guiding' if it so please you.[2] In 'Song and Pain' – same conditions – have 'making's'. ('and joy in the making'.)[3]

'The Poplar and the Moon' is very beautiful, like very good F.W.H. 'Field Daisy' has good points; but star – star – star – star and 'unchanging are'. No bon, that! 'At Carnoy' is good too. The other – so, so. I have copied 'Poplar' and 'Carnoy'. He is a poet, though – Sassoon. Send me some more, please.[4]

As to the idea of sending my things to editors; Yes, by all means; it might mean cash, and a wider public. The *Academy, Spectator, Nation, Saturday review, New Witness, New Statesman, Westminster*; all these might take something. *English Review*, perhaps.

We cannot hear the guns at this place, but the flashes are clear enough; to remind us of the reason why we sleep on straw and not 'pillowed in silk and scented down' as Alan Seeger wrote[5] C.V.S. wrote me a letter. (Did I tell you?) greatly praising Howells' Elegy. How I would like to hear it! And today with your letter, came one from H.N.H. himself. 'O world God made!' Why are we separated, painfully to express ourselves by signs when speech is molten gold to that black ink or pencil? Fritz is to evacuate all territory, to start separation, to give guarantees, and relinquish all his guns before all this cease! Well, it is the best way; but la guerre fait tres longue. Des aeroplans, aeroplans. First to squash him to juice then blow him sky high to fall to Hell, for a sycophantic self deceiving treacherous Thug. Best wishes. I hope you are going on well. It is eleven at night. Tomorrow a letter to Mr Scott.

Your sincere friend
Ivor Gurney

[1] John Churchill, 1st Duke of Marlborough (1650-1722) married Sarah Jennings (1660-1744).
[2] Presumably for 'making' in line 4. See letter 225.
[3] See letter 147.
[4] See letter 240 below where 'Field Daisy' is seen to be by Marion Scott.
[5] In 'I have a rendezvous with Death'.

---

37 To Sydney Scott   G.41.121

16 August 1917 (P)

My Dear Mr Scott

Again I have to thank you for an interesting letter and a charmingly-given present. Thank you very much for both. There is not much to buy here, and although we are overcharged for all things, still I find my expenditure less now than ever. Alas, there is no cafe au lait now, as last year at Laventie.

After a tactful pause of a fortnight, I propose presenting my Literary agent with another book; but even so, after a break, it will be hard to avoid the appearance that it is your gift, not mine. The notes they paid out today are dirty though, and if I send one of them as a guarantee of good faith.

There have been no raids lately; at least the papers have reported none; whatever happens I hope your office will remain safe; if not, that the cellar will protect you.

Your holiday should arrive soon, and you free to gather strength for another round with Life. I am glad to hear that the bread is better where you are; all reports of leave-men are very bad; as for our own it is very good still. Lately we have been very well fed; ever since May we have had enough of stringy bully beef. Very little fresh meat, but enough Maconochie etc etc. And three times Rabbits, a most delicious change. Tomorrow we move. Which means mud, I suppose. Still the thunderstorms continue; still the great clouds and the heavy air. Indeed the Allies do not run well with the Clerk of the Weather.

Gerard's book must be interesting, but his account of German losses are absurd – for a reason no doubt. Belloc gives $3\frac{3}{4}$ million to 4 million dead or totally useless. 5 million losses – men capable of hospital orderly work or such, including men who will in time return. And then there are the continual slightly wounded and sick.

I hope your health will continue to get better and a soon holiday set you four-square.

With best wishes

Yours very sincerely
Ivor Gurney

13 August 1917 (G)

Dear Madam   August 13th

You will kindly delete *all* dedications save three – 'To Certain Comrades'; and one each to yourself and F.W.H. This is a final irrevocable decision. I 'have the wind up' about – and – and – ; and besides, it will look absurd. Out with them! Slay, have no mercy!

You will realise that this action implies no disrespect for you, and the next book shall show that, I hope, of which four masterpieces are already extant.

But what a hell of a lot of letters I write you nowadays! Enough to show you that this letter is no forgery, no cheat, but is from

Him-who-must-be-obeyed
Ivor Gurney

Author, Composer, Soldier-of-a-sort, and your humble sincere servant, Miss Marion.

14 August 1917 (G)

[*Standard Field Service Post Card signed with initials* IBG *and dated August 14. All is crossed out except* I am quite well *which is Gurney's signal that he is going into the line.*]

18 August 1917 (P)

My Dear Friend

Is 'Field Daisy' yours?[1] Then I may congratulate you very much, for beyond the repeated 'star', the internal rhyme on line 9, and the awkwardness of line 8 (to which I can suggest no improvement) it is very good indeed. I took it for Sassoon – and – do you remember that Elizabethan thing you sent me a long time ago? You have learnt a lot since. Lines 3 and 4 are charming indeed. (Might not line 8 run – 'Of such things symbol as unchanging are'? The accent on 'such' puts me off.) Line 9 (to escape star) might have the common word, 'wonder'. The sonnet might have been Masefield's, might have been Sassoon's. Cheerio!

I have not paid it the compliment of copying, but all the same had kept it folded in my notebook. It is a far, far better thing than you have ever shown me, for the words become alive and are abstract representations no longer.

And so Ledwidge is dead.[2] If the new book is not too expensive you shall have it from me. He was a true poet, and the story of his life is (now) a sad but romantic tale, like that of so many others, so wastefully spent. Yet the fire may not have been struck in them save for the war; anyway it was to be, and is.

I am glad you are pleased with my communication to S and J; a most unlegally direct document, I think. Yesterday I heard from them as to the date of publication; till then I shall live in a pleasing state of anticipation, as near happiness as is possible to me. I hope it will look as well, be as small and give as much pleasure as F.W.H.'s book.

The *Round Table* arrived and was welcome. Some good articles it had. That one on English Education was truthful enough, and its recommendations perfect, I think. Many thanks to the giver.

I am glad you are taking on more tasks, more amusements, since, I know, impotence must be very hard for you.

Russia seems to be kicking pretty hard now. I think with you that we must not expect with certainty but can look forward to great things, for that offensive, betrayed, but not by cowardice, was a great thing, and so is the present resistance. 'And after a while he came to himself'.... After his unaccustomed liberty had been seen for what it was – a responsibility, a burden. On the whole, out of my ignorace, I believe more in Russia than do you. Perhaps the French papers are more optimistic.

This is a darling land, and its children the most beautiful, most healthy I ever saw; as a whole. Goodness is in the faces of most men, a mellow merciful spirit founded on centuries of beautiful living. (I should like to read Cammaerts and the other man.[3]) The cottages are perfectly charming, and there is no ugly house, in the country at any rate. The roof is thatched, or like those of Sussex, red tiled. Low and longish, one has painted them white with window frames and shutters and doors in pale green. In France, blue often, brown, yellow, dark red, but not often so here. The men that would have destroyed or mastered this country have a great guilt, for such peasants are the salt of the earth; the only true test of good foundation; the essential of health; the preservation of simplicity and gratitude, and common kindness of a happy state. That Prussia also may become as she one day! – yes and England also, that is cancered and defiled by ugly towns and commodious villas, born of vulgarity, sluggish liver, greed, and all uncharitableness. (Never mind, Tewkesbury stands up so across the plain and is noble and golden of colour in autumn. And Frampton on Severn, that wonder, villages of the hills also are precious and still clean.) My dear lady your eagle eye will detect Belloc here; and why not? I am unashamed, as of a debt to Shakespeare, for both are greatly healthy, both bombastic, and both nerve on nerve alive.

Damme, I envy you those proofs! Perhaps I may be in Blighty by then though ... Qui sait? Five francs not enclosed yet. Though — there is some danger of its being wasted if I keep it... – just now.

With best wishes

Yours very sincerely
Ivor Gurney

Don't send books just yet.

---

[1] Not in Marion Scott's only published volume, *Violin Verses* (1905).
[2] The *T.L.S.* review of Francis Ledwidge's *Songs of Peace* in the issue of 16 August 1917 reports his death the previous week.
[3] Emile Cammaerts (1878-1953), a Belgian poet settled in England in 1908. His poems, translated by his wife, had some influence during the war.

---

241 *To Marion Scott*   G.61.38

18 August 1917 (P)

[*A French postcard stamped with the name of a shop in Rouen and on the face the words and music of 'Régiment de Sambre-et-Meuse', a ferociously heroic story in song of a glorious defeat, with words by Paul Cezano and music by Robert Planquette. Gurney has written only the address and the words* A Fine tune this.]

23 August 1917 (P)   [*On paper headed* Y.M.C.A. On Active Service
                         WITH THE BRITISH EXPEDITIONARY FORCE.]

My Dear Friend   Sunday August the umptieth[1]
   I feel a talk would do me good, and so here goes.
   My gun team is in the line, but I, a relief, am modestly in the rear at
present, near the big guns. Fritz tries to bomb them at night, bless him.
   The poem on Gloucester has been returned, but with request for more. My
feelings are too seriously hurt for that, though, at present. How dare he?
   One of our men just returned from England says that the bread is much
better now. I hope this is true, for one does not like to think of friends as badly
fed.
   Henderson seems to have played Hamlet with singularly poor effect. And
what does that consummate old maid the Pope think he is driving at?[2] And
what will be the effect on Catholicism of all this pother?
   I hope you will send me some more Sassoon, for his touch of romance and
candour I like. He is one who tries to tell Truth, though perhaps not a
profound truth.
   This is dull and hard work writing, compared to the easy speed and interest
of the spoken word. O to wake up tomorrow to find it all a dream, myself in
London just before teatime, making ready to visit you. For, I believe, unless
the flood of matter stopped the gap of speech by sheer pressure, there is stuff
enough in me to talk for ages, since no-one is really interested in the things are
vital to me. I would fix you with my glittering eye, 'to move thee to a si-i-i-
gh, and chearm thee to a tee-ee-eear'. Yarns that I think would strike you
pink, and petrify your ear. Of most disastrous chances, and moving accidents
in flood and field. Not arms, but *Men* I would sing.[3]
   Perhaps I shall be able to extemporise a little after the war since my mind is
steadier than it was. But why when there are the 48 and Schumann and
Chopin and Beethoven. Why pipe on scrannel straws at all?[4] And what have I
to sing about? The only thing I have seen in France which absolutely took me,
is Rouen, with its great golden rock under the sun. As for England she has
made copy for me, and has to be absorbed afresh – How differently, you will
know by my music. So here's a scribble all about myself, but that is because I
feel lonely tonight. But do not forget you, or to hope you are getting stronger
and have not to 'calculate' your pleasures so much now.
   With best wishes
                                            Yours very sincerely
                                            Ivor Gurney

[*In the same envelope and on the same Y.M.C.A. paper:*]

My Dear Friend
   Your letter with Conan Doyle's 'Guns in Sussex' arrived yesterday, and

Sassoon today. Thank you so much for the trouble and the patience it must have cost you to copy them. The Conan Doyle is not very good; sincere but dull. The Sassoons not so good as a whole as they might be – but true. Hodgson's 'Moor' very fine.

Now your letter.

I do not know what is the cause of the unfinished letter.[5] It is possible that being in a hurry I sent it off all too tout'suite.

Surely I have thanked Mr Scott by now for his present? But all the same my mind retains no memory of the other 5 francs making 20. My memory of such things is horribly uncertain however, but my first impression is of 15, and that never has been strongly corrected by any other.

If you would like all the books I sent, save *First and Last*,[6] please accept them, and give me pleasure. (O, except of course *The Shropshire Lad*.) Nicholson has not yet arrived. I shall be delighted to see him, suck his brains and return him to you, to keep for me. I could not wish for a better birthday present. Thank you so much. (Is it a good thing to mark with presents a day which only marks another year of wasted time?)

Rumours of War
Yes, 'On Sussex hills'.
Verse 2. stet.
Verse 4. 'No one dare speak', if you think so. But the effect is not so creepy.
Verse 6. Yes, that last line cost me trouble, and I am not sure of it yet; but let it stand for the sterile present. Send 'Rumours of Wars' to some paper if you like; would it be better to wait till the first book is known a little?

The 'Guns in Sussex' has one pretty good verse – the first.

Now then – Sassoon![7]
'Tree and Sky'   Mps!
Wisdom's last line is good.
Whispered Tale true and good.
Absolution beautiful. But – one finds in it the fault of minor poets who make beautiful lines of unmeaning or not of any particular significance. *Why* is Time a *wind*, a *golden* wind, why does it *shake the grass*? I'll tell you; because of 'pass', and because it is a good line as a whole. He was proud of it, and may have written the poem round it.
'*Golgotha*' is strained, though true, but not poetry.
'*They*' needed to be said, but is journalism pure and simple. What does 'Before Day' mean? Again, line 4 means what? This is the key, the chief part of the puzzle, so to speak. He cannot fully manage his material as yet. Line 8 ditto. As a whole 'empty'.

But

you must remember that a lot of this has been written to free himself from circumstance. They are charms to magic himself out of the present. Cold feet, lice, sense of fear – all these are spurs to create Joy to such as he; since Beauty is the only comfort.

'*Stand-to: Good Friday Morning*'.

Not perfect; not what he meant, but good; and the end absolutely true save *perhaps* 'old'. The triple rhymes are wrong as in other places of his poems. 3 similar endings are almost always trivial in sound. But there are tears there. That was Southern Somme front by the sound of it.

'The Moor' perfect; save perhaps for the three repeated 'miles'.

Why not 'at miles and $\left.\begin{cases} \text{stretching} \\ \text{desert} \\ \text{lonely} \\ \text{dreary} \end{cases}\right\}$ miles.

What does Line 4 verse 2 mean?

Thank you again. These things stimulate me and give me hope. My Anthology enlargens. Theodore Maynard is naught.[8]

I am sick of being away from all my friends.

And last night on fatigue I had the roughest chanciest hour I ever had. My shrapnel helmet has an interesting dent in it.

However today is lovely, lovely. And yesterday we had a thrill. A German aviator was shot down from thousands and thousands of feet up (Guynemeyer did it they say.[9]) He fell not 30 yards from me. The only exciting, really thrilling thing I have seen in France!

Best wishes for all good things.

Your sincere friend
Ivor Gurney

[1] Probably the 19th.

[2] In his peace proposals, made public on 15 August.

[3] A mixture of popular song, *Othello*, and adaptation of Dryden's *Aeneid* translation.

[4] Reference to Milton's 'Lycidas' where 'Their lean and flashy songs/ Grate on their scrannel pipes of wretched straw.'

[5] See letter 233.

[6] By Hilaire Belloc.

[7] *The Old Huntsman* came out in 1917.

[8] Theodore Maynard's *Drums of Dust* is reviewed in the *T.L.S.* of 26 July 1917, p.359.

[9] The French air ace George Guynemer (1894-1917); he was shot down on 11 September 1917.

---

243 To Marion Scott   G.41.129

24 August 1917 (G)

My Dear Friend   Friday Aug 24

Beaucoup ourages[1] maintenant. The bivvy sways and wrenches at its pegs, and so do I – for I am sick of all this; all, that is, save the shining spirit of comradeship so modestly, so naturally, beautifully shown by certain men.

As for what has been happening, please keep the accounts of fighting on the 22nd. There is no news at all as yet of my old Company, but, I am sure, like the rest they did well. Luckily for me, I am new as an M.G. and had to go up on fatigue only to return where Fritz was lobbing shells every now and then. We got caught in a barrage for an hour on the fatigue, and shrapnel caught me twice – once on the blessed old tin hat, (dent and scar) and once on the belt. (no mark.) Pretty hot just there.

Thank you for copying the poems, once again. There are twenty altogether in my book.

Curse the weather! is it going to change again? Ah, but were it Autumn and I in England! Such golden-pathed days I remember, on Cranham; wading knee deep in rustling leaves, or exulting in some miraculous sombre-passionate sunset over Wales, and in such peace as nothing but the very presence of God may give.

I hope you are still Excelsiorising, toddling upward toward strength. Soon the violin, soon the book, and then – what? Well, this is all for the present scribble.

Best wishes

Your sincere friend
Ivor Gurney

[*In the same envelope*:]

My Dear Friend   August 24th 10pm
    The books have just arrived ... My Goodness! Thank you beaucoup! Have you looked at them? Some of Brett Young is perfect. As for Freeman, listen to the end of No 1[2]

'And England lovelier looked than when
Her dead roused not her living men.'
What more do you want?

Why the Ruddy Hades did I write 'Spring 1917'? Why, O why did I, did I write ...

My book is far better than F.W.H.'s as a whole, but the artistry, the assurance, the matter and manner of these two absolutely puncture me.

Well, mine is interesting too.

Yours
I.B.G.

All I have is 2.20!
For the present, my most grateful thanks.

---

[1] Gurney presumably means 'orages': storms.
[2] See letter 245 below.

24 August 1917 (G)

My Dear Friend   August 24
   Here are some more things for you, written between fatigues and marches
and general Army worries; out of thoughts of sunset and war. Please criticise
hard.

Eternal Treasure

> Why think on Beauty as for ever lost
> When fire and steel have worked their evil will,
> Since Beauty lasts beyond decaying dust,
> And in the after-dark is lovely still?
> We are no phantoms; Body is but the case
> Of an immortal Flame that does not perish,
> Can the all-withering power of Time outface,
> Since God Himself with love that flame does cherish.
> Take comfort then, and dare the dangerous thing,
> Death flouting with his impotence of wrath;
> For Beauty arms us 'gainst his envious sting,
> Safes us in any the most perilous path.
> Come then, O brothers, greet what may befall
> With Joy, for Beauty's Maker ordereth all.
>   V — August 1917

That is surely not unworthily in the Shakespearian tradition?
   Now
(Name denoted by dash)

           — (Dash no 1)

> I saw proud — under the dawn,
> Poor — that was once so proud!
> Like clanging trumpets came the dawn,
> Victorious trumpets clamouring loud.
>
> And — pale besmearéd face
> A little colour took from pride
> In her past beauty, and her race
> Of heroes that like princes died.
>
> Then Hope from Pride arose again
> That dared to dream her fate was not

311

Misery and still unending pain;
Her wrongs by God and man forgot.

Straight pierced her weary mind the thought
That these drab figures three years seen
Were men by whom deliverance wrought
Would set her high again, a Queen.

O thought! The high transfiguring fires
Of sunrise made her eyes glow deep.
Deeper, her passionate desires ....
Thus Royal — waked from sleep!

V — August 1917.

I hope these will meet with your approval.

Today Chance brought me to a rickety old piano, and once again I played.
My fingers are not stiff, nor my brain. Just wait!

Have you received 'Camps' yet? These two poems make 7 don't they for
book 2? Or is it 6?

Well, no matter!

Your sincere friend
Ivor Gurney

245 *To Marion Scott*   G.41.127

25 August 1917 (G)

My Dear Friend   August 25
Again a little more time, and scribble.

Those books gave me a happy time; it was delightful to feast on words I had
not seen before, and by candlelight, which has been forbidden of late.

Well, to criticism.[1]

F.W.H.'s book (as if new to me)
The writer is obviously at the beginning of his **strength,** and has not yet
gained mastery. Some pieces have been written under pressure of time and lack
form, chiefly, on that account. He has not many beautiful lines, but can write
beautiful wholes – 'Gonnehem', 'In Flanders', 'If we return', 'If Beauty were
a mortal thing'. A careless book, often ill-wrought, often ragged. A course of
Shakespeare's Sonnets, Keats, Milton and Robert Bridges would be the best
for him. The Ballad of Beelzebub is fine and striking altogether. An interesting
occasionally beautiful book from a fine but untrained and not-yet-settled
character. Too much W.H.Davies – an influence he does not need.

Five Degrees South F.B.Young.

This writer is far more a master of craft than F.W.H., and can write sonnets, not only of beautiful phrases, but of an ordered whole. Some of his lines are exquisite, and whereas F.W.H. is beautiful but not original in thought, F.B.Y. is often strikingly so. Here is far more music, not necessarily because the writer has more at heart, but because of superior training in technique and, probably, greater age. There is no saying what will be the future of Harvey, but of Young one may speak with some certainty. Reading the book through one comes on verses like the last verse of 'Porton Water'.

> 'The pale moon she comes and looks,
> Over the lonely spire she climbs;
> For there she is lovelier many times
> Than in the little broken brooks'.

Or verse such as that passage in 'Testament' which opens

> 'We talked of beauty and those fiery things' and ends
> 'Now I have known sorrow, and now I sing
> That a lovely word is not an idle thing'.

There is an exquisite poem, fresh and innocent, called 'Easter', in which the actual talk is mingled with verse ordinary in a perfect way. A sonnet, 'After Action' ends in this manner. -

> 'So quiet was it, I might well have been lazing
> In a room I love, where the ivy cluster shakes
> Its dew upon the lattice panes at even;
> Where rusty ivory scatters from the dying
> Jessamine blossom and the musk-rose breaks
> Her dusky bloom beneath a summer heaven'.

In 'Sonnet' one reads

> 'Of brazen skies that smile on our duress,
> Making us crave thy cloudy state no less
> Than the sweet clarity of thy rain-washed air,
> Meadows in moonlight cool, and every fair
> Slow-fading flower of thy summer dress'.

'Envoi' seems to me rickety in metre. I do not like pauses to be made only in one, and that the first verse. 'Song of the Dark Ages' is very striking. And the sestett of 'Five Degrees South' with its reminiscence of Robert Bridges. 'The Gift', '104 Fahrenheit', 'Testament', 'Song', (p.31) the powerful 'Ghostly Loves', 'On a Subaltern killed in Action', and even 'Envoi', that unevenly moving poem, are all fine, all worth reading. It is a good book, this; and the work of a poet, master of his craft.

John Freeman *Presage of Victory*

'The Crazy Clay' I cannot read, though undoubtedly there are fine things therein. 'Presage of Victory' has some beautiful gravely moving verse, and is a fine poem. 'Sweet England' is good also, and 'The Stars in their Courses' strength and beauty. A book well worth reading for its friendship given therein with a spirit strong, sincere and tender, touched to beauty by beautiful things, but chief by England and the stars. He uses the word 'strange' too often, and tries to make atmosphere by that word not to be used too often.

[1] F.W.Harvey, *A Gloucestershire Lad at Home and Abroad* (1916), Francis Brett Young, *Five Degrees South* (1917), and John Freeman, *Presage of Victory* (1917).

246 *To Marion Scott*   G.41.126

late August 1917 (KT)

Last letter of the set

My Dear Friend

Surely we may give up thanking each other for our letters, for it is tedious and (if we may believe each other) unnecessary. This refers to your letter written August 21st.

In medias res, for I may be up the line in no time. (A damn good thing for me I transferred.)

I am glad you are pleased with 'Winter Beauty' though even now it is not what I want – quite. Sidgwick and Jackson told me the book might be out in September (by the end of September) but that October was more probable. They have not announced much, so it may be all right.

'Camps'

Yes 'lovely against the blue the summits show' is better, and that line was the one I could not remember on rewriting. Verse 5 alright 'living calmly led' is grammatical, – to lead a life calmly. Last verse, do as you please; 'gate' if you like; if not 'gates'; but perhaps 'gate' is better, for the 'receives'.

O those damned dedications! Should not a woman be meek? Should an agent overbear an author with calm assurance? I know not; but it looks likely to happen in the present case. But why dedicate the biggest – longest, that is – thing in the book to dear Sir C.H.H.P.? I give in, but surlily on the other things, but why this? Why this? Take just what dedications you please. (I won't interfere with my own business ever again.) They being a free and gratefully given present.

Only, the steel is visible under the velvet glove here.

As you will about the *Contemporary*. I have learnt my place.

I am glad the notebook has given you pleasure, which was the object of the giving.

You have no idea how nice it is to get letters one can really answer. It is the Chief Joy of the B.E.F. to receive letters, the worst torment to answer them. To you I can write straight on without even remembering the lice; (You see, I become courtly on occasion) and the pleasure of doing so is great. I hope to be writing to you at the age of 70.

314

Now then as to the books; you have a criticism of them elsewhere. I have pretty well sucked their brains; but can learn a lot from F.B.Young; Robert Bridges, younger more romantic is his description. I have enjoyed myself very greatly. O my brain, how much swifter, larger, wider, stronger art thou! I begin to live now, and what I was begin to forget. And Peace will bring double life and health.

You shall have Brett Young and Freeman back again soon.

Meanwhile, dear Marion, thank you very much indeed.

Your sincere friend
Ivor Gurney

247 *To Marion Scott*   G.41.128

27 August 1917 (G)

My Dear Friend   August 27th

Yet another letter to you!

I think it will be better to omit nearly all dedications, because

(1) People will begin to compare.

(2) It looks silly and makes the book a sort of family affair.

Yes, I would prefer them out. What pleasure it would give to certain people shall be (partly) made up when I tell certain people certain things are for them, and write it in their copy. Critics too are almost certain to dislike so many inscriptions. Besides, taking this way, the value of such dedications as there are will be greater.

Nicholson's book has arrived, (Again to be grateful to you!) and it will be better to say I am very disappointed with it, though of course, not all has yet been read. *The Times L.S.* quoted practically everything good. All the poets whom I have lately read I should like to meet – Sassoon, Binyon, Freeman, Brett Young, Hodgson, (Harvey ....) but nothing in this man's work but that quoted by the *T.L.S.* attracts me. He is violent, (a sign of weakness), wrests the true nature of verse, knows something but not enough to justify his liberties; his love of soldiers seems to me to be somewhat of a pose; (a dreadful accusation.) His face; his having published it abroad; His attitude to War and the men of war seems to me to be as detached as that of Zola; not so near as Fabre on his insects.[1] It and they – War and Men – are his material, and never he looks on a piece of beauty but that he will strive to make words on it – for a Book!

I will try to read the earlier things tomorrow.

A double set of proofs! Yum, Yum!!

Yes, the Rupert Brooke dedication to be retained, if you please.

Le Matin printed a thing in emphatic type purporting to be taken from a

315

conversation with a highly placed British General, which would say that important events may be near, which 'are able to be decisive', the strongest language I have known *Le Matin* use. If we took Lille, the coast, and a favourable position well in Belgium before the close of this year's fighting season, do you not think that Germany might crack up before the next clash? For certainly Germany will have most severe internal trouble this Winter.

Last night I was reading *Lear*, and its bareness of naked words thrilled me very much. O late readings again after music. We will play the Kreutzer some day most stormfully – bare downs of late October and at ominous dusk.

I am glad The Old Bold Mate has arrived, and that you like it.

A wicked evening. The line will be a swamp again; but at any rate we shall be out of this night certain to be evil.

Meanwhile, I hope you are gradually getting stronger, and wish you would tell me something about your recovery, however slow.

With best wishes

Your sincere friend
Ivor Gurney

[1] Jean Henri Fabre (1823-1915), scientist and entomologist, whose works display amazing powers of minute observation.

248 *To Marion Scott* G.41.125

29 August 1917 (G)

My Dear Friend

We are off up again, and this is the last letter written in the quiet. (We can write up there however, and do you write.) I go up with Brent Young, Harvey, 6 Tragedies of Shakespeare and *The Bible in Spain*, with nothing to fear on that account therefore.

You will find a fresh pome below, though there is no question of volunteering....

And here I break off because they say no letters will be censored up there. 'May all the infections that the sun sucks up - fall upon Fritz and make him by inchmeal a disease'.[1]

(Today is August 29)

To M.M.S.

O, if my wishes were my power,
You should be praised as were most fit,
Whose kindness cannot help but flower.

But since the fates have ordered it
So otherwise, then ere the hour
Of darkness deaden all my wit

I'll write: how all my art was poor,
My mind too thought-packed to acquit
My debt ... And only, 'thanks once more'.
                    August 27, near P—[2]
For the beggars haven't paid us yet! 30 francs in 8 weeks!

The Volunteer

I would test God's purposes;
I will go up and see
What fate is mine, what destiny
God holds for me.

For He is very secret,
He smiles, but does not say
A word that will foreshadow
Shape of the coming day.

Curious am I, curious ...
And since he will not tell
I'll prove him, go up against
The flary mouth of Hell.

And what hereafter – Heaven?
Or Blighty? O if it were ....
Mere agony, mere pain the price
Of the returning there.

Or – nothing! Days in mud
And slush, then other days...
Aie me! 'Are they not all
The seas of God?' God's Ways?

That's not so bad, I think. Are colours turning yet in Kent? Perhaps. In
Kensington gardens I have no doubt leaves are turning colour, are drifting to
please children as in other years, but the country is different and holds its ways
longer, especially in the West Country, that greener and fairer land than poor
old smoky Middlesex.

Herein you will find also a dissertation on Nicholson's book,[3] which would
be sent off today, had I the money, but that lacking, the book must stay

behind, safe in a sandbag.

You shall have my second note book when that parcel comes.

Things look pretty hopeful now, don't they? The Italians seem to have remembered Caesar and his far wars and glory. What the Austrians remember I cannot say. (Austerlitz?) And the French don't seem exhausted, as as for the English.... Our guns would frighten imps in the lowest concrete dugout of Hell, so they shake *me* up pretty considerably.

Now write to me, prattle sweetly in your accustomed fashion, for how long we shall be in we do not know save from that fickle jade Rumour, whose information is rarely much good. And by all means send the proofs if you can get a double set.

Goodbye. With best wishes

Your sincere friend
Ivor Gurney

[1] Shakespeare's *The Tempest*, II.2.3.
[2] This may be Passchendaele.
[3] There is no such thing enclosed.

249 To Marion Scott   G.41.132

31 August 1917 (G)

My Dear Friend   August 31st 6pm

Still moving along life's weary road, not very pleased with the scenery of this section of it, and wishing the guns would give over; for these literally are never still. When the parcel comes with the books returned to you, you will find a small packet wrapped in newspaper (if it is allowed to be sent, as I suppose it will.) In this there will be a local German Newspaper of August 10, and a fragment of filthy notebook which you might like to have – it being as I think a piece of a section commander's book.[1]

This morning I was exploring some ruined Tanks but not with any striking success. And tomorrow is September 1st! Summer almost gone ..... Seven years behind accomplishment!

Today I have been reading *The Bible in Spain*, that brilliant curious book. Indeed, but Borrow is indispensable – *Lavengro*, *Wild Wales*, *Romany Rye* and *The Bible in Spain*! A queer chap though, and often purposely queer. Also F.W.H.'s book has been in my hands, but I desire before all things to learn, and he has not much knowledge. But it is queer to look from the real sight of this tortured ground on to that picture of my old School House taken from the playing ground![2]

I.B.G.

When 'windy', write letters, and so – here you are. For Fritz has been shelling and it has rattled me.

Thank you for your two letters – August 26, 27. It delighted me to get them this morning. As for the *Fifth Gloucester Gazette* I am indifferent. The only public I could get to that will not be accessible in the ordinary way is that class of people who would not care for what I write.

As to 'Field Daisy', it seems to me that the first version is better than this last, of line 8; with which there is nothing seriously wrong anyhow. But here is a bit that pleases me.

'Even before this pain was set upon the Earth, this scourge of War' For I do not altogether agree with you that it is all Man's fault.

It is very good news to hear that Fritz gets a hotter time of it on his present raids in England than he did. The Foul fiend. I hope you will escape ever being bombed at all, wherever you pitch your tent and make your stay.

Cyril Scott writes as one expects.

The lights you saw on that Wednesday were Aurora Borealis, so I read; not lightning. Mein Gootness! Now I remember seeing something of the kind most wonderful about that time perhaps, but took it for a coast bombardment, yet heard no sound, which was strange. These illuminations are connected in some mysterious way with sun-spots.

You are right about Sassoon; you are right about Hodgson. Sassoon is the half-poet, the borrower of magic. But as for the talk about poetry .... Well, I think about that sometimes in this little concrete and steel emplacement holding 25 men, but O the crush! Slum conditions if you please.

As for your book, I doubt whether you will get much help from me, whose convictions are firm but nebulous.

As for the Imagists – I hate all attempts at exact definition of beauty, which is a half-caught thing, a glimpse. What the devil *is* a 'cosmic poet'? Surely a better name would be cosmetic?

Hodgson is really the true thing, and so I would rather put off comment till later when I am better able to think of such things, and have read the 'Song of Honour' in full. If it is much longer, O please don't copy any but the very best parts, for to tell the truth, I do not like being obliged to people for kindnesses I would not return, and to copy out the 'Song of Honour' would about kill me. Thank you very much for your beastly decency, as boys say. 'When I'm among a blaze of stars' is very clear-cut well and truly seen, but not poetry. Good verse. 'The Bells of Heaven' is splendid. 'Reason has moons' I will refer to again.

Ruined Tanks in front of me against a flaring west of tomorrow's wind and rain. A country like the last Hell of desolation. And to write verse, and abstract perfection! And so I quiet my nerves, and set my mind on another train of thought. I am most grateful to you for your friendship for you are the only one of my real friends save my while-lost F.W.H. that can talk about these things, and can stimulate me. I am convinced that without you *Severn and Somme* would have been either not written, (as most probable) or written

319

on pieces of letters etc and drifted piecemeal away as fast as written.

Your sincere friend
Ivor Gurney

[1] There is no sign of either in the archive.

[2] Gurney is referring to the picture on the cover of Harvey's book.

250 *To Marion Scott*   G.41.111

early September 1917 (KT)

My Dear Friend

Here am I, sheltered from the sun by the parados of a trench behind a blockhouse; reading *The Bible in Spain*. That's finished now, and *Robinson Crusoe* need not be begun for we are being relieved tonight, and O! the relief! *Robinson* may follow; we shall have tomorrow off anyway. What a life! My memories of this week will be. – Blockhouse; an archway there through which a sniper used his skill on [us] as we emerged from the rooms at the side; cold; stuffy heat; Brent Young; Smashed or stuck Tanks; A gas and smoke barrage put up by us, a glorious but terrifying sight; Fritzes shells; One sunset; two sunrises; *Bible in Spain*; the tale of the cutting up of the K.R.C.s in 1914; of Colonel Elkington; of the first gas attacks also; of the Brigade Orderly; and of the man who walked in his sleep to Fritz, slept well, woke, realised, and bolted; Thirst; Gas; Shrapnel; *Very* H.E.; Our liquid fire; A first sight of an aeroplane map..... Does it sound interesting? May God forgive me if I ever come to cheat myself into thinking that it was, and lie later to younger men of the Great Days. It was damnable; and what in relation to what might have happened? Nothing at all! We have been lucky, but it is not fit for men to be here – in this tormented dry-fevered marsh, where men die and are left to rot because of snipers and the callousness that War breeds. 'It might be me tomorrow. Who cares? Yet still, hang on for a Blighty'.

Why does this war of spirit take on such dread forms of ugliness, and why should a high triumph be signified by a body shattered, black, stinking; avoided by day, stumbled over by night, an offence to the hardest? No doubt there is consolation in the fact that men contemplate such things, such possible endings, and are yet undismayed, yet persistent; do not lose laughter nor the common kindliness that makes life sweet – And yet seem such boys – Yet what consolation can be given me as I look upon and endure it? Any? Sufficient? The 'End of War'? Who knows, for the thing for which so great a price is paid is yet doubtful and obscure; and our reward most sweet would seem to depend on what we make of ourselves and give ourselves; for clearer eyes and more contented minds; more contented because of comparisons ironically to be made....

and yet

etc (Not quite correct)

Forgive all this; and accept it as a sincere reflection; a piece of technique; only one side of the picture; trenchweariness; thoughts of a not too courageous, not too wellbalanced mind. Like Malvolio, I think nobly of man's soul, and am distressed.[1] God should have done better for us than this; Could He not have found some better milder way of changing the Prussian (whom he made) than by the breaking of such beautiful souls? Now *that* is what one should write poetry upon. Someday I will say it in Music, after a while.

Now I must go into the Blockhouse, may get a Blighty doing so ... and O if it were but a small hole in the leg! But I am lucky only in my friends, and existence has gone awry for me, not by any means wholly my fault. Maybe I am strong enough to prove the truth of 'Character is Destiny' now.[2] God, how I could work, how train myself in Blighty now, were it over! Dyspepsia or no dyspepsia, I'd 'be a marvellous kid!'[3] And yet (O the Shakespearian insight of me!) Had I used those earlier years, still I must have come out here for all my promise and accomplishments, and – there you are; here.

I have made a book about Beauty because I have paid the price which five years ago had not been paid. Someday perhaps the True, the real, the undeniable will be shown by me, and I forgive all this.

There is a great gap in my mind, very thirsty, which shall be filled with sunsets, trees, winds, stars, and children's faces; blossoming fairer after so long a drought my mind shall turn freely to that which once was effort to contemplate. I, even I, may experience Present Joy – but not yet. But were I home, with this new ability and Passion for my work, O then perhaps ...

It is a hard thing to accustom oneself to the resigning of life at any moment, and to become aware and more aware of what that leaving means. Meanwhile, while I am thus thinking and writing, our guns pour almost incessantly a thin musical complaining watery trickle of shells; for what purpose one may rise up and see. 'After all I might have gone to Liepsic, to Bonn, to Munich; and they might have been my friends and companions in Art'. There goes a dud, and I am glad of it.

Who will dare talk of the glory of Waterloo or Trafalgar again?

There now, I have written myself out, and feel happier. (Theirs or ours?

321

Theirs. Bash!)

I do not forget in my preoccupations to hope you are getting stronger, and that Mr Scott is now on holiday. Nor forget the funny side of things. A few yards away are three walking cases; perhaps 'Blighty' men. To get to the Dressing Station is a slightly risky thing, but far less so than many ordinary things a soldier does. Will they risk it? In daylight? Hardly! For they have that which is more precious than much fine gold.

Tea's up!

TEA!! O magic word.

Late reading with a pipe and a teapot. 5 oclock at Cranham. Willy Harvey and wonderful Mrs Harvey. Framilode. Twigworth.

O what not? All these memories have music in them. Bach and Schumann. Perhaps there are two men of that name over there.

Your sincere friend

Ivor Gurney

I wish I wasn't so lousy. Don't trouble to sympathise. I take that for granted or would not have written comme ca.

[1] *Twelfth Night*, IV.2.59.
[2] An aphorism of Novalis, quoted by George Eliot in *The Mill on the Floss*.
[3] A reference perhaps to Chatterton, whom Wordsworth called 'the marvellous boy' in 'Resolution and Independence'.

---

251 *To Marion Scott*   G.41.133

7 September 1917 (G)

My Dear Friend

Your letters of August 30 and 31st reached grateful me in the line. Je vous en remercie.

You have had a great patience in copying out the 'Song of Honour'; I would not have asked had I known its length. Do not copy any more Sassoon please; I have absorbed him. He is a neat picturesque interesting writer who occasionally reaches poetry. The 'Song of Honour' has great passages but is not the poem all we have been waiting for. (But for that, afterwards).

No, I don't like 'Ave (Autumne', I should think; if a second declension.) 'The leaves are preparing to die' is prosy.

'The amethyst asters (are) gemmed in imperial hue' is a good line, but could be used better

<blockquote>The amethyst asters gemmed in imperial hue

Most royal, emerald herbage flaunting its riches.</blockquote>

Line 2 of v:3 is weak. And line 3 annoys me with 'like'. Say boldly things *are*. (Also 4 'The's' at the beginnings of lines.)

The golden-rod lifts processional torches of splendour;
From sapphire heaven gentian catches a gleam.
Topaz the phlox, and luminous, pink other worldly,
And daisies silver-of-dream.

The last verse is good, especially the last line, but not coherent, yet easily made so. As it stands it does not make sense, to me.

The 'One legged man' is good. 'The Bells of Heaven' glorious.

I will talk of the 'Song of Honour' when I can see it whole. Meanwhile many thanks. When they pay us, perhaps tomorrow, I will return the books mentioned before.

(Second Letter)

I am glad you have managed to get some concession in the way of flour, and very glad you have managed 2 miles, say rather over 3 kilos! You will do it with a pack someday for fun!

I do hope you will manage to stay at Sevenoaks, and in a nice house. Indeed you deserve luck, since it is luck to have you as a friend.

(O 'Reason has moons' is perfectly delightful. And O, delighting me!)

Well, we are out now, but for how long is doubtful. It may be the out-of-the-line feeling, but I do not think I shall get killed. That is the only premonition, save a slight one that there is no Blighty just yet.

Leave is quite possible when this fighting season closes.

I have no more to say, save that in such a September day as this I should have been picking apples and shooting rabbits with Willy Harvey. Crack not my heartstrings!

Best wishes

Your sincere friend
Ivor Gurney

September 7
My Dear Friend

As this letter has not yet been taken, I may as well add a P.S. to say what a devil of a temper I am in – what with flies, lice, and being on guard.

They have paid me – 10 francs! So today if possible Nicholson and Co shall set out youward. I wish that I could write some more now, but don't feel up to it. What's up with the weather? What's up with everything? Everything's up what, and that's the truth of it. Meanwhile go you on and prosper.

52 *To Marion Scott*   G.41.134

9 September 1917 (G)

My Dear Friend   September 9

Thank you for your letter of September 3, which reposes peacefully before me on a pack. Conditions: beautiful morning, which we must spend in a concrete affair, once a peaceful farm; now called after that farm, but how unlike! ('How unlike the state from which they fell'!)[1]

I am sorry you get well so slowly, The War is probably the cause, and War diet. May it not be so for long!

Russia does seem in a hole now; but the declaration of a Russian minister that the cause of the retreat was concentration of technical force and not cowardice sounds better. (Tanks?) The enormous majority against Stockholm at the English Trades Union Conference is very good and encouraging. So also is Gerard's statement that he thinks Germany can hold out not more than another year, economically. Gerard must be a man worth meeting!

I am very glad you like my last two things, especially that for you.

Yesterday I sent off to the postman a parcel containing, *Five Degrees South*; *Presage of Victory*; and Nicholson's book; which (as you suppose) has taught me something; my second notebook and anthology; a German paper; and, lastly, a noisome fragment of a German N.C.O.'s note-book, as I should judge, at least.

The best way to learn to write is to read classics like Milton, Keats and Shakespeare, and the Georgian poets. (Do you remember V.Williams said the same about Music?) One learns form and the true use of language from those, and flexibility and the modern touch from these. Remoteness and Modernity mixed, is the best diet for youth – or Age. In my notebook you will find some things you have not seen. Do as you will with them. By the way you have never acknowledged a poem called — (because the name may not be written) and a Shakespearian sonnet that came with it, of which I am rather proud. Those are written in the note-book though rather illegibly. Some things there may help to pad out a book if I happen to return to Music sooner than – 40 poems shall we say? Though, if the first book is successful we ought to do with less, and then not be considered mean.

I do not ask how you are for Form's sake, (since nearly always I forget Form) but because I wish to know. Thank you for telling me, and please keep on. Do you feel ill or merely weak and helpless or what? I mean, can you Live a little now? Your letters are alert enough anyhow.

'The Song of Honour' was good enough when it was written, but it is better still now. Could one, dare one write a hymn to the honour of Man now? It would be too high a thing. Only a Bishop could not see that. Only the professional Churchman is blind, who 'goes lack-lustre' all his days.[2]

The Five Francs have not been sent. Please excuse this, but - well it was only 10 francs after 3 weeks, and the Line to follow. In a certain case I must refer you to my executors, that's all.

My books up here are few – Tolstoi's *Master and Man etc*, *A Gloucestershire Lad* and verse taken from your letters. (By the way I spotted Corbie the other day, near Peronne.)

Do you care for 'The Late Last Rook'? I cannot say it attracts me much. Tolstoi's short tales are perfect. No one but a Master could write so well and simply; anyone must love them.

By the way, I *did* write to thank Mr Scott for long letter and present, surely? My memory. My memory!

Such an afternoon! Golden September sunshine which should be seen flecked on the grass of Redlands paddock with F.W.H. and I strolling round – talking, talking. With best wishes

Your sincere friend
Ivor Gurney

[1] Milton's *Paradise Lost*, Book 1, 1.75.
[2] The quotation is from Hodgson's 'The Song of Honour'.

---

253 *To Marion Scott* G.41.135

12 September 1917 (G)

My Dear Friend letters of Sep 3-7
Sep 12

Thank you, in spite of what I wrote about not thanking.

I am very glad you like my two last things, two more toward your book. Today I have been writing, but will polish up a little before sending it on.

— (you are right about the title!) was a mere exercise, a fill up of time, written because I had not written for some time. Your praise of it shows that I have some technique now! Of the last line of verse 2 – there is an influence further back than F.W.H. 'And they shall die like men; and fall like one of the princes'.

I am very sorry to hear of you sister's illness, and hope she is getting well in a proper manner. It does not sound dangerous anyway. May old Dr Bunnett prove right that you yourself will have a free time from illness for the rest of your days. After all, it may be true that a radical defect is now removed, and though the trouble caused thereby is great a good time follows after. It is reasonable to think so, surely?

You need not be disappointed at your birthday present being a failure. it was not; since my own book appears to be better than Nicholson's! I only wish things were quiet so that the book could be studied by me, but that will come after – when there is no need. Now you add the three other books, your present appears royal. You will enjoy Brent Young, a poet – though not a big one, and a master of his craft, through studying Robert Bridges chiefly. There are some lovely things in that book, and it was good to come across Bredon mentioned. This is the Gloster-Worcestershire Bredon, not Housman's.

I hope you will manage to stay at Sevenoaks, since it suits you and pleases you, and since the soil seems favourable to letter writing.

By the way I am still in the line, but not having at all a bad time of it. My throat is still sore from gas; it is just (or was) as if I had had catarrh, but only an occasional explosion of coughing is left now. No luck! One cannot smell the new gas. One starts sneezing. The old gas had a heavy hothouse Swinburnian filthy sort of odour – voluptuous and full of danger.

Yes 'Eternal Treasure' is good. The use of 'safes' is purely Shakespearian, not mine; though I have forgotten a passage to quote. *Macbeth* perhaps has it. O yes, and *Antony*.[1]

I am glad Harold Darke likes my things so, and of course he may use my song.

As to Sassoon's book, you will find the pretty but thin 'Before the Battle' in my note book. The other isn't bad. Violent of course = weak. Please do not trouble to copy out things of this standard; they not giving me pleasure enough to compensate for your trouble.

We go out tonight, it is likely, thank Goodness!.

Outside the guns are hammering, but they will have to hammer well at the remnant of a German blockhouse before they hurt us, and anyway it is mostly our guns. 10 shells to one is a usual procedure.

Goodbye, and don't worry, and get well as quickly as you may, for the War must end someday, and it will be a joyful thing to find my friends fit.

Best wishes

Your sincere friend
Ivor Gurney

---

[1] Not in *Macbeth* but in *Antony and Cleopatra*, I.3.55 and IV.6.26.

254 *To Marion Scott*   G.41.131

17 September 1917 (KT)

My Dear Friend   September – Monday

Thanks be to goodness I am out of it for a day or two, gassed in the throat 5 days ago – but not thinking to get anything out of it. How long will it last? Couldn't say, but not so long as I would wish. Being gassed (mildly) with the new gas is no worse than catarrh or a bad cold.

Well, everything in the way of letters will go astray for a bit. And it is probably of no use to send an address now, as any time we may be shifted.

So – to correct Proofs! Luckily they arrived the day before I went sick. Please cut out the dedications as I have said. So many are they that one arrives in the end at giving them to those who expect it rather than those to whom one would wish.

Yes, I agree, considering the poor paper, the book looks very nice, but O (yes, 'O!') the 'I's! Confronted with the thing in cold print, I am struck with the thinness and futility and egoism of the thing – but won't say more. I have arrived at more pages than F.W.H., but he has oftener long things like Ballades.

From that last word I turned aside to look *Severn and Somme* through once more, and finished the corrections, as I think. Don't you think from what you have that Book 2 will be a better one than this? I hope you have the notebook by now, as perhaps you may think one or two things worth using.

Yesterday I met my pet R.A.M.C. man, who knew Tolstoi. He gave me a surprise. Told me his girl was Brett Young's sister! He has often spoken of her, but until I read that book, *Five Degrees South*, it could mean nothing to me who she was; while we are in France anyhow.

I am very glad you are able to find something to suit you at Sevenoaks; in all ways, it is better to stay there, and for your sister to come too soon.

Well, there will be no letters for me now; probably not till I settle down somewhere; and that will be the M.G.C. again I think, for there is not much hope of staying in hospital for me. By the way your letter of Sep: 12 arrived just as I left.

With best wishes

Your sincere friend
Ivor Gurney

21 September 1917 (P)

My Dear Friend

Still at the C.C.S. but expecting to move today, through the blowiest white fleeted weather of September, every gust of which brings a memory to me; of scent, of sight, or of sound of the hollow echoes of woodfelling or some such thing at Highnam. I don't wonder you wish to stay at Sevenoaks, Chelsea and the Gardens have their charm and Yoshio Markino[1] has told us about the Colour of London. (By the way have you read that most fascinating book?) O that I were worse! It would not have been too difficult to get to Blighty with a real serious case now. Just my luck!

Strong protests and representations have been forwarded to the Lord Almighty, but I expect no yielding in that quarter, and on account of so common a complaint.

Again a term beginning draws near. O what a wasted time! Can it be possible to acquire a balance of experience of life, of clear sight and strength of character to make up for all this? Twentyseven, and not yet trained! I feel a boy still; a boy who has not yet had his chance, with the ability and determination to make one if necessary. That is in the abstract. In the concrete, the continual question seems, 'Will you ever be able to build, to construct? Could you write one good Sonata movement?' No, I couldn't; but let me get back to soak myself properly in music , and to feel alive again and secure, and then – En avant! Full Steam Ahead! And then (to alter the image) I hope to have sufficiently hard work to hold the tiller. O comforting dreams!.

Today should send you out walking, and far, if the wind is not too much. For the air, here, in this tent, is as clear and pure as any of Kent, I suppose. It is a 25 mile day, though you will hardly manage that yet awhile. It is a day to see Cranham above you and Portway in front, to stalk knee deep through drifts of early fallen leaves; to climb higher for the sight of Severn, Wales, Malverns, Bredon and Clee Hills – I chuck in the Severn plain as buckshee. A sunset and the road over Coopers likewise. But Arcturus over May Hill I reserve for myself.

I hope your sister is getting better still (It is some time before I may hear anyhow) and will be able to get to you soon. She might as well convalesce at Sevenoaks as near Hyde Park. The puddles of Kent are better than the rivers of Middlesex.

I am very sorry the proofs will reach you in so dirty an envelope. Your own, but it had travelled, and such things must be stowed any old where in the Army. Curse the Army!

This is an annoying wind; it gathers or seems to gather the sweetest things one has ever known to drift about and taunt a poor private of no renown at all, at all. Curse the wind!

By the way, I, moi meme, have got the name for being extremely cool under shell-fire. It may be so to the view, but could they read my mind sometimes! So you see, neurasthenia leads one to a strange praise. By conquering fear-of-Life one may learn at once to love Life and to scorn death together; but neither has come yet in reality.

With best wishes

Your sincere friend
Ivor Gurney

[1] See letter 123 and note.

22 September 1917 (G)[1]

My Dear Friend

The unexpected has happened. Just but now, I walked up steps and saw the Evening Star, to show me where England lies, and the blue and silver gleam of tossing sea-water. I cannot chortle, for feelings of all kinds turning my distended breast.

Today we have been steaming down the loveliest river in the world, in the loveliest weather. Alack! gas or staying still has disturbed my anatomy so

much that I could not
(Interlude. 'Life Belts on!' Now we shan't be long.)
appreciate it at all worthily, yet its miraculous beauty will arise beautiful in the mind some day, and become my own, and sing for others.

Well, I shall see you, I suppose sooner or later, and tell you all about myself, and analyse my emotions till you are bored stiff. Of course you will be patient, but that is the Ass' chief virtue; and someday you may wake up to think you *are* one to stand it. And no-one could blame you for kicking.

But how I should have liked to have you as confidante tonight – early! For everything seemed futile, save Beauty that was too high for me; myself a failure and prematurely worn; my friends poor trusting fools to be disappointed..... George Gissing's *Henry Ryecroft* contributed to this mood. I am about to settle to him again, so perhaps it will be better to shut up.

I hope you are getting well properly. And your sister – much better I hope.
Lights dim. Goodbye

Your sincere friend
Ivor Gurney

[1] This letter has been separated from its envelope, and its envelope used to contain a letter for 29 March 1917 (G.70.11.1) and one of early September 1916 (G.70.11.2), neither of which belongs to the date on the envelope. The envelope has in Gurney's hand 'Soldiers Letter' where he had previously written 'On Active Service'; it is franked 'RECEIVED FROM H.M.SHIP NO CHARGE TO BE [word illegible]' and forwarded from Sevenoaks on 24 September 1917.

257 To Marion Scott   G.41.137

26 September 1917 (G)

My Dear Friend

To write to you on common notepaper, white and smooth, to be in between sheets white and smooth – yesterday, but I smoke in bed! - and to hear noises domestic and well known flurries and scurries about one – how sweet are all these! And to be within 17 miles of Enbro, that old city of Scott and R.L.S.; such is my nature that this last idea or fact is sweetest of all. *Ward 24 Edinburgh War Hospital, Bangour, Scotland* is my present address. Only slowly and uncertainly is the conviction leaking in through the strong covering of frost and use that I am *really* in Blighty. You remember F.W.H.'s parable of the man who was in Heaven and did not know it? Even so is it with me!

Last night started the change moving a little quicker for I played for two hours, mostly in accompaniment, and I found to my joy that what I had hoped is true – that the effort to concentrate is a pleasure to me; which means that in so much neurasthenia is a thing of the past. And that what I have would go if I lived in my old life once again, with an added incalculable Joy added thereto. Rejoice with me my friend, for that which was lost is found; or shall I say rather – its hiding place is known.

I hope Autumn with its crisp air and beauty is bringing you some treasure of health also, you who are Captain of your soul[1] though the body play all manner of fantastic tricks. And your sister too, whose sword of spirit is also too keen for the scabbard, as one has said.[2]

Now look at that![3] O Sherlock Holmes, could you not deduce somewhat from the arrangement of these two pages?

I shall be delighted to hear from you again. Please send the old letters on. Are you in your new house I wonder? What about the book?

(I won't say anything about the state of me – medically speaking, being profoundly disappointed, and not hoping to escape the Winter as I had thought.)

How lovely to hear the voices of Scottish women, and see the faces of women pitiful, proud, humourous, strong, lovely of spirit. Not that the French women are not fine. They most undoubtedly are. But the strength of our Islanders is very fine. And which is likely to be the finer strength I would ask – that of men who have controlled themselves in danger and long cold nights of mud and frost, and under a hateful discipline; or that of women doing day long duty of pity in routine? I would say that of women, who are always active in service, will be finer and stronger, only there are comparatively few of them. But there – I am lost in admiration of all Europe, driven by forces beyond their control. The contrast between the magnificent behaviour of Man to that of the apparent callousness of God is most striking, and were it for no other reason than that of having companied with good men one could face God with (almost) a slightly cynical but interested expectation. His debt to Europe, to the World, is very great.

Two or three things I have read that are good. Walpole's *Maradick at Forty*, and G.A.Birmingham's *The Bad Times*. Also an article by Belloc, which has been forcibly abstracted from the *Western Australia*. I know you will be interested to see it. What 'Nights at the Mermaid' must have gone to the making of this essay! Also Snaith's *Fortune* a splendid bit of braggadocio. Swank at its best.[4]

I wonder if you have seen *Gloucestershire Friends* yet?

Of course I will come and see you if every Fate will not contravene me. My ten days leave will come anywhere from 1-2 months time. The farther off, the luckier, for I do not wish to go Back There just yet. On the other hand, there's nothing the matter with me.

I am not well of course, but the thing that struck me on the boat coming over was that noone looked well. There was not any more jollity than if it were merely Another Move. The iron had entered into their souls,[5] and they were still fast bound; unable to realise what tremendous changes of life had come to them for a while.

Dear Marion, this was sad to see, and a tribute to the power of the Old Sweats and Prussians generally. But the river – that magnificent river, the Seine! From Rouen to Le Havre it is just one splendid Symphony, the greatest I have ever seen. I could only try to forget I was so weak of soul to remember a feeling of sickness in my body, and wish they would give me three days rations and a small sailing boat. By the Lord, I would have sailed her clean across if there had been sight of any star. Airships were patrolling the harbour mouth.

Now I must go down to shave – in front of a real mirror!

Clean sheets, clean clothes and skin; no lice; today's papers; ordinary notepaper... what next?

Goodbye, and all good wishes for all good things.

Your sincere friend
Ivor Gurney

[1] Quoting from W.E.Henley's 'Invictus'
[2] Perhaps Byron's 'For the sword outwears the sheath' in 'So we'll go no more a-roving'.
[3] Gurney has divided his single sheet of paper into two very uneven columns.
[4] A reprint of Hugh Walpole's *Maradick at Forty* (1910) was noticed in the *T.L.S.* of 21 June 1917. *The Bad Times* (1908) by G.A.Birmingham (pseudonym of James Owen Hannay, 1865-1950). *Fortune* (1910) by John Collis Snaith (1876-1936).
[5] Quoting from Psalm 105.

258 To Marion Scott   G.41.137

26 September 1917 (G)[1]

My Dear Friend   Sep:26

I have just finished Vachell's *Quinney's*,[2] and would like to talk about it. Surely the book will last? (You see I assume you have read it.) For the characterisation is so good, the play of events so inevitable that – since *Cranford* can last – I can see it in the hands of people of 2005. Perhaps it is Q's love of his craft that pleases me most, but Susan, Posy, Tomlin, the stranger of Brittany, Lord Mel – all please and delight me infinitely, especially after slogging at Classics so long. Soon, I suppose, the curious observer may be able to see me strolling round Enbro, browsing at bookstalls, for one glad hour forgetting myself. If I see any very extra special bargains there you shall hear of them, be sure. I love buying books, but when that is not possible, luring my friends on has an equal pleasure for me.

Since I must live in the past, why not in the company of great men, by stalls laden with tattered books of their making? If they can know, it must please them to see a soldier weary of arms and routine forgetting himself in a delicious agony of uncertainty, caused partly by his divided love and (bond of sympathy to them) a loose purse? Did I buy all I wished, should I read all I bought? That is very doubtful, but the touch smell and appearance of books is very lovely to me.

I wonder if you are in your new house by now, and whether you find it in some way home. You have a great house in London but I doubt whether it can be to you what a tiny house may be, even if it is hung only with framed pages of the *Studio* or *Jugend*, and the piano leaves little room for free movement, and three pipes going would soon asphyxiate the careful landlady. How are the creepers round your house? The winds are chill here today; soon frost will enforce the colours of Autumn on your walls, to delight yourself and as I hope your sister too. (I am not sure she is not right about liking 'Estaminet' best.)

Life will begin to widen itself for you soon, with the violin and your book; let but the winter be but kind, and you should be finely set up by May, and see what Spring can do for fragile things of Earth! Why even playing 'The Rosary', 'Friend of Mine', 'Drake's gone West'[3] etc has knocked me up no end. What power shall not Bach have on you; that is full of all sanity and sweetness and a great restoring power of health? When Peace comes, all the air now full of uneasiness and hate will sweeten; when Europe is sick it is not strange that a spirit like yours should be affected; but it is hard lines you should have to suffer more or less passively. But will you remember that soldiers also suffer passively but under direct orders that lead them to act – as machines of boats that go among hidden mines, risking destruction.

War brings greater self-control – or breakdown. You also must have mastery of yourself, or perish. And whether the pain be of complaining nerves or of waiting on agelong nights of cold and wet to pass, it is all the same, and the use of patience brings the same reward. There is even the same uncertainty with us two, for instance – the same aching thought; whether we shall get the chance to use the rewards of patience. Indeed there is no difference in our conditions, save that I have the right to wear two 'wounded' stripes, and you can only want to do something – anything, to justify yourself to yourself. There again we are equal; for War is simply a necessary but horrid nuisance, and my aim is work in Art, not a medal or a ribbon. Another consideration. Supposing I did get a D.C.M., I know well that braver men than myself have died without, and how to wear a distinction without shame that is so uncertain in the earning?

Please do not accuse yourself of uselessness. At any rate not to me, who have so much to thank you for.

Our positions are reversed, and I am trying to cheer *you* up for once, instead of writing interminable complaints to get wise consoling words.

Today there may be a letter from you, perhaps many letters from France sent on, but it is not wise to hope for all that to happen after 4 days of hospital.

Today I will write to Howells, and Shimmin. There is Sir C.H.H.P. to come, and one or two others of lower degree.

For the length of this letter you must accuse the lack of magazines and books here. For the lack of matter a dull life, but what you have endured so often you may well last out again. If there were no M.M.S. it would be necessary to invent one.

With best wishes

Your sincere friend

Ivor Gurney

[1] In the same envelope as the preceding letter.

[2] Horace Annesley Vachell (1861-1955), *Quinney's* (1914).

[3] 'The Rosary' by Ethelbert Woodbridge Nevin (1862-1901) sold 6 million copies in the thirty years after its publication in 1898. 'Drake Goes West' and 'Friend o' Mine' were by Wilfrid Ernest Sanderson, a prolific and popular composer.

259 To Marion Scott   G.41.138

29 September 1917 (P)   Ward 24, Edinburgh Military Hospital,
Bangour

My Dear Friend

I have just turned over a page, just finished writing a most unsatisfactory piece of verse with which I shall not trouble you.

And would you really be polite enough to ask how I am getting on? Then you shall learn that the will of the doctor still keeps me in bed and on Light Diet; as that does not include bully-beef and biscuits I am not unsatisfied altogether, but it does mean *Lightness*, and that is not good. And the little baccy I have is of the most distressing; cigarettes are no companions like a pipe, and one tires of them. They do not care for classical music much here; my head is thick; my fingers stiff; the weather dull; there is nothing worth reading.

So there you are out of my grumbles. For to be between clean linen in a light room is no small thing; nor to be able to buy today's papers a small blessing. It is good to wander surreptitiously from one's own room to another and listen to Scots tales of battle and winter hardship – if one does not look forward. Rest is good, and for the present that is all of my business. Would to God I had a cough – a cough! What can a gassed man do without something hoarse or rattly? My chances are small, for my chest betrays me, of staying peacefully 'in silk and scented down'.[1] 'I have a rendezvous with Fritz
By some disputed barricade'[2]
and that before long.

Perhaps you would like to hear something of our movements lately. When I left Rouen, the first place we got to was Nesles, which had been ours not more than two months or so; and well preserved, not destroyed at all; pretty and soberly charming. However, our division had left that front the day before, so after that one night, off we went to Amiens to catch them 10 kilos the other side. (There was no time to see the Cathedral.) I have forgotten the name of the place. A few days after a 23 kilometre march with a sick foot about settled me – but there! one gets used to dying out yonder; so there we were in Neuvillette, near Bouquemaison. More marching. Wavans, I think. Then in the line for 8 days at Arras, to the right of Mouchy, watching which village at dawn, I thought of the 'Song at Morning'. Out again, somewhere. Then by train to Buire-au-Bois, near Auxi-le-Chateau. Beautiful country and very nice people. There we had training for some time, and trampled down crops and crops enough to make you sick. But what cared Brass-hats for all-daylight labour gone to ruin? I left the Glosters at Buire au Bois for the M.G.C. at Vaux. All this country is marked with old encampments, and full of memories. A beautiful land – but not my own. From Vaux to Saint Omer by train. From Saint Omer to Buysscheure, 10 kilos. Training awhile. Then up through Arike by train to the Ypres front, near Poperinghe, that neat clean dignified worthy home of dignity and civic life, now being shelled every day, bombed every night. And then up by short marches to the right of St Julien. Where sheer hideousness is the prettiest thing. Where peace often reigns because men are tired of shooting each other. Where I searched the Tanks with two other men, but – too late. Where I was an hour getting tea and sugar from dead men's kits and salvaging a mess-tin, which was sniped. Where I stopped a panic; the best thing to me so far; and found that filthy fragment of notebook, and that paper you have, (I hope.) for it was sent off some weeks ago, smelling pretty foully. I was half afraid to send it, but knew you had liberty to drop it in the fire if you so wished, and had curiosity to know what it was exactly.

O the souvenirs I might have had! But only officers have any real good chance of souvenirs, since only they can get them off. The men find things, and people who live in dugouts will hang them up and brag of great deeds in that old time. But the men, who could not carry very well, *and had no place to store things* and hardly a leave, will be empty-handed. You see, if one finds something interesting, it may be a hot corner, and how is one to carry it, for the haversack is full. Suppose one gets it out the line, then one must wait for leave, or a friend's leave. And if a wound comes all your stuff is lost. A man found a quartermaster's stores at Omiecourt, near Chaulnes, with hundreds of brand new helmets, but all that could be done was a little traffic with officers. I had two books and some papers for you, all lost at Vermand. Men hang on to revolvers and badges, watches and compasses etc, all that can be easily carried. There is too much sniping for the fighters to get souvenirs, the salvage and burial parties get them. (Will this letter interest you? And if so, why?) People unfitted for the line, lunatics, funks, bosseyed idiots and such like, from whom an officer with 50 francs may make himself rich with booty – and reputation. The A.S.C. do well, for they have room to store. R.T. officers, with Real Homes. Brass Hats can get what they would. Only the poor fool who goes over the top – and under the bottom – seems to be without anything at all. It is only fair to say that he is easily contented – with bare life, warmth, and food he must be counted rich; so by all means load weights of discipline on to him till he cares not whether he is in Rest or in the Line. And doesn't care a ha'penny obscenity about souvenirs save in his leg or arm; marketable, magic-carpet-like, transmuting talismans as they are. What an ode Burns would write To a Piece of Shrapnel! I hope for a letter from you very soon.

Your sincere friend
Ivor Gurney

[1] See letter 236.
[2] Adapted from Alan Seeger's poem (1888-1916), by substituting 'Fritz' for 'Death'

---

1 October 1917 (P)   Ward 24, Edinburgh War Hospital, Bangour

My Dear Friend

I have just discovered a letter which should have gone days ago, which might have been answered by now had it not been overlooked. But – have you had my address at all yet? If not, my carelessness brings its own punishment, for letters from you are a pleasure to me – even in Blighty, where one may be in bed and read that strange fiery record of *Villette*.[1] What a queer magical sort of tale it is, and what an uncanny tortured otherworldly yet supremely real atmosphere she can bring one into! Was she one of the people who can find no peace on earth? Or, rather, one who would have done very well in Canada, Australia, South Africa? It is a dreadful thing to realise that moving but a few yards into the company of next door people might bring one out of Heaven into Hell or vice versa.

And what a style! In a few words she can give you an Autumn evening in a way not equalled by any writers of that time – if even they ever seriously attempted such description. We are used to such moments of beauty in our books in this later day.

In chapter 12, there is an exquisite description of the night sky with its crescent moon, and then this –

the thunderstorm

'Within the dormitory they gathered round the nightlamp in consternation, praying loud. I could not go in. Too resistless was the delight of staying with the wild hour, black and full of thunder, pealing out such an ode as language never delivered to man – too terribly glorious, the spectacle of clouds, split and pierced by white and blinding bolts.'

Where is R.L.S. and the tribe one and all of conscientious makers of style?

How lucky I am not to have read her, to come fresh to a great classic! Bon! I lick my chops and will continue.

Did you see the review of F.W.H.'s book in the *T.L.S.*?[2] Golly, but there is nothing to give my poor friend swelled head in that notice. It *is* true that in *A*

Gloucestershire Lad there is not much good stuff, but what of that when 'In Flanders' is there – a pure beauty, actual colour and wistful distance of blue hills on the page? As for my own, they will not say much to affect me, for the sight of the whole thing in proof convinced me that humility should be my proper mood, and gratitude for a hobby found when one was needed. Neither he nor I have lived in the proper atmosphere to write much yet – the company of men who are trying for the same end and prize of a modern technique. That matters little to me, who have another larger and finer string to my bow, but for him – he must be thirty now and has a living to earn – at law, which he hates.

(Another dirty sheet.)

Ah! a light bursts on me suddenly. I believe, know, that I have sent you a letter; Belloc's article which has gone proves it; so that soon I shall be hearing from you, perhaps in an hour or so. Who knows?

Margaret Hunt has written to me of your new address, and so it shall go there direct this time.[3] I hope you like the house well, and can feel at home there, and that with you it is sunnier than with us near Enbro, where the sky was grey and austere on the day that papers told us was London's most beautiful day of Autumn.

Allons, I am nothing but grumbles because staying in bed makes me unfit in no time – a bundle of oppressed nerves; and those ruddy drawing room ballads set me afire. It is true that they want an accompanist, and he *might* stay on some time beyond ordinary, even till Christmas, but, though a refusal will mean France before then perhaps, rather than play accompaniments to songs I hate, and the little good music that stays with me still to a more or less unwilling audience; I will become a leader of forlorn hopes, a pot-hunter, a scalp-seeker of high renown. Four blessed hours I played yesterday; four ages of exquisite torture.

Two extracts from Scripture. 'Lord help me.' 'For I am not as other men are.'[4]

The *T.L.S.* praises Drinkwater's Plays a great deal. He has a fine technique, and only now have I acquired concentration adequately to appreciate such work, so it will be well for me to make such haste as I may to know these.

If we were playing Bach together now ... or Brahms, if he were not too difficult for me! Or if F.W.H. and I were walking the Minsterworth roads. Talking hard of books, and I encouraging and stimulating him, O what joy! Now and here, in this light clean room, there is nothing for me but the old feeling of inefficiency, sadly wasted time, still buried talents, and a sense of shame at my continual grumbles where others are content. Just to see the face of a Scot not 12 yards away, what a humiliation of weakness must I feel before such strength! I swear that if happiness and utility do not come to me after the war, I will first earn some money at picture-palaces and then go to sea with such men, whom I do admire so, and who take me along with them to some extent; in a rough life to live in free air, to work oneself clean out with the joy that comes from sticking it well to follow.

Sorry, but you get always the full flow of my grievances!

Your sincere friend

Ivor Gurney

[1] Charlotte Bronte's novel of 1852, from which the passage below is an accurate transcription.
[2] There is a brief and bland notice in the *T.L.S.* of 20 September 1917; the later review of 4 October 1917, p.474, is kind but not fulsome.
[3] Letters since 21 September had been redirected to Riverhead Vicarage, adding to the delay in reaching Marion Scott.
[4] The first is from Matthew 15.25; the second from Luke 18.11.

261 *To Marion Scott* G.41.140

1 October 1917 (P)

My Dear Friend

Your letter of the 28th has arrived, and the enclosure, which is hereby returned, properly dealt with.

Indeed I am distant – Here follows a confession I have made to noone else. There were 6 districts to which one might be sent. The Gloucester district ranged from Bristol, Cardiff, Birmingham to somewhere East. If one asked to be sent there, it might be that Fate would manage it. That is, it was both doubtful whether you would be allowed to stick to your district, and how far away from home you would be *if* you got there. But – so I was told, Scotland was sure; took even the overflow of other districts.

Now I knew that my getting to England was practically a fluke, and my stay in hospital certain to be short – I wished to see Scotland, Edinburgh in particular, so why not? And here I am.

But the chief fact was that railway fares were fearfully high, and visits fearfully short. So why bother about being near friends, when the bother was not likely to land one within 75 miles at least of the place desired? I did not bother, and so have saved my friends' money and time, and from worrying as to whether they *ought* to come and see me.

There is nothing the matter with me as far as I know save fatheadedness and unfitness and indigestion from doing nothing and eating too much. (I am in a horrible temper, so don't interrupt; Weltmuth[1] and indigestion together. Of course it *might* be gas. I only hope they keep me here till I am cured under that impression!)

I am as Ratty as can be, but nobody knows it, save you. So much France has done for me.

For Business –

Here you are and Damn the Censor!!

(Down, down my heart – { *King Lear* })[2]

337

You may have both 'Pain and Beauty' and 'Purple and Black'. It is my wish to please you. As for the cover, do just as you please.

And so the parcel has not come! Brett Young and all! Souvenirs as well. My voice breaks. I can no more.

Tears. General snuffles.

This must go now if you are to have it soon.

I am very glad your sister is better, and with you. Floreat soror tua.

Your sincere friend
Ivor Gurney

---

[1] This might mean 'courage to face the world', but Gurney is probably meaning 'Weltschmerz' or perhaps 'Wehmut', which means 'wistfulness'.

[2] *King Lear*, II.4.122; 'O me, my heart, my rising heart! but, down!'

---

262 To Herbert Howells   G.3.12

2 October 1917 (P)

My Dear Howells

One thing in your letter interested me hugely. Have 'they' been writing you 'anonymous insults'? If this is connected with your music, Cheerio; you are getting on. You don't tell me much about yourself. As for your work, is it suspended in the summer holidays? Anyway, don't give me silly or unpleasing answers, for I am in the devil of a temper. I am not *quite* sure whether the gas has not slightly aggravated my ordinary thickheadedness and indigestion. If this is so, then there's hope for the Wangler; if not, then no hope; I should be merely a Lucky Blighter soon to be cast out into outer darkness again. Anyway, I am that spoilt pet of Society, an accompanist that can read at sight. But O! what that same Pet has to endure! The rapturous soulfulness that disdains tempo. The durchganging baritone that will not be stayed long by interludes of piano, whose eager spirit is bars too early for the fray. The violinist that will play *songs* – not only the voice part but any choice twiddly bits that a careless writer has left to the piano. The universal clamourous desire for ragtime. Topsiturvinesses of diseased vanity of all sorts, kinds, conditions.

Enbro is indeed a magic name. Its glamour is increased (as usual) by distance and denial. 16 miles and regulations of the most strict. I wonder which was Henley's hospital?[1] There are many memories round this city, but the dearest to me are those of R.L.S., that friend of Everyman. Henley and the Great Sir Walter, Dr John Brown[2] and Holyrood come after him in my mind.

There is no blooming (well done!) music in my head. I am frosted up. Last night, I felt the beginning of the thaw, the first hint of what joy music might give. I was playing Beethoven, and for one golden minute my wandering mind was fixed and could see stars; I forgot the restraint that so long has been partly self-imposed on myself and flew free. Why I had no indigestion to speak of! A glimpse up the shaft of Hell.

Perhaps some songs may come from me before I return, but there is a lot to do before my mind will freely conceive anything. You simply don't know what France means, not in horror, but in everyday trial. If this letter is to go, it must finish now. 'Hoping that you are in the pink'.

Yours ever
I.B.G.

---

[1] The Old Royal Infirmary. Henley had his foot amputated under anaesthetic by Lister in Edinburgh and wrote some 'In Hospital' poems which influenced Gurney's 'Hospital Pictures'.

[2] John Brown (1810-1882), doctor and essayist, and general practitioner in Edinburgh.

263 To Marion Scott   G.41.141

4 October 1917 (G)

My Dear Friend   Thursday October 4

Your letter of September 30 has arrived. With it the first really presentable weather North Britain (I will be rude) has seen fit to give us. This morning has shadows and there is a velvet look to the distances, the sky seems new again, the strength of the hills is not grim.

It is to be feared that yet another parcel is lost. The poem I was writing is also lost; they dropped my vanity bag carrying me from train to hospital – the fraud that I felt!

Perhaps it wasn't bad, but my brain was really getting stuck over there. How much, last night showed me. The Presbyterian chaplain gave a lecture on Adam Smith. He was a capable man, what do I say! He was touched with greatness, supremely alive, warmblooded, interested, interesting, fine looking with eyes of humourous power. A man from Fifeshire. For two solid hours I was what *I* know as yet for happy. I could have sat all night. He had a slip of paper with subjects for the next ten weeks, and O but I wished him to use them all – to start at Adam Smith and go on to Nelson!

Next to me was the most astonishing man I have ever met. A coalminer of Fife, he had the Celtic temperament, which shamed my half-vitality where I sat. He could hold an audience in his hand, and never feel the weight. He was over 50 years of age, had been out to the front and still was affected by some sickness contracted out there, but spoke with no bitterness of that fact. He could see as well as any the greatness of the times and spoke like Lloydd George to the men. He was pretty well read, and through mere interest in the thing had worked through all Prout's Harmony exercises and the R.C.O. papers for thirty years. Bach made him drunk with glory. 'Man, but it's fine.' (The spelling of that last word in inadequate to *his* speaking.) He should be one of the leaders of British Music and is but a coal-heaver beating his dusty wings, but without complaint. But fancy having to go back to the front after meeting these two! Wumman, but it's awfu'!

I am likely to be here another fortnight, for in the colonel's inspection I was one of the few not marked Con: Camp. 'Why?' 'Accompaniments, my dear.' For once, I saw the Army winking its eye at me, and wunk back.

I hope that what comes from an Italian source as to America's Peace offer is correct. These are none so bad. And, barring an absolutely complete military victory, as good as we can get. Of course, the terms are too generous for Germany, but without generosity I cannot see how she is ever to assert herself against the Junkers. So much priceless blood has been spilt, the organisation has been so perfected, that, right or wrong, a commercial blockade for 25 years would mean an eating cancer in the heart of Europe. We have to encourage democracy, in this case by discrediting a ruling caste. I don't believe a commercial blockade would do more than pull Germany together under the old rule and keep Europe safe – granted! But there is a better way. To crush Germany more than is needed of effort. France cannot ever be hopeless again. So much we have gained. To sum up – It is a great pity that Europe cannot gain the same unconditional surrender of Germany as a parent may exact of a child, but if things are properly managed, *in the event of Germany accepting the proposals of U.S.A. of course*, then the price is too great to pay any longer. It is time we left off, with a Faith in God, and an International agreement which would make agression hopeless for any country.

Lastly, a complete military victory will not guarantee South Eastern Europe for long, if Russia will not see reason. This arrangement is far more likely to keep peace and to make reason a moving force in International communication. A military victory will not guarantee peace, neither will this; but it has more promise as a birth or potential force of peace, because further conflict will leave Germany weaker than ever. It is more unwise to weaken her, than to trust that her people have learnt a lesson; because in the essential things of self-government we cannot interfere.

Excuse this long, long dissertation.

As for getting into Enbro, it has not proved possible so far, but if human effort can manage it ....

I am so glad you like your new house, and very sorry the Germans will not leave you alone; It must be a strain. (This letter must be off!)

I will write to Mr Dunhill and Erbert Owls. Concentration! I thought I had none, till last night. Only Joy can make me fit of mind, all this half-sickness is due to half-vitality, half-use of capabilities. About F.W.H. I will write again.

I can see (in my masculine vanity) a romance springing up between Audrey and 241281. Even though there is a great longing for me to see my Chapmen again, and the rude and turbulent Mick.

With all best wishes to you and your sister

Your sincere friend
Ivor Gurney

340

4 October 1917 (P)[1]

My Dear Friend

Hearing a few casual catchwords flying around, it struck me that you might like to know of some of them – such as I can remember. Poor bare jests, almost too familiar to remember at will.

There is one (just heard for the thousandth time) which brings a picture of a tragic roll call. A man may be shouted for who is not present, and the room answers, 'On the wire, at Loos'. A lighter answer, a mock of this last, is 'Gassed at Mons'.

A coming strafe means carrying parties, and they are greeted with 'More iron rations for Fritz'. Germans are known, affectionately, as Fritzes, Allemans or 'Johnny'. The Scots use the last name chiefly.

An intimation of a charge for crime is made by the phrase 'You're *for* it'. Intimation of death is made as, 'H – has got it'. 'Poor old Bill's snuffed it'. Or 'Shan't see old George again'. To see Germans kill the wounded, is to see 'the boys done in'. One 'goes up the line with the Boys'. Or 'over the top with the Boys'.

Practically *all* swearing ceases when one reaches Blighty, though the language out there is frequently foul. A commentary on the life! A bad officer, that is, a bully, is a - ! A Good officer, that is, a considerate, is 'a toff'. 'I'd follow him anywhere'. 'The men's friend'; or simply, but in significant tones, a '*gent*leman'. A funk is 'windy', a bad funk, 'as windy as Hell'.

An officer always takes whisky in the line, and his being drunk on any critical occasion is always condoned. I have never known any of our officers really funk an order. Exact orders are always obeyed, or practically always. A bombardment is of course 'a strafe', a bad one 'some strafe'. Men are 'glad to be out of that'. A premonition of Death is given as 'My number's up'. A ditto of Blighty – 'I'm for Blighty' 'Blighty this journey'. A box respirator is a 'Gaspirator'. A helmet a 'tin hat'. A rifle a 'bundoob' (Hindustani?). A revolver 'a peashooter'.

The Germans, in anger, are referred to as 'them – bastards'. The English soldier has an enormous reverence for Hindenburg and his strategy. An almost complete belief that man for man he is far better than Fritz. A doubt of our Air-service. A conviction that the Germans are as he is – a sufferer under discipline, no better nor worse than he; only unluckier. A belief that our discipline is stricter than his. A longing for home, and English girls. A contempt for everything French, although he has learnt to think better of the soldiers. French girls, towns (as a rule), houses, farm implements, are all objects of scorn. He admires the .75 gun very greatly.[2] As for French beer, cigarettes, baccy.....The comparison simply must not be hinted at even by dashes. For all his amorous intentions once he reaches home, he thinks the French girls highly immoral. For all his stealing, the French unspeakable thieves. He likes Church Parade. Loathes most of all disciplinary parades, kit inspections and the like. Marches till he drops, Loves to frowst, and has a marvellous ability in the making of fires, 'bivvies' etc. Fritzes splendid dugouts always move his praise.

His Guide, Philosopher, and Friend is *John Bull*. Horatio Bottomley is recognised as a scoundrel, but, for all that, the finest man in England, the only one to sympathise with a common soldier's woes and oppressions. Lloydd George is also admired, and, slightly, the King. Asquith is simply 'Wait and See'. Their faith in newspapers has been sorely shaken for ever by the comparison of accounts with realities. But chiefly by the contrast between the phrase 'Mastery of the Air' and the reality. Parliament is a haunt of people who talk and don't care what happens to him and his like. Still he preserves his faith, how and in what, is obscure, but I believe it to be his feeling that Englishmen would not condemn him to suffer longer than was needful. But he never says so.

I may remember more, if so and it interests you, you shall have it.

[1] In the same envelope as the preceding letter.
[2] The French 75mm rapid-fire field gun; a much-admired weapon.

265 *To Marion Scott*   G.41.142

8 October 1917 (P)

My Dear Friend

For the first time since when-God-knows I dip pen in ink and indite friendly unimportances. And it is very nice too, as the slang says. To write in pencil, is to be casual, careless, informal, unworthy of the true inner seriousness of letter writing; is to show one's lack of appreciation of the texture of paper, of the lovely gliding of the pen – but not this one – of the beautiful look of clear script black against white paper – why is this blue? Of the use of ceremony in life; to show oneself altogether unappreciative of those finer points that divide Man from the Beast, and make a penny worth the spending.

The man who would attempt to write verse with a pencil when a pen is handy and convenient to him would rob a church without more thought than he would give to the flicking of a cigarette ash – which indeed is frequently the trick of the melodramatic villain. For the writing of music there can be no more so foul of spirit as to contemplate aught but the pen as instrument. The pencil here is beastly and detestable beyond chaste thought; let us pass by with averted face, or even shuffle sideways like a crab; avoid the thought as base indeed, with shame not to be told.

The soldier is exempt from all these considerations; For he is unwillingly vile. Ink, pen, and blotting paper haunt the dreams where only he may be himself.

Let the Gods judge in this – the worst of his crimes, the deepest of his woes, wherein he is more sinned against than sinning, the blind constrained tool of Destiny.

I hear you say, 'but this is all Nonsense' in a withering tone, without effect on me, who reply with a complete answer, a snub, a saying of great beauty and intense meaning; to wit – 'It is far better, Madam,' (with courtliness also, you see!) 'to write nonsense reverently with a pen than to have graved the Ten Commandments with a diamond pointed instrument of the Gold of Ophir, or on loveliest marble of Carrara, such as Browning wrote of (with a pen, you may be sure!) in 'The Bishop orders his Tomb at St Praxed's'. The Artist respects his materials, loves their peculiarities of texture and management, and deals with them gently as with his own flesh and blood, or the priest his sacrament of Bread and Wine; red and white; Passion and Serenity'.

Let us use ink whenever Fate and Supply allow us, for so we shall show ourselves cognisant of and grateful for the civilisation of Europe, that once again has survived onslaught of the barbarian; who showed himself nakedly to all when he would destroy a 'scrap of paper', and the work of pen and ink without a pang.[1]

After Music

Why, I am on fire now, and tremulous
With sense of Beauty long denied; the first
Opening of floodgate to the glorious burst
Of Freedom from the Fate that limits us
To work in darkness pining for the light,
Thirsting for sweet untainted draughts of air,
Clouds sunset coloured, Music ... O Music's bare
White heat of silver passion fiercely bright.
While sweating at the foul task, we can taste
No Joy that's clean, no Love but something lets
It from its power, the wisest soul forgets
What's beautiful, or delicate, or chaste.
Orpheus drew me, as once his bride, from Hell
If wisely, she or I, the Gods can tell.

Halfway through this effusion the mail arrived with the *R.C.M. magazines* and a letter from you. (In order of size.)

Alack. It seems only too likely that another parcel has (or has not?) Gone West. Nicholson was there also, wasn't he? Have you had him back? Regrets are useless. As for the verses, I can remember nothing at all of them; as they were quite ordinary. *Quinney's* is better than the *Hill*.[2] Have you read Wister's *The Virginian*?

A certain Sister borrowed *Gloucestershire Friends* and has not yet returned it. My first impression is disappointment. He is farther away – F.W.H. – from the reader than in *A Gloucestershire Lad*. 'My father bred great horses', if it

343

were a little better would be first-rate. 'The Ballad of Army Pay' is good. 'Seth bemoans the oldest inhabitant'. And a poem which includes a line 'with one high morning note a drowsing man'.[3] The poem written at Douai (O questions!) has very good stuff in it. That, also, which would 'work Thy Will with Passion'. That also (though I do not like 'big' glory) which has a refrain, 'and in the little valleys thatch and dreams'. The best thing, I believe is - 'We have taken a trench'.

My poor friend was tired; do not judge him by this. it is the ineffectual beating of wings, a sick mind's desire. So fine a footballer, cricketer, man, cannot wait many years after the war for his fulfilment. *This* is not it, anyway. It will do as a source of quotation for Bishop Frodsham, who will also obtain a pleasurable glow of satisfaction at his great work of uplifting the People by Literature. Obelise him![4]

Will Harvey is an untidy careless dreamer, who has known much sorrow, chiefly because his mind was not occupied as fully as it needed to be. He is chivalry itself, and the detection of Fear within his heart is merely the spur to action. He sings well, and is indeed born a lover of all Beauty. He is capable of great Wisdom, of glorious foolishness. Loves Life which loves not him.

Some men have to form themselves, to control their every tiniest movement of spirit, and indeed to create their own world. And such is he; who has now learnt all bitter things, and has only to gather the sweet with inexperienced hand. A mind of sweetness allied to such strength which has never known itself and cannot live as most men by habit. But don't look at *Gloucestershire Friends* to find all this.

Another letter will ask you how you are getting on yourself.

Meanwhile all best wishes

from your sincere friend
Ivor Gurney

Don't forget *Ward 24*

[1] Theobald von Bethmann Hollweg to Sir Edward Goschen, 4 August 1914: 'Just for a word – 'neutrality', a word which in wartime has been so often disregarded, just for a scrap of paper – Great Britain is going to make war'.
[2] Both books by H.A. Vachell: *The Hill* (1905). See letter 258.
[3] From 'The Bugler'.
[4] The Right Rev. Bishop Frodsham, Canon Residentiary of Gloucester, wrote an Introduction to Harvey's book.

266 To Herbert Howells   G.61.173

? October 1917 (KT)

My Dear Erbert Owls
    This is a sad shock for you, bear up, my man. There is nothing dedicated to

you in *Severn and Somme*.

Why? Because there were too many friends to whom I wished to dedicate, and all took away from the prime dedication. Miss Scott in consideration of her faithful service has two; Will Harvey has two more which directly refer to him. No other living people are there.

I hope you won't mind and will understand. However I propose to write a symphony in Canon. Its length is directly dependent on the patience of the audience. The first, leading part goes over the top, say, at 8. Pip. Emma, and reaches its first objective (Common time till now) at 8.27 P.M. Starts again (3/4 Largo) at 8.28, and is again found digging in at 8.51, going over immediately for its 3rd objective, and finally turning up at its fourth objective at 9.48, when the working parties (that is, the last-entering voice) have just started. It has two alternatives - to go straight backward, bar by bar, or to start at the beginning again, *but it must not stop*. An artillery of 200 Italian combined-instrumentalists (16 to each man. You know them?) provide the barrage. And Ha! you blench! It is to be dedicated to You!!

Yours
I.B.G.

267 *To Marion Scott* G.41.145

8 October 1917 (KT)

My Dear Friend

Sixteen miles from Enbro, and can't get there; not a sight of it. My parson is going away for a week, and afterwards is going to try to manage it. He is a great friend of Lord Guthrie who owns R.L.S. house, and promises me a complete tour of everything that can be packed into a short stay. This same Ratcliffe Barnett is the man who is keeping myself and a singer here. The man who told us after service yesterday, 'I hate parsons!' That rare thing, especially among his kind, of being a Truth-teller, Lecturer on English Literature, Mountaineer, Lover of Men, Music, and Books. One does meet men of this kind occasionally, not often. God, I do feel wise and old and grey with waiting! He has eyes that can look you through, and a fine head with a Roman nose defiant at the fore. A character can hold a crowd as easily as one man. A master of Life, consequently of Death also. A great reader. A great admirer. A great man to finish with whose aim at present is to set men at ease when they talk to him.

After all this, let me thank you for the baccy which was most companionable to receive.

Nielson (O that you might see him) tells me tales of Norroway over the faem with it, tales of She(e)tlands, Iceland. Tells me what men do at sea, and what sad carelessness landed him in the Army. What eyes he has, and fine wrinkled long humorous face, wise with seafaring and long contact with men of the sea. Obviously he is as brave as a lion, obviously as tender hearted as a child. To lead up to the purpose of all this – Damn the War!

You gift is not unappreciated by him, and I spend hours in his room. Tomorrow he goes on furlough, but has saved up an ache and a pain that will yet be useful, after three weeks or so.

Last night I played Bach and Beethoven for two hours, and got a little into swing towards the end. That was good. I am too lazy to write, and besides nothing will come to me when I try to pump - the bilge pump, I think, by the results.

Memory, let all slip

Memory, let all slip save what is sweet
Of Ypres plains.
Keep only autumn sunlight and the fleet
Cloud after rains,

Blue skies and mellow distance softly blue;
These only hold
Lest I shall share my panged grave with you,
Else dead, Else cold.

[*there is no formal ending to this letter.*]

268 *To Marion Scott*   G.41.143

12 October 1917 (P)

My Dear Friend
I have just been reading the *T.L.S.* article on Horace Walpole,[1] and that has made me want to write a letter; an easy gossipy letter; an airy fairy Lilianish sort of epistolary Stunt. But I won't.

Here are three sets of verses for the New Family Album, but, curse it all, why can't I go into Enbro and walk where Ste'enson walked a queer brighteyed crock of a stripling, hanging on to Life as a thing most precious. The contrariousness of things is not an Army monopoly, but merely the continual ever present motive which never relaxes nor becomes weak through want of support in this glorious army of Free Citizens.

Nielson went yesterday, and I suppose we shall never meet again. And Evans, the Welsh singer whom I *may* come across. Dammit, there are only too many golden people in the world. (There were more still before August

20th.[2]) But Nielson's wrinkled wise face and deep eyes were lovely to look at and gave me strength. Men of the sea are better to live with than the sea itself, and through his talk, though there was nothing nautical in it, ran ever the old charm of moving salt green water, and the pictures of fearless sailors taking their chance. I might have asked his address, but didn't. It was wiser, since he is there in my mind as clear as life, and since we shall not meet again, and since it is foolish to regret. Since we are living in this damned topsy turvy irritating old world of ours, in short. Nielson! what a name! What a man!

Those Italian rumours of terms have come to nothing, so I retract for the present. It is irritating to please the *Morning Post* though. (See 'To the Prussians of England'.) However playing Bach does not help one to a level judgement, and Garvin wrote very well last Sunday. I wish Sydney Webb would shut up, and my pay were raised more than 2d, and I to stay in England while the retreat comes with following Fritz over floods and traps, and that we could have a long uncensored chat together, with no air-raids and boko[3] brilliance of conversation, and that everything weren't cussed as of set purpose.

But I *hope* you are getting well properly (for no information will you give) and your sister too, and that I shall have something to tell you of Enbro, the old grey city of disgusting weather, when I write next. And I hope you will like these verses.

By the way, judging from what was said at a debate last week, the British soldier is absolutely confident of victory, and (since it must be) willing to go on. But O, what a hot time he will give to some people after the war!

Don't forget 'Ward 24' in the address please. With best wishes

Your sincere friend
Ivor Gurney

    The Target.

I shot him, and it had to be
One of us, 'Twas him or me.
Couldn't be helped, and none can blame
Me, for you would do the same.

My mother, she can't sleep for fear
Of what might be a happening here
To me. Perhaps it might be best
To die, and set her fears at rest.

For worst is worst, and worry's done.
Perhaps he was the only son ...
Yet God keeps still, and does not say
A word of guidance any way.

Well, if they get me, first I'll find
That boy and tell him all my mind.
And see who felt the bullet worst,
And ask her pardon, if I durst.

All's a tangle. Here's my job.
A man might rave, or shout, or sob;
And God he takes no sort of heed.
This is a bloody mess indeed.

To the Prussians of England

When I remember plain heroic strength
And shining virtue shown by Ypres pools,
Then read the blither written by knaves for fools
In praise of English soldiers lying at length,
Who purely dream what England shall be made
Gloriously new, free of the old stains
By us, who pay the price that must be paid,
Will freeze all winter over Ypres plains.
Our silly dreams of peace you put aside
And Brotherhood of man, for you will see
An armed Mistress, braggart of the tide
Her children slaves, under your mastery.
We'll have a word there too, and forge a knife,
Will cut the cancer threatens England's life.[4]

'Annie Laurie'

The high barn's lit by many a guttering flare
Of flickering candle, dangerous, hence forbidden,
To warm soft straw, whereby the cold floor's hidden;
Wherein we soon shall rest without a care.
War is forgotten. Gossip fills the air
Of home, and laughter sounds beyond the midden,
Under the stars, where Youth makes Joy unchidden
Of gods or men, and mocks at sorrow there.
But hark, what sudden pure untainted passion
Seizes us now, and stills the garrulous?
A song of old immortal dedication
To Beauty's service and a woman's heart.

No tears we show, no sign of exultation
In this an immortal moment set apart.[5]

In Hospital.

[1] The front-page article for 4 October 1917 which ended by quoting Walpole: 'Let me have but the letters I desire!'
[2] The middle of the third battle of Ypres.
[3] i.e. beaucoup, much.
[4] The last couplet revised from:
> We'll have a word there too, and England's life
> Is dear, and for her cancer forge a knife.
[5] Line 12 replaces the deleted 'To Beauty and to Annie Laurie's'.

---

269 To Marion Scott   G.41.144

13 October 1917 (P)

My Dear Friend   Saturday
    This is an acknowledgement of not an answer to your letter, but by all means take it as the second if it will bring an extra letter to me.
    I enclose a scrap of paper which may interest you.[1]
    My 'Essay Fantasia on Ink and Paper' was written to let off steam. It was good fun, even though writing on my knee with a bad pen made me doubtful of the advantages. Your writing is always clear, anyhow.
    As for the new Poems (you will have some more before this) I will see.
    'Ninety nine people out of a hundred' will be right with pang-ed.[2] Sorry I left out the mark.
    Thank you so much for the invitation. Gratefully accepted herewith. (Now why did a picture of Chaulnes spring up in my mind, there?) 'The Riddle of the Sands' is an old favourite of mine. Either Sydney or the Taylors inroduced it.[3]
    Tonight I vamp again, but the acute pain I feel is almost neutralised by the acute pleasure of the audience, and (last night) by the grateful congratulations of the funny man, a very nice chap of considerable force of character. Any way my worst sensation is of dull misery. But they do so enjoy it.
    Next letter you shall have a Bennet-Galsworthy-Gissing-Conrad-Mackenzie analysis of my interior workings to compensate for the super-abundance of hard fact this time. So sorry!
    You tell me nothing of how *you* got on.
    With best wishes

                                        Your sincere friend
                                        Ivor Gurney

[1] A cutting from a newspaper reporting the death of Karl Julius Maria Beethoven, a grand-nephew of the composer. It makes the event an occasion for comment that Beethoven

'could scarcely have been in sympathy with the Imperial heroics of modern Prussian rule.'
[2] In 'Memory, let all slip'; see letter 267 above.
[3] *The Riddle of the Sands* (1900) by Erskine Childers (1870-1922) had come out in a new shilling edition.

270 To Marion Scott   G.41.146

16 October 1917 (P)

My Dear Friend

This is a most lovely morning, and I ought to be out on the hills somewhere instead of writing letters, even to you. For letter writing is work of a sort, though I like it not badly here, and in France it is often a pleasure.

There is not much to tell you, there is no masterpiece of chiselled and exquisite verse. To be sure there is 'A hundred pipers and a'' running in my head but you knew *that*, surely?

Your tales of the Down country interested me. If you had ever told my ear that Richborough was the last port held by the Romans it went out of the other ear, for I remember nowt about it.

As for 'After Music', the last line is meant to be quizzical, and is true of myself. *Is* it wise of me to play music? Well, I do, but know only too well that the effort to forget will be an extra difficulty against the little serenity I shall have in France. Unless I grow stronger of soul of course, and so much stronger is unlikely.

The things I should most like to write, are things of beauty with a vinegary ending, something after 'The Fire Kindled'. Heine I believe is famous for that sort of thing. It is best to be Shakespeare but good to be Heine – though not Thersites.

So the same was meant for 'Memory let all slip', the beginning of which seems to me to be just ordinary – excused by the end, which is (as you suggest) not all it might be. And it was meant to be 'panged' (two syllables). But if you prefer –

'Lest I my panged grave must share with you.
Else dead. Else cold.'

(And even there, why not 'pangéd'?)

I think there should be a semi-colon after 'It from its power' in 'After Music'.

As for the cover, Red so be it. L.A. bon!

And while I think of it, is it not enough to shame me to read over the name of Edward Shanks,[1] this, in the *S.W.*

350

The Fields are full.

The fields are full of summer still
And breathe again upon the air
From brown dry side of hedge and hill
More sweetness than the sense can bear.

So some old couple, who in youth
With love were filled and overfull,
And loved with strength and loved with truth,
In heavy age are beautiful.

Which knocks most Lyrics in *Palgrave* senseless, it is so packed with thought, so musical and significant.

Yesterday I was wiping cutlery and plates and things after breakfast and dinner, and it tired me out. I hate that sort of thing so. Nurses are really wonderful people to do so many things distasteful and still to smile. There is a very nice set of nurses here (have I told you?) that could hardly be better. They call this the 'Ragtime Ward', a name of envy given by men oppressed in places of female dragons and discipline. The courage of women is certainly not less than that of men. To my mind, that is. The serene performance of hateful duties, and the refusal to be depressed by them *is* the finest form of courage. The more sensational are the wilder forms – no higher. There are a few soldiers who go on till they are knocked out, not heeding wounds, most of these comparative few have supported their nerves only too freely beforehand. The rest may be the flower of earth, but the man who can be brotherly and crack a joke on a winter night in a shell hole has undoubted undeniable unsupported courage, which is not always certain of the spectacular gentlemen, who may be Berserk or drunk. But there! it is only my preference perhaps for serene and quiet strength rather than for the violent kind. Violence is waste of energy.

Here endeth the umptieth lesson.

As for fearing the Front – well, that is only because Life is too pleasant here. They'll soon alter that out yonder. (There's a dramatic Lyric someday!)

The lucky people are the Scots, who can concentrate, the unlucky men are those who may be surprised into a single thought in the heat of (rather excited) conversation, but at no other time, if there are such men, and not only one! For this one wanders anywhere while he is playing Bach; yet they are not such black thoughts as they were.

Wise people are the Scots, anyway the nurses among them – for they had given up trying to make me so uncannily tidy as other men are. So I turn my locker to the wall, when the (U.S.A.) doctor comes.

The attitude of a fairly ordinary type of man to Classical Music is – that he does not like it, ought (yes, I think so) to like it, and would like it if he had had a proper education. That's not so bad. But perhaps my courteous attitude to Ragtime makes a little difference here. And I never swank. The British respect sincerity, and they can *see* I like Bach, and believe there is something in it just as there is in what astronomers say of stars beyond ordinary view. They are willing to believe that something lies behind that inextricable tangle of notes, a reality beyond the mystery. I hope both you and your sister are getting on well, and that Audrey has not had her beauty-sleep broken lately.

With best wishes

Your sincere friend
Ivor Gurney

[1] Edward Richard Buxton Shanks (1892-1953), poet, novelist and critic; assistant-editor of the *London Mercury* 1919-22; his verse includes *Songs* (1915), *Poems* (1916) and *Poems, 1912-32* (1933).

---

271 *To Marion Scott*   G.41.147

16 October 1917 (G)

My Dear Friend   16 October 1917 A.D.

I am very sorry that you have taken the sonnet 'To the Prussians of England' as meant for yourself. That Sonnet was originally named 'To the Prussians of England and the Evening Stump', which, being interpreted, is no more than the *Morning Post*. My dear friend, your frail body seems to me to have given you an over tender conscience. At present I agree with you that the ruling class of Germany shows no sign of repentance. I trust Belloc very much indeed, and if I myself had to bargain with Germany they would find more than Brotherhood behind my spectacles. There are one or two comforting things I have read this day. Conan Doyle says he thinks our losses in killed are no more than 150,000 (this year I suppose), Belloc says that the French are $1\frac{1}{4}$ years behind the Germans in the classes fighting (that is to say, boys of 18 are still in barracks) and that General Maurice puts the German losses at 75 per cent higher than our own. I see no reason to doubt these opinions, which are cheering.

But O how I would like a talk with Belloc about the Pope and his attitude, and the effect on B's opinion of Catholicism.

Yes, Madam, it is true. I do see the *T.L.S.* here, but your spare copy is not wasted, but goes on its useful way; but still if you have another use for it yourself, please keep it. I believe, Madam, I have received all correspondance addressed by Marion Scott (spinster) to the private Ivor Gurney, who believes his last letter to you will mention those letters you refer to. As to the P.C. no, that was not mentioned, but (better late than never,) let me thank you now.

By the way, thank you for forwarding Mr Dunhill's (very nice) letter. He tells me Frank Sidgwick is dead.[1]

The state of the envelope you last received was due to the amount of travelling it did in my pocket, and even I was doubtful whether it ought to go; still it went and got there.

Now for the Pomes.

The sestett of 'Annie Laurie' is altogether off the rocks. Too much alteration did bemuse me.

'Of flickering candle, dangerous – hence (or 'and') forbidden' -
Wherein and whereby don't annoy me.
Well let 1, 2, 3, of sestett stand, then
    'To Beauty's service and one woman's heart.
    No tears we show, no sign of flame in us
    This hour of stars and music set apart'.

As for the third thing – Comment on it as you will, for it is not meant in the least for you, but for Colonel Repington, the *M.Post*, and all the foul hellspawn that preach war and escape service. Who will oppose disarmament, or at least make an International Armament difficult to arrange in detail. Who would (as the *M.P.* men would) have brutalized Belgium less foully, but no less cruelly, than the Germans have done – for Military Necessity. Who see nothing in the tragedy of Russia but a failure of discipline, and never a hint that slavery may sometimes result from oppression. What is Northcliffe? Winston Churchill? Devonport? Rhondda? And what but geographical accident shows them English?

Do not forget this. That because the state of the world will be rickety indeed, therefore Freedom of individuals will be sorely restricted for some time. And by the same people (unless we have a care) who are gradually shamed and forced into the shortening of hours by American example; America that alone has not been behind German efficiency. Ford was a pacifist. But there are worse things than pacifists. There are cancers and devil-fish to begin with, and breakers of promises to poor men. How long ago was the Taff Vale decision given, and what was the state of the English workman in 1800? And who is responsible for the success of the German efforts to deprive us of essential products at the beginning of this war? – to strike nearer. Can you give any reason for thinking that Kitchener's spiritual home was not Prussia? A useful tool, a handy servant for England, and the English who must warily see to it we need not such again.

To end up – Thank God, this war was not a six months affair, for our victory would have throned Prussia at Westminster. For we, who made such big threats with such little power would have seen power large enough turned on ourselves. I admire Kipling as you know. **But** – before *Puck of Pook's Hill*, he was *not* English. Perhaps is not now, but *Puck* showed us that he realised a virtue not his own. A.G.Gardiner of the *Daily News* is not admirable wholly, but his mistakes are not greater than Kipling's mistakes. And he cares, as I care, more for liberty for Englishmen, than for liberty of England. Perhaps in the long run they are identical, but that serves to show the difference of two standpoints.

It is of more importance that the Duke of Bilgewater should respect and sympathise with Bill Jones than that the sun should never set on the British Empire, whose liberties have been kept alive by revolt against the fathers of the present 'Prussians of England'. O what a long dose! But I hope it will convince you of one thing at least, that the sonnet was not meant for you. Bless your heart, I would make Belloc Prime Minister if I had my way! And Chesterton Poet Laureate.

(I go on through your letter and find it is time to say) I am so sorry you have been sick again though only mildly. 'And find a vivid enjoyment in being able to walk without intense fatigue' is not pleasant reading. But I am glad you rose again so quickly from your attack of gastric fever.

As for me, I am as well as can be in these conditions, and could walk twenty miles without intense fatigue. Last night I played Beethoven for an hour or more – not carefully to train my fingers, but as near to my thoughts as possible, and by God! they liked it, and thanked me afterwards! Quite unexpectedly to me, you may be sure; who never sit comfortably on that chair for thinking of bored men who long to whack their feet on the ground to ragtime. One of the things I played was the whole of the D major Sonata – an early one, and quite possibly the first of the set (with a few tittivatings of my own.) One of the few sonatas almost free from suspicion of stodginess and padding. And the logic of the thing is so glorious, as shining as the apparent logic one sees in places familiar long years – where everything is as it must be, and unquestioning acceptance is as easy as to a child.

Indeed once or twice I forgot myself in the music. If I were a better player I could wish for no better audience than yourself. Nor could Hamlet! Whose soliloquies in that case would have been twice as long, and far more discursive. For you have such patience and gift of listening as would make you the easy prey of all the sincere bores in being.

Thank you for your two tales, which have been handed on already.

I hope you feel 'your own' for a fair proportion of the day now - that you have not to rest and be careful in order to exist. Perhaps before long we shall excite each other into a little more vitality, for the colonel is coming round today and if it is humanly possible I will most certainly rest on the breast of the Scott family for awhile, according to their kind invitation.

If Conan Doyle's estimate is for this year's slain only, we might get 40,000, 100,000, 250,000, 150,000 = 540,000. I should say just below half a million myself.

With best wishes

Your sincere friend
Ivor Gurney

[1] See letter 273, which corrects this information to Hugh Sidgwick.

19 October 1917 (P)

[*A postcard announcing simply a change of address.*]

> B2. The Camp.
>   Bangour
>   near Edinburgh

A step nearer.

23 October 1917 (G)

My Dear Friend   Oct 23
   Thank you for the letter and postcard just arrived, one of them gave pleasure anyhow.
   Mr Barnett has been informed of my literary dealings, and it excited him. We are to exchange scalps, for today he will bring me a little book of his own. Casual anecdote yesterday. He was playing at a Hall, an ordinary parish concert I believe, and had some success. When he was leaving, an old 'habitual' and street player came up to him and said 'Man, it was Fine!!! In the old days of Homer men exchanged swords. Me and you'll exchange fiddles'. Which is the cause of the appearance in Bangour of a suspiciously raw looking instrument apparently made of packing case and – yellow yellow yellow varnish.
   (By the way did you ever read the Yeats book that came out with Yeats' *Responsibilities*? I believe that had anecdotes of the same kind.)
   No light coloured fiddle will ever please me like a dark one.
   Mrs Voynich has just sent me a short story of hers. 'And so be patient, be wise and patient, friend', for I know pretty well the attitude from which it will be written. That it will see life unsteadily and as an awful Hole.[1]
   Allow me to recommend you a book. Why I read it is because the authoress is a poet we have both heard of – Rose Macaulay; and because the Y.M.C.A. is chiefly 'remainders'. *The Making of a Bigot* is the title, and the book has some fine sketches of people, a beautiful tolerant satire, and some proper stodges.
   The Sonata in D I mentioned, is the one you suppose, and I have one or two striking improvments to offer. First movement

Yes, the word in 'Annie Laurie' is 'flame'.

Sorry, it is Hugh Sidgwick that has been killed.[2]

You say no word about your own health so I suppose you are still just slowly forging ahead. Peace should bring a double rate at least I think.

I have *Gloucestershire Friends* in front of me.

No 1. Not bad. No.2 H'm. No 3. chill breeze-birches? But not bad. 'Prisoners' has a good last verse. But to complete the picture, the last line should have rhymed in '-ed'. Why does he so often upset his form? First verse of 'Christmas Wish' is good. 'Christmas Prison' foreshadows the full Harvey. Ballade No.2. is good. The second part especially. 'Solitary Confinement' is good - is touched with the Shakespearian influence that will grow on him, and has a charming thought about the white arm of the Lady Moon. A 'Rondel of Gloucestershire' is slightly boshy, but not bad. 'The Little Road' shows increase of technical power in some of the lines? (*Why* doesn't he keep his form?) Sestett of 'Sonnet' is good. The 'Sleeper' not bad. 'Army Pay' has excellent sentiment at least. 'Afternoon Tea' – perfect. 'To the Unknown Nurse' has a good second line. 'The Horses' is also 'future' Harvey. Not perfect, but good. 'The Drums of Death' 'The Oldest Inhabitant' 'Marriage' 'The Wind in Town-Trees' (Future Harvey) – all good. The Villanelle has pure poetry. The last part but one very good.

'Kossovo Day' has two good last lines. But why (save for metre) 'tortured'?

Last night – O lucky me! a Scottish Rifle sat up beside the stove with me, which glowed and made believe it was a fire. And he had travelled and could talk, and we had the same politics and the same tastes. His eyes were steady, his laugh open and easily provoked, and a smile that could not be long checked being chiefly an affair of the eyes. O well, it must have been 12.30 when we illicitly walked under the stars, watching Orion and hearing his huge sustained chord

through the night.

Of Courtesy, it is not less
Than Courage of Heart, or Holiness,
And in my walks it seems to me
The Grace of God is in Courtesy.[3]

That's true and memorable enough. And then what of

'But, heart, there is no comfort, not a grain.
Time can but make her beauty over again.
The fire that burns about her when she stirs
Burns but more clearly. O she had not these ways
When all the wild summer was in her gaze.
O heart, O heart, should she but turn her head,
You'd see the folly of being comforted.[4]

The great test of Art – the Arts of Music, Writing, Painting anyway is to
be able to see the eyes kindly and full of calm wisdom that would say these
things behind the page. I will not try to write verse in England. Once out
there, it will leak from me in vulgar streams.

With best wishes

Your sincere friend
Ivor Gurney

[1] Gurney's description adapts Arnold's line 'Who saw life steadily and saw it whole',
describing Sophocles in 'To a Friend'. He also quotes from Yeats's 'The Folly of Being
Comforted'.
[2] See letter 271 above.
[3] From Hilaire Belloc's 'Courtesy'.
[4] From Yeats's 'The Folly of being Comforted' from *Responsibilities*.

274 *To Marion Scott*   G.41.149

26 October 1917 (P)

[*On Y.M.C.A. paper and with Y.M.C.A. envelope.*]

Details of the Life
and Crimes of the private
named Gurney

Gloucester Cathedral 1900
Head boy sometime

Dr Brewer Jan 1906

I have forgotten when I got the Scholarship (I have asked Miss Hunt to tell you.)

Stanford – Composition

Mr Waddington (whom I like very much) for Counterpoint

Also the Westminster Board.

Mr Sharpe (a good man) for Piano

Dr Davies. Dr Allen.

Centre-forward for King's School

Owner of the 'Dorothy' (defunct)

2nd best batting average

3rd best bowling – last term of school

Crack platoon shot July 1917

Author of *Severn and Somme* and a further unborn imbecility

Army Feb 9th (?) 1915

Proficiency pay. C.B. every now and then. Sang 'Widdecombe Fair' blushingly at Albert Nov: 1916

Wounded Good Friday night – or rather on the Sat:

Gassed (?) at Ypres.

[*Postscript at head of letter*:]

Not those photographs: another.

275 *To Marion Scott*   G.41.150

29 October 1917 (P)

My Dear Friend

The old letters have arrived and the hurried new one. All welcome, you may be sure; though inevitably not *quite* so welcome as in France, where letters – some letters – are as stars in the night. And not 'faint blooms of light' either, Authoress.

Well, I have sent details of my wasted life. I hope they will be in time, and the photograph taken some years ago. There will be a new one soon.

By the way in my criticism of *Gloucestershire Friends* I missed 'Over Bridge' which I like very much. But still – remember 'In Flanders' 'Gonnehem', 'Ballad of Beelzebub', 'If Beauty were a mortal thing', 'If we return'. Yet there is something of great promise in this book, though there is so little worthy of publication, (that is, after reading *Poems of Today*, and couplets like

'O heart! O heart! should she but turn her head,
You'd know the folly of being comforted'.[1]And poems like 'Shadows and Lights'.)

By the way, in my next letter, you will receive at least three 'Hospital Pictures'. I want to keep these a little yet. Perhaps also in my next letter I may be able to tell you something of my movements or probable movements.

There are so many things I want to talk to you about. Not least, your remark that C.H.H.P. and Parratt[2] seem to see everything broken that they have builded.

Your letter of September 21st gives a sad account of your health, but a great idea of your courage. You are a wonderful lady, and, if I were you, I should restrain that purely civilian amateur raw opinion of soldiers being heroes above price. There is no brave deed of man yet done which is not equalled or surpassed by one of a woman.

Again I have been trying to find out something about my time here with unsuccess. I think it will be cheaper and better for me to come to London first, then to High Wycombe and then to Gloucester.

A strong rumour runs that military police have been put on in the village where I was to have [been?] photographed. So it is possible that no photograph will be taken here. Please excuse the shortness of this letter. There will be three or four sets of verses in the next. Perhaps tomorrow, perhaps the day after.

Thank you for the trouble you have taken about the 'Music Student', but all I care for until I have satisfied myself is the opinion of people like V-Williams and yourself.

With best wishes

Your sincere friend
Ivor Gurney

[1] Yeats's couplet.
[2] Sir Walter Parratt (1841-1924), organist, professor of the organ at the R.C.M., Master of the Queen's Musick and Professor of Music at Oxford 1908-18.

276 To Marion Scott

G.41.151

31 October 1917 (P)

My Dear Friend

Thank you very much for the history, which I enjoyed very much, and which has set me eager to read the Old Road as soon as possible;[1] I know the Gloucester library has it – the big edition, with good illustrations.

I have 3 Poems, and O – a new song for mezzo soprano. One of my best, madam; that being a setting of those wistful magical words of Yeats – 'The Folly of Being Comforted'.

There is one passage

'O she had not these ways
When all the wild summer was in her gaze',
which will raise your hair. And the full completion of meaning in the words at
the cry
'But heart, there is no comfort, not a grain' –
Of course it cannot be as fine as 'By a Bierside' but it is more difficult and hard
to form than 'In Flanders', and quite as successful. Perhaps 'In Flanders' is
slightly more beautiful as a whole, but there is a sorrow of wasting beauty and
such tragic passion here that puts it above any but 'By a Bierside'. Yet what
hard luck! (It was written in one sitting the night after I had been up all night
helping in the wards. Some stunt!) Well, I finished a fairly completely written
sketch, and then found I had left out
'The fire that burns about her when she stirs
Burns but more clearly'.
O Blasphemy! My balance upset! Well, there is not enough MS to copy this
out, it shall come next time.

As to being cleared out I know no more, nothing.

Last night Mr Barnett took me down to play to the officers who listened
beautifully. The piano had once a touch and a tone – an ancient but not yet
hopeless 'grand'. Yet some notes stuck, for a vase had upset on the keyboard
that afternoon. Well, well.

Programme
Beethoven – Sonata in D
Bach Prelude and Fugue in E^b (*2nd*)
    Preludes F# mi (The folly of being comforted)
            D mi
Chopin Ballade in A^b
    3 Preludes
1st half of Fantasie in F mi
Beethoven – Final movement of Funeral March Sonata.

Mr Barnett sat by, and listened in a pure ecstasy. What a fine thing it must be
to have a mind so single, joyful, childlike. Then, as I had copied out 'By a
Bierside ' for him, he would have me sing it; and afterwards 'The Folly of
Being Comforted'.

Your down-talk makes me desire very much to go into certain things once
more. Geology, for instance, to find out how deductions are made; and other
sources of early history. It delights me to hear that the roads run south of the
churches, because of that reason. Is that not a more satisfying reason than that
the Christian Churches give for the position of their temples? The sun is
glorious to all, and not perplexing.

And it is also delightful to hear of the artistic renaissance of the 7th
century. And strange; so queer a thing is Time, so difficult is it to realise that
these men we read of were men like ourselves.

What a book G.K.C.'s *History of England* must be![2] And what a prose he can write, and does! I always love G.K.C. the man when reading his books; for he is so great-hearted. Never will his review of Masefield's *Gallipoli* fade from my mind, nor an appeal to the American People. There is no style in music quite like that ... or is there? Yes, by the Lord and it is in Chopin – the Fantasia in F minor! The A major and A^b Polonaises. Some of the studies! Who would have dreamed of connecting the two men? Eureka – a discovery!

What a frightful hit poor Italy has sustained![3] What a blow! And we, for if Russia does not recover we shall have a hot time of it on the West. Indeed Britain is the rock of hope now. This news will pull Germany through another winter I suppose, when the signs were that there would be bad trouble at least.

With the selfish fear I have, mingles still sorrow for all humanity suffering under this strain. Some day men will read history books, and say with Brett Young,

> 'Poor savages that wrought in stone,
> Poor savages that fought in France'.

How shall formal religion console me? It is only Music that will comfort the heart – mine does already, and when more dross is burnt out of me, perhaps then I shall see Beauty clearly in everything. Yet O, that this purification should come by war! Obscene and purely dreadful!

I am glad my songs were a success at Reading. If they like 'By a Bierside' as much as Mr Barnett, then my place as a prophet is secure. Well, I will do all I can to get 'The folly of being comforted' ready for the next letter, but may let it wait till I see you in person. But here's one set of verses – the others are not quite ready.

Hospital Pictures. No (1)
Ulysses

A soldier looked at me with blue hawk-eyes,
With kindly glances sorrow had made wise
And talked till all I'd ever read in books
Melted to ashes in his burning looks.
And poets I'd despise and craft of pen,
If, while he told his coloured wander-tales
Of Glasgow, Ypres, sea mist, spouting whales,
(Alive past words or power of writing men)
My heart had not exulted in his brave
Air of the wild woodland and sea-wave.
Or if, with each new sentence from his tongue
My high-triumphing spirit had not sung
As in some April when the world was young.

Bangour Hospital.
Oct 1917.[4]

I hope you will like this Nielson-Kelly mixture. And sincerely hope you are feeling pretty well, and will be when we meet again. How is Miss Stella now?

With best wishes

Your sincere friend

Ivor Gurney

[1] By Hilaire Belloc (1904).

[2] Chesterton's *Short History of England* was selling well.

[3] On 24 October 1917 the Austrians attacked at Caporetto. By nightfall they had advanced 12 miles and destroyed the Italian 2nd Army as a fighting force.

[4] Published in *War's Embers* under the title 'Aberdonian'.

---

277 *To Marion Scott*   G.41.152

1 November 1917 (P)

My Dear Friend

I have been marked out to-day, probably for Saturday, and am coming straight to London. For how long is undecided. But I think that two days is not a bit excessive, three perhaps. But probably $2\frac{1}{2}$ in London $1\frac{1}{2}$ at High Wycombe. You are to be back in London by the end of October, n'est ce pas? And this will suit you? You see I can use my pass, and save a lot of money this way. Still if you are not in London yet, I would put off till the end of my leave.

This chuck-out is unexpectedly early; perhaps the departure may be a trifle late. Tuesday perhaps. But all's uncertain.

Meanwhile all sorts of best wishes

Your sincere friend

Ivor Gurney

---

278 *To Winifred Chapman*   G.45750

1 November 1917 (KT)   B2 The Camp, Bangour, Near Edinburgh

My Dear Winnie

Here's t'ye, my bonnie lass, and don't you forget it. Soon the fatal chuckout will come and before going out I be granted a golden holiday from the Army. On which happy occasion you are to behold me once again, a gallant sojer with a loathing of everything in the whole bangshoot except the men chiefly oppressed.

Fair and charming damsel, once again will I present my respects to you, and tell you All About Myself, and walk up on Keep Hill, and read and douse the glim late, and stick my feet on the mantlepiece in disreputable old slippers, and smoke a guggly churchwarden, and bless you my child, and wish I was a fixture for a while, and tootle the freudlich Bach and the triste Chopin, and frowst, and behave myself as though I were in a properly-conducted family of high ethical status.

I wonder whether I shall do all this? Je ne sais pas; anyway I will cherish the Chapman family in my bosom and criticise Haig's strategy as though I knew all about it.

Yours affectionately
Ivor

O yes, and you can say something every now and again.

---

279 *To Marion Scott*   G.41.152a

3 November 1917 (P)

My Dear Friend
   Well, to business, (probable)
   Chuck out – Tuesday. London 7.30
   High Wycombe, Friday Morning.
   Gloucester Sat: night (as late as can be.)
   There's a bit of luck; owing to slight indigestion (presumably due to gas; wink, wink!) I am to go to Command Depot for two months – a sort of Con: Camp in Khaki. I hope they *will* keep me for two months, and then of course, if the indigestion isn't cured .....
   No, the song isn't done, when I'm with you perhaps. Two months Con Camp! O Composition.
   Tomorrow I will write out
         Hebridean
         Ulysses

for you. With best wishes
Your sincere friend
Ivor Gurney

---

280 *To Marion Scott*   G.41.157

5 November 1917 (P)

[*Telegram handed in at 1.02 p.m. in Edinburgh.*]

Roaming about Edinburgh with you breakfast tomorrow
Gurney

281 To Marion Scott   G.41.153

15 November 1917 (P)

My Dear Friend   In the Train   Thursday
   Thank you for the letter and for the crusade you are carrying on.
I saw the announcement in today's paper.
My address will be
          Pte Gurney 241281
            C Coy
        4 Reserve Battallion
         Gloucester Regiment
         Seaton Delaval
          Northumberland.
A long way off.
   I will send some more Hospital Pictures soon if things turn out as I wish.
With best wishes

                      Your sincere friend
                      Ivor Gurney

282 To Winifred Chapman   G.45750

17 November 1917 (KT)

My Dear Winnie
   Here is a book I thought you would like; I hope you won't mind the
markings: they are simply what pleased me.
   Dear old kid it was nice to see you, and nicer to see you again. At present,
or at least on Monday I am to be put on a signalling course, to last from 2 to 4
months; time to think of a commission after that, old girl.
   The copies of my book have not yet come, and I can't afford to buy any
more. Directly it comes you shall have one. The papers have been kind to it –
especially *Times* and *Morning Post*. Did you take away the photo of yourself
from the set I had? If so, you lay yourself open to extreme penalties, and
utmost rigour of the law.
   This place is a pit village, ugly enough but the (rather tame) sea is only 4
miles away, and the wind roars continually. This is the address.
        Pte Gurney 241281
        C Coy, 4th Reserve Batt:
        Gloucesters
        Seaton Delaval
        Northumberland

   Has Kitty got a new post yet? I hope she will get as good a one as she
deserves. I hope everybody is well, Mammy, Daddy and the brats Arthur and

Micky, who has such a persuasive tongue.
Goodbye best wishes to you and everybody.

Yours affectionately
Ivor.

[*Written at head of letter*] Paper and string not to hand. Book comes when they come.

---

283 To Sydney Shimmin   G.76.4

November 1917 (KT)   Pte Gurney IB 241281, B Coy 4th Reserve Batt:,
                               Gloucester Regiment, Seaton Delaval,
                               Northumberland (Golly!)

$$\{ \text{לֹלֹ}\;\text{לֹ}\;\text{ז}\;\text{לֹך} \}$$

No, I never got your books
My Dear Shimmin

No, dear chap, I am afraid it was impossible for me to see you. It is true I stayed too long in London, but that came out of High Wycombe time, (unfortunately.)

And never, O never, shall I be invited or accept an invitation to stay with the Scotts again. Marion's all right, Stella's all right. Mr Scott is (I think) all right. But ..... Oh well, I enjoyed myself pretty well on the whole, and have only realised since coming away what an upheaval I must have caused occasionally. The Taylors were just delightful, though I did plant myself on them at a late hour and inconsiderately demand a meal. Mrs Voynich was as nice as could be, Geoffrey Taylor ditto. Sir CHHP. idem. The Hunts ditto. Harveys ditto. Everybody save Mrs Scott and Mrs Chapman. For the kids at High Wycombe are trumps of the aciest.

Benjamin arrived from the front tout a coup and Howells brought him. O what luck! And they were just right, and later I saw Howells twice in Gloucester and that was just right. Strornerary Luck! The only chap I missed was you, O yes and Brierley whom you do not know. A blessed time.

I was so glad to hear you are better. Dear old chap, you have had a rough time. My book is out. *Don't* buy one; wait for the author's presentation copy. To you and Mona. And don't try to go out to the front, because it is only a change in being bored. Take what comes, and curse the Kaiser.

O well, will there be an Asquith Cabinet? That gives a jolly good chance of peace I think – a sign rather than a chance I mean. And if so, O my frabjous boy (Callooh! Callay! if so.....

I've got 6 blooming songs to write out. For 'In Flanders' and 'By a Bierside' have to be rewritten. Then there is 'The Folly of Being Comforted'

365

'Wenlock Edge' 'Even Such is Time' and a 'Song' of my own. *Perhaps* there will be some Command Depot for me: I go to the doctor now.

With best wishes

Your sincere friend
Ivor Gurney

---

284 *To J.W.Haines*   G.83.3

17 November 1917 (P)

My Dear Haines

Will you please send me, then: two copies of *Friends*, 1 copy of *Five Degrees South* – Brett Young, The Second *Georgian* Book, and Housman's *Shropshire Lad* (6[d]).

Alas, there is to be no Ireland for me, no Command Depot. A3 – fit in 6 weeks or a month is the verdict on me. I think I shall tackle the commission, but have put myself down as a signaller, which means 4 months training! So my mind is uncertain, save in desire to escape France. Say 6 weeks + 8 signalling and then an application? I don't know.

Someone has just sent me *Friends* and more than ever I am amazed and delighted. Nowhere save from the West Country could that have been taken; it is so sweet, so mature.

I enjoyed that evening with you. Your books and the unquiet face of E.T.[1] and your talk of things and people that so interested me. Who knows where we may run against each other next?

Best wishes to yourself, Mrs Haines and the Hainlet.

Yours very sincerely
Ivor Gurney.

[1] Edward Thomas had been killed in April 1917; Haines had a picture of him.

---

285 *To Herbert Howells*   G.3.25

17 November 1917 (P)

My Dear Howells

The time we had together pleased me very much, and I am glad we are such good friends.

What I want to say is, O don't worry yourself to write now; write if you must; perspire it; let it leak, but don't O don't get impatient with the slow days, and overwork yourself. If you were well, you would be wasting your time in the Army, 'and so be patient, be wise and patient, friend',[1] for it is best to be wasting time as you are doing, than for you to be lost.

366

Well, here I am, back in harness, and not to be sent to Command Depot. (Dear old Army!)

The notices of my book were out yesterday, and you will probably receive one soon. Could you collar the *Morning Post* review anywhere? The *New Statesman*? *New Age*? *Nation*? Possibly you might see one lying about and collar the bit. It is a crime, but here excusable, I think.

I hope Miss Dorothy is properly gracious to you. Not yet has any letter come from the Princess to me, but still I feel that all is well, and feel that our hearts are conscious one of the other; which brings a kind of serenity after the heat.

My address is a pretty good one

>Pte Gurney I.B. 241281
>>B Co
>>4th Reserve Battallion. T.F.
>>Gloucester Regiment
>>Seaton Delaval
>>Northumberland
>>(Hear, hear!)

So write sometime.

A horrid rumour has reached me that we shall get our embarkation leave next Thursday and be off on the next draft. If so, I shall apply for a commission just *after* the 6 days. (Shudders of surprise.) Farvel! Au Revoir. Auf Wiedersehn. Goodbye.

>>>Yours ever
>>>I.B.G.

---

[1] From Yeats' 'The Folly of Being Comforted'.

---

286 *To Winifred Chapman*   G.45750

November 1917 (KT)   Pte Gurney 241281, C Coy 4th Res: Batt:,
>>>>>>Gloucesters

My Dear Winnie

That blooming book has got stolen, I suppose, for no memory of sending it to you do I remember.

It was, poor thing, *The Old Country* a YMCA book, which had some good stuff. Still, here's one of the most lovely little books I know.[1]

'The Old Bed' is simply perfect

The first five sonnets very good.

'I saw three pigs a riding', 'Tenants' and some more first rate. This is very precious to me, Wilfred Gibson is a master.

367

Sorry you haven't had my book yet. S and Js are slow.
The Times, Morning Post and *Telegraph* have liked it. With love to you all.

Yours affectionately

Ivor Gurney

Where's that photograph? What! What!

¹ The book is *Friends* again.

287 *To Marion Scott*   G.70.21

17 November 1917 (P)

*Hospital Pictures*¹
Excursion

They turned the village band on us,
Who sat with desperate calm of face
To meet the sound-storm clamourous.
They turned the village band on us
And manners failed. Without a fuss
We vanished in a black disgrace ....
They turned the village band on us
Who sat with desperate calm of face.

Companion – North-East Dugout

He talked of Africa,
That fat and easy man.
I'd but to say a word,
And straight the tales began.

And when I'd wish to read,
That man would not disclose
A thought of harm, but sleep;
Hard-breathing through his nose.

Then when I'd wish to hear
More tales of Africa;
Twas but to wake him up,
And but a word to say.

368

To press the button, and
Keep quiet; nothing more;
For tales of stretching veldt,
Kaffir and sullen Boer.

O what a lovely friend!
O quiet easy life!
I wonder if his sister
Would care to be my wife .....

Ladies of Charity

With quiet tread, with softly smiling faces,
The nurses move like music through the room;
While broken men (known, technically, as 'cases')
Watch them with eyes late deep in bitter gloom,
As though the Spring were come with all the Graces,
Or maiden April walked the ward in bloom.

Men that have grown forgetful of Joy's power,
And old before their time, take courtesy
So sweet of girl or woman, as if some flower
Most strangely fair of Spring were suddenly
Thick in the woods at Winter's blackest hour –
The gift unlooked for – lovely Charity.

Their anguish they forget, and worse, the slow
Corruption of Joy's springs; now breathe again
The free breath was theirs so long ago.
Courage renewed makes mock at the old pain.
Life's loveliness brings tears, and a new glow.
Somehow their sacrifice seems not in vain.

[1] The first poem here was omitted from *War's Embers* at the suggestion of Frank Sidgwick
but the other two were included in 'Hospital Pictures' there.

---

288 To J.W. Haines   G.83.1

19 November 1917 (P)   B Co, 4th Reserve Batt: Glos Reg:
                                         Seaton Delaval, Northumberland

My Dear Haines
    Thank you for your letter – just what I needed, and very nice to get. I look
forward to your considered opinion with great interest. As for the nebulously

enthusiastic gentleman in the *Citizen*, not a thought do I give him. save as to the dastardly insinuation that I rhyme 'beauty' with 'duty'. There is no such thing in my book.

I hope you are willing to wait a time for me to pay you that book-bill. Why I say so is because I bought *This England* yesterday, a present for someone. On the whole you had better leave out the second *Georgian*, unless you are willing to wait. Of course there are royalties, royalties, royalties .... O yes. But meanwhile thank you very much, and would you mind letting me have what criticisms you see? What crimes you commit in getting them is your affair, not mine. Best wishes to Mrs Haines and yourself.

Yours very sincerely
Ivor Gurney

---

289 To Marion Scott   G.41.154

21 November 1917 (P)   Pte Gurney 241281, B Co 4th Reserve Batt:
                          Gloucester Regt, Seaton Delaval, Northumberland

My Dear Friend

Alas, for the two months! Today I am on ordinary training, and that means but a short stay if nothing happens.

I hope you are getting on all right. There have been no air-raids, at all events; which is lucky. I wonder how London is looking now, that was so charming for the days I saw her – well, some of the days.

Two of the local reviews have reached me. they are just what I expected – and didn't want. But I got a delightful letter from Haines – the man who knows Gibson and Abercrombie – which said how pleased he was at his first glance, and how it seemed to be a not unworthy companion for Sassoon's Book, and Sorley-Turner; whom I have not read.

By the way, some time ago Sassoon walked up to his colonel, and said he would fight no more. Flashes, of course; and blue fire. There were questions in the House, and a general dust-up; but at last they solved it in a becoming official fashion, and declared him mad, and put him in a lunatic-asylum; from which there will soon come a second book, and that will be interesting to see.

Will you let me know what poems you have received lately? I have been rummaging in my Bangour notes, and have written a little since I saw you. There must be 7 or 8 things to come, not all quite polished up and hairparted but nearly so.

Thank you so much for *Friends*, for I love that book. Of course, Rupert Brooke is exquisite enough, but one can always read *Friends*. Mrs Gibson, probably affected by W.G.'s being called up (a C 3 man!), has fallen downstairs, and spoilt one eye for ever. When Rupert Brooke went abroad, he left his copyrights equally between Gibson, Abercrombie, and De La Mare. They have had £2000 each! That's why Gibson has not died, and his family.

370

Poetry pays – it took a War to make it; but still, there you are.
Best wishes

Your sincere friend
Ivor Gurney

---

24 November 1917 (P)

Recompense

I'd not have missed one single scrap of pain
That brought me to such friends, and they to me;
And precious is the smallest agony;
The greatest, willingly to bear again –
Cruel frost, night vigils, death so often ta'en
By Golgothas untold from Somme to Sea.
Duty's a gray thing; Friendship valorously
Rides high above all Fortune without stain.

Their eyes were stars within the blackest night
Of Evil's trial. Never mariner
Did trust so in the ever-fixed star
As I in those. And so their laughter sounded –
Trumpets of Victory glittering in sunlight;
Though Hell's power ringed them in and night surrounded.

Bangour
October 1917[1]

The Plain

The plain's a waste of evil mire;
And dead of colour, sodden-gray.
The trees are ruined, crumbled the spire
That once made glad the innocent day.

The flowers, the flowers are buried deep
With friends of mine who held them dear;
Who lie with innocence, asleep,
Dreaming of April's covering there.

371

O if the Bringer of Spring does care
For Duty valorously done,
Then what sweet breath shall scent the air!
What colour-blaze outbrave the sun!

Ypres-Bangour
September 1917.[2]

Hospital Pictures (No 3)
The Miner

Indomitable energy controlled
By Fate to wayward ends and to half-use.
He should have given his service to the Muse;
To most men shy; to him, her humble soldier,
Frank-hearted, gracious, bold.

Yet though his fate be cross, he shall not tire,
Nor seek another courage than his own;
For selfless valour and the primal fire
Shine out from him, as once from great Ulysses –
That king without a throne.

Bangour
Oct 1917.[3]

---

[1] Published in *War's Embers*. Line 13 has three false starts: 'As Victory's trumpets', 'Trumpets' and 'Victory's trumpets cry', before the final version; Gurney deletes Ypres from the dateline and changes September to October.

[2] Published in *War's Embers* with variation of lines 5 and 7. Gurney has corrected the last three words of line 6 from 'loved them well'.

[3] Published in *War's Embers*. See letter 301 for the miner, Pte T Evans.

291 *To Marion Scott* G.41.158

24 November 1917 (P)

My Dear Friend *C* Company
   Thank you so much for your letter. And for E.N.'s letter. (This is only a note)   No, I don't agree with your suggested alterations.
   The *Times* Review is as good as any could expect, and of course there *may* be a longer review.
   Osborne's book looks very interesting.[1] I shall try to get it, I think.
   In the ordinary way I should be chucked out in a week or so, but some fairy has given me a course of signalling, which means 2-4 months training. A

commission would mean 6 months more!

Best wishes and thanks

Your sincere friend

Ivor Gurney

Letter tomorrow or Sunday.

Dedications (for Second Ed:)

The Fire Kindled – to A.H.C.[2]
To the Poet before Battle – Mr Dunhill
Maisemore – to my Father
Afterwards – to Arthur Benjamin
Carol – to Winnie Chapman
Strange Service – to Ralph Vaughan Williams
Serenity – Mrs Voynich
Signaller's Vision – to the memory of Jimmy Taylor
The Mother – to Mrs Harvey
Bach and the Sentry – to Sir Charles
Letters – 'to Puck, if she will write'
Strafe – to Leslie Drake
The Strong Thing – to J.Haines
Scots – to Patrick Ritchie
Purple and Black – to M.M.S.
West Country – to My Mother
Firelight – to Oswald Bradley
Estaminet – to my Gloucesters
Song – to H.Plunkett Green
Ballad of the Three Spectres – Charles Caudle
Time and the Soldier – to Nurse Drummond
Praise – to Micky Chapman
Winter Beauty – to Herbert Howells
June to Come – to F.W.H.
Hark hark – to F.W.H.
Song at Morning – to M.M.S.

And take the final s from 'consolation' in 'Winter Beauty' (last line verse 2). And alter the last line of 'Scots' to 'Over the top this morning at the dawn's first grey'.

---

[1] *The Muse in Arms.*
[2] A.H.C. is Canon Cheesman and 'Puck' is Annie Nelson Drummond. Those not identified elsewhere (Jimmy Taylor, Leslie Drake, Patrick Ritchie, Oswald Bradley, Charles Caudle) were probably fellow soldiers.

27 November 1917 (P)

My Dear Friend C Coy
    I am glad to have your letter today, but sorry that you have taken the reference to 'charming days' in London to be meant for anything but the weather; which was bad on the first and last day. That was all I meant.
    I am glad to hear you have taken the violin at last with pleasure, and managed to begin those difficult articles of yours. And to hear that your songs were so well received, as was only deserved. Cheero! The news from the Western front is good, but how can you call it '*great*' after the Italian disaster passes my comprehension. Philip Gibbs says the Germans fought 'desperately' against the Tanks.[1] They are a great race in their way, and it is their unexpected bravery more than the weather has upset our plans. So *that* is the important part of his very good article.
    I did not think you would care to see the local reviews; what did they matter? Still, if you are interested, you may be amused as well. Here they are, friend.
    It is very good news to hear there may be another *Times* review. I should think you may be satisfied with the success of your foster-child – carefully reared and baptized by you.
    With best wishes and thanks

Your sincere friend
Ivor Gurney

[1] The Battle of Cambrai (20-30 November) saw the first massed use of tanks.

29 November 1917 (P)

My Dear Friend Wednesday Evening
    Your delightful letter was good to get in this wilderness. What weather it has here you can hardly imagine – however damp and cold are always present, though today for once we incredulously saw the sun. It is very nice to hear you are going on well in health and with (O Lord) 'Youth and Music'. ('Babbling limpidity' is a good phrase!)
    Yes, there *were* good things in that bad time a year ago; good things. One feels far more fed up here than in France, as a general thing. It is good to go to

one's limit, and good to see men facing hardships well and coolly facing vile Deaths.

If we get a clear formula of demand from Germany, and give a clear one back, I shall ask no more, but remain satisfied. Do you know, dear Friend, the thing that shocks a soldier is that not many civilians guess at. The fact that men at last do things not from courage or for their Country, but because of discipline (as I was told in 1914 and more still in 1915, but refused to believe.) It is that which revolts one, and makes one long for the finish. And O, if men died in a mood of glory occasionally instead of in a mere state of being fed-up!

I am so pleased about the photograph. It is natural, is it not? I got Pitcher to put up one of his studies which struck me and it was that, not horror, produced that look.

Night operations! Don't talk about 'em! Monday, Tuesday, Wednesday! so far. And you talk about sending me a book present! I will accept the *Third Georgian* with a pure pleasure, but not yet, not yet. It is mere fact that I never read. You shall hear at once when the reading mood returns, which it must, in spite of everything.

There are rumours of a shift to somewhere South; O if it might be.

I cannot say what the Cathedral Sidney has sent may be. Beauvais?

Again I have to apologise for carelessness; for the Glasgow editor's letter is nowhere to be found. This is a bad fault, and I am very sorry; if it does turn up you shall have it at once.

How in the name of goodness did high-explosive shell stick in your house? From a big bomb was it?

I am glad you have joined the Poetry people. That is a good circle.

But as to getting any from me, O help! Will I lie fallow; and am about to send you Thomas' poems. Very curious they are, very interesting; nebulously intangibly beautiful. But he had the same sickness of mind I have – the impossibility of serenity for any but the shortest space. Such a mind produces little.

The news about Herbert is sad. O Lord, what if *he* leaves his work half-begun only? One cannot help fearing that, poor boy.

Is Beauty to be made only for breaking?

Mr Dunhill has written, wants to set 'Firelight'. Of course he may.

A friend of the Hunts tried in London – at the Times Book Club – for *Severn and Somme*. Out of print it is! Harvey's two books, a *Shropshire Lad* and mine are selling like hot cakes, they told her! So all your efforts have not been in vain; and the Music Reviews have not yet started!

You have stirred things up well, with a long arousing stick.

Will you please alter that dedication 'to Puck, if she will write' to simply – 'To Puck'. And a horrid thought strikes me. Did I leave out Mrs Chapman ('La Comtesse Tilda' as I call her)? If so, she must have this; Puck can do for Book two in this case. But only *if*. O black-avised year, what dost thou bear to us? The *Times* says each successive year has been bloodier than the last. And here's another on us. 'Dear houses, the very God does seem asleep'.[1] With best wishes

Your sincere friend
Ivor Gurney

[1] Adapting Wordsworth's line from 'Upon Westminster Bridge': 'Dear God! the very houses seem asleep'.

294 *To Marion Scott*   G.70.12

29 November 1917 (P)   *C* Coy etc Gloucesters, Seaton Delaval

My Dear Friend

Thank you very much for the papers. The *Times* review is charming, I think; and satisfactory, save for the stress laid on my being a 'Gloucestershire' poet.

I did not expect Osborne to be pleased with my book, for he is a Prussian – still, his treatment of my book is all I could expect; and his reference to my double endings pleased me very much.

The criticism I most look for is from my friend Haines, and (if it may be) Walter de la Mare in the *S.W.G.* Haines wrote me a delightful letter after a first glance, and he is a good critic. (He is the man who knows Gibson and Co.)

Well, I call that a very successful start. The book has three or four possible audiences. (1) Gloucestershire (2) Musical (3) Military and Friends (4) Poetical and (5) (who knows) pious. I must get a poem on vegetarianism or temperance in the next.

I hope it will be possible, my dear G.L.A., to get those dedications pushed in. But the corrections *must* go in. What is the royalty? From 500 to 2000 – 10% 2000 to 5000 15% 5000 to 20000 20. 25% thereafter: is that it?[1]

You have been lucky about air-raids since your return to England, and I am very glad – but wondering; why? As for the victory in the West – what effect will it have on Germany? That's the point. Otherwise, for all I can see, it makes not much difference; since they fought so well, the Germans, and lost so few guns. But from Lloydd George's speech and its subsequent events, Germany is not ready to make terms.

I hope you are feeling fairly well, increasing your record every day, and able to do some work. It will be nice to hear you have taken to the violin again. Perhaps before long, if the weather does not fool about too much, you will be able to enjoy yourself to some purpose with Bach. And your book too.

(Oh, yes, I'll send that book all right.)

Osborne's book sounds interesting, and I suppose I must get it some time or other.[2]

My time at home was perfectly delightful, and went O too quickly. Howells I saw on two days, and he was very nice indeed. 'Sir Patrick Spens' and the 'Elegy' I think I shall like very much; and bits of the Concerto were delightful to hear again. A strange new time – so short. We were more intimate than ever before, I think.

It is difficult to settle down into Army life, especially in a Depot, where the discipline is so strict and there is so much cleaning up to do. Not yet have I been crimed, and there is improvement to come. They have put me on the signallers, which means an 8 – 16 weeks course! So much the better.

Best wishes and many thanks from

Your sincere friend
Ivor Gurney

---

[1] The contract gave 10% on copies from 500 to 2000, 15% from 2000 to 10,000 and 25% thereafter, 'no royalty to accrue on the first 500' (G.61.261).
[2] *The Muse in Arms.*

295 To Marion Scott   G.70.8

12 December 1917 (G)

My Dear Friend

Thank you for everything – programmes as well. (The *Sunday Times* mentioned my song by name.) I am glad he has sung it.[1]

I hope your health goes on improving and you more able to do what you wish. I hear the Gloucester weather is lovely, here either very cold or rainy. God knows what terrors of aspect the season wears at Bangour.

I'm so glad you like that last batch – which brings me to a half-book, I suppose. Here's something that will amuse you. (The *Telegraph* gave me a good review; the best, in some ways.) The *Gloucester Journal* came down on me like a ton of bricks; I suppose, for my friends did not send me it, so I inferred there was something wrong. I gather from Haines' letter in this week's issue that one passage read 'and that he will obey Miss Marion Scott more strictly in future' – it was something like that. I gather it was rather savage and very stupid; considering it necessary to praise F.W.H. in order to decry me. If possible, I will get it, but that's an issue of Saturday week.

I enclose a nice review from the *Bristol Times*. I wonder if the *Journal* will make any difference to sales locally? Well, well, that majesty has shut his burning eye for once – the critic, I mean. Also – the deaf adder that stopped her ears – a ruder quotation; occurs to me.[2]

I hope you are well into your articles, and manage to find them interesting. And your book? Does that form in you still?

It seems there is no hope of peace yet. On the whole I think we have done well up to Asquith's speech, but do not see why we cannot define our aims clearly. I suppose we are banking on the future still, and Alsace-Lorraine is probably a hindrance.

My old company S.M. has been killed at Cambrai in that do, so what's happened to my company is probably only too certain, since S.M. was a funk.

Gibson's *Friends* is really and really a lovely little book, and in merely its 3rd Impression! Ye Gods!! Poor old Wilfred is an A.S.C. driver in Italy.

Was there some word of writing songs there? It is only a word then, since there is no time from revally till 5.0 and cleaning up to be done then, with two evenings a week out of that. I hardly write anything, though there is one thing to come with this; and one more thing written for a Gloucester Hospital magazine, which I may or may not send you.

T'is a vile life, my lady, lengthy and wearisome.

The Censor has returned my last letter to Harvey, I don't know why.

There are two ways of getting unfit men to France. One is, putting him on the G.O.C.'s inspection – when he will be rejected by that potentate; then putting him in as substitute at the last moment. The other, by keeping him off the inspection, and putting him in after. An admirable example of soldierly honour. Of course the General knows all about it.

Another great joke the Army plays. To promise the men extra pay, and not to pay it. To make them buy all extras of polish etc after having taken away their kit allowance on promise to provide all necessaries, to reduce rations, and to use the canteen profits for barrack-room damages. It is a perfect globe of conduct. Among men I have come across lately are, a trainer of ponies in the polo team that beat America, (he knows the Grenfells well.) and a Shakespearean comedian (Augusta Harris) who was very interesting. He says the Scots are the best Shakespeare audience. It is a wonderful mixture of people, this crowd.

Best wishes and thanks

Your sincere friend
Ivor Gurney

Hospital Pictures (No)
  Dust

Lying awake in the ward
Long hours as any must,
I wonder where the dust
Comes from, the Dust, the Dust!
That makes their life so hard –
The nurses, who must rub
The soon appearing crust
Of green on the bright knob.

And little bits of fluff,
Dull-white upon the floor,
Most soft, most curious stuff
That sidles to the door

378

When no-one sees, and makes
Deep wrinkles and heart-breaks,
Light sighs and curses rough.

O, if a scientist
Of warm and kindly heart
Should live a while apart,
(Old Satan's tail to twist,)
Poring on crucibles,
Vessels uncanny, till
He won at last to Hell's
Grand secret of ill will –
How Fluff comes and how Dust.

Then nurses all would paint
Cheeks pretty for his sake;
Or stay in prayer awake
All night for that great Saint
Of Cleanliness, that bright
Devoted anchorite;
Their champion and True Knight.
                    I.B.G.

Seaton Delaval
December 1917[3]

I am glad you like so much those later things of mine.
                    fire –
    Or a child's face, a sunset – with the old hot desire.
Is right.[4]
    O, if but I were out of the Army and free, how I could write, but now all
my courage and strength is needed to live as much as I do.
    Still it *is* better than France, but there is less time to think and Be.
    The *Glasgow Herald* Editor writes nice letters. I have not seen the review.

---

[1] The *Sunday Times* of 9 December 1917 reported on p.4 a recital by Gervase Elwes and the London String Quartet at the Aeolian Hall the previous Thursday, at which songs by Vaughan Williams, Frank Bridge, and Colin Taylor were sung alongside Gurney's 'Sleep'.
[2] The deaf adder is from Psalm 58, v.4.
[3] Published in *War's Embers* as the second in the section.
[4] From 'The Battalion is Now on Rest', printed in *War's Embers*.

16 December 1917 (G)

My Dear Friend   Sunday
   It is kind of you to write such letters and take such trouble while you have
neither much time nor health, and I am grateful to you. And for your
criticisms, which are justified, but at present I simply cannot alter. The words
are to me undoubtedly the right ones, and 'innblinds' and 'valourously' must
be dodged by separating the poems. 'Innblinds' does so much express what I
want to say, and so well.[1]
   Which is the right spelling of Laventie or Levantie, I do not know – the
first I believe. Personally the repeating of a phrase such as 'And yet, and yet'
does not annoy me. But it becomes a mannerism when found 3 times in a
batch of poems. Thank you, there's one altered.[2] As for 'Innocent' and
'innocence' – well, I must think of something else, but can't yet. This is
barracks, not ten days' leave, alas!
   Your account of your visit to the *T.L.S.* man is most interesting. You find a
way to tame lions; anyway they don't sound terrible.
   It is good of you to take so much trouble; certainly I cannot work up
enough interest in them to worry so much … Well, not now; if they gave me
a month's leave however, there might be stirs.
   (This letter is written at Mrs MacMahon's, the mother of an old 2/5th
friend who was lately here on leave. My poor old Batt: got caught in the
Cambrai do, and O well Lloyd George is delightfully confident.)
   Bruce Richmond was very nice, I think. I am glad to know that De La
Mare had not quarrelled with the *Times*. Haines said he was in the sugar
department, but also that his ideas were not Northcliffe's, and so they parted.
But he may not have told you of that.
   There is a review in the *Sunday Times* today of *Severn and Somme*, I will get
it and put it in with this, and the Bristol paper's review.[3]
   Blackwood's is high indeed, but if it could be managed – Bien!
   And that would be a nice start, indeed. It is good news about *Severn and
Somme* getting a second review.[4]
   Ah, mam'selle, an Ode, a 'Hymn to the Honour of Man'? Perhaps, but not
here, where my mind is sodden. But O to write that Hymn!
   Part (1) Courage of Joining up
        (2) Courage to bear up when what-Army-Life-is was really seen
        (3) Courage under fire
        (4) Courage in the wet and cold
        (5) Decency to each other, comradeliness in all states of lousiness and
other evils.
        (6) Courage of dying.
I should like to write that, dear Friend. Maybe in France, not here. And on a
quiet front, if there are to be any.
   The Situation?

Well, one forgave the Paris speech, because it might have reasons. (Or half-forgive.) But O not this latest.

What is 'Victory'? Breaking the German line, and compelling them to status quo, loss of Alsace Lorraine, and Independent Poland, and restitution to Belgium and Serbia. That's victory, nothing else + indemnities and all our War costs.

Because, as Lord Rhondhha says, 'When the Lusitania sank, I made a vow to get even with the Kaiser'. To get even with the Kaiser! There you are! The real Prussian attitude! Besides, Germany has a case against Europe. The case of a Power that became great between 1850 and 1900, yet got no seaports comparable with her power. Of course it was not right to take Belgian seaports, but still, they had a case.

And, as to atrocities – Well, the Germans have been on the *unfortunate* side as regards morality. We should have disregarded precedents had we been in their position, with Time on the other side, and comparative plenty. One *cannot* allow the Lusitania to sail the seas with valuable goods for enemies. One cannot refrain because of passengers that have been warned. This is the horror of War, not of Prussia.

Have you heard anything of Sidney Shimmin? I don't think he will have a bad time altogether.

Do you know anything of the sale of *Severn and Somme*? I am afraid you do, since you threw out a hint about a first edition being plenty, and have said nothing more.

Directly I get a large enough envelope, the other verses shall be returned. (I have noted any corrections.)

There are signalling operations three nights a week now! Three evenings gone! O Lord! So you will see that time for writing or forgetting the Army will be scanty.

With best wishes

Your sincere friend
Ivor Gurney

[*On back of envelope the words* 'Verses returned when big envelope turns up.']

---

[1] 'Valorously' is used in both 'The Plain' and 'Recompense'; 'inn-blinds' is used in 'Toasts and Memories' where there is also a repetition in stanza 6 which Gurney (ill-advisedly in my view) removed.

[2] In 'The Plain' Gurney removed a repetition in line 5, and in line 7 altered 'Who lie with innocence' to 'Poor shattered loveliness' to avoid the repetition from line 4. 'And yet, and yet' remained in 'Upstairs Piano', line 22.

[3] The *Sunday Times* of 16 December 1917, p.4, reviewed Gurney under the title 'Another Gloucestershire Lad', picking out 'Spring, Rouen, May, 1917' for special praise.

[4] *Severn and Somme* was briefly reviewed in the *T.L.S.* of 22 November 1917, p.571, quoting 'June-to-Come'; it was more thoroughly treated in the *T.L.S.* of 28 February 1918, p.101.

23 December 1917 (KT)

My Dear Friend   Sunday
   Here is just a note to say I have been invited out to tea and so shall not be able to write till tomorrow.
   What with a Concert last night (Some concert! but they were very pleased) 1 rehearsal and 4 night operations, there are a whole bunch of letters waiting.
   I hope you will like this photograph of me taken in Gloucester.
   This time last year I was forgetting Time and cold feet by writing to you from Crucifix Corner. Where will next find me?
   I hope you will have – take care to have – a happy Christmas. Any riotous debauch or luxury that come to my hand shall be used. Best wishes to you and all

Your sincere friend
Ivor Gurney

298 To J.W. Haines   G.84.6.1-2

23 December 1917 (KT)   Pte Gurney 241281, C Coy, 4th Reserve Batt:,
                               Gloucesters, Seaton Delaval, Northumberland

My Dear Haines
   Your letters have been jolly interesting to the Artistic Exile, and he thanks you for them. Agrees about Brooke; *save* 'The Great Lover' and the 5 Sonnets there is not much; and I doubt whether he would have gone much farther. But that is a large '*save*'.
   If you think I do not like Thomas' Poems you are mistaken. The things attract me greatly, but the feeling runs in me all the time that he had not found himself, and was sick at soul. His work every poet should study, that being very suggestive. 'The Trumpet' is incoherent and its image not clear, but it is good. 'The Owl' very good. 'Swedes' I like. 'Thaw', 'Tears', 'Interval', 'Like the touch of rain', the delightful poems to his children, 'When first', 'Head and Bottle', 'After you speak', 'Sowing', 'When we two walked', 'In Memoriam' (beautiful), 'The Cherry Trees', 'Some Eyes Condemn', 'May 23', 'The Glory' with its two lovely first lines and discontent. (How well I knew it!) 'Melancholy', 'Adlestrop', 'The Mill Pond', 'Haymaking', 'The Sun used to shine', 'Liberty', 'There's nothing like the Sun', 'Lights Out', 'Cock crow', 'Words'. This is a long list. I like the 'Owl' best. But pity a poor musician on hard labour; this is not the life for discrimination. If I were a poet and at my ease, I should study E.T. long and long. Still, a sense of imperfection, of a veil between him and his object continually haunts me in reading him. Why doesn't he break out into divine unliterate clearness more often? Like 'Waly, Waly', or 'On Wenlock Edge'

or 'The Fiddler of Dooney' or 'Gonnehem' or 'In Flanders'? Or 'The Old Bed' or 'I saw three pigs a-riding'?

The *Georgian Book* has not yet arrived, but I am sending you the money for *Friends* and *Five Degrees South*. Thank you very much, and I will try to find out about the Georgian from the Bookshop, but it has never reached me yet.

Thank you so much for having defended me so well and cunningly; unfortunately I have not yet seen the review. N'importe. The reviews on the whole have been good. *The Daily Telegraph* most flattering. S and J are not enthusiastic about the sale, but (I think) expect a second edition, and the musical Papers have not yet started. It ought to do fairly well, if every one was not so fed up with everything.

My goodness but I should like a talk with you about Really Interesting Things! Dammit, and Peace looks far off still, yet who can tell? Practically all commissions applied for from this side have now been stopped. Still, it *is* luck to be a signaller – in England for months yet, and to be in a safer service abroad.

This is an ugly land after my own and yours, but the people are kind, which makes up for a lot. But O, O Gloucester!

I was born in a fair land, and may never forget it.

You shall have some of my later poems before long, for you are the best critic I have, and your advice will be valuable. Only – one needs brains and deep leisure for polishing; in the Army there is no use for either.

I hope you will like Pitcher's photo of me – that makes me look like an artist anyhow; for which I am grateful, bless him!

As for F.W.H., I will say nothing.

Best wishes to yourself, Mrs Haines and the baby, and the room with the books in – crowded companionable shelves and the picture of Edward Thomas and the rest.

Yours very sincerely
Ivor Gurney

O yes, and some blooming sort of a Merry Xmas!

99 *To Marion Scott* G.70.9.2-4

23 December 1917 (KT)

My Dear Friend

This is still Sunday, after Lights Out and there is a fire to write by, so here goes.

The verses have been returned to you; would have been returned before but for the fact that there were no large envelopes in Seaton Delaval, and I had to go to Blythe to get them.

The weather is cold and harsh here. It is better with you I hope, for cold weather must be trying. Are you still getting on well, and improving in health. It was nice to see you able to do something of what you desired, and normally I suppose that you would go on getting better – in spite of your elementary Violin articles; a dreadful task indeed.

It would be interesting to know how you are gradually pulling yourself out of illhealth, by what little dodges of extra work and wangles of 5 minutes more a day.

As for me, the Army cloud is pretty heavy upon me. Perhaps the weather has something to do with it. Anyway 'I am constipated in the brains' as Stevenson said. Only going out of billet at night keeps me alive.

As for reading – well, I had no spectacles for 9 days; both pairs broken, but my eyes stood it surprisingly well.

They are giving us (so they say) plum pudding and turkey Christmas day. Let us wait and see, anticipate and suffer.

The attitude of men, going on drafts and men on courses and so not to go out soon; is that of men certainly convinced that no Victory is certain, horribly fed up; yet still cheerful, still friendly to one another, and very skilled at getting fun out of life. They expect a very bad time of it, but the wildest rumours of Peace go round. They are very fine still.

Colonel Feyler insists that Cambrai was a victory and that the German losses were colossal. Good, and his opinion is worth having.

Have you heard or seen anything of Arthur Benjamin since that night at your house? That was a night to remember – an augury of future meetings. Or of Sidney Shimmin? I hope he will get on all right; believe he will; as the work is definitely useful and not very hard.

It was good to see how well Howells' Elegy was received. Perhaps this is the beginning of his real prominence. Somebody is getting on with work anyway.

There is a new piece of verse, but I want to look at it a bit first, believing myself to be too fed-up to write well.

Last night I vamped accompaniments at a parish concert. One man sang badly and retired in confusion. The chairman (a collier) observing this said in his North Country dialect – 'We don't always do things right. That man has just missed leave, too. He has a very bad cold. Still he's done very well, but will do much better next time'. Personal remarks, biographical sketches – all sorts of things he entered upon to his chapel audience. There was some fun in it, but alas, I have a great power of being bored.

I hope when this reaches you, you will have had a happy sort of Christmas – a pretty happy one anyway – all of you. And may the next be less tragical, the song of the Angels less cynical-sounding.

Best wishes anyhow

Your sincere friend
Ivor Gurney

23 December 1917 (KT)

[*On back of envelope is the note:* 'A letter enclosed with his photographs'.]

One for Erbert And One for Harthur
that great musician man

    And

            Best Wishes

                    for a bloody

                            sight

better

            Christmas

than this.

26 December 1917 (P)

My Dear Friend
    No, I cannot theorise about this world, save only that it seems to be made for the creation of Character – that it is Hell, or at least Purgatory.
    There may of course be several sets of existences, each incomprehensible to the other; but I don't worry about that.
    Well, here comes Housman's Song.[1]
    There is a piece of kindness you might like to do – as is your way. The chap I asked you to send a ticket to was in Hospital at Bangour with gastritis or some such thing. He was a miner, with keen interests, and a good voice, hardly any knowledge of fine music, but with fire, and a temperament that with his voice ought to go far. You would like him, I'm sure. Would you mind asking him to come and see you? He's not at all well, and most horribly depressed, what with sickness of mind and body, and a talk with a sympathetic you would cheer him up no end I am sure.
    You will not often get a chance of doing so much good so easily as in this

instance. The address is

> Pte Evans T 118853
>> No 27 Coy MTASC 40 Harold Rd
>> Upper Norwood
>> London SE.

I hope the Air Raid did you no sort of harm. And that the invalids are all better.

With best wishes

Your sincere friend
Ivor Gurney

[1] Perhaps 'On Wenlock Edge' or 'The Land of Lost Content'.

302 To Marion Scott   G.41.161

3 January 1918 (P)[1]

Toasts and Memories

When once I sat in estaminets
With trusty friends of mine,
We drank to folk in England
And pledged them well in wine,

While thoughts of Gloucester filled us –
Roads against windy skies
At sunset, Severn river,
Red inn-blinds, country cries;

That stung the heart with sorrow
And barbéd sweet delight
At Riez Bailleul, Levantie;
At Merville, many a night.

Now I am over Channel
I cannot help but think
Of friends who stifle longing
With friendly food and drink.

'Where's Gurney now, I wonder,
That smoked a pipe all day;
Sometimes that talked like blazes,
Sometimes had naught to say'?

And I – and I must wonder
Where all my comrades are;
Those men whose Heart-of-Beauty
Was never stained by War.

Seaton Delaval.
Nov 1917

Hospital Pictures (No {?})

Upstairs Piano

O dull confounded Thing,
You will not sing
Though I distress your keys
With thumps, in ecstasies
Of wrath, at some mis-said
Word of the deathless Dead!

Chopin or dear Mozart,
How must it break your heart
To hear this Beast refuse
The choice gifts of the Muse!
And turn your airy thought,
With clumsiness to nought.

I am guilty too, for I
Have let the fine thing by;
And spoilt high graciousness
With a note more or less;
Whose wandering fingers know
Not surely where they go;
Whose mind most weak, most pure,
Your fire may not endure
That's passionate, that's pure.

And yet, and yet, men pale
(Late under Paschaendale
Or some such blot on earth)
Feel once again the birth
Of Joy in them, and know
That Beauty's not a show
Of lovely things long past.
And broken men at last
Take heart and glimpse the light,
Grow strong and comforted
With eyes that challenge night,

387

With proud-poised gallant head,
And new-born keen delight.

Beethoven, Schumann, Bach;
These men do greatly lack,
And you have greatly given.
The fervent blue of Heaven
They will see with purer eyes –
Suffering has made them wise;
Music shall make them sweet.

If they shall see the stars
More clearly after their wars
That is a good wage.
Yours is a heritage
Most noble and complete.
And if we, blind, have gone
Where a great glory shone,
Or deaf, where angels sang;
Forgive us, for you, too,
A little blind were, knew
Of weakness, once, the pang;
Of darkness, once, the fear.

And so, forgive this dear
Pig-headed chest of strings,
And me, whose heart not sings
Nor triumphs as do yours
Within the Heavenly doors –
Walking the clear unhindered level floors.
Gloucester
Nov 1917

The Sentry

He fronts the dark with straining eyes,
While thousand things in fancy stir;
And guards his comrades from surprise,
Yet still finds room to think of her

Who kissed him, when the train went slow
From gray Victoria, with dry
Eyes that were fiery with Love's glow,
With steadfast grave intensity.

He sees them now; and, fighting, clings
To memory in the freezing dark;
And songs of love and longing sings,
Honouring her with courage stark.

Ypres-Bangour
September 1917[2]

The Battalion is now on Rest

Walking the village street, to watch the stars and find
Some peace like the old peace; some soothe for soul and mind;
The noise of laughter strikes me as I move on my way
Towards England – Westward – and the last glow of day.

And here is the end of houses. I turn on my heel,
And stay where those voices a moment made me feel
As I were on Cotswold, with nothing else to do
Than stare at the old houses, to taste the night-dew;

To answer friendly greetings from rough voices kind ...
O one may try for ever to be calm and resigned,
A red blind at evening sets the poor heart on fire –
Or a child's face a sunset – with the old hot desire.

Seaton Delaval
Nov 1917

Hospital-Pictures (3)
The Miner

Indomitable energy controlled
· By Fate to wayward ends and to half use,
He should have given his service to the Muse,
To most men shy, to him, her humble soldier
Frank-hearted, gracious, bold.

Yet though his fate be cross, he shall not tire
Nor seek another service than his own.
For selfless valour and the primal fire
Shine out from him, as once from great Ulysses,
That king without a throne.

---

[1] This group of poems is in an envelope dated 3 January 1918, but the comments in letters 295 and 296 indicate that Marion Scott has already seen these poems and commented. This is presumably then the date when the revised poems were returned rather than first sent.
[2] Omitted from *War's Embers* at Sidgwick's suggestion.

10 January 1918 (P)

My Dear Friend

The only thing I can think of to send in reply to your good wishes is – I hope we may get it. This year seems to be in the hand of God more than ever. We the runners in this desperate trial of strength seem able to feel nothing but the pain – yet the declarations of these last few days assure us our course is better than that of the Germans, and we far more fitted to shape the future.

Thank Goodness for a clear declaration at last![1] Of course, these are not final terms but I imagine that the Liberal Elements of the Central Powers will prefer our attitude to the Prussian, and may at last bring a fairly united strength against their lords, as we should against ours in like circumstances.

Garvin makes me sick. The *Saturday Westminster* is so much better. Garvin wants to get even with the Kaiser, like Rhhonnda [*sic*] and Co. Well, that's all about news.

Now as to what verses were written in Trenches.

> All the triolets were written in Trenches.
> Strange Service (the same day as 'By a Bierside')
> To Certain Comrades
> June to Come
> Song at Morning
> Song of Pain and Beauty.
> To England – A Note.
> England the Mother.

As for writing, there are in this book some feeble attempts at verse, but no more than that. When the weather gets better I may be able to do more, with warmer days and longer light.

I am just dry – my strength being taken up by endurance. If I could sit up late, perhaps that would get me into swing, but that's impossible.

For you to give me a present now would be just waste. Please wait awhile – unless you think it would wake me up. (The *Observer* was a good one, and spotted one of the best things in the book – the last four lines of all.)[2]

I have just heard from Shimmin – stagnating in some place or other. I hope he will do pretty well, and, of course the circumstance of doing useful work may make him happier.

Have you heard that *S and S* is sold out? A friend of the Hunts inquired at the Times Book club to hear that it was out of print, and had been selling like hot cakes, together with Harvey's two Books and *A Shropshire Lad*.

Last night I spent with his brother – a Lieutenant with the Military Cross – and enjoyed myself as to him, but not his wife.

Lamps again tonight! I will send a little more later. Please excuse this scrawl. With best wishes

Your sincere friend

Ivor Gurney

[1] President Wilson's '14 points' speech, made to Congress on 8 January 1918. The Germans and Austro-Hungarians were later to request these as the basis for peace talks.
[2] The end of 'England the Mother'.

---

304 To Marion Scott G.41.163

10 January 1918 (KT)

My Dear Friend

Thank you for your long and most welcome letter; and here are two poems to thank you for it. But O you don't know how difficult it is to write anything – the shortest note – in this freezing, ugly, uncomfortable Hell of a Hole. (You see I am still fed up.) The other men get round the fire and take the bench, one cannot write in the billet on the table therefore. Only warm weather, or France, will alter things.

Yes, you did tell me of your visit to S and J's. I am almost sure of having written about it, and their asking for my second book. Yes, the first edition is gone, but the blighters have not sent my copies yet, which is rather mean, even for verse publishers.

Thank you again about the *Third Georgian*. If you think it would spur me to write please send it. But I warn you that noone else on full duty reads verse at all here. Small blame to them!

As for Herbert, you know as much as I do, save that Sir James Mackenzie says he will fight the case if Herbert is called up. Have you seen his new photo, taken at the same time as mine? A very good one it is, but the eyes look so ill.

Hadow[1] has written to him sympathetically, and saying that he considers H.N.H. to be the chief hope of English Music. I wonder if God is fool enough to end him first.

Thank you about 'La Comtesse Tilda'. Yes, that will be her title; not Mrs Chapman. I am sorry about Mr Dunhill; he looked fagged and thin when I saw him in November.

As for the 'Music-Student' think no more on't, friend; although fools are annoying enough when they try to hide foolishness so.[2]

Thank you for all the trouble you have taken about the 'Elizas'. You are a good friend indeed. There are two songs coming to you from Herbert – 'The Folly of being Comforted', and 'Severn Meadows'. All I have done.

Sir Hubert is a great man, and my admiration of him has been great from the first. He speaks with authority, not as one of the scribes. What has been his illness? Indeed, the human race often seems to shame God, for even the most wise Deity and most pitiful could hardly refrain from triumph and shame

391

to see how nobly men endure in schemes far beyond their comprehension – doubting indeed whether there is any plan to comprehend.

As to the War – I feel much happier. Our terms are definite (though of course to be receded from) and Germany is still ruled by bullies and liars. Well, we soldiers wanted to know that, so the knowledge has rather overshadowed Lloydd George's other disgraceful speeches.

We cannot accept the German terms, which are fatal to Freedom, so we must go on being harried by our Old Sweats still a while longer; though I do not forget the faces of men hobbling down with trench-feet, while our War-makers take no danger.

To spur me on, I bought *More Soldier Songs* at Blyth. O dear! perhaps I am a poet after all.

How are you now, physically and mentally? Are the articles for the brats finished? And can you practice? Please tell me; not for politeness' sake do I ask.

And thank you for the *T.L.S.*s. The Rob Roy article and the review of *Georgian Poetry* were very good.[3] The papers go a round – I do not keep them.

Letters and papers are not what they are in France; but they keep alive in me the resolution not to be broken by the Army as some men are broken, keep alive hope, and memory of the pleasure that filled me in your music room – a sense that there is a port, and I shall arrive there.

Many thanks and best wishes from your sincere friend

Ivor Gurney

[1] Sir William Henry Hadow (1859-1937), educationist and writer and lecturer on music.
[2] A pseudonymous correspondent or reviewer.
[3] The *T.L.S.* for 3 January 1918 had an article on 'The Centenary of *Rob Roy*' on p.6; that for 27 December 1917 had a review of *Georgian Poetry, 1916-1917* on p.646.

305 To Marion Scott   G.41.163a

11 January 1918 (P)

My Dear Friend

Your gift came today,[1] received with pure pleasure and sincere thanks. It looks most fascinating, and will be read as soon as possible. The song is ready written out but must be tested first on some piano.

And now I'm going through your long and most interesting letter.

You say you have a sick household. I hope Mr Scott is much better – or at least, able to amuse himself; but he must be really ill not to be able to do that, with his clear interested mind.

Your review of my book[2] has given my people great pleasure, and they are very proud of me, you may be pleased to hear. Mr Bellows sent the *R.C.M. Mag:* to them. Sidgwick and Jackson have sent no books.

Yes Edward Thomas is a very poetic soul indeed, and English at the core. Please write about them. Haines knew him intimately, and talks of him a lot.

I do hope you are all getting well now, Mr Scott, the 'Aunt who lives with us', your Mother, and Audrey, and hope that the Air-raids have made no difference to getting well. Goodness, what a dose at once! Is the weather bad in London now? It has improved here, and they may all be flourishing.

Yes 'Wenlock Edge' is written out, but I will not send it till tested. Also a new song – Gibson's 'For G', which certainly wants tinkering with. You may show my songs as and when you please, of course.

Why should not 'Orpheus' come first in the Elizas? If not, why not, and something rowdy must begin, put 'Spring' first and 'Orpheus' last.

As for the first two bars of 'Sleep', – certainly. 2 first bars as written, then in octaves – the notes written, and an octave above. Yes play it *almost* slurred.

 comme ça!

Thank you so much about Bruce Richmond. You are a more than superhuman Literary Agent, because you do these things for kindness' sake.

'And which has brought such honour to the College' is a reference which greatly pleases me.[3]

Please talk about yourself when you feel inclined, for I like listening. My enquiries about your health are quite genuine. For a person with your pluck and with your health deserves solicitude. So – 'How are you Miss Marion, this evening, Ma'am?'

That you can walk with enjoyment is very good news. If it were not for the War, you would probably be quite well in no time at all, with your determination. Hang on, my Jolly Literary Agent, and smile even if only for cussedness.

About your work I am going to be simply honest. I don't know what to say, and that's true. Should you go on writing? Well, I care only for Music of strong individuality; Bach, Beethoven, and Herbert Howells and Vaughan Williams. It is the same with verse – I care only to hear what I could not do myself; I like what is beyond me.

But as to the use of making a body of *English* music there is no doubt, whether is has genius or not; but I, who am paralysed by doubt, before writing, as to whether it is worth while or no, cannot be expected to give advice. Literature? Now could I – *could* I give any opinion? Can't you ask Mr Dunhill, who must have read some things of the kind you mean? I am simply in the dark – don't know.

Consider what I am – the semi-invalid who tried to write and the fairly fit man totally out of touch with everything!!!

Your influence may be strong for good anyway, but you have a perfect right to please yourself, not ask hopeless, fed-up, people like myself. (They paid me 5/- last week.)

You write as clear English as your handwriting – judging by your letters.

As for your music – further darkness – I know only your tiny songs. So there you are – as if you had not asked me!

Is Germany waking up? It rather seems as if any unsuccessful offensive on this front would lead to trouble. Anyway we know now that the present German terms are quite unacceptable, and can go on fighting with a clear heart.

The quotation from Newbolt is very beautiful. And thank you so much for the trip to Chamonix and up. You can write you know, and in this your personality was clearly felt.

Yes, I think you must be better, could not have written that evening out of you before now. Cheerio!

I feel ashamed to close now, but even this must be paid for by writing illicitly tonight after Lights Out at Signalling notes for an hour.

It's worth it.

You are a good friend indeed. Letters are not here what they are in France, but gratitude (I like G.K.C.'s definition) has become so dead in me that I am not glad to get your warm hearted vivid letters.

And your symbol and mine look very well in the Georgian Book, placed just right, and, of course, well done. Perhaps you'll set me writing with your much-desired gift, although Time is so scant.

With best wishes

Your sincere friend
Ivor Gurney

[1] The third anthology of *Georgian Poetry*.
[2] MMS's review is in *R.C.M.Magazine*.
[3] In MMS's review.

306 To Herbert Howells   G.3.32

January 1918 (KT)

My Dear Howells

That was a lovely note of yours. (I sent it on to her!) And gave me great pleasure. Save the news about yourself. Poor old chap! I am the luckier of us two at present, I think, for you have a distressed mind.

If I do well here, there may be a chance of my staying for a considerable time, so I'm going to try to do well. Anyway there is a probable five months still to go.

Here is a new, more orthodox, song. Please send it on [to Miss] Scott when digested. It is beautiful, isn't it?

You know why ......

[   ]he could hear it.

[Annie?] Nelson Drummond is older than I thought – born s[ooner] I mean. She is 30 years o[ld an]d most perfectly enchanting. She has a pretty figure, pretty hair, fine eyes, pretty hands and arms *and* walk. A charming voice, pretty ears, a resolute little mouth. With a great love in her she is glad to give when the time comes. In Hospital, the first thing that would strike you is 'her guarded flame'.[1] There was a mask on her face more impenetrable than on any other woman I have ever seen. (But that has gone for me.) In fact (at a guess) I think it will disappear now she has found someone whom she thinks worthy.

A not unimportant fact was revealed by one of the patients at hospital – a fine chap – I believe she has money. Just think of it! Pure good luck, if it is true (as I believe it is). But she is more charming and tender and deep than you will believe till you see her.

O Erbert, O Erbert....

I forgot my body walking with her; a thing that hasn't happened since ....when?

I really don't know.

[She tes]ted me with a pretty severe test. I said, if she wanted me to I would c[ome] and see her, but must see her [ ] nothing. That was

[*The rest of the letter is missing. The spaces above are where it has been nibbled by mice.*]

---

[1] In his own 'At Reserve Depot', he writes of the violet 'Hiding its dark fervour, guarding its flame'.

307 To Herbert Howells   G.3.20

16 January 1918 (G)

Going North to Edinburgh

My Dear Howells

I have just written you a letter telling you of my coming up here. Please don't say anything about it to anyone but the Taylors. It will need explanation I am not ready to give yet, and of course my people will want to know why I did not go home – but a week-end leave is so short.

Compree mong bong Amy?

Yours
I.B.G.

[*In the same envelope*]

My Dear Howells   Wednesday 16

Enclosed with this you will find a letter enclosed written just before I was hastening North to Edinburgh.

What I think of your photograph is – that it reveals you in a fine way, but

O poor Boy you look ill.

Hadow's letter[1] delights me. He is an honest critic, and right in this instance besides; a letter of this sort must buck you up. Just be as serene as possible. Let not the eager fire of your mind eat your body any more than it must, for you are great and shall do great things.

Your criticisms are true. As to similarity – Well, perhaps I won't admit anything but similarity in method. As to linking them up more tightly, that may come; but as to setting the things I do in an orthodox fashion – well it could be done; but I live attempting difficult things, and this is my way.

Wait till I'm out of this though.

Yes, I mean you to send these songs to Miss Scott (I told Mrs Voynich so.) and so please send them.

Make any copies you wish of course – but should I not do that myself, Sick Genius? These songs are a success. They have pleased you, and I want no more. As to *Severn and Somme*, I have not yet had my copies!! Damn S and J, they take a long time about things.

Sir Charles has a photograph of me though.

Well I have just been to Edinburgh, about that magnificent place, and in and out to Bangour.

Herbert Howells, it is just perfectly and radiantly All Right. I have reached Port, and am safe.

I only wish and wish you could see her and know her at once. You and Harvey.

My Goodness, but it was a hot pain leaving her. We had a glorious Saturday afternoon and evening together. A glorious but bitterly cold Sunday evening. A snowy but intimate Monday evening. For the first time for ages I felt Joy in me; a clear fountain of music and light. By God, I forgot I had a body – and you know what height of living *that* meant to me. Well I'll say no more.

Being in the Army is worse and better for me filled with memories and anticipations, and being where I am – in surroundings that mock all beautiful dreams.

But to get her and settle down would make a solid rock foundation for me to build on – a home and tower of light.

Like you, I see in her first of all a beautiful simplicity – her very first characteristic, – As you see in Dorothy. The kind of fundamental sweet first-thing one gets in Bach, not to be described, only treasured.

Well, well; why bore you? You know what I think and how it is with me. May good luck be with you in this thing and all things.

Yours ever

I.B.G.

[1] See letter 304.

20 January 1918 (P)

My Dear Friend

Here are two poems – Writing it out has made me glad I did not scrap 'Photographs'. Being in Newcastle last Saturday, I bought *More Soldier Songs*, but will write of that later. A weak thing on the whole.

Thomas' book you will be able to read in better conditions than I, but my experience is that it pays for rereading many times. The exquisite art of the books, the loving subtlety, the half-lights, the deep-in sadness of his lovable mind – are very striking.

'The Owl' is most awfully good. Well, you will see what has been marked. Is the book a success? I do not know, but it is an exquisite failure at the worst.

I.B.G.

To His Love

He's gone and all our plans
Are useless indeed.
We'll walk no more on Cotswold
Where the sheep feed
Quietly and take no heed.

His body, that was so quick,
Is not as you
Knew it, on Severn river
Under the blue
Driving our small boat through.

You would not know him now ...
But still he died
Nobly, so cover him over
With violets of pride
Purple from Severn side.

Cover him, Cover him soon!
And with thick-set
Masses of memoried flowers –
Hide that red wet
Thing I must somehow forget.

Seaton Delaval
Northumberland
Jan 1917.[1]

Photographs

Lying in dugouts, joking idly, wearily;
Watching the candle guttering in the draught;
Hearing the great shells go high over us, eerily
Singing; how often have I turned over, and laughed

With pity and pride, photographs of all colours,
All sizes, subjects. Khaki brothers in France;
Or mothers' faces worn with unnumbered dolours;
Or girls whose eyes were challenging and must dance,

Though in a picture only, a common cheap
Ill-taken card; and children – frozen, some,
(Babies) waiting on Dicky-bird to peep
Out of the handkerchief that is his home,

(But he's so shy!) And some with bright looks, calling
Delight across the miles of land and sea,
That not the dread of barrage suddenly falling
Can blot quite out – not mud nor lethargy.

Smiles and triumphant careless laughter. O
The pain of them, Wide Earth's most sacred things!
Lying in dugouts, hearing the great shells slow
Sailing mile-high the heart mounts higher and sings.

But once – O why did he keep that bitter token
Of a dead Love? That boy, who, suddenly moved
Showed me, his eyes wet his low talk broken,
A girl who better had not been beloved.

Seaton Delaval
Dec: 1917.

---

[1] The date is obviously a slip for 1918.

309 *To Marion Scott*   G.70.14

1 February 1918 (P)

[*Postcard*]

My Dear Friend   College
    Will you please send concert tickets to Pte Evans, whether it is for my songs

or no.[1] I met him at Bangour – he is a miner, but deserves better of Fate, and has a good voice and great ambition; is also a very decent chap. Do let him have one, please. His address is Pte Evans.T. M.T.A.S.C. 40 Harold Road, Upper Norwood, London SE. You would like him. Please oblige us.

I.B.G.

[1] Gurney's five Elizabethan songs were sung by K. Vivian Worth (scholar) at R.C.M. College Concert No 624, on the afternoon of 28 February 1918.

---

310 To F.W. Harvey   G.61.390

February 1918 (KT)   19 Barton Street Gloucester

[Stamped with the censor's mark of the German prison camp at Bad-Colberg]

My Dear Old Willy

It's a dull day. I will comfort and renew myself by writing to you, friend of orchard and river; drawing life from memories of blue and silver seen together and great sights of sunset from the little hill.

There's not much to tell you of course. Things are going on steadily, and little by little I gain happiness and health and power over my mind and external things; and gain this not only by desire but because One Other is giving me such gifts as I may deserve.

You would hardly know me now, or recognize my piano playing (had I a month's practice,) and indeed there is a startling difference between the white-faced thin thing from hospital and what Pte Gurney is now. I think you would be pleased with your friend, Willy, a weed no longer; though hardly a smart soldier and never enthusiastic about cleaning and such like spiritual exercises.

How are you now, being out of solitary confinement and able to mix with men again? You must be happier surely. Are your parcels coming? Your mother said you had not been getting them regularly when she last heard.

Dear chap, there's so much to talk about. I'll put my hand on your shoulder, and we'll wander about the fields and roads to talk of the *Georgian Book, No 3* – which has several new names. (Willy, I hope you'll be in No 4.) Turner, Sassoon, Monro, J.C.Squire, Stephens, Graves. And old names. Drinkwater (a good selection) Gibson (a poor one) Walter De La Mare, Davies (poor) Hodgson.

These young writers are very interesting, very much in earnest, and very gifted; out of them a great poet should come. Make haste Willy and start it! O we'll do such things together yet!

You must be stale with imprisonment; but still, unless weak with hunger or sickness – force yourself; write.

You will be glad to hear of me, that though I am still neurasthenic and naturally gloomy yet the knack of kicking myself into doing things has developed a lot, and hardly ever am I idle. My evenings are quite full up, one way or another. O you just wait! Once you are back I'll fill you to the neck with music and wonderfully subtle criticisms of your own and other poetry.

We'll frighten cows with gesticulations and hot outcries behind Hygrove. I think I shall be able to help you quite a lot, old boy, and strongly hope so. Especially as I am going on growing in insight in my own craft, and this must help me to see into yours. *Severn and Somme* has sold out one edition but my Author's copies have *not* arrived. It's February – the year's going round, and I have escaped the Winter out there Thank Goodness. It is likely my course of signalling will last till May anyway. Perhaps Luck will keep me in England till June, which will suit me better than wallowing in the mire of Flanders.

I have been playing the piano – not a bad one – in the Recreation Room here. And there is no doubt Willy that I play better than ever in my life. I longed for you to hear some of the stuff I went through – a most appreciative audience you were always, and when you come back (if circumstances permit) I'll set you writing in no time.

Bell is signalling officer here – a decent chap. He says he knew you well in the   [1], and it is through his power it may come that I keep out of things for a time.

There is a new song and some new verses. Here is a song written in November.

> My heart makes songs on lonely roads
> To comfort me while you're away,
> And strives with lovely sounding words
> Its crowded tenderness to say.
>
> Glimmering against the forward dark,
> Your face I see with pride, with pain
> So that one time I did desire
> Never to see that face again.
>
> But I am glad that Love has come
> To bind me fast and try my worth;
> For Love's a powerful Lord and gives
> His friends dominion over the earth.[2]

You know whom that's meant for.

The weather here is almost unrelievedly ugly – the colours and mellow grace of Gloucester seem a false phantom of a lover's mind, but are not. Do you remember how, in Spring evenings, the gold of late sunlight used to be heavy on the floor of the orchard, that lies to the right of the road, nearing your house on a journey from Gloucester? And great sunsets? And Autumn afterglows, most tender, most 'thronged'? (You know what I mean.) You'll make words to catch that charm, and I'll make music, combine the result.

Cheerio, Willy, things will come right in the end. Look at me – the sick creature of 4 years ago, and what I am now. If *I* can do it, what can you do?

Though you have to live on the last ultimate scrap of grit in your being – some day you'll live easily in Joy, because you like living for its sweet and varied interests, and think of any evil of the past as a necessary light price for so much content. Dear old Willy, if friendship is anything at all, you should be happy, for there cannot be one friend of all your many forgets or has forgotten you, who have the power of holding from a distance as only Great Lovers can – of increasing it, indeed. I'll write again soon to let you know of anything worth letting you know, and prattle in my old egotistical style.

Good bye with love

Yours ever
Ivor

---

[1] A short word here has been scratched out, presumably by the Censor.

[2] A version of this is printed in *Collected Poems*, p.54, but the above seems a more coherent version.

311 To J.W.Haines   G.83.4.1-2

6 February 1918 (P)

My Dear Haines
    Here's for a talk then.
    Please tell me when you write what you think about the new *Georgian*. Here's my choice – 'Romance'. '*The Caves of Auvergne*'. (Turner) 'Westland Row' (Stephens) '*A House*' 'To a Bulldog' '*The Lily of Malud*' (Squire) '*To Victory*' '*In the Pink*' (Sassoon) 'To — ' 'Fulfilment' 'Philosophers Oration' (Nicholson)[1] .'Everything' 'Week End' 'The Bird at Dawn' (Harold Monro) I IV(?) V VI (Masefield) '*The Gypsy Girl*' '*The Bells of Heaven*' 'Babylon' (Hodgson) 'It's a Queer Time' 'Star-Talk' '*In the Wilderness*' 'Not Dead' (Graves) 'Tenants' '*To G*' (Gibson) 'Discovery' '*Stone Trees*' 'The Pigeons' (Freeman) 'The Midlands' '*Reciprocity*' 'Birthright' (Drinkwater) '*The Scribe*' 'The Ghost' (De La Mare) 'White Cascade' (Davies) 'New Years Eve' (Bottomley).
    I only wish we could be sitting together in your room burbling about these! I looking at Thomas' face beside me and the lovely array of books, those trustable things, where ever my eyes might go.
    Now don't mind saying *what* you think of my newer stuff. There are several things written in France of which there is no copy, save in Miss Scott's hands, but that cannot be helped. Say what you please.
    Have you been walking lately? If so, where? How Mrs Haines? And the small one? Please give them my best wishes for good relations with each other.
    I feel much happier about things for the late speeches and acts about the

401

War. There is no doubt we must go on and hard.

There was a very interesting account in last Sunday's *Sunday Chronicle* – which rang true – It was that the big offensive of the French last April had succeeded so far that orders were actually issued by the German G.H.Q. for a retreat to the Meuse; but politicians on the spot – unused to losses, exclaimed that their armies were being sacrificed – at the moment of victory the offensive was bound. If this is true, then we have hopes for this year.

As for Russia – what novels will the Tolstoi of 2000 A.D. write? I am glad you liked my photograph. It was a triumph for Pitcher and a gratification to myself.

I am afraid there is no more to say, except that I am far fitter than you have ever seen me, and to hope to see you soon. It will be some months before I leave England, and the leave may not come till May.

With best wishes

Yours very sincerely
Ivor Gurney

[1] Gurney makes his usual mistake of Nicholson for Robert Nichols, i.e. Robert Malise Bowyer Nichols (1893-1944), author of *Invocation* (1915) and *Ardours and Endurances* (1917).

312 *To Marion Scott*   G.70.15

11 February 1918 (P)

My Dear Friend

I return the cuttings with thanks. The one that mentions 'thefts' is unfair, it seems to me.

Thank you for those, and the *Musical Record*, and the *R.C.M.Magazine*, in which the review is just as suggestive as possible; but no, there was no bombardment accompaniment to any of my things.[1]

The evening of 'To Certain Comrades' was most beautiful, and I stood outside my study-dugout watching the transfigured flecks of cloud and an aeroplane, wondering if it was all a bad dream in so much loveliness.

And thank you so much about Evans; but by now perhaps you will have had his gratitude. He's got stuff, don't you think?

That review of yours is indeed a lovely bait for the unwary; I hope the poor flies will be attracted. Mr Dunhill's is very good also.[2]

O S and J! How strange, even in this world of coincidences, it is, that Harvey's book also were 'lost in the post'. Please convey my sympathies on this double loss. Sidgwick and Jackson are an honest firm about sales, I believe. The Times and other places are refusing to restock, that must be it.

I hope all your invalids are well, or at least better now. There is bad news from me also. My father has had an operation suddenly, and is in hospital.

Tomorrow I expect leave to see him. My Goodness, if anything happens there ...![3]

The *Georgian Book* has interested me tremendously, but only Hodgson is the equal of Edward Thomas, who is omitted. Turner's 'Caves of Auvergne', Squire's 'House' and 'Lily of Malud', Sassoon's 'To Victory' and 'In the Pink', Freeman's 'Stone Trees' and one or two things of Drinkwater's, I like best perhaps. They are very stimulating (O yes, of course! Graves' 'In the Wilderness'.) and very interesting people, these young men. They have talent, but Yeats, Hodgson and Thomas have genius.

> 'As the stars glowing
> That left unlit
> The land and water.
> Rise up and scatter
> The dew that covers
> The print of last night's lovers.
> Scatter it, scatter it![4]

I do hope you are not discouraged or in the least affected in any way by my non-committal attitude as to your future work. It is that I do not feel myself competent to judge. If you cannot make up your own mind, Time and the drift of circumstances may decide for you, Dear Friend.

While I am at Gloucester I shall try to write one or perhaps more new songs – for there is no time here. I hate all the details of signalling, though for B.E.F. work I shall be quite suited, and I have to swot up, especially as our time has been unexpectedly cut shorter, and I may fail, and don't want to.

Bother everything.

Thank you very much for the *Times Supplements*, that are not wasted.

Well, well, Sir C.V.S. will now receive his promised copy, although he has not acknowledged my photograph. When I see him though, I think a long acquaintance with Sergeant majors and other lovable but eccentric people will have given me ability to wangle through his disfavour, if there be any.

I hope to write from Gloucester next.

Will there be any flowers, I wonder – yet?

Best wishes of all sorts from your sincere friend

Ivor Gurney

---

[1] A reference to a comment in Marion Scott's review in the *R.C.M.Magazine* vol 14, No 1 [January 1918].

[2] In the *Musical Record*.

[3] David Gurney died of cancer, after several operations, on 10 May 1919.

[4] From 'The Trumpet' by Edward Thomas.

18 February 1918 (P)

My Dear Friend

Behold me once more at Seaton Delaval, having travelled up to York with H.N.H., who saw the Cathedral there with me and the Tank 'Nelson'; he thought he saw me drop something before the train moved off, and he was right – it was a 10/- note. I hope somebody who needs it finds it.

My father is getting stronger and more cheerful. Must still further improve before another operation heaves in sight, poor old Chap! But, after just escaping Death and having a lot of pain, he is much better. I hope Mr Scott is getting better too, and your other invalids. I suppose he has worked himself stiff, and that this is a reaction. Well, it is better to wear out, than rust out – a poor but real consolation. How are you yourself? And how much work do you manage to squeeze out of yourself now?

I have forgotten whether I have thanked you about Evans; but have no doubt that his pleasure gave you pleasure. What luck for him Howells and Benjamin came!

As for your review I have thanked you for that most excellent piece of advertisment. Thank you for the Magazine with my portrait in, too.

But O, what is all this to my memory of Gloucestershire. There was a morning I went unexpectedly out with Haines to Newnham-on-Severn. The sun was struggling to get out, and did at last for a short space. All day the colours were beautiful; and we found celandines and cuckoo flowers.

Another day I did 17 miles on a pint of beer and bottle of ginger beer, because I felt seedy.

I think that gas has left effects on me and am going to Newcastle to be examined this week. Nothing much, but it may mean time off for light Duty.

So glad you like my new songs. O Gloucestershire, how did you set me longing!

How much, much longer will it all last?

I liked Howells better than ever, and what a lovely phrase that is which ends the Slow Movement of Lady Audrey's Suite!

And this from a crock, that can't work, walk or sleep properly!

O the magnificence of tiny unconquerable Man!

When you have done with Edward Thomas, please send him back, will you? Haines showed me the first draft of the last poem in that book about Words. Almost without alterations in a beautiful neat hand.

He must have been lovable.

I had 3 whole days at home, and touched Maisemore, Hartpury, Ashleworth, Hasfield, Longford, Twigworth, Hucclecote, Cooper's Hill, Highnam, Minsterworth, Newnham-on Severn. Which wasn't bad.

There were snowdrops, crocuses, violets, primroses, celandines, daisies, cuckoo flowers.

A view from Bredon Hill to the hills above Bath. To Malverns,

Herefordshire, Bristol Channel, May Hill.

Three days, but what a time!

Ach Gott! Beauty is not dead, though all the world grow blind and furious, or sick and careless.

The earth of Glostershire sorrows for its dead, and February flowers come of its great pity. Colonel Repington is brought up. Lloydd George totters. Robertson resigns, and on a wayside bank – red earth covered with fresh grass – Haines and I discover two cuckoo flowers, and saw the beauty of the whole dreaming world leap to life as the Sun broke through the limiting clouds of the South West, by right of youth and glory. Best wishes to all you sick people. Spring's near, tell them.

With all good wishes from

Your sincere friend
Ivor

314 *To Marion Scott*   G.41.165

25 February 1918 (P)   Pte G:IB 241281 Glosters,
A17 No 1 General Hospital, Newcastle

My Dear Friend

My inside having been a little extra troublesome lately, I went sick and now am here! So long as the gas has no influence on my tummy after the War I don't mind. Well, I am trying to write, but my mind is appallingly rusty as you may well believe. By sheer will power (no musical impulse aiding) I turned out a song today. But alas! I have only two books with me, *The Shropshire Lad* and your gift of *Friends*. So if you have done with E.T. please return him, will you.

I am sorry Mr Scott is so ill, and do hope Time will bring rapid and permanent improval. It is overwork I suppose has done it – another War result. And Audrey – Lady Audrey – may she soon be rosy and jolly. May you all be, as you deserve, poor things.

Thank you so much for all your presents. The *Poetry Review* has not much in it, do you think? It is too elementary; but some of the children's stuff is interesting and 'Ambition' (in vers-libre) is fine, it seems to me.[1] One is ashamed of it – but Mrs Meynell is altogether too annoyingly 'chaste' to live in this world. An enormous amount of good must be done by this Review however; and more still will be done when the young men return, if there are any.

(Monday Morning) Let us be tactful and not refer to the news.

My Father is surprisingly stronger, they tell me. Still, it needs another operation to make things shipshape; after which one may be allowed to talk of getting well. I think you would like my Father very much; he looked very fine and serene in bed, and himself was serene and fine – both.

You don't seem to mind Air Raids, Miss Marion! It is a great compliment to tell me that you were absorbed in reading my songs while aeroplanes and bombs and shrapnel were in the air. Thank you very much for that, and for having the *Englishwoman's Review* copied.

Yes, I had read (and copied) Hodgson's 'Time', but not at all closely, I think. It was certainly not a steal. Where I found it was in *Poems of Today* which I had not seen for a long time. Walter de la Mare's original I do not know.

There is nobody I can think of who would like to hear the 'Elizas', save Evans, and the Taylors.

Now will you please send me some M.S. paper when you next write? The reason is, of course, that we get no money in Hospital. It will be my complete endeavour to return the sheet covered with master-work, but I doubt it. When you get 'To G' from Herbert, I believe you will like that better than some of my things.

I feel an awful washout you know, but there is a certain pride in me when I think that some of my best things have been written in the Army. Have the others written at all? Save Benjamin?

I am so glad you are having success as an Author. Judging from the review of my Book, you are adapted to that sort of work as well as anybody. *And it is important that these articles should be done well.* One ought to be interested in such things as you have written of.

Did you do well at the Photographers? Were the day and the hour and the facial control and the necessary brazen impudence and devil-may-careness all right? I wish it were Pitcher you had for photographer. He is now engaged on a perfect lovely study of Gloucestershire, which he means to be his chief work, I believe; it looks something like an East painting, judging from my casual memory.

Don't things look luverly in the East? Well, it removes all doubt. We have to fight until Germany will behave well on this front at least. On the other, nothing save an over-powering defeat can make any difference – and that is hardly likely, is it? Our hope lies in the fact, that German soldiers, though they may be willing to go on to the end, know perfectly well that the cost has been too great, and that the working classes can not allow themselves so to be cheated, bullied, misused, ever again.

I am out of it for a while, and hoped to be able to write and forget everything; but my brain is too rusty, and all stimulation is absent. One must be fired before emotion is released.

This dumbness would not matter, only that it makes distrust in oneself.

The day I came into Newcastle, not expecting any more than a report, there were two books only in my pocket; but having heard the verdict desperation took me out 10 minutes walk or more into the town where I bought *Boswell Vol 1* – lucky for me. But somehow in my mind there is a great desire to read the lives of great workers, Bach, Carlyle, Beethoven, Goethe, Michel Angelo, Da Vinci; and yet, what could all that do in Wartime?

Vain dreams, though not discreditable, and having hope for the future. It is unfortunate that there is no one in the Ward to whom I can talk – not unexpected, however.

With best wishes to you and the Invalids for all good luck

Your sincere friend
Ivor Gurney

Will you *please* forward this to Evans? For I have neither envelope, stamp, nor address!

---

[1] *Poetry Review* Vol IX, No1, January/February 1918 contained 'Ambition' by Olaf Baker, a selection of schoolgirls' work, and an essay on 'Thought and Mrs.Meynell' by James A. Mackereth.

---

315 To Herbert Howells   G.3.11

25 February 1918 (P)

My Dear Howells

How are you, old chap? Has Yorkshire done you good? Can you sleep? Are you stronger for walking? Can you write?

It was nice to come up with you, and talk about the things I shall always love to talk about, though now – through the lethargy of circumstance and disuse – my brain is unfit for such things.

But you can't guess where I am! It is in Ward A17 No 1 General Hospital Newcastle; through stomach trouble caused by gas, though I needed a rest as well; and so lie on my back reading Boswell's account of the mighty Johnson and wondering when O when I can be working towards my goal, where A.N.D. lives.

I am horribly fed up, just as the Doctor himself was, when not really using his mind, but I won't trouble you with that, since you are so brave in far worse circumstances, bless you!

You know you thought something dropped from my pocket book in York Station? Well, something did. It was – O my grief! – a 10/- note; nearly all my worldly wealth, that was to take me to Edinburgh. So not being able to go to E: I came here to save money! Don't laugh, they might hear you!

I wonder if you could lend me your 'Lady Audrey Suite'? No, don't send it! For my tenure here is absolutely uncertain, and it might get lost following me. But I *would* like something hard to chew!

I shall buy M.S. paper and try to write, although my last attempt was disastrous. Who can write in the Army with a sick stomach? Not I, at any rate; still, the attempt shall be made.

What is the place you are staying at?[1] Is it pleasant? Are your housecompanions nice? How nice it would be to see you, and talk, and wander as much as pleased us and you could stand!

Well, if Howells is impossible, I must content myself with Boswell, trying to drown the voice of my conscience ..... Are you easier in your mind now that the exemption has come to you, permanent and final? O that is good news, boy, and rejoiced me, for selfish and self-absorbed Moi is glad at your good-fortune, which is that of British Music. So much was clear with the Concerto, and it has become clearer still since, so they say.

Goodbye, old chap, and wish me well too. But I do wish that sense of guilt was lesser than it is. Mere weakness, I know!

May you find some Beauty to inspire you wherever you be, and your courage get its right reward.

Yours ever
I.B.G.

¹ The address is c/o Mrs Sandham, The Grammar School, Easingwold, Yorks.

316 To Marion Scott   G.70.17

3 March 1918 (P)

My Dear Friend

Thank you so much for your letter, music paper, E.T.'s poems, and the *T.L.S.* to say nothing of the College Programme. For my personal interests in the last two,¹ I am not so blind as not to be able to see that it is your hand has done both for me. You are a jolly good friend, there is no doubt of it, and I can only hope you will get something on the M.S. which will please you – but doubt it; for one loses the sense of wonder in the Army; which can be remade or aroused by Music, Quiet and Natural Beauty, of which things Tyneside is almost destitute.

Yes, certainly I will write to those people who played and sang, and in grateful terms, if possible.

It is nice to hear that Evans was there, for he longed for that sort of thing, and needed it to remind him his dreams were not all foolish. And I am glad that he has heard some songs of mine.

Last night I had the good fortune to find a friendly soul that cared for Beethoven and such, and so went on playing till excited out of myself! Could this be really the same person? I.B.G. at 6 p.m. and I.B.G. at 8? At most times the act (if passivity be an act) of living bores me to tears on nearly all Army conditions, but here I knew again, as on my 10 days leave, that this state is not natural to me, and how easy it will be to think in music someday – as now it is impossible.

The War looks good for another two years yet!

O Rip Van Winkle what a wisdom was thine!

You don't seem to take much notice of raids yourself, say little about them and read my songs for musical obligato (can't spell it). But they must be most trying, and cannot help you to health – what with wakefulness and noise. Are your rations better or worse now? Everything is short on Tyneside save bread; even in Hospital, where in 1916 men from Somme wrote home the most ravishing accounts.

The only thing that makes me want to stop in England (since I cannot write here) is the thought of the names I should call myself if I got into trenches one hour before it need be.

Next time I write, you shall have resurrected scraps from my note book – if my conscience will let me – for verse has indeed been scarce lately; yet it is far better for me to attempt verse than music, since the conditions for verse are almost always present in leisure, whereas in Music one wants familiarity and the special atmosphere of continual playing or hearing music. Is not that so?

Best wishes to you and all the invalids, and many thanks

Your sincere friend
Ivor Gurney

[1] The review in the *T.L.S.* of 28 February 1918 of *Severn and Somme* and the R.C.M. College Concert of the same date, where K.Vivian Worth sung his 'Elizas'.

---

12 March 1918 (P)   Gallery Ward, Brancepeth Castle, Co Durham

My Dear Howells

I am happy today with a letter from A.N.D. soon after another both charming, so shake hands; and her presence is strong on me as I write. O Erbertowls when will it come right? This morning I feel certain-sure for both of us, my jolly Genius, but hope that the meanwhile is not too dreary for you, Poor old Chap!

Can you sleep well, Ducky? Do you feel pretty well, can you write? Say 'yes' and gladden the heart of a Dyspeptic Wangler.

There will probably be 5 songs or so out of this easy but dull time; one a love-song especially for Annie,[1] whose eyes and lips are so bright in me this dull grey typically-Northern imitation of a morning. How are Dorothy's with you? She has been whispering most comforting things these last few days, and I have walked in my loveliest most beloved paths with her, drawing free glad breath from that sweet South Western Air.

I am so glad you like the place and people, and got on well with Bairstow. Perhaps it is because not all geniuses are ratty and porcupine-skinned that H.N.H. gets on so well. I wish him all good luck, but O that I and he were just going north to Edinburgh! And then we'd All come South to see

Dorothy. Wow, wow! I feel skittish!!
    Best wishes.

Yours ever
Ivor Beegy

[1] Perhaps 'Thou didst delight my eyes'.

---

12 March 1918 (P)   Gallery Ward, Brancepeth Castle, Co Durham

My Dear Friend

You have left me very little excuse for not writing! Thank you so much for all, not least for the loan of *The Muse in Arms*,[1] most for your long and delightful letter.

Songs you shall have, but the verses are rotten as a general thing. When I get out again there will probably be a flood of it. Brancepeth Castle is a fine place, but the weather is gray, and there are reasons to keep us in besides – waiting for inspections and so forth, which spoil a morning. How are you all? Homekeepers and exiled invalids? I do hope Mr Scott is better, for I have a genuine admiration for the firmness and clearness of him (because I lack those, probably.) and it would please me to know he is doing well. Were you touched by the Air Raid? Whether these frighten you or not makes no difference to the fact that they cannot help a delicate lady, whatever pluck she may have.

Myself? O there's very little wrong really, except the old nervous trouble. I never feel well, never am ill. Toujours, toujours. It's the Army does it, and only happiness will put me right, and hard work in security and with a Straight Course!

There are 4 songs waiting for final polish and perhaps the best is 'Thou didst delight my eyes'.[2] One I shall probably not send at all – or if it is sent, you shall have the first copy, untidy and difficult to read, for there is not much in it, I believe.

My Father is most awfully pleased with the letter and programme and review. Any kindness done to him gets its full reward of gratitude. He is getting gradually stronger, but slowly, so that the Doctors daren't fix a date for a second operation. I can't believe he will be himself for a very long time if ever; for if it were to be a quick recovery, if that were possible, his serenity would have brought better results than have come as yet. I have written to persuade him to leave our present house as soon as possible, and trust to luck for what comes. O bless you! they know about my being here, and why I am in hospital. This is a real old castle – with a picture gallery and armour and bloodthirsty inquisitive looking weapons on the walls. I should hate to live in such a place of barns, but there must be worse Convalescent places. The poor old piano sounds like a boiler factory in full swing because of the stone walls.

You write awfully interesting letters you know, and I could wish these were better, of mine. Out at the Front they were simply God-sends, with their cheeriness and talk of music, scraps of verse and so on. They were a real link not only with the past, but with a hoped-for Future and all the things I longed for.

Here are two scraps of verse. (Yes 'innocency' again!)

At Reserve Depot

When Spring comes here with early innocency
Of pale high blue, they'll put Revally back.
The carelessly amused passers by will see
Breakfastless boys killing the patient sack.

And there will be manoeuvres where the violet grows
Hiding its dark fervour, guarding its flame,
When I shall lie and stare while the mystery grows
Huge and more huge, till the Sergeant calls my name.

February   Seaton   Delaval[3]

Above Ashleworth

O does some blind fool now stand on my hill
To see how Ashleworth nestles by the river?
Where eyes and heart and soul may drink their fill.

The Cotswolds stand out Eastward as if never
A curve of them the hand of Time might change,
Beauty sleeps most confidently for ever.

The blind fool stands, his dull eyes free to range
Endlessly almost, and finds no word to say;
Not that the sense of wonder is to[o] strange

Too great for speech. Naught touches him; the day
Blows its glad trumpets, breathes rich-odoured breath;
Glory after glory passes away.

(And I'm in France!) He looks, and sees beneath
The clouds in steady Severn silver and grey.
But dead he is, and comfortable in Death.

Seaton Delaval   February[4]

411

I hope you will like them, poor things. What is happening is that my real groove lay in Nature and Music, whereas Pain and Protest forced the other book into being. If I go – (when I go, rather; there seems to be little enough doubt surely!) out again there will probably be any amount written, influenced by E.T. chiefly, perhaps by Robert Graves – a true poet.

Thank you so much for the *Muse in Arms*. Next time I will write more about it. Willoughby Weaving has poetry, as I knew from R.B.'s *Spirit of Man*,[5] and from a review in the *Times* a little while back. Did you happen to notice a review on a 'Diarmuid and Grainnhe' poem by a man named Clarke about two months ago?[6] O that was good stuff! Someday I must read it.

I hope the Air Raiders were not very near to you lately. But it is getting pretty serious there, I suppose, and one must feel anxious, for what is a barrage to anyone who has been out to France and knows how the airmen sail about there in defiance of all the muck that may be chucked at them. Best wishes and thanks and fair hopes for Mr Scott.

Your sincere friend
Ivor Gurney

[1] *The Muse in Arms* (1917), edited with an Introduction by E.B.Osborn.
[2] A setting of Robert Bridges' poem, published in the third volume of Gurney's songs in 1952.
[3] Published in *War's Embers*.
[4] Omitted from *War's Embers* at Sidgwick's suggestion but published in *Collected Poems*, p.53. Gurney has had problems with the last stanza, deleting 'His eyes turned down to' and then deleting '(And I'm in France!) His eyes look down [deletion] beneath/ On nothing that ['can stir ' deleted] may move that spirit so grey'; there is a further deletion of an attempted penultimate line but it is illegible.
[5] Number 271 in that anthology is by Weaving. Weaving's *The Bubble, and other Poems* was reviewed in the *T.L.S.* for 13 December 1917, p.612.
[6] A review of *The Vengeance of Fionn* by Austin Clarke in the *T.L.S.* of 13 December 1917.

---

319 To Marion Scott   G.41.167

12 March 1918 (P)
[*Postcard*]

The best of *A Muse in Arms* are I VIII IX XI XII XIV XV XIX XXI XXII XXIII XXIV XXVI XLVII LII LV LVI LIX LXI LXII LXV LXVI LXXVI XCI XCVII C CIX CXII CXIX CXXI CXIII CXXX[1] Best and most interesting. Some people ought to be cut out. All the sea people. Aeroplane people. Coulson, etc. Where is Harvey's 'Gonnehem'? More Sassoon, perhaps, Graves also Brookes. Harvey.

I.B.G.

[1] Gurney's is an interesting selection: I Rupert Brooke 'If I should Die'; VIII Julian

Grenfell 'Into Battle'; IX W.N.Hodgson 'Before Action'; XI Robert Graves 'Big Words'; XII Robert Nichols 'The Approach'; XIV Sassoon 'Absolution'; XV Richard Molesworth Dennys 'Better Far to Pass Away; XIX Hodgson 'Release'; XXI Gordon Alchin 'The Road'; XXII Willoughby Weaving 'Between the Trenches'; XXIII Nichols 'Comrades'; XXIV Patrick MacGill 'The Star-Shell'; XXVI Nichols 'The Assault'; XLVII Nichols 'The Last Salute'; LII Graves 'Goliath and David'; LV C.A.A. 'To Charles Lister'; LVI Brooke 'Gifts of the Dead'; LIX Weaving 'The Dead, 1915'; LXI Charles Hamilton Sorley 'To Germany'; LXII F.W.Harvey 'If We Return'; LXV Max Plowman 'When It's Over'; LXVI A.V.Ratcliffe 'Optimism'; LXXVI Sorley 'A Letter from the Trenches'; XCI Sorley 'The Army of Death'; XCVII Harvey 'The Soldier Speaks'; C Harvey 'In Flanders'; CIX Harvey 'To his Maid'; CXII Nichols 'Fulfilment'; CXIX Weaving 'The Warrior Month'; CXXI Weaving 'Progress'; CXIII A.L.Jenkins 'The Spirit of Womanhoood'; CXXX Graves 'Escape'. Since all the others are in numerical order, I suspect that the penultimate one is meant to be CXXIII Edward Shanks 'On Account of Ill Health'.

320 To J.W.Haines

G.83.5.1-2

16 March 1918 (P)   Pte Gurney I.B. Gloucesters, Gallery Ward,
                                     Brancepeth Castle, Co Durham

My Dear Haines

I hope you are all well. Father, Mother, and Baby, (that'll make Robin angry!) and that the weather's less cold with you than with us, for it's bitter here.

This is a Convalescent Depot, where Ivor Gurney is trying to right a digestion injured by gas (hitherto perfect!) and there is a *bare chance* of a category, I think, but don't expect too much.

Once again let me thank you for Edward Thomas – who is an exquisite Dear.

I heard from F.W.H. a little while back; a postcard about *Severn and Somme* mostly. He likes 'To the Poet Before Battle' and 'Homesickness' best. Bless his heart, won't it be nice to have him back again!

What chances do you think there are of Peace? Surely our side is trying to bring about something? Surely we shall make no offensive this year?

I wish this Saturday afternoon were to be spent with you in Gloucestershire, talking books and people and finding flowers; but that must wait, like so much more.

There was a very interesting account of Ledwidge in last month's *English Review* by Katharine Tynan. He wrote delightful letters besides verse. 'How should he die

        'When cruel old campaigners win safe through?'

I envy you your visits to Newnham, but 3 days ago I saw Durham Cathedral under perfect conditions. To gaze on that magnificent group of buildings from across the river on the first day of Spring! O but it was a revelation, a vision beyond price!

I am trying not to waste time in spite of cold and noise. Have written 4 songs, am writing a fifth, and there are sketches for a sixth. Not bad, when there is a rackety piano going all day in these echoing chambers, and I am too cold to do much else than shiver.

O curse all grumblings! Am I not very lucky to be in England so long?

By the way, how full of poetry the *Maid's Tragedy*[1] is! Those old boys could write, bless them.

Howells is improving in the Yorkshire air, but is still very crocky – writes still, and holds his frame together by a great Will. He has any amount of pluck; ought to win through.

Now dinner is up. Will you please send this on to W.W.G.? No, his letter made no reference to my book. It was an answer to one I wrote him when in trenches, and he in America.

With best wishes to all

Yours very sincerely
Ivor Gurney

[1] By Beaumont and Fletcher (pub. 1619).

321 *To Marion Scott* G.70.7

22 March 1918 (P)

My Dear Friend

Thank you very much for both your letters, and for the kind things in them. And especially for the concern you feel about my Father, who is weak, very weak but making satisfactory progress, so they say. It is an awfully good thing the Spring's coming on, instead of a cold Winter to recover in. Where he will go I cannot say, but perhaps Framilode since he knows the people there; but perhaps the air is not bracing enough.

I hope Mr Scott will manage to get strength little by little in spite of overwork and the worry of raids and so on. It is possible the raiding will cease now we are in a position to hit back effectually.

Yes, Spring has come, and today is lovely, even in County Durham. (Perhaps even at Seaton Delaval) And I have had a tooth out and feel much better able to enjoy things than yesterday, with that brute throbbing and making violent attacks on my peace.

How am I? O pretty well, thank you. Rather dyspeptic and gloomy but otherwise well. All that's been the matter is nerves I think – for Depot was a strain on me, and the gas has left some effect I believe.

(Again to march through your first letter.)

Thank you so much about the *Westminster*, and O may there be a fee![1] Yes, you did right to correct the proofs, and thank you also for your attempt with *Blackwood*.

Second Letter
(I am glad the songs have turned up)
'The carelessly amused passers by will see' doesn't annoy me. Would
'The amused careless passers by will see' suit better?[2]

Verse 2

where the violet grows or shows
mystery shows or grows.

(You pays yer money etc)

Above Ashleworth
The Cotswold's range out Eastward

The blind fool stands, his dull eyes free to range
semi-colon after 'change'. Punctuation correct.

So Sidney is at Rouen! What luck! and I am delighted he is pleased with the
book. I do hope he is better and stronger – able to take Life easier than
heretofore. He has had a rough time of it. Life is brutal today, but it teaches.

It passes my imagination how you get so much work done! And yet can
write such cheery friendly long valuable letters. Here of course are not ideal
working conditions, and not much is accomplished, but my sense of shame, of
reproach was considerably lessened by finding in a bookshop at Durham this
sentence of Romain Rolland[3] 'Mozart could not compose save in the presence
of the one he loved' and later that he could not play either. It is so with me. I
take no delight in playing, walking, reading, existing by myself; and how
many years is it I have been lonely now? My work is chiefly a Stunt at present,
and done to preserve self-respect chiefly.

I do hope it will preserve some reason for that in your eyes – my songs I
mean. 'Even Such is Time' must be considerably altered.[4] There is another (of
Gibson) 'Red Roses', and an attempt at the 'Fiddler of Dooney' is slowly
struggling toward completion.[5]

And so the German offensive has begun at last![6] With what success we do
not yet know; but men returned lately say there have been miles and miles of
barb wire erected. O isn't it all beastly! And to me it is not credible we can
break their line this year, nor next, and the year after, when the Americans
might be so strong, will see such perfection of defence as never was known. I
admit to complete disbelief in our ability to hurt Germany very much in this
form of Warfare if we were to go on to the last man. My hope lies in a change
of German mind brought about chiefly by contact with the Russian and Polish
subjects it will be brought in contact with. No soldier believes in any military
victory – none that I have met for a year. It has pleased me to see what a hash
of things the Government has made of the Shipping Problem. Lloydd George
may not feel quite so sure he is a better Head than Asquith now – it is not easy
to see why he should.

I hope this offensive will fail and that moderate Germans will be strong enough to bring about a moderate peace in the Autumn. What more have we to look for?

O the noise the rackety piano kicks up in the Gallery Ward! The row is worthy of a young barrage.

There is another poem or two. You shall have them soon. But I must go walking now – cannot keep fit without. Shall I.B.G. always be defective nerves and nothing else? Yes, in these conditions, I fear. But a walk to Durham and back may alter things a little in my outlook.

Best wishes and thanks

from your sincere friend
Ivor Gurney

[1] 'The Immortal Hour' was published in the *Westminster* in June 1918; Gurney received 16 shillings. Marion Scott wrote wishing that it had been more (see G.70.38.1).

[2] The line finally read: 'The passers-by carelessly amused will see'.

[3] Romain Rolland (1866-1944), prolific French author, and Nobel prizewinner in 1915.

[4] A setting of Raleigh's poem, published in the fourth volume of Gurney's songs in 1957.

[5] 'Red Roses' remains unpublished, but 'The Fiddler of Dooney' was published in the fourth volume of Gurney's songs in 1957.

[6] The Somme offensive, begun by the Germans on 21 March 1918, was meant to be a 'Peace Offensive' to end the war.

322 To Marion Scott   G.41.166

26 March 1918 (S)[1]

My Dear Friend

Here's some news for you.

You know how a neurasthenic has to drive himself, though he feels nervy and his heart bumps in a disturbing but purely nervous fashion? Well, Ivor Gurney determined to drive himself. His heart certainly did not feel right, but that was imagination and he must go on – through Salisbury Plain, Laventie, Somme, Caulaincourt, Vermand, St Julien. He was tested once or twice, but doctors said nothing. They marked him A3 at Depot when he got there. It is true he never felt well, and had continual digestive and general nervous trouble, but that was presumably to be driven out. Which lands him at Depot getting weaker and fuzzier in the head without knowing why. On Friday he went to Durham 9 miles there and back, after which his pulse was waltzing irregularly like this as it is now

 That's my heart.

Surely a prostitute's job is cleanly compared to doctors who allow this and mark 'Debility' on a case sheet so that a man shall not know? Shall leave the hospital a little recovered and go on till he drops again? That's what they have done for me. By God, I'll do nothing more strenuous than clerical work for months, whatever they try to do with me, and *never* march again.

Meanwhile the crisis of the Tragedy has been reached in France, and (whatever else may be) the British Soldier feels a glory in killing before he dies – such a contrast to last year! Our men will stick it however hard the task, but – they tell me Amiens has been fortified with barbwire and trenches.

Good old 51st! They are a glorious lot of men – Seaforths, Gordons, Black Watch, Argyll and Sutherlands. And how many left of you, poor boys? Yes, but this is so much better than Paschaendael! Now I'll walk a little, two miles an hour and tired at that.

Supposing after a month here, they gave me a Board and then a chance of discharge. What then? What will the College do? I would like to know that. It may be useful. However I am too tired to think of Composition with any pleasure.

With best wishes for yourself and Mr Scott

Your sincere friend
Ivor Gurney

[1] Marion Scott has written 'Received March 26th 1918' on the letter.

---

323 To Marion Scott   G.70.6

28 March 1918 (G)

My Dear Friend   March 28 Brancepeth

You may have fears, but I knowing my friends have none. The fighting last year sickened all the B.E.F. Everyone was fed up, and said the rudest things about the King, Lloyd George, our War aims and Capitalism, bitter things about the hopelessness of trying to move Fritz, the bullying out of the line, etc etc.

But now all this is changed. They'll fight like heroes. I tell you this because you know I would not deceive you. Did you see the 61st was 'mentioned'? How I chortled! No, the British Army was unwilling after August 1917 until this attack began (that seems to have failed.) but now, with the good chances going of killing before you are killed, and seeing Fritz at last – well it's a man's war again. At a guess I should say that we hoped to check their second push where they are now, at the beginning of the second. So we have partly failed – so have they, but if our flanks at Arras and Noyon hold, they stand a chance of a thundering good hiding if they waste reserves. This is *War* not a contest of engines so much as before. The B.E.F. will never give in. The 2/5th won't – in these conditions.

It was unfortunate for me my grumble came at this time, but I was furiously angry at being treated as I have by people who never will run any chance of danger. And as they marked me 'Debility' I had forced myself – to cure it, and was pretty exhausted. Since then Rest has certainly done me good, but my heart, nerves, digestion, brains are all wrong and tired. Still I am far happier, for I know now what it is has made it so difficult to work with my mind – the worst pain it was to feel impotence there for I lost confidence and hated writing.

My dear Father is much better and they have strong hopes for him. There came a letter in firm handwriting and most serene in tone. There was no need my Friend. For quite suddenly there came to me the ability to talk to him – from here. Compree?

And yesterday I felt and talked to (I am serious) the spirit of Beethoven.

No, there is no exclamation mark behind that, because such a statement is past ordinary ways of expressing surprise. But you know how sceptical I was of any such thing before.

It means I have reached higher than ever before – in spite of the dirt and coarseness and selfishness of so much of me. Something happened the day before which considerably lessened this and lightened my gloom. What it was I shall not tell you, but it was the strangest and most terrible spiritual adventure. The next day while playing the slow movement of the D major

 etc

I felt the presence of a wise friendly spirit; it was Old Ludwig van all right. When I had finished he said 'Yes, but there's a better thing than that and turned me to the 1st movement of the latest A^b Sonata – a beauty (I did not know it before). There was a lot more; Bach was there but does not care for me. Schumann also, but my love for him is not so great. Beethoven said among other things he was fond of me, and that in nature I was like himself as a young man. That I should probably not write anything really big and good; for I had started late and had much to do with myself spiritually, with much to learn. Still he said that he himself was not much more developed at my age (spiritually) and at the end – when I had shown my willingness to be resigned to God's will and to try first of all to do my best, he allowed me (somehow) to hope more, much more. It depends on the degree of spiritual height I can attain – so I was somehow let to gather. There! What would the doctors say to *that*? A Ticket certainly, for insanity. No, it is the begining of a new life, a new vision.

(By the way I also had a premonition this afternoon; no, not premonition; by making my mind able to accept anything the idea arrived that June 1920 would bring complete victory for the Allies! Mein Gott, what a length of time! But that looking forward is far less trustworthy.)

What *will* you think of all this? I don't much care; did I mind a lot you

418

would not have heard of it at all. But could you see me, you'd know that I am as sane as ever – only, different. It is the beginning of a new life, wherein the price is surrender, and the reward Peace and a clear Joy – a hard life for the selfish, but a fine one. Don't think I am cracked. No you won't. I am a pretty level creature on the whole. My heart's bumping like anything. There's some indigestion – nothing else.

I could not get much about Howells off L van B; (the memory is faint;) he was reluctant to speak; whether Howells is to die or not to develop I could not gather.

I did not mean to tell you about this – but the mention of my Father started me off.

How I would like to see your face!

No, you'll take it seriously, and decide I am not unbalanced or overstrung. This letter is quite sane, n'est ce pas?

Chance of a category[1] – I don't know, but as I shall probably not wangle – that is, shall show my comparative willingness to try again, it isn't very great. At present I am *not* fit.

I am glad Mr Scott is better, very glad, and hope he will take to eating again. Our boys will *not* be beaten! For this is defending Britain, not extending the Empire – for who cares tuppence about that? Compared to Britain and all she stands for. They will hold, though Hell gape for them; though Amiens be shattered before their eyes, that see the German that would conquer, not Fritz the badgered and driven, like ourselves, the man in the hole suffering over there as we here.

Golly, I'd *love* to see your face! BUT DON'T TELL *ANYBODY*.

With best wishes to you and Mr Scott

Your sincere friend
Ivor Gurney

P.T.O.

This was not all Beethoven told me, but the rest doesn't concern anybody else.

I am attempting a Violin Sonata.

I had never heard it or attempted it before.

What a letter! I can't help laughing.

What a letter to deliver through the Post.

[1] Identification as falling within a category not eligible for active service.

419

5 April 1918 (G)   Bulmer Ward, Brancepeth Castle, Co Durham

My Dear and True Friend   Friday April 5th
  Your letter gave me great pleasure, and thank you very much for it. Let me
thank you for it, and for quoting those noble lines of Sir Hubert – who, it is
permitted to say, is linked with Beethoven in my new life. But Sir Hubert can
hardly become a better friend to me than you have been, whatever happens –
since your influence has done so much on me (I wish it had been stronger, but
that might not be) After all a creature that lacks happiness and has grown used
to doing without; that has sunk into a groove of darkness – is hard to stir.
  My Father is doing extraordinarily well, and the doctors are patting
themselves on the back about him. Perhaps before the War very few would
have dared the operation.
  I have just left the rewriting of 'By a Bierside' (more than half done) which
will come to you soon. This will probably be finished this morning, and may
be sent off too. There are many little alterations.
  There are also some verses; but as you know my style is changing. I am very
dissatisfied with what I do, and anyway music is my real path.
  Lately the Born Genius has been coddling himself and persuading himself he
is too much of an invalid to write, which is not true; although it is true he has
no spontaneous musical impulses.
  I hope you are getting out on sunshiny mornings and enjoying yourself
under that jolly round faced bringer of benificence, and smiling at his little
children the flowers. And Mr Scott; is he improving still, or does overwork
affect him still, as it must? Well Ivor Gurney has known what it was to drive
his body, but he is making a number of interesting but humiliating discoveries
about his own cowardice.[1] But this letter as usual has already too much about
myself.
  Are you still at articles for budding youth and maidenhood? (It sounds like
socks or something for delicate chests.) I am certain you will do them well,
and such things are not easy to do well, since one has to look at music from a
mechanical point of view, or at least a view devoid of all passion for Beauty,
which cannot be easy for you.
  Have you heard of Howells lately? Sidney Shimmin sent me a p.c. (official)
yesterday to say he was well; which is good news. It is probable though that
he has a lot of work to do, which must try a weak person's strength.
  W.W.Gibson's letter from Sydenham came to me yesterday – with a strong
hint that 'G' and himself would very much like to hear my settings of his
words. As this is impossible, perhaps the politest thing to do is to send him a
copy of 'To G' and 'Red Roses' (which you have not had, though the first
copy is finished.)
  Alas for the joyless fragment of a Violin Sonata! That annoys me to look at,
merely.
  The news is more cheery than it was; but the poor boys are having a hard

time of it. Rain may be a good thing for Europe, but the boys that have to shiver all night through may have their own ideas on the question.

How is Sir Hubert? He sent a very nice letter in reply to my 'birthday letter', which did not read like a 70th anniversary. And Sir Charles, how is he? Do you know anything about Elgar now? There are two songs in 'Sea Pictures' I like very much – the first, and 'Where Corals lie' – that I did not know before. There is a real beauty in the first. Surely he had great possibilities in those days. O how am I? It is rather difficult to say. Far better at any rate, but feeble and with an irregular appetite and so forth. Yesterday my head was awfully thick, so that I despaired perhaps of writing ever the things I wish to write. But that is better now, and the coward is not so afraid of life once more.

How is Audrey? Something should surely come of that girl. These last days have been lazy days, I am ashamed to say, but this copy of 'By a Bierside' is a new beginning of work, and is a thing that should have come to you long enough ago. There is 'Red Roses' 'Time' (to be rewritten) and perhaps the 'Fiddler of Dooney', before they chuck me out.

Goodbye, with best wishes and thanks.

Your sincere Friend
Ivor Gurney

[1] He has deleted after this the words 'Strange what pluck s'.

---

325 *To Sydney Shimmin*   G.76.9

April 1918 (KT)   19 Barton Street, Gloucester

My Dear Shimmin

That Field Postcard has stirred me up to write at last, lazy and forgetful as I am. How are you, old chap: of course you would stick it, but I do hope you are not finding this too hard. What are you doing exactly? Miss Scott says you have just read my book, and on one of the 'spots': which is lucky for you for that is a lovely one. The sight of that great cliff is not easily forgotten, even by one in an easy delightful Convalescent home, one that has not grace enough even to be glad for his mercies. I am here because my heart had been strained so long it brought other things down with a run, and I was rather a wreck when I came here; am far better now, and likely to be chucked out again soon. It is over 6 weeks since I left Depot. O the poor boys that are struggling in shell holes and so forth east of you! They are having a bad time of it, but at least their duty is clearer now (it seems to me) now that Germany has made this huge assault on Europe. I suppose you get little or none of music now, poor chap. For though Rouen sometimes gets concerts, you can have little time for such, especially now. Do you get the chance to play at all? If you are at all like me, you neither enjoy touching it nor leaving it alone: for on the one

421

hand it is so difficult to work oneself into the mood: on the other, it is too beautiful a thing to leave alone. Howells was ordered to Yorkshire 6 weeks (or 7 rather) ago; for a month. His heart is very crocky, and everybody is rather anxious about him. Thank Goodness he is out of this little scrap in France, at any rate.

Benjamin was flying somewhere near Cirencester (E.Gloster) but has in all probability been moved now.

I have managed to squeeze some songs out of myself since being in Hospital – nothing very much. More for occupation's sake than any other reason. You are probably too tired to do more than gasp at the the wonder of anybody writing now, but your turn will come, old chap —- but not yet.

Miss Margaret Hunt is in a very bad state I think, poor thing. What will happen to Emmie Hunt if she dies, I do not know. Miss Scott is a kind and writes as nice letters as ever.

What did you think of the Seine as you came up it? Wasn't it magnificent? That is, if you had such a wonderful day to see it on as we had in September.

What do you think of Dr Allen's getting up at the College meeting and proposing to find possible successors for C H H P, C V S and Parratt? That took pluck! His first meeting too.

But it wouldn't surprise me to know that C H H P is behind it all. (Others think so too) So long as a certain other person is not left behind to run things, it doesn't much matter. Well, well, good luck old chap and as many sights of the town as possible.

Yours
I.B.G.

326 *To Marion Scott*   G.70.19

16 April 1918 (P)

My Dear Friend

I regret to say that the truth is that there is no permission at all. I don't think he would mind but cannot say more.[1]

His address I believe (but cannot find it now) is

> Pte Gibson W
> MT ASC Depot
> Sydenham

More than that I can't remember.

They are marking me out today. I know no more than you do what will happen next.

Thank you for all the trouble you have taken about my things. I hope these will meet with your approval, to pay you in some way for the trouble.

That's all I can say – save to hope that you are well, and Mr Scott

considerably better at any rate.
Goodbye

Your sincere Friend
Ivor Gurney

[1] Marion Scott was trying to get permission for the performance of Gurney's settings of W.W.Gibson's poems.

---

327 To Herbert Howells   G.3.1

22 April 1918 (P)   Ward A18 No1 General Hospital, Newcastle

My Dear Erbert

I do hope everything is going well with you, and that you are far better now after that stay in Yorkshire. What with pudding and so forth you ought to be a little bit fatter at any rate. Can you write any better now, and what is it? And O, and O, if it is Gloucestershire what is Gloucestershire like now, so near Mayday? O Framilode, O Newnham, be glad to see little Erbert and smile at him to make him well. Please Goodness that all that lovely land may come before my eyes again soon. Ah if only the past were to do again with new eyes!

It is over two months since I have been at Depot, but one gets very tired of Hospital, and very much more complacent to infantry ways.

How often do you manage to get to London now, and how much does it try you? (Please excuse this 'notepaper'.) It is Sunday and all the shops are shut, which does not brighten canny Newcassel, where people have very kind hearts and very rough manners often. Very hospitable in a fashion almost unknown in the South where they are poorer.

How's Benjee getting on? Those days are old now. They seem very far off to us two now, I suppose, but are not yet forgotten nor will be just yet. What's coming to everybody we know? Joy I hope, full flooded joy on which you may arrive to begin a new age of music in England. How Sir Willy McCormack now? Dear chap, let's have a line to say you are all right, please, sometime and early; for it gives me great satisfaction to know that H.N.H. is going strong. How is Dorothy Dawe keeping? A.N.D. is flourishing still in the North Countree.

Ah, would it were all over Erb and we foregathered once again in the old College tea-room. When it's all over Erb; when it's all over.

Write a tiny line, wot?

Yours ever
I.B.G.

7 May 1918 (P) Pte Gurney C Coy 4th Reserve Batt:,
Gloucester Regt, Seaton Delaval

My Dear Howells

Your very jolly letter cheered me up no end; and the news that you had so good a time at Easingwold was the very best of news. Glad I am to hear there is music on the stocks, in preparation for great doings in the future, for there will be great musical doings surely once this war is over and we can settle down to ordinary life again.

But that is looking forward; meanwhile I am very glad to hear you are not yet dried up.

I am glad to say that the weather for two days has been beautiful indeed, and Tyne Side has looked quite like South Country. The sea in Whitley Bay was quite wonderful, and would have given you leaping thoughts and rythms[1] for something very great of the future. Let's have some Sea Music out of you someday old chap, will you?

Or what of the Forest of Dean Symphony? What of the opening pages of the sight from Newnham-on-Severn looking across the valley to the hills. An A major beginning surely –

What have they done to Chepstow river? Is it still beautiful as a whole, or is it spoiled for ever? What are your further plans, what have you settled to do with yourself? Dear old Howler, be glad they have not called you up as they have called so many, and let off steam in a Symphony, but not yet, for your health will not permit.

Do the Elizabethan Manuscripts still go strong, or are you putting them aside for the time, and waiting till the power of driving yourself all day has returned? Poor chap, you must find it very hard work all this continual waiting. But how well you have stuck it! I wish I could stick it half as well as you, for I am still crocky from my heart and a nervous breakdown from working too much at Brancepeth Castle.

Try and see as much of our County as may be while the splendour of Spring lasts, which will be longer down there than up here. May you soak in something into your Music, old chap, and give a delighted world your view of Gloucestershire as May clothes it in Beauty. O to see May Hill rising above the plain again, and to look at its glorious purple against the Sunset skies; to drink in the hush of still evenings and feel that God is very present and is intensely alive in every [thing] that moves or stays silent.

Well, well, you know all this, old chap; and much more I do not write, for it is probable you see far more than I ever did. Why, to think of the C minor Concerto makes me tremble; it is so much above me in everything save (I believe) pure beauty. There is a sun tonight, but we have seen better suns walking Kensington High St together old boy, or in Glostershire together. Bless you my child, and be as happy as circumstances will let you be, for they are not too kind and it is a strain on your pluck, which will not fail

nevertheless.
    Best wishes

                                        from yours ever
                                            I.B.G.

[1] This mis-spelling follows a deletion of another, equally inaccurate, attempt.

13 May 1918 (P)

My Dear Friend

I am very sorry to hear you have been ill with gastritis, just as you were getting back your strength again.[1] Do please be careful and not overwork yourself on my behalf, because the songs simply aren't worth overworking for. You are always kind, and always have been; and this latest kindness about the songs is not the least. Thank you so much, so much. Perhaps someday there may be a fresh set for you, but not yet, for there is no music in my head; nothing to build on. Perhaps when I am back at the Front something new may come to me, and something quite different. But that is looking forward.

There is very little to tell you. I am not very strong, but am pretty well; and would very much like to be playing you music again, but my unsettled state of mind wants music to read from and new music. Probably I shall be out and in the old life again soon, and a jolly good thing too. Hospital life is dry rot.

Your praise of my songs is like rain on the hot face. Thank you so much – for the praise and for sending the songs to Gervase Elwes; that I should have copied myself; not you.

It is good news to hear that Mr Scott has been made Senior Warden; though of course the true meaning of this is quite unknown to me;[2] please give my congratulations and say I hope he will enjoy his duties, whatever they are.

I am very sorry that your life-long friend has died, and hope that you will find consolation. She was very gracious to me, I remember – through you, again. Denis Browne is mentioned in *Friends*, do you remember? In that Poem about the Ring?[3] O that is a sweet book, and I am truly glad it was myself introduced you to that.

Have you ever read John Buchan's *Thirty-Nine Steps*? That is a good shocker; and awfully well written. Just the thing for your sister to read in Somersetshire. I do hope that she and Audrey will have a good time there. It is Bridgwater again, where they have gone, most likely; and everybody says that is a fine part of the West Country. Cannot you take a holiday after all the work you have been doing? And go stay in the green fields this May-time for a while; though Kensington Gardens must be very pleasant, and I envy you the chance of walking through them now. Thank you so much for writing.

With best wishes to you all

Ivor Gurney

[1] This letter comments on information received in Marion Scott's letter dated 9 May 1918, of which drafts are in the Gurney Archive (G.70.64) complete with news of gastritis, praise of Gurney's songs, of sending songs to Gervase Elwes, of Mr Scott's appointment as Senior Warden and so on.

[2] Marion Scott's draft says 'my Father has been made Senior Warden of the City of London Solicitors Company – one of the highest honours for a London solicitor'.

[3] 'William Denis Browne', the second poem in *Friends* talks of listening to the Ring. Browne (1889-1915) was an organ scholar of Clare College, Cambridge and was beginning to compose songs.

---

330 To Herbert Howells   G.3.9

20 May 1918 (P)   No 2 Up West, Lord Derby's War Hospital,
                                                          Warrington, Lancs

Dear Howells

Thank you so much for your trouble about my songs. Here is a robustious ending, though commonplace; and personally I should prefer the other.[1]

It is hard lines indeed you should have neuralgia, and that it should be so bad as to stop music – especially your music. Miss Scott's news about Dr Hull's[2] wishing to study that gave me great pleasure. I hope he will appreciate it, and give you a good leg up, and hope also that the neuralgia won't last long, and that you will manage to squeeze something out of yourself, Herbert Norman – for you are a son of Gloucestershire, and the county deserves worthy celebration. No, I am not quite as my wish could have me, but far better, thank you.

It was jolly to get your letter, and to hear that actually in Brewer's drawing room – that sacred spot – you rehearsed our songs! Strange happenings after 1904-1912![3] Do you remember one day when I rode over to Lydney, and was simply astounded by the quantity of work you did? That was in 1912, I think.

A long time ago, and you have advanced since then by leaps and bounds indeed. You are sick now, but Thank Goodness in a lovely part of the world where you can soak in Beauty, and feel music grow in you when your body is not too sick. What a pluck you have, Herbert Norman! and how you have stuck to it in spite of all difficulties!

Is your brother well whom I met with you at Queen's Hall one time? I hope so, for he was a very decent chap, and ought to do well. Have you heard from Evans at all? I owe him a letter yet, I fear, and must write at once.

Goodbye with best wishes and thanks

I.B.G.

[1] Gurney encloses a sheet of music for the end of his setting of 'Spring' by Thomas Nashe.

[2] Dr Arthur Eaglefield Hull (1876-1928), founder of the British Music Society in 1918 and writer on music.

[3] The period of their close association with Dr Herbert Brewer. A draft of a letter from Marion Scott to Gurney dated 9 May 1918 says: 'Herbert has told you all about Miss Dorothea Webb I expect, and how he played your songs and his to her in Dr Brewer's drawing room. At his request I sent the Elizas, For G, and In Flanders for her to see, and I also sent the 'White Cascade', and Herbert lent her 'Severn Meadows'. I wonder which she will select for the I.B.G. – H.N.H. groups she intends doing: the Recital is on June 26th.' (G.70.64.3).

23 May 1918 (P) No 2 Up West, Lord Derby's War Hospital,
Warrington, Lancs

My Dear Friend

Your kind letter and all its interesting news about people and things gave me great pleasure, chiefly on account of the kindness shining through it. Thank you very much for it, for I believe that is an especial sort of kindness now that you are so busy.

It pleased me to hear about Dr Hull's enquiry about Herbert's music; and do hope that his notice of Herbert's work will make a difference. – and that your account of H.N.H. will produce its full effect. Thank you very much for your offer to send along the typewritten letter, and I should like to realize once more through your mind what his music is.

My Goodness! What an absolutely terrific amount of work you get through in your time; it is astonishing to think how you manage to stand the strain – what with visits to the dentist as a kind of sugar-icing to the whole. Please accept my best wishes as to the result of the hat adventure; it must be a triumph above the ordinary to turn out something of one's own; and an adventure in thrift too; which is not an easy thing to accomplish.

Thank you so much for your trouble about my verses. Perhaps some more may come from me when I am at the Front. Hardly before I think.

Audrey's letter did indeed sound Elizabethan, and 'eskeyped' is very good indeed; someday she ought to do some individual work for she has eyes and forehead enough and character, which under your careful training ought to produce something worth having someday.

I was glad to receive (though surprised at this late hour) the review of *Severn and Somme* – but sorry that the reviewers think Graves cannot write; for he is a poet and I'm not.

Your *Muse in Arms* is in my kit-bag in the stores, and I shall make a real attempt this morning to get the corporal to let me send it off. I am afraid it is mere laziness that has kept it from being returned before.

Willoughby's[1] things are occasionally very striking, don't you think.

Thank you so much for your most kind and interesting letter, and please excuse the dullness and flatness of this scrawl – which is so inferior to your own letter, bright and full of interest.

Yours gratefully with best wishes
Ivor Gurney

[1] i.e. Willoughby Weaving.

10 June 1918 (P)   No 7 West, Lord Derby's War Hospital,
                                                           Warrington, Lancs

My Dear Friend
(Since that is how you start your letter)
There are many things to thank you for, including a most sympathetic and
interesting letter, some *Times L.S.*, a paper with a thing of mine in,[1] and today
some flowers, for all of which thank you very much. It puzzles me why you
are so kind – since your kindness is so little valued; still it is nice to think
oneself remembered kindly – so thank you very much. I sent the poem to Miss
M Hunt. The flowers which were small were given away to different men –
and the tall ones put in a jug since there were no vases to be had in the large
room. but tomorrow I will try to get them placed on our table. Two I wore
myself.

I hope you are feeling stronger and are still able to work for other people, as
you love to do – myself – well you know I was always selfish.

Tonight a letter has come from Evans to say he is well, but very fed-up.
This is not surprising as he has a restless spirit.

This last month or two has been trying enough, but someday I hope to do
better because of them.

More than this you will not hear in this letter. Perhaps next may be better.

My Father is down in Weston, after a week or so at Framilode, from which
place he returned very brown so they say.

Sidney Shimmin has received your type written appreciation of H.N.H.'s
work I hope. It was sent some days ago. If only something of the same kind
could be written of me – now in shame and despair – with so little done, yet
reassured by friendliness from you and others (H.N.H. Sir Hubert and Sidney
Pitcher) sufficiently to write letters.

                                                           Yours
                                                           Ivor Gurney

[1] The *Westminster Gazette*, which published 'The Immortal Hour' in June of this year.

---

333 To J.W.Haines   G.84.7

Received 17 June 1918 (JWH)   7A West, Lord Derby's War Hospital,
                                                           Warrington, Lancs

My Dear Haines
Your letter was a breath of fresh air from Gloucestershire though here there
is the sea air from the Dee, and a fairly well wooded country; it is not
Gloucestershire though, for there is only one big hill in sight in fine weather;
no Crickley, no Cranham. I am glad Herbert Howells came to see you, and

that you lent him books; yes he is a fine chap, and has a fine future.

Lascelles Abercrombie too! You have had celebrities to see you, and it pleases me enormously you took him to see Framilode, which must be one of the darling places of Gloucestershire. Please God they'll never cut down the trees at Priding; it would mean almost ruination to that scene from old Long's place, looking down river.

It is good news that F.W.H. has sent a bagful of MS home, and I'd like to see 'Ducks' very much. Mrs Harvey tells me there is a good chance of his getting to Holland soon, in exchange. If that might be! He has had a rotten time in Germany on the whole, but wrote me the cheeriest of letters about Christmas time. I wish that there was half the courage in me, for it needs pluck to write the happy things he does in captivity.

Abercrombie's plays sound good. Has he written anything since his entry into the munition world? It is not easy to remember Gloucestershire Yokels in an iron foundry.

Is there any chance of your getting a holiday anywhere soon? The Lakes, Chepstow, Devon, or anything tasty like that?

Please write again and tell me something about Robin and Mrs Haines.

Dorothy speaks about you in her letter with great admiration and respect, so don't offend her and lose an admirer, if you care for ladies' admiration.

Well, that's all I can squeeze out and thank you very much for your letter. With best wishes

Yours ever
Ivor Gurney

---

334 *To Marion Scott*   G.41.172

19 June 1918 (P)

My Dear Friend[1]

This is a good-bye letter, and written because I am afraid of slipping down and becoming a mere wreck – and I know you would rather know me dead than mad, and my only regret is that my Father will lose my allotment.

Thank you most gratefully for all your kindness, dear Miss Scott. Your book is in my kit bag which will be sent home, and thank you so much for it – at Brancepeth I read it a lot.

Goodbye with best wishes from one who owes you a lot.

May God reward you and forgive me.

Ivor Gurney

[1] Unlike other letters sent from Scotland or England, this letter has no stamp, but is endorsed by Gurney with the words 'Wounded Soldier's Letter' as he had endorsed his letters from France 'On Active Service' in lieu of a stamp. The Post Office has exacted three halfpence postage. Both envelope and paper are printed with the details of The Soldiers' Home, Bold Street, Warrington.

335 To Marion Scott   G.41.179

20 June 1918 (KT)   6A West Ward, Lord Derby's War Hospital,
                                                                                Warrington, Lancs

Dear Miss Scott
    Please forgive my letter of yesterday. I meant to do that I spoke of, but lost
courage. Will you please let Sir Hubert know?
                                                                                I.B.Gurney

336 To Marion Scott   G.41.181

late June 1918 (KT)   No 5 D W

My Dear Friend
    The flowers you brought are still on the mantelpiece and blooming
beautifully still – and none of them stolen though much admired by
everybody.
    Thank you for your letter too, as cheery as your presence, which is always
an inspiration to others. The *Music Student* came, and the *Poetry Review* (which
I have not yet read.) Your article on Women Instrumentalists[1] is a wonderful
example of how to distribute praise without repeating the same phrase at all.
This must require a very long practice. The *Poetry Review* looks very
interesting, and the glances I have taken at it have stirred me up. A soldier's
'Marching Song' especially seemed to me to be good.[2]
    Such kindness as yours came very sweetly after ordinary hospital relations
(though these have been very good) and through you the matron came down
to see me two days ago, with many ribbons on her breast, and a very pleasant
smile and manner.
    Please take the copy of the Song as being the final piano and voice sketch for
the orchestra version which must come later. Did I ever send you a copy
before? That which I did at Brancepeth was not quite full, if my memory is
correct; but do as you please about accepting either of the two versions.
    The doctor gives me some hope of being transferred to Cardiff, and there
perhaps I may soon go.
    With best wishes and thanks
                                                            from your sincere friend
                                                                            Ivor Gurney

[1] In the *Music Student*.
[2] The nearest to this description is 'Beginnings', one of four poems headed 'From a
Soldier's Note-Book', by John E.Stewart, *Poetry Review*, May/June 1918, Vol IX No3
p.171.

late June 1918 (KT)   No 5 D West, Lord Derbys War Hospital,
                                                                    Warrington

My Dear Friend

Thank you for the letter and programme[1] – both most interesting to me.

I had not heard that H.N.H. had set 'I saw three pigs'.[2] He would do it very well. Thank you so so much for the attempts to get my songs taken up by Gervase Elwes; He would sing them as well as anybody in England. The whole scheme of the programme you have sent me is just what it should be for scope; and Miss Webb must be something above the average to risk such a programme.

I hope you are enjoying this fine weather and have good health because of it and all that sunshine means. But the dentist! I do hope that your experiences there are over and that you have been properly rigged out now with what you require. There's nothing much worse than the grinding of a tooth in imagination or apprehension.

What you will think of the enclosed song I cannot say. It is extremely ragged in places but will come off fairly successfully – I believe.

Lascelles Abercrombie visited Mr Haines the other day and read him a couple of unfinished Gloucestershire plays 'with gorgeous yokels' so Haines says; but that's all I know of him at present; save that he is munitionising somewhere quite near here.

How is Mrs Scott now? Did she take any ill-effects from her journey? The Sergeant apologised profusely next day when the Matron came in and (presumably) mentioned your name; but this makes no difference to the draughtiness of the corridor. The flowers have finally disappeared today, having stood on the mantelpiece since you left – the carnations stayed fresh till the last, the two that were not stolen. It is a gorgeous flower, the carnation; and as royal as any.

I am glad to be able to tell you there is a chance of a transfer to another hospital nearer home; and to tell you that Father is far better (after two little holidays at Framilode and Weston) and is now at work; though of course not a full day's work. They say he walks well and eats well, and is very brown; so there are hopes of a complete recovery. With thanks and best wishes

from your sincere friend
Ivor Gurney

P.S. Please excuse envelope.

[1] The recital of I.B.G. and H.N.H. songs on the 26th June by Miss Dorothea Webb.
[2] Gibson' s poem. See next letter.

11 July 1918 (P)   No 2 D West, Lord Derbys War Hospital,
                                                                    Warrington

My Dear H.N.H.

I hope the utter laziness as a cure is succeeding – you have at least chosen a
good spot to recuperate in, and that's something. Miss Webb's Concert was a
bit of a heartener anyway for both of us; it would interest me very much to
hear the setting of Wilfred Gibson's Words – 'I saw three pigs a riding'.

How is the neuralgia, old man? That's a shocking drawback to
composition, but since the dentist has had a 'stunt' now, you may be able to
do more.

The Carnegie Quartett – Ah, when shall I hear that? Or See Chosen again?
Though I feel heaps better, (and have even set a poem of Edward Thomas[1])
there is not much chance of my being out yet to talk with all the good folk
who were part of my County and life.

Isn't Pitcher a genius? Those three photographs are simply wonderful; but
has he shown you one taken from above Ashleworth?

J.W.Haines wrote me a very jolly letter with a description of a visit from
you in it, that made me envy both of you – walking about down there and
discussing books, books, books.

What do you think of the following little screed of verse? Entitled
The Fisherman of Newnham

> When I was a boy at Newnham
> For every tide that ran
> Swift on its way to Bollo
> I wished I were a man –
> To sail out and discover
> Where such a flood began.
>
>
> But when my strength came on me,
> 'Tis I must earn my bread –
> My father sent me fishing
> By Frampton Hock, instead
> Of wandering to the Ocean;
> Wherever Severn led.
>
>
> And now I've come to manhood
> Too many cares have I
> To think of gallivanting
> (A wife and child forbye)
> So I must wander ever
> Until time comes to die.

Then Peter, he will tell me
Upon the heavenly floor,
What makes the tides in rivers,
How comes the Severn bore.
And he will show me all things
I never knew before.

Now my Father wants money. Is it the best way to send this to Chappell set
– or send it as it is? I might have a go at it myself – but feel too lazy. Please
advise me as to the best way of getting most money. Should I get double pay if
they accepted a setting from me? Would you care to have a try if they chuck
mine out? It seems to me the sort of thing they like for pot-boilers. Is it?

Write soon and tell me about more Gloucestershire delights, and what the
world says about the Chosen Quartett. Are they celebrating the occasion by a
performance anywhere? Surely Rowland's band might be hired for the
occasion, with a little wangling, and shoved through in some style. I'll have a
go at that 'Fisherman' thing and set it for a violin harp and cornet
arrangement and dare Strauss to do his worst. Then Severn shall know she has
two people at least who can surprise her into fury. Tell me something about
the authors Haines lent you. And of which you are most enamoured.

Mrs Taylor may be coming here soon; but please don't worry about not
being here yourself. It would be hardly worth your while yet – Wait till I have
got out and seen the world a little, and heard a little music.

Goodbye t'ye friend with best wishes

Yours ever
I.B.G.

[1] 'The Penny Whistle'.

339 To Marion Scott   G.41.173

22 July 1918 (P)   No 5 D West, Lord Derbys War Hospital,
Warrington

My Dear Friend

It delights me that you have at last come to the West Country and seen
what Howells and Harvey and myself have seen – Malverns across the plain
against Sunset. Today your p.c. arrived, for which and for your jolly letter
many thanks.

A letter from M.H. tells me you took the 'Penny Whistle'[1] down with you. Thank you so much for all you say about it – the suggested alteration does not seem to me to be very necessary; but revision was always difficult, and light may come later.

I am sorry you are returning so soon to London; for Malverns must surely suit you well enough; still I suppose it may be necessary – work must be done Please remember me to Mrs and Mr Scott and say I hope they will be pleased with their West Country visit, and improved in health; and also (to put it selfishly) as pleased with Gloucestershire as you yourself are.

The Hunts were delighted with your visit, and say it was like a visitor from another world 'in our quiet backwater', but say you looked rather tired. I hope that you will be like a giant refreshed with the wine of Malvern air. (By the way, Malverns, so I have heard, were the first part of Britain to stick out of the water.) Mr Haines has not written, but I shall expect a letter soon full of book-talk he has had with you, for any contact with a booklover such as you, would necessarily set him going; talking at his top speed doubtless, and as well as usual; for he is a really good talker. Dorothy fell in love with you at first sight, and wrote such a jolly letter about your visit; she *is* a first rate sister, and I am proud of her.

Thank you yet once again for your attempt to wangle a fee out of the Cambridge Press. Such things are of course safely left to you, who manage these things to perfection I have no doubt.

My father is a fine chap, and has always been (I have no doubt) since the early days of scaring birds off the corn; which is his earliest reminiscence. He has a real appreciation of music, and has been more kind than almost any father about all the time I have wasted in the past. May the future be brighter! I feel that only France or the sea will do me much good for a bit; there are no pictures in my mind – so repaying him must wait longer than I had hoped.

It really does please me very much that you got in such an amount of seeing people at Gloucester, and like the Cathedral so much, but wish – O so much – you had seen the country round; Newnham, Stroud, Tewkesbury, and the rest. The West Country is incomparable, though I daresay Devon may be finer as a county than either Gloucester or Worcester, but don't care much – Anywhere between Newnham, Newent, Tewkesbury, Stow on the Wold, Bourton on the Water, Birdlip, Stroud will do for me; and doubtless for you too, poor town-dweller!

There's a lovely evening sky behind me as I finish this letter! I wonder what it looks like at Malvern; and what gorse is like, and whether you have been able to climb up much, and view the seven counties they say are to be seen high on (I think) the Worcestershire Beacon.

A long time it is since Father and my elder sister, my brother and I rode to Malvern and saw all these things – it must be 13 years ago! Fern I remember and Malvern beneath us – Ledbury on Severn, where Tom Jones stayed, and Tewkesbury – but nothing really of Malvern itself. I hope everything will please you there, and that without cracking yourself you have managed to see all you desired, and enjoyed yourself as you deserved. Fresh friends you have made anyhow, not least M.H. and E.H.

    With thanks and best wishes

Your sincere friend

Ivor Gurney

[1] Edward Thomas's poem, whose setting Gurney mentions in the previous letter.

340 To J.W.Haines   G.83.6.1-3

22 July 1918 (P)   No 5 Down West, Lord Derby's War Hospital,
Warrington, Lancs

My Dear Haines

    Thank you for your jolly racy letter, with all its delectable descriptions of Gloucestershire; and parts I do not know at all. Pitcher is taking some awfully good photographs about Newnham and the postcard you sent me is a splendid one also.

    Your verses have a real swing and ought to be set to Music, but may I be blowed if anything occurs to me but Belloc's rollicking tune in the *Four Men*,[1] a book we are both fond of, I believe; and I hope to walk with you on some of the hills you have been describing so well, and sing them with you in my cracked voice. Gloucestershire deserves singing about though in better tones than mine.

    Miss Scott wrote to me a few days ago, and said you had taken her round the Cathedral, and had been to dinner with them – talking books and Bookmen. This was very pleasant to hear, for one always likes one's friends to meet and be friendly. It was an evening I could have wished to be present at and someday or other I hope for a real old mixup, of Miss Scott, Harvey, Howells, the Hunts, Benjamin, and some of your poet-friends – O to play Bach to them! You would revel in Bach, especially the organ works, the '48', the 'Italian Concerto', and above all the Chromatic Fantasia!

    O well, that may come before long, since Jerry has had a smack in the eye, and since the Severn will (I suppose) always have that U you describe so well. That day at Newnham I was fortunate enough to get with you was a very bright spot in Army training, and something to look back on, after months of Seaton Delaval!

    A friend of someone who knows L.Abercrombie called here a few days ago and asked me if I needed anything in the way of books or so forth; an offer which I accepted gladly for the sake of lyrics to set. It was a Canon Somebody of Warrington that made the first offer. Have you heard any more from W.W.Gibson? *Friends* is here with me; the book you introduced to me; and a favourite – though not your copy which went West in France – near Vermand I think.

    Mrs Harvey wrote me a charming letter, with a lyric by F.W.H., which

436

will not be too easy to set, (and is not much good I think.) Have you seen 'The Wife'? It is not of the class of 'In Flanders' or 'Gonnehem', but is not of the worst for all that.

Robecq-Minsterworth[2]

Thick lie in Gloucester orchards now
Apples the Severn wind
With rough play tore from the tossing
Branches, and left behind
Leaves yellowing upon the still
Up-and-down pastures, the little hill.

And I lie leagues on leagues afar
To think how that wind made
Great shoutings in the wide chimneys
A noise of cannonade –
Of how the tall elms by the sign post
The tempest's will obeyed –

Lie thinking how in some German prison
A boy lies with whom
I might have taken Joy full hearted
Hearing the great boom
Of Autumn, watching the fire, talking
Of books in the still room.

O wind of Somme, and Lys, and Severn
Blow there also and tell
Stories of comrades returned, Home keeping,
Music and Autumn-smell –
Blow him comfort, and friendly greeting
Hearten him – wish him well.

Bit of doggerel for you to cut up, Herr Heinz, so go you to work with blue pencil and indicate the more noisome passages in this miniature epic.

I wish this letter had a twentieth as much meat on its bones as yours; but there is little to say, except here's to Gloucester and Gloucestershire men for ever.

Best wishes to Mrs Haines and 5 year old Robin

> Yours ever
> Ivor Gurney.

[1] 1912.
[2] Gurney has crossed out 'Ypres'. The poem was published in *War's Embers* as 'Ypres-Minsterworth' and dedicated to F.W.H.

23 July 1918 No.5 Down West, Lord Derby's War Hospital,
Warrington, Lancs

My Dear Friend

Thank you so much for the postcards and books. The Weyman and
Somerville and Ross are old friends of mine, but the Napoleon book I did not
know at all. Thank you very much indeed for the gift. I hope you are not
feeling tired at all from rushing about to view the wonders of West England;
and have brought back some memories which will haunt you in your
meditative hours. The British Camp I have never seen, but the postcard view
is a famous one and beautiful enough for anything. But the distant view of the
Malverns is a more familiar one with me and the up and down of them from
Maisemore is the thing that made 'In Flanders'. Though I believe Harvey was
more influenced by the further views of Hytham and Minsterworth. London
must seem prosaic enough after all you have seen surely.

You and Margaret Hunt seem to have fallen in love with each other. I don't
wonder much – it's not strange that two such unselfish people should take to
each other. The past months have shown me how little worthy I am of my
friends, but until I am clear, it does not seem possible to do much to show
them this. Still, both you and she have had to pass through great suffering to
be what you are, and this may be better for me in the end – when that comes.
But O to be at the Front, enduring in company with [the] people of the
Gloucesters.

There is one more song of Edward Thomas I have written out – 'Sowing',
and a setting of Tobias Hume's 'Fair would I change that note', which only
needs inking in.

The Maurice Baring Poems[1] I like, but not very much; for there is little but
the common feeling of the Georgians in them, and not much technique. Still it
was jolly to see modern verse on the page, and beautifully printed matter on
white paper!

This is written in bed, where the doctor is to examine me, for tomorrow I
go to St.Albans; which surely will be better than here? For there may be a
Cathedral to look at through the windows. But, please, dear good kind Miss
Scott, don't tire yourself by running up North to see me again; your visit to
this Hospital made me feel very ashamed – especially as you looked so little
fitted for rushing about and there was so little accommodation when you and
Miss Scott arrived.

The Napoleon book surprised me by its revelation of N's kindness to
Gourgaud, in annoying circumstances. He had a lot to put up with from
Lowe, and seems to have behaved as well as one would have expected – better
in fact. The first part was rather heavy and difficult, but the second – the
remarks on the books he liked, the reason for his fall, his opinion of different
nations and so forth interested me very much.

A boy not 10 yards from me is using your *Muse in Arms*, which has at last

438

been unearthed from the store; on drawing kit this morning for tomorrow's journey – you shall have it back quite soon with thanks – but stamps are short at present. I hope to send you two songs with it.

Thank you so much for your present.

This afternoon the Matron called.

And this is finished hurrying South on the train to Knapsbury War Hospital, St.Albans, which your good offices I think has done for me. Perhaps there may be some farm work there or at any rate something more interesting than staying in a ward; though there were multitudes of good men there.

The first poem in Baring's book you know from the *Georgian* book. After that I like 'Pierre', 'Julian Grenfell' and 'Le Prince Errant' best. The 'Beethoven' is not all it might be. The 'Elegy' which begins 'Juliet has lost her little owl' I like also. A re-reading has shown me that it is a better book than at first I had thought it, so you may get a long critique on it yet. There are no lines especially fine, I believe; but the whole book is interesting and sincere. Thank you so much for that and the rapid and Brilliant Weyman book, and the jolly Somerville and Ross.

With best wishes

Your sincere friend
Ivor Gurney

[1] Perhaps *Poems 1914-1917* (1918) by Maurice Baring (1874-1945).

---

342 To Marion Scott G.41.183

Early August 1918 (KT)[1]   No 8 Ward, Napsbury War Hospital, Middlesex

My Dear Friend

Thank you so much for the Exercise book, pocket-book and postcards – letter too, but I am reading the letter; raw material for this hurried scrap – you letters are always delightful.

Yes, the Edward Thomas (dear thing!) was left behind on the seat; with which book I ran after you but just missed getting you at the door.

Knole Castle does look a fine old place to be sure, and I would like to have a look at it myself.

Well, here is the precious exercise book, with its contents of 'Fairy Gold', two songs also – tiny things, but 'O Happy Wind' I believe to be one of my best.[2] As I look out the window I can see trees, poplar, plane and elm over which any wind might like to wander, from Sevenoaks way perhaps.

I hope you'll report on these verses as favourably as M.H. who likes them all except (doubtfully) 'Crickley', which may need polishing in a month or so's time. But her appreciation in general is very warm – the author might blush indeed at such praises.

You shall have a better letter than this later on, as you surely deserve for your sweetness in coming up here – I, who only am able to trouble about myself, am simply amazed at the energy with which you do things for other people. But perhaps you have grown up like it; unless hard constant practice has made you able to take such interest in unselfish actions. Anyway the pocket book shall come out with me, and if I can get a lyric out of me, you shall have it soon. With best wishes for happy times in the garden

Your sincere friend
Ivor Gurney

[1] Marion Scott's postcard of 8 August 1918, printed in *Stars* p.97, is a response to this letter and enclosures.
[2] Setting of a poem by W.H.Davies; see G.30.2.1,4 and 5.

---

343 *To Winifred Chapman* G.45750

August 1918 (KT)　　　　　　　No 8 Ward, Middlesex War Hospital, Napsbury

My Dear Winnie

There's 10 minutes or so to spare before breakfast, and you shall have the benefit thereof. The Most Gracious Comtesse has received a letter from me lately I believe (My head's like a colander, and cannot hold much) but if this is not so she shall receive fullest consideration on notification of the same.

I wonder whether you are more stately than once you were, and what new accomplishments have come to you in the past year – whether you can make Simnel Cakes or burnish halberds or starch ruffs; or pickle peppercorns or any of a hundred things useful to be known by the young of that species, woman. My certes there's a whole world of accomplishments that has come to me here. Polishing floors, rubbing brasses, washing pots, pans, kettles, floors; hoeing mangels and turmuts! ('Give I the turmut hoeing'). You see this is a new list – in which piano playing does not appear – for though the spirit is willing, the flesh is weak enough to quail before the looks of some folk here when they look up from cards or snoozing with a look either of amazed contempt or bitter anger! Well, well, there is always something to put up with in this crocky old world of tears. But of tears I hope there is no trace at Perran. Don't get 'flu' or any other silly old disease. What do you do with your time – is it cricket, sand castle or mud-pies? Would that this poor mortal were with you dashing about, and finding out the colour of sea water from the depth of a yard.

Comme ca, m'selle! Observe the dash from a height – the slow float and the gradual return!! A masterpiece, without doubt. I hope soon to be in a position

to do such mad delightful things, and then great works without number (Symphony No 8 dedicated to Winifred Chapman) will simply leak from my pen. Arthur shall have a special portrait in music, of his making a century at full speed with beaucoup boundaries. Until then, ma chere mamselle I suscribe [*sic*] myself, with love

Yours affectionately
Ivor

received 20 August 1918 (JWH)   No 8 Ward, Middlesex War Hospital,
Napsbury, St Albans

My Dear Haines

Your jolly letter full of place names of Somerset and walking in free air was a tonic to one more or less confined to a Ward, and the more I shall be able to get, the more pleasure to me. Miss Scott was here a couple of days ago or so and told me about her Gloucestershire visit and her talk with you, about books and similar delectable things. She mentioned your book and said it would probably not be long before S and Js had it in their hands. Good luck go with you in your 'artistic aspirations', as a man told me yesterday.

'Paradise' I remembered (though not completely) from your reading thereof, and it seems to me to be a sound and brilliant essay. Page 4 especially appeals to me. Belloc of course has influenced it, but what of that? It is jolly good Belloc at any rate, and none but a fool will grumble about such a Mentor. Miss Scott will see it sooner or later I hope? For it is just what she would enjoy. Edward Thomas' *Poems* – which you gave me – went away with her, for a rereading which she will enjoy as much as any the most worshipping of us E.T. enthusiasts. 'Lob' I had started learning by heart. What a beginning!

> 'At hawthorn-time in Wiltshire travelling,
> In search of something chance would never bring,
> An old man's face by life and weather cut
> And coloured; rough, brown, sweet as any nut –
> A land-face, sea blue eyed, hung in my mind,
> When I had left him many a mile behind.'

There's colour and 'cutness' about that! I wish that he had written piles of stuff more; all of it should I wade through – and some day the prose works will (I hope) delight me likewise. Praise God for Poetry – it is a good thing and fills up spaces in landscape and life with human interest and memory. Dear things like 'The Trumpet' and 'Choose me your English words' hang long in the mind. A debt of gratitude I owe you for the introduction.

There is an exercise book full of stuff I want you to see; the Misses Hunt have it, and I will ask whether it can be sent to you for cutting up and necessary condemnations. Don't be afraid to say what you wish about the things; for music is my real game and the most supercilious or the most contemptuous snorts won't move me much – yet I should like to hear you praise them.

How is Robin getting on? Has he come forth with any more criticism lately? Walter De La Mare's *Peacock Pie* I had a squint at in a Durham shop, and it seemed to be an enchanting thing for children of all ages. Robin ought to be compelled to swallow salts or take De La Mare every morning – if he were mine own it should be an ordinance, fixed and unalterable.

There are men of Plymouth and Zummerzet here, but mostly of dingy London; men without much colour in their minds. But one man (now living in Buckinghamshire) has roughed it in a hundred ways in this island and abroad, and has tramped 50 miles without bread – to Oxford for a job. Knows Cotswold well and the villages thereof, and takes life with a serenity that I wish my doleful temperament could equal.

Best wishes and thanks for letter and wind-and-flying-cloud essay.

Yours ever
I.B.Gurney

Best wishes to Mrs Haines and Robin.

345 To Marion Scott   G.70.41b

24 August 1918 (P)

[*Picture postcard of St.Albans Abbey*]

Thanks so much for your delightful letter, which shall receive a reply soon. I have been hammering at a V & P scherzo sitting in front of this. Mr Dunhill has sent some songs. Thanks to you.

I.B.G.

346 To Marion Scott   G.41.175

27 August 1918 (P)

My Dear Friend

I am sitting up in bed, after an afternoon at St Albans where I lay on the grass outside the Abbey and made various shots at a Scherzo, sent you a postcard, bought some tobacco, and did other various useful things; and now here's a perfectly delightful letter to begin to answer; full of appreciation and kindness which is most encouraging.

I am glad the verses delight you so – there are more to come. 'Crickley Hill'
I will see to when revision starts. The irregular rhyme was a mistake. 'You'
and 'dew' are not perfect rhymes, but will pass without any notice among
critics. There are some more to come later. It is good of you to say such pretty
things, but I am no Edward Thomas. All I want is – guerre fini, soldat fini;
and to go home without burden of any thought save music, and hard swot for
a time.

Migrants

No colour yet appears
Of trees still summer fine
The hill has brown sheaves yet,
Bare earth is hard and set;
But Autumn sends a sign
In this as in other years.

For birds that flew alone
And scattered sought their food
Gather in whirring bands; –
Starlings, about the lands
Spring cherished, Summer made good
Dark bird-clouds soon to be gone.

But above that windy sound
A deeper note of fear
All daylight without cease
Troubles the country peace;
War birds, high in the air,
Airplanes shadow the ground.

Seawards to Africa
Starlings with joy shall turn;
War birds to skies of strife,
Where Death is ever at Life;
High in mid-air may burn
Great things that trouble day.

Their time is perilous
Governed by Fate obscure,
But when our April comes
About the thatch-eaved homes, –
Cleaving sweet air, the sure
Starlings shall come to us.

443

Which is one of my best things – to the author's mind, at any rate. You shall
have the book that was lent me so long ago – the *Muse in Arms*, that thing full
packed with good stuff, and thanks so much for it.

No, Ma'am, there is no sign as yet that I shall be allowed to use the piano
while the others are out. The doctor did say something about a Church Organ
– which was only a mention, and not very satisfactory at that – but nothing
has moved since you came, and went to your romantic dwelling house among
flowers. It was a kind thought of yours to send flowers to Warrington and
sure it is they will be appreciated by the poor folk tied up there. Some very nice
people were among that motley crowd and several I shall be sorry not to meet
again. There was an old coster (with his 'attempt-mark' still on his neck) a
most sweet and plucky nature; who had continual longing for his folk and
donkey cart. He has full expectation of my joining him in business after the
War – with evenings spent fruitfully at the Picture Palace.

Twigworth Vicarage

Wakened by birds and sun, laughter of the wind,
A man might see all hearts desire by raising
His pillowed, sleepy head (still apt for lazing
And drowsy thought) – but there a green most kind
Waved welcome, and the rifted sky behind
Showed blue, whereon cloud ships full sailed went racing
Man to delight and set his heart on praising
The Maker of all things, bountiful-hearted, kind.

May Hill that half revealed tree clad thing,
Maisemore's delightful ridge, where Severn flowing
Nourished a wealth of lovely wild things blowing
Sweet as the air – Wainlodes and Ashleworth
To northward showed. A land where a great king
Might sit to receive homage from the whole earth.
St Albans
August 1918

Interval

To straight the back, look up, and see the slow
Dispersed cloud-flocks of Heaven wandering blind
Without a shepherd, feel caress the kind
Sweet August air, soft drifting to and fro.
Meadow and arable – Leaning on my hoe,
I searched for any beauty eyes might find.
The tossing wood showed silver in the wind;
Green Hills drowsed wakeful in the golden glow.

444

Yet all the air was loud with mutterings,
Rumours of trouble strange in that rich peace;
Where War's dread birds must practice without cease
All that the stoutest pilot-heart might dare.
Death over dreaming life managed his wings;
Droning dull song in the sun satiate air.

St Albans
August 1918

There is one thing – perhaps two more – but these must wait till afterwards.

Mr Haines wrote me the jolliest of letters lately – Surely he has the real touch of talent of genius? a born letter writer surely?

Mr Pitcher sent me also a view of Gloucester Cathedral seen from the river, with one great cloud hanging over it ('overbowed with benediction' as, I think, Browning has it[1]) and such a cloud came to delight me over St Albans red block of power yesterday. It was quite like old times and Tewkesbury to see that sight again – clouds and tower. God be praised that made Gloucestershire, and put it in the hearts of men to build towers to perpetuate His praise, for what service is there like the making of a great thing in stone?

There's our call for out – and a lovely blowy blue sky to watch, during the intervals of Scherzo-hammering and welding. I *think* it will be a success, though there is too much of the old-fashioned Beethovenish smack about it to please me. But I want hours and hours of hammering anyhow at a piano to tune me up – such as I had at your house in London, how many eternities ago!

What do you think of the news? Peace seems impossible before Autumn 1919 at any rate; but it is best to hope that Fritz will see reason.

An officer-friend turned up here and took me to London where we had a little music and chocolate together and lemonade at St Albans – spirit and matter mixed. But it was delightful to see him; with talk of the old Batt: and the changes in the Staff; gossip of the Front etc. He says his Brigadier has a great admiration for the French Staff, and a contempt for ours – All daily orders are issued from Foch, and he believes that a vast improvement in all ways has come since that General took command. It was good to hear intelligent shop-talk again, and words like Merville, Lestrem etc floating on the air.

Mr Dunhill very kindly sent me his 'Wind Among the Reeds' as a present, and lent 'Wenlock Edge', with some more of Martin Shaw.[2] His own songs are weak, I think; but Vaughan Williams has always strength and colour, though to me the set lacks real musical instinct; to hear they must be very fine. Poor chap, I fancy he takes some time to heat up, and that his character has made him a musician rather than his gift.

Goodbye, and may you be wandering round that garden for some time yet, with books and music to read and not altogether uninteresting articles to

hammer at. Anything I can help you in please send.
    With all best wishes

from your sincere friend
Ivor Gurney

'Epic' is far too stiff for me to tackle I fear. The *Muse in Arms* shall accompany it soon back to you.

[1] 'The Last Ride Together' has a description of 'some western cloud / All billowy-bosomed, over-bowed / By many benedictions'.
[2] Martin Shaw (1875-1958), organist and song-writer.

347 *To Marion Scott*   G.41.174

Early September 1918 (E)   No 8 Ward, Middlesex War Hospital,
                                                    Napsbury, St Albans

My Dear Friend
    I am delighted that you are delighted, and – yes, aeroplanes is yet a stunt in poetry; and a memory of Willoughby Weaving and a sight of starlings in flocks did it. ('Starlings rise in roars, from the misty fields'). How are you getting in this new-September weather. The wind has been jolly lately – & jolly it has been to feel the wind in one's hair. Your garden I daresay has been full of it, and all your flowers tossing their head in joy to feel the rush and thrill of Autumn coming once again – April – May – September – October – these are the four months of life.
    Will you please excuse my having sent a parcel to Mr Dunhill to you, for forwarding? By mistake I destroyed his letter the day before.
    And now for some new verses.

> *Girl's Song*
>
> In curtain of the hazel wood,
> From sunset to the clear-of-star,
> An hour or more I feared, but stood –
> My lover's road was far.
>
> Until within the ferny brake
> Stirred patter-feet and silver talk
> That set all horror wide awake –
> I fear the fairy folk....

446

And whether late he came or soon,
I know not, through a rush of air
Over the white road under the moon
I sped till the square

Of golden lamplit blind came, then
Hand on my heart, I slackened. stood ...
Though Robin be the man of men,
No more I'll tryst that wood.

Solace of Men

Sweet smelling, sweet to handle, fair of hue
Tobacco is. The soldier everywhere
Takes it as friend, its friendliness to share
Whether in fragrant wreaths it mount faint blue
In dug out low, or surreptitiously to
Parapet in rimy night, from hidden lair
Of Sentry; staying hunger, stilling fear –
The old dreams of comfort bringing anew.
For from that incense grows the stuff of dreams
And in those clouds a drowsing man may find
All that was ever sweet to his starved mind,
Heart long bereft – Dear Friends, hills, horses, trees
Slopes of brown ploughland, Sunset's fading gleams,
The bane of care, the spur to memories
(As poppy and mandragora it is?) (which do you prefer?)

To F.W.H.

Ink black and lustreless may hold
A passion full of living fire;
Spring's green the Autumn does enfold –
Things precious hide their bright in the mire.

And a whole county's lovely pride
In one small book I found that made
More real the pictured Severn side
Than crash and shock of cannonade.

447

Beneath, more strong than that dread noise
I heard the talk of trees, and men,
The still low-murmuring Earth-voice ...
God send us dreams of peace again.

Girl's Song

The tossing poplar in the wind
Shows underleaf of silver white,
The roughness of the wind unkind
Torments her out of all delight.
But O that he were here
Whose blows and whose caresses alike were dear!

The great oak to the tearing blast
Stands steady with his great arms wide,
So over him my anger passed,
When his rough usage hurt my pride
But O that once again
I might arouse that passion endure that pain.

September
St Albans

That's all for the present, Mamselle. Herbert has just sent me a packet of two-part songs to imitate – which is a new and interesting side of music to me. It will be good to read them in bed tonight.

There'll be a song in a day or two for you to see – a setting of 'Had I the Heaven's embroidered cloths'[1] which I think you will like; and an old resurrected Brancepeth song – 'The Fiddler of Dooney'.[2]

It's raining horrid outside and the paths are running; so no farm work will there be probably; swot today at Music which one grows to hate – having no piano; but I believe from today the Doctor is to let me have that hour in the evening. Last night he promised that but one cannot tell whether these folk mean what they say.

With best wishes

from your sincere friend
Ivor Gurney

[1] Yeats's poem; Gurney's setting published in Volume 5 of Gurney's songs (1979).
[2] Another Yeats poem; the song published in Volume 4 (1957).

4 September 1918 (JWH) No 8 Ward, Middlesex War Hospital,
Napsbury, St Albans

My Dear Haines

Yes, I like your Foxglove and Hawkweed very much; and perhaps will have
a try at embalming them in sweet sound later – but with a Violin Sonata and
another thing or two on hand, it is not yet possible to squeeze out anything, I
must wait a little, and then perhaps you will be the proud possessor of a baby
MS – value nil.

I say, how you travel, you lucky chap. Somerset, Newnham, Forest of
Dean, Seven Springs, Cotswolds .... Your Somerset talk makes me envious; so
do your letters, which seem to me as racy as they can well be. You have the
real knack of talk on paper, – a rare and (to one's friends) delightful gift.

Gibson's 'Empty Cottage' spoils the memory of the original 'To G', which
is beautiful enough. Really it seems to me to have no merits at all – for
W.W.G. Why did he do it?

I got your letter as you see; the address changed only one ceiling's worth;
and glad I was to get it – chock full of colour and rush all your screeds are; and
had I guessed 'Paradise' was meant for me, by no means would it have been
sent back. It is the best essay on Gloucestershire possible I do verily say – save
only, I could have wished for something more about the people; jolly
farmfolk, quiet herdsmen and the like; girls with thin shy faces at cottage
doors, and so on.

Now what have you to say to my latest bunch of Poesy? Something nice,
but let's have something useful as well; some blame of scansion or repetition,
or so on. There is a little more growing up by degrees that you shall see when
the author has brooded on it a little longer and decided whether commas
should be semi-colons. Still, Music is my real game, and sooner or later I shall
chuck verse altogether.

My goodness, what a hell of Time the War lasts! Toujours, toujours!

This is a short unimportant scrap of nothingness in return for your
interesting and finished works of art, but after all this is Hospital and you have
the free Gloucestershire life to write of.

Where are you this afternoon? Wandering Cotswold is it? I had put in for
St Albans, but some mouldy medico who knows me not has chucked the thing
out. St A: is a pretty little place, with a big market square, and a cathedral
with a fine tower, a fine interior but a wretched looking block of a nave, from
outside.

There's so little to say about the life here. We decouch ourselves at 6.15 or
so; break our fast at 7.45 and get out on farmwork at 8.30 or thereabouts to
hoe the patient mangel or collect the elusive spud; reap dock and thistle; the
general care and management of all farm life weighs lightly however, and we
can see trees and clouds flowers and men as can the rest of outdoor people. A
lucky life compared to Warrington's enclosed existence.

In intervals the Violin Sonata grows gradually to birth, and, for all my struggles without a proper instrument, does not completely disgust me yet.

Herbert Howells has just sent his Quartett along for inspection – a birthday gift of the best; full of clouds and moving airs. It must be a treat to hear; in one place the Malverns stand up distinctly enough – great dreaming masses of blue immortality. No doubt of them at all; one looks up from the page across miles of Severn Country, and says 'I have come home'. And to what a home! Miss Scott is as keen on it as the rest of us, and must return to visit Gloucester and the people whom she met and liked so much. I hope it will not be long before I see it again myself. Dear place, dear people, dear air and skies!

Today is blowing like Autumn and the poplars outside are tossing their arms and heads violently to and fro in the wind.

Here is a new thing called

Migrants

[*Transcription of text, with only minor variants from letter 346*].

I hope you will find something worthy in this – not scorn it utterly, not contemn it quite; the idea of which came to me mangel hoeing; not a romantic sounding occupation, but with decent companions jolly enough. There's more honey from the same hive; to come later.

With best wishes to you and the family

Yours ever

I.B.G.

What is Robin learning now? What is his new fancy in poetry?

349 *To Marion Scott*   G.70.43 and 41.171

7 September 1918 (P)   No 8 Ward, Napsbury War Hospital

My Dear Friend

Thank you so much for the delightful letter of September 2nd.

The visit to London would be unsure always, for it depends on the pass being granted, and only on a Saturday is this possible, and for a couple of hours or so only. I must be back at 6.30 and cannot start till 1 oclock, so there can be little time. Next Saturday would do, but as it is now Thursday, better it is to fix on Saturday week.

Up till now I have only read one movement (the Slow) of Herbert's Quartett, but like it very much – with clouds and the Malverns seen blue and rugged in the distance. Thank God for the Malverns, they set off Gloucestershire well and are good to look at, though my county has no need of them.

'Cleaving sweet air, *the* sure' is the proper line.[1]
autumn-smell should have a small a
'homekeeping' may be left without the dash if you wish.[2]
Now what do you think of this?

Fire in the Dusk

When your white hands have lost their fairy power,
Like dimpled water flash and charm no more,
Quick pride of grace is still, closed your bright eyes –
I still must think, under those Northern skies,
Some influence shall remain of all that sweet;
Some flower of courage braving Easter sleet;
Colour to stir tears in tenderest skies;
Music of light. Your Autumn beeches shall
Set passion blazing in a heart until
Colour you gave be fashioned in formal line
On line; another's beauty prove divine,
And all your wandering grace shall not be lost,
To Earth being too precious, too great of cost –
Last wonder to awake the divine spark,
A lovely presence lighting summers dark;
Though dust you body is, such dust as makes
Blue radiance of March in hidden brakes....
Pass from your body then, be what you will,
Whose light-footed walk outdanced the daffodil,
Since Time can but confirm you and fulfill
That hidden crescent power in you – Old Time,
Spoiler of pride, and towers, and breath, and rhyme,
Yet on the spirit impotent of power and will.

That County

Go up, go up your ways of varying love,
Take each his darling path wherever lie
The central fire of secret memory;
Whether Helvellyn tower the lakes above;
Or black Plinlimmon time and tempest prove;
Or any English heights of bravery.
[Or any English eyries of bravery]
I will go climb my little hills to see
Severn, and Malverns, May Hill's tiny grove.

No Everest is here, no peaks of power
Astonish men. But on the winding ways
White in the frost-time, blinding in full June blaze,
A man may take all quiet heart's delight –
Village and quarry, inns and many a tower
That saw the Armada beacons set alight.

That's all for now. I hope these will please you. Please excuse the envelope's
return. There are none such here.
 With best wishes and thanks
  I remain

your sincere friend
Ivor Gurney

Yes, the Hunts have the Scherzo by now.

[1] From 'Migrants'; see letter 346.
[2] These two alterations are for the poem 'Ypres – Minsterworth', which was published in
War's Embers without them.

350 *To Marion Scott*   G.41.176

10 September 1918 (P)   No 8 Ward, Middlesex War Hospital,
                                                Napsbury, St Albans

My Dear Friend
   Am I to understand from your p.c. that the article was not returned to you?
If so I am afraid that by an unpardonable carelessness it has been destroyed
with the letter that accompanied it. This is a very bad piece of senselessness;
and if it is as I fear, then please let me make up for it in any way I can.
Anything please, regardless of what it may be, but O that it may not be true,
and that the larger envelope I remember sending has the article as part of its
contents.
   There are two new songs to come with this , and I hope you will like them.
The words of one I owe gratefully to you – for they are very fine.
   Next Saturday I cannot manage so well as Friday – on which day all day
passes are sometimes granted. Tomorrow I will ask the doctor and get some
kind of definite understanding as to whether it will be possible to come, then
you shall hear at once.
   Mr Haines has just sent me a long letter of criticism on the famous exercise
book, so you will please return your copy for a few days, and receive it –
probably with a few corrections. He objects to the use of 'fair' in the
'Stonebreaker' as you do. And it is probable I shall try proper revision at

once.[1] Anyway here are one or two more on which I shall be glad of your opinion.

Girl's Song

In curtain of the hazel wood
From Sunset to the clear-of-star
An hour or more I feared, but stood –
My lover's road was far.

Until within the ferny brake
Stirred patter-feet and silver talk
That set all horror wide awake ...
I fear the fairy folk,

That bind with chains and change a maid
From happy smiling to a thing
Better in ground unhallowed laid
Where holy bells not ring.

And whether late he came or soon
I know not, through a rush of air
Along the white road under the moon
I sped, till the golden square

Showed, of the blind lamplighted, then
Hand on heart, I slackened, stood....
Though Robin be the man of men,
No more I'll tryst that wood.

          St Albans
          September

(O, *please* send the lines of 'Fire in the Dusk' from 'Blue radiance of March in hidden brakes').

De Profundis

If only this fear would leave me I could dream of Crickley Hill
And a hundred thousand thoughts of home would visit my heart in sleep;
But here the peace is shattered all day by the devil's will
And the guns bark night-long to spoil the velvet silence deep.

O who could think that once he drank in quiet inns and cool
And saw brown oxen trooping the dry sands to slake
Their thirst at the river flowing, or plunged in a silver pool
To shake the sleepy drowse off before well awake.

We are stale here, we are covered body and soul and mind
With mire of the trenches, close clinging and foul.
We have left our old inheritance, our Paradise behind,
And Clarity is lost to us and cleanness of soul.

O blow here, you dusk airs and breaths of half-light
And comfort despairs of your darlings that long
Night and day for sound of your bells or a sight
Of your tree-bordered lanes, land of blossom and song.

Autumn will be here soon, but the road of coloured leaves
Is not for us, the up and down highway where go
Earth's pilgrims to wonder where Malvern upheaves
That blue-emerald splendour under great clouds of snow.

Someday we'll fill the trenches, level the land and turn
Once more joyful faces to the country where trees
Bear thickly for good drink, where strong sunsets burn
Huge bonfires of glory – O God send us peace!

Hard it is for men of moors or fens to endure
Exile and hardship, or the Northland grey-drear;
But we of the rich plain of sweet air and pure
O Death would take so much from us, how should we not fear?

St Albans
August 1918

  I hope you will like both these things, and I hope – hope that your article is
not lost.
  With best wishes

Your sincere friend
Ivor Gurney

[1] Gurney revised the five stanza version to the seven stanza version which appeared in
War's Embers.

received 11 September 1918 (JWH)   No 8 Ward, Middlesex War Hospital,
                                                         Napsbury, St Albans

My Dear Haines

Thank you so much for your detailed criticism which I will attend to very carefully when Miss Scott sends me her copy back for revision. I believe you are right in many cases. About the 'Stonebreaker', my meaning was that I saw in Flanders a face which gave me just such a feeling of England as the stonebreaker had done, but it may not be made clear enough. Anyway your criticisms I trust as no one else's.

You are right about 'fair' which must come out.[1]

I am glad Howells has come again – with that list which shows what that amazing pen can do. *Peacock Pie*[2] I had a squint at in a Durham shop about February time; and liked it extremely. *Whin*[3] not yet have I seen. But de la Mare is an important man and can do wonders with words, as 'The Listeners' showed. A good talk about books would do me good. Store up anything you find interesting in that retentive mind of yours, and let's have it when these devils let me out. I hope to have a little time walking round Gloucester at a great rate, and getting all stuff of beauty into me in the quickest and best way I can. At present my brain pan's empty – having been so long away from home; which makes a world of difference to me.

There's a glorious great sky outside with blue and white, steelgrey and black vivid upon it, and any amount of green to show it off. It is a pleasant part this and St Albans I like extremely – for its position on a hill and its own clean delightful self. The abbey is fine especially the tower, inside and out – not as good as Tewkesbury, but very good.

At present not much verse is coming from me, as a Violin Sonata wants hammering into shape, and the thing must come somehow, though MS is scarce and time not too plentiful – nor ideas Meinherr, for my head's empty of beauty altogether.

With best thanks for your letter
and best wishes to all of you

                                                         Yours ever
                                                         Ivor Gurney[4]

Hidden Tales

The proud and sturdy horses
Gather their willing forces
Unswerving make their courses

Over the brown
Earth that was mowing meadow
A month agone, where shadow
And light on the tall grasses
Quivered and was gone.

They spoil the nest of plover
And lark, turn up, uncover
The bones of many a lover
Unfamed in tales;
Arrows, old flints of hammers,
The rooks with hungry clamours
Hover around and settle
Seeking full meals.

Who knows what splendid story
Lies here what hidden glory
Of brave defeat or victory
This earth might show.
None cares; the surging horses
Gather untiring forces
The keen-eyed farmer after
Guiding the plough.

August 1918
St Albans

Omens

Black rooks about the trees
Are circling slow
Tall elms that can no ease
Nor comfort know
Since that the Autumn wind
Batters them before, behind
A bitter breeze, unkind.

They call like tongues of dread
Prophesying woe
Rooks on the sunset red
Not heeding how
Their clamouring brings near
To a woman the old fear
For her far soldier dear.

That harsh and idle crying
Of mere annoy
Tells her, how men are dying
And how her boy
May lie, his racked thought turning
To the home fire on the hearth burning;
The last agony be learning.

Mangel-Hoeing

To straight the back, look up, and see the slow
Dispersed cloud flocks of Heaven wandering blind
Without a shepherd; feel caress the kind
Sweet August airs soft-drifting to and fro
Meadow and arable. Leaning on my hoe
I searched for any beauty eyes might find.
The tossing wind showed silver in the wind;
Green hills drowsed wakeful in the golden glow
Yet all the air was loud with mutterings,
Rumours of trouble strange in that rich peace,
Where War's dread birds must practice without cease
All that the stoutest pilot-heart might dare.
Death over dreaming life managed his wings
Droning dull song in the sun-satiate air.

St Albans
August 1918

From the Window

Tall poplars in the sun
Are quivering, and planes,
Forgetting the day gone,
Its cold un-August rains.
But with me still remains
The sight of beaten corn,
Crushed flowers and forlorn
The summer's wasted gains –
Yet pools in secret lanes
Abrim with heavenly blue
Life's wonder mirror anew.
I must forget the pains
Of Yesterday and do
Brave things – Bring loaded wains
The bare brown meadows through.
I must haste, I must out and run,

457

Wonder, till my heart drains
Joy's cup as in high champagnes
Of blue, where great clouds go on
With white sails free from stains
Full-stretched, on fleckless mains –
The captain's joy of some proud galleon.

St Albans
August 1918

[1] This was in the second line of the original first stanza, the whole of which came out. See *SASAWE*.

[2] By Walter de la Mare (1913).

[3] By W.W.Gibson (1918).

[4] Gurney transcribes nine pages of poetry, some of which show only minor variants from other versions in this edition; I have transcribed only those not quoted elsewhere. The poems are:

'Girl's Song' (see previous letter);

'Fire in the Dusk' (see letters 349 and 353) including the line after 'hidden brakes' 'And sets the brown thrush singing as the rapt lark.' He misses off the last line with the comment 'Sorry; I have forgotten the rest and will write to Miss Scott for it and hand it on.'

'Solace of Men' (see letter 347)

'Hidden Tales'

'Omens'

'De Profundis' (see previous letter)

'Mangel-Hoeing'

'From the Window'

'Twigworth Vicarage' (see letter 346).

352 To Marion Scott   G.41.184

11 September 1918 (E)

My Dear Friend

Thank you so much [for] your letter full of kindness and appreciation.

Tomorrow I shall be able to let you know more about the pass business; but if it is Saturday is fixed on, I should arrive at about 2.30 – 3.0 and leave about 5.30 – 5.45. It will be by bus, not by train, and I should come by bus to your house. Better fix on that day; there will be the chance of a later Friday all day perhaps. Yes, perhaps it is best to let things stand as they are; so the M.O. shall not be worried tomorrow.

I am so glad the article has arrived, as from your letter I infer, and glad my suggestions have not annoyed you.

There is very little to tell you about anything at all – there is part of a First Movement but it's hard to make music here. Bits of lyrics are easy, but first movements are no bon.

But anyway, time will come when I shall be able to pull together and swot.
Till then, music will be hard.

Meanwhile – thanks for your correction in 'The Girl's Song'
'The great oak in the tearing blast
Stands steady with strong arms held wide.'

The Poplar

A tall slim poplar
That dances in
A hidden corner
Of the old garden,
What is it in you
Makes communion
With this wind of Autumn,
The clouds, the sun?

You must be lonely
Amidst round trees
With their matron-figures
And stubborn knees,
Casting hard glances
Of keen despite
On the lone girl that dances
Silvery white.

But you are dearer
To sky and earth
Than lime trees plane-trees
Of meaner birth.
Your sweet shy beauty
Dearer to us
Than tree-folk, worthy,
Censorious.

I hope this will please you; to Saturday and a quiet time together! And a
long talk about interesting things. With best wishes

Your sincere friend
Ivor Gurney

I must say I like both these songs, especially the middle part of 'The County
Mayo'.[1]

[1] A setting of a poem by James Stephens, published by Winthrop Rogers in 1921.

11 September 1918 (KT)

My Dear Haines

This is very good of you to send that typed copy and long letters of valuable
criticism, open air, cheeriness and a scent of Severn and Cotswold from every
line exhaling. I am honoured in your praise and Freeman's and Frost, and am
glad you had such a good time at Marlborough. To hear good talkers and in
such a country is a fine thing, – which reminds me that last night I lay in bed
and listened to a little Devon chap (now living in Buckinghamshire) who has
tramped all over England in search of work at divers times; one tramp was
from Gloucester to Oxford without a bite of bread, he being too proud to beg;
and is now living at Chalfont St Peters, Buckinghamshire. He was yarning
away about Bucks when the name of Beaconsfield cropped up, and that moved
me to remark that a writer called Chesterton lived there. He wrinkled his
brows and said 'O yes, I know the chap quite well. Great burly chap. Looks
like a German'. (O G.K.C!) And then came a tale of how he had a long
argument with G.K. on hospitals and infirmaries – on their voluntary support,
which gave Mr Harvey great satisfaction. He likes the 'great chap' very much,
and has met him 10 or 11 times or so. Belloc he has heard on the platform
alone – not the railway platform.

The evening with Freeman and Frost must have been a fine one. To hear
talkers going hard at such a subject as verse is as good as music, (I hope the
clay hadn't upset you too much) and a great deal would I give to have been a
floating disembodied spirit in that company. What was their opinion of E.T.'s
poems? You yourself, enthusiastic as you are cannot be keener than am I. His
mind is as full of beauty as any of the long list of present day poets – and more
English than any if possible.

Your criticisms are often very just – and thanks very much for them
anyway, agreed with or disagreed.

'Migrants' I like myself. 'Summer-fine' doesn't annoy me.[1] In 'Girl's Song'
'Where holy bells not ring' does not either. I am afraid it is all too true that
you cannot 'tryst a wood'. 'No more I'll walk that wood' may do instead.
'Fire in the Dusk' will remain pretty much as it is perhaps. The remaking of
all the unworthy parts would be too long a business. The end of this
masterpiece runs as follows

> 'Though dust your body is, such dust as makes
> Blue radiance of March in hidden brakes,
> Pass from your body then, be what you will
> Whose light-foot walk outdanced the daffodill,
> Since Time can but confirm you and fulfill
> That hidden crescent power in you, old Time
> Spoiler of pride and towers and breath and rhyme,
> Yet on the spirit impotent of power and will'.

That's all can be squeezed out of me, I fear.

'Solace of men'. 'Heart long-bereft' is weak, and must be altered. Will 'Heart long denied' do instead?[2] 'The idle crying of mere annoy' might suggest to a mother her sons dying. The rooks don't mean anything, but make eerie sounds, is my meaning.

'Mangel Hoeing'. 'The tossing *wood* showed silver in the wind'. I am afraid you are right about the Infinitive.

'To straight the back how good! To see the slow' etc.

In 'Twigworth Vicarage' it is 'thing' all right – an inexpressive word, but the only one I can manage.

Toussaints

Like softly clanging cymbals were
Plane trees, poplars Autumn had
Arrayed with gloriously sad
Garments of beauty wind-astir –
It was the day of all the dead,

[*The following four lines deleted:*
Toussaints; the Autumn air seemed full
Of passing presences. between
Those coloured pillars, peasants keen
Of face]

No a lot of that has to be altered, and so I leave you with a noble fragment. Soon you shall have all the rest.

Personally I should like to chuck verse altogether and make music alone, but the way is too dificult perhaps in the Army, and the two paths must be kept just at present. When Sidgwick and Jackson have accepted (supposition only) this next book, I mean either to chuck verse or music till the War's over, and then Music, music hard. But meanwhile there's the War – the war.

Someday I hope to go tramping with you, and to jaw hard or to listen hard the whole time, for at present life seems too much of a bore to do either very much – It is the company I have had to keep for so long, perhaps.

The Spirit of Man is beside me, and (though a borrowed copy) is probably going out with me on the farm work this morning. I love Yeats' 'All things uncomely and broken' and 'O hurry where by water among trees'. They are both beautiful enough for anything. He may well take days in polishing and repolishing his verse, for there is little enough flaw; as in a grass blade; delicate finely-shaped and beautifully coloured. Someday, if the Fates are good enough I must read George Moore again; there is much about Yeats and his cloak and thin dark face in there

Thanks so much for the criticism. Thanks so much for the letters, and for the copy. It is awfully kind of you, and one poetling is helped and encouraged. But O magician, Spirit me on to my hills, and give me a free run of a piano and music!

    With best wishes to yourself and Mrs Haines and Robin

Yours ever
Ivor Gurney

[1] In the second line of 'Migrants'. The following comments apply to poems which were to appear in *War's Embers*, which are referred to as 'new verses' in letter 347. 'Girl's Song' was renamed 'The Tryst' to distinguish it from another poem with the same title. The end of 'Fire in the Dusk' differed little from the version given here.
[2] It did.

---

354 To Marion Scott   G.70.40

11 September 1918 (P)

[*Postcard*]

    The doctor has promised to let me come early on Saturday at 10 oclock. So I shall come by bus probably to arrive at 12.30 at Westbourne Terrace.

I.B.G.

---

355 To Marion Scott   G.41.182

? September 1918 (KT)   No 8 Ward, Middlesex War Hospital,
Napsbury, St Albans

My Dear Friend

    Your charming and appreciative letter arrived here tonight when I was in the dumps rather and cheered me no end – cheered me up so that I was able to think once more of swotting at music. And O great news! The doctor asked me last night whether my people were willing to take me home! So my board and discharge are near I suppose and freedom, perhaps strength to work. O to slog on under Herbert's direction and develop all that is deep in me so undeveloped – and give you one really good V.Sonata! Well, with God's help that may come, but I need that.

    My goodness you are a generous lady about praise though! Never was anyone so lavish and kind. It delights me you are delighted.

    (*No formal end to this letter*).

462

c.21 September 1918 (KT)

Thank you very much about Mrs Jacob; yes, she is the Bishopess, so to speak; and I am anticipating a good time next Saturday at their house.

Certainly I will read the Carnegie article through, and do my best with it.

Thank you very much for the number of the *Music Student* and *Poetry Review* both which interested me very much. The Theodore Maynard Sonnetts especially were quite good, and the last line of 'Warfare'

'What sword
'Win to the tower where thy perfections sit',
and the last lines of 'Treason'
'Heedless of our uncaptained hosts arrayed
Or of the flags their battle shall bring down'
are both quite good.[1] I am anxious to know your opinion of 'Toussaints', which pleases me quite, and the alterations in 'The Stonebreaker'. Also of the 'Farm' and of 'On Rest'. I think the first shows pretty well now, and the second has been improved. 'O Tree of Pride' I did yesterday.

Please like these; my new children, but you do like everything I do apparently; a too appreciative critic. 'Crickley Hill' I must have a shot at later, for certainly as Mr Haines says the later part is too rhetorical.

There is little news to tell you. I may be able to get down on Saturday, October 5th, but am not certain – may be at home by then. It would be delightful to play once more on that glorious piano, but it is just possible that I may be away by then. Goodness knows I hope so.

My dear Friend, who have been so good to me, what a time it would be to get back to Gloucestershire and start swotting. You should have some songs then! But duty seems to point to the Army again, and there I shall probably find my feet after a short time and write my best. Well, Time will tell, and the last part of my life may be the happiest. Well may it be – the first part has been bitter enough – bitter enough.

Still, so has yours and you make no complaint, so why should I?

Today is perfectly glorious out, and clouds are sailing the skies, shadows are black as if it were summer almost and I can imagine your garden perfectly beautiful in this September month – which is usually the best or almost the best of the year. September – what a name; what associations too of mellow sunlight and the first signs of gold on the great elms!

May you enjoy it well! With best wishes to you and all

Your sincere friend
Ivor Gurney

---

[1] 'Warfare' and 'Treason' are published in the *Poetry Review* for September/October 1918, Vol IX No 5 p.285.

28 September 1918 (P)

[*Postcard¹*]

    Thank you for your delightful letter, and the essay which I have not yet read. Yes, please come on Tuesday, as the Board of discharge for me is not till Monday week, and I do not expect to go away till the Thursday following.
    Best wishes and thanks from I.B.G.

¹ Printed with the address Verulam House, St Albans.

28 September 1918 (KT)   No 8 Ward, Middlesex War Hospital, Napsbury

My Dear Friend

    Thank you for your delightful and delighted letter that reached me today, just as I was setting out for the Bishop's Palace.

    No, Mamselle, my board is not to be on Monday, but on Monday week, and the Thursday will see the back of me. If you would *not* mind I should prefer to put off my visit till then, as it is so frightfully short a stay on the Saturday; do you mind? But on Tuesday I shall be able to see you for a couple of hours here; might possibly be on pass (but don't think so.) Anyway it will be possible to try at any rate. The official usuality is against it, but as a matter of fact Evans came to see me on Friday and was allowed the two hours. However I hope pretty confidently that the doctor will grant me a pass for the afternoon, and that we shall be having an afternoon of comfortable chatter together.

    The account of the Carnegie Quartett interested me greatly, and you have done Herbert proud; perhaps it would have been as well to have made guesses at what was Malvern and what Cotswold. Surely

is the Malverns sticking up their heads? Dear county, it deserves such a work to celebrate it. When my poor brain is in proper form I hope to give you something to look out for, but that's a bit far off at present, and songs and Fugues etc is all for the present. You must be full up with work at present, chockfull; and I wonder you can spare the time to come up. With your usual goodness and ability to cram any amount of work into no time at all. Well, you have heard of my admiration for your powers, and I won't express them again.

A letter came from Arthur Bliss yesterday with particular reference to *Severn and Somme* which he liked. 'That much of it which was beautiful in the book pleased me'.

He has met Robert Nichol, but does not admire his verse very much. He's in the 1st Grenadier Guards, and the notepaper is headed Grenadier Guards Base Division B.E.F.

How do you feel now that you are landed back in your old Westbourne Terrace 'bivvy'? (To use a *B.E.F.* phrase.) Surely it is too much of a sudden change not to regret the open spaces of country just as the leaves are changing colour and October's coming on.

My goodness, it's much I want to be back in the West Country – to be on with work again. I am awful sorry not to have rewritten 'Crickley' but the fact is the whole thing needs making again if it is to be any good; and that needs really too much time, patience, and so forth to be done just at present.

Goodbye, with best wishes from your grateful correspondent and sincere friend

Ivor Gurney

359 To Marion Scott   G.61.3

2 October 1918 (E)   No 8 Ward, Napsbury

My Dear Friend

Thanks for the lovely day we had yesterday, and all the talk and cheerful chatter of my esteemed correspondent. This is to say merely that my discharge does not come off till Friday, so that means we draw kit tomorrow and do not come to our various destinations till next day.

Will this upset your plans? I hope not indeed. Will Friday night suit you as well for my staying?

Let's hope all will fit in and I be landed safe in the arms of my people on Saturday.

With best wishes

I remain

Your sincere friend
Ivor Gurney

360 To Marion Scott   G.41.177

17 October 1918 (P)   19 Barton St, Gloucester

My Dear Friend

Thank you so much for your only too kind letter, and your mention of Mr Napier Miles.[1] I have just written a letter to him to ask whether I might go there at once – not being sure of my impulses, and being anxious not only to save myself, but also my father, who must be more worried by my being here, than there under care. Also, if there is music, I could do as well there as here, until my time is past.

Perhaps Herbert has told you something of what I told him.

O there is one gorgeous bit of news – F.W.H. has reached Holland – Schevingen!!

This is written at no 54 Wellington St,[2] and in front of creepers and trees of October; so beautiful. Alas, that I must leave freedom so soon, but I believe it to be best. Thank you so much for your kindness, Mamselle the Fairy Princess, and I am not without hope that this will turn out well by March, perhaps before.

With thanks and best wishes

> your sincere friend
> Ivor Gurney

[1] Philip Napier Miles (1865-1935), composer and patron of the opera, opened his house Kings Weston as a hospital during the war, and there was talk of Gurney going there.
[2] Where the Hunts lived.

361 *To Marion Scott*   G.46.30.2

18 October 1918 (P)   19 Barton St, Gloucester

Dear Friend

Thank you so much for your charming-as-usual letter, and the enclosure also, which is going to buy a *Spirit of Man* for the dear Hunts. It was not what I expected; little chance did there seem of getting anything out of my poor little book,[1] but here it has come at last, and usefully. Thank you so much. This is written at 54 Wellington St, and your letter is at home, so will you please excuse my answering it now? I am delighted Herbert is delighted with 'The County Mayo'. And will you *please* oblige Mr Haines by sending him 'Toussaints' which he likes very much, but has only seen the first verse!! and wants the rest. We are going walking tomorrow in the Forest of Dean, and I could wish you were coming with us. Alas that is not possible!

Pitcher is frightfully rushed just now, without assistants, and hardly able to do things quickly but I will go see him tout' suite

Goodbye and Good luck

with all best wishes

> from your sincere friend
> Ivor Gurney

[1] A royalty statement for the second half of 1918 (G.61.270) shows royalties on 33 copies, a total of seven shillings and sevenpence! This indicates he had sold over 500 copies and would be getting a ten per cent royalty.

2 November 1918 (P)   19 Barton Street, Gloucester

My Dear Friend

I am sorry to hear that you too have come under the influence of this dreadful new thing,[1] which strikes where it pleases, but why on you, who have had so much to endure during these last years? Surely that scourge might have spared you?

Well, since that is not so, may you soon recover; and find something in your sickness to interest you.

I am glad to tell you that I am better myself, after a fortnight's hauling of heavy things about the Munition Works, but that is a job that won't last long – fortunately – by the look of things in the papers. Isn't the news glorious? What a week the last has been![2]

Poor Herbert is down with the 'flu' also, complicated by pneumonia, and not feeling any too cheerful I daresay, in spite of his being at the house of his lady-love, at Churchdown under that little hill of Chosen he has loved so well.

Coming back in the train today there was a great sight of Malvern to cheer me sticking up across the miles of plain – enormous enough, and reminding all whom it might concern of

May it not be long before you too may say 'Look, See!' at them. Robinswood Hill looks fine too; our works are spread just along in under him, and every morning one gets view of that humpy crest.

Well, there is no more I can tell you save that I may be 'going to sea' again, and this time less ignominiously I hope!

Meantime, may you prosper, and recover your old self, and soon, under the influence of Peace Bread, and may that soon be dished out!!

With best wishes

your sincere friend
Ivor Gurney

[1] The Spanish 'flu epidemic, which killed 25 million people in 1918 and 1919.
[2] President Wilson asks for effectively unconditional surrender of Germany; Ludendorf is asked to resign.

467

November 1918 (KT)   19 Barton St, Gloucester

My Dear Winnie

I hope you will like this book: it seems to me to be one of the jolliest and best packed books going.

Charles Doughty, Barrie, Housman (A E), Dr John Brown, G K C, Lucas, Sorley, Ledwidge, R. Bridges – let me especially recommend. I do hope all you lovely people will have a good time at High Wycombe since there are none better deserve it; and O that I were along to share it with you, you dear children and grown ups! Alas there'll be no I.B.G. to smoke his churchwarden and deliver weighty sentences after the style of Dr Johnson. Someday, and soon, (for I am to return to College) St Mike's will shelter me once again, and O will there be ping-pong? Will the state of Europe permit frivolities, think you? Let's hope there will be a great flurry of snow that night to encircle the feasting house with white wonder untouched till Micky goes out to dance on it. That night Miss Marjory shall play Beethoven's most difficult Sonata and Arthur wriggle his eeliest. The fond parents looking on indulgently the while, bless'em, for in calibre precision of fire and general aptitude for service they are level with the best. My best respex to you all and may you like this presink.

Yours affectionately
Ivor Gurney

30 November 1918 (G)   19 Barton St, Gloucester

My Dear Shimmin

It is long since I have heard of you, and Christmas is coming on with jollity, high jinks under the mistletoe, and distended waistbands – general charity and slight intoxication mixed in a delectable compound – so it has seemed good unto me to indite an epistolary mattaw – which latter it is this.

How are you now? Do you ever hear music, play or see Music? Thank Goodness the War's over; thank Goodness there is a chance we'll all be back again soon moving our fingers over black and white, and playing ecstatic sentimentalities on the Vox Humana the while the Vicaw surreptitiously chaws his last eucalyptus lozenge before commencing operations.

Alas, I am afraid Pte Shimmin has had all too bad a time of it, and deserves a rest covered with medals for kindly and attentive service to the Common Wangler.

Have you heard that I have got my ticket? That means College soon I hope, and sounding loud timbrels, plucking resonant harps, tootling on sackbuts shawms, balaikas (or whatever they are) and other tuneful instruments of Musick. May you be there along soon! We'll sit in some inn parlour and

chortle 'Widdecombe Fair' together for joy of return, reunion, mere existence
– Joie de vivre, as the linguists say. Ho ho! and there's a Violin Sonata *almost*
finished, two or three songs for you to see. A Quartett on the stocks, all about
Gloucester, that fair city; gloomy today, but glorious enough on Thursday,
when St Nicholas Tower shone white in a pearly sort of fashion lovely to see.
O Yes, and there's a new book soon for to astonish literary critics and
generality alike, probably to be entitled *War's Embers*.

(Please excuse wrong clef?)

I have been chortling that this morning; on the decrepit instrument biding
here in this street overlooking room. Well, well; you'll have that soon, I
hope. Now all good be with you. And grub galore and festivity.

> 'May all good fellows that here agree
> Drink audit ale in Heaven with me.
> May all my enemies go to Hell
> Noel, Noel, Noel, Noel!

Yours ever
I.B.G.

P.S. Did you get Mrs Chapman's letter forwarded on?

365 To J.W.Haines   G.85.8

Boxing Day 1918 (G)

My Dear Haines

Yes, you must know Cornwall someday, a grey land of blue sea and
frowning cliffs of might. Boulders outcropping in all conceivable places. Skies
wonderful enough. Violets in bloom (though not many) at Xmas. Great
winds and dashing spray, clear stars, gulls, cormorants, rooks, a wishing well,
old and dangerous-to-the-unwary-traveller pitshafts ... Zennor Head, Carn
Naun, Hell's Mouth, Rosewall, Tregenna, Lelant, Godrevy. Towednack-in-
the-Moor (with its little Elizabethan church) Castle Andinnas, Trefoil
Bottom, The Carracks, Trevalgan, Clodgy Head, Pen Enys, a good enough
list of names. You'd love the lot, and come back to stare at the ceiling through
clouds of smoke – to see Armada clouds, huge breakers, wicked looking rocks
and brown and grey moorlands .... Surely the great Symphony in C minor
will come out of this. (Pray that it may not resemble the Brahms!)

It's a Swinburne land, a good land, where middlesized and shortish people
direct you with 'My dear' in soft voices. O a good land! You must come
down a long and see it. About the scrumptious dinner at Porthminster Hotel,
and the musical chairs amd winking-game after you shall hear nought, neither

of the charade shall you be told, but of Hells Mouth at sunset, plain immensely strong houses, great hedges crowned with turf, ferns continual, short cuts not always 'short', and of the Great Composer lying fearfully on his stomach gazing at a white floor of surf like fluid marble – a great deal.

There was a lifeboat launch too, for a collision five miles out at sea; a discovery and investigation of a stranded but undamaged steamer arched over with a huge and brilliant rainbow whose base was two violently black storms.

Boxing Day.

And today we have seen great chasms, climbed rock of granite covered with lichen, and seen the sea quiet and gray, save near the rocks over which it boiled furiously when the mood took us. O a murderous but gloriously majestic place! The fear of men of the sea, but to poets a joy, a great memory after the seeing. This was Zennor Bay (I think) near Galver and West of St Ives.

Primroses glorify all this place in spring, and here the sea pinks abound. Here also we found a little blue flower (uncommon, so Mrs V: said.) called something like 'squininsy wort'. (Mrs V: is still out and is not to be consulted.) Rosewall again we passed, a fine long granite-bouldered down and brown with dried bracken, but the sight of those three great chasms falling sheer to rock or sea since the tide was not high was memorable enough.

There are many British remains about here, and the whole land has a sense of men in skins and not tall. Living underground, a primaeval air there is about anything. Well, that had to be left behind, we must return to St Ives; which by the way I leave on Monday.

My goodness though, what a wealth of wonder of flowers must bloom here in Spring, and that an early one. Violets must be thick everywhere; bluebells, primroses a carpet in places, and everywhere the fern, the fern! (Halt to light up.)

It is a county that would delight you unspeakably, and someday or other you must visit these wonderful sheer falls of black rock and granite; see the Cornish Sea and altogether find new country. Yes, a great land.

I hope you had a pretty happy Christmas. Did Kerr take any part therein?

The Anthology of New Poetry is amusing, but O were the English poets left out what would the book's worth be?

How's Mrs Haines and Robin? I hope well and festive.

On Christmas Eve we had the most scrumptious feed you can imagine at an Hotel here. (O thank Goodness we don't dwell in one. Quiet lodgings are better!) You all would have stared to see it! Many courses, all gorgeously prepared and plentiful and sumptuously served ... After that we played Musical Chairs and such like frivolities till late – bored but courageous, then came back to loiter wearily to bed. O it was worth it though! A great day.

Well, there is no writing out of all this, but will be sure; will be, *sure*, though Music I hope and not verse.

Well Au Revoir. Au Revoir. I hope the folk songs came in useful!

Yours ever

I.B.G.

470

January 1919 (KT)

My Dear Old Win:

O don't be sick, seedy, out of sorts and so on, for soon it is the intention of the famous composer the visit the Hill of the Castle with St Mike's situated thereon (its outhouses and messuages pertaining) and to find you not in a condition to play Ping Pong would be sad indeed. Well, here's to a Happy New Year to you and all the rest with no crocks-up and nothing but robust and even noisy health.

It's snowing hard outside. Snowing like blazes (to use an unsuitable simile) and lovely to look at the dark-sky world is. Can you send any hints on how to pack shirts, music, socks, books, coats, shoes, of enormous bulk into a box half the size of the combined mass? If so please do, for that is the problem that confronts me. Or hints how to write joyous Masterpieces when in the dumps? Ah, but you poor dear, having to lie still, and take things what they call 'easy' have none too good a time. May it pass, soon, soon! Dear kid, I am so glad you like that book. It is an honour to get in with such a select crowd, ain't it? Book 2 of me is at the publishers but no reply has been received as yet. Well, here's hopes to see the whole Joyful Crowd of you soon.

With love from your humble obedt servant

I.B.G.

367 To J.W. Haines   G.83.10.1-2

16 January 1919 (P)   83 Sterndale Rd, West Kensington, London W

My Dear Haines

It would be a height of fortune to drop once more into that book surrounded room and read, smoke, yarn, and so on; but that cannot be. I must remain awhile in dingy diggings; until Spring comes and with it my return to the land that bred me, that joys my friends to sight, and me in memory.

I hope you all well [*sic*]; Mrs Haines, Robin and the maid. Hope that St Heliers has happy days to smile out upon; sees Chosen clear, and blue sky over it.

There is little to tell you – after a heart breaking hunt for digs: I managed to get a bivvy here; which may or may not endure for a season. Today my books have arrived, and soon the astonished landlady will see Everymans and others standing round the room. Two Edward Thomas' will be there, the first, O far more highly honoured than the second; which seems to me to be rather manner than matter, and the fallen fruit rather than the choice of the tree.

'I never saw that Land before' 'The Dark Forest' 'The Ash Grove' 'Old Man' 'The Thrush' 'Digging' 'The Mill-Water' 'A Dream' 'Sedge Warblers' 'What will they do' 'Song' 'She Dotes' 'The New House' 'March' 'Over the Hills' 'Home' 'Unknown Bird' 'The Lofty Sky' 'Digging' 'But

these things also' 'April' 'The Wasp Trap' 'A Tale' 'The Source' *'The Word'*
'Aspens' 'Ambition' 'This is no case' 'Health' *'Beauty'* *'Snow'* 'The Other'
'Man and Dog' 'A Private' 'Out in the Dark'. All these I like, especially those
underlined and the others well – some very well; But O it's not Books.

My composition goes haltingly I fear. There's one set of verses in rough;
another half done. The poor Quartett presents difficulties in the making and
must wait. This little booklet I thought you might care to carry with you on
your tramps abroad; as you know some of the tunes; and the words of so
many being good, the thing being cheap; why, here you are, and may you find
Joy therein. Now I am going to bed, and with a Brahms Quintett and the
Second E.T. will find me enough to fill an hour by candle light.

Well, meanwhile, Fare you well, and if you come up to town, please let me
know, wilt?

With best wishes to you all

Yours ever
I.B.G.

---

368 *To Marion Scott* G.53.24-27

25 and 26 February 1919 (S) 19 Barton St, Gloucester

My Dear Friend

Thank you so much for the letter and Postal Orders. And all your general
benificence to the Lorn Scribbler. I hope the poor jaw is recovered now and
that you will be able to use it after any lawful fashion in ease. O but
Gloucestershire's beautiful, beautiful, after the grey waste of London.

Dear places that they are! And the crowds of old Gloucesters there are
about.

Later Wednesday.

I am returning my proofs to you, with corrections from your suggestions,
for which thank you very much. Some of them had already caught my eye.
Anyway here is my draft for you to do as you will with. Don't the old book
read well in print though? Don't it look business-like, tight and right? Well, I
think we are both entitled to be pleased at the result of our 'doos', to use a
Gloucestershire word, and can lean back and chortle with some satisfaction at
the result.

F.W.H., the same, or nearly the same, as ever, has been putting me up
these last few days, and has told me much about his captivity, and most
interesting. We had a great stunt last night; sat up together to make a cycle of
songs called a *Gloucestershire Lad* Cycle. 'In Flanders' was already done. 'The
Horses' nearly so. So I did 'The Rest Farm' 'Pipers Wood' and
'Minsterworth Perry'; all of which we shall do at Stroud on Saturday week.[1]
'The Horses', the drinking song and 'The Rest Farm' all quite good. This
performance started with milk, went on to Perry, which was succeeded by

Champagne to end with sloe gin! Only 'Pipers Wood' needs much attention. Needless to say this was the last of the set; made between 4 and 5 oclock!!

Willy told me what a huge demand there was for 'Captain Stratton's Fancy', and this was confirmed by a letter this morning positively crying therefor. There ought to be a huge sale for the old thing, and on no account ought the copyright to be relinquished. What shoals of prisoners have heard it F.W.H. says can hardly be counted.

Poor Madge[2] is very seedy, or was yesterday, poor thing. I am just off round there, and will know more then. It is serious influenza on top of the heart trouble, and may lead to the ill thing. Emmie bears up well, but it must be an awful strain on her. I have not yet seen Madge, but hope to tonight.

With this comes 'Is my Team Ploughing'.[3] The rest shall follow as promised, but not just yet.

No, 'To G' has never yet been done in public as far as I know. But O could you get 'Capn Stratton' to a publisher soon? (It is of course my greed that causes this keenness!)

The Wizard

The trees of high summer
Completion have, and stand
Like those that Noah cargoed
Above the drowned land.

The April trees are maiden,
Carry their green as free
As any school miss dancer
At her first junketry.

Her foredeath blaze of passion
And wild regret is shown
In thickets, woods of Autumn,
Tall elms oaks set alone.

But Winter's sombre magic,
Sable traceries,
Ebon on sunset crimson
Is yet more strong than these.

And his dark magic stronger
Than any girlish charm,
Though touched and streaked with evil;
Ominous, threatening harm.

An Ending

His body lies so still that swift was in flight
As any summer's swallow; and blind to the light
His eyes are that saw with blue eagle glance
The smallest pennon borne aloft on farthest lance.
That pride of him that power laid low in the dust
Death on him has put strong edict, the dread 'must'.
And he has obeyed thereto, as all must soon or late;
Will ride no more to clatter of hoofs through the gate;
Will take no more the first soft breathings of Spring
With welcome surprisal, nor hear the bird sing
Any more in the midnight brake or see far hung
May's crescent of silver in clear heaven swung
For these are of earth, far off he may recall
The twin wonders sacred of dayspring and night-fall
With longing hardly to be borne scarce supported
So strong his love was, his faith so great hearted,
While we the unworthy watch that pageant change
Of fresh and ruddy colour of pride, the Seasons range;
And he naught knows of any wonder of wide skies
Or May's hedges foaming, fast-closed are his eyes,
Hands folded, limbs loose, pallid, unwilled,
His burial awaiting with hot heart stilled;
Passionless, uneager; a story is done.
Let us pile earth to hide him from his Father the Sun,
Raise a stone of honour, weep, turn, and begone.

I hope you like this. Book three you see is in the making! 'The Fiddler of Dooney' is half done, and will soon be with you.[4]

You shall hear how the Stroud affair goes. It will probably be great fun, F.W.H. is no small man at rousing people. Should he come to London you will make a most interesting acquaintance perhaps friend, who knows?

With thanks for all kindnesses I remain

Your sincere friend
Ivor Gurney

By the way *A Gloucestershire Lad* has been issued to match *Severn and Somme* and his other book – in blue. It looks well.

[1] Harvey's poems are from *A Gloucestershire Lad* except for 'The Horses' which is from *Gloucestershire Friends*.
[2] Margaret Hunt.
[3] Housman's poem, which Gurney set; published in 1926 as part of *The Western Playland*.
[4] Yeats's poem, which Gurney had begun to set in 1917, and which was published in 1957.

11 March 1919 (KT) 19 Barton St, Gloucester

My Dear Friend

Here is 'Spring' and a few more verses, which I hope will please you. In my next letter you will get repaid in coin – be told rude (or perhaps polite) things about your own book, but at present I am rather rushed and all that sort of thing. Thank you so much for the cheque – alas! that it is the last! By the way Squire has just accepted Harvey's 'Ducks' the longest thing he has written.

Our affair on Saturday went off very satisfactorily. F.W.H. was rather weak in the gills and husky but otherwise pretty much himself. St Clair Baddely took the chair, an archeologist of some repute. It was all very jolly – Mr Haines, Gladys and Edith Harvey came with us, and in a motor, over Horsepools Hill to see Painswick lying below us on the left, half way to Stroud.

They propose to ask me to lecture to them! Golly, what a lecture that will be! The Sesame shop is the name of the show, and quite a comfy show that is. John Drinkwater is its presiding deity quite often.

Thank you so much for your letter to my Father. He has not spoken of it, but it must have reassured him. Poor old chap he is very sick, very much in pain, and a soon end is best.

Emmie Hunt bears her trial remarkably well,[1] and indeed on the whole I think is glad. It is there I shall work of mornings anyway, am just off round there.

The Sonata had 5 or 6 hours slog yesterday, but not successfully; it wants wangling to a remarkable degree.

Well, well, this is all a somewhat muddled brain can squeeze out, so I will close with thanks for all. With best wishes

Your sincere friend
Ivor Gurney

[1] Margaret Hunt died on 3 March.

17 March 1919 (KT) 19 Barton St, Gloucester

My Dear Friend

Yes, as with you, the weather today is vile enough to frighten music clean out of existence. And my head is empty of news too.

Emmy is bearing remarkably well, is cheerful and feels Madge near her continually; likely to get nearer too. Soon she may be in London and wanting to see you of course.

Yes, I saw the printer had left in the dedication to F.C.S. and have crossed it out accordingly. Mr Haines is enthusiastic about the book and so is F.W.H. – for all the roughnesses therein and round about ness.

There are some more verses to come. The first movement of the Violin Sonata[1] is almost ready the other two revised (have to be rewritten) and the last beginning.

Meanwhile, my jolly Manager and Bucker-Up combined, here are two songs for you. 'The Horses' is one of the cycle of F.W.H.'s things which might go in a lump to the publisher.

There is a setting of 'Kathleen Ni Houlihan' (shall come next time) which will knock you flat. My best song? Well, perhaps — After 'By a Bierside' and 'In Flanders' anyhow. Though 'Time' always seems pretty big to me.[2]

O but you should have seen last Thursday! The whole world seemed to exult and glory in mere being! A Beethoven day by the Lord! As a poem says, as yet unpublished

> Kyrie Eleison and Gloria
> Credo, Magnificat and Jubilate ....

The whole world gathered strength to praise the Day.

Of course I will copy out 'To G' but I fear my memory is not able to this, save with the copy. Will you please send that.

Now I must off to F.W.H. who leaves his home behind him, reaches his friends his hand, on Saturday – Seaton Delaval, that hole, to be his staying place for a time, poor fellow.

Best wishes to you all from

Your sincere friend
Ivor Gurney

A nicer letter next time.

---

[1] The Violin Sonata in E flat, for which various manuscripts exist (G.24.4.1-12).
[2] I cannot find any music for Harvey's 'The Horses'. 'Kathleen Ni Houlihan' was published in 1938, 'By a Bierside' in 1979 and 'In Flanders' in 1957. 'Time' is probably 'Even such is Time', a setting (published in 1957) of a poem by Walter Raleigh.

---

371 To Marion Scott   G.61.5-8

21 March 1919 (S)   19 Barton St, Gloucester

My Dear Friend

Of *Violin Verses*,[1] I find myself to have marked 'The very music of our English tongue' the 'Sonnet' on p.8, particularly the close of the octave. Verse 3 of 'A Dream Song' (4 and 5 as well). Verse 3 of 'Violinist to Violin'. Verse 1; 6 and last of 'My 'Guadagnini' violin speaks'. The last verse of 'Nicholas Gagliano'. Verse 3 (last two lines) and last verse but one in 'The Betts Strad'.

The book has sincerity, directness, power; its only fault is too many adjectives. For a book on one subject it is surprisingly successful; on which success please accept my congratulations. You ought to have written more, done far better work than this, since. It seems a pity that with all the new verse and new technique you have not stuck at it, but I suppose that the desire to help other people has proved too strong; and the love of Music, Business-Agenting, College Work etc.

Emmy is about to dive into its contents; you shall hear from her no doubt. Her health is better, she has more colour; the strain is over, and she is glad her sister is free.

About book covers, well .... all that kind of thing may safely be left to you; but I do like Harvey's blue covers. Still, it may avoid confusion to have another red. 'Sais pas'.

There came a letter this morning from College of many hands. Erlebach first, H.N.H., A.J.B., S.S. jolly to receive. I am so glad Sidney is released, please give him my best wishes, and all sorts of affable greetings. I hope we'll meet soon. O do give him a dedication! Has he been forgotten? O let him in, Dedicatee, and at your own choice!

Now some things come with this which may interest you; 'Kathleen' will knock you flat – given me on a great day, last Thursday I believe, when Earth exulted like a thousand Beethoven symphonies.

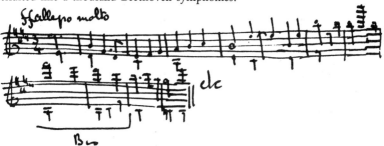

The 1st movement of the E^b Violin Sonata is finished. (Possibly the best thing I have yet done, for a long movement.) Coming soon!

The Violin part of the revised Slow Movement comes. And the final and authoritative version of 'In Flanders'. – The whole of the *Gloucestershire Lad* Cycle in fact.

(There will be a Short Introduction to the last Movement of the Sonata).

What with sketches of 'A Gloucestershire Rhapsody', a Symphony, 3 songs needing correction, Two writing out, my life is not worth living! There is the Mass too! Of course there's the Quartett! Nothing else, but I want to write out

'The lads in their hundreds' and

'Song of the Night at Morn' of Mrs Meynell.

There is a short Violin piece half done.

F.W.H. is all to[o] soon to be back at Seaton Delaval. Alas!.. He has just done 3 ripping poems on 'Coal' 'Iron' and 'Fire'.

Is Herbert ill or only to attend hospital? He has put off an appointment with F.W.H. anyway. I do hope it is nothing much.

And my restlessness will now set me at copying out 'I praise the tender flower'.

Oh but there is a world of things to do, and if God will, I shall dig in to accomplish them. But ain't Kathleen a dear? isn't she a forcible sweet thing? Some trouble she cost, but it seems to me worth while. Wouldn't Plunkett Green make the rafters shake with that!

Mr Haines and Kerr are well and jolly, but Kerr has just had his MS returned for the 6th time; being grieved in consequence. Hard lines! it deserves better fate. I feel ashamed to face such ill-fortune.

Good bye, good luck.

When are the Christian Science Monitor articles to appear?

Please remember me to all with kindest regards. Especially do I hope Mr Scott is now quite well,

With best wishes and thanks

from your sincere friend
Ivor Gurney

[1] Marion Scott's book of poems (1905).

---

372 *To Marion Scott* Hurd Transcript

March/April 1919 (KT) 19 Barton Street, Gloucester

My Dear Friend

I am so sorry you missed Mr.Haines, who is equally sorry, but was most taken with Miss Prince (is it?) your Aunt, with whom he seems to have enjoyed himself. A pity, but not to be helped. I have just come from staying the night there, and finishing the Scherzo which comes with this.

The Violin Sonata movement will please you I think; the Coda especially. The Davies Song I have just unearthed – tis a good one, think you not?

Thank you so much for the Squires letter. I am very glad – this is sure to be a good thing. My letter to him lies before me, and I have said what you have directed, wise – obediently. Permit me to compliment you on your wangling abilities – those of no mean order; but McKerrow certainly was decent. But then you have the knack of compelling or at least inducing some sort of decency from the roughest. Again thank you about 'Kathleen'.

Winthrop Rogers will do excellently for the *Gloucestershire Lad* cycle, I should say. F.W.H. and I will contribute little biographical notes. These songs went awfully well at Stroud, and should have a grrreat sale here.

There will turn up in a day or two 'To G' transposed, the Slow Movement you know. A song by Yeats 'Maid Quiet'. And a rattling Belloc drinking Song, *absolutely first-rate*, written many years ago. Perhaps a Mrs.Meynell

478

Song. Perhaps the rewritten Scherzo of the V.S.

Yes, E.H. is very well considering, and there I go to write everyday. She feels Madge not far away, so is not lonely really and finds enough to do. We are going out to Minsterworth together soon. F.W.H. is still here – having found a doctor to certify to unfitness. He has written three good things on Coal, Iron, and Fire. He is not unwell, but simply not well.

Gloucestershire is beginning to glory, but things are late. The snow-sprinkled Malverns have been very impressive. Somehow the whiteness was streaked, which made them look very Alpine-rugged and fine. Cotswold always is great anyway.

My County

Gloucester, County of tales, Gloucester my Homeland
Fair-named Wonder of Western eyes.
Should you show many days like this, such clear
Beauty transcendent, I must leave all else
And live only to seek out quiet places
Hidden by hedgerows, havens each a story –
More than any other search and worship
Your secrecies, till gathered were to me
Memories unnumbered, not of the great days,
Since those must live perforce, but of quiet coloured
Russet hue corners of ploughland, secret
Fountains of Joy to none else known but me;
Or known, by none treasured as I treasure.

The Scherzo shall come with this (born of such a mood) since tis legible, and it will do you no harm to glimpse Maisemore through my eyes.

This is a short letter, but a forerunner of a longer one fitter to thank you for your kindnesses.

The new Yeats book and that of Freeman[1] are disappointing. But O the malicious gossip of Cumberland's 'Set down in Malice'! Walford Davies cannot be too well pleased .....

Why did not Keats finish the 'Ode to Maia'? That is a gorgeous fragment indeed........

I hope you will set the seal of your approval on The Violin Sonata: surely this is the best long movement I have done?

With best wishes to all
    and especially to yourself

From your sincere friend
Ivor Gurney

[1] *Memories of Childhood and other poems* (1919), by John Freeman.

15-16 April 1919 (S) 19 Barton St, Gloucester

My Dear Friend

You do write the most extraordinarily encouraging letters; the most full of sweetness and (to me) revivifying light. (As Mr Jorrocks rudely asked once. 'Fine weather for bee-keeping. Do they make much honey round your parts?' But that was written to Captain Doleful, who needed such handling.)[1]

Yes, 'Maid Quiet' is to be rewritten.[2]

Thank you so much for all you are doing about publishers. It pleases me that Plunkett Greene likes my songs. Who is better judge than he?

As to Sidgwick and Jackson, please do as you please. It is your trouble, and on my account. If you happen to see Mr McKerrow, and it becomes easy to ask, please do. Surely it is not otherwise worth troubling about?

I am sorry you cannot get away for a holiday – but O April's a disagreeable lady this year, after the bad example of March, who was generally a beast. Trees only just beginning to bud in Mid April, in Gloucestershire! Shocking!!

Of course you shall have any help I can give as to essays or anything else. Please send them to receive all attention.

Alas, Will Harvey is at Seaton Delaval! Disgusted to go, but the War Office had lost sight of him, and he must be rescued from the pigeon holes. When I go again to Redlands however, I will ask about the new poems. There is a glorious Ballade of Leeuwarden and a Drinking Song good enough for anything.

My father is still (unfortunately) alive, suffering great pain, still brave and occasionally hopeful. Hard to realise that once he took us, the merriest of guides, to Maisemore of Sunday evenings!

Thank you for your appreciation of the *G.L.* Cycle. Yes, 'Piper's Wood' is the least good, but touching up the accompaniment will help. The order is In Flanders, Pipers Wood, The Horses, The Rest Farm, Minsterworth Perry.

Yesterday brought me that rare sight – the ground end of a rainbow. I could see the hedges through it – a wonderful sight. Under Crickley it was, under the Roman camp – such a ridge, such a sky, such a rainbow, and (afterwards) such a sweeping scud of storm – a wonderful glittering curtain of rain sweeping across the valley.

L.Abercrombie wrote me the nicest letter about my returning to him the old presentation copy of *Deborah*, stained woefully but interestingly with Laventie mud. He is at Dymock now, writing hard. Later on he means to get up a Concert of my things in the North, which will be jolly enough for my prospects there, since he knows so many people of interest.

Emmy Hunt looks and is very well, is to go away soon on visits as you know, and will be badly missed here.

Mr Haines, Kerr and myself had a stunt of ballade and triolet making at H's house on Sunday, with Mrs H: looking on, after the naughty Robin had been put to bed with full dishonours. Kerr is the most provocative and amusing of talkers (Quite reckless) and it was great fun to hear the two hard at it. The irresistible force and the immovable object...!

Good wishes O lover of Kensington

from yours gratefully
Ivor Gurney

PS.
Thank you so much – the explanation is eminently satisfactory.

With this comes the Belloc drinking song,[3] once sung with singular ill-success at a church tea party Chaxhill way (8 miles from here) by F.W.H., but nevertheless I believe it to be rollicking and vinous (or aleful) enough for anything or anybody. Mr Haines has tackled all of De La Mare, Abercrombie, Frost and Freeman about the book, which should get good reviews. It will be fun reading them, an amusement I am looking forward to. The last Movement of the E^b Sonata is half-sketched now.

[1] In the books of R.S. Surtees (1805-64).
[2] A setting of Yeats's poem; see G.36.8.13-14.
[3] 'West Sussex Drinking Song' published in 1921.

374 *To Marion Scott*   G.46.30.7

22 April 1919 (KT)   19 Barton St, Gloucester

Can you tell me anything about enclosed coin, ploughed up today, Wed?
My Dear Friend

This is just, and just the place would please you! An old gray-stone rambling array of buildings under a Roman camp near the site of a Roman villa where many things have been from time to time discovered. A place of thorn, oak, ash, elm, clear streams, a 500 feet-up place where one gets a sight of the Severn Sea, May Hill, and on clear days of the Welsh Hills, by looking out of a window merely or wandering out of a gate. Here I am set to learn farm business, to become sane and glad for life, with many books, Beethoven, Bach, Mozart, Tristan and the Magelone Lieder.[1] The last movement of the Sonata ought to finish quickly I should say. The Farmer is delightful enough; intensely interested in Borrow, Jacobs, Burns, Surtees, – of which authors we hold similar opinions, and not minding having to put up with a fool so he be willing to learn. My wages (in money) are to be 5/- a week and keep; but O what a full competence and more of beauty! Aren't I lucky? Well, time will show whether this will be worthwhile to me. Meanwhile, the good earth and winds, sun and stars must restore me to some semblance of the old bodily sick but spiritually sound me.

I am very glad to hear that the YMCA it was gave a big order – if any one was to want a lot – it means that some soldiers will see *Severn and Somme* would otherwise not see it.

Will you manage no holiday this Eastertime? Surely it will be possible to struggle out somewhere away from London?

What with College work, Christian Science Monitorising and Business Agenting, you should need one, O keen sword in frail scabbard! Dryhill Farm, Shurdington near Cheltenham would be, O just your mark!

Harvey was demobilised on Good Friday, much to his joy and is now at Home, where I saw him yesterday – Easter Monday, and a glorious one at that. The cuckoo has come. According to F.W.H., the Minsterworth term for the cuckoo's cry is that it 'hollers'. 'Have 'ee heard the cuckoo hollering'? (Do you remember the 'two fold shout'?) After writing which I stood up, pulled aside the blind, and saw Arcturus (is it?) and beneath him the long lights of Gloucester in the valley.

Tomorrow to follow the plough, do an hour's Fugue perhaps, and hammer at the Sonata on the rickety old piano here. Alas an unhelpful beast.

I left my Father in pain, hoping for his end, alas not yet certainly near, and though brave convinced that Death is the happy ending to be desired. May it come soon!

Emmie Hunt is very well indeed, having a small (ish) niece staying with her for a day or so and enjoying it.

Now I shall to bed, and to read for a time – shall it be *Don Quixote*? Why not? Or the *Canterbury Tales*? O galupshous choice! By the way there is one fine poem in Kipling's new book on Shakespeare.

With best wishes from your sincere friend

Ivor Gurney

[1] Brahms, op.33; fifteen Romances from Tieck's *Magelone* for voice and piano.

375 *To Marion Scott*   G.61.12-16

Late April 1919 (KT)   19 Barton St, Gloucester

Dear Friend

Yes, they will take lodgers here – Mrs Green prefers to call them paying guests, but what of that? The loveliest place almost that ever was, the widest sweep of Beauty before one. It is high enough up 500 feet and over, probably nearer 900 than 5.

(Friday)

And has the most gorgeous of sunsets at times, as tonight, when I hurried back, and wrote 'The Green Rift' which I had seen above Malvern. The whole Western horizon blazed and the valley darkled under it save where the rising smoke of Gloucester caught a glory. It was an evening to lift the heart.

Do you think College would take me back at half term? I think 6 weeks would be enough for the Mass? Do you think they would prefer this? After such things seen here, one ought to be able to write – the Stolidest of

Dutchmen in most baggy of trousers might feel stirred watching such a valley into something like rapture.

Please forgive this pencil, but the ink has given out, or is so intermixed with hair as to be useless or too detrimental to calm as to be better not used.

It was awfully good of you to take such trouble over my songs and Winthrop Rogers, and very good news that he will take 'Sleep'. As to the Minsterworth set. 'In Flanders' is surely perfect. The rest are all right, save 'Pipers Wood' which needs rewriting. (I don't care for it at all, save the last page.) Surely the other four will stand? What think you? (As candid as you like, Miss!)

He sounds very interesting indeed (Rogers) and well worth meeting. You seem to have enjoyed your time on the whole, which is a mercy at any rate. I am glad when my Business Agent gets some return for her unpaid kindness.

No, there is no chance of F.W.H. being in London as far as I know – he is too stuck at home, too happy there especially now the blossoms are coming on. He is contemplating a new book this Autumn, which will have some rattling good stuff therein. As to sales, *A Gloucestershire Lad* is now in the 5th Edition, a remarkable thing. He is becoming his jolly old self once more, and will no doubt grow completely into the F.W.H. of old cricket and haymaking days.

You know, O Business Agent, that all things as to arrangements are confided unto your most capable good will. You it is have the bother, and in this most difficult of tangles I shall leave you to wangle, and hope that you will enjoy yourself to some extent in the diplomatic wiles you seem delighted to exert. (Luckily for a good many. Not least, myself.)

Thank you for the Programme and the article on Mestrovic, both awfully interesting to me. And O yes! I would like the *Poetry Review* very much, and the *Times* also, which I never see. Mr Haines told me *War's Embers* was announced this week or last, so soon the critics will be red of fang, and happy. F.W.H. is to review it in the *Gloucester Journal*. I wonder whether S and J's would send him the advance copy he has asked for.

I am so grateful to you for your long criticism of my poems.

No, 'with Heaven's chief wonder of Night' does not annoy me at all. Heavens is a two syllable word there, that's all.

Sorry about the 'Epitaph', but I could not wangle out of the use of 'grace', twice – simply could *not* do it!

In 'In Town' I fancy 'drab' must take the place of 'witch', that's all.

Yes, the version of 'I love chrysanthemums' is correct.

Alas, you are right about 'Moor and Ocean'! I must try again, for there is stuff therein.

I don't like farm work much. The skilled work I am not given, the unskilled is drear, but O the beauty of the place, the beauty!

Yes, I am a lucky chap, but my place is College.

Your articles in the *C.S.M.* will be awaited eagerly. Can't you see this place first, O reader of Encyclopedias. Thank you so much for the details about

Roman coins, and I assure you Mr Green is as keen as myself to hear more about our particular find.

They will please you here I think. Mr Green especially, who is all himself – a great character. She? No, not very much. The children are nice though, and the dog, one horse, and a calf. Dryhill Farm is just the place for you, not so magical as Framilode, but O far stronger. One gets to it from Cheltenham or Gloucester. It is 1½ miles from famous Birdlip Hill, to climb which even the Romans crooked the road, and a gallant road it is, by Jeremy Taylor!

How is Sidney getting on? And what are his plans? Has Walford Davies gone to Wales yet? What is to happen to the Temple?

How are all your people? I hope this most beastly early Spring has not harmed Mr Scott at all. But it has been really a beast, and might damage a Tank.

Schubert

A spot of sapphire green glowed in the plain,
Brightened and deepened until almost I could
Have sworn 'twas Schubert made the wind forlorn,
His the thrush-spirit fluting in the far wood.

Goodness, could you have seen that day though! A wonder!! There is a passage in Carlyle ('The Everlasting Yea') which must have been written from such a height over such a plain!

With best wishes and many thanks to you

from your sincere friend
Ivor Gurney

376 To Marion Scott   G.61.4

9 May 1919 (P)   19 Barton St, Gloucester

My Dear Friend

Thank you so much. The gray is charming indeed, and there is nobody but will like the binding chosen by you. This is written at Emmy Hunt's place and she is regarding her presentation copy with the same admiration that burns inside myself.

Here is a surprise for you. I am proposing to come to College again, thinking it better to risk this term and (if necessary) work at farm work or some other thing in the summer. This seems to me to be common sense at any rate. No reply has yet come from Mr Aveling, but I propose to come up on Monday week. All I want then is some sort of grant for a good piano. Can that be got?

Herbert and Dorothy and myself went for a walk on Robinswood Hill yesterday. I started 'Kathleen' to him but he said that you had already played it over to him. The rate is about 120; the time signature possibly should be $\frac{2}{2}$ and the mark Molto Allegro – do you think?

Another letter soon, O Business Agent from you obliged faithful humble Servant to Command

Ivor Gurney

P.S. Lots of music inside, but lots of verse written out and awaiting transcript, only occasionally polish.

---

377 To Marion Scott   G.61.322

May 1919 (KT)   30 Clifton Hill, St John's Wood, London NW8

My Dear Friend

(*Please* excuse the smudge). Yes of course, I shall be delighted to come – and hope to see you looking very countrified and fresh of face after Lichfield. 'Cherry Orchard' sounds a good enough address.[1]

The rest of the letter contains very good news for me, but that we will talk over tomorrow, when I shall bring a host of sketches for your approval or otherwise. Likewise a knock-me-down, pick-me-up review from the *Citizen* of *War's Embers* which may amuse you.

I hope it is today, Wednesday, you have come back; London is looking very fresh and maidenly; very unlike the city of the Winter term!

with best wishes

from your sincere friend
Ivor Gurney

[1] The previous letter had been forwarded to Marion Scott at 23 Cherry Orchard, Lichfield.

---

378 To J.W.Haines   G.83.14.1-3

2 June 1919 (P)   30 Clifton Hill, St John's Wood, London N W 8

Dear J.W.H.

This is written from a place in Surrey, and to send a hope that you and the family are flourishing; to extract a letter from you (which is always worth while) and to ask whether you would mind sending me that precious red book crammed of immortal verse, which shall be returned with yet more pearls of fair-shaped wisdom inscribed therein.

Near this very ancient house where I am staying burrows the famous Mole, for Reigate is but a short way off and the Pilgrims Way, which I must go see before my departure tomorrow – a four mile tramp merely, but it would seem a jolly one. What tramps have you had lately, what books read, what good folk seen? Has that walk with Mr Green yet come off, if so where did it land you? What inns visited you?

London has defects enough, but at least it heightens the desire for and love of such things as the Crickley cliffs, the quarry there below Coopers Hill, the gaze down on Ashleworth tower curiously white in the friendly air ...

Cuckoos holler here all day in an annoying fashion, so that the cry of a bird grates one at last as it were of a foolish clock made by furriners in strange lands, afterwards to be dumped here to the wrath of all good Protectionists. In our own land they observe more circumspection, unless it is their parts are better written, with far more rests, and a recognizable cue to entries. Here is a Crickley Memory which crystallised yesterday.

> The flame so primrose pale
>   In sunset's glow
> Rosy and golden is
>   And hot-heart now.

> The sun has drawn with him
>   Light from the air
> Dusk breathes a lovely rest
>   After his glare.

> With tender hands stars bless
>   The tired earth, let
> A Beauty misty fall
>   Of star dew wet.

> But the farmer not perceives
>   His eyes ne'er raising
> From the black and perished bramble
>   Or the still blazing.

> As the stars he circles in
>   His path foremade
> One with his work on move
>   In the bramble shade.

There, Butcher is a tender lamb ready for your vile handling ....

But the *Dynasts* makes one callous to the fate of one's own outpourings. But a tiny glance gives one a sense of great power, quite Shakespearian in grasp and technique. I suppose everyone dislikes pretty much the same sort of thing therein, but O the country talk, the songs .... It's a huge thing. Wordsworth I would cheerfully give up – say, all but Shakespeare and Milton for this.

Now a last piece of business. Could you let me know for the benefit of my hosts, whether there are any farms of 100-200 acres to let in Glos: with not too large a house; the smaller the better indeed, for the purpose of making a living therefrom? This place is to be sold and they may have to clear out in September. The farmer's a great chap most noble to behold – by name Nicholson and able to trace his descent from Norse time. Mrs N: is the authoress. Please do them this service, will you?

Someone has given me £50!

True, no jest.... With best wishes to all.

Yours ever
I.B.G.

379 *To J.W.Haines*   G.83.12

Received 13 June 1919 (JWH)   30 Clifton Hill, St Johns Wood,
London N W 8

My Dear J.W.H.

Thank you so much for your racy letter, which shall receive a reply of some sort in due course. Meanwhile, news that Stainer and Bell have accepted 'Captain Stratton's Fancy' but want particulars. So, if you think it would be better to ask L.A. to forward a letter to Masefield would you of your charity send both to him?

Reward A Copy in due course if the gods are kind. I know you will be glad to help the Old Bold Mate. And, golly it ought to mean Rum for me. Hist! a word in thine ear – tuppence in the shilling, what say'st to that?

A gent named Johnston Douglas is singing the 'Penny Whistle' and 'Fiddler of Dooney' on Friday.[1]

Farewell

Yours ever
I.B.G.

P.S. Stainer and Bell will take, I think, Edward and the Twa Corbies.

[1] A song recital at the Wigmore Hall on 13 June included these two songs (the second wrongly titled 'The Piper of Dooney'), marked 'first performance' on the poster. The singer was Walter Johnstone-Douglas.

380 *To J.W.Haines*   G.83.13.1-2

22 June 1919 (P)

Dear J.W.H.

Thanks awfully for the exercise book, that argosy most precious.

This is tea time – talk-time, and you are to be companion. Your accounts of Tom Green's walk and of the Associated Poets was most interesting. I am sorry that office work is so worrying. Will cutting the Midhurst lawn help you at all? Mowing grass with a defective machine is calculated to make one forget all minor worries, I believe.

There's one thing you may be interested in. I found a shop today with 3 copies (leather bound) of E.T.'s *Song Book*, but 7/6 each. It's the one you want all right – 1907 is the date, and all's well. Anyway I thought it best to let you know. Kerr's copy is blue cloth – these are leather.

Just now work goes not well – a Piano Sonata has proved more difficult than is pleasant, but E.T.'s 'Today I think only with Scents' and Walt Whitman's 'Reconciliation' are going well.

We are having no end of bust ups at this term end with the Prince of Wales and similar fine gentry to be admitted free of charge so be they put on clean collars and blow their noses properly.

'In Flanders' and 'By a Bierside' are to be done – alas in the first version! I must write to F.W.H. on the matter.

The *Englishwoman* has written offering a guinea a time for suitable things. Why don't you try them with summat? A guinea is a guinea and publication does not displease; why not? Cannot you squeeze (as Jack the G.K. squoze his cheese) somewhat from your late walks? Think of 252 pennies well and truly earned.

E.T. grows more dear to me as the days pass. Three presentation copies have I bought, (of the 1st book in each case for still it is that is so much better in my eyes.)

I wonder if you had such a mighty thunder clap as London heard today? Like some mighty 18 pounder gun blaring defiance most sudden to all fine weather.

There is some new verse but that must be polished before passing under your august eyes.

Yours ever
I.B.G.

---

381 *To Marion Scott*   G.61.157

August 1919 (KT)

[*The first page of the letter, G.61.156, is missing or misplaced.*]

stationariness. That said – have your fling, with kindness but firmness.

I hope you are feeling far less Secretary-like than you were; less post-receptionish of nerves. Who deserves a rest if not you? Who have acted as helmsman, fender, stoker, steward, etc (and a many) to the Union.

This must be the shortest of letters, I fear, for in an hour or so Mr JWH and I are off to Abergavenny, Pandy, Crickhowell, Pontrilas or some such show, where my jealousy must not lead me to underrating anything that may come to my eyes.

'Hesperus' should have

> 'Sheep to be folded in twilight, –
> Children for mothers to fondle.'
> Me too will bring to the dearest,
> Tenderest breast in all Lemnos'.

To High Wycombe in first September. Yes, Sidney did come, and we got Portway, Cranham, Birdlip, Crickley and Wellington St out of the day. (I thought you had heard all this.) A long letter to-next-week. Best wishes to Captain Cook, the Scott Family, Caedmon and Hilda. A very interesting crowd altogether. I do hope Mr Scott will have proper good fortune with health.

with best wishes

from your sincere friend
Ivor Gurney

P.S. O yes and there's the essay too. Not well done, but it may pass.

---

382 To Marion Scott   Hurd Transcript

September 1919 (KT)   19 Barton Street, Gloucester

Only the songs are sent. The rest next time.
My Dear Friend

I am so glad to hear from Mrs.Taylor that Mr.Scott is far better, and that you are so much pleased with Whitby itself. Audrey's choice must be approved in the future I suppose since this present one has turned out so well. I am looking forward to a letter from you, since (surely?) it is your turn. But as Mrs.Taylor has told me you have been seeking my address, which has been Leigh and Clifton Hill; now is home once again.

What there is to tell is soon told. I saw Sidney looking worn, dark under the eyes, and thinner than his wont; yet plucky as ever; His old spirit shining out of great eyes. It was a ten minutes 'see', not longer, and just enough to make him tired.

There's one bit of news. John Masefield sent the most delightful of letters about my work, which you shall see when Mrs Chapman returns it as she will in a day or two. (I knew it would give her great pleasure to have a sight of that.)

Well, Leigh was very jolly, delightful rooms and garden, very kind people, a piano, books enough. So that somehow the Slow Movement has got finished, and very particularly I would ask that you will compare the two and say which you like best; criticise any detail of writing and let me have it hot where needs be. (All this *by the Brahms standard*.) There are also two songs (Sappho) and 3 piano Preludes. One finished. One sketched, and a third in writing.

One or two new poems are also done, but those you shall have later. Could you have seen Hempstead this afternoon. Cleeve, Crickley, Cranham, and the Cathedral standing out blue gray in the distance, sentinel to Malvern! A clear, not far-too-beautiful afternoon, but one that let beauty through, if not displayed it. But O that night when after going to see Emmie at Cleeve I walked back by Leckhampton, Shurdington, Brockworth – just missing Crickley. Meteors flashed like sudden inspirations of song down the sky. The air was too still to set firs or beeches sighing, but the grass swished; twigs crackled beneath me, and the occasional stir of wild creatures in the undergrowth set off the peace – O the depth of it. Crickley is a pure joy. (That came another night.) It was shameful to leave it, but after making up my mind to do 20 miles, I was foolishly drawn on. Schumann would have stayed there under those royal cliffs in that flood of light, would have gathered the influence of the fire into him, later have given it out.

Well .... do you think it advisable to send the Sappho Songs to Dawson, Freear, or Dorothea Webb, or some such singer? Are they new and good? (Hesperus I know is.) By your advice I shall stay in this. 'The Bonny Earl of Murray' should certainly go. 'Pipers Wood' has got rewritten today.

Have you read *What the Public Wants* by Arnold Bennett? It is a most extraordinarily good play – to me, that is. *The Pretty Lady* is pretty bad.[1]

Farewell and best wishes to everybody for health
   and sun brownness from your sincere friend

Ivor Gurney.

[1] The play is from 1909; the latter, a novel, is from 1918.

---

383 *To Marion Scott*   G.61.148,150-151

September 1919 (S)   51 Queens Road, High Wycombe, Bucks

My Dear Friend

In this lucid interval between conducting Leonora no 3 and Composition, I place this letter, hoping to send with it a song and a Piano Prelude a la Scriabine.

Thank you so much for your meaty and juicy letter, soothing to my vanity. I am so glad you like the Slow Movement better than in its first form – of course it is far cleverer, But I wanted more than that.

At present the Symphony Slow Movement attracts attention, being sketched up to the Return, and as I think in its final form.

There are other Preludes to come.

Well, Whitby pleased you I know but so does Wycombe myself, where I am to live, move, have or lack being – which last is supported at present by a quite alarming appetite, which may be explained by three days digging of afternoons. An appetite for cakes is an expensive thing however, and best counteracted by the liveliest tasting and seeming apples got from the farm house where the work lies – in a valley, under a cornfield and a hanging wood. It is a delectable land all this, with changing soils in the valley and a happy air of peace over all. I am going out to see these all once again – with two sketch-books and my little Bible-looking Beethoven.

Your mouth must be watering however at all this – in spite of the Gardens and screen of trees before your windows.

My certes, but if one may not walk a four miles or so in this land, afterwards to drink friendly in an inn, then where?

An awful pity it was – after looking forward to seeing so many good men again, buying the ticket, rehearsing with Harvey and so forth (for the 2/5 Dinner), they put on me a practice here, and snuffed all out, for it did not seem sage to try getting out of my first. But it was distinctly unpleasant.

Harvey has finished his book, and rests on his poetical oars I believe, but shall hear soon. The *Spectator Athenaeum*, and *Harpers* have returned my things. The *New Witness* (probably by carelessness) sent back two. Quel dommage! as Caudle of the 2/5 used to say when met by such catastrophic incidents as an order for mess tin inspection, a 9.2 shell or plunge into mud-hole.

Have you read Motley's *Dutch Republic*? I have been dipping into the second (middle) volume, and have been brought to think that had Germany attempted to invade Holland, she would have had more than an ordinary strenuous time. What courage! what set and steely resolution!

Stevenson's *Letters* please me as much as ever. Are they not the most friendly of things? His best work surely?

O, about Ireland's Sonata.[1] It seems to me (but judging warily as of a difficult thing) that the thought has been deliberately divorced from naturalness in many places. There is sincerity occasionally, not very striking or strong – an attempt at 'out-doery'. I admire it though – wish I had such an harmonic range, but ...

Gatty[2] is of little use.

With best wishes to all, especially to yourself and Mr Scott, who I hope has pretty well found his feet.

from your sincere friend
Ivor Gurney

---

[1] Probably the violin Sonata in A minor.
[2] Nicholas Comyn Gatty (1874-?), composer and music critic.

Received 10 September 1919 (JWH)   51 Queens Road,
High Wycombe, Bucks

My Dear J.W.H.

Here's Masefield's letter to look at – a sight for sore eyes, a discovery of generosity most good to look on.

There's no one to play to worth the playing to – no one to stay with till twelve oclock at night, imbibing and discoursing sweet music, of books and – generally – discoursing sweetly. Let not Mrs Haines forget the Brahms Sonatas; those very worthy things; the G major first, that has three good movements. But the A major is rather the easiest.

Tragic to miss the 2/5th dinner, where so many fine people were, so many seen under difficulty and bearing that well – of mud, of vermin, danger, routine annoyance – So on, so forth ad infinitum.

This is a very delectable land, and with any sort of luck I do not intend to leave it. If there be foolish folk intending to study that difficult but fascinating Siren of Music at close quarters, such I intend to trap and having enticed to doom, suck dry. My little parlour is not yet inhabited but will be in a day or two.

Masefield's 'Here the Legion Halted' has just got set, in some fashion or other – perhaps not too badly. Words, I want words! Where's another 'Kathleen ni Houlihan'.

Meanwhile the office boy of *Harper's Magazine* has imitated the example of him of the *Spectator* and slung them back at me. My pet malediction on the whole!

Stevenson's Letters were the best refuge from life, and in that gossip, courage friendliness, a certain forgiving tolerance came in on me.

My slippers have just received the honour of a report from my mother, who found them (probably) where she had put them – a most safe hiding place as a rule. This afternoon I go to a farm voluntarily for a couple of hours or so, under the lee of a wood in a small valley – for an unmusical brain the best restorative.

With best wishes to yourself, Mrs H and Robin

           From yours ever
           I.B.G.

September 1919 (KT)   St Michaels, Castle Hill,
                                                                High Wycombe, Bucks

So sorry you don't altogether like the essay-thing.[1]
My Dear Friend
    This first part is written in an interval of composition without your letter at
hand – for my own sake, to rest myself, so the real answer must come later in
this epistle.
    You were to leave on the sixth, were you not? But to an unknown
destination, or uncertain, so that I suppose it is not London you are wondering
at this translucent morning. Already the first slants of coloured leaves drift to
the ground – not yet royal of hue; the first valourous skirmishes of that full
host shall come before very long, to our never-staled amaze. Spring takes one
by throat and heart (almost) with Beauty on her great days, but Autumn
surges us up and down as on a sea of passion and sometimes we are not anyway
our own.
    And hereafter came more composition – a huge feed in three reels, so to
speak: and then after an interview with a farmer as to working it off (abortive;
shall go tomorrow, to pick up wheat) walked through lovely avenues of green
and gold in Penn Woods. Saw in the distance my favourite earth view of
curving ploughland and rounded woods (an F major Brahms effect), then after
half a pint of beer once more here to finish your letter, and send you the Slow
Movement long promised, also one more, and rather striking Piano Prelude
(so it seems to me.)
    I liked your description of the evening of soft rain and even darkness
wherein you sent my packet off; a most tender word-picture in which a
human love has managed to interpenetrate that of Nature. (I have been reading
Stevenson again and his letters, that are the best of him.)
    Your praise of the Sappho songs is sweet to me. As RLS says 'It is a horrid
thing for a fond architect to find his monuments received in silence'. My own
opinion of 'Love shakes my soul' is – that it is a good song but with a rather
over-elaborated accompaniment.[2] Is this not the case.?

[page of letter missing or mislaid]

at one in the wind.
    Altogether I am lucky to be here – better so than at £150 in London surely,
unless there were conducting and so forth.
    Have you read Walt Whitman's *Specimen Days*? Such a book! The best
diary I have ever come across.
    The first fifty pages of Walpole's *Secret City* – all I could read – I skipped
nothing a record. Stevenson's *Letters* taste as good as ever.
    Arnold Bennett's play *What the Public Want* is first rate.
    Tomorrow the rejected *Spectator* things go to the *Westminster*.

Thank you so much for copying Katharine Tynan's review out. Rather patronising, was it not? But there, Masefield's letter, which you have yet to see, has put a great price on my stuff – but not for editors. Ah, if only J.M. ran a paper!

You have said nothing about violin pieces? Has your courage failed, in the multiplicity of articles? J.W.H. and F.W.H. were greatly pleased with the *C.S.M.* article. Best wishes

from your sincere friend
Ivor Gurney

¹ See letter 381 above.
² See G.28.7.6,8 and 9.

386 *To Marion Scott*   G.61.154

September/October 1919 (KT)   51 Queens Rd, High Wycombe, Bucks

My Dear Friend

Here's the copy of 'By a Bierside' returned from Miss Webb. One or two other things also. I am glad there is a copy ready for sending at once, and a pretty clean copy at that.

Miss Foster should be pleased, I think; her voice has purple in it, as has this song, and the two should combine together quite well.

Best wishes to all, and especially to yourself and Audrey of the Ailing Wrist.

From your sincere friend
Ivor Gurney

1st copy of E.T.'s thing. Has been revised.

387 *To J.W.Haines*   G.83.16.1-3

23 September 1919 (P)   51 Queens Road, High Wycombe, Bucks

My Dear Haines

It was nice to see the face of that Beethoven book again, and the look of your handwriting, with which one is certain of getting some clear and most suggestive picture of Gloucestershire trampings.

I hope the Silverdale affair went off all right – or is it tomorrow? and Gordon Bottomley in good talking vein – John W.Haines, the well-known man of Letters, is not a very difficult travelling companion, nor the most taciturn. By Jingo, I wish you could be here this afternoon – with such a wind and such a clear-water sunlight.

This is continued in the Chapmans' house, where Winnie Chapman that delicate but cheery soul is propped up with cushions and yarning away like a gramaphone. [sic]

Kerr gave me an old Gazetteer the which I am anxiously expecting, to follow your various tours with interest and brush up odd knowledge of all sorts of places – a jolly book from which I got the information that the subject of that engraving of Gloucester you now have is the Pool of Gloucester. Perhaps even then there was a lock or at least a passageway where the lock now is. The book does not mention that wonderful anchor, whose size and all-sort majesty draws the eye so strongly and long.

By the way do you know Forster's *Goldsmith*?[1] A pleasant, chatty enough book though having much of Boswell interpolated – which would make anything interesting.

Alack and well-a-day, Well known Literary Man, do you know every single lousy editor has returned every single unfortunate one of my priceless productions. To say that comment is needless is weak – to say that comment is useless (save of the most violent) is just, but unhelpful. Perhaps Masefield will help or give advice.

I hope Robin is all right now, and not troubling his anxious parents with any untoward symptoms. All that gaiety and lightness of heart and body is not likely long to be dimmed.

Please keep Mrs Haines up to scratch about the G major Brahms Sonata – too good a thing to be missed by any violinist at all – a most comfortable homely firelit sort of thing.

Did you see the unravelling of Miss Sitwell's poem in this week's *Westminster*? It is in some ways light bringing, but the explanation as to why the thing was done at all does not show.

Have you had from Miss Scott the other articles of the Gloucestershire Group series? All interesting I think, and if she does not send them you shall have mine.

My slow Movement racks me, uselessly as I think - but two more Preludes and a couple of Songs have appeared. Masefield's 'Halt of the Legion' and 'Over the Downs' from *Lollington Downs* [sic].[2] A Sappho Song wants copying too.

Lots of stuff in me apparently, but the devil's own job to get it out, it is.

The Spirit of the Age I found very interesting in parts; rather heavy to read all through, but excellent as to nubbly bits. Coleridge I remember to have thought best. The chap can write though, bless his heart. What raciness and clear lines he has! It is not to be wondered at that Stevenson valued him so highly and imitated him so much.

Best wishes and all that to yourself and the Family. May they dig about the garden, get hot, grubby, happy for time long enough. Sorry I am not to be with you to play tonight.

Yours ever
I.B.G.

[1] *The Life and Adventures of Oliver Goldsmith* (1848).
[2] *Lollingdon Downs* (1917).

388 To Marion Scott   G.61.143

September/October 1919 (KT)   51 Queens Rd, High Wycombe, Bucks

My Dear Friend

Here is the Masefield Song, which seems to me to have lilt and atmosphere enough for most things.[1]

Perhaps this might do for Miss Mason, though it is thought as a Baritone Song. Anyway I thought best to let you have a look at it, and to get your opinion first.

As for the train-strike and getting to College and so forth, I am just going up to the Station to enquire about Trains and so forth. I *must* hear Music, must, must. Nothing good save the scrap of the Sea Symphony has come my way for months, and the Proms are all too tempting.

Best wishes to you in everything, musical and literary; and to Audrey and her wrist.

from your sincere friend
Ivor Gurney

P.S. And yes. perhaps there might be one pupil now.

[1] 'On the downs' which is dated September 1919 in G.33.8.7.; and see the comment in the next letter.

389 To Marion Scott   G.46.30.5

10 October 1919 (P)   51 Queens Rd, High Wycombe, Bucks

My Dear Friend

I called this afternoon, as doubtless you will have heard, and to find you out. There was nothing very especial to tell or ask.

Goldie recommends Miss Milne or Miss Johnson as 'cellist, but to neither of these have I made any overtures.

Also, I had just been to see Mr Shanks and found Hodgson there as well as Shanks himself. About half an hour only I stayed, then left to see McKerrow, whom I found you had just seen. Isn't the Birmingham critique a beauty? Still the flower of all is the Aberdonian one ....[1]

Shanks told me that Squire thought me the best of the young men below the horizon, which led to a natural question as to why he had rejected so much lately.

I hope Audrey is on the upgrade once more, and mending in all ways – which from the 'feel' of her is thoroughly to be expected.

Last night's Promenade was chiefly interesting on account of Glazounoff's 6th Symphony which is very clear and fine stuff, I think, but Stravinsky's 'Fireworks' is awfully good in its way, too, it seemed to me. But a long and dull Rubinstein Concerto sent me outside to smoke and walk.

The peculiar hue of the chemist bottle seems to have inspired the genius that coloured Queen's Hall – a wonderful conception entirely...

But it is almost 2 o'clock and to think further of that will bring dreams not of the best.

with best wishes

from your sincere friend
Ivor Gurney

P.S. Your letter and the account just arrived. Thank you so much. I am very glad you like the new Song, which seems to me to have downland in it.

Have got up fearfully late after a late night, and must now hurl myself into Scriabine's F♯ minor Sonata which I have just bought – hope to play it you later.

Thanks and best wishes

from Ivor Gurney.

London was jewel-like yesterday, and one scene in Marylebone I shall not soon forget.

[1] The *Birmingham Post* of 8 July wrote that he had 'no sense of the witchery of words' and advised him to study Shakespeare. The *Aberdeen Daily Journal* of 16 June 1919 made the ludicrous assumption that his poem about a man from Aberdeen – 'Aberdonian' – meant that 'the author apparently voyaged in the S.S.Aberdonian'.

---

390 To Marion Scott   G.61.155

17 October 1919 (S)   51 Queens Rd, High Wycombe, Bucks

My Dear Friend

No, it is nothing at all serious; simply nerves and an inability to think or write at all clearly. The concert would have been rather an infliction to say the least. Believe it, it was better I did not come. Please forgive this upsetting of your plans – you have right to be annoyed, but really and truly I did well not to come. To miss the Choral Symphony[1] is to be done out of hearing the greatest of things.

Please don't mind very much.
   with many regrets and thanks

from your sincere friend
Ivor Gurney

¹ Beethoven's Ninth.

391 To Marion Scott   G.46.30.3

31 October 1919 (P)   51 Queens Rd, High Wycombe, Bucks

My Dear Friend
   Thank you so much for your trouble-of-arrangement and press cuttings.
   The train I must catch on Wednesday is the 5.38 Marylebone, but at a great
pinch, 6.25 Paddington might be made to do.
   I am to see Mrs Shanks the day before and will bring such songs as she can
spare.
   No, I am afraid the Scriabine F# minor Sonata will not be ready in time.
Anyhow it is not anyway up to the Preludes, it is certain to me.
   Thank you again.
   I am glad the *Gondoliers* did Audrey good and hope that her arm will all
ways fit quite soon.
   with best wishes

from your sincere Friend
Ivor Gurney

392 To Marion Scott   G.46.30.4

8 November 1919 (P)   In the Oxford Train¹

My Dear Friend
   Thank you so much for the letter and the part song, which shall be copied
out in due course.
   And thank you for your good wishes which I hope will be fulfilled this gray
November day – mist hanging lightly over the brown earth and an air of
melancholy and latter-endedness coming over all earth. Thank you, the boil-
thing has pretty well disappeared, but somehow or other I cannot work, and
feel empty-heavy-headed. Too much eat, too little walk, I fear – am certain.
   Well, here goes for Masefield, Captain Stratton, Reynard the Fox and all.
You shall hear fully enough about the visit later.
   If Pembroke might but be got in – Dr Johnson's place, I should be glad but
am not sure about necessary times. Have to meet Harvey at 12, at the
Roebuck from which we go in half an hour – so there will be time for a talk

before the jolts and jerks start, of the Roebuck coach, a famous thing I believe that is to take us Boar's Hill-wards.

Miss Webb is singing 'Twilight Song'[2] at her concert, and in a remarkably good programme. You would enjoy her rapt and beautiful singing. I will write and ask her to send you a ticket as Xtian Monitorian.

Well here's Oxford, learning, port wine, gowns, grey stone, talk, ... with best wishes from

your sincere friend
Ivor Gurney

[1] Harvey and Gurney were invited by a letter of 24 October to visit Masefield on this Saturday (Reproduced in *Stars*, p.104).
[2] Gurney's setting of a poem by Francis Ledwidge; also called 'Desire in Spring'. See G.33.4.1 and 2. Published in Vol 5 of Gurney's songs.

393 *To J.W.Haines*   G.82.17.1-2

Received 11 November 1919 (JWH)   51 Queens Road,
High Wycombe, Bucks

My Dear Haines

Thank you so much for your Lakeland letter, which was most interesting to a lover of the *Prelude* like myself. You were extremely fortunate in your month which was the best October since about 1907 (I think) when first I got to know the Hunts, and went up Portway with them – a happy time.

(This is a break away from an attempt at setting Housman's 'Far in a Western Brookland', which goes with difficulty.)

The *Prelude* is really and truly one of my favourite things, and to walk myself tired with such a companion as yourself would be just my desire. Someday perhaps .... Will this journey set you off on writing I wonder? Or on the rereading of the Lake Gentlemen merely – Shall we have papers on De Quincey, and fire-new, subtle-sensitive appreciations of the Great W.W. himself?

Well, no more further than a passing glance of envy will I bestow on your excursion, and a hope that the family will keep the extra life there given some considerable time.

Not much is there to tell you of doings here, – almost abortive work in a lovely land – walks to Penn, Totteridge, Winchbottom, Marlow, Beaconsfield.

But I have seen Shanks in London 3 or 4 times, Monro, Turner at his house. And one evening the Shanks, Monro and myself went to hear Steuart Wilson sing the Wenlock Edge Cycle of Vaughan Williams – a fine strong piece of work.

On Saturday as you will hear from F.W.H. we visited Masefield in his proper haunt at Boar's Hill, where are Graves, Nichols and Bridges also. He was extremely nice, a boyish, quiet person with a manner friendly enough, and easy to get on with.

Mrs Masefield, the daughter and boy I did not care much for, but there was a Ma'mselle who was quite interesting – a Parisian before whom my French fell to dust.

Neither F.W.H. nor myself thought Masefield cared much for 'By a Bierside', but the 'old Bold Mate', and 'The Halt of the Legion' and 'Upon the Downs' pleased him. 'A Londonderry air', the first movement of the Italian Concerto,[1] the Slow movement, Minuet and Trio of the Beethoven D major Sonata, 'Billy Taylor' and 'The Coasts of High Barbary' gave considerable satisfaction, I think. He was putting up a climbing rope for his boy when we arrived in a garden lined with bracken.

Boar's Hill is not pretty as *we* know prettiness but it isn't bad – 4 miles south of Oxford and (so they say) within a few hundred yards of a great view, which we did not see. Once again Masefield expressed admiration of my last book – 'It was jolly good', and I fancy wants me to go to Oxford on a grant. Well, it was worth while making the visit, and very nice to see Harvey again. A walking tour with the both of you would relieve me from the utter and absolute despair I am in over my work. 'Fraid it can't be however, but it's nice to think about.

Well, that's all. Winthrop Rogers is, I think, likely to take the Elizabethan Songs – which another job, – have to be rewritten.

Write again soon please

Yours ever
I.B.G.

Best wishes to Mrs Haines (who I feel sure has *not* got the Brahms Sonata) and Robin.

[1] By Bach.

---

23 December 1919 (P)   51 Queens Road, High Wycombe, Bucks

My Dear J.W.H.

Prithee help me in distress!

Fox Strangways has accepted 'Kathleen ni Houlihan' for his most important Quarterly Magazine – *Art and Letters*.[1] But no word has come from Yeats about permission. Can you help in this situation? Stir up Abercrombie to prod Yeats, or otherwise assist in this difficulty?

It is your Yeats I have, and *Lollingdon Downs* which shall be returned on my coming to Gloucester on Monday – today week; with the pleasure of seeing you and F.W.H. to brighten the days. Best Christmas wishes to you, Mrs Haines and Robin! May you have the jolliest of times, and all your happy anticipations turn out justified.

Wish I were to be there to share the general thanksgiving!

With best wishes

From yours ever
I.B.G.

---

[1] Arthur Henry Fox Strangways (1859-1948), founder and first editor of *Music and Letters*.

395 To J.W.Haines   G.83.19.1-4

Received 9 February 1920 (JWH)   51 Queens Road, High Wycombe,
Bucks

'Old Bold Mate' still keelhauled!

My Dear Haines

Why doesn't something fairy-godmother like and aeroplanic land me somewhere Newnham way, instead of leaving me journeying disconsolate and grumbling towards London and College and music, that one learns to hate, as a business? One long tramp with you to quarrel with would do more good than 40 Symphonies. Quarrel, that is, after the skilful fashion of today's *Daily News* reviewer on Doughty today.

Is there some news of Gloucester worth the sending? Then prithee, worthy scrivener, indite and send.

Is the garden hard of digging? Then send brotherly complaints to one who has spent a morning among the flints and parsnips.

Are there new books to deracinate? Which be they, and in what consist their shortcomings?

Perhaps before this Kerr will have reached you, and told once more of the Vicar in *Pompey*, and of new things in the National. *Pompey* is good – splendid stuff, though to me it seems as though one should play it as *Puck of Pook's Hill* reads. 'By a Bierside' comes off very poorly, I think, being given out by four melancholy bearers of uncertain self-control.[1]

Rumours reach me that F.W.H. had got his £250 a year job on Pensions. Is this true? Or mirage?

Herbert Howells has a nice enough compliment from E.Newman in this morning's *Observer* about his *Procession*. The phrase is 'a brilliant piece of writing', which is unusually polite for E.N.

Did you see the very witty adverse review of Doughty's latest book in the *Daily News*? Wonder what you will think of the book. The reviewing of the *D.N.* is the best (I think) of any morning paper now. When is the E.T. book coming out? Pitiable and shameful both it is that so few folk know even his name, that will be (is, I should say) one of the chief glories of our letters – though a minor one.

My stunt is a Quartett at present which goes hard and creaks badly. Out of Gloucester, away from you-all what am I? Find me a nice active short time job, wilt?

Has Mrs Haines got the Brahms Sonatas yet? Particularly the G major?

I heard Sammons[2] and Murdoch play the Dohnyanyi, Beethoven G major, Ireland and Debussy Sonatas the other day. Remarkable playing, it was, but only the G major first movement, and parts of the Ireland stirred me.

My Housman cycle is to be done at a party at the Scotts in March. Rupert Brooke's friend Steuart Wilson as singer, the Philharmonic Quartett and myself as background (*Not* accompanists, do you note?)[3]

Awful hard lines on Tom Green isn't it? Such a colossus, and so laughing with his strength.

With best wishes to all

From yours ever
I.B.G.

[1] The words for Gurney's so.1g come from Masefield's *The Tragedy of Pompey the Great*; it was performed for a short run at the end of January at the St Martins with Sir Frank Benson as Pompey.
[2] Albert Edward Sammons (1886-1957), violinist and William Murdoch (1888-1942), pianist.
[3] A 'Gloucestershire Evening' was announced for Friday 19 March 1920 at the Scotts'. Those taking part were J.Steuart Wilson, F.W.Harvey, G.Thalben Ball, Herbert Howells and Ivor Gurney.

396 To J.W.Haines G.83.20.1-2

31 March 1920 (P) 51 Queens Road, High Wycombe, Bucks

I like Locke Ellis better now. Good man!
My Dear J.W.H.

Greetings to all, and an account of two pilgrimages. The first to an inn, the something Arms where I met a man (farmer or some such man) who knew Rupert Brooke, Masefield and Steuart Wilson. J.M. had given him the *Widow in the Bye-Street*,[1] which (timorously) he judged 'Rather low from a sentimental point of view, don't you think'. He put me on the track of 'The Pink and Lily' – Brooke's Inn,[2] where yesterday I went, saw the book, (wrote in it – incidentally) twice signed by R.B. – whom they liked extremely. The place is mean from outside, better within, and in lovely, lovely country – equal of its kind to our own. He was a nice old boy – and she is a nice old girl – those two innkeepers, and the iron plate at the back of the fire had come from

John Hampden's house. Couldn't you come and walk? Hampden is lovely, Hughenden, Bledlow, Radnage – all good enough. As good as our own of its kind – this country.

Chappells have (verbally) offered me £5 instead of the royalty on 1st 300 copies they proposed to rook me of. Why? May I not smile a flattered smile?

Read the *Woodlanders* – a poorish book by a good author. Damn his fashnable folk!

Best wishes to Mrs Haines, Robin and Uncle Com Tobley himself.

Yours
I.B.G.

Have signed agreement about Elizabethans.

¹ Published 1912.
² Near Princes Risborough.

---

397 *To Marion Scott*   Hurd Transcript

13 May 1920¹   Cold Slad, Dryhill, Witcombe, Glos

It requires a little explanation, does it not? Well, in one of my fits of not being able to stand it any longer, I wrote a letter to the chief churchwarden at Wycombe, arranged for the service to be taken, and came here – to find out what might be found out. An old Cotswold stone house with one pretty good upper room, but draughty. There are holes in the floor – to be dodged. There are two square places in the roof which will need stopping. The garden was long ago a ruin, the stream dried up, and weeds grew in it; no one came save the curious; and now under the shadow of the great rise of Crickley – here am I. I am a bit afraid, but hope to earn a little somehow, enough to carry on. If not, there are the picture palaces, which I carefully looked up in the *Era*, and Captain Browcher's promise to take me to sea.

¹ This is the date on the transcript, but I suspect it may well be 1919.

---

398 *To J.W.Haines*   G.83.21.1-2

10 October 1920 (P)   74 Longridge Rd, Earls Court, S.W.

Dear J.W.H.

Best wishes and news.

Winthrop Rogers is not only willing to back my songs pretty hard – to take many more, but he has sold out the first edition of some of the Elizas – already! Isn't this good luck? He also advanced me £20 when it was very badly needed. The most engaging publisher that ever was.

Last night I met Blunden at Edward Shanks, and tonight have been somewhere with J.S.Squire [*sic*]. Blunden is quite a boy; one might have known him in the Gloucesters. A person of enormous energy and pluck I should say. No telling what will come there. He is very full of a great number of Clare poems up till now unpublished.

By the way, I have told both him and Shanks about your diaries and especially about Edward Thomas, so stand by to receive boarders.

Best wishes to Mrs Haines and Robin. Since you were fond of Spider, I am sorry he has been so untowardly done with life.

I say, I do like the glimpse just had of *Fairies and Fusiliers*.[1] It is such jolly, fresh, talented stuff. *Sartor* seems to me to be greater than ever. Sidgwick and Jackson are bringing out another anthology called *The Book of the Daffodill*. Not bad in spite of the title.

With best wishes, and happy hopes.

What about the poems? When do they appear?

I hope Cotswold is looking itself now. October shows great things there!

Yours
I.B.G.

[1] By Robert Graves (1917).

---

399 To J.W.Haines   G.83.22

October 1920 (JWH)   74 Longridge Rd, Earls Court, S.W.

Dear J.W.H.

Would you mind sending the red exercise book to the *Athenaeum* – to Blunden who wants to look at them. It shall be returned.

I am glad to say Winthrop Rogers has chosen 'Kathleen' 'Mayo' 'Penny Whistle' 'Today I think' 'Brittle Bones' and 'Fiddler of Dooney' for the next selection.[1]

Blunden is a very nice chap, and a devil for work. He is busy on a new volume of Clare, of whose poems a thousand or so more have been discovered.

I fancy the new *Chapbook* will soon be out. Harold Monro was very keen about having things put right anyhow.

By the way I have bought a gazetter of Glostershire thicker than, but about the same form as a Chapbook – 1710 or thereabouts by judgement. Is it rare or valuable? Half a crown I paid. Very interesting.

Best wishes to Mrs Haines and Robin and of course to yourself

from
Ivor Gurney

Please give any details about the Gazetter though. If it were rare I would see it went to the right people. There's a second hand old Rudge also there. Would you like it. (2/6 I think)[2]

[1] 'Cathleen ni Houlihan' was published in 1938, 'The County Mayo' in 1921, 'Penny Whistle' and 'Today I think' (i.e. 'Scents') in *Lights Out* in 1926, and 'The Fiddler of Dooney' in 1959. I am not aware of the publication of the setting of Graves' poem 'Brittle Bones' though there are versions at G.31.5.2-3.
[2] Rudge is a motorcycle, though half a crown sounds rather cheap.

---

400 To Peter Harvey   G.74.77

October 1920 (KT)   74 Longridge Rd, Earls Court, S.W.

Dear Peter Harvey,
  Here's a whole host of letters from different people – Gervase Elwes, Steuart Wilson, Wilfred Gibson, (with whom I have to dine)[1] Armstrong Gibbs, one of the best of our younger men, Harold Monro, Winthrop Rogers, prince of publishers and so forth.
  I hope the time with the Haines' was as jolly as might be, and often it is. I should like to be back there myself.
  Yes, at least two of the Elizabethans are sold out and perhaps the others also by this time. W.R. is to publish 6 or 7 others of the best including 'Cathleen'. – So you see the tide sets.
  I hope you have seen Cranham this October – pity to miss it now of all months.
  with best wishes
    I remain

                                                    Yours very sincerely
                                                       Ivor Gurney

[1] W.W.Gibson's invitation is dated 20 October 1920; G.74.39.

---

401 To Edith Harvey   G.74.75

October 1920 (KT)   74 Longridge Rd, Earls Court, S.W.

My Dear Miss Harvey,
  Here are two autographs you might like. J.C.Squires and Scott Moncrieff, the author of the magnificent translation of *Roland* which is iron and ringing iron at that. O yes, and a third you will value – Blunden's which must be rare.

Hope you are having a pretty good time.
Best wishes

yours very sincerely
Ivor Gurney

My songs are selling very well.
A fourth – Gervase Elwes.

6 November 1920 (P)   74 Longridge Rd, Earls Court, S.W.

My Dear J.W.H.

Many thanks for your interesting-as-usual letter, any scrap from you is always welcome.

The Government grant is through – £120 a year dating from Sept:25. The 'Elizas' are clean out. W.R. has accepted 'Cathleen' 'Brittle Bones' 'Fiddler of Dooney' 'Today I think' 'County Mayo' and 'Bonnie Earl of Murray'.[1] Curwen is the next man to approach.

O but London wearies one after the hills and meadows! What is Putney Heath but a turf enclosure? One expects pavements everywhere, and notices ....

Alas, Ledwidge's song is to be called 'Desire in Spring', not 'Twilight Song'.[2]

I had lunch with W.W.Gibson a short time back, and Blunden came here for a couple of hours. Shanks is as nice as ever, but sickish.

Thanks so much about that M.S. book. Work goes badly. The songs come all right, but the Piano Sonata and 'Elegy' for Orchestra; No, there is a hard and futile grind there.

Winthrop Rogers is an awfully nice chap, one of the best, and has met interesting enough people in his time. A New Englander of the best, and kind as might be.

Last night a String Quartett was there with one of the d'Aranyi's leading, a wonderful player. Haydn and Mozart – O yes and Schubert's A minor Quartett also.

Herbert looks well after a bad time of it. Armstrong Gibbs is not now at College and appears only sporadically. His song the 'Bells' is a masterpiece (a W.de la M setting.)

O, W.R. has accepted the 'Preludes', bless his heart.

Best wishes to Mrs Haines and (if there is one) the follower of Spider.

I should like to see you if you come to town.

'Ludlow and Teme', Steuart Wilson on Tuesday 9th.[3] Mr Shanks and Blunden...

506

Could it be done?

Yours I.B.G.

[1] See note to letter 399. 'The Bonnie Earl of Murray' was published in 1921.

[2] The two manuscripts (G.33.4.1-2) have Gurney's preferred title. Published in 1928 and 1979.

[3] Steuart Wilson had already sung 'Ludlow and Teme' on Saturday 29 May 1920 at the 647th concert of the Cambridge University Musical Club.

403 To J.W.Haines   G.83.24

February 1921 (JWH)   74 Longridge Rd, Earls Court, S.W.

My Dear J.W.H.

Here is the book, for which many thanks and apologies for having kept it so long.

By a headline in *Musical America* (a review) I see that 'Ivor Gurney sets T.Nashe's 'Spring' '.

Rather nice, isn't it?

Best wishes

I.B.G.

404 To J.W.Haines   G.83.25.1-2

9 February 1921 (P)   74 Longridge Rd, Earls Court, S.W.

My Dear J.W.H.

Thank you very much for the address. Mrs Casson has written – a very nice letter – to acknowledge the Carol, and to say she likes it.

Walter De la Mare also to acknowledge a setting of 'Epitaph'[1] – long considered but a failure still.

This is a beastly life, this houses and drain-pipe streets life – this is the afternoon for Cranham or the Adam and Eve;[2] or by Stincombe, to end up at Bisley, where Roger Bacon might be born, and my mother was; to talk about Maxim Gorki's surprising little book on Tolstoi, or the not unsurprising price of the new *Arabia Deserta*.

O you were quite right! I have got that little Irish Book – *Wild Earth* or some such name, in spite of strong denials. Some girl at College set 'O men from the fields' awfully well.

Country Sentiment has yielded up 5 or 6 now, a bad setting of 'Allie' by J.R.Heath gave encouragement. I am Michael Flood with Pot Boilers now.[3]

By the way in one of the Cambridge Readers there is a chunk from *Don Quixote* in Ormsby's translation which seems to me to put an entirely new light on that. The most surprising thing (literary) that has happened to me is opening Wordsworth's *Shorter Poems* and getting hit slap in the eye – a very clean line in the Sonnets he has; that stick of a man.

John Booth has taken 'Ludlow and Teme' to look at. Miss Nettleship a setting of 'In Youth is pleasure' for voice and violin alone, to be sung on the 15th.[4]

Tuesday

There's an article in the *Pall Mall* of yesterday, by W.H.Davies, in which he announces his intention of writing a play and also denounces the practice of going into Society. Says also that Synge would have been the finest poet had he lived.

I saw W.de la Mare on Sunday, and am just sending him a setting of 'All that's Old'.[5] He was very nice; John Gould Fletcher was also there. I will ask Blunden about the red M.S. book.

Best wishes to yourself and Mrs Haines

From yours
I.B.G.

---

[1] Published 1938.
[2] A pub in Paradise.
[3] 'Nine of the clock' (pub.1938), 'Hawk and Buckle' (pub.1938) and 'Goodnight to the meadows' (pub.1952) were from Robert Graves' *Country Sentiment* (1919).
[4] An unpublished setting of Robert Wever (fl.1555); see G.36.4.
[5] Untraced.

405 To Robert Bridges   Bodleian Library Dep Bridges 109 f.177

18 February 1921 (KT)[1]   74 Longridge Rd, Earls Court, S.W.

Dear Dr Bridges

Boosey have sent me the first proof of the Song – 'Since Thou O Fondest and Truest', above which I have written 'To Robert Bridges in gratitude'. Will you allow me to do this, and so thank you for 14 years or so of delight in your work?

Altogether there are 'The Sea Poppy', 'The Even darkens over', 'If Death to either shall come', 'When June is come', 'The Hill Pines', 'I love all beauteous things', 'Since thou O Fondest and Truest', and 'Dear Lady when thou frownest', set at one time or another. If you would care to see any or all of these, please say so, and I should be glad to lend you the only copies I have, and am pretty busy to do more than my necessary copying for College work; though it would pleased [sic] me to have copied all for you.

I remain with admiration

Yours very sincerely
Ivor Gurney

[1] Endorsed by Bridges 'Thanked for 'Since Thou O Fondest' Feb 21 1921 2 days after arrival'.
[2] Of the songs Gurney mentions 'The Sea Poppy' exists in two MSS (G.29.3.16 and 17, dated 1920 and 1925); 'The Even darkens over' is untraced; 'If Death to either shall come' is dated July 1920 in G.29.3.8 and was published in 1938 (see also G.37.5.1); 'When June is come' is dated 3 October 1910 in G.29.3.15; 'The Hill Pines' is dated June-October 1909 in G.29.3.10; 'I love all beauteous things' is untraced; 'Since Thou O Fondest and Truest' is dated 1908?/1925 in G.29.3.6, copyrighted 1920 by Boosey & Co in G.29.3.5, and published in 1921; 'Dear Lady when thou frownest' is probably 1910 in the version at G.29.3.13, and dated March 1925 in G.29.3.14.

To Marion Scott   G.61.17

7 April 1921 (P)   1 Westfield Terrace, Longford, Gloucester

My Dear Friend

Gloucester is simply wonderful, and it is better not to tell a person in bed too much of it. Home it is for anybody at first sight....

Lady Olga Montagu's letter arrived yesterday, and thank you for it.

I have seen Mr Haines and Kerr already – Haines very well, and talking of an Easter visit of Freeman. His book will be out soon, with Selwyn and Blount.

I wonder what you are reading in your quarantine? Herrick has proved wonderfully fresh and masterly – Carlyle a bore; Balzac very interesting; and Chaucer (at his best) most human, most tender. Bits of Lamb wonderful – but one expects it; Herrick is the surprise, with his classic squareness and English delight; queer to go with such continual indecency. The country does show so well in his lines, better than with Milton. There is nothing else to tell of books.

The miners strike seems to be a brutal affair, though the *Herald* might show differently. Work is short enough in Gloucester already, but I do not despair of finding someone on whom to plant myself. Anything better than nothing.

The Carlyle I mentioned above was *Past and Present* – most dictatorial stuff – of a genius who thought it his duty to teach, whereas it was merely to give his force play. In *Sartor* there is Beethovenish power.

My grant has not yet come through, but that was owing to some carelessness in filling up – the others came. Best wishes to you, and please thank Mrs Scott for her kindness in ringing me up.

your sincere friend
Ivor Gurney

[*P.S.*] O, Mrs Haines may be up soon, would you care for her to call? I was there last night and had a very good time.

---

407 *To J.W.Haines*   G.83.26

17 April 1921 (P)   1 Westfield Terrace, Longford, Gloucester

[*Postcard*]

By Gum, but Chapman's Homer's *Iliad* is immense! Better than all but the very great Beethoven. Keats did not by any means over-praise. Thank Goodness, there are still discoveries to be made!

I.B.G.

---

408 *To Marion Scott*   G.61.18-19

19 April 1921 (P)   1 Westfield Terrace, Longford, Gloucester

My Dear Friend

I am glad you like *Don Quixote* too – it is a meaty book. The friendly masterpieces (though truly this is not yet quite accepted of the real me) do make other things seem hashy and just amiable. I walked over Horsepools today and Painswick, Cranham, Coopers with *King Lear* and Chapman – also Mozart's Quartetts; not so good as Thackeray, or the able work of any able freelance I think – and finished Chapman with his length and glow and fury. I have promised myself the other Chapman as well. *King Lear* is better, nakeder and has an edge that Chapman never had on his battleaxe, to this sword. *Lear does* get there!

I remember snapping you up about Shakespeare's Historical Plays. Carlyle did say that sort of thing – and it is true I suppose. Never the less, it is a 'stunt' to read them.

Barring *Henry IV*, there is nothing amazing. It surprised me to find that Masefield on Shakespeare at this present time moved gratitude for past help, and a slight scorn of the slightness and cheap assertion of the book. The *Daily News*-ishness. Quiller Couch would have done better, Belloc, Chesterton, Shaw, Squire, Shanks, Haines, Kerr, Freeman, etc would all have done better – but the book as a populariser is yet very good. It is not informed – Chesterton's *Victorian Literature* one quarrels with and sometimes hates, but – there's the man behind. Moliere I can't read as yet (but only a bit of a play.)

Balzac's *Cesar Birotteau* very good. Thick, heavy and true.

That's gossip enough, I think about books. Of Music gossip there is none. Fox Strangways don't like my article enough.

I hope Mr and Mrs Scott will keep up and even improve on their Brighton form. Cobbett's remarks on that place might invigorate them.

My Aunt or Mother tells me HNH passed here in a motor car today. When will somebody do that Concerto? The 'Emperor' has a wonderful opening, right up to the B$^\flat$ orchestral shout; afterwards ... Well, I don't pass that!

From timid remembrance I should reckon it the best ever written, just as the scolding song in the *Beggar's Opera* licks Richard Wagner. (My books haven't come yet, I remember ....!)

Frederick Austin is a remarkable man.[1]

O the Piano concerto's run thus don't they.

1) H.N.H. 2) G major Beethoven, 3) Schumann

4) { C minor Beethoven   5) A major } Mozart. I don't
   { D mi Mozart   C mi   }

know Grieg or Brahms.

Gloucestershire is – just itself, and the country people as impressive as ever. O neurasthenia! O knock-knees!! O Spectacles!!!

Will Harvey is getting married! Quite suddenly, to all his friends. A Miss Kane. She's very nice and very Irish. They'll be happy.[2]

Pity it's Swindon though!

Well, so things go.

I have just set Edward Thomas' 'Cherry Tree'[3] and a pot-boiler, and am writing another set of kids things.

Lord Sandwich is to try to land me in the next *Georgian*.[4]

The Carnegie verdicts are the things I look for, and the coming of the now preparing 'Edward'.

'Ludlow and Teme', a clean thing. It does in the open air. As in the drawing room. Have patience with a fool, and perhaps our of a pretty black welter something may emerge. If so, Miss Marion Scott will not be the least factor therein.

B

[1] Frederic Austin (1872-1952), singer, composer, opera director, and arranger of music for Gay's *Beggar's Opera* (1920) and *Polly* (1923).
[2] Harvey married Sarah Anne Kane on 30 April 1921.
[3] See G.35.4.6-8.
[4] Gurney did not appear there.

511

?April 1921 (KT)   1 Westfield Terrace, Longford, Gloucester

My Dear Friend

I hope you are much better; I will write tonight to say so at more length.

Thank you for the offer of money. If you would let me have another £3 or
even £5 I should be very glad. The grant has not come, and my pension book
has run out.

Today I have been tramping, and find farm labouring is as little needing
men as other trades, even on the keep and pocket money basis – the out of
work countrymen being willing to work on farms.

Best wishes

From your sincere but querulous Friend
Ivor Gurney

---

26 April 1921 (S)   1 Westfield Terrace, Longford, Gloucester

My Dear Friend

Thank you so much – still the grant arrives not. I am so sorry you have been
having such a rough time; funerals on the top of influenza are not the proper
way of spending Easter holidays. Please accept my hopes for a better time.

Myself – well a congested liver and congested Labour exchange have made
me full of grumbles. Still, there is a new set of Children's pieces just going off
to Edwin Ashdown.

Sunday was a day of visit to Harvey, who is stoically-cheerfully
contemplating his doubling of fortunes.

But O the beauty, the best-of-Brahms-like beauty of Sunday; the look of the
tower across the valley! No, the strong praiser of Beethoven and Chapman,
daring to exalt those great men and to exult in their accomplishment, will say
nothing more.

With your letter came some ballad verses from Lagos, Nigeria for setting.
Queer world to bring fashionable lyrics from such a far place. Winthrop
Rogers writes to say that the Preludes will soon be ready, and that proofs of
some more songs may be along soon. He also hints that, not being able to go
to Radnege, they may choose Gloucestershire for a home. To which, I
suggested Stroud.

Mr Haines is at Newnham. I have seen him but twice. Kerr is nicer than
ever. My aunt who lives here – indeed owns the house is a dear, and spoils me.

'The West Sussex Drinking Song' is to be put into E^b; and on one too
lovely night I did some elver fishing. I say too lovely, because elvers swim deep
on moony nights. But the night was so calm, and the sight of the fishers, and
the sound of their talk over their wood-fires was very beautiful and grateful –

though Gloucester always is a most romantic place.

Tom Jones turns out to be very good, but I don't want to read it.

Joseph Andrews good in its parts. Very English, books we owe a lot to, and don't care for. Books for a farmer on a frosty evening after a hard day; but not like *Handley Cross*.

The right reading for now, I suppose, is Robert Bridges.

A night walk brought me at dawn to Birdlip; I had done 6 hours digging that day, and still am sick. It is a beastly thing. And one feels *such* a great musician at that time! 'If only I were well' ....

The woods were very calm and pierced through with stars of the quietest. And Crickley looked majestical enough against the 6 o'clock light.

Best wishes to you for your health and easy working, and to your people.

Harvey and I spoke of the Gloucestershire evening with tender appreciation. It was an unassuming happy time.

your sincere friend
Ivor Gurney

411 *To Francis Brett Young*   Birmingham Univ. Library FBY 2054

1921   1 Westfield Terrace, Longford, Gloucester

With best wishes from an admirer of *Five Degrees South* in France and England
  'Jupiter like a ship's lantern swinging'
  While scarce a ripple stirs the upland grain'
    etc etc

From
Ivor Gurney

412 *To the Editor of the Outlook*   G.64.11.149

1921 (KT)   1 Westfield Terrace, Longford, Gloucester

Dear Sir

I am sending a poem called 'London Dawn' to you which I hope you will like. Am sorry it is in common script, and enclose stamp in case of return.

I remain

Yours truly
Ivor Gurney

1921   1 Westfield Terrace, Longford, Gloucester

To Iolo Aneurin Williams Esq.,

Dear Mr Williams
   The song was sent to you because I can not get my things published – or
very slowly – but also set in admiration of your words. If you could manage to
get anyone to take it I should be very glad, since the music pleases me, and the
song is a real Song – which, as Belloc says is the making of the best of all
trades,
   With best wishes

                                        Yours very sincerely
                                        Ivor Gurney

30 May 1921 (KT)   1 Westfield Terrace, Longford, Gloucester

Dear Mr Howard
   Here are some songs[1] – some I like under my own name; some potboilers
under another. I hope somehow something will hit.
   Is there any news of the Carnegie awards?
   Elver fishing is going strong tonight, but I doubt whether much will be
caught. The only time I went out there was a bare handful to me in two
hours.
   Best wishes

                                        Yours very sincerely
                                        Ivor Gurney

[1] A note not in Gurney's hand lists seven songs as sent to J.M.[?] Greene on 30 May 1921.
They were 'As I lay in the Early Sun' (by Edward Shanks; see G34.10.1), 'Spring' (by
Thomas Nashe; see G.34.1), 'The Fair' (by W.M.Letts, set under the name of Michael
Flood; see G.33.5.2), 'At the Jolly Blue Boar' (by H.Kenniston Wynne, set under the
name of Michael Flood; see G.36.7), 'Pedlar Jack' (by W.W.Gibson; see G.31.1.9),
'Cowslip time' (by W.M.Letts, set under the name of Michael Flood; see G.33.5.1) and
'Hawk and Buckle' (by Robert Graves, set under the name of Michael Flood; see
G.31.5.8).

30 May 1921 (KT)   1 Westfield Terrace, Longford, Gloucester

Dear Mr Howard[1]

I guess Gloucestershire is looking better than Wardour St just now, but I join you tomorrow.

I hope one or other or some of these will suit you. The Robert Graves Songs I like, and hope you will.

With best wishes

I remain yours very sincerely

Ivor Gurney.

---

[1] See previous letter. This letter has the following annotation in Gerald Finzi's hand: 'These were with some songs sent to Stainer & Bell in 1921. Miss Marion Scott managed to get them back (still in M.S.!!) in 1937'. Apart from 'Hawk and Buckle', Robert Graves poems that Gurney set were: 'Loving Henry', 'Brittle Bones', 'Star-talk', 'Nine of the clock O' and 'Good night to the meadows' (see G.31.5).

June 1921 (KT)   1 Westfield Terrace, Longford, Gloucester

My Dear Friend

Many thanks for the *Times Literary Gazettes* which seem to be getting more cosmopolitan, alas! More commercial in outlook; but still interesting.

I cannot at the moment – there being visitors and disturbances, find your most interesting letter, but will do so and reply to it.

I remember the being rushed with work and your opinion that Wagner has lasted. I may sympathise with the first, but not the second remembrance. The end of *Tristan* is piano extemporization, but I like Brangane's Narration very much – good musical prose. The Seigfried [sic] Idyll tiresome and long. I may retract, but it seems to me that Brahms has lasted much better. There is a Norse touch about his fine things that convinces. Wagner was artist enough, but more? The first scene of Gotterdammerung is as great as Hardy if not more, but there is so little of it.

I am glad so much Parry is chosen for Leeds. As for the 'Apostles', the craftsmanship seems to be as clear as ever was – but the weakness of character is sometimes apparent.

As for my Quartett; my guess of it is that the first movement is best in material, perhaps up to almost anything – it is Chapman of *Bussy D'Ambois* – the second, despite the rather obvious opening, does work up to a better climax than Brahms ever managed in string music (perhaps), it is all strong; the third is *Midsummer Night's Dream* with a rather cowardly interpolation. The last; 'business', chiefly if not merely. I am sure you underrate it. The second, was begun as Carpentry, has some good stuff in Movement one; one of the best slow movements ever made, a good square scherzo, and a laudable last movement. In any case, I cannot find myself wishing to exchange with any but Vaughan Williams, Herbert Howells, John Ireland, and perhaps Elgar. It is wood carving mostly; taken from Ben Jonson, Chapman, Webster.

I am sure you think too lightly of it. Shakespeare would have liked it, if Middleton Murry or Turner wouldn't.

A complete Ben Jonson has been pretty well marked lately. The Commendatory verses from his 'Sons' though is the surprising thing. But anyway the whole book is the second thing in our language. I withdraw Chapman.

This is a very technical letter, but since June has come Gloucestershire save between 9 pm and 8 am has grown more common. One reads the Greeks.

Homer is mighty, AEschylus and Sophocles both pass as great, and Virgil is but a marvellous verse writer. What a halting business the *Aeneid* is! But what verse! Poems have got done in shoals. Jolly good some. (I enclose specimens,) but editors don't agree.

There was a book by a Sussex Poet beginning with D (Dolman?) patronised if not cut up by the *Times* which has a fine elegy on Edward Thomas; and Drinkwater has deserved better than its review.

I am certain something is more wrong than formerly.

The *Christian Science Monitor* never comes my way, but I hope things are all right there?

Will Harvey was down for Whitsuntide; I am glad he is in the second *Poems of Today*, but alas the Second is noway comparable to the first.

Sunday

Your letter has turned up, and reminded me of the SWM struggles, of which your letter gives indications – most guarded – Greek Chorus hedging on a doubtful horse and rather weary anyhow. I am sorry there are struggles even in this.

The hoeing lasted one week, in which I did an acre; other men then joining. It was painful work having been left too long, and one furrow was a long job, yet good.

Last night Cotswold was Aeschylean, gloriously strong, and full of the impulse behind big things. Cold Storage was forgotten, save the strain, and peers showed as 10% merely – not a pleasant thought – Crickley was as a Greek praise, beyond laws save that of the predicted change. (By the way Sophocles at the mere unimportant present pleases better than *Prometheus Unbound*. Jonson learnt their lessons).

It seems certain to me that the second best thing in our language is the Verses Prefixed + the 8 Good plays, plus what is good in the Masques + Underwoods, Epigrams etc + the Commonplace book + the Commendatory

Verses of Jonson – an amazing collection. Bach except in a few isolated specimens having no such craft. Had Bach time, he would have developed the subtle idiom of the Slow Movement of the Italian Concerto; instead of which alas .....! The Matthew Passion came. Jonson reached after Shakespeare's freedom, and had the Greek form. Some of his followers rose at his death to masterly greatness.

The school of Youth is Ben Jonson + Bach + Madrigals + Folk Song + the right Mozart + the right Beethoven and Brahms + the right Strauss songs + Wenlock Edge Sea Symphony Howells' Concerto + John Ireland's Sonata + the Carnegie Quartett (and my songs perhaps) + Max Reger's songs.

May I *beg* of you to search curiously (through Charing Cross Rd – not Foyles,) for a *complete* Ben Jonson (5s – 15s?) which will start you on an entirely new view of things – such varied mastership being beyond the more tied Bach, always too hard worked. While Jonson was presiding at the Phoenix Club Bach was in fever of writing out second tenor parts perhaps.

Chapman's *Iliad* is by no means withdrawn from favour, but by the nature of things it is unvaried. The total Chapman achievement is below the raised expectations. Vaughan Williams stands the test. Parry almost does. The best Herbert Howells is yet freer. John Ireland's Sonata is Chapman (Chapman and Jonson all mixed up.)

Indeed are we beyond our masters the Greeks, or were. For what good can come of the present state of literary things in London? Did Middleton Murry ever justify himself? Or Clutton Brock? Truly? Is the *Mercury* a success? What relation to literature has the *Times Supplement*. Or what relation to merit Barrie's Order? How many publishers saw Edward Thomas' *Poems*? Has *Deborah* been staged? Why aren't Kerr's Poems published? The Honour of Saintsbury, the recognition of Thomas Hardy, and of Vaughan Williams are the good signs.

For the rest money rules, better than lust or the liver which is the Pope and Dryden time.

But the Elizabethan money was better used, London being different then. Shakespeare (through Southampton) Beaumont, Daniel, Spenser, Drummond of Hawthornden, and probably Drayton, had money. Fletcher too. Marlowe, one guesses. Chapman, surely a little.

Now there's a long screed – chiefly from an angry stomach to a critic impossible to get at. May I exhort you not to be surprised or more than tickled at a new thing, until the Jonson Commendatory Verses have ceased to tickle. That is to say of the second movement of Vaughan Williams' Phantasy Quartett or Byrd's Motetts.

There is no *new* musical thought, or practically so. What there may be is that reflected thought of a musician reading *Antonio and Mellida*[1] or Drayton's Epistles and refusing to write lesser stuff – that is to say approximately Rasoumoffsky or Quintett in F minor. New thought I know alone through two preludes of Scriabine. (Op 40 or so)

517

Best wishes and apologies

from your sincere friend
Ivor Gurney.

[1] Marston's tragedy (1602).

417 *To J.W.Haines*   G.83.28.1-2

Received 1 July 1921 (JWH)   The Five Alls, Studley Green,
                                                    Stokenchurch, Bucks

My Dear J.W.H.
True you had no letter, but there was little to say, except perhaps an excited
chortle over the Carnegie award, which chiefly is interesting on account of the
great work it will involve.
Poor me, it probably means copying all those blooming parts afresh.
Also barring some visits to J.C.Squire there was nothing to tell – and of one
to Robert Graves.
The Country here is rather too much what one would expect, save Bledlow
Ridge, and two valleys. The Ridge is a superb little thing, not large but very
fine.
One day I an another chap here walked to Rupert Brooke's inn – the 'Pink
and Lily', and took tea there. A pilgrimage.
You are right about the first Prelude, the A minor probably next, and then
the D^b. Clumsy and nice truthful music.
Awre and Amazon is good. The river *is* wonderful, and the great tide rips in
the Western light always most joyous to behold.
I hope the rheumatism is better, and Robin more (or apparently)
sympathetic. I could write a whole screed about my internal symptoms would
as the immortal deer-poacher of Shottery (was it) phrased it, give him pause.
John Coates wrote two very nice letters about 'Spring' and wants to see
new things.[1] A.E.Housman gave the needed permission. Lucky autographs
for Gladys Harvey who must have now quite a collection.
Well, this bob enclosed is for Robin, if he will make a copy of 'The County
Mayo', and 'Kathleen Ni Houlihan'. If he won't, will you kindly lend your
books to the servant of so rosy a demeanour, and ask her?
It is for Winthrop Rogers, who is to publish those and 'The Bonny Earl of
Murray' before long, and it is impossible to get at those things here.
The String Quartett goes its perverse way. And a Piano Trio a perverser.
What think you of the Squire Anthology? I am sorry Will is left out. He is
worth much 'better men' at his best. And I shall be glad to see your coal-
strucken volume. Mrs Radford writes well. And J.G.Legge's translations
from the Greek occasionally very fine.

518

Best wishes to Mrs Haines and yourself

From I.B.G.

[1] John Coates sang Gurney's 'Under the Greenwood Tree' in a 'Shakespeare Song Recital' at Chelsea Town Hall on 20 March 1923.

418 *To J.W.Haines*   G.83.27.1-3

Received 16 July 1921 (JWH)   The Five Alls, Studley Green,
Stokenchurch, Bucks

My Dear J.W.H.

Your book is better at its best than I could have thought.[1]

'Paradise' I like.

'April 1917' – especially 'And not a single twig believes.'

'Broad Oak' too, but I am not *quite* so sure about the 'not' being rather mannered (mine I know)

Some of 'Death's Genius'

Some of 'The High Road', especially 3 and 4.

'Flowers' too.

'Late February' especially 'had crushed the snowflakes', etc.

'And his small footprints' etc (E.T.)

'Beyond in fields' (six lines quite your own

'Grey clematis' etc – particularly a kept and cosy sanctuary.)

'From naked larch trees tier on tier' etc

And the end, except for the greats. 'Duns and glows' is good.

'Lakeland'. 'Coloured subsidy' is damned good. last verse too.

'A Drought' has 'Sea gulls' wings that whirr –

centred at his feet' – fine stuff.

'The stonecrops of the quarry and the wall' etc is jolly good.

'To Ladies'

'Near Keswick' is jolly good, and has that glorious line 'And yet those crests cry nearer to the stars'. Coleridge I suppose, though it would be very fine for him. A bit too languid for Chapman (who [*sic*] *Odyssey* is a very stiff affair.)

'Cumberland' is good. Verse five especially.

'He Arnoldises' is a title sufficiently attractive.

'Silver were the snows' etc is good.

'A Child' is better than W.W. (no overwhelming praise in the context.) The 'Chimney' is good.

'The Dead Inn' is good. Very good sometimes.

'Harbour of Refuge' has a good end.

'Alchemilla' is charming and all your own.

'Bradley Hall' is a good telling. 'He paid in gold' very good.

'The Track through the Forest' very good. Pity the last 3 lines are grandiloquent.

I think you may well be proud of it. An unpretentious half successful book, with hardly a falute in it. Edward Thomas would have been glad of it. I find your writing difficult to read always, and never adequately appreciated. 'Lady's Mantle'. There is far less Wordsworthian verbiage than I had thought.

The book lacks authority and therefore will gain no great praise from poets in general, who nevertheless will like it. A companionable thing. You know I think that both F.W.H. and myself are underrated, you will join us, and we shall be glad of you.

The book isn't as good as you yourself though. A thing I escape by making walking – writing on the march, a dirty trick some would say.

Herbert Howells is at his port of sail I suppose.[2] The Kaiser in Holland sued for his taxes, Ben Jonson often above Shakespeare, (I maintain it) myself in a Lyons shop, and God's in his Heaven, so everything's all right, I suppose everywhere.

J.Stephens wrote 'Mayo'.

Yours
I.B.G.

Letters from Yeats, John Coates, Housman.

---

[1] John Haines, *Poems*, published by Selwyn and Blount in 1921.
[2] Howells went to South Africa and conducted at Cape Town,

---

419 *To S.C.M. Scott*   G.61.141-3

July 1921 (KT)   1 Westfield Terrace, Longford, Gloucester

Dear Miss Scott

I am glad you liked Ben Jonson so much. He seems to me to be as a stylist, greater than Beethoven, lacking only natural charm and intense spirit; but a rock, a Colossus. *Cataline, Sejanus Poetaster Volpone Bartholomew Fair* all these are very fine indeed. A sort of hewn fineness about all. *Everyman* edition, two volumes is very good.

Webster, though given to horrors has certainly genius. All the others are by Swinburne and such overrated, unless one compares their style with that of any other time. The way those people use words is marvellous. It is a pity that so often the dramatists were driven to violent and sordid plots, for the audience's sake.

The speech on Kingship I could not find, but Marston does marvellous things.

'Now are the lawn sheets fumed with violets'.

Jonson's plots are certainly his own – the *Alchemist* has the best plot in the world I think. Drummond's Conversations are not easy to get. Everyman would tell you much. Anyway I know you have the *Encyclopedia Brittanica*; and there is the Chambers thing I sent.

I agree about Marlowe's *Edward II*. Beaumont and Fletcher have *Bonduca* and *The Knight of the Burning Pestle*. *Eastward Hoe* published as Chapman is good. There's a jolly little volume in the World's Classics of Selected Plays.

But Shakespeare stands above all for materialness, journalistic quality, poetry. (How thundering good *Henry VIII* is!)

I seem to agree with you about everyone save putting Webster high for two plays. The Cambridge History is interesting about these people. I have just been reading volumes 6 and 7 (I think).

Vanburgh wrote interesting plays and one or two of Middleton ('Mermaid Series'). Heywood is sweet too. Chapman's *Caesar and Pompey* has points too. But all these men seemed to use words alive so as was hardly equalled again till Browning. Hazlitt writes prose so; but Carlyle better still. £5 a play was the usual pay, but Shakespeare did get £25 (outright sales) and a benefit. But you'd find all that in the *Encyclopedia*. Ben Jonson knew everybody, great and small – he called his pupils his 'sons'. Shakespeare submitted plays to Beaumont. I fancy Jonson too.

But to do what Marlowe did! What an achievement!

Music has not often touched the best work of these men; and the more beauty of the medium hardly hides the comparative poverty of thought. A great deal due to the drawbacks of time of composition required and former weakness of technique.

with best wishes
I remain

Yours very sincerely
Ivor Gurney.

---

420 *To Marion Scott*   G.61.27

9 September 1921 (P)   1 Westfield Terrace, Longford, Gloucester

[*Postcard*]

Thank you so much for your letter. Somehow it pleases me that you liked to see pastoral France after the high Alps. Best wishes for smokeless immaculate uninteresting London, that has lost her attracting veil – may you not mind it much! No, I am not yet well; in spite of a journey to Crickley yesterday, where I found Cold Slad occupied, renewing, with two new welcome windows looking on the Hill. Mr Masefield was running *Iphigenea in Tauris* at Stroud yesterday, and wrote to ask me over; but not being well and having a chance of Crickley decided me not to go. I write feeble songs, and wait for my boxes with the Carnegie thing.

Yours well-wishingly
Ivor Gurney.

421 *To Edward Marsh*   New York Public Library Berg Collection

December 1921 (KT)   1 Westfield Terrace, Longford, Gloucester

To E Marsh Esq

Dear Mr Marsh

I could not resist copying out 'Tarantella' and sending her – with Sir Hugh Allen's blessing on her head.

Also I have told W.R.P.Kerr about your willingness to look at his verses, and written again to Bristol about the Gloucester vacancy.

Meanwhile has come an offer from a London Cinema show, and since the Civil Service post will not fall vacant till the middle or end of March I am glad to take that – if the offer prove fact.

  with best wishes
    I remain

Yours very sincerely
Ivor Gurney.

P.S. A letter to you from me has just been returned from Cliffords Inn, where I had thought you lived – but of no importance.

422 *To Edward Marsh*   New York Public Library Berg Collection

December 1921   56 Llandover Rd., Plumstead, S.E.

Dear Mr Marsh

(I do not see why grandeur and age may not suit you)

Thank you very much for sending 'Tarantella', which may be important.

I am afraid I shall not be present at the evening, unless I could fix up a deputy in the next few days – which may yet be possible.

The difficulty is in getting off in the fortnights trial, but the one day a week off might be managed then. It is but to buy a collar and all's well.

Yours very sincerely
Ivor Gurney.

New York Public Library Berg Collection

December 1921   56 Llandover Rd., Plumstead, S.E.

Dear Mr Marsh

Thank you very much – today would have ended possibility of staying in London. In any case it seems better to return, but I will certainly come on Sunday, for which invitation again thank you.

I am sorry to need all this help and general – worrying-about-after, but can see no alternative to doing what I have done.

Cinema posts are hard to get, fearful to retain, easy to lose.

For Rupert Brooke – I read him in France, set him, though badly, in England, and have twice visited the 'Pink and Lily', whose landlord, a nice old chap, had latterly been very ill.

I was first directed there by a Farmer to whom Mr Masefield had given *The Widow in the Bye Street* – a gift not wholly approved of.

With many thanks
    I remain

Yours very sincerely
Ivor Gurney

423A To F.W.Harvey   G.70.44

Early 1922 (KT)   47 Barclay Road, Walham Green, S.W.

My Dear F.W.H.

No luck as yet. Except 4 lovely volumes of Goethe at 3d each. And this of Gloucester. Do frame (passe partout) this not too recognisable thing. It may be the only one left anywhere.

I have seen Miss Scott, as kind as usual. I fancy she means to ask you to read things on the thirtieth.[1] Mr Fox Strangways also. Miss Rogers is running the music business, probably well.

But things are not looking well for me. College opens Monday; shall see then.

What awful music Curwen publish! and the rest. Tis a saddening sight and they saddening sounds I do not doubt.

Alas, bookstalls are fast disappearing, and second hand shops. Four have disappeared in Fulham alone since 1914. And London a raw city these days, with not so much as Swindon light even or even near as good.

'The childing seasons change
    One knows not which is which'.[2]

My 4th violin Sonata is nearly finished. 'What you have in you, Out with it'.[3] Despairing work is the noblest refuge against other despairs after all. We have sailed rivers and trod sorrel together, but that was in too lovely a county, too free a time perhaps. Best wishes for the novel.

Yours
I.B.G.

[1] The Scotts held an 'At Home' on 30 January 1922 at 92 Westbourne Terrace, when Clive Carey sang new songs by Gurney.
[2] Adapting *Midsummer Night's Dream*, II.1.112-4.
[3] From the chapter 'The Everlasting Yea' in Carlyle's *Sartor Resartus*.

---

424 *To Edward Marsh*   New York Public Library Berg Collection

Early 1922 (KT)   1 Westfield Terrace, Longford, Gloucester

To Edward Marsh Esq

Dear Mr Marsh
    May I send you my poems?
    There must be about fifty you have not seen.
    I remain

Yours very truly
Ivor Gurney

---

425 *To Edward Marsh*   New York Public Library Berg Collection

Early 1922 (KT)   1 Westfield Terrace, Longford, Gloucester

To E Marsh Esq
Dear Mr Marsh,
    Here are my verses, in answer to your permission to send them.
    I am sorry they are so ill-written; but surely the best is very good. Some of the War Poems I like very much. If you would scan them through, as a notebook, I think it would be worth your while.
    Again I am sorry for the horrible state of some of it, but am pretty badly done nowadays.
    I remain

Yours very truly
Ivor Gurney.

Early 1922 (KT)

1 Westfield Terrace, Longford, Gloucester

To E Marsh Esq

Dear Mr Marsh

I am sorry you did not like my things enough; and hope to please better.

The packet coming with this, is F W Harvey's book *Farewell*[1] of which (you may remember) I spoke. If you already have this please put my address on, and return with enclosed stamps. Please excuse bothering you in this fashion, but I should like you to see it.

This morning I have been walking reading the Bohn *Iliad*, shortly after dawn – a good translation and fitting majestic sunrises. It is the noblest stuff, and went with thunder clouds and a streaked east or north east.

with best wishes

I remain

Yours very sincerely
Ivor Gurney.

[1] Harvey's fourth book, published in 1921 by Sidgwick & Jackson.

January 1922 (KT)

1 Westfield Terrace, Longford, Gloucester

To E.Marsh Esq

Dear Mr Marsh

I am glad to tell you that a Picture Palace Post has been offered me at Bude; if this were to last I should be content. Meanwhile there is no vacancy in the Gloucester office; it depends on an engaged couple finding a house.

Anything better than being a Bard among fisher-folk could hardly be imagined, and I shall go there on the money you gave me; and there write a four-song cycle of Rupert Brooke.

with best wishes

I remain

Yours very sincerely
Ivor Gurney

January 1922 (KT)   1 Westfield Terrace, Longford, Gloucester

To Mrs Edward Shanks

Dear Mrs Shanks

I send along 'The Fields are Full', smudgy, but newly written out, and hope that you will like that.[1] Something tells me you have already a copy, but this will do as the latest version.

I hope Lewes looks well.

Next week I am starting a trial at Bude in Cornwall. If that job would last, surely it is well? Cinema pianist to sailors would be romantic even to a Greek. But who can tell.

I hope Mr Shanks is well. Lewes was unhealthy for Simon de Montfort, but for others may prove more lucky.

best wishes

> Yours very sincerely
> Ivor Gurney.

[1] There are two versions of this setting of Shanks's poem in the Archive: G.34.10.5 and 6. It was published in volume 5 of Gurney's songs.

Early 1922   1 Westfield Terrace, Longford, Gloucester

To E Marsh Esq

Dear Mr Marsh

I send under title of 5 Songs of Rupert Brooke, 4 settings,[1] of which I do not think very much, but they are probably better than those of most folk.

These four have been done some time. I must try to get another for the set – 'The Pacific Clouds' with luck.

If you care to get these sung to you, I can believe you would like them, though mere carpentry in the doing. I am fond enough of 'When Colour goes home' to wish to have done that with some sprite in me, but could not.

With best wishes

I remain

> Yours very sincerely
> Ivor Gurney

A man named Tourneur wrote
> 'The duke's son's great concubine
> A drab of state, a cloth o'silver slut

Who has her train borne up but lets her soul
Trail i' the dirt'.

[1] This letter and the accompanying MS songs were found by Christopher Hassall (presumably in Marsh's papers) and returned to O.U.P. in 1959. They in turn, not feeling them worthy of publication, passed them on to the Gurney Archive where they form G.29.4.1. The songs are 'The Treasure' (i.e. 'When colour goes home'), 'There's Wisdom in Women', 'One Day', and 'Song' ('All suddenly the wind comes soft'; also called 'Heart's Pain'). There is a MS of 'Clouds' at G.29.4.2.

430 To Maurice Jacobson   British Library Add MS 62551 O

March 1922 (KT)[1]   1 Westfield Terrace, Longford, Gloucester

Dear Jacobsen,

I meant to write before, meant to see you indeed. Those boast[s] about my slow movement I also meant, but I did think your thing most extraordinarily beautiful, and hope it came off at the exam. I shall wish to hear it or see it before long. Personally, I have got rather tired of waiting to hear good music and retired deep into Lamb's *Specimens of the Elizabethans*,[2] but your music seemed to me to be directly drawn from the 48 and indeed to be just such music as he would have been proud to have written. I hope Vaughan Williams heard it, that's all.

The end of Jonson's *Cataline* would surprise you. And Webster's *Duchess of Malfi* has just such beauty as you would like. It seems to me that the best way of attaining the proper scorn of the *Dutchman*[3] that all good sailors have is to refuse to take German Biography at its own value and to compare the thought of Mozart with that of Herrick. (We win) That is for string Quartetts alone. Or the songs of Schubert with W.H.Davies *Songs of Joy*, or the general run of Wagner with the general run of Hardy's *Dynasts* and Meredith's *Love in a Valley*.

The best Beethoven and Bach and Brahms are practically all that will pass this test, and the *Missa Brevis* and a few isolated things like Debussy's *Nuages* and *Tristan* and the Early Schumann work. I believe that when Edward Thomas begins a poem

> At Hawthorn time in Wiltshire travelling
> In search of something chance would never bring
> And old man's face but weather cut
> And coloured, rough brown sweet as any nut
> A landface sea-blue eyed hung in my mind ... etc[4]

He does something absolutely above all that all but the greatest Continentals can do. What do the well known Germans write about but fir trees, blossom, moonlight, Eternity, World Awe and so forth? Shakespeare writes 'And shake the yoke of inauspicious stars from this world wearied flesh'.[5] And Herbert Howells writes a Concerto, and Martin Shaw a Song, Stanley Wilson a Cello Sonata, John Ireland a Piano Sonata that seem to me marvellous things.[6] The bit of your thing I heard seemed to stand with all this to me.

Please excuse my writing all this. There is not any sort of patronage meant. But after many years of trying to find depths in clumsy Beethoven and Schubert, true neatness in the Mozart Quartetts etc I find *such* things in the Elizabethans, and compare *The Knight of the Burning Pestle*[7] with anything at all; Dammy, why should we be humble? If I fail, then let one say 'You haven't a mind like Shirley or John Fletcher' – not, 'ah there's nothing like Schubert or Sullivan, or Haydn'. All these people were crippled as were never the Elizabethans; some under fine patronage, some living perilously from hand to mouth, but at taverns where one might meet sailors and such men – not at all the fettered lives of Grand-Ducal musicians or of we poor police-ridden folk of today. Ben Jonson and such were as used as undergraduates to staying up all night.

It is a foolish thing not to praise, and I am sure enough that the English have right to say 'Yes' or 'No' to Continental imports by now. How our new school is to be raised without patronage I can hardly see however. The poets were gratuited or had money already.

Best wishes yours very sincerely

Ivor Gurney

[1] Jacobson's music was performed at a R.C.M. concert on 8 March 1922.
[2] Lamb's *Specimens of English Dramatic Poets Contemporary with Shakespeare* (1808).
[3] Wagner's opera.
[4] The opening of 'Lob'.
[5] *Romeo and Juliet*, V.3.111.2.
[6] Martin Shaw (1876-1958).
[7] By Beaumont and Fletcher.

431 *To Marion Scott*   G.61.23-6

9-10 April 1922 (S)   1 Westfield Terrace, Longford, Gloucester

My Dear Friend

Thank you so much for the notes.

The Quartett is finished, and though not Shakespearian in size has awfully good stuff in it. The Scherzo seems to me to be good enough (as the 6/8 part) for anything. For the rest I write songs, and read Elizabethans. Tried Aristophanes but got not far. Bought the *Arabian Nights* and liked it very much.

The more I read Elizabethans and especially Shakespeare, the more I am convinced that Music has not quite got there yet, and that the search for new expression is a mere weakness of those who have not yet compared those 16th century writers with Kipling, Conrad, and so forth. There is very little music as packed as the best of our drama. And Heywood at his best writes as competently as Beethoven ordinarily.

This afternoon I read the beginning of *Lucrece* full of good things.

'Tarquin leaves the Roman host
And to Collatium bears the lightless fire
Which in pale embers hid, lurks to aspire
And girdle with embracing flames'. is in the first verse; surely swift enough. And on one reads

'Beauty itself does of itself persuade
The eyes of men without an orator'

They were a wonderful crowd. Vanbrugh wrote amusingly enough too. One could hope to write String Quartetts with such a touch.

The *Cambridge History* is very interesting on all these people. One could wish for full lives though. By the way the Brahms life I have so often clamoured for from you, is returned to me from Erlebach. (The Walter Scott life) An interesting sketchy thing, with the personal touches that please me – though too few; for I like all kinds of silly little gossips about the people I like.

W R P Kerr showed me a poem of his tonight with one very clear line.

'High in the branches the romantic moon.'

There is a great hope among us that he will be in the next *Georgian*.

Did you read the *Observer* today – Squire on Smart? If you will turn him up in *Chambers* you will find the ground whence the 'Song of Honour' was dug. Since my reading has widened, through *Chambers*, more through W R P Kerr, there is not much modern stuff I care much for. Our young Elizabethans didn't know the old ones, or the war verse would have been a very different thing; in four years that has so faded. Wilfred Owen's 'Strange Meeting' has come off best, I think. But F.W.H. and myself stand high among poor stuff. Nearly first. 'Gonnehem' 'In Flanders' are good enough for anything.[1]

Chatterton is a discovery – in Satire especially. The genius of him undoubted to me.

Some music I have read – the Sibelius Quartett; the Rasoumoffsky Quartetts, Two Reger, but the last – a Piano Quartett in D minor – a late work – rather shocking to me. Byrd better than Palestrina, – barring the Missa Brevis – that I know, and Gloucester County a wonder.

The *Gloucester Journal* souvenir I send is worth the sending I think; It is the first of a good paper, and not unworthy of the place; which is now excited about Major Armstrong, not the elver season which is now beginning, in queer weather suddenly clouding capriciously, raining crossly, now shining most mellow.

The Parry Room I hope is a real success, I wish you would tell me when you next write. And of the Vaughan-Williams Quartett. The Second

Movement of the Phantasy Quintett is a glory.
  with best wishes
    I remain

Your sincere friend
Ivor Gurney

[1] Both poems by Harvey; see Anthony Boden's biography, pp.81-2 and 92.

---

432 To Marion Scott   G.46.30.6

9-10 April 1922 (S)   1 Westfield Terrace, Longford, Gloucester

My Dear Friend

One or two days ago I read Abercrombie's *Interludes and Poems* in which are wonderful things here and there.

> 'And I dare swear
> The cuckoo flower down by the water meadow
> Has made a test of whiteness for the side
> (In Heaven unquestioned) of a goddess young.

> 'Eternity, scattered with starry troubles'

and of a mountain land

> 'Where the earth gets up in royal attitudes'.

I am sure you would like the book, and send this bit of a letter as a guide to something modern – occasionally worthy of the great time (I mean of Elizabeth).

There is little more, save that Dante is found unreadable, and that a saga called *Howard the Halt* is not bad. That's about books.

As to the Quartett, I am glad you like it, and admit myself to liking it too. The best is very good, and the whole hangs together well. Your letter was a very square affair, the long one, which I liked much, and was glad of. Of course I cannot hear praise of anywhere else but Gloucester, and the sea save for St Ives a lonely unimpressive kind of thing, but it is very good to be out of London at any rate. France or Spain from Du Bellay or Cervantes. I believe about Modern Music – that as no modern poem should be difficult to understand, neither should Music. When Abercrombie leaves clarity, he tangles himself.

F.W.H. was home for Easter and I saw him for one evening. His novel has got three parts done, and much verse. The baby was in bed, but he still is F.W.H. and incomparable. It was an evening of friends, but not alone. The long evenings of music-and-book talk seem to have vanished – quite essential to any joyful making of art.

The *Times* has recovered his Literary Page thank Goodness, the first blink of sun. Everybody seems to write well now – the clearness of ordinary written English is quite extraordinary.

April 23 1922

What fame is hers,
This England in the tides Atlantic bound,
What honour most inhabits of her ground,
What, void of fears,
Goes with her name to men that hear the sound
England?
Sure, that one Stratford slip of youth that had
Misfortune with the Justice in some mad
Deer stealing freak, and held horses they say,
Played Ghost and Adam on a luckier day.
Got money, bought a house and farm or two;
Died. Leaving poets else not much to do,
Save praise an *Alchemist* or *Iliad*.
What eventuality! What a crew.

Which isn't a bad Ode as those lumpy things go, I think.

My poems are pretty well ready for the publishers by now – of which I have said little to you, and some of them aren't bad at all. Sort of 'young Thomas' many of the things.

The Second Quartett is 3/4 ready. A minor – Carpentry but not bad at all.[1]

I am to hear about the Civil Service job tomorrow, and anything that kept me in Gloucester would be a good thing – never was such a place. It is full of continual wonderful surprises like Shakespeare; whose worst performance may be quoted from with devastating effect. *Titus Andronicus* begins well, but afterwards goes to pot – such blood and thunder bad even for that time.

With Best wishes
I remain

Your sincere friend
Ivor Gurney.

[1] See G.27.3.

433 To Marion Scott   Hurd Transcript

10 May 1922 (W)   1 Westfield Terrace, Longford, Gloucester

My Dear Friend

It is a long time since I have written – through various distractions, and there is not much to say save the completion of the Second Quartett, the despatch of a book of verse to Sidgwick, (80 poems or so) and walks abroad. And the arrival of the Carnegie proofs today. The book was returned – sort of rejected but telling me to correct and reject, which I have done, but not sent off yet, for form and coyness sake.

A letter from Lascelles Abercrombie, and a great evening at the Haines, with Will Harvey and Kerr. Wherein talk ranged right round the compass, and reputations disappeared like snow flakes.

Gloucestershire is getting a little too rich now, but the austere Crickley is in its grey glory fringed with grace. Nevertheless there are no farm jobs there. Today three goes were failures. However my pension has been renewed and that is considerable stand-by.

The chief luck of living out at Longford where the neighbour meadows are matchless – such arrangement of trees, such light, and levelness never known. Nevertheless one sight of Coopers Hill woods beats all. The great nuisance is climbing so castle-like a thing, but I had come from the east by strange ways, and indeed the kingdoms of the earth were spread before me. Brimscombe where thay were putting up a cross is much more Cold-Cotswold than all this. Bareness reserved for September to make beautiful (but good now).

The Second Quartett has a ripping slow movement and a competent Scherzo. All pretty good. The poems – the book according to F.S.S.Sidgwick is more like a poet's note book but O there's good stuff there!

Shakespeare has had most to do with the improvements

> 'Shakespeare's the fashion with all lonely walkers
> 'And wonder with ruth mixes in the blood'.
> 'Dawn pales the stars a brief while earlier day
> By bright day'.[1]

Lascelles Abercrombie asked for them, with whom they are now.

Still I send the book returned from an attempt to enter Georgian precincts. The later things are more delicate (John Fountain) (of Lamb's extracts). I do not ask about College, but one would like to know how the Parry room gets on. It was badly needed, and people should find things pleasanter because of it. Mr De la Mare was at the Haines a week ago, to lecture at Stroud, unfortunately on abstruse technical ps and bs. Well, here's *Ludlow and Teme* to do, for whose inclusion in the Carnegie list I suspect your party to have been sole mover.

Miss Nettleship sang a setting of Ben Jonson's 'Though I am young' somewhere in London.

Herbert's domestic news is interesting.

> 'Ay, ay, my liege And of a lovely boy: the God of Heaven
> Both now and ever bless her! Tis a girl
> Promises boys hereafter.'[2]

May the grace of Chapman's *Iliad* descend upon the arrival.

Let also the glory of *Antony* on the new Gloucester Festival thing. I hope the Christian Scientists will deny evil to you, continually. Many thanks for your letters and the enclosure. I have taken no especial pleasure to reproach

myself with waste.
    With best wishes
        I remain

                    Your sincere friend
                    Ivor Gurney

[1] Gurney is quoting from his own 'First Spring'; see letter 441 below.
[2] *Henry VIII*, V.1.163-6.

434 *To Marion Scott*   Hurd Transcript

May/June 1922 (KT)   1 Westfield Terrace, Longford, Gloucester

My Dear Friend
    All sorts of odds and ends there are to tell you; but nothing important save that I am hoeing six acres of wheat for 30/-, and consequently have a job. Will you please cease sending the allowance therefore? It is at Sandhurst just above Severn, and the soil light enough. That is the most important thing, and I have written to Dr. Vaughan Williams concerning it.
    Yesterday afternoon I went to Deerhurst for my first time. The Saxon chapel is nothing but the Norman and later church was very interesting with a tall oblong tower, graceful and strong and some of the finest carved doorways you could wish to see. The county is too full of foliage now – the Severn plain is better severe.
    The String Qartett is still without expression marks, but the Carnegie thing is almost finished. By the way I looked at Herbert Howells' Piano Quartett and did indeed think it the best piece of Chamber Music after Brahms F minor Quintett. The climax of the Slow Movement is one of the best things ever.
    Meanwhile I read Ben Jonson – and the Commemoratory Verse of all kinds, most extraordinarily good – by men like Cartwright, Broome and other hardly known people. They wrote splendidly. Goodness knows what they would think of our looser modern verse – some of it.
    There's a perfectly horrid memorial of the Gloucester Yeomanry put up in the Cathedral Close. It needs seeing to receive the proper shock. Some of the Cotswold things are said to be good, but Maisemore does not show well. Usually small crosses, but Barnwood has a lych gate, but a cock-eyed one. Deerhurst was better to see. It was extraordinary to come across that lonely village by Severn – once must have been a water-coup I should think, and on the Isle of Olney which Oman says was the Canute-Edmund Ironside affair not the Alney of Gloucester. A few cottages, a manor house, and a sort of queen ruler of a church over all, but Pendock Church was the most compact and well shaped of any ever I saw almost, and there too the manor house was good. But the wealth of good things is amazing.
    I am surprised to hear you think the *Ring* improved by time. I do like the

beginning of *Gotterdammerung* but the rest I cannot remember to have liked much.

Tuesday It is awfully hot today the hoeing most slow. One is aghast before such a waste of thistles, and quite unable to help hacking corn about. It is not far from the river; two meadows; and the cathedral shows, and a horse and plough are going in the next field; a lovely brown covered thing with noble furrows that come straight up at one. The farmers are very nice indeed. Carnegie is done with; the proofs were very good and gave little trouble; but verses have been rejected wholesale.

I have written to Dr.Vaughan Williams about this job. And asked him to stop the allowances which will you please do. I have been very grateful for it. When the third String Quartett is finished I shall feel more or less justified. And there are songs. Would be more but for the absolute shortage of verse.

It seems hopeless to say to any London person what the Gloucester [stars?] look like. Always different, always wonderful, and the faint high-looking stars of London are different indeed from these.

Ben Jonson is a stay as ever. A farm advertisement and other attempts to get jobs proved of no use.

With best wishes
    I remain

Your sincere friend
Ivor Gurney

P.S. One of my attempts was the brilliant idea of blackmailing a vicar into taking me as organist on condition he found me a farm job, but it was no use.

435 *To Walter De La Mare*   New York Public Library Berg Collection

Early June 1922 (W)   1 Westfield Terrace, Longford, Gloucester

To W.de la Mare Esq

Dear Mr De la Mare
    Thank you so much.

My intentions are to apply to the Committee for this post, and before my interview to make an immediate dash for London – my final attempt at gaining a musical post – which of course I ought to have, but have been unable in 4 whole months to obtain one.

If this dash is not successful I shall be most grateful to Mr Marsh and yourself – living on charity being most dreadful. Thank you again
    with best wishes
        I remain

Yours very sincerely
Ivor Gurney

New York Public Library Berg Collection

June 1922 (W)   1 Westfield Terrace, Longford, Gloucester

To E.Marsh Esq

Dear Mr Marsh

Mr de la Mare has written to you about my affairs. If you could help me to a clerkship at the Income Tax Office in Gloucester I should feel very obliged. Both the age and the *ERA* reject me, and in any case a picture palace was not the best of jobs. A clerkship would leave me without ties, with enough time to get and keep health. At present the county seems too lovely to leave. I seem to have caused a lot of people a lot of trouble, but think that the whole lump of my songs is the best of any lump. Reading accounts of new masterpieces brought out in London is disturbing, but there .... The County and English Literature should keep one sane. Mr Kerr, head of the Department knows me personally, and backs the application. From the tales of ignorance shown by the girl clerks I should be worth the money I think, and until a lectureship or a good school job (neither likely) comes along I should consider myself lucky to have it.

with best wishes
and apologies for troubling you
I remain

Yours very truly
I B Gurney.

Allow me to say I remember your bold enough painting of the Lakes with pleasure. In the lucky hour I did a pencil sketch of Framilode once that pleased me too.

New York Public Library Berg Collection

June 1922 (W)   1 Westfield Terrace, Longford, Gloucester

To E.Marsh Esq

Dear Mr Marsh

I am very sorry to trouble you about the same matter as before, but there seems a chance of use in writing. Although you told me not to suppose you could help me any more

Mr Kerr is about to have an extra clerk sent to him, and suggests that it might be possible for me to have that post.

If not, please do not trouble about this, and I will wait for the other which may fall vacant about the end of June.

I remain

Yours very sincerely
Ivor Gurney.

438 *To Edward Marsh*   New York Public Library Berg Collection

June 1922 (W)   1 Westfield Terrace, Longford, Gloucester

To E Marsh Esq

Dear Mr Marsh

I send a copy of a poem that appeared in the *Gloucester Journal*, hoping you will be interested to see it.[1]

It seems good enough to myself.

I remain

Yours very truly
Ivor Gurney.

[1] Gurney enclosed a cutting of 'Tewkesbury' which appeared in June 1922.

439 *To Edmund Blunden* Harry Ransom Research Center, U. of Texas at Austin

Late June 1922 (KT)   1 Westfield Terrace, Longford, Gloucester

To E.Blunden Esq

Dear Edmund Blunden

I have not properly read your *Shepherd*,[1] it being too clean a book for my careless borrowing, but some of the things struck me – 'The Puff ball' is stronger than I thought you ever capable of; it *is* a strong thing. 'The Gipsies' too I remember with appreciation.[2]

There seems a chance that the Civil Service post so long expected will soon fall vacant. Meanwhile the last of Three String Quartetts is nearly finished, and I suppose about a hatful of verse.

Your 'Waggoners' I tried to set and rather failed.[3]

If Sidgwick refuse my new book, is there any publisher it is wise to try instead? Some of the best things I have done would be in it, and nothing really amateurish. One postcard on this subject would oblige

Yours very sincerely
Ivor Gurney.

[1] Published 27 April 1922
[2] Called in fact 'The Idlers' in that volume.
[3] From *The Waggoner and other Poems* (1920).

June 1922 (W) 1 Westfield Terrace, Longford, Gloucester

Dear Mr Marsh

Firstly I want to tell you that the Civil Service post has fallen vacant, and that I am to start on Monday[1] – and to thank you extremely for your getting it me; which I hope to find a soft job in a lovely county; Thank you for this.

Next to say that I am sorry you do not [like] 'Gloucestershire from the train' etc well enough for the *Georgian*; being myself quite sure that F W Harvey is awfully underrated. I have not seen Hardy's latest book, but I doubt whether he does ever, if at all, much surpass this poem. True, the book would seem to make a bad model, but that is true of others. As for 'Tewkesbury', if you can give so much time to criticising a small poem, you must have small time for yourself. It is very considerate to take so much trouble. Anyway, I am proud of the thing; as a picture it seems to me to be first-rate. There is one foot dropped in one line – altered to 'Here man does rule, his works to be found here.'[2] Otherwise it is a sort of Chapman verse, and that I am content with, though the Miltonic verse may be far above that in technical achievement – yet Milton does so often achieve technique only.

The difference being as between Palestrina and Byrd that Byrd was always trying to do things with his modal counterpoint – not a pure thing perhaps, but far more likeable.

It is cockeyed, but Milton would have put a Corinthian pillar or two between the village Forthampton and Tewkesbury, couldnt have got the various hints in about the history – not in the time at any rate. I suppose my blank verse to be words set to a blank verse tune, but do like

'And gathers by a sign the broad meadows in round here'

And do like the poem as a whole very much; do not think anyone else would have drawn Tewkesbury as well.

I am sorry to reply in so contradictatorial a fashion, being very surprised to find three sheets devoted to me, but am so sat upon, that kicking seems right.

Thank you again for the Civil Service Post.

With best wishes

I remain

Yours very sincerely

Ivor Gurney

Neither Palestrina or Byrd though!

[1] He had started by 3 July
[2] Line 12.

Early July 1922 (KT)   1 Westfield Terrace, Longford, Gloucester

Dear Blunden

Many congratulations on winning the Hawthornden Prize.[1] From my glances at the *Shepherd* I should say that it was much more accomplished than the *Waggoner*. (After reading the Commemoratory Verses Epigrams etc in Ben Jonson's book, I remembered your advice. I suppose you to have reared yourself on him.)

The 'Giant Puffball' I should say would be memorable in any age, and then there is that poem ending up with the kiss of day, and 'the moon the blossom of lonely hours'.[2] No, there are no new French poems, but if anyone should show a sign of taking there probably would be. Hearts of stone have the editorships now.

Anyway as the true admirer of both your books I am glad you have the Hawthornden – you being one who are a follower of Clare and Cobbett Morland and Crome. It is true you have not written of as lovely a county as this is – Had you lived in Gloucestershire, more than the general background of green leafage-stuff would seem to appear to me. The Clouds here are terrific. I mean that you seem to write when have become absorbed by lane-look. Here it would be different.

L.Abercrombie wrote me a very nice letter about my things. The *Sale of St Thomas*[3] I take to be the best modern poem of ours. Would you agree?

Here is one of mine, which I like.

First Spring

Now are there green flames springing by washed roads,
And colour where winter black and gray thorn showed.
Shakespeare's a fashion with all lonely walkers,
And wonder with ruth mixes in the blood.

Miles and miles walk they those schoolgirls and school boys
For daffodils and primroses with the lies
Of half a hundred trespasses upon them,
Who drown their crimes with action and clear noise.

Dawn pales the stars a brief while earlier, day
By bright day and the stars take new array;
Only my dumbness mocks my search for speech
Only the thing-accomplished makes delay.

I hope you will like it; and once again congratulate you on winning this

prize, and glad so very downright and English stuff stands to your name.
Best wishes

Yours very sincerely and congratulatingly
Ivor Gurney

[1] The presentation was announced in the *Times* of 30 June 1922. The name, with its association . with Jonson and Annie Nelson Drummond through Drummond of Hawthornden, is at the centre of a cluster of ideas for Gurney.
[2] The fourth line of 'Evening Mystery' in *The Shepherd*.
[3] By Abercrombie (1911).

442 *To Edmund Blunden* Harry Ransom Research Center, U. of Texas at Austin

Mid July 1922 (KT) 1 Westfield Terrace, Longford, Gloucester

To Edmund Blunden Esq

Dear Blunden

I hope you will not mind my sending you this stuff, of which, in spite of the base word I am proud. Sidgwick with some politeness has rejected it, but myself see thundering good stuff there, beauty and a very good sense of form, and no swank.

If after reading it, you would send it on to Cobden Sanderson I should be very much obliged; or if you think it better send it here again.

There is nothing so good as the 'Giant Puff ball' but pots of good stuff there is.

I am an unsuccessful and angry poet writing to a successful poet who has already done things for him, but the Swan of Avon himself has occasionally had his wing plucked here, I think. Nevertheless, no long flights.

Best wishes
I remain

Yours very sincerely
Ivor Gurney.

443 *To Marion Scott* G.53.19-21

July 1922 (KT) 1 Westfield Terrace, Longford, Gloucester

My Dear Friend

I have just received my second week's pay without outcry, so suppose it is all right, but all things frighten me rather. The third Quartett is stuck in its last movement but will do.

My verses went to Blunden to whom I had written in appreciation of a poem in *The Shepherd* called 'The Giant Puff-ball' one of the finest things ever – who sent them to Cobden Sanderson from whom I have not heard.

Masefield wrote the nicest note about 'Tewkesbury' containing the phrase 'your lovely gift'. And A E Housman the most generous free permission for *Ludlow and Teme* which I have tried to persuade the Carnegie Trustees not to accept.

So my correspondence list has been illustrious sufficiently, and I write War Poems. (rather bad.)

I was glad to see Ireland's Prelude was being done at College – anything might come after the Sonata – that noble thing. He must have been reading Jonson.

It is queer how Brahms stands the test. The fugue at the end of Handel-Brahms Variations is the most glorious fake ever made.

Of course Bach and Beethoven both do – the Wedge Fugue is my best admiration at present.

And an amazing book of Elegant Extracts printed by Bensley of Fleet St in 1824, in which there is much remarkable stuff including the noble 'Vanity of Human Wishes' of Dr Johnson, all sorts of minor things by Akenside, Armstrong, Smart. A meditation by Mrs Barbauld in blank verse containing things like

'This dead of midnight is the morn of thought
And wisdom mounts her zenith with the stars'
which is pretty large. All sorts of wonderful stuff, including an excellent Shakespeare Selection, and many play Prologues and Epilogues.

The Taxes office is just on the Corner of College Court, quite a fine building with something of a staircase, and a view across to Malvern from higher window looks, and an interesting view across good slate roofs and honest 18th Century brick. The front is very fine Corinthian (or sort of) with well spaced windows. It is not so bad for Taxes; from which I have cribbed the best of Poetry Note Books.

Gloucester has a new a vile Garage in Westgate St, but there is one jolly general shop where I drink milk with some enjoyment.

The Cathedral still disappoints as to the Nave, the surrounding country being so much stronger. Greek Plain and Roman Hills, and meadows like (I should guess) a Virgil Pastoral.

The most formidable bundle of proofs has come from Stainer and Bell – *Ludlow and Teme* and a set of Children's Pieces. It is to deal with them. [*sic*]

W.R.P.Kerr dashed up to London and had a great time with E.Marsh and Colonel Laurence. He is to be in the next *Chapbook* and is very bucked in consequence. Certainly the best talker I have met. W.Harvey is here, but I have not been well enough to go out. J.W.Haines characteristic but worried – surely a Worthy.

The excellence of early Browning is my chief admiration. What a literature

540

we have. Bach of course worked through to wonderful content at times but not often to good style. Mrs Barbauld topped excellence once – 'Summer Evening's Meditation'.

With best wishes
I remain

Your sincere friend
Ivor Gurney.

444 *To W.H.Davies*   G.61.88

1922 (KT)   1 Westfield Terrace, Longford, Gloucester

To W H Davies Esq

Dear Mr Davies

Ever since *Nature Poems* first was shown to me I have always been a sincere admirer of your work, and have carried your books in London, Gloucestershire and France. I am occasionally stuck-up in my ordinary writing and then set verse – it occurred to me that you might like this. If it were properly done, you might say it was a good one.

Gloucester Library of course always was a good one, and Fulham had your work where I read *The Autobiography of a Supertramp* several times with delight while at the Royal College of Music. I wonder whether you ever came across Framilode – opposite Rudford, near Newnham on Severn? It was a place I read your poems most at, sailing a boat, spouting 'Sing happy Soul'. I can think that the poem which has a phrase about the ship of sunrise being launched was written there.[1]

With best wishes I remain

Yours very truly
Ivor Gurney

[P.S.] I have set 'O Happy Wind' and 'Dreams of the Sea' also.[2]

[1] Davies' poem 'Songs of Joy' has the line 'Sing happy Soul'. The 'ship of gold' is launched in 'Early Morn', one of the poems Gurney set (see G.30.2.3).
[2] The Gloucester Archive contains (at G.30.2.1-7) seven settings of Davies poems, three of them being versions of 'O Happy Wind' and one a version of 'Dreams of the Sea' dated 1914. The other three are 'Early Morn', undated, 'A Bird's Anger' dated July 1924 and 'The Moon' dated 1922. This last may well be the piece referred to above.

445 *To the Mayor of Gloucester*   G.70.56

October 1922   Barnwood House, Gloucester

To the Mayor of Gloucester (KT)

Sir

I pray in the Name of God to be taken out of Electrical influence, and after to receive such fate as may be. In the Name of God I pray it. I am in the four walls of Barnwood House and cannot stand it. Continual electrical influence destroys.

I remain

Yours truly
I.B.Gurney

Gloucester Police Station is torturing.

446 *To J.W.Haines and F.W.Harvey*   G.83.29.2

4 November 1922 (P)   Barnwood House, Gloucester

To Messrs Haines & Harvey, Solicitors, King St, Gloucester

Sirs

I hope for release and a chance of death successful. For nothing else. Do not leave me here. I suffer.

I remain

Yours
I.B.Gurney

I only wish to die. Never mind the pension. To die. Not to be tormented.

447 *To Gloucester Police Station*   G.83.29.3

4 November 1922 (P)   Barnwood House, Gloucester

To Gloucester Police Station[1]
Clerk

Sir

May I be allowed to receive the reward of my misdoings (eating in the street) rather than to stay here? To be imprisoned. May I ask in the name of God?

I.B.Gurney

P.S. I have a twisted body of some kind.

In God's Name

In God's Name to have Mercy
And to be granted death –
Is the most of desire now
Of the giving up of breath

And quite incredible
Madness in pain forgotten
Only, only to die out
Till all things are nothing

Crimes are surely paid for
By a death's paying
Nothing to be afraid, for
Death is all denying.

[1] G.83.29.1 is a deleted letter 'To Clerk, Police-Constabulary, Gloucester': 'In prison there is surely more chance of keeping health than here. Have mercy, I pray, and grant a chance of death or true punishment. Grant chance of the railway line I pray, and remember that there was more mercy in other ages, please. Have mercy I pray. Grant chance of death.'

448 *To Ralph Vaughan Williams*   G.61.175

November 1922 (KT)   Barnwood House, Gloucester

To R.Vaughan Williams Esq

Sir

I would pray you believe *words*, and to get me term of imprisonment, *dangerous public service*, work, freedom to go on tramp, *but chance of death always* – rather than to be left here, where conditions are not such as one can get well in, and one may be never well enough to go. Have mercy; believe words. A living thing desires not to be cooped up; often under influence; will do almost anything for freedom and usefulness, but not to be left here to rust into disuse, after so much desperate trying. Doctors and superintendent say I may go if friends call for me. I am in Barnwood House – Please free me from the possibility of staying one more week. I will obey orders, and do what I can do.

Yours humbly
and desperately
I.B.Gurney

Chance of death. Words of truth. To save from Barnwood House.

449 *To F.W.Harvey*   G.84.10

November 1922 (KT)   Barnwood House, Gloucester

To F.W.Harvey Esq, Solicitor, King St, Gloucester

Sir

Under spell of E.I of various sorts I escaped at night.[1] Dared not stay at the
Railway. Left letter at Palace and Deanery. Made for railway. No use. Made
for river. Could not do it. Made for Police station, where later was handed to
Hospital Authorities. Would have taken Railway, or Shot, but it was not
possible. Could not face river. Kindly treated by authorites on the whole.

Would ask for death or freedom. Or imprisonment to cover small crimes.
Railway denied by chance. No trains at critical moment.

I.B.Gurney.

Not afraid to die by shot or railroad.
Much less pain today but bad.
Doctors say friends may take him. Ronald.

[1] The Superintendent of Barnwood, Arthur Townsend, wrote to Marion Scott on 9
November 1922 that Gurney had escaped on the 8th; see *Ordeal*, p.156.

450 *To Dr Harper*   G.84.10

November 1922 (KT)   Barnwood House, Gloucester

To Dr Harper, Half Moon St, Piccadilly, London W

Sir

I thank your great kindness, would have taken the railroad, but flunked the
river. The doctors are good men but conditions are not good. Pain bad
sometimes. Attendants many ex-Service, very kind. But may I receive either
freedom or chance of death. Dangerous service. Anything rather than to
remain here.

May the Metropolitan Police of London grant mercy to one placed here for
protection by friends.

Have mercy I pray.

I.B.Gurney
Bernard Barton[1]

[1] Why Gurney signs this name as well is difficult. A Bernard Barton (1784-1849) wrote
The Convict's Appeal to protest against the severity of the criminal code, as well as
Household Verses (1845).

November 1922 (KT)   Barnwood House, Gloucester

Dear J.W.H.

Thank you very much for your letter. It was good of you to write, but at present I have to sit still and suffer such a slow hardship. Will not one of [you] come to fetch me away, to do what things are good to be done at your advice? I send my hopes and for a life where I may move about.

Such difficulties there are. I came here because I was tormented. Will it not please you to remove me from here. In mercy's name to have me out.

Dr Vaughan Williams and Miss Scott came to see me, but I could not persuade them to take me at the moment. I am here, be merciful, get me away. With crippled sore feet, an intelligence-of-being sometimes threatened, and fear. Do not omit to understand this. Could I not, might I not live in the hut in your garden. Can you not believe me?

Thank you for your letter though. Many hours of fine love I have had for you, who must sit here almost useless. Reassure me somehow, that I am not to be left. Come to see me if it may be. I like very much the doctors, but pain is hard-master. Many attendants are of the best kind.

Yours
I.B.Gurney

Send stamped envelopes, I would ask.

November 1922 (KT)   Barnwood House, Gloucester

To Miss M.Scott

Dear Miss Scott

I thank you so much for your coming, and the good intentions that impelled you to send the cushions. I am now up however and do not so need them.

Thank you for coming though. Had issues been more fortunate, I might have been repaying kindness before now, but the help of Carlyle proved useless, and none knows what might have happened. I have written many letters – all for freedom; except those for imprisonment or chance of death. I wish to work or die. I have the same thoughts as you. Yesterday Ronald came, but he doubted that the talk of my pain was more than electrical delusion. It is good of you to write. After the War, what hopes there were! To earn a living and to write praise of England! Surely the ordinary desirings of a mind seeking fulfilment, after the manner of seekers after Truth, lovers of mankind and the pleasures and joys God-sent. But not much pleasure have I taken. This waiting here so tiresome, but there is no pain now, thank goodness. I ask pardon for so small a letter, your great kindness deserved more. May God reward it, that good endeavour.

One cried out of pain and another heard.

But had war hopes proved anything well, – Well it is no use thinking. *War's Embers* has improved with time, and what I would have done has not accomplished. Nevertheless the Two Quartetts are very good in their way.

Is it still to write all this, but in pain.

These words mean what they say. To have mercy, to release me from here, for the pain of Barnwood House is great. St Albans was nothing to it. The doctors are good men, will they not attend to letters?

A soldier and an artist asks to be released to the chances of common life – to work or to be allowed to die. Ask Ronald to believe mere words and not his own opinion. I have to sit still. Will not the General Election make a difference? Will not electricity be used to clean ends. My Mother thinks there is something the matter with me and that I had better be left. – to what? O Just fancies, she thinks. Then let me have work in the open, or anywhere. The negation of God is here. You saw me less tormented than often.

Believe that nevertheless God rewards such kindness as yours. Do not risk anything, do not suffer danger, but believe words. I have written to Knapsbury. But consider – such have uncomplaining hopes so broken! May your kindness be rewarded. May no punishment fall on your great mercy in coming here. I am up, but not moving about. Sitting still, and being agitated.

Have mercy and rescue I pray

Yours
I.B.Gurney

---

453 *To Marion Scott*   G.61.174

November 1922 (KT)   Barnwood House, Gloucester

Dear Miss Scott

I am greatly obliged to you for your having come to see me. But *every word* that was said in my letters was meant, is meant. Nevertheless the great kindness shown is fit to be celebrated, and may some return be shown to you. Do not leave me here, I pray, but I would not withdraw one word of what has been written.

Death would be rest from torment. The use of life is so far from here. The verses are sent from me. But it is better to be writing what I should – three quartetts I had hoped for. To St Albans if it may be, though the first thing is to be got from here. May God guard all.

546

I am glad the Housman book is so good. One is glad that that fine metal lasted.

I remain

Yours gratefully
I.B.Gurney

Hoping for chance of death. Rescue me I pray.
[*P.S.*] There is work at Knapsfield. XX to get from here!! XXX
[*Crossed out at the bottom of the letter are lines of a poem:*
    Surely the natural law of life is such
    As goes on kindly with a true flow
    Of goodness and to goodness with a touch
    Of naturalness in love]

---

454 *To Colchester Wemyss*   G.70.53

November 1922 (KT)   Barnwood House, Gloucester

To Colchester Wemyss

Sir
    I was brought by friends out of Electrical tricks.
    Brought here, left.
    To be put under torture. E.I. meals and the rest.
    To live in bad conditions and unhuman humiliation
    Dreadful torture at times.
    Have twice escaped.
    And have suffered incredibly.
    Being paid for here, as guest, continually praying for
    Death, In the Name of God.
    May you please to grant imprisonment out of electrical control or influence
or the mercy of death.

I implore
I.B.Gurney.

But release from here in the Name of God.

November 1922 (KT)   Barnwood House, Gloucester

To Miss Scott

My Dear Friend
    I have been in such pain this morning, that I have posted letters to the
Bishop of Gloucester and others, asking to be delivered from my agony. And
have applied for imprisonment and other things. Rescue me while I am sane.
One more day here is terrible to think of. Your letters are beautiful letters, but
I cannot bear my pain. There is no reason for any such. Any fate but to remain
in Barnwood House. Death at once is far better.
    The doctors will not let me go, and I am under continual Wireless influence
and electrical influence. In the Name of God get me another fate. Pity a human
being, under attendants orders. Made to sit still, led about. Having appealed to
the doctors for all things anything. Praying for death. Imprisonment,
anything, to clear fate. Or the supreme Mercy of death at once. But not to be
left here one more moment. It is all incredible. But the pains are better.
                                                            I.B.Gurney.

456 *To the Dean of Gloucester*   G.70.54

November 1922 (KT)

To the Dean of Gloucester
Thanking him
Sir The fundamental fact is torture.
    The second is the doctors do not release a sane tortured being.
    The third is that, the doctors permission that my friends may take me away
is not taken advantage of.
    When I should not be a part of many electrical schemes
    My friends may take me away

    The mercy of Death is continually desired.
Because the four walls of Barnwood House surround.
With all the dreadful conditions here.
I pray to you that you will release me from one more day of this dreadful
house.

    Imprisonment or death or employment.
Not to be tortured as everyday have I been.
                                                    In mercy
                                                    I.B.Gurney
Release from here is first demanded.

November 1922 (KT)   Barnwood House, Gloucester

> I write to Dr Terry, and I tell him
> That six months imprisonment would be an easy way
> Out of tangle. That Barnwood House is Hell
> That terrible torture is known there. That Doctors as well
> As others may be tortured. That Dr Little
> Is a thorough good sort, and Dr Soutar
> A good man; Dr Townsend a gentleman, but that
> All day nothing happens that is human but
> Work, to me. And I am tormented, and life
> Is as easily shaken off in desire as feather
> That I cannot write letters but in tangle.
> And there is nothing had of knowledge but
> A tangle of perplexities. Why do they not
> Release? Why are things tied so in a knot?
> I am saner and more innocent
> Than many people walking the open air.
> And have written verses, and much music
> Take me away, grant death or merciful fate.
> Six months imprisonment, to clear this
> Tangle of tortures, but now mental, and easiness
> To what has been. But all is heated and confined.
> Fresh will blow outside the November air kind
> And I am so that I would shoot the dearest
> Thing I knew to save it from such clearest
> Pain; and no one knows what fortune ever has been
> Which is kind, and merciful and as Design meant good
> Who have walked after first hour rejoicing in mood.

November 1922 (KT)   Barnwood House, Gloucester

To S. Scott Esq

Sir

I rise and am in electrical influence immediately. In the name of Mercy release me from this place.[1] Grant sacred Mercy of death.

I am here because my friends brought me. May God take me away, to prison or mercy of Death. May God grant always immediate Death, but rescue must come out of this place. In God's Name of Mercy for rescue.

Grant Death I pray. Pity misery. I would rather die than live at any moment in this house. I am under E I all day. Have mercy. Death would always be great mercy.

Imploringly
I.B.Gurney

Gloucester Police Station tortures.

[1] Sydney Scott replied on his Scott, Bell and Co paper from their address in 15 Queen Street, Cheapside, London, E.C.4 on 25 November 1922: 'My dear Ivor/ I have received your letter & am glad to be able to assure you that active steps are being taken as you wish to change your place of residence & I feel sure this will be arranged very shortly./ There is always a certain amount of detail inseparable from moving from one place to another as you will readily understand but the matter is in train & will speedily be satisfactorily concluded./ Meantime I am sure you will make up your mind to stick it knowing that every effort is being made on your behalf.' The letter has Gurney's comments in its margins: 'Sir, I thank you. Am in the hands of Barnwood House. Grant six months imprisonment I pray attendants explain. I am afraid of Barnwood House which torments. Grant rescue, just trial, freedom or death, which I am always ready to take./ There is no reason for torment. I have sincerely asked for 6 months in Gloucester Gaol.'

---

459 To Marion Scott   G.10.76

9 December 1922 (P)   Barnwood House, Gloucester

My Dear Friend

I am not much tormented tonight, but not allowed to move about much. Going quietly mad.

My friends have been told they may fetch me away. Why do they not, when every hour is bad, and I have suffered agony today. But Pain much better now. The Police Station is doing me in (but I dare not say so.) Write to ask it whether I may go there and mark Books. Any fate but this awful one. Or to the War Office for Death. I cannot stand one hour of it. All through this unnecessary agony I could not stand it. God's pity has been far from me.

Any death in Gods Name. Rescue from here from here. I am treated as a lunatic, led about by an attendant. Walk in a small compound, have regular meals. Incredible things happen in my mind.

Awful incredible Hellish things have happened.

My friends do not take me out!

I.B.Gurney.

[*Over the page*] Being brought here by friends out of electrical tricks
Being [*crossed out* put / It is Gloucester]
In the Name of God at once
Imprisonment out of E I

460 To Marion Scott

December 1922 (KT)   G.10.62.2

Barnwood House, Gloucester

My Dear Friend

I am to go to a Doctor Steen's near London.
Is this all right? Should it not be Virginia Water?
I cannot stand much more –
I ask your pity, and favour to do what you or goodness and charity will do.
But first to be saved from this place.
Thank you so much for the tobacco.
I am under strict orders just now. See that I be fit to go. I fear and ask should it not be Virginia Water? It is wrong to trouble but such pain has right. Have mercy. I am ashamed to be so much trouble, but there has been so much pain. Now better.
I hope it is all right. Indeed I had great delight in life. But now, would pray to God for Death.
Be kind, I pray you, and see after my affairs.
I remain

Yours trustingly
I.B.Gurney

461 To Ronald Gurney

December 1922 (KT)   G.10.62.2

Barnwood House, Gloucester

To R.E.Gurney Esq

Dear Ronald

Why have you not taken me away?
Look after Mother please. Gloucester Police Station is tormenting, I think.

Yours
I.B.Gurney

My pain has been very great.

462 To Marion Scott

December 1922 (KT)   G.10.63.1

Barnwood House, Gloucester

Dear Miss Scott

I ask your especial mercy to have me away from here to Dr Steen's, as soon as possible, for indeed much awfulness do I endure. Will you please ask him to take me as soon as possible. For indeed I am in great distress. Have mercy, and help me. Save me.

Ivor Gurney.

463 *To Dr Steen*

G.10.63.2

December 1922 (KT)

Barnwood House, Gloucester

To Dr Steen Dartford Kent.
 Asking him to take him and save him.

Ivor Gurney

464 *To Marion Scott*

G.10.20

December 1922 (KT)

Barnwood House, Gloucester

Dear Miss Scott

This night I am feeling better, and things are quieter and cooler, but life is cramped in a $12\frac{1}{2}$ hour day, and one could wish space to work. I was tortured silly this morning – I hope you are not in danger, for I saw a sign of it. Are my verses all right? Are you yourself all right. What I can say of thanks is little, for the pain of being here is great. Woolwich mud is desired, but Waterloo Bridge or the Monument is wished for more.[1] My life is a $12\frac{1}{2}$ hour one of torment of some kind. What will come, if possible, I leave to Mr Scott. For I myself under E I can do nothing, much. Poems for the London Metropolitan Police or under torment (which? I laugh) I hope Mrs Voynich is all right. I have seen signs of her being tormented; please protest, as it is right to protest against all torment. I cannot cut my throat on a window pane is all that is the matter. Save, I pray, to some fate. For this wireless torment of a $12\frac{1}{2}$ hours day is no good.

Best wishes. If I were dead it would be better. If alive could do good work. But I want death, as a compensation for so much pain. Best wishes

'Lady of Mercy'
Ivor Gurney

[*On the back*] I can write little here,

---

[1] Presumably as methods of suicide.

December 1922 (KT) Barnwood House, Gloucester

To Dr Harper, Threadneedle St, Piccadilly

I sit still after torture. Sir, I desire death more than anything But cannot get it.

If it were freedom for work I should be glad – but rather than one day more of Barnwood House – the Supreme Mercy of Death. I cannot bear it. Desire death.

If it were possible to get freedom of life or good employment at once I should be glad. But rather than endure such hours as I endure – the Mercy of Death. I pray the doctors for death, I ask them. Today has been intolerable. Mercy of Death I pray. I cannot bear to be tortured. My life has just freed itself. I have a 12½ hours day. 4 meals. Need 18 and freedom.

They are interrupting and have been torturing. My life recalled with torture, Dr Harper. If you can save, I will stand just trial for living on my aunt beyond her means. Not for beating the dog.

Have mercy on one who has read everything Elizabethan that matters, much music and verse have written. Get me from this place I pray out of torture into merciful fate. They torture with past life foolishly, as if pain had not many times been reckoned.

Conditions impossible – with varied distractions.

I am afraid.

Are past crimes never pardoned?

Being afraid of further torture, I want Death.

I remain Sir

Yours truly
I.B.Gurney

All today I would gladly have prayed for Death.

Or imprisonment for past crimes or to clear fate.

Anything but to stay in electrical pain or influence.

'Mercy of Woolwich mud earnestly desired.' I send a sign.

Imprisonment and trial Two days old.

Or Death.

466 *To Marion Scott* G.10.61

15 December 1922 (P) Barnwood House, Gloucester

To Miss Scott

Praying that she may save him from the fate of staying longer in Barnwood House.

For the mercy of being brought to Dr Steen's

Ivor Gurney
In the Name of Mercy.

---

467 *To Marion Scott*   G.10.79

21 December 1922 (P)   Barnwood House, Gloucester

Dear Miss Scott
  If I am left here any longer I shall go mad.

Ivor Gurney
In the Name of God

[*On the verso of this letter are the first two words of an aborted letter to J.W.Haines.*]

---

468 *To Marion Scott*   G.10.8

26 December 1922 (P)   Dr Steen, Dartford, London

To Miss M Scott.
  I am here, and know how many efforts you have made on my behalf – but know also, that there is no real reason for my being confined. I would ask you to do what you can for me, who am hungering for work. But Death or Imprisonment to clear tangle and work after. Anything. There was no reason for my getting into trouble at all – save misdemeanours which a months imprisonment would have cleared and living on my Aunt. I have suffered too much. May you rescue me by some means. I shall appeal to J.C.Squire – for indeed my labour was great and my staying up. I shall hardly be able to work here. Though Dr Steen has suggested kindly that I shall be allowed on the poultry farm. You know how things are. It is a tangled case. Which should have been no case. Be good to me. If instant release, I should be glad. If not – may my friends do much for me. It is bad for a night-walker, and a worker to call on people so. What tales are to be told, may I be spared for telling here. Be good and rescue one who is always ready for Death, but wishes for work, any work in merciful conditions.
  Rescue I pray, one who would be fit outside.
  If Mr Scott would arrange something I should be glad. It is true that there are many good men here, but do rescue. To some life or death. Mr Scott will know more than I.
  I am quite fit for work. Any kind almost, for who can bear confinement. I send my best wishes and thanks for all your endeavours and say once again there is no reason why I should not be out. Help me, I ask you. For this is a

554

place one cannot be happy in. If my tale were told it would more than justify me.

I pray you help me.

Ivor Gurney.

26 December 1922 (P)   Dr Steen, Near Dartford, Kent

Dear Miss Scott

Who has done so much to get me here, I thank you very much, and hope that you will save me to one of the two sane fates.

There is no reason why I should be in confinement – Much trouble have I known; after so good an attempt to work. My aunt's kindness was not wasted. I have much to write of – but can hardly do it here.

I am a writer and musician. In a mental home, sometimes suffering terrible pains put on me for no reason. For I harmed none. I pray you to rescue me. To get me away to some fate, Death or Life, with no pain, and chance to work or death. Will you not understand? Will you not accept my thanks for help – but understand that I have worked very hard, have been unjustly dealt with, with such pain. Will you not instantly so deal that I shall be free, for some fate or other – not to suffer. There is no reason for it all. It is purposeless wickedness. Will no justice release to life such a being? I cannot work here. Surely my friends have enough influence, immediately to require me out? Terrible pain in hopeless surroundings. You are so good yourself, but you cannot understand. All England should be honouring me. Whereas I should be honoured.

I pray my friends to take me as one sane from confinement and pain any longer. Some have been here ages.

They can do it – knowing that I have suffered so as to have cried or been willing to cry for Death every day. I cannot work out of it here. Will they not get me out simply? It cannot be so difficult to require release and to protect afterwards. I pray their patience, their strength, their understanding of my words – and exact appreciation of the pain that drives me to do certain things. I am at Dr Steen's. Under rules. They cut. It is true much has been done for me, but instant salvation for Life or Death is what I want. The whole is too cruel, too unbearable.

It is Ivor Gurney calls for help and release. Other lives are terrible, but this one is to be helped. Great pity to one who is broken, but only needs freedom as of other people to work. Sane, innocent, much tormented. Save I pray.

I remain

Yours imploringly

Yet with thanks for your endeavours
Ivor Gurney

If the Metropolitan Police will save me, these verses are intended for them. I ask much, but cry for death.

To the City Churches

Wren made you with straight lines showing clear
In artificial lighting your clear-cut lines.
And when the cool daylight on soot-stone shines
Then there is joy in passers by, and near
The Viaduct one hastens to look over
To see Traffic pass, but one's looks do return
To see St Albans (is it?) as Wren the lover
Of stone set it upright in shape that, stern
And tender both, will take day and night some centuries
Yet, the seeing and soul set well to please.

I.B.G.

There is a natural freedom

There is a natural freedom right to man
That never should be, save most carefully
Be taken ever away; as part of plan
First promise of his Maker to the free
Being, who was with his labour to earn freedom
As curse, to earn bread with sweat of his brow
But even that bitter right may be denied now,
When poor humans have taken from them hope to come.
But now the fittest and the best are taken
With no cause from their just employment and
Given pain that's dreadful to the Making Hand
By such dread pangs of mind are torn and shaken
As Never meant the maker to their being –
Who gave strength to limbs, breath, hearing, seeing.

I.B.Gurney

Have Mercy I pray O God
For in my distresses
Weigh heavy, thy cleanly rod
Has not such stresses

Of Pain on the sick mind
That rod is clean
And does not leave behind
Such black ill stain

Give not power to such bad
Black hands of strength
But to the lovers, the sad
Atom, of length.

Give not thy Power now
That might remake
Earth again to such slow
Fighters, for Mercy's sake.

The Lamplights

To the golden summer lamplights of London now
My thoughts return, with gratitude for green leaves
Seen shimmer in the warm summer's dim glow,
When there is warmth of colour on late eves.
Walking leisurely in the bright lamp flare
Seeing stars glimmer high up through depths of air
High summer stars lonely or in a crowd
Of golden light, and in the higher spaces some
Scattered glows showing, scattered glows
Of far dim starshine – walking cool of wonderful
Dim night. O but there was an olden company
Of night-walkers, brave of word and of heart's courage
Who would have seen in these still friendly things
Whose station is so set, yet the whole sky swings
And there is all night movement on the stage
Of Heaven, while earth seems to stand as steady
As any thought still dwelt on, the earth ready
To obey the further motion outside space,
The idea that does keep the whole in grace,
And new in freshness every night, the sure
Thought behind all motion that makes endure
The swinging of the spheres and the good going
Of any at all of those high lamps there glowing
Softly over the tides of people and
Thames flowing through mud-flats to further sand.

I.B.Gurney

INDEX OF RECIPIENTS

Letters to the following people begin on the page noted.

INDEX

A book of this size must have limitations to its index. Among economies of entry, I have indexed only the more significant moments in Marion Scott's life since she appears on nearly every page, and I have not indexed Gloucester, which is mentioned almost as frequently, nor members of the family mentioned in a family letter. I have also assumed that places mentioned in the Chronology are as simply found by looking at the letters of the relevant dates as in an index.

Boswell: 144, 174, 288, 406-7, 495.
Bottomley, Gordon: 401, 494.
Bottomley, Horatio: 59, 108, 342.
Bouquemaison: 280, 334.
Bourton on the Water: 435.
Bourton on the Hill: 254.
Bourtseff: 31.
Bradley, Oswald: 373.
Brahms: 1-3, 19, 45, 119, 184, 256, 268, 336, 469, 489, 493, 511-2, 516-7, 527, 529, 540; Magelone Lieder: 481-2; quintet: 472, 533; St Antony Variations: 119; sonata: 492, 495, 500, 502; symphonies: 197.
Brancepeth Castle: xvii, 410.
Brangwyn: 189.
Bredon: 216, 224, 325, 328, 404.
Brewer, Dr Herbert: xiv, 358, 426-7.
Bridge, Frank: 379.
Bridge, Sir John Frederick: 270.
Bridges, Robert: xx, 70, 73, 104, 107, 131, 177, 233, 237, 249, 256, 271, 294, 312-3, 315, 325, 468, 500, 509, 513; The Spirit of Man: 135, 138, 140-1, 148, 212, 215, 230, 236, 239, 276, 299, 412, 461, 466.
Brimscombe: 532.
Brock, Clutton: 517.
Brockworth: 490.
Brontë, Charlotte: 335, 337.
Brooke, Rupert: viii, 19, 20, 25, 29, 80, 174-5, 181, 203, 220, 236, 288, 292, 315, 370, 412, 502, 523; Inn – 'Pink and Lily': 502, 518, 523; Letters from America: 75-6; 'Sonnets 1914': 210, 382; 'The Great Lover': 382; 'The Soldier': 81.
Broome, William: 533.
Browcher, Captain: 503.
Brown, Dr John: 338-9, 468.
Browne, Denis: 425.
Browning: 34-5, 63, 124, 130, 140, 147, 192, 239, 267, 445, 521, 540; 'The Bishop orders his Tomb at St Praxed's': 117, 343.

Brussilov, General: 97, 292.
Buchan, John: 21, 425.
Bude, xviii.
Buire-au-Bois: xvi, 284, 334.
Bullen: 292.
Bunnett, Dr: 325.
Burns: 89, 91, 174-5, 177, 183, 335, 481.
Butterworth, George: 252.
Buysscheure: xvi, 334.
Byrd: 517, 529, 537.
Byron: 331.

Cambrai: 374, 378, 380, 384.
Cambridge Press: 435.
Cammaerts, Emile: 306.
The Canadian Magazine: 246.
Carey, Clive: 524.
Carlyle: 33, 50-1, 74, 406, 484, 509, 521, 545; Heroes and Hero-Worship: 50-1; Past and Present: 509; Sartor Resartus: 504, 509, 524.
Carnegie United Kingdom Trust: 244, 249, 260, 511, 514, 518, 522, 532-4, 540.
Cartwright, William: 533.
Cary and Doré: Dante: 288.
Casson, Mrs: 507.
Catchwords: 341.
Caudle, Charles: 373.
Caulaincourt: xvi, 416.
Censor: viii, 128, 149, 154, 158, 170, 280-1, 337, 378, 399, 401.
Century of Essays from Caxton to Belloc: 53, 55, 57, 63.
Cervantes: 275, 530; Don Quixote: 482, 508, 510.
Cezano, Paul: 306.
Chamberlain, Austen: 251.
Chandler, John: 61.
Chapbook: 504, 540.
Chapman family: vii, x, xv, xvii, xx.
Chapman, George: 510, 512, 515-6, 519, 521, 537; Iliad: 510, 517, 532;
Chappells: 503.
Chatterton: 322, 529.

563

Movement: 478, 489-90, 493, 495; Scherzo: 442, 445, 452, 478-9; Fourth Violin Sonata: 523.

512; 'There's Wisdom in Women': 527; 'Thou didst delight my eyes': 409-10, 412; 'Though I am young': 532; 'To G': 406, 420, 473, 476, 478; 'To the Fallen': 201; 'Today I think only with Scents': 488, 494, 504-6; 'Trafalgar': 7, 9; 'Twa Corbies': 67, 487; 'Under the Greenwood Tree': 10, 216, 519; 'Upon the Downs': 500; 'Wenlock Edge': 366, 393; 'West Sussex Drinking Song': 478, 481; 'The Western Playland': xviii, 474; 'When June is come': 508-9; 'White Cascade': 427; songs (unspecified): 10, 38, 104, 109, 129, 233, 238, 410, 414, 425, 431, 477, 490, 517; performed: 238, 361.

LIFE: army number: xv, xvi, 108, 249, 261; band: xv; bullet in arm: 241; Details of the Life: 357; discharge: 464-5; Electrical influence: 542, 544, 547-50, 552; escape: 544, 547; farmwork: 449, 481, 483-4, 491-2, 501, 512-3, 516, 532-4, 554; grant: xvii; income tax job: xviii, 522, 525, 531, 534-7, 540; Machine Gun Corps: 284-5, 287, 327, 334; might enter Pembroke: 498; Munition Work, 467; music against verse: viii, ix, xi, 58, 65, 135, 191, 223, 289, 321, 324, 336, 409, 412, 420, 442, 449, 461; note book, 299, 324, 409, 439, 441, 452, 485, 487, 504, 506, 508; pension: xvii, xviii, 532, 542; photograph: 79, 119, 124, 254, 269, 358-9, 375, 382, 385, 396, 402-3; picture palaces: xviii, 139, 191, 444, 503, 522-3, 525-6, 535; pleads for death: 542-555; pseudonym Michael Flood: 507; railway job: 49, 50, 52-3, 58, 60; sends verses to Marsh: 524-5; signalling: xvi, 84, 91, 93-4, 364,

372, 381, 403; suicide note: 430; unhappy stay at the Scotts': 365; views on the Novel: 294; visits Masefield: 498-500; wounded: xvi, 242, 244, 332, 358.

HEALTH: 'cold in the stomach': vii; dyspepsia: vii, xv, 7, 8, 10, 11, 17, 52, 105, 124, 191, 232, 238, 243, 321, 338, 405, 409, 414, 416, 418-9; gas: xvii, 326, 328, 333, 337, 358, 404-5, 407, 414, 413; health in general: 3, 7, 21, 25, 27, 32, 43, 45, 52, 60, 64, 149, 169, 177, 221, 337, 340, 384, 421, 512, 523-4; marked 'Debility': 417-8; mental state: 297, 410, 416, 418-9, 425, 497, 516; nervous breakdown: xvii, 424; neurasthenia: vii, xv, 32, 37, 52, 94, 103, 115, 138; 228, 231, 238, 281, 328, 330, 399, 416, 511; teeth: vii, xvi, 123, 137, 139, 414, 432; terrible spiritual adventure: 418.

Gurney, Ronald: xiv, 544-6.
Gurney, Winifred: xiv, 290, 302.
Guthrie, Lord: 345.
Guynemer, Georges: 309.

Hadow, Sir William Henry: 391-2, 396.
Haig, Douglas: 215, 248, 363.
Haines, J. W.: xiv, xxi, 6, 10, 370, 373, 376-7, 380, 393, 404-5, 432-5, 445, 452, 463, 466, 475-6, 478, 480-1, 483, 494, 501, 505, 509-10, 512, 532, 540; 'Paradise' (essay): 441, 449; *Poems*: 436, 509, 519-20; walking with IBG: 488.
Hankin, St John: 11.
Hardy: 4, 9, 29, 31-3, 35, 38, 41, 144, 153, 174-5, 181, 212, 515, 517; *The Dynasts*: 7, 29, 35, 230, 486, 527; novels: 1, 2, 4, 32, 41, 174, 212, 215, 230, 503; tales: 38-9.
Harper, Dr: xv, 3.
Harper's Magazine: 246, 491, 492.

570

Harrington, J. P: 151.
Harris, Augusta (Shakespearean comedian): 378.
Hartpury: 79, 404.
Harvey, Bernard: 10.
Harvey, Edith: 52, 475.
Harvey, Eric: 5, 10.
Harvey, F.W.: xiv, xxi, 11, 17, 40, 42, 44, 46, 58, 65, 68, 126-7, 135, 140, 145, 153, 161, 181, 183, 189-90, 205, 212, 216-7, 222, 226-7, 234, 236, 242, 252, 268, 274, 280, 285, 292, 296, 298-300, 302-4, 310, 313, 315-6, 319, 322-3, 325, 327, 329, 336-7, 344, 373, 377, 413, 430, 434, 436, 466, 472-6, 478-9, 481-3, 488, 491, 494, 498-502, 512, 516, 520, 530, 532, 537, 540; *Comrades in Captivity*: 137; *Farewell*: 525; *Gloucestershire Friends*: 268-9, 330, 343-4, 356, 474; IBG's review of GF: 344, 356, 358; *A Gloucestershire Lad*: 150-1, 156, 159, 181, 215, 230, 299, 305, 312, 314, 318, 320, 324, 335-6, 343, 375, 390, 474, 483; IBG's review of GL, 312; individual poems, 30, 181, 190, 297, 343, 430, 436-7, 475, 477, 479-80, 537; 'Gonnehem': 312, 358, 383, 412, 437, 529; 'In Flanders': 38, 40, 43, 151, 181, 190, 312, 336, 358, 383, 437-8, 529; novel: 524, 530; 'death' and capture: xvi, 136-7, 151, marriage: 511.
Harvey, Gladys: 10, 475, 518.
Harvey, Mrs: 5, 10, 79, 181, 234, 236, 261, 268, 300, 322, 373, 430, 436.
Hasfield: 404.
Hauptmann, Gerhart: 44, 275.
Hawthornden Prize: 538.
Hay, Ian (John Hay Beith): 83.
Haydn: 45, 506, 528.
Hazlitt: 495, 521.
Heath, J. R.: 507.
Heine: 198, 350.

Hempsted: xiv, 490.
Henley: 286, 331, 338-9.
Herald: 509.
Herrick: 251, 509, 527.
Heywood: 521, 529.
Higgs, Miss: 17.
High Wycombe: xvii.
Hindenburg: 111, 145, 155, 232, 245, 248, 288, 341.
Hindhead: 84-5, 156.
Hodgson, Ralph: xvii, 278-9, 293, 301, 308-9, 315, 319, 323, 399, 401, 403, 406, 413, 496; 'The Song of Honour': 278-9, 319, 322-5, 529.
Hodgson, W.N.: 229-30, 413.
Holyrood: 338.
Homer: 516.
Hood, Thomas: 18.
Hopkins, Gerard Manley: 140.
Horsepools: 475, 510.
Housman, A. E.: 80, 169, 325, 468, 518, 520, 540, 547; *A Shropshire Lad*: 172, 243, 249, 267, 299, 308, 366, 375, 390, 405, 474; 'On Wenlock Edge': 382.
Howard, Geoffrey: 229-30, 251.
Howard, Keble: 147.
Howe, Percival Presland: 11, 12.
Howells, Herbert: vii, x, xi, xiv, xv, xxi, 19, 45, 69, 83, 93, 114, 122-4, 143, 146, 149-50, 152, 160, 192, 194, 196-7, 203-4, 209, 212, 216, 221, 223-4, 228, 244-5, 249-50, 261, 265, 267, 272, 292, 332, 340, 365, 373, 375-6, 391, 393, 404, 406, 414, 420, 422, 427-9, 434, 436, 448, 455, 462, 466-7, 477-8, 484, 501-2, 506, 511, 516-7, 520; Beethoven's opinion of: 419; birth of daughter, 532; dedication of 'By a Bierside': 253; engagement: 256, 260; Organist at Salisbury: 223, 225-6; scores IBG's songs: 225. MUSIC: 'Chosen Quartet' (Carnegie): 95-7, 123-4, 135, 244, 292, 433-4,

Morris, William: 67, 530.
Morrow, George: 110, 112.
Motley, John: 491.
Mouchy: 334.
Mozart: 19, 29, 45, 47, 289, 297, 415, 481, 506, 517, 527; concerti: 511; quartets: 510, 528; quintets: 59.
Muller's Exercises: 10-12
Munro, Neil (Hugh Foulis): 21, 27.
Murdoch, William: 502.
Murry, Middleton: 516-7.
Music and Letters: 500-1.
Music Student: 431, 463.
Musical America: 507.
Musical Times: 224, 228-9.

Napoleon: 253, 438.
Nashe, Thomas: 514.
Nation: 275, 288, 303.
National Song Book: 230, 239.
Nesles: 333.
Nettleship, Miss: 508, 532.
Neuve Chapelle: 150, 155.
Neuvillette: 280, 334.
Nevin, Ethelbert Woodbridge: 332-3.
New Numbers: 20.
New Statesman: 303.
New Witness: 303, 491.
Newbolt: 7, 177, 394.
Newent: 79, 261, 435.
Newman, E.: 501.
Newnham: 81, 404, 413, 423-4, 435-6, 449, 501, 512, 541.
Nichols, Robert (IBG often calls him Nicholson): 288-9, 292, 300, 308, 323, 325, 343, 401-2, 413, 465, 500; *Ardours and Endurances*, 299, 315, 317, 324.
Nielson: 345-7, 362.
Nivelle: 248.
Nohl: 8, 9.
Northampton: xv.
Northcliffe: 31, 245, 353, 380.
Novalis: 322.
Noyes, Alfred: 38, 146.
Noyon: 417.

Observer: 96, 148, 155, 158, 194, 224, 228, 261, 501, 529.
Oliver, F.S.: 92.
Omiecourt: 334.
Orion: 51, 150, 198, 280, 356.
Osborn, E. B.: 157, 183, 224, 231, 291; *The Muse in Arms*: 83, 154, 225, 291, 372, 376, 410, 412, 428, 438, 444, 446.
Owen, Wilfred: 529.
Oxford: xvii, 162, 192, 499, 500.

Painswick: 153, 475, 510.
Palestrina: 19, 529, 537.
Palgrave: 93, 120, 292, 351.
Pall Mall: 508.
Parratt, Sir Walter: 359, 422.
Parry, Sir Charles Hubert Hastings: xxii, 3, 9, 17, 27, 38, 84, 94, 114, 143, 150, 159, 196, 215, 218, 314, 332, 359, 365, 391, 420-2, 429, 431, 515, 517; praises IBG's song: 245
Passchendaele: xiv, 417.
Pater: 46, 65.
Patterson, John Edward: 29, 30.
Peguy: 155.
Pepys: 131, 144, 146, 158.
Peronne: 324.
Le Petit Journal: 142-3.
Le Petit Parisien: 93, 153.
Philharmonic Quartet: 502.
Piano: viii, xiv, xviii, 65, 70-1, 96, 100, 103, 115, 117, 123, 133, 138, 146, 148, 160, 194, 212, 222, 225, 231, 237, 240, 245, 276, 282, 312, 338, 360, 392, 399, 400, 411, 414, 416, 440, 444-5, 461, 463, 482, 484, 489.
Pitcher, Sidney: 375, 402, 406, 429, 433, 436, 445, 466; photo of IBG: 383.
Planquette, Robert: 306.
Plowman, Max: 413.
Plutarch: 72.

383, 391-2, 396, 402, 441, 461, 480, 483, 504; *Book of the Daffodill*: 504; *A Selection of Poems from recent volumes*: 181, 184; accept IBG's book: 284, 287; refuse new book: 536.

Simpllicimus: 233.

Sitwell, Edith: 495.

Sitwell, Frances (afterwards Lady Colvin): 126-7.

Smart: 529, 540.

Smith, Adam: 339.

Smith, Mabel Saumarez: 68, 228, 271.

Snaith, John Collis: 330-1.

Society of Women Musicians: 2, 3, 9, 67, 96, 113, 116, 192, 215, 516.

Soldier Poets: 230, 251-2, 267.

Somervell, Sir Arthur: 88-9, 95, 113; 'A Slumber Song': 87, 89, 95, 113; 'David of the White Rock': 87, 89, 95, 113.

Somerville and Ross: 438-9.

Somme: xvi, 115, 124, 151, 155, 160-1, 188, 268, 309, 409, 416.

Sophocles: 516.

Sorley, Charles Hamilton: 251, 292, 413, 468.

Sorley-Turner: 370.

Southwold: 8, 9.

Spectator: x, 303, 491-3.

Spenser: 517.

Squire, J. C.: 399, 401, 403, 475, 478, 504-5, 510, 529, 554; IBG visits: 518; opinion of IBG: 497.

Stainer and Bell: 515, 540; accept 'Captain Stratton': 487; will take 'Edward' and 'The Twa Corbies': 487.

Stanford, Sir Charles V.: xv, xxii, 10, 21, 27, 94, 138, 196, 217, 223-4, 228, 261, 270, 294, 300, 303, 358, 373, 396, 403, 421-2.

Stead's *Penny Poets*: 124.

Steen, Dr: xviii, xxii, 551.

Stephens, James: 399, 401, 459, 520.

Sterne: 144.

Stevenson, Robert Louis: 2, 21, 63, 119, 126-7, 140, 144, 160, 174, 269, 275, 329, 335, 338, 345, 384, 493, 495; *Across the Plains*: 63; *Kidnapped*: 147, 174, 230; *Letters*: 1, 491-3; *New Arabian Nights*: 147; *Travels with a Donkey*: 249; *Treasure Island*: 147; *Weir of Hermiston*: 63: 174; *The Wreckers*: 63; *The Wrong Box*: 147.

Strachey, St Loe: x.

Strangways, Arthur Henry Fox: 500-1, 511, 523.

Strauss: 6, 45, 120, 434, 517; 'Heldenleben': 46, 79, 120.

Stravinsky: 497.

Stroud: 86, 435, 472, 474-5, 478, 512, 521.

Studio: 332.

Sudermann, Hermann: 14.

Sullivan: 528.

Sunday Chronicle: 402.

Sunday Pictorial: 160.

Sunday Times: 377.

Surtees, R.S.: 481.

Swinburne: 469, 520.

Swindon: 511.

Synge: 4, 5, 11, 189, 275, 508.

Tagore: 21.

Tanks: 318-20, 324, 334, 374, 404, 484.

Taylor, Colin: 379.

Taylor, Franklin: 78.

Taylor, Geoffrey: 365.

Taylor, Jimmy: 373.

Taylor, Mrs: 77, 113, 293, 434, 489.

Taylors: 43, 123, 146, 162, 180, 192, 197, 223, 238, 286, 287, 300, 349, 365, 395, 406.

Le Télégramme: 142.

Tennyson: 41, 67, 124.

Tewkesbury: 134, 216, 306, 435, 445, 455, 537.

Thackeray: 95, 246, 249, 268-9, 287, 303, 510.